AMERICA'S POLITICAL

A Text with Cases

FIFTH EDITION

AMERICA'S POLITICAL SYSTEM

A Text with Cases

Peter Woll
Brandeis University

Robert H. Binstock
Case Western Reserve University

McGRAW-HILL, Inc.
New York St. Louis San Francisco Auckland Bogotá Caracas Hamburg Lisbon London Madrid
Mexico Milan Montreal New Delhi Paris San Juan São Paulo Singapore Sydney Tokyo Toronto

AMERICA'S POLITICAL SYSTEM
A Text with Cases

1 2 3 4 5 6 7 8 9 0 DOC DOC 9 5 4 3 2 1 0

ISBN 0-07-071584-X

This book was set in Palatino by the College Composition Unit
in cooperation with Ruttle Shaw & Wetherill, Inc.
The editors were Bert Lummus and Fred H. Burns;
the designer was Gayle Jaeger;
the production supervisor was Friederich W. Schulte.
The photo editor was Rita Geffert.
R. R. Donnelley & Sons Company was printer and binder.

Part Opener Photo Credits:
Part I: Jonathan Wallen
Part II: UPI / Bettmann Newsphotos
Part III: Paul Conklin / Monkmeyer
Part IV: Owen Franken / Stock, Boston

Cover Photo Credits:
Front cover (counterclockwise from top):   Michael Heron / Woodfin Camp & Assoc.,
Dennis Brack / Black Star, Catherine Karnow / Woodfin Camp & Assoc.
Back cover: Lisa Quinones / Black Star

Library of Congress Cataloging-in-Publication Data

Woll, Peter, (date).
   America's Political system: a text with cases / Peter Woll,
   Robert H. Binstock.—5th ed.
      p.   cm.
   Includes Index.
   ISBN 0-07-071584-X
   1. United States—Politics and government.   I. Binstock, Robert H.   II. Title.
JK274.W73   1991
320.973—dc20   90-42968

About the Authors

PETER WOLL is professor of politics at Brandeis University. He received his A.B. degree from Haverford College, where he was elected to Phi Beta Kappa, and received his Ph.D. degree in political science from Cornell University. Professor Woll has written extensively in the field of American government, and his works include *American Bureaucracy, American Government: Readings and Cases, Behind the Scenes in American Government,* and *American Government: The Core.* He has been a consultant to a presidential campaign, a congressional committee, and to administrative agencies. He has also been a recipient of a Social Science Research Council grant and had actively participated in American Political Science Association and other professional association meetings over the years. He has taught the introductory American government course during his entire professional career.

ROBERT H. BINSTOCK is Henry R. Luce Professor of Aging, Health, and Society at Case Western Reserve University. He received his A.B. and Ph.D. degrees in political science from Harvard University. A former president of the Gerontological Society of America (1975–1976), he served as director of a White House Task Force on Older Americans in 1967–1968 and as chairman and member of a number of advisory panels to the United States government, state and local governments, and foundations. Professor Binstock is author of more than 100 articles on the politics and policies affecting aging. His sixteen books include *"Too Old" for Health Care?, The Politics of the Powerless,* and three editions of the *Handbook of Aging and the Social Sciences.* Among the honors he has received are the Donald P. Kent Award from the Gerontological Society of America, the Brookdale Prize Award, and the Arthur S. Flemming Award from the National Association of State Units on Aging.

v

This book is dedicated to MONICA WOLL and JENNIFER BINSTOCK

Contents

PART FOUR / THE NATURE AND DISTRIBUTION OF GOVERNMENT RESPONSIBILITIES   505

Maps and Charts

Tables

Preface

America's Political System is a comprehensive mainstream introduction to the whole landscape of American government. An examination of our rich constitutional and political traditions is complemented by an analysis of contemporary political institutions and practices. American politics is examined within the context of the Constitution, giving students the background to compare American democracy today with the Founding Fathers' intentions and hopes for a balanced, representative, and effective national government.

THE TEXT'S MAJOR FEATURES

Here are the major features that distinguish the fifth edition of *America's Political System:*

1. The text is published in paperback and it is under 600 pages. This means that the cost for the student is considerably less than that of many hardcover mainstream texts. This means that instructors can easily augment this text with supplements and monographs if they choose.
2. Like earlier editions, this edition continues the strong focus on the basics—constitutional foundations, political institutions, political processes, and public policy.
3. Each chapter concludes with a case study contributed by a political scientist, a journalist, or a historian. The cases are an integral part of the chapter.
4. Extensive use is made of boxed inserts, cartoons, tables, and figures. We have sought to make *America's Political System* interesting and visually attractive.
5. The fifth edition continues to include the popular annotated Constitution at the end of the book for easy reference. An extensive bibliography follows ("The Student Researcher"), which is designed to help students carry out research projects and pursue topics of special interest. The "Researcher" includes a listing of primary source materials available from both government agencies and private groups, as well as the titles of secondary works of particular importance and usefulness. In addition, the popular glossary of political terms remains in the appendix for student reference.

An expanded instructor's manual for *America's Political System* continues to be available to teachers on request. McGraw-Hill also publishes a study guide, which can be ordered through the college bookstore.

WHAT'S NEW IN THE FIFTH EDITION

The fifth edition of *America's Political System* retains four classic case studies: Tocqueville's analysis of democracy (Chapter 2); *Marbury v. Madison* (Chapter 3); Theodore Sorensen on presidential decision making (Chapter 12); and essays by Oliver Wendell Holmes, Benjamin Cardozo, and Felix Frankfurter (Chapter 15). The remainder of the cases are new to this edition. The new cases take into account recent political trends and developments and give students the most contemporary materials possible. The chapter titles with their corresponding new case studies are:

CHAPTER 4
The Rights of Citizens: Civil Liberties and Civil Rights
CASE STUDY 3 *Freedom of expression and the American flag*

CHAPTER 5
The Structure of Federalism
CASE STUDY 4 *Federalism in the 1990s*

CHAPTER 6
Political Attitudes
CASE STUDY 5 *Political issues and attitudes in the 1990s*

CHAPTER 7
The Organization and Functions of American Parties
CASE STUDY 6 *Party alignments in the 1990s*

CHAPTER 8
Nominations, Campaigns, and Elections
CASE STUDY 7 *Choosing a president*

CHAPTER 9
Interest Groups and Their Demands
CASE STUDY 8 *The emergence of professional interest-group politics*

CHAPTER 10
Congress: Its Framework and Members
CASE STUDY 9 *Congress in crisis*

CHAPTER 11
Congressional Policy Making
CASE STUDY 10 *The senate of the 1990s*

CHAPTER 13
Presidential Policy Making
CASE STUDY 12 *The president and the press*

CHAPTER 14
The Bureaucracy: Organization and Power
CASE STUDY 13 *Administrative decision making*

CHAPTER 16
Judicial Policy Making
CASE STUDY 15 *Judicial self-restraint versus judicial activism in the 1990s*

CHAPTER 17
The Media: The Fourth Estate
CASE STUDY 16 *The media revolution and the new politics*

CHAPTER 18
Government Policies: Their Nature and Scope
CASE STUDY 17 *The politics of targeting tax payers*

CHAPTER 19
The Distribution of Government Responsibilities: State and Local Governments
CASE STUDY 18 *The changing role of state legislators*

New boxed inserts, graphs, and tables illustrate important points and trends. Boxed inserts include, for example, a congresswoman's lively account of her relationship with constituents; a sample from the oral arguments presented to the Supreme Court in the seminal abortion case, *Roe v. Wade* (1973); and many other illustrations of government and politics in action. Tables and graphs depict emerging voting patterns; how political opinion differs among groups and on important public policy issues; partisan trends and party identification; categories of political action committees and how they contribute and spend in national election campaigns; and a wide range of other topics that help to explain how the political process works.

The book is generously illustrated with over ninety political cartoons that present different and often provocative perspectives on the political process. Newly drawn figures help the student understand the structures and processes of politics and government.

We greatly appreciate the sage guidance and patience of our long-time editor, Bertrand Lummus. As in past revisions, he skillfully pinpointed needed areas for change, and was a steadying influence throughout the revision. We would also like to thank our editing supervisor, Fred Burns, who adeptly guided the book to completion on time. A long-time friend of the book, Martin P. Sutton of Bucks County Community College in Newtown, Pennsylvania, also skillfully pinpointed needed areas for change, and was a steadying influence throughout the revision. My colleague Sidney Milkis revised "The Student Researcher" in the appendix to keep it in tune with the times and to make it an invaluable research source for undergraduates. Neil Sullivan continues to take an active interest in the book and we highly value his contributions. Melissa Feldman and Jodi Golinksy served as our research assistants and made many useful suggestions. Finally, we wish to thank Elaine Herrmann who over the years has skillfully and professionally processed the manuscript.

Peter Woll
Robert H. Binstock

AMERICA'S POLITICAL SYSTEM

A Text with Cases

An Overview of the American Political System

The United States of America is the beacon of democracy throughout the world. Over the course of American history millions of people have uprooted themselves from their native lands to journey to freedom and what they hoped would be prosperity in the United States. They came to a land incomparably rich in natural resources, a nation that was the first to promise liberty and justice for all.

THE SIGNIFICANCE OF THE CONSTITUTION

The system of government created by the Framers of the Constitution reflected the revolutionary ideals of the eighteenth-century Enlightenment: All men are created equal and are endowed with natural rights. Government must be responsible to its citizens and cannot abridge their inalienable rights. Moreover, the Framers shared the eighteenth century's burning faith in progress, an almost unbridled optimism about the future of the new republic. They sought to create a perfect government, in the words of the preamble to the Constitution, "a more perfect Union," that would "establish justice, insure domestic tranquility, provide for the common defense, promote the general welfare, and secure the blessings of liberty to ourselves and our posterity."

Creative, poetic imaginations have helped make the Constitution far more to us than a simple political document. The literature, drama, and poetry of the nation have romantically portrayed the founding of the republic as the beginning of the American mission to promote individual liberty, foster progress, and serve as a model of democracy for the world. But the true significance of the debates over the Constitution was explained at the time by one of the leading Framers, Alexander Hamilton. In the first of a famous series of newspaper articles written to persuade the state of New York to ratify the Constitution, Hamilton wrote

It has been frequently remarked that it seems to have been reserved to the people of this country, by their conduct and example, to decide the important question, whether societies of men are really capable or not of establishing good government from reflection and choice, or whether they are forever destined to depend for their political constitutions upon accident and force. If there be any truth in the remark, the crisis at which we are arrived may with propriety be regarded as the era in which that decision is to be made; and a wrong election of the part we shall act may, in this view, deserve to be considered as the general misfortune of mankind.[1]

While the Framers were idealists, they were also realists. They had studied history and were aware of the mistakes of past repub-

---

[1] *The Federalist*, No. 1.

(Drawing by P. Steiner; © 1982 The New Yorker Magazine, Inc.)

"Remember, gentlemen, we aren't here just to draft a constitution. We're here to draft the best damned constitution in the world."
The Founding Fathers believed that the American mission was to set an example for the world.

lics which had led to their replacement by despotic regimes. Above all they understood the frailties of human nature. Thus, in constructing the new American government, they let themselves be guided by the practical lessons of the new science of politics. As Hamilton observed,

The science of politics, . . .like most other sciences, has received great improvement. The efficacy of various principles is now well understood, which were either not known at all, or imperfectly known to the ancients. The regular distribution of power into distinct departments; the introduction of legislative balances and checks; the institution of courts composed of judges holding their offices during good behavior; the representation of the people in the legislature by deputies of their own election; these are wholly new discoveries, or

have made their principal progress toward perfection in modern times. They are means, and powerful means, by which the excellencies of Republican governments may be retained and its imperfections lessened or avoided.[2]

The Framers recognized both the opportunities and the perils of their task. John Adams, later to serve as our second president, undoubtedly spoke for all politically aware Americans of his time when he wrote

The institutions now made in America will not wholly wear out for thousands of years. It is of the [utmost] importance, then, that they should begin right. If they set out wrong, they will

---

[2]*The Federalist*, No. 9.

never be able to return, unless it be by accident, to the right path.[3]

THE NATURE OF POLITICS

Wherever there is government, there is politics. Politics concerns power, who gets what, when, and how. As the political scientist and philosopher Harold Laswell has written, "The study of politics is the study of influence and the influential. The science of politics states conditions; the philosophy of politics justifies preferences."[4]

The Constitution and the Arenas of Politics

The Constitution, especially its provisions for the separation of powers and checks and balances, created a number of independent but overlapping political arenas. It formally established three distinct branches of government—the presidency, Congress, and the courts—each with different constituencies, powers, and politics. It accommodated the emergence in the twentieth century of the federal bureaucracy as an unofficial fourth branch of government, with powers and a politics of its own. Also, in creating a federal system, it guaranteed a rich diversity of state and local politics. And finally, through its First Amendment freedoms of expression and association, the Constitution has sustained the politics of political parties and interest groups that have become a vital part of the democratic process. Citizens are free to organize for political purposes, provided they respect the constitutional rights of others and do not present a threat to the government itself. The freedom to petition government for a redress of grievances

is fundamental. Freedom of the press protects the independence of the media, without which democracy would be meaningless.

Contemporary Politics

The game of American politics has rules and a flavor all its own, which only its participants fully understand and appreciate. Journalist Jimmy Breslin has captured some of its flavor in his description of politics in Massachusetts, where the game is played with relish and for keeps.

There is in this country no place that could even be suggested as being anywhere near the Massachusetts State House for bone politics. . . .In Massachusetts, the legislators prefer to sit forever. They usually have to be driven out of the building, practically at gunpoint. If a Massachusetts legislator is removed from his game, his sport, his very life, then all that is left for him to do is return home to his wife and family, and in Massachusetts anybody can have a family, but the true goal of life is to be a politician; or, true term, a Pol. It is not uncommon for the Massachusetts Pols to sit in the State House throughout the summer, arguing, spreading rumors, using the phones, and—true glory—plotting against each other.[5]

The pluralism and freedom of American politics make it unique and exciting. The game is played with great intensity, and its outcomes are important to every citizen. All those who have the desire and skills can participate. For those who do not wish to be directly involved, politics remains a great spectator sport carried to the nation through the mass media. But most spectators cannot appreciate its internal "politics,"—the constant machinations and striving for power—the game the participants are *really* playing for themselves, not for the outside world. The participants and insiders in the different political arenas convey

---

[3]John Adams, *A Defense of the Constitutions of Government of the United States of America* (New York: Da Capo Press, 1971), p. xxv.

[4]Harold Laswell, *Politics: Who Gets What, When, How* (New York: Meridian Books, 1958), p. 13.

[5]Jimmy Breslin, *How the Good Guys Finally Won* (New York: Viking, 1975), pp. 136–137.

(Drawing by D. Fradon; © 1968 The New Yorker Magazine, Inc.)

"How many times have you asked yourself, 'What can I, as a single person, possibly do to help shape the destiny of mankind?' Well, I'll tell you what you can do. You can vote for me."

Each person's wishes, wants, and needs should be the principal concern of his or her elected representatives.

the flavor of politics best when they speak for themselves.

Congressional Politics

Congress, from its lofty position on Capitol Hill, oversees the White House and the bureaucracy to the west and looks eastward to the Supreme Court. Congress is the keystone of Washington politics, having the sole authority to make the nation's laws. It shapes policy also through its exclusive authority to authorize and appropriate money for all federal programs. The Constitution pits Congress against the president in a never-ending battle for supremacy, while in the meantime the House and the Senate check and balance each other.

Capitol Hill politics weaves complicated webs of relationships on the outside with the president and his staff, the bureaucracy, special interests, political parties, and of course the voters who choose the members of Con-

gress in the first place. Politics is equally complicated within Congress, as members vie with each other for power and status (represented by choice committee assignments and congressional party leadership positions). Above all, Congress is not as it is usually pictured—an institution that simply reflects the pressures of voters and special interest groups.

Committees. Approximately 300 committees on Capitol Hill divide legislative power and are the lifeblood of the legislative process. Some committees have more authority and status than others, and there is keen competition to obtain seats on them. In the House the Ways and Means and Appropriations Committees, and in the Senate the Judiciary and Foreign Relations Committees, are at the top of the power hierarchy.

Committees shape the federal budget, formulate legislation, hold investigations, oversee the bureaucracy, and, in the Senate, conduct special hearings on executive nominations. As the late Congressman Clem Miller of California astutely observed, "There are all sorts of ways to get things done in Congress. The best way is to live long enough to get to be a committee chairman, and be brilliant enough to be a good one. Chairmen complain to me that they are frustrated too, but this is really beside the point. If things can be done, they can do them; we are very sure of that."[6]

Congressional staff. Congressional staffers play politics as assiduously and are as conscious of power and status as their bosses. Those who hold important positions on personal or committee staffs are surrogate members of Congress, who can be highly influential in the decision-making process of Capitol Hill. (They have been quite appropriately called "the unelected representatives.")[7]

---

[6]Clem Miller, *Letters of a Congressman,* ed. John W. Baker (New York: Scribner's, 1962), p. 39.

[7]Michael A. Malbin, *Unelected Representatives: Congressional Staff and the Future of Representative Government* (New York: Basic Books, 1979).

The House Armed Services Committee is one of many that illustrates the power of staff. One observer commented: "The members of that staff are the high priests of the legislative process." The staff director, noted one military lobbyist, "is the de facto chairman of the committee."[8]

Members of Congress and their aides, once they leave Capitol Hill, either on their own initiative or buffeted by shifting political winds, generally want to stay in the highly charged and exciting political environment of Washington. They have caught "Potomac fever," the term applied to addiction to the politics of the nation's capital. Retired members of the Capitol Hill community often seek positions with interest groups, law firms, in party and campaign organizations, and in the bureaucracy.

Presidential Politics

A sign that always stood on the desk of President Harry S. Truman read: "The Buck Stops Here." Truman believed, as do all strong presidents, that the White House should be the focal point of political leadership. The nation expects it. Presidents who want to take their place in history with the great leaders of the past, as almost all do, must be capable of making difficult and often unpopular decisions in the national interest as they see it. Truman commented, "There's always a lot of talk about how we have to fear the man on horseback, have to be afraid . . .of a strong man, but so far, if I read my American history right, it isn't the strong men that have caused us most of the trouble, it's the ones who were weak."

Presidential power is not omnipotent, but it is awe-inspiring. One of Lyndon B. Johnson's chroniclers, Ronnie Dugger, described his first-hand impression of presidential power during the Johnson administration.

One night, after meeting with Johnson, he wrote:

I walked the streets of Washington, which are well known to me. Huddled in my overcoat against the cold, looking through the bars of the iron fence at the power-glowing White House, I thought about Johnson in there that night. Half a million Americans were fighting in Vietnam at his command. He personally, at that exact moment which I was also living, could destroy hundreds of millions of people. He personally could destroy human civilization from this venerable old house.[9]

The power of the president, however, is exaggerated. Although his finger may be on the nuclear button, he cannot press any other "button" that will automatically result in decisions. President Harry Truman, before he left the White House in 1952, remarked to an aide, as he thought about Eisenhower in the Oval Office: "He'll sit here . . .and he'll say, 'Do this! Do that!' and nothing will happen. Poor Ike—it won't be a bit like the Army. He'll find it very frustrating."[10]

The president's extraordinary authority in foreign and military affairs is not duplicated in the domestic sphere. His power, as political scientist Richard Neustadt has pointed out, reaches only as far as his ability to persuade others that their interests coincide with his. Presidents must confront and master Congress if they are to achieve their policy goals. They must understand the arcane ways of the bureaucracy, over which they have no automatic control. They must not run afoul of the courts, as Harry S. Truman did when he unilaterally seized the steel mills on the basis of his constitutional authority as chief executive and commander in chief. (The Court ruled that neither the Constitution nor Congress had authorized the president to take the seizure action.)

---

[8]Richard Halloran, "Military Panel Staff: Roots of Power," *The New York Times*, June 28, 1982, p. A13.

[9]Ronnie Dugger, *The Politician* (New York: Norton, 1982), p. 22.

[10]Richard E. Neustadt, *Presidential Power* (New York: Wiley, 1960), p. 9.

The president's staff. The presidency is often thought of as being one person who makes all of the decisions and is held responsible for them. But no one can deal single-handedly with the multiple responsibilities and complex politics of the White House. The White House staff is the president's "right arm," and he is assisted too by a presidential bureaucracy that has the Office of Management and Budget (OMB) at its apex. Presidential aides play politics as they strive to maintain or to increase their power within the White House and in the broader political establishment of Washington. Many presidential decisions are actually those of aides who have persuaded him to accept their viewpoints or, in some cases, acted on their own initiative. The White House staff has been called the "invisible presidency" that exercises power behind the scenes and without direct accountability to anyone but the president himself. Former presidential aide George Reedy wrote:

The trouble with the White House—for anyone who is a part of it—is that when he picks up a telephone and tells people to do something, they usually do it. They may sabotage the project after they have hung up the phone. They may stall, hoping that "the old son-of-a-bitch" will forget about it. They may respond with an avalanche of statistics and briefing papers in which the original purpose will be lost and life will continue as before. But the heel click at the other end of the wire will be audible and the response—however invalid—will be prompt. There will be no delay in assurance, however protracted may be performance.[11]

The personal presidency. The president's personality and style determine how much he will rely upon his staff and how much leeway he will give to them to shape presidential policies and politics. The White House decision-making process varies from one incumbent to the other. Presidential politics is played differently from one administration to the other. A president

makes his decisions as he wishes to make them, under conditions which he himself has established, and at times of his own determination. He decides what he wants to decide and any student of the White House who believes that he is making a contribution to political thought when he analyzes the process is sadly mistaken. At best—at the very best—he can only contribute to human knowledge some insights into the decision-making process of one man.[12]

Bureaucratic Politics

Top-level bureaucrats play politics in many ways. Some, like J. Edgar Hoover and Admiral Hyman Rickover, become political entrepreneurs, using their agencies, positions, policies, and personalities to build constituencies outside of the executive branch. They cultivate close relationships with the congressional committee chairman who oversee their operations and determine their budgets and programs. They appeal to special interest groups and even to the broader public for support, using the most effective public relations techniques. In this way successful bureaucrats and entrepreneurs eventually become invulnerable to political attacks and see their programs enacted, even over strong opposition within their own departments (as Admiral Hyman Rickover saw his nuclear submarine program carried out).

Not all ambitious bureaucrats are political entrepreneurs, however. Some, with survival as their primary goal, learn nimbly to serve many masters. They develop expertise in critical areas of public policy, budgeting, administrative procedures, and congressional relations to a point where they become indispensable to their politically appointed bosses. Their skills tide them over from one administration to another, resulting in the same continuity of power that bureaucratic entrepre-

---

[11]George E. Reedy, *The Twilight of the Presidency* (New York: World Publishing, 1970), p. xiii.

[12]Ibid., p. 31.

neurs achieve in a more flamboyant way. Bureaucrats, whether entrepreneurs or quiet survivors, often determine the shape of government policies. Their expertise and political interests that their departments and agencies invariably represent are taken seriously on Capitol Hill and in the White House. The Framers of the Constitution did not foresee the development of a politically powerful bureaucracy, which has become an important "fourth branch" of the government.

Judicial Politics

The Supreme Court appears at first glance to stand majestically above the political system, providing equal justice under the law to all who come before it. The Court presumably interprets rather than makes the law, and reasoned judgments rather than political passions supposedly determine judicial decisions.

The courts, however, have always been deeply involved in politics. The original advocates of a strong judiciary wanted the courts not only to have the authority to review congressional laws (as Alexander Hamilton stated in *The Federalist*, No. 78) but also, more importantly, to be able to uphold national power over the states. In the Republic's formative years, and much to the chagrin of the advocates of states' rights, Justice John Marshall's bold decisions unequivocally upheld national authority and supremacy. Marshall and his colleagues, Federalists and Republicans alike, adopted an active and interventionist stance that put the new national government on a firm foundation.

The Supreme Court has often helped to shape national policies. In the late nineteenth and early twentieth centuries, for example, it became deeply involved in economic policy, handing down decisions that favored large business corporations. In the 1930s, however, it came into direct conflict with President Franklin D. Roosevelt, when it ruled that major parts of his New Deal legislation were unconstitutional. This led to Roosevelt's ill-fated

scheme to make the Supreme Court more subject to political control by expanding presidential appointment authority to name new justices to supplant those over 70 years of age. (There were six septuagenarians on the Court when Roosevelt was elected, all of them opposed to the New Deal legislation.) Roosevelt's outspoken secretary of the interior, Harold Ickes, recalled in his memoirs the Cabinet meeting when the attack on the Court was launched. "The disposition of the Court always will be to whittle down all powers except its own," he wrote.[13] (Ickes wanted the president to go even further by seeking a constitutional amendment to curb the Court's "usurped" power of judicial review over Congress.)

The political controversy swirling around the Supreme Court subsided after 1937, when it decided to exercise judicial self-restraint in reviewing economic legislation. The period of relative tranquility was broken, however, when the Warren Court of the 1950s and 1960s took an unprecedented initiative in cases involving civil rights and civil liberties. The Court continued to be politically controversial even after the appointment of Chief Justice Warren Burger in 1969. President Richard M. Nixon, like Eisenhower, hoped to turn the Court in a conservative direction through the appointment of conservative justices. Nixon, however, again like Eisenhower, found that a justice, once appointed, is no longer beholden to the White House. Eisenhower had thought he was appointing a conservative in Earl Warren. Nixon, who had the opportunity of nominating four justices, was more successful in shifting the Court to a conservative viewpoint; but he could only have been shocked when one of his appointees, Harry Blackmun, wrote the Court's controversial opinion upholding the right to abortion.[14]

---

[13]Harold L. Ickes, *The Secret Diary of Harold L. Ickes*, Vol. II, *The Inside Struggle, 1936–1939* (New York: Simon and Schuster, 1954), p. 65.

[14]*Wallace v. Jaffree* (1985).

Reagan appointees, Sandra Day O'Connor, Antonin Scalia, and Anthony M. Kennedy, generally adhered to his conservative philosophy; however, even they did not always toe the conservative line. For example, Justices Scalia and Kennedy supported the majority opinion of liberal Justice William J. Brennan, Jr., in the controversial *Texas v. Johnson* (1989) case which held that flag-burning is a constitutionally protected freedom under the First Amendment. In other cases Sandra Day O'Connor, for example, wavered on the issue of abortion and sometimes appeared to lean toward the freedom of choice position which Reagan publicly abhorred. She also joined with liberal justices to overturn an Alabama law that authorized a moment of silence in public schools for "meditation or voluntary prayer," on the ground that it violated the First Amendment's establishment clause.

A majority viewpoint, expressed in a single opinion, is not easily attained on the Supreme Court. The justices often jockey among themselves for position and power. Associate Justice Harry Blackmun candidly commented:

[The nine Supreme Court Justices are] all prima donnas. . . .Somebody, perhaps it was Holmes, described us as "nine scorpions in a bottle." But whether they are prima donnas or not, at least the nine justices are necessarily, I think, by the time they arrive here, persons of fairly strong conviction and they're not going to be pushed around. They've had experience in the law and each of them feels that his attitude probably is the correct one.

Blackmun observed that in the process of reaching decisions,

I'm sure that we all play hardball a little too much on occasion. But the friendship and the mutual respect [among the justices] I believe continues. But if someone's going to play hardball with me, I'll play hardball back, if I firmly believe in the position, although I

suppose that if I were completely a gentleman I wouldn't.[15]

CITIZENS AND GOVERNMENT

Most citizens stand apart from the games political insiders play. But America's political system is a *constitutional democracy*, which both limits government and provides for popular participation in it. The Constitution makes the government dependent upon the people through elections and provides the basis for political pluralism in the First Amendment's protection of the freedoms of expression.

The Need for Government

Governments are organizations that have the authority, whether given to them by the people or not, to make and carry out laws that are binding upon the community. Through their courts governments decide individual cases and controversies arising under the law. Governments are necessary in the most fundamental sense to enable society to engage in collective or group action to accomplish goals that could not possibly be achieved by individuals acting alone. The need for national defense and for the regulation of commerce among the states were major reasons for the creation of the new national government under the Constitution.

While constitutions formally establish governmental institutions, defining their authority and the limits upon their powers, informal forces also have a profound influence upon government.

Informal Forces

The purposes for which a government establishes its authority and the scope of that authority are determined by political behav-

---

[15]Cable News Network, "A Justice Speaks Out, A Conversation with Harry A. Blackmun," December 4, 1982.

ior. People react to situations and problems in various ways, because they have different motives for doing things and many varied interests and concerns. They also have different standards on which they base their lives. Some people are religious, some scorn material things, and some place a high value on social position. These are all personal factors that influence people when they ask the government to do something for them or when they select representatives to act for them. These representatives, whether they be mayors, governors, Congress members, or the president, are subject to the same personal factors as the rest of the people.

It is these *informal forces* of politics that activate, restrain, and reshape the government and its authority. Indeed, they frequently have more to do with the nature and impact of government than do the formal institutions. Therefore, these informal forces should be examined carefully, along with the formal structure of government.

Unequal representation in elections. The importance of informal forces can be seen in the difficulties that will arise when a government attempts to set up a *formal mechanism* guaranteeing equal representation to each citizen. This mechanism is important to a *democracy* such as ours, where the authority to govern, or *sovereignty*, is shared equally, in principle, by all the people. If this guarantee were carried out to the letter in the United States, it would mean that 250 million people would decide just how the government should act in every instance. To make government a practical operation in this country and still enable the people to retain ultimate authority, a mechanism has been devised by which the people delegate their authority to a few representatives.

Consider a simple example of such a formal mechanism, a popular election, in which all the citizens of a community select a single chief executive invested with all the powers to run the community's government. If each citizen has the same opportunity to participate in the election, equal representation will have been accomplished. All the citizens will have had the same chance to determine who will exercise the government's powers on their behalf.

The informal forces that play on a voter as well as on a candidate will almost immediately confront this simple mechanism and cause it to break down. Due to personal motives, each person is going to want different criteria for setting up the election procedure. Are all the people to have a voice in the selection of candidates? If so, is it not then possible that there will be too many candidates? (In an extreme case all the citizens might select themselves.) Perhaps one candidate for each group of citizens? If there is to be a nominating committee to select candidates, then which qualifications should the members of such a committee have? Are all citizens to vote, regardless of age?

Unequal influence on governmental decisions. To carry the example a step further,

(Lou Erickson, *The Atlanta Journal*)

"Do you sometimes get the feeling . . . ?"
Citizens sometimes feel they have been run over by the government they are supposed to control.

once candidates have been elected and are in office, what guarantee is there that they will do what the people expect of them? And when they have decided what to do, how will they carry out their decisions?

It should be clear to everyone, from the items in the news or from personal experience, that the citizens of a community (local or nationwide) do not all participate in the decision-making process of government. There are few formal arrangements in our country, or anywhere in the world, for the direct participation of the people in making or applying governmental decisions. The candidate for a position in the government usually makes many vague promises, and some specific ones, as to the decisions he or she will make if elected. But commitments made in the heat of an election campaign are rarely fulfilled and are soon forgotten by most voters; in any event, they are certainly not binding.

The participation of citizens in governmental decisions is apt to be haphazard, unpredictable, and unregulated. Some people are invited by governmental officials to participate in policy deliberations. Others seek to inject themselves into the governmental process and do in fact influence the decisions of legislators and administrators. Still others, the vast majority of citizens, do not participate at all, and in many cases they do not even want to.

Expert citizen participation. In 1982 a National Commission on Social Security Reform, which had been appointed by President Reagan, held hearings on proposals to revise the financing of the social security system. The system was threatened with bankruptcy, and the Commission, which included prominent members of Congress such as Senator Robert Dole (R., Kan.) and Florida Congressman Claude Pepper (D.), wanted to know how the problem could best be solved. The changes that were being considered in the social security taxation system did not equally affect all groups; those in the middle- and upper-income levels in particular would be forced to pay large tax increases. The Commission invited to these hearings a few private citizens and governmental officials to give their opinions on what should be done. Most of these people were invited because they were regarded as experts on the subject by the members of the committee. No doubt there were other citizens, equally knowledgeable on the subject, who were unknown to the committee and thus not asked to participate. Thousands of other citizens would have liked to express their own views if they had been asked. A great many others who knew about the hearings would not have had any views to express, even if they had been invited. Still countless others were not even aware that the hearings were taking place.

This, then, is an example in which the participation of citizens in the governmental decision-making process was unequal. The invited persons, because they were regarded as experts, were able to participate in policy deliberations and possibly to influence a major congressional decision. Yet no one can claim that these were the best experts on social security; they merely happened to be known to those on the Commission.

Organized citizen participation. Another type of unequal representation takes place when private individuals or groups feel that their vital interests are affected by the government's action. Unlike the situation in which officials seek out the participation of citizens, in this case private citizens inject themselves into the process by trying to alter, block, or encourage official decisions. The factors that determine which type of informal influence is needed to obtain a desired government action, of course, vary from one situation to the next.

Much of this activity is undertaken by organized groups representing economic, professional, social, and ideological interests. Labor unions attempt to influence government decisions affecting wages, working conditions and hours, fringe benefits, strike regulations,

(Drawing by D. Fradon; © 1976 The New Yorker Magazine, Inc.)

As government expands, private interests seek to preserve their independence.

collective-bargaining procedures, and other such matters that are of importance to them. For example, while members of the United Auto Workers talk with congressional representatives, administrative officials, and White House aides, the Washington representatives of the auto manufacturers try to sway the same people toward their point of view.

Organizations that represent professional groups—the American Medical Association, the American Bar Association, the National Education Association, and others—also try to influence governmental decisions that may have an effect on the practice of their respective professions. One notable example has been the continuing interest of the American Medical Association (AMA) in the federal government's health insurance and health care programs. Under Medicare, for example, es-

tablished through legislation in 1965, all of the nation's older citizens are insured by the government for a substantial portion of their medical expenses. Naturally, physicians would be vitally concerned about such a program, and the AMA was actively involved, on their behalf, in the deliberations and legislative debates that took place before the enactment of Medicare. The AMA has continued its interest in health policy debates through the 1990s.

Other organizations, working on behalf of social and ideological causes, are continually aware of governmental policy that might concern their members. The National Association for the Advancement of Colored People, the Congress of Racial Equality, the National Urban League, and other groups that work to better the lot of black Americans try to affect policy, too. The American Legion, the Daughters of the American Revolution, the Veterans of Foreign Wars, and other patriotic organizations become active when they feel, for one reason or another, that fundamental American values and ideals are being threatened.

The Moral Majority and other evangelical Christian groups became an active political force in the 1980s. The Reverend Jerry Falwell and other fundamentalist Christian leaders organized the participation of their followers in the political process to achieve the goals they wanted—the defeat of candidates who disagreed with them; the election of those who supported their positions favoring a ban on abortion; prayer in public schools; the abolition of sex education; the defeat of the Equal Rights Amendment; the elimination of tax penalties for segregation in private education; and the rollback of school busing. Joining the Moral Majority on many issues was the National Conservative Political Action Committee (NCPAC), the vanguard of the New Right organized by Richard Viguerie, the master of direct-mail techniques for political advertising and raising funds.

Corporate, labor, trade association, professional, and many other groups organized Political Action Committees (PACs), beginning in the 1970s and expanding in the 1980s and early 1990s, to channel money into politics. PACs multiplied at an astonishing rate, growing from 608 in 1974 to over 4,000 in 1991. Corporations, labor unions, trade associations, cooperatives, and a host of nonconnected groups have organized PACs to spend in behalf of and make direct contributions to political candidates.

There are thousands of organized groups, representing almost every conceivable cause, interest, or concern, seeking to influence governmental policy. By gathering vocal and concerned people together, these organizations have a greater influence on policy than an equal number of unorganized individuals might have.

The impact of organized groups. The influence of special interests in government at all levels far exceeds individual influence in the political process. Not only have powerful groups been increasingly able to sway legislators due to their PAC contributions, but such groups are also directly represented in the bureaucracy. Most administrative agencies have been created because of the demands of special groups for representation and protection. The Departments of Agriculture, Commerce, Labor, Health and Human Services, and Transportation represent special clienteles. These departments generally look out for the interests of the groups they represent, fighting with both the president and Congress to increase budgetary allocations to "their" special interests. Departments and agencies want to bolster the groups within their jurisdictions because those groups provide the support that determines the clout—and perhaps even the survival—of agencies in the political arena.

Congressional committees are also often tied to special interests. Chairmen of committees constantly seek to protect their power within the legislative process, which requires the preservation of their committees. A sup-

portive relationship develops between committees and their outside constituencies—the groups within their legislative jurisdictions. The names of committees such as Agriculture, Armed Services, Aging, Veterans Affairs, Indian Affairs, Merchant Marine and Fisheries, and Post Office and Civil Service illustrate the groups they represent. Close ties often develop among committees, administrative agencies, and pressure groups within the same policy spheres as they strive to mutually support one another. Some political scientists have called this arrangement the "iron triangles" of power due to the solidity and permanency of the relationship.

Special interests are a legitimate and integral part of the Washington power establishment. Nevertheless, members of Congress, top-level bureaucrats, and the press periodically engage in rhetorical attacks on what is labeled "excessive pressure-group influence." Interest groups are favorite whipping boys in the political process. (Senator Edward Kennedy of Massachusetts once charged that the U.S. Congress is "the best that money can buy," referring to the growing PAC influence in congressional campaigns.) Congress has passed lobbying-regulation laws requiring the representatives of interest groups to register with the clerk of the House and the secretary of the Senate if they are directly attempting to influence legislation. The Campaign Finance Laws of the 1970s, passed due to Watergate revelations that interest groups (particularly corporations) were secretly channeling millions of dollars into the Nixon campaign chest, were designed to reduce the influence of money in politics. Ironically, the finance laws spurred the tremendous expansion of PACs, which became under the law the only legitimate channels through which groups could make substantial contributions to campaigns.

Presidents and their aides have often joined the chorus of criticism against the excessive influence of special interests. From the vantage point of the White House, interest-group power is often seen as a major obstacle to the enactment of the president's programs. Even before Congress had the chance to act, President Jimmy Carter remarked in a nationwide speech announcing his new energy program, "We can be sure that all the special interest groups in the country will attack the part of this plan that affects them directly." Carter was correct, as hundreds of lobbyists from oil companies, utilities, and other groups that would be affected by the new energy program deluged Capitol Hill to plead their causes. These in turn were joined by the legislative staffs of executive departments in the agencies whose interests were also affected. An energy program finally emerged after months of congressional debate, but many of the original proposals had been dropped or substantially modified.

Ronald Reagan's proposals for sweeping changes also met the opposition of special interests. Budget Director David Stockman, who developed most of the administration's budget-cutting proposals and represented the president on Capitol Hill, found that it was not easy to change the traditional ways of doing things in Washington. Stockman's proposed budget cuts deeply affected departments and agencies as well as their clientele groups. Convincing Cabinet secretaries that they would have to "bite the bullet" on budget cuts was no easy matter. Stockman commented on his proposals to cut deeply in the Department of Agriculture's subsidy programs: "I sympathize with Jack Block [the Secretary of Agriculture]. I forced him into a position that makes his life miserable over there. He's on the central team, he's not a departmental player, but the parochial politics of that department are fierce."[16] As it turned out, Agriculture was only a minor obstacle in the path of the enactment of Reagan's programs. Spe-

cial interests of all kinds had to be accommodated before budget and tax cuts could be passed. And the most powerful "iron triangle" of all—formed by the Defense Department and the Armaments Industry and Armed Services Committees—was left untouched. Reagan thus remained committed to an increase in defense expenditures, although Stockman saw defense cuts as necessary to reduce the federal deficit in a meaningful way.

President George Bush confronted the same problem as Reagan when he attempted to reduce the defense budget. Special interests from around the country mobilized to oppose cuts, and many congressmen joined in to oppose reductions in defense expenditures that would affect their districts, particularly the closing of military bases.

Only a very small proportion of all citizens are represented by organizations that express their views on any given issue. Few individuals spend much time considering how governmental policies could, or do, affect them, and most of those who think about these matters do not want to express themselves or do not know how to go about it. Consequently, a small minority of persons who do know how, and who are organized to pressure officials, have a far better chance of achieving their purposes through governmental processes.

Unequal application of the law. Just as citizens are represented unequally in the formulation of policy, policy, in turn, may be applied unequally to the citizens. Here, once again, informal forces are working upon the structure of government.

Sometimes policy is applied unevenly due to the motives of and pressures on officials who implement the law. Consider the application of laws against public inebriation in the case of a man who has had too much to drink and is wandering the streets at 3 a.m. If the man is white, neatly dressed, and in a middle-class residential area, a policeman will prob-

---

[16]William Greider, "The Education of David Stockman," *The Atlantic Monthly*, December 1981, p. 35.

ably see that he gets home safely so he can "sleep it off." If, instead, the man is black, unshaven, poorly dressed, and in a skid row area of the same city, he may very well be charged with disorderly conduct and thrown in jail. The two citizens have received different treatment under the same law and from the same police force.

Federal law-enforcement and regulatory agencies also have a great deal of discretion in the way they apply the law. Policy considerations and constraints of time and money often determine government actions. The Justice Department and the Federal Trade Commission, for example, are among the agencies that enforce the antitrust laws. Whether or not they seek to prevent business mergers is up to them. During the Reagan administration the Justice Department settled a major antitrust suit against the International Business Machines (IBM) Corporation for violation of antitrust laws that had been initiated years before, taking a decidedly more lenient view toward business mergers than had existed in most past administrations. The Federal Trade Commission, too, although it questioned some mergers, generally adopted a hands-off attitude as large corporations pursued profitable business combinations. Government policies produced the "merger-mania" that characterized the 1980s and profoundly affected not only business competition but also the entire financial structure. Corporate debt used to finance mergers increased to a point that alarmed some experts who saw in the possibility of a business slowdown a potential financial catastrophe if victorious corporations in the merger game could no longer meet their debt obligations.

The Reagan and Bush administrations' lenient attitude toward antitrust law enforcement contrasted with the strict enforcement that had characterized many past, particularly Democratic, presidencies. Presidential policies and the "tone" of different administrations often determine the way in which laws will be enforced, making their applications seem uneven over a period of time.

The seemingly unequal application of the laws may also result from limits on agency time and money. The Internal Revenue Service (IRS) cannot enforce the tax laws in the same way with respect to every individual and group. Some taxpayers are selected for audits, while others escape. The IRS, seeking to use its resources in the most efficient way, targets some groups of taxpayers for stricter enforcement than others. The law remains the same for all, but its impact differs due to administrative necessities.

Although government policy is frequently applied unevenly without any conscious or deliberate intent, at other times unequal treatment is actually sought and received by private citizens. Usually these are attempts to have officials overlook the law. Everyone has heard of someone who has had a traffic ticket "fixed." The individual may have done this by offering a bribe, by making a threat, by asking for a favor, or simply by drawing upon a personal friendship.

The use of influence to secure special application of the law takes place at all levels of government. In local government it extends beyond traffic violations to violations of gambling laws, sanitation, building, and fire codes, and so on. This kind of activity flourishes because the vast majority of citizens are usually indifferent to or uninformed about these matters. However, when an official has been too obvious in granting special favors or in his or her relations with underworld characters, informed citizens who have been following the case through the news media can express their displeasure at the ballot box, although they do not always do so.

The use of influence at the federal level, when it is exposed, is often quite dramatic. Although it is often assumed that corporate finances and contacts are intimately involved with daily political life in Washington, the exposure of specific instances often shocks the American public. The media quickly picks up scandals and gives their lurid details on the nightly news and the front page. *Time* featured one of Ronald Reagan's top aides, Michael Deaver, in a cover story about corruption and influence peddling in Washington. The Reagan administration produced more than the usual number of White House staffers, cabinet secretaries, and top administrative officials who faced charges of corruption in office. During Bush's first term it was not the White House but Congress that became embroiled in ethics and corruption controversies. House speaker Jim Wright (D., Tex.) was forced to step down from his exalted position and resigned from the House because of allegations that he had improperly accepted gifts and failed to report income in violation of House ethics rules. Other House members faced similar charges. On the other side of Capitol Hill five prominent senators faced allegations of unethical conduct and became known as the "Keating Five" after the name of a prominent savings and loan official in whose behalf they had intervened with government regulatory officials to prevent action against practices that led to one of the largest savings and loan bankruptcies in history.

Ethics controversies during the Reagan and Bush administrations were not unprecedented. As disclosures of corporate influence in the Nixon administration mounted during 1973, public disaffection with the President grew apace in public opinion polls. Public disillusionment with Nixon spread to Congress and to the government generally. The post-Watergate years saw Congress trying to restore public confidence in government by passing stricter laws governing campaign financing than had existed previously, to eliminate, among other things, the unequal influence of large contributors in political campaigns. Congress also attempted to get its own "house" in order through the passage of ethics codes governing its members, designed in part to prevent legislators from being more influenced by powerful outside groups than by their broad public constituencies. One proposal enacted for this purpose limited the outside income that Congress members and senators could earn from speaking engagements, so that particular groups could not sway members of Congress by offering large sums for appearances before them.

Although government uses its powers unevenly, many citizens do not take advantage of their own powers. Those citizens who are knowledgeable about their rights usually acquire the benefits that are offered. Some know, for example, that certain expenses can be deducted from their income tax, that when apprehended by a policeman they have the right to a lawyer, and that they are eligible for social security when they retire and workmen's compensation if they become disabled. Others do not know these things. They do not fully enjoy the benefits they are entitled to simply because they have never been informed about these opportunities. Other citizens may be unable, due to lack of money or personal connections, to take advantage of their rights in the courts. The person who can afford a highly skilled lawyer has an advantage over someone who cannot. Many people do not even vote, thus depriving themselves of any representation in the system.

The Meaning of American Government

The Framers of the Constitution carefully provided for effective but limited government. They recognized that a strong national government was essential to do what the states and the people could not accomplish separately and individually. But they also knew that constitutional limits, checks and balances,

(Drawing by Stevenson; © 1974 The New Yorker Magazine, Inc.)

"I guess he must have a lot of political pull."
If personal influence were allowed to be carried to extremes, such exaggerations might be more common.

were essential to prevent arbitrary and possibly despotic government. The Constitution and the formal institutions it creates have been complemented by informal forces that make American politics a rich mixture. The government is ultimately responsible to the people, and constant vigilance remains the price of liberty.

PART ONE

The Setting of the American System

It must not be assumed that the American political system, with all its strengths and weaknesses, bloomed overnight in a flurry of activity and debate during the Constitutional Convention at Philadelphia in 1787. The heritage from which Americans drew the ideas for their government was an old one—beginning with Plato and continuing through John Locke and Baron de Montesquieu. The Framers of the Constitution thus had a fairly well-developed body of political theory from which they took the ideas they incorporated into the Constitution.

Although the American democratic system is partly a product of the Revolution and of the political philosophies prevalent at that time, it has been developing ever since. With the remarkably flexible Constitution as its cornerstone, the American system has been constantly expanding to meet the needs of the people. Yet most of the basic principles that are still adhered to in the present system were born of solutions to problems the nation had while it was still new. Federalism, for example, was a response to the desires of the new states to retain some of the sovereignty they enjoyed when they first broke away from Great Britain. Defenders of states' rights today trace their arguments to these early battles for state sovereignty.

Other features of American democracy as it is known today were responses to changes in the political climate of the nation. The expansion of suffrage, for instance, came about in two steps. First, the Constitution was strengthened by adding certain amendments granting the vote to all citizens regardless of race or sex. But this proved to be not enough. The right to vote was guaranteed only after the passage of legislation enforcing these amendments.

Over 200 years have passed since the American Constitution was written, yet the document is still workable. Some amendments have been added for the purpose of defining phrases or statements in the original work. Others have been added in response to changes in American life. One amendment, the Twenty-first, was even added to negate a previous amendment, the Eighteenth, which was the product of a social outcry—Prohibition. Despite changes, the basic principles of the Constitution still stand.

The Ideological Foundations: Philosophies of Constitutional Democracy

The American democratic system has certain important general characteristics. Some of the more familiar are majority rule, government by the people, government conducted by delegates of the people, and a society that accepts the principle of equality. But no one of these characteristics, nor all of them together, can adequately suggest even the broad outlines of American democracy. The American political system is a blend of many features that cannot be labeled with a single term.

THE MEANING OF CONSTITUTIONAL DEMOCRACY

The most accurate phrase to describe the American political system is *constitutional democracy*. The American system of constitutional democracy is based upon an acceptance of certain basic and inherent rights of the people, such as the right to property, the right to freedom of speech and press, the right to freedom of religion, the right to assemble peace-

ably, the right to seek redress for grievances against the government, and the right to due process of law in criminal proceedings. The acceptance of these values of freedom and democracy leads to the participation in government, directly or indirectly, of those who uphold these values; it also makes possible the removal of leaders, as well as changes in the forms of government, if it is found that they are not serving the people.

Above all, constitutional democracy is based upon the rule of law. It is a government of laws, not of people, in which the personal aspirations of political leaders are to be kept within channels carefully designed to harness individual political ambition to the public interest. Within the broad forms of constitutional democracy leaders, interest groups, and political parties play a key role in shaping public policy. The informal balance of power among these political forces complements the formal separation of powers and the system of checks and balances of the Constitution.

The political values and governmental procedures implied by the term "constitu-

20

tional democracy" suggest the complexity of the American political system, which is at once both constitutional and democratic. To understand the philosophy of the system, each of these components must be examined separately.

A Definition of Democracy

The distinguishing feature of a democratic society is that sovereignty rests equally with all the people. (*Democracy* derives from the Greek word *dēmokratía, demos* meaning "people" and *kratos* meaning "power.") This does not mean that popular consent is required for every law, amendment to the Constitution, administrative regulation, or other action of government. What it does mean is that the whole structure of government rests on a foundation of popular support.

The principle of having sovereignty rest with the people means that governmental decisions are tested and evaluated by how well they meet the people's interests. Since a democratic government is established to meet the needs of the people, it acts properly and legitimately only if its actions are directed toward those needs.

There are other means by which a government can obtain results. Some societies, during times of religious fervor, have accepted the actions of their king and his government because they were certain that the sovereign acted in accordance with the word of God. Other governments have succeeded by threatening the people with physical force. In the United States, however, the government's performance is measured by the people according to how well it meets their needs.

America's democratic system is also called *constitutional* because governmental authority is limited first by the Constitution and then by other factors. These limitations prevent the government from controlling the people.

(From *The Herblock Book* [Beacon Press, 1952])

"We now bring you more late election returns."

(© Norris, *Vancouver Sun* /Rothco.)

" . . .Tomorrow a citizen can walk into this humble station, proud in his democratic right to choose his government, secure in the privacy of his choice, profoundly thankful for this hardwon freedom . . .and louse up his ballot."

A basic democratic right—the right to vote—may operate differently under contrasting political systems.

An Explanation of Constitutionalism

To call the American system of government simply a democracy, then, is to neglect one of its key distinguishing features—*constitutionalism*. A *constitutional system* is one in which the power of the government is kept in check by certain principles inherent in the system. These principles may be based on unwritten customs, traditions, and social facts, as in Great Britain, or they may be set forth in a written document, as in the United States.

One of the major checks on the power of American government is the guarantee of certain rights to individual citizens. Some of these rights are set forth in the Bill of Rights—the first ten amendments to the Constitution—which guarantees such basic freedoms as speech and press. The Constitution erects numerous obstacles to governmental action so that citizens are free to pursue most activities without interference from or control by the government. Moreover, there are only a few circumstances when the government can deny Americans their full rights as citizens. (Prisoners, for example, can be denied the right to vote.)

Another important restraining feature of American constitutionalism is the *separation of powers* among the different branches of the national government. As powerful as the president is, there are many things that he is not authorized to do. And even in the areas where he *is* authorized to act, he can be checked by the actions of Congress or the Supreme Court. These two branches of the national government are in turn checked by the president and by each other.

Similarly, the power of the national government is restrained by the *federal structure* of the political system with its division of authority between the national government and the fifty state governments. In fact, the national government's authority is limited to those powers expressly enumerated or reason-

ably implied in the Constitution; all other powers remain with the states.

Each of these checks on governmental authority in turn prevents any abuse of governmental power by a majority. The separation of powers and the federal structure serve to prevent the representatives of the majority from misusing the authority of government. The purpose of these restrictions is not only to protect the minority from being tyrannized by the majority but also to make governmental policy reflect a balanced expression of popular preferences. Thus, a narrow majority—such as 51 percent of the votes in Congress—cannot easily commit the society to a course of action that is severely in conflict with the wishes of a large minority.

Constitutional restraints also tend to check the swift execution of a policy that may have the backing of virtually everyone in the nation. This is sometimes desirable because policy may be an expression of emotionalism and may be regretted when passions have cooled and new information and ideas have become available. If the government were able to commit itself effortlessly to popular courses of action, it would often have to reverse policies and try to correct mistakes.

Despite the basic importance of constitutional restraints on governmental activity, the term *constitutional* alone is inadequate to describe the American system. Constitutionalism can be *monarchical*, as it was for many centuries in Great Britain when authority—divided between the king and Parliament—was restrained by some guaranteed rights such as those expressed in the Magna Carta. Constitutionalism can also be *aristocratic*, as it was in certain states during the early years of the American Republic when only adult males who were not slaves and who owned a certain amount of property could vote. However, the words *constitutional* and *democracy* both are needed to portray adequately the complexities, strengths, and weaknesses of the American political system. Our system is a constitutional one because of its sources of limitation; it is a democratic one because it responds, within limits, to the needs of the people.

The Dilemma of a Constitutional Democracy

In a constitutional democracy people evaluate the government's performance by asking: How well does it accomplish the public interest or work for the common good? Since each person has many interests that might conflict with the interests of others, it is difficult if not impossible to know how all these personal elements combine to form a "public interest" on any given matter. The strongest challenge to a constitutional democracy is that it must preserve the freedoms and interests of individuals while convincing them to act collectively for the benefit of all. This challenge is particularly difficult because it is impossible for both basic objectives to be fully realized at the same time. No action can be taken on behalf of the public interest without sacrificing someone's private interest or freedom. It would be impossible for any public policy to be so broad that it could answer every individual's demands. This perpetual dilemma of a constitutional democracy is solved only by compromise. Government must balance private and public interests. For example, part of the tax money of most citizens goes toward providing other citizens with food, shelter, and clothing. As long as the balance reflected in government policy remains tolerable to the majority of people, the system remains workable.

Styles of Representation

The mechanism of *representation* is probably the most important device for ensuring

(Drawing by Ed Arno; © 1982 The New Yorker Magazine, Inc.)

"Monarchy, while perhaps not necessarily the best form of government in principle, has always seemed the best form of government for me."
A person's interests, including occupation, often shape his or her views on government.

that both public and private needs are met. There are two styles of representation employed by elected officials, and the combined use of these styles makes balanced policies possible.

Direct representation. One style of representation commonly used by members of Congress and other legislators might be called *direct*, or *transmission-belt, representation*. Representatives who follow this style vote or express views in accordance with the dominant desires of their constituents. They serve as direct conveyors of these interests to the representative assembly. In the assembly these interests are registered and weighed against the preferences of the other represented constituencies.

If this method were employed by all members of Congress, the output of the legislative subsystem would be policies that are consistently weighted in favor of powerful interests. Overall balance among the many different needs and interests of the citizens would be difficult to achieve, and no one would be paying attention to matters of general concern.

Indirect representation. The other style of representation used in the American political system is *indirect*, or *virtual, representation*. Here representatives do not simply register the dominant views of their constituents. Instead, they assume that they have been chosen as representatives on the basis of their judgment as politicians and not because of their reliability as transmission belts. Thus they interpret their responsibility as requiring them to weigh carefully all issues of public policy in order to decide which course of action is in the best interests of the total society.

The concept of indirect representation was described particularly well by Edmund Burke in a speech to his electors in Bristol while he was campaigning for election to the British Parliament in the late eighteenth century:

To deliver an opinion is the right of all men; that of constituents is a weighty and respectable

opinion, which a representative ought always to rejoice to hear; and which he ought always most seriously to consider. But *authoritative* instructions; *mandates* issued, which the member is bound blindly and explicitly to obey, to vote and to argue for, though contrary to the clearest conviction of his judgment and conscience; these are things utterly unknown to the laws of this land, and which arise from a fundamental mistake of the whole order and tenor of our constitution.

Parliament is not a *congress* of ambassadors from different and hostile interests; which interests each must maintain, as an agent and advocate, against other agents and advocates; but parliament is a *deliberative* assembly of *one* nation, with *one* interest, that of the whole; where not local purposes, not local prejudices ought to guide, but the general good. . . .

Certainly gentlemen, it ought to be the happiness and glory of a representative, to live in the strictest union, the closest correspondence, and the most unreserved communication with his constituents. Their wishes ought to have great weight with him; their opinion high respect; their business unremitted attention. . . .But his unbiased opinion, his mature judgment, his enlightened conscience, he ought not to sacrifice to you, to any man, or to any set of men living.[1]

Mixture of styles. The operation of both styles of representation on all levels of the political system results in a reasonable balance of public and private interests. In this way specialized needs and desires as well as the welfare of the entire community are both taken into consideration. Direct representation enables legislators to help their own, smaller constituencies achieve goals that might otherwise be overlooked while protecting rights that might otherwise be violated. Indirect representation, on the other hand, helps produce policies that are designed to benefit the total

---

[1] Edmund Burke, *Burke's Politics: Selected Writings and Speeches of Edmund Burke on Reform, Revolution, and War,* eds. J. S. Hoffman and Paul Levack (New York: Knopf, 1949), pp. 115–116.

community, regardless of the advantage or disadvantage to any single constituency.

In Congress there is a continual struggle within most legislators as to the proper balance they should strike between constituent and national interests in their support of legislation and in other activities, such as investigations and case work arising out of complaints from constituents about government action. Freshman members of Congress, and senators in particular, are more attuned to serving their constituencies than to adopting stances independent of their constituencies in favor of national interests. More senior members of Congress feel freer to be Burkean representatives, exercising leadership on important issues of public policy even though

(Copyright © 1966 *The Chicago Sun-Times*. Reproduced by courtesy of Wil-Jo Associates, Inc., and Bill Mauldin.)

"Here, consensus! Here, consensus! Here, boy!"
No matter which style of representation a delegate chooses, can he or she discover what the public is thinking?

influential individuals and groups within their constituencies might have opposing points of view.

For example, Utah Republican Orrin Hatch, after becoming chairman of the powerful Senate Labor and Human Resources Committee in the 97th Congress (1981–1982), found himself acting more as a Burkean representative than he had in the past. After being elected in 1976, Hatch had voted with the coalition of conservative senators over 90 percent of the time. Since Utah is overwhelmingly Republican, Hatch's almost fanatical conservatism had been in line with the views of the mainstream of the state's voters. Thus they were happy with his stands against a nuclear moratorium, against fair housing, against federal funds for abortions under any circumstances, and against an increase in the windfall profits tax on oil companies. (The conservative Americans for Constitutional Action gave him a 96 percent approval rating, while the AFL-CIO Committee on Political Education [COPE] gave him only a 10 percent favorable mark.)

Hatch, like most members of Congress in powerful positions, found that as a committee chairman he could not please all sides. Even more importantly, to be an effective chairman he could not simply "rubber stamp" the positions of his conservative constituents on all issues. He developed a cordial relationship with the committee's ranking minority member, Senator Edward Kennedy of Massachusetts, who was diametrically opposed to him on virtually every issue coming before the panel. Hatch began to moderate his conservative views. On the issue of abortion, for example, instead of proposing an absolute constitutional ban he shepherded an amendment through his committee giving the federal and state governments joint regulatory authority. Antiabortion groups, which had always supported the Utah senator, were furious, calling him "a symbolic Hamlet miscast as Horatio-at-the-Bridge, with the enemy poised to pour across."[2] Hatch acted as a statesman rather than as a "transmission-belt legislator" on other issues as well. He worked out a compromise that prevented social welfare programs from being handed intact back to the states under block grants. Hatch was somewhat uncomfortable as a Burkean legislator, however, lamenting, "I have a difficult time in Utah. My folks out there don't realize I'm chairman of two of the most volatile committees [Labor and Human Resources; Constitution Subcommittee of the Judiciary]. This places me in the middle of controversy. . . . Utahans don't like controversy, but I cannot avoid it. I have to take positions."[3]

Admittedly, where legislative constituencies express strong feelings on particular issues of public policy, their representatives in Congress usually follow. Michigan Congressman John Dingell, a Democrat who has represented a heavily industrial, primarily automotive, manufacturing district in the Detroit area since 1956, is the undisputed voice of General Motors and Ford in Congress. For decades he almost singlehandedly defeated, stalled, or watered down environmental laws that would have imposed strict pollution controls on automobiles. Only when he saw the handwriting on the wall in 1989, in the form of strong presidential and congressional support for effective environmental legislation, did he agree as the decade of the 1990s opened to tone down his attacks and stop blocking environmental legislation in his powerful Energy and Commerce Committee.

The Burkean-trustee mode of representation comes into play most frequently where constituency opinion is divided, ambiguous, or even nonexistent on a particular issue. Given the scope and complexity of the issues before Congress, legislators often find that their constituencies do not give them concrete guidance on how they are to deal with many of the issues they confront. Legislative "statesmanship" can be exercised in a broad arena of public policy because when constituencies are divided, as is most often the case, legislators do not suffer retribution. Only the outright defiance of a clear majority in their constituencies is likely to lead to their defeat at the polls.

Government officials who are not legislators also employ two styles of representation. The president, for example, continually acts as both a direct and an indirect representative. On the one hand, he tries to pursue policies that coincide with national public opinion; on the other, he has the responsibility of doing whatever he feels is best for the nation, regardless of an action's immediate popularity. Naturally, each president, like each legislator, develops his own mixture of styles of representation, goals, and understanding of public needs. Presidents more than members of Congress, however, often find themselves propelled toward defending unpopular positions that they feel they must take in order to uphold the national interest. Characteristically, presidents tend to view their office more as a trusteeship than as a simple conduit for the expression of popular views. The flexibility of presidential decision making is heightened by the ambiguity of public opinion and by the inevitable conflict of views among the large number of interests in the president's national constituency.

President Ronald Reagan faced the same problem as other presidents when he found his popularity rapidly declining to a 43 percent approval rating before he had been in office even two years. His principal program, "supply-side economics," which consisted of large tax cuts and reductions in federal expenditures, seemed to be failing as unemployment rose and the economy stagnated. Senate Republican leader Howard Baker commented at the end of Reagan's first year: "I have not witnessed the sort of anger and indignation I am seeing today in a long time. Some of this is [even] coming from

[2]*Congressional Quarterly Weekly Report*, Vol. 39, No. 41 (Oct. 10, 1981), p. 1956.

[3]Ibid.

Republicans."[4] Reagan's response was that of a Burkean trustee: "I'm determined to stick with it ["Reaganomics"], and I will not be deterred by temporary economic changes."[5] Although the public's rating of President Reagan's performance had dropped more quickly than the ratings of most of his predecessors, his difficulties in the polls were characteristic of the modern presidency. Reagan, like most presidents, had essentially followed Lyndon B. Johnson's advice: "Every President must act on problems as they come to him. He must search out the best information available. He can seek the counsel of men whose wisdom and experience and judgment he values. But in the end, the President must decide, and he must do so on the basis of his judgment of what is best—for his nation and for the world."[6]

In many ways it is remarkable that American constitutional democracy has survived and flourished in spite of the problems that challenge it. The Americans who framed the Constitution deserve much credit for the strength and endurance of our political system, despite its flaws. They embodied certain principles in the Constitution that have enabled the system to work effectively throughout the varied stages of this nation's growth and development.

THE ORIGINS OF AMERICAN POLITICAL PHILOSOPHY

Throughout history examples can be found of political systems that have evolved without the guidance or adoption of any particular set of ideas or systematic philosophy. Governments established by force or by a personal claim to power have often been justified later by a philosophy created solely to support the already existing government. In the case of the United States, our government was deliberately designed by men who had already studied the writings of others on the philosophy of government. Furthermore, they were familiar with the experience of government in the colonies, in England, and on the European continent. The individuals who shaped the beginning of American government not only were students of philosophy, history, and government, but also were themselves deeply involved in politics. This firsthand experience of politics made a major contribution to the effective integration of theory and practice that was ultimately reflected in their design for the future of American government—the Constitution of 1787.

Historical Influences

Since the beginning of Western civilization, political philosophers have been concerned with an extensive range of questions about the processes of government. They have considered such matters as the nature of the state, the role of constitutions and other forms of law, the relationship between the people and their government, the best form of government to attain various goals, and the meaning of concepts like "the public interest" and "the common good."

Most of the issues of political philosophy were raised in one form or another as early as the fifth century b.c., first by Plato and later by Aristotle; and almost all of these issues remain important today. The emphasis of concern has shifted, of course, throughout history, fluctuating in accordance with economic and social changes. The issue of the relationship between church and state, for example, formed the core of much medieval philosophy, especially in the writings of Saint Augustine and Saint Thomas Aquinas. During this long period of Western history, most political thought was expressed as theology.

---

[4]Michael Kramer, "Reaganomics after Stockman," *New York,* November 30, 1981, p. 38.

[5]Ibid.

[6]Lyndon B. Johnson, *The Vantage Point* (New York: Holt, Rinehart and Winston, 1971), p. 531.

Later, after the bond between religion and politics had been weakened by the Reformation, political philosophy took on a more secular aspect.

The American political tradition was strongly influenced by the eighteenth-century Enlightenment in Europe and particularly in France. The "Enlightenment" refers to a time when philosophers turned away from total reliance upon Christian principles to explain the universe and human behavior. The "enlightened" philosophers based their theories on reason and the scientific method. The Enlightenment was the "Age of Reason," a time of great optimism that embodied the idea of progress in human affairs. Some of the great minds of this period, such as Turgot, Voltaire, and Condorcet, echoed the beliefs of eighteenth-century Americans, who conceived of progress as freedom.

The Science of Politics

The American Enlightenment reflected the same beliefs as its European counterparts in reason and the scientific method as the basis of progress. Americans of the eighteenth century applied the scientific approach when composing the Constitution in 1787. This approach was also used by Alexander Hamilton, James Madison, and John Jay in a series of 85 newspaper articles written during 1787 and 1788 to champion the cause of the Constitution. Addressed principally to the voters of New York, these papers were later published as a book, *The Federalist Papers,* in the spring of 1788. Hamilton and Madison took this opportunity to advance numerous arguments and to cite evidence supporting the principles embodied in the Constitution.

Much political writing in eighteenth-century America was "political science" in the sense in which the term is used today. However, the evidence used to support and justify political propositions was often crude, consisting of vague and unconvincing references to history and philosophy. At the same time, American political thinking could also be persuasive and logical, especially when

based on the practicality of the colonial experience. The fundamental principles of the American Constitution, such as the separation of powers, came from a combination of philosophy and experience.

Because American political thought is derived from many sources, it is a mixture of viewpoints. Thus it is difficult to speak of a unified American approach to political theory. The frontier environment, the maturing political life of the colonies, and the ensuing struggles with Great Britain and its agents in the colonies all produced lively political discussion leading to the evolvement of an American philosophy.

A Universe Governed by Science

Among the more widespread political ideas in eighteenth-century America was the concept that people can shape their governments, their societies, and their communities in accordance with the laws of nature. The source of this idea was a belief in the superiority of science, the scientific nature of the universe, and human ability to use reason to ascertain scientific laws that govern both physical and social behavior.

The American revolutionaries were particularly optimistic. They were men like Thomas Jefferson, who believed that human beings can better themselves through education and that societies can and should form governments in order to preserve liberty and the natural rights of all.

The Declaration of Independence clearly illustrated the prevailing assumptions. Even though the document was drafted by one man, Jefferson, it strongly mirrors the views of the period about government, the nature of the universe, and even the nature of humankind. Consider the opening paragraph:

When in the Course of human events, it becomes necessary for one people to dissolve the political bands which have connected them with another, and to assume among the Powers of

BOX 2.1　　　　　The Declaration of Independence　　　　29

The unanimous Declaration of the thirteen united States of America, In Congress, July 4, 1776

When in the Course of human events, it becomes necessary for one people to dissolve the political bands which have connected them with another, and to assume among the Powers of the earth, the separate and equal station to which the Laws of Nature and of Nature's God entitle them, a decent respect to the opinions of mankind requires that they should declare the causes which impel them to the separation.

We hold these truths to be self-evident, that all men are created equal, that they are endowed by their Creator with certain unalienable Rights, that among these are Life, Liberty, and the pursuit of Happiness. That to secure these rights, Governments are instituted among Men, deriving their just powers from the consent of the governed. That whenever any Form of Government becomes destructive of these ends, it is the Right of the People to alter or to abolish it, and to institute a new Government, laying its foundation on such principles and organizing its powers in such form, as to them shall seem most likely to effect their Safety and Happiness. Prudence, indeed, will dictate that Governments long established should not be changed for light and transient causes; and accordingly, all experience hath shown, that mankind are more disposed to suffer, while evils are sufferable, than to right themselves by abolishing the forms to which they are accustomed. But when a long train of abuses and usurpations, pursuing invariably the same Object, evinces a design to reduce them under absolute Despotism, it is their right, it is their duty, to throw off such Government, and to provide new Guards for their future security. — Such has been the patient sufferance of these Colonies; and such is now the necessity which constrains them to alter their former Systems of Government. The history of the present King of Great Britain is a history of repeated injuries and usurpations, all having in direct object the establishment of an absolute Tyranny over these States. To prove this, let Facts be submitted to a candid world. . . .

The Declaration of Independence, written by Thomas Jefferson, proclaimed the right of a people to dissolve its government when that government fails to protect the rights of individuals to life, liberty, and the pursuit of happiness.

---

the earth, the separate and equal station to which the Laws of Nature and of Nature's God entitle them, a decent respect to the opinions of mankind requires that they should declare the causes which impel them to the separation.

Note in this passage the phrases "Laws of Nature" and "Nature's God." They show a belief in a law higher than that of man—the law of nature. And emphasis is given to the idea of a god who is the source of that law. This "Nature's God" is not, however, a specific supreme being who is worshiped through a particular religious sect or institution.

Natural Rights

What is the content of the natural law that Jefferson mentions in the Declaration of Independence? This is clearly set forth in the second paragraph: " . . .all men are created equal . . .they are endowed by their Creator with certain unalienable Rights, that among these are Life, Liberty, and the pursuit of Happiness." (See Box 2.1, p. 29.)

Since the framing of the Declaration of Independence, there has been controversy over why Jefferson included "happiness" and not "property" among the natural rights. Clinton

(From *Cartoons* by Herbert Johnson. Copyright 1936 by Herbert Johnson.
Reprinted by permission of J. B. Lippincott Company.)

A Fine Old American Family
This cartoon from the 1930s shows the right of personal property as
one of the American system's fundamental ideals.

Rossiter, a modern historian, claims that Jefferson

was more than a felicitous penman when he proclaimed the "pursuit of happiness" to be a natural right of man, for by the time of the Declaration most thinkers agreed with him on this point. He was, however, something of a non-conformist in substituting this right for that of property. He alone flirted seriously with the advanced view that property was a social rather than a natural right.[7]

This interpretation notwithstanding, "property" rather than "happiness" would probably have been the more accurate reflection of the eighteenth-century view. Property

rights have always been considered by Americans to be among the most fundamental of all rights, and despite Jefferson's innovation the Founding Fathers did recognize the importance of the concept of private property. The Fifth Amendment to the Constitution, adopted in 1791, stipulates that private property cannot be taken by undue governmental action. Property was thus placed on an equal level with "life" and "liberty." And again, the Fourteenth Amendment, adopted in 1868, reaffirms the right of all citizens to "life, liberty, and property."

The influence of John Locke. The American concern for property is clearly traceable to the philosophy of John Locke, the seventeenth-century British political theorist. Locke based his theory of government on

---

[7]Clinton Rossiter, *Seedtime of the Republic* (New York: Harcourt, Brace & World, 1953), p. 380.

sources similar to those used by other political thinkers of the time, and he formulated his opinions during a period when the English were fighting for parliamentary supremacy.

A similar urgency to overthrow what was felt to be a despotic English government existed later in Revolutionary America. It was thus quite natural that Locke was read by educated colonial Americans, although he probably did not enjoy as wide an audience as is postulated by some historians. In any case, the colonists drew on the same tradition of political thought and experience that underlay Locke's thinking, and the similarity of his ideas to those espoused in eighteenth-century America is striking.

Certainly Jefferson and a number of his contemporaries studied Locke. In fact, one of Locke's works, *Second Treatise of Civil Government* (1690), was used by Jefferson in drafting the Declaration of Independence. (See Box 2.2, p. 32.)

A summary of Locke's treatise reveals the parallels between Locke and Jefferson. Locke believed that all men were reasonable enough to recognize the general principle, which he termed "the Natural Law," that no one ought to harm the life, liberty, or property of another. However, Locke also thought that in the absence of government each man would be continually exposed to uncertainties and fears for his safety, liberty, and possessions. Each man would then apply Natural Law to suit himself when his own interests were involved. And without government there would be no recognized, unbiased judge to turn to for an impartial settlement of resultant disputes. According to Locke, men therefore establish governments for their mutual protection and to settle their differences.

The real influence of Locke, however, goes far beyond the impact he had on Thomas Jefferson. There is little question that American political life has adhered to the fundamental principles contained in Locke's the-

ories about relations among people, society, and government. For example, Locke emphasized the sanctity of private property, and the strength of this principle in the American political tradition undoubtedly accounts in large measure for this nation's rejection of communism's central principle of collective ownership.

Of particular importance is the extent to which we Americans share Locke's views on the nature of humankind. All our governmental institutions, processes, and traditions are based on these views. Such concepts as the primacy of the individual, our inborn ability to exercise reason to discern truth and to arrive at the higher principles of order and justice, and political and social equality among people are all values Americans accept as Locke did. Although our belief in these ideals and values has not always been borne out by experience and practice, America is theoretically committed to them.

Montesquieu: the separation of powers. Eighteenth-century Americans admired many other political philosophers in addition to Locke. Probably most influential was the French Baron de Montesquieu, who wrote in the first half of the eighteenth century, during the reigns of Louis XIV and Louis XV. Clinton Rossiter says that "every literate colonist could quote [Montesquieu] to advantage, and . . .[his] exposition of the separation of powers was already making perfect sense to American minds."[8]

The most prominent feature of Montesquieu's political theory, the separation of powers, is contained in his famous *Spirit of the Laws*. In this work he points out the need for a government of law that incorporates a separation of powers to protect individual liberty. Montesquieu argued that by granting some authority to each branch of government—legislative, executive, and judicial—the

---

[8]Ibid., p. 359.

There is, therefore, secondly, another way whereby governments are dissolved, and that is, when the legislative, or the prince, either of them act contrary to their trust. . . .

Whensoever, therefore, the legislative shall transgress this fundamental rule of society, and either by ambition, fear, folly, or corruption, endeavour to grasp themselves, or put into the hands of any other, an absolute power over the lives, liberties, and estates of the people, by the breach of trust they forfeit the power the people had put into their hands for quite contrary ends, and it devolves to the people, who have a right to resume their original liberty, and by the establishment of a new legislative (such as they shall think fit), provide for their own safety and security, which is the end for which they are in society. What I have said here concerning the legislative in general holds true also concerning the supreme executor, who having a double trust put in him, both to have a part in the legislative and the supreme execution of the law, acts against both, when he goes about to set up his own arbitrary will as the law of the society. . . .

But it will be said this hypothesis lays a ferment for frequent rebellion. To which I answer:

First: no more than any other hypothesis. For when the people are made miserable, and find themselves exposed to the ill usage of arbitrary power, cry up their governors as much as you will for sons of Jupiter, let them be sacred and divine, descended or authorised from Heaven; give them out for whom or what you please, the same will happen. The people generally ill treated, and contrary to right, will be ready upon any occasion to ease themselves of a burden that sits heavy upon them. They will wish and seek for the opportunity, which in the change, weakness, and accidents of human affairs, seldom delays long to offer itself. He must have lived but a little while in the world, who has not seen examples of this in his time; and he must have read very little who cannot produce examples of it in all sorts of governments in the world.

Secondly: I answer, such revolutions happen not upon every little mismanagement in public affairs. Great mistakes in the ruling part, many wrong and inconvenient laws, and all the slips of human frailty will be borne by the people without mutiny or murmur. But if a long train of abuses, prevarications, and artifices, all tending the same way, make the design visible to the people, and they cannot but feel what they lie under, and see whither they are going, it is not to be wondered that they should then rouse themselves, and endeavour to put the rule into such hands which may secure to them the ends for which government was at first erected, and without which, ancient names and specious forms are so far from being better, that they are much worse than the state of Nature or pure anarchy; the inconveniences being all as great and as near, but the remedy farther off and more difficult.

Thirdly: I answer, that this power in the people of providing for their safety anew by a new legislative when their legislators have acted contrary to their trust by invading their property, is the best fence against rebellion, and the probablest means to hinder it.

John Locke, in 1690, argued that governments can be dissolved if they fail to protect the rights of citizens to life, liberty, and *property.*

power of one branch would offset or check the power of the other branches. Under such a system liberty would be protected from the excesses of government. He assumed that those who governed would use their power to the fullest but that the distribution of power would prevent tyranny.

Although Montesquieu attempted to use the British constitution as a model, the example was not a successful one because the British did not have the kind of separation of powers that he advocated. Nevertheless, his concept of a constitutional government founded on a separation of powers was important to the Americans.

Basic acceptance of the theorists. Although many political philosophers had an impact upon the American political tradition, Locke and Montesquieu can be considered the two principal exponents of the political philosophy adopted by Revolutionary America. Certainly there have been various divergent trends in American political thought. For example, Alexander Hamilton, James Madison, and John Adams—three major figures in the construction and development of our political system—did not share with Jefferson the optimistic Lockean view of human nature. They did, however, share a faith in the effectiveness of constitutional democracy, a faith that has been maintained since the formulation of the Constitution. Essentially this is a belief in government by the people under law.

In accordance with both Locke and Montesquieu, Americans have recognized that government can be too big and that some restraints must be imposed both on the will of the majority and on the government itself in order to preserve individual rights. Principally, these rights are expressed in the Constitution, which also provides that neither the power of government nor that of the people as expressed through government should be absolute.

CONSTITUTIONAL RESTRAINTS ON POPULAR SOVEREIGNTY

The American constitutional system is based on ideas, tradition, and political experience. These three factors have enabled the complex but flexible system to meet its many challenges successfully. On the one hand, the constitutional system has been a potent instrument for the execution of the popular will; on the other, it has been sufficiently fragmented and restrained to avoid the dangers of unchecked governmental power.

The merits of the American system can be assigned in part to the wisdom and judgment of the Framers of the Constitution. These men blended their knowledge of political philosophy with their own experience to compose a complex legal mechanism as the basis of a constitutional democracy.

The essays of *The Federalist* reveal the thinking that went into the process of justifying the Constitution. By examining some of these ideas it is possible to come to a better understanding of the fundamental structure of American government.

The Problem of Faction

The reasoning employed by some of the Framers is illustrated by James Madison in *The Federalist*, No. 10, in which he explored the problem of faction. In this paper, Madison defined *faction* as "a number of citizens, whether amounting to a majority or minority of the whole, who are united and actuated by some common impulse of passion, or of interest, adverse to the rights of other citizens, or to the permanent and aggregate [collective] interests of the community." In other words, Madison was implying that a faction was a special-interest group or party. He foresaw the development of factions through the inevitable conflict between individual and public interests. It was Madison's goal to construct a system of popular government that could overcome factions in promoting the general welfare. "The friend of popular governments," he said, "never finds himself so much alarmed for their character and fate, as when he contemplates their propensity to this dangerous vice [faction]."

One of the sources of faction that Madison identified was the unequal distribution of property. In *The Federalist*, No. 10, he said:

Those who hold, and those who are without property, have ever formed distinct interests in society. Those who are creditors, and those who are debtors, fall under a like discrimination. A landed interest, a manufacturing interest, a mercantile interest, a moneyed interest, with

many lesser interests, grow up of necessity in civilized nations, and divide them into different classes, actuated by different sentiments and views. The regulation of these various and interfering interests forms the principal task of modern legislation, and involves the spirit of party and faction in the necessary and ordinary operations of the government.

According to Madison, once a faction was able to influence government, serious consequences would result. This was because a faction, as he defined it, was opposed to the national interest. He felt that legislators and other members of the government would naturally act in accordance with the particular interests they represented and that gave them support. Madison clung to a skeptical view of human nature—namely, that politicians strive

(Burr Shafer. Copyright © 1965 Evelyn Shafer. Reprinted by permission of Evelyn Shafer and *Saturday Review*.)

Through History with J. Wesley Smith
"But I have my own well; why should I be taxed for Croton Reservoir?"
Of concern to all factions and interest groups, taxes have often been a source of political division.

for maximum power and the promotion of their own interests.

Controlling the effects of faction. It occurred to Madison that there were two possible ways to remove the causes of faction: first, "by destroying the liberty" that a faction needs in order to survive; and second, by making all citizens conform in their opinions, passions, and interests. However, he rejected both alternatives. The first method was of course unsatisfactory to Madison because he was committed to freedom and popular government. The second was because he was a realist and believed the "causes of faction"—fallibility and "self-love"—were inherent in human nature.

Having determined that "the *causes* of faction could not be removed," Madison concluded that "relief is only to be sought in the means of controlling its *effects*." One way to control the effects of faction, as he saw it, was to federate a number of popularly governed communities into one large representative republic. By doing this, Madison believed, the strength of any single faction would be diluted and the factions would balance out one another. He reasoned that some "factious leaders may kindle a flame within their particular states" but would "be unable to spread a general conflagration through the other states." In like manner, "a malady" might be contained within a country or district without spreading to the whole state.

In addition, Madison felt that a government of representatives would further control the effects of faction by refining and enlarging the views of the public. He thought that special interests would be watered down "by passing them through the medium of a chosen body of citizens, whose wisdom may best discern the true interest of their country, and whose patriotism and love of justice, will be least likely to temporary or partial considerations."

However, it is clearly not enough, Madison continued, to rely only on the federal structure and on the principle of representa-

tion to protect against faction. For "men of factious tempers, of local prejudices, or of sinister designs, may by intrigue, by corruption, or by other means, first obtain the suffrages, and then betray the interests of the people." Madison thus recognized that factions could develop within the governing body as well as among the citizens of the nation. What was to be done to check the power of special interests within the federal government itself? Consideration of this problem led him to support a separation of powers among the executive, legislative, and judicial branches of the national government.

THE DOCTRINE OF THE SEPARATION OF POWERS

Although the doctrine of the separation of powers had been tested to some extent during the colonial and post-Revolutionary periods, it was accepted largely on faith. Its effectiveness had not been proven. In *The Federalist*, No. 51, Madison noted that

the great security against a gradual concentration of the several powers in the same department [of government], consists in giving to those who administer each department, the necessary constitutional means, and personal motives, to resist encroachment of the others. . . . If men were angels, no government would be necessary. If angels were to govern men, neither external or internal controls on government would be necessary. In framing a government, which is to be administered by men over men, the great difficulty lies in this: You must first enable the government to control the governed; and in the next place, oblige it to control itself.

The government, then, should have two characteristics. First, it should have the power to govern the people; and second, it should be motivated to control itself. The delegates to the Constitutional Convention of 1787 had to decide which fundamental powers would be needed to govern the people and how these powers should be divided among the branches of government.

The Framers developed a practical arrangement of the separation of powers. First, the government had to be able to make laws, or legislate. This power was thus given to the legislature—the Congress. Second, it had to be able to administer or enforce the laws once they were made. This power was given to the executive—the president. And, third, the government had to be able to settle disputes that might arise either among the branches of government or between the people and the government. This power was given to the judiciary—the Supreme Court and the inferior courts under it. All this was not accomplished, however, without some debate among the Framers over just how this separation of powers was to be incorporated into the government itself.

Importance of the Legislative Branch

Of the three branches of government established by the Constitution, the legislative received the most attention from eighteenth-century American political theorists. This attention was an outgrowth of the emphasis placed on legislative bodies in Great Britain and in the colonies. The principle of parliamentary supremacy had been firmly established in Great Britain. And, although the colonies had been initially subject to strong executives (the royal governors), colonial assemblies had assumed increasing power during the eighteenth century. The belief that great power should be invested in legislative bodies was heightened when the state constitutions, written after the Revolution, granted even more formal power to the legislatures than had been held by the colonial assemblies. (In many instances these new state constitutions merely recognized legally what had already been practiced in fact.)

After the Revolution began, it soon became obvious that some form of national government would be necessary. In 1781 the Articles of Confederation, reflecting the strong belief in legislative power, set up a weak national government in which there was no executive or judicial branch. Although most legislative authority was retained by the states during the period from 1781 to 1787, the central government did manage to obtain some power in the national legislature.

When the Framers were forming a federal constitution in 1787, it was clear to them that significant authority had to be assigned to an executive if the new government was to have any strength at all. A great deal of effort was thus expended in convincing the populace of the various states that the new executive branch would not usurp essential power from the legislature. Since the power to govern had only recently been acquired by the states, they were jealously guarding this hard-won right.

Balance of Legislative and Executive Power

Eighteenth-century attitudes about an appropriate balance of power between the legislature and the executive were unclear. Some of the Framers felt the legislature should have a great portion of governmental authority. Since it would have the widest range of representation possible, the legislature would be the branch continuously responsive to the wishes of the people. Other Framers of the Constitution felt that the amount of authority required by any legislature for a popular form of government would almost certainly result in an abusive exercise of power. There were, then, conflicting opinions among different groups at the Constitutional Convention, and even within the minds of some individuals, over the extent of legislative and executive authority.

Thomas Jefferson, who did not attend the

Convention but who held ideas similar to those of many delegates, was known for his cautious approach to executive power. One of Jefferson's principal objections to the Constitution was that it did not limit the number of terms a president could serve. He feared that without such a limit any one man holding the office for a long time could make the executive far too strong. At the same time Jefferson was wary of placing too much power in the hands of the legislature. In his *Notes on the State of Virginia*, finished in 1782, five years before the Constitutional Convention, Jefferson expressed his dissatisfaction with what he considered a defect of the Virginia constitution.

All the powers of government, legislative, executive, and judiciary result to the legislative body. The concentrating of these in the same hands is precisely the definition of despotic government. . . .One hundred and seventy-three despots would surely be as oppressive as one.

Jefferson was equally concerned over the possibility that too much power would be delegated to the legislature by the national Constitution. He saw a separation of powers as the means of controlling the legislature.

The best eighteenth-century expression of the view that a constitutional democracy should have a dominant legislative branch is found in *The Federalist*. Although in these letters, both Madison and Hamilton favored a strong executive, they also explained the strength of the legislature. After all, they were trying to sell the Constitution to the newly formed states, where opposition to the document was largely centered on the fear of a powerful executive.

While the authors of *The Federalist* emphasized the power of the legislature, they also stressed the need for a strong and independent executive authority to balance this power. They coupled their emphasis on this need to control the legislature with an argument for the desirability of an independent and unified executive.

Over the years, many statements made in *The Federalist*, especially those regarding the potential of the legislative and executive branches, have been invalidated. Yet Madison and Hamilton, regardless of whether they believed in what they said, mirrored the opinions of many of their contemporaries. In *The Federalist*, No. 48, Madison expressed the view that legislative power is based on the fact that the legislature represents the people both directly and indirectly. The people are ultimately the greatest source of power. But according to Madison, there are also important reasons why legislative power is to be feared in a representative republic. The constitutional authority of the legislature is necessarily extensive. Tradition dictated, for example, that it would have control of the nation's purse strings. Thus the legislature would both appropriate money and possess the authority to levy taxes. Madison believed that these powers could not be taken from the legislature without subverting the very firmly established principles of constitutional democracy.

Contrast of the Three Branches

A highly revealing passage in *The Federalist*, No. 48, contrasted the potential powers of the legislature with those of the executive and judicial branches. Here Madison states that since the constitutional authority of the legislature is more extensive than that of the other government branches and "less susceptible to precise limits, it can, with the greater facility, mask, under complicated and indirect measures, the encroachment which it makes on the [other branches]."

The balance of power among the three branches of the American government has changed drastically since the Constitution was adopted. While Congress remains powerful, it can no longer be considered dominant. The powers of the president and the Supreme Court have grown enormously since the early days of our republic. And an administrative branch adds yet another dimension to our constitutional system. The balance of power among the branches of government is dynamic and changes over time to accommodate shifting political forces.

CASE STUDY 1

THE WAY DEMOCRACY WORKS IN AMERICA

In the 1830s Alexis de Tocqueville, a French statesman and aristocrat, visited the United States. Imbued with liberal ideas, he came to examine and write about American democracy. Everything he saw went into his two-volume masterpiece *Democracy in America*.

According to Tocqueville, political equality was the way of the future. But at the same time, he was frightened by what he had seen in Europe—the disintegration of the traditional social restraints of church, crown, and class. He was fearful that Americans as well as Europeans, hungry for the promises of the new democratic age, would create a "tyranny of the majority" far worse than the injustices of the old regime in France.

Unlimited Power of the Majority in the United States, and Its Consequences / *Alexis de Tocqueville*

In my opinion, the main evil of the present democratic institutions of the United States does not arise, as is often asserted in Europe, from their weakness, but from their irresistible strength. I am not so much alarmed at the excessive liberty which reigns in that country as at the inadequate securities which one finds there against tyranny.

When an individual or a party is wronged in the United States, to whom can he apply for redress? If to public opinion, public opinion constitutes the majority; if to the legislature, it represents the majority and implicitly obeys it; if to the executive power, it is appointed by the majority and serves as a passive tool in its hands. The public force consists of the majority under arms; the jury is the majority invested with the right of hearing judicial cases; and in certain states even the judges are elected by the majority. . . .

If, on the other hand, a legislative power could be so constituted as to represent the majority without necessarily being the slave of its passions, an executive so as to retain a proper share of author-

ity, and a judiciary so as to remain independent of the other two powers, a government would be formed which would still be democratic while incurring scarcely any risk of tyranny.

I do not say that there is a frequent use of tyranny in America at the present day; but I maintain that there is no sure barrier against it, and that the causes which mitigate the government there are to be found in the circumstances and the manners of the country more than in its laws. . . .

In the United States the omnipotence of the majority, which is favorable to the legal despotism of the legislature, likewise favors the arbitrary authority of the magistrate. The majority has absolute power both to make the laws and to watch over their execution; and as it has equal authority over those who are in power and the community at large, it considers public officers as its passive agents and readily confides to them the task of carrying out its designs. The details of their office and the privileges that they are to enjoy are rarely defined beforehand. It treats them as a master does his servants, since they are always at work in his sight and he can direct or reprimand them at any instant. . . .

. . .But in a nation where democratic institutions exist, organized like those of the United States, there is but one authority, one element of strength and success, with nothing beyond it.

In America the majority raises formidable barriers around the liberty of opinion; within these barriers an author may write what he pleases, but woe to him if he goes beyond them. . . .he is exposed to continued obloquy [censor] and persecution. His political career is closed forever, since he has offended the only authority that is able to open it . . .and those who think as he does keep quiet and move away. . . .He yields at length, overcome by the daily effort which he has to make, and subsides into silence, as if he felt remorse for having spoken the truth.

Fetters and headsmen were the coarse instruments that tyranny formerly employed. . . .Such is not the course adopted by tyranny in democratic republics; there the body is left free, and the soul is enslaved. The master no longer says: "You shall think as I do or you shall die"; but he says: "You are free to think differently from me and to retain your life, your property, and all that you possess; but you are henceforth a stranger among your people. You may retain your civil rights, but they will be useless to you, for you will never be chosen by your fellow citizens if you solicit their votes; and they will affect to scorn you if you ask for their esteem. You will remain among men, but you will be deprived of the rights of mankind. Your fellow creatures will shun you like an impure being; and even those who believe in your innocence will abandon you. . . ."

Absolute monarchies had dishonored despotism; let us beware lest democratic republic should reinstate it and render it less odious and degrading in the eyes of the many by making it still more onerous to the few.

. . .But the ruling power in the United States is not to be made game of. The smallest reproach irritates its sensibility, and the slightest joke that has any foundation in truth renders it indignant. . . .The majority lives in the perpetual utterance of self-applause, and there are certain truths which the Americans can learn only from strangers or from experience. . . .

It is important not to confuse stability with force, or the greatness of a thing with its duration. In democratic republics the power that directs so-ciety is not stable, for it often changes hands and assumes a new direction. But whichever way it turns, its force is almost irresistible. The governments of the American republics appear to me to be as much centralized as those of the absolute monarchies of Europe, and more energetic than they are. I do not, therefore, imagine that they will perish from weakness.

If ever the free institutions of America are destroyed, that event may be attributed to the omnipotence of the majority, which may at some future time urge the minorities to desperation and oblige them to have recourse to physical force. Anarchy will then be the result, but it will have been brought about by despotism.

Mr. Madison expresses the same opinion in *The Federalist*, No. 51. "It is of great importance in a republic, not only to guard the society against the oppression of its rulers, but to guard one part of the society against the injustice of the other part. Justice is the end of government. It is the end of civil society. It ever has been, and ever will be, pursued until it be obtained, or until liberty be lost in the pursuit. In a society, under the forms of which the stronger faction can readily unite and oppress the weaker, anarchy may as truly be said to reign as in a state of nature, where the weaker individual is not secured against the violence of the stronger: and as, in the latter state, even the stronger individuals are prompted by the uncertainty of their condition to submit to a government which may protect the weak as well as themselves, so, in the former state, will the more powerful factions be gradually induced by a like motive to wish for a government which will protect all parties, the weaker as well as the more powerful. . . ."

Jefferson also said: "The executive power in our government is not the only, perhaps not even the principal, object of my solicitude. The tyranny of the legislature is really the danger most to be feared, and will continue to be so for many years to come. The tyranny of the executive power will come in its turn, but at a more distant period."[9]

I am glad to cite the opinion of Jefferson upon this subject rather than that of any other, because I consider him the most powerful advocate democracy has ever had.

---

[9]Letter from Jefferson to Madison, March 15, 1789.

What Are the Real Advantages Which American Society Derives from a Democratic Government?

The political Constitution of the United States appears to me to be one of the forms of government that a democracy may adopt; but I do not regard the American Constitution as the best, or as the only one, that a democratic people may establish. In showing the advantages which the Americans derive from the government of democracy, I am therefore very far from affirming, or believing, that similar advantages can be obtained only from the same laws. . . .

Democratic laws generally tend to promote the welfare of the greatest possible number; for they emanate from the majority of the citizens, who are subject to error, but who cannot have an interest opposed to their own advantage. The laws of an aristocracy tend, on the contrary, to concentrate wealth and power in the hands of the minority; because an aristocracy, by its very nature, constitutes a minority. It may therefore be asserted, as a general proposition, that the purpose of a democracy in its legislation is more useful to humanity than that of an aristocracy. This, however, is the sum total of its advantages.

Aristocracies are infinitely more expert in the science of legislation than democracies ever can be. They are possessed of a self-control that protects them from the errors of temporary excitement; and they form far-reaching designs, which they know how to mature till a favorable opportunity arrives. Aristocratic government proceeds with the dexterity of art; it understands how to make the collective force of all its laws converge at the same time to a given point. Such is not the case with democracies, whose laws are almost always ineffective or inopportune. The means of democracy are therefore more imperfect than those of aristocracy, and the measures that it unwittingly adopts are frequently opposed to its own cause; but the object it has in view is more useful.

. . .The great advantage of the Americans consists in their being able to commit faults which they may afterwards repair.

. . .It is easy to perceive that American democracy frequently errs in the choice of the individuals to whom it entrusts the power of the administration; but it is more difficult to say why the state prospers under their rule. . . .As the people in democracies are more constantly vigilant in their af-

fairs and more jealous of their rights, they prevent their representatives from abandoning that general line of conduct which their own interest prescribes. . . .If the democratic magistrate is more apt to misuse his power, he possesses it for a shorter time. . . .It is no doubt of importance to the welfare of nations that they should be governed by men of talents and virtue; but it is perhaps still more important for them that the interests of those men should not differ from the interests of the community at large; for if such were the case, their virtues might become almost useless and their talents might be turned to a bad account. I have said that it is important that the interests of the persons in authority should not differ from or oppose the interests of the community at large; but I do not insist upon their having the same interests as the *whole* population, because I am not aware that such a state of things ever existed in any country.

No political form has hitherto been discovered that is equally favorable to the prosperity and the development of all the classes into which society is divided. These classes continue to form, as it were, so many distinct communities in the same nation; and experience has shown that it is no less dangerous to place the fate of these classes exclusively in the hands of any one of them than it is to make one people the arbiter of the destiny of another. . . .The advantage of democracy does not consist, therefore, as has sometimes been asserted, in favoring the prosperity of all, but simply in contributing to the well-being of the greatest number.

The men who are entrusted with the direction of public affairs in the United States are frequently inferior, in both capacity and morality, to those whom an aristocracy would raise to power. But their interest is identified and mingled with that of the majority of their fellow citizens. . . .

The maladministration of a democratic magistrate, moreover, is an isolated fact, which has influence only during the short period for which he is elected. Corruption and incapacity do not act as common interests which may connect men permanently with one another. . . .The vices of a magistrate in democratic states are usually wholly personal. . . .

In the United States, where public officers have

no class interests to promote, the general and constant influence of the government is beneficial, although the individuals who conduct it are frequently unskillful and sometimes contemptible. . . .In aristocratic governments public men may frequently do harm without intending it; and in democratic states they bring about good results of which they have never thought.

. . .But I maintain the most powerful and perhaps the only means that we still possess of interesting men in the welfare of their country is to make them partakers in the government. At the present time civic zeal seems to me to be inseparable from the exercise of political rights. . . .

How does it happen that in the United States, where the inhabitants have only recently immigrated to the land which they now occupy, and brought neither customs nor tradition with them there; where they met one another for the first time with no previous acquaintance; where, in short, the instinctive love of country can scarcely exist; how does it happen that everyone takes as zealous an interest in the affairs of his township, his county, and the whole state as if they were his own? It is because everyone, in his sphere, takes an active part in the government of society.

The lower orders in the United States understand the influence exercised by the general prosperity upon their own welfare; simple as this observation is, it is too rarely made by the people. Besides, they are accustomed to regard this prosperity as the fruit of their own exertions. . . .

. . .As the American participates in all that is done in his country, he thinks himself obliged to defend whatever may be censured in it; for it is not only his country that is then attacked, it is himself. . . .

After the general idea of virtue, I know no higher principle than that of right; or rather these two ideas are united in one. The idea of right is simply that of virtue introduced into the political world. . . .The man who submits to violence is debased by his compliance; but when he submits to that right of authority which he acknowledges in a fellow creature, he rises in some measure above the person who gives the command. There are no great men without virtue; and there are no great nations—it may almost be added, there would be no society—without respect for right; for what is a union of rational and intelligent beings who are held together only by the bond of force.

. . .In America, the lowest classes have conceived a very high notion of political rights, because they exercise those rights; and they refrain from attacking the rights of others in order that their own may not be violated. While in Europe the same classes sometimes resist even the supreme power, the American submits without a murmur to the authority of the pettiest magistrate.

. . .The government of a democracy brings the notion of political rights to the level of the humblest citizens, just as the dissemination of wealth brings the notion of property within the reach of all men; to my mind, this is one of its greatest advantages. I do not say it is easy to teach men how to exercise political rights, but I maintain that, when it is possible, the effects which result from it are highly important; and I add that, if there ever was a time at which such an attempt ought to be made, that time is now. . . .When I am told that the laws are weak and the people are turbulent, that passions are excited and the authority of virtue is paralyzed, and therefore no measures must be taken to increase the rights of the democracy, I reply that for these very reasons some measures of the kind ought to be taken; and I believe that governments are still more interested in taking them than society at large, for governments may perish, but society cannot die.

But I do not wish to exaggerate the example that America furnishes. There the people were invested with political rights at a time when they could not be abused, for the inhabitants were few in number and simple in their manners. As they have increased, the Americans have not augmented the power of the democracy; they have rather extended its domain. . . .

It cannot be repeated too often that nothing is more fertile in prodigies than the art of being free; but there is nothing more arduous than the apprenticeship of liberty. It is not so with despotism; despotism often promises to make amends for a thousand previous ills; it supports the right, it protects the oppressed, and it maintains public order. The nation is lulled by the temporary prosperity that it produces, until it is roused to a sense of its misery. Liberty, on the contrary, is generally established with difficulty in the midst of storms; it is perfected by civil discord; and its benefits cannot be appreciated until it is already old. . . .

In the United States, except slaves, servants,

and paupers supported by the townships, there is no class of persons who do not exercise the elective franchise and who do not indirectly contribute to make the laws. Those who wish to attack the laws must consequently either change the opinion of the nation or trample upon its decision.

A second reason, which is still more direct and weighty, may be adduced: in the United States everyone is personally interested in enforcing the obedience of the whole community to the law; for as the minority may shortly rally the majority to its principles, it is interested in professing that respect for the decrees of the legislator which it may soon have occasion to claim for its own. . . .

. . .Among civilized nations, only those who have nothing to lose ever revolt; and if the laws of a democracy are not always worthy of respect, they are always respected; for those who usually infringe the laws cannot fail to obey those which they have themselves made and by which they are benefited; while the citizens who might be interested in their infraction are induced, by their character and station, to submit to the decisions of the legislature, whatever they may be. Besides, the people in America obey the law, not only because it is their own work, but because it may be changed if it is harmful; a law is observed because, first, it is a self-imposed evil, and secondly, it is an evil of transient duration. . . .

It is not impossible to conceive the surprising liberty that the Americans enjoy; some ideas may likewise be formed of their extreme equality; but the political activity that pervades the United States must be seen in order to be understood. No sooner do you set foot upon American ground than you are stunned by a kind of tumult; a confused clamor is heard on every side, and a thousand simultaneous voices demand the satisfaction of their social wants. . . .

The great political agitation of American legislative bodies, which is the only one that attracts the attention of foreigners, is a mere episode, or a sort of continuation, of that universal movement which originates in the lowest classes of the people and extends successively to all the ranks of society. It is impossible to spend more effort in the pursuit of happiness.

It is difficult to say what place is taken up in the life of an inhabitant of the United States by his concern for politics. To take a hand in the regulation of society and to discuss it is his biggest concern and, so to speak, the only pleasure an American knows. This feeling pervades the most trifling habits of life; even the women frequently attend public meetings and listen to political harangues as a recreation from their household labors. . . .

In some countries, the inhabitants seem unwilling to avail themselves of the political privileges which the law gives them; it would seem that they set too high a value upon their time to spend it on the interests of the community; and they shut themselves up in a narrow selfishness, marked out by four sunk fences and a quickset hedge. But if an American were condemned to confine his activity to his own affairs, he would be robbed of one half of his existence; he would feel an immense void in the life which he is accustomed to lead, and his wretchedness would be unbearable. I am persuaded that if ever a despotism should be established in America, it will be more difficult to overcome the habits that freedom has formed than to conquer the love of freedom itself. . . .

When the opponents of democracy assert that a single man performs what he undertakes better than the government of all, it appears to me that they are right. The government of an individual, supposing an equality of knowledge on either side, is more consistent, more persevering, more uniform, and more accurate in details than that of a multitude, and it selects with more discrimination the men whom it employs. If any deny this, they have never seen a democratic government, or have judged upon partial evidence. . . .Democracy does not give the people the most skillful government, but it produces what the ablest governments are frequently unable to create: namely, an all-pervading and restless activity, a superabundant force, and an energy which is inseparable from it and which may, however unfavorable circumstances may be, produce wonders. These are the true advantages of democracy.

. . .If, in short, you are of the opinion that the principal object of a government is not to confer the greatest possible power and glory upon the body of the nation, but to ensure the greatest enjoyment and to avoid the most misery to each of the individuals who compose it—if such be your desire, then equalize the conditions of men and establish democratic institutions.

CHAPTER THREE

The Constitutional Framework

The core of a nation's political philosophy is usually expressed in its constitution. In some countries, such as the United States, the nation's political philosophy has been set down in a single written document. In other countries, such as Great Britain, the substance of the nation's political philosophy consists of separate laws and judicial decisions made over hundreds of years. Thus Great Britain's "constitution" is simply all those laws and court opinions that are still in force. Regardless of whether a country's constitution is found in a single document or in many, it is usually extended through interpretation, customs, and traditions.

To endure over a period of time, a written document must contain thought and language so flexible as to be interpreted differently by succeeding generations to meet new governmental requirements, changes in social customs, and technological advances. This does not mean that a particular principle stated in a constitution will be ignored when it is no longer needed. It means the principle will simply be redefined to fit the new situations as they come into being. For this reason, *interpretation* of a constitution is often as important as the formal document itself.

The United States Constitution is a lean document that has been expanded substantially both through judicial interpretation and political practice. As the oldest written constitution in existence, it has proved well able to withstand the test of time.

THE CONSTITUTIONAL CONVENTION OF 1787

Although an examination of the constitutional document itself will not yield an understanding of our system today, it is helpful to view the Constitution in its original historical context. The lesson to be learned from such a historical analysis is that there had been no obvious, clear-cut governmental goal prior to the Constitutional Convention of 1787. Rather there were many conflicting ideas about what should be included in the nation's system. These divergent interests were compromised through a series of hard-bargaining sessions, and the final product was a "patchwork" of many views.

Autonomy of the States

American politics in the period immediately preceding the Constitutional Convention was characterized by a firmly embedded tradition of state sovereignty or self-government. Even before they became independent the states had exercised a substantial autonomy within the loose framework of British controls. One of the major causes of the American Revolution was the fact that when the British mercantilist system was tightened it clashed head-on with the spirit of self-government that had developed in the colonies. And during the Revolution each state tended to regard itself as a separate entity, recruiting its own militia and negotiating separate treaties.

43

"It is unthinkable that the citizens of Rhode Island should ever surrender their sovereignty to some central authority located way off in Philadelphia."
The issue of states' rights has been perennial in American politics.

This condition continued throughout the period of national government under the Articles of Confederation. Having no authority to raise taxes or duties, to provide a national currency, regulate interstate commerce and trade, or to enforce its laws, Congress thus had little power over the states or the American people. In 1786, for instance, Daniel Shays led a rebellion of Massachusetts debtors who were irate about being threatened with prison and the loss of their property. Massachusetts had to put down the rebellion by using a private army supported by individual contributions. It had thus become evident that a stronger national government was the only alternative to complete anarchy.

The desire for state sovereignty, however, was still prevalent when the Constitutional Convention met in 1787. Alexander Hamilton, in addressing the Convention, pointed out that the states "constantly pursue internal in-terests adverse to those of the whole." A new national government, continued Hamilton, would require the "habitual attachment of the people," but the "whole force of this tie is on the side of the state government. Its sovereignty is immediately before the eyes of the people; its protection is immediately enjoyed by them."[1] Hamilton's views reflected those of many other convention delegates. James Madison, for example, declared that "In spite of every precaution, the general [national] government would be in perpetual danger of encroachments from the state government."[2] The majority of delegates agreed with the nationalistic views of Madison and Hamilton and voted for the creation of a national government that would have complete authority to carry out

---

[1]Max Ferrand, *The Records of the Federal Convention of 1787*, 4 vols. (New Haven: Yale University Press, 1911), 1:284.
[2]Ibid., p. 356.

specific enumerated powers. The Constitution, however, did not settle the issue of the balance of national versus state power, which continued to be fought in the courts, on the battlefields, and in the political process itself.

Convention Disputes

Although the Framers of the Constitution were primarily dedicated to the establishment of a stronger national government, there were also regional interests that had to be incorporated into this new governmental system. The Constitution, drafted in 1787 and subsequently ratified, was an attempt to satisfy the needs for a strong central government without offending regional concerns and advocates of state sovereignty.

The key to the drafting of the Constitution was compromise. Without this compromise between different personal, political, and economic interests, the national organization would never have been possible. Because each state had interests that it wanted to protect against encroachment by the others, disputes arose at the Convention over the proper structure and powers of the new government. The large states were pitted against the small states, the Southern slave states opposed the Northern free states, and the merchant states were in conflict with the agrarian states.

Large versus small states. Delegates from the large states maintained that representation in the national legislature should be apportioned according to the population of each state. A plan to organize the government along these lines was presented by Edmund Randolph of Virginia. The Virginia delegation, which included George Washington and James Madison in addition to Randolph, had originally provided much of the impetus and guidance for the Convention. As a member of the assembly that had framed Virginia's constitution, and as attorney general and governor of the state, Randolph was a man of extensive political experience. But he was still only 34 years old when he put forward the plan upon which the Constitution ultimately,

with many compromises, was based. As he rose to present his proposal on May 29, 1787, he "expressed his regret that it should fall to him rather than those who were of longer standing in life and political experience, to open the great subject of their mission; but as the Convention had originated from Virginia, and his colleagues supposed that some proposition was expected from them, they had imposed this task on him."[3] Under the Virginia Plan (as Randolph's proposal became known), there was to be a *bicameral*, or two-house, legislature. Representation in the lower house would be according to each state's resident population. The upper house was to be selected by the members of the lower house. This arrangement would have given the larger states such as Virginia, which was the most populated, a dominant role in the new government.

The interests of the smaller states were stated in the New Jersey Plan, devised under the direction of William Paterson. Whereas the Virginia Plan was designed to establish a strong national government, the New Jersey Plan would have allowed continuation of a government more akin to the confederation already established. The Articles of Confederation would have been maintained, and a few amendments would have been added that would have only slightly increased the powers of the national government. The *unicameral*, or one-house, legislature of the Articles of Confederation was to be retained, with each state having the same number of representatives. Paterson also proposed that the legislature be authorized to request state revenues in proportion to the population of the states and to regulate commerce among the states. Undoubtedly the New Jersey Plan would have resulted in a weak national government with real power retained by the states.

Historian Max Ferrand has commented that "It would seem as if the New Jersey Plan

---

[3]Charles Warren, *The Making of the Constitution* (Cambridge, Mass.: Harvard University Press, 1947), pp. 139–140.

more nearly represented what most of the delegates supposed that they were sent to do." Had Paterson's plan been presented at the beginning of the Convention, the delegates might well have adopted it. But, comments Ferrand, "in the course of the two weeks' discussion, many of the delegates had become accustomed to what might well have appeared to them at the outset as somewhat radical ideas."[4] Paterson argued that his plan "accorded, first with the powers of the Convention, and second with the sentiments of the people." He did not want a radical departure from the Articles of Confederation that would undermine the powers of the states. "Our object," he said, "is not such a government as may be best in itself, but such a one as our constituents have authorized us to prepare and as they will approve."[5]

Alexander Hamilton, however, expressed the views of a majority of the delegates who rejected the New Jersey Plan. Addressing the Convention several days after Paterson's proposal was presented, he declared:

We owed it to our country to do, on this emergency, whatever we should deem essential to its happiness. The states sent us here to provide for the exigencies of the Union. To rely on and propose any plan not adequate to these exigencies, merely because it was not clearly within our powers, would be to sacrifice the means to the end. . . .The great question is, what provisions shall we make for the happiness of our country?[6]

Amazingly enough in light of the emphasis on the separation of powers eventually written into the Constitution, both of the original plans advocated selection of the executive by the legislature. Supporters of the New Jersey Plan reasoned that a weak executive

would mean increased power for the small states since under the plan these states would be equally represented with the large states in a unicameral legislature. Backers of the Virginia Plan believed that if their plan was accepted the large states would hold sway in both branches of the bicameral legislature and would thereby control the executive.

Economic disputes. The other two basic arguments during the Convention set the Northern states against the Southern states. Most of the Northern states were concerned with manufacturing, and they needed to import raw materials for their factories. They therefore wanted imports to be favored. Southern plantation owners, however, wanted the government to favor exports and to allow continuation of the slave trade as a source of cheap labor so that their products would have an advantage with overseas buyers. Naturally, each region wanted to control the government that would make the decisions about treaties and taxes.

Slave versus nonslave. The South was also concerned about how slaves would be counted in the population. It would make a tremendous difference if representation in the new government were based on population. Northerners, who did not possess the great numbers of slaves that the Southerners had, wanted slaves counted only as property for tax purposes.

The Compromises

The differences between the large and small states, and between free and slave states, as well as contrasting commercial and agricultural interests, threatened to dissolve the Constitutional Convention as the heat of the Philadelphia summer intensified. During a particularly acrimonious session on June 30, James Wilson, a prominent Philadelphian, who had been a signer of the Declaration of Independence and a member of the Congress of the Confederation, admonished the delegates, "Can we forget for whom we are form-

---

[4]Max Ferrand, *The Framing of the Constitution* (New Haven: Yale University Press, 1913), p. 89.

[5]Warren, *The Making of the Constitution*, p. 223.

[6]Ibid.

ing a government? Is it for men, or for the imaginary beings called states?"[7] Madison suggested that the major dispute was not between the large and the small states but between the free and slaveholding states. Benjamin Franklin, the oldest delegate at 81 years of age, attempted to smooth the "ruffled feathers" of the younger delegates, a role he played throughout the Convention. He told them, "When a broad table is to be made, and the edges of planks do not fit, the artist takes a little from both, and makes a good joint. In like manner, here, both sides must part with some of their demands, in order that they may join in some accommodating proposition."[8]

The tension among the delegates was at a peak by July 2, when a compromise was suggested by Oliver Ellsworth, a Connecticut lawyer and member of Congress, who had also served as a judge on the highest state court. To accommodate the interests of the small states Ellsworth proposed that there be equal representation of states in the upper house of Congress, the Senate. The vote of the Convention was tied, with five states on each side. It is an irony of history that if all the delegates had attended that day the proposal would undoubtedly have been defeated and the Convention dissolved by a walk-out of the small states. As historian Charles Warren has written:

The absence of two men changed the fate of the Constitution and the whole future history of the country. William Pierce of Georgia had gone to New York to attend Congress (and incidentally to fight a duel) [Alexander Hamilton served as a second to Pierce's adversary in the duel], Daniel of St. Thomas Jenifer of Maryland was late in taking his seat that morning. Both of these men were opposed to equality of representation. Had Pierce been present, the vote of Georgia would not have been equally divided and would have been cast with the large states. Had Jenifer been

more prompt in his attendance, the vote of Maryland (actually cast by Luther Martin with the small states) would have been divided, and the large states would have prevailed on the motion.[9]

So the Convention was not dissolved, but it was still at an impasse. South Carolina delegates Charles Pinckney and General Charles C. Pinckney proposed the formation of a committee composed of one member from each state to study and make recommendations to resolve the disputes. Although Randolph, among others, had little hope for its success, the committee was duly appointed. Drawing and elaborating on the Ellsworth proposal, the committee quickly arrived at a solution known as the "Great Compromise" (or the "Connecticut Compromise"). The plan called first for a bicameral legislature, which most of the Framers had already accepted. Delegates to the lower house would be elected by the people from each state in proportion to the population. As a compromise between Northern and Southern interests, each slave was to be counted as three-fifths of a person for representation and taxation purposes. All states would have equal representation in the upper house, with two members chosen by each state legislature.

The Great Compromise carried on July 16 by a vote of five states to four. The Massachusetts delegation was evenly split and therefore did not cast a vote. Had Massachusetts voted no, the Convention would have dissolved. Maryland delegate Luther Martin later commented, "We were on the verge of dissolution, scarce held together by the strength of a hair, though the public papers were announcing our extreme unanimity."[10] Charles Warren notes that:

The acceptance of the compromise by the Convention was not only a victory for the

---

[7]Ibid., p. 256.
[8]Ibid., p. 257.

[9]Ibid., pp. 261–262.
[10]Ibid., p. 309.

smaller states; but it was a deserved victory. Writers on the Constitution have been prone to regard the leaders of these states as a somewhat fractious minority, to pacify whom the nationalists were forced to yield their more valid principle of proportional representation. But the fact is that the small states were entirely right in believing that no such form of government as the nationalists, at that stage in the Convention, were supporting would ever be accepted by the people of the states—a government in which the national legislature was practically supreme, having power to elect the executive and the judiciary, and to negative all state laws which it deemed to infringe on its own and practically national powers. Students of the Constitution often forget now that at the time of the compromise the form of the government proposed was radically different from that which was finally adopted. The degree of the change marked the wisdom of the delegates in modifying their views after repeated discussions of the effects of their proposals upon the varying needs and conditions of the different states and the country at large.[11]

The Great Compromise saved the Convention, but other compromises were required to settle the controversies between the commercial interests of the North and the agrarian ones of the South. These controversies involved the powers to regulate commerce and to tax, as well as the procedure for admitting new states. The "commerce compromise" provided that the national government would have the power to regulate commerce, but that it could not tax exports nor could the states tax imports. The South exported agricultural products and feared that federal power to tax exports would be harmful to Southern economic interests. This part of the commerce compromise thus answered a regional need.

On the other hand, those who favored a strong national union won a victory in this compromise by adding the provision prohibiting state taxation of imports from other states or from abroad. Undoubtedly such a power

would have been used by many states against the products of their neighbors as well as against foreign goods. The ability of Congress to regulate commerce later became a potent weapon in the arsenal of those who favored the expansion of national power over the states.

Opposing views over the ability of the national government to tax were finally settled by providing that direct taxation would be apportioned according to population and that all excise taxes were to be uniform. Arguments over methods for admitting new states were resolved by passing the problem on to the new Congress.

Finally there was the issue of slavery. In addition to the three-fifths compromise of the Great Compromise, a series of other accords dealt with this issue. The Framers agreed that the slave trade could continue until 1808 without interference, that fugitive slaves would be returned to their masters, and that whether or not slavery would be extended to the new states would be determined by Congress.

The Signing of the Constitution

Monday, September 17, 1787, was the historic day when the delegates to the Convention, with three exceptions, placed their signatures on the document which they had worked so hard to produce. Benjamin Franklin, the Convention's sage, sought the unanimity of all in support of the Constitution in an opening address that he had written but that was read by James Wilson:

I confess that there are several parts of this Constitution which I do not at present approve, but I am not sure I shall never approve them. For having lived long, I have experienced many instances of being obliged by better information, or fuller consideration, to change opinions even on important subjects, which I once thought right but found to be otherwise. It is, therefore, that the older I grow, the more apt I am to doubt my own judgment, and to pay more respect to the judgment of others. . . .Thus, I

_____
[11]Ibid., p. 310.

(Drawing by Weber; ©1988 The New Yorker Magazine, Inc.)

"As a matter of fact, I have read the Constitution, and, frankly, I don't get it."

consent, Sir, to this Constitution, because I expect no better, and because I am not sure, that it is not the best. . . .On the whole, Sir, I cannot help expressing a wish that every member of the Convention who may still have objections to it, would, with me, on this occasion doubt a little of his own infallibility, and to make manifest our unanimity, put his name to this instrument.[12]

Thirty-eight of the forty-one members present in Independence Hall signed the Constitution, and the signature of a thirty-ninth, John

Dickinson, who was absent, was affixed at his request by one of the other delegates. Ironically, in the end Edmund Randolph refused to sign the Constitution. He felt that it granted too much power to the national government and would cause the new political system to "end in tyranny."

Benjamin Franklin appropriately closed the signing session as he looked toward the painting of a sunrise behind the chair at the front of the chamber, which had been occupied by John Hancock as president of the Continental Congress and by George Washington

_____
[12]Ibid., p. 709.

in presiding over the Convention. "I have," he said, "often and often in the course of this session, and the vicissitudes of my hopes and fears as to its issue, looked at that [painting] behind the President, without being able to tell whether it was rising or setting; but now at length I have the happiness to know that it is a rising and not a setting sun."[13]

Ratification

After the Constitution had been drafted and accepted by the Framers, it had to be ratified by the states that would make up the new Republic. Ratification by nine states was required to put the document into operation. Conventions were called in 12 of the 13 states in 1787 and 1788. (Rhode Island, the only state that refused to call a ratifying convention at the time, finally ratified the Constitution in 1790 after it had been accepted by the other states.)

Extensive debates over ratification took place within the states. Objections were made that the Constitution lacked a list of individual freedoms, that the executive was too powerful, and that the proposed new national government would be able to submerge state interests. Many, but certainly not all, Federalists, as nationalists, agreed with the anti-Federalists, the opponents of the Constitution, that a bill of rights should be added. A tacit condition for the ratification of the Constitution in many state conventions was the promise of such a bill that would limit the authority of the national government to curtail the civil liberties and rights of citizens. The anti-Federalists also proposed numerous other amendments. Among these were an amendment to prevent the reelection of the president, the requirement of a two-thirds vote of both branches of Congress to ratify treaties, and a provision to restrain the power of the federal judiciary. However, debate and objections notwithstanding, the opponents of the

strong and effective national government that would later be established by the Constitution lost their battle primarily due to the skillful political compromises already worked out by the delegates to the Convention. The ninth state convention (New Hampshire) ratified the Constitution on June 21, 1788.

THE MACHINERY OF CONSTITUTIONAL LIMITATION

The Constitution was seen primarily as an instrument to strengthen the national government, but the Framers were wise enough to realize that certain provisions would also have to be made to protect individual rights from an overwhelmingly powerful government. The power of the government, then, would have to be divided, and no one branch would be allowed to gain an excess of authority over the others.

As conceived by the Founding Fathers, the mainstay of constitutional limitation was to be the separation of powers. To this end, they set up three distinct branches of government with independent constituencies. (One of these branches, the Congress, or legislative, was further divided into two parts—each with a different constituency and, in some instances, separate authority.)

A System of Checks and Balances

The Framers of the Constitution did not consider it sufficient, however, merely to separate the legislative, executive, and judicial functions of government from one another. They felt that despotic or arbitrary government could be prevented only through a system of *checks and balances* by which each branch possessed the ability to curtail excessive power by either of the other two. Consequently, an essential ingredient of the separation of powers was the sharing of some powers among

---

[13]Ibid., p. 717.

the branches of the government. Without some shared functions, it was feared that each branch would possess unlimited authority in its respective sphere.

For example, with a complete separation of powers, an uncontrolled judicial system could be unjust in deciding cases and controversies. Likewise, the legislature could make laws and expect them to be obeyed, even if they deprived some citizens of their freedoms. Equally, the president, if unlimited, could appoint incompetent ambassadors or negotiate unreasonable treaties without any restraints.

The Constitution, then, created a relationship of restraints among the three branches of the government. In *The Federalist*, No. 47, Madison outlined the arguments that were made against the Constitution by those who thought that it blended the functions of government too much. He answered these arguments in this same paper and elsewhere in *The Federalist*.

First, Madison recognized that "the accumulation of all powers, legislative, executive, and judiciary, in the same hands, whether hereditary, self-appointed, or elective, may justly be pronounced the very definition of tyranny." He then went on to point out the debt that the Framers owed to Montesquieu, whom he thought should be credited with the authorship of the doctrine of separation of powers. According to Madison, the French theorist had never envisioned that the three branches of government should be completely separated. Rather, he interpreted Montesquieu as implying that the principles of a "free constitution" would be lost only in the extreme situation where "the *whole* power of one department is exercised by the same hands which possess the *whole* power of another department." Thus some interlinking of responsibility, or sharing of functions, among the branches of government had to be expected.

Illustrations of shared functions. The sharing of functions among the branches can be demonstrated in several ways. (See Figure 3.1.) For example, the president's power to

veto, or refuse to sign, a bill is essentially a legislative function. This means the president can stop a bill from becoming law. Presidential responsibility for recommending legislation and providing general information about the state of the union are other examples of the executive's legislative function. And over the years the responsibilities and powers of the president in these areas have increased.

Likewise, Congress can interfere at many points with the exercise of the executive function. For example, although the president has the authority to write treaties and appoint ambassadors, the Senate must approve all treaties and appointments.

Congress is also empowered to decide the nature of the federal judiciary's organization— the number of courts and judges, their location, and the way they operate. Congress can decide which types of decisions made by the lower courts can be appealed to the Supreme Court. Thus Congress shares some of the judicial function.

All these provisions set up the machinery by which legislative, executive, and judicial branches check and balance one another's power, with no one branch dominating the government.

Implications of the Separation of Powers

It is easy enough to understand the concept of separation of powers with its system of checks and balances. But how has this doctrine actually worked?

Legislative implications. For many observers, the most potent limitation resulting from the Constitution is the Supreme Court's power to overrule Congress through judicial review. However, historically this power has been sparingly enforced. Since the drafting of the Constitution the Supreme Court has ruled unconstitutional only about 80 acts of Congress, and since 1937 the Court has so ruled only once. The latter unusual case involved congressional removal of American citizenship

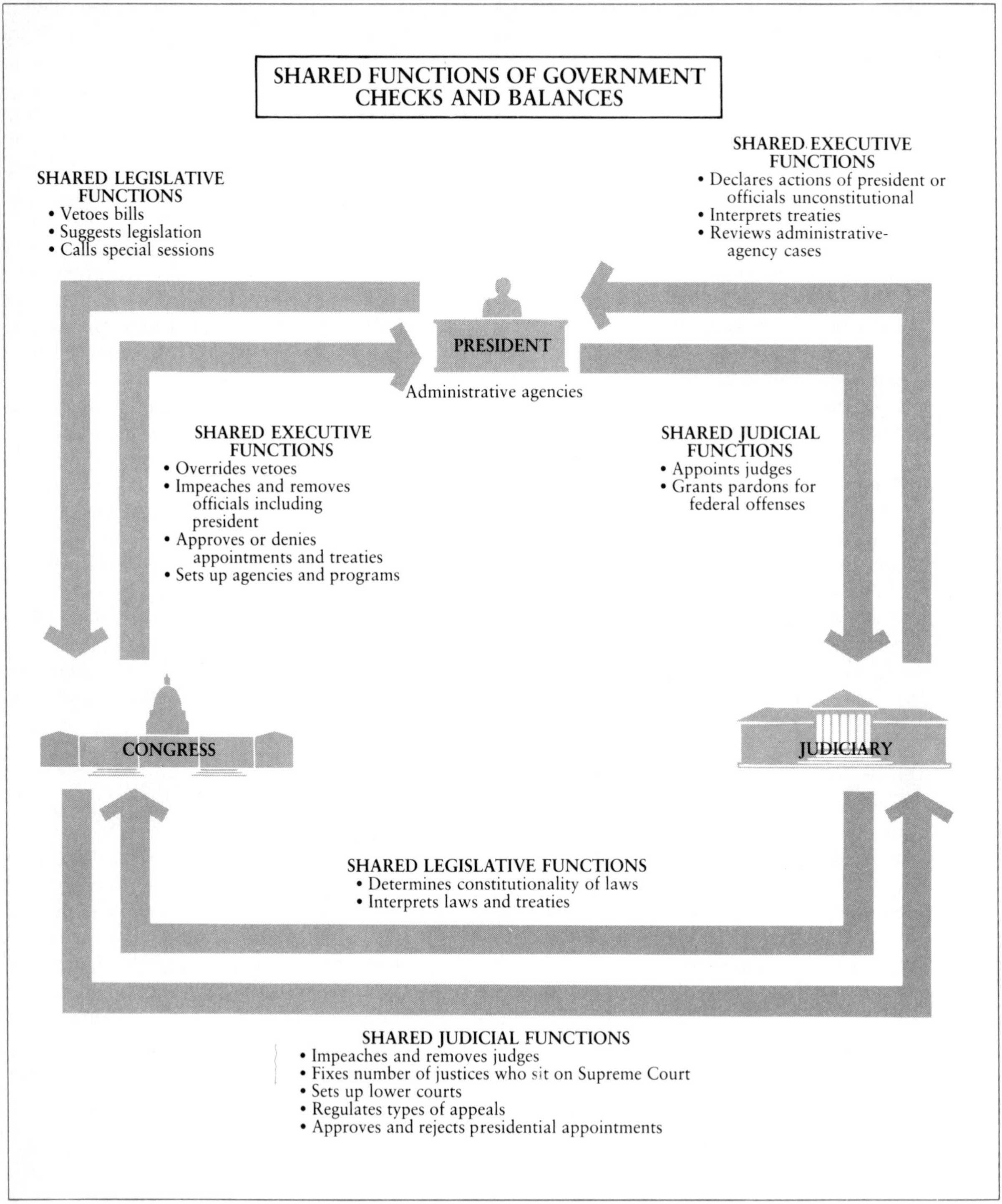

SHARED FUNCTIONS OF GOVERNMENT CHECKS AND BALANCES

SHARED LEGISLATIVE FUNCTIONS
- Vetoes bills
- Suggests legislation
- Calls special sessions

SHARED EXECUTIVE FUNCTIONS
- Declares actions of president or officials unconstitutional
- Interprets treaties
- Reviews administrative-agency cases

PRESIDENT

Administrative agencies

SHARED EXECUTIVE FUNCTIONS
- Overrides vetoes
- Impeaches and removes officials including president
- Approves or denies appointments and treaties
- Sets up agencies and programs

SHARED JUDICIAL FUNCTIONS
- Appoints judges
- Grants pardons for federal offenses

CONGRESS

JUDICIARY

SHARED LEGISLATIVE FUNCTIONS
- Determines constitutionality of laws
- Interprets laws and treaties

SHARED JUDICIAL FUNCTIONS
- Impeaches and removes judges
- Fixes number of justices who sit on Supreme Court
- Sets up lower courts
- Regulates types of appeals
- Approves and rejects presidential appointments

FIGURE 3.1

from draft evaders going to other countries.

As far as the lawmaking process itself is concerned, the most significant constitutional limitation has been the requirement that the president and Congress agree on major legislation. If they do not, the president can use his veto, and the Congress has recourse to a number of delaying tactics. This has caused many stalemates in the legislative process. The nature of their legislative functions alone—with the president asking for the passage of certain legislation and the Congress debating its value—frequently puts these two branches at loggerheads.

In addition, the separate branches of government draw their supports and demands from different constituencies. As a result they often work for separate interests. The president represents the welfare of the nation as a whole, whereas the senators are responsible for the interests of their states, and the representatives are responsible for local interests within their states.

Disagreement between the president and Congress may be even greater when they represent opposing political parties. Usually one party controls Congress with a majority of members in both houses. However, occasionally there is a party split between the House and the Senate. This was the situation after the 1980 election, when the Senate became Republican for the first time since 1953 while the House remained Democratic. As a result, President Ronald Reagan found that his programs encountered far smoother sailing in the Senate under his own party than in the opposition-controlled House. There is always tension between the two sides of Capitol Hill, regardless of party lineups. The Framers of the Constitution clearly foresaw that the division of power in a bicameral legislature would be an important check upon Congress.

The bureaucracy as an outgrowth. There is little doubt that the separation of powers has encouraged the development of the federal bureaucracy, which consists of the many administrative and regulatory agencies that enforce most government legislation. Ordinarily it is thought that since the president appoints agency directors and commission members the administrative agencies are under his legal control. Since he also has the power to appoint cabinet members and is commander in chief of the armed forces, it would appear that a unit such as the Defense Department would report to him. However, this is not entirely true.

The Constitution endowed Congress with the power to create and structure the organization of the bureaucracy. When this right is coupled with the jealousy of Congress towards presidential power, it is only natural that Congress should place the administrative agencies outside the direct supervision of the

(Copyright © 1966 *The Chicago Sun-Times*. Reproduced by courtesy of Wil-Jo Associates, Inc., and Bill Mauldin.)

Top Hat
Although it is under civilian control, the Pentagon does make some decisions on military matters by itself.

White House. Actually, although Congress can provide for agency control by the president, it has relinquished its power only in special circumstances. In any case, Congress retains control of the agencies' budgets and can call for investigations whenever it feels agencies are overstepping their bounds. In addition, the decisions of independent agencies are subject to court review, and the judiciary can overturn agency decisions that it considers unconstitutional or beyond the legal authority of the originating body. In this way the administrative agencies are checked by two other branches of the government.

Over the years, the presidential-congressional separation has brought about the development of a diversified bureaucracy without very definite lines of responsibility. As a result, some commissions are considered the agents of Congress, some are directly under presidential supervision, and some are a combination of both. The freedom of administrative agencies to act within their own spheres of authority stems directly from this uncertainty in the line of control. The Constitution did not establish any clear lines of authority over the bureaucracy. Instead it simply empowered the Congress to oppose the president in this and other areas. As a result, the bureaucracy is not clearly responsible to any one of the three branches and in effect has become a "fourth branch" of the government, often acting in a semi-independent fashion. The development of this semi-autonomous authority is undoubtedly one of the most far-reaching consequences of the separation of powers.

CONSTITUTIONAL OBSTACLES TO MAJORITY RULE

A very important benefit of the separation of powers is its tendency to prevent the accumulation of political strength by an overpowering majority or faction at the national level. If a political party or faction, or even a popular majority, were to acquire too much power it might monopolize the government and suppress any disagreeing minorities.

Because the various branches of the government are based on different constituencies and have different sources of authority, each branch has reason for and the means of resisting encroachments by the other branches. There are several constitutional obstacles to the superiority of the majority, or *majority rule*, whether it be by a party, a particularly large interest group, or a popular consensus.

Passage of Legislation

First, the bicameral nature of the legislature itself is an important limitation to majority rule. To become law, a bill must pass both houses of Congress. Therefore, two majorities—one in each house—are needed for passage. Since the House of Representatives and the Senate have different constituencies, passage is not always easy, and often the two houses are in sharp disagreement.

The President's Veto Power

Second, once a bill has been passed by both houses of Congress it must be signed by the president. If the president vetoes the bill, its chances of becoming law are slim. A presidential veto can be overridden only by a two-thirds majority of Congress in both houses, and since most members of Congress who belong to the president's own party are reluctant to override his veto, two-thirds majorities are very difficult to achieve. In the nineteenth century, Henry Clay, the colorful Speaker of the House of Representatives, expressed the view still held by many legislators on Capitol Hill when he proclaimed that the president's veto power would very likely make him the "ruler of the nation."[14] (Clay

---

[14]Wildred E. Brinkley, *President and Congress* (New York: Vintage Books, 1962), p. 86.

proposed a constitutional amendment that would have enabled Congress to override a presidential veto by a simple majority vote.)

Presidential clout notwithstanding, when the partisan "pull" of the chief executive is counteracted by contrasting forces in the separate congressional constituencies, a veto can in fact be overridden. In 1973 a resurgent Congress, weary of unilateral presidential initiatives in committing American troops to "police actions" abroad, easily overrode President Richard Nixon's veto of the War Powers Resolution (1973) that limited the president's authority to make war. At the time Congress was solidly Democratic and highly partisan in opposition to the president on the eve of the Watergate revelations. Even during the Nixon administration, however, only five out of a total of forty vetoes were overridden.

Under the terms of Article I, Section 7, of the Constitution, the president must return a bill to the Congress within 10 days after it is passed if he wishes to veto it. The only exception to this rule is if Congress adjourns within 10 days after the passage of legislation. In such cases the president can resort to a *pocket veto*. This means that he can refuse to take action on the bill, or "pocket" it, in which case it automatically dies.

In recent years the pressure of business in Congress has been so great that much legislation has not been passed until the end of a session. This situation substantially increases the ability of the president to control the outcome of legislation by making use of the pocket veto.

The Administration of Laws

Third, in almost all cases, after legislation has been approved by both Congress and the president, the authority to carry it out is delegated to a particular administrative agency. Since administrative agencies have acquired a certain amount of independent responsibility, they are generally able to *interpret* policy without referring back to Congress or the president for guidance.

Because an administrative agency is for the most part able to ignore the broad constituencies of the branches that originally approved the legislation, a bill may be given a shape not foreseen by its original proponents. Thus whereas majority rule may have been expressed on the presidential or congressional level, it may be reshaped by the enacting agency, which responds to its own particular constituency, which includes special congressional committees more than Congress as a whole. Administrative constituencies, therefore, can actually limit the effectiveness of majority rule. For example, the Department of Agriculture tries to protect the interests of farmers by maintaining high price supports, even though the majority, who are consumers, would benefit from lower prices.

Extraordinary Majorities

Fourth, the Constitution also limits majority rule under certain circumstances by insisting on *extraordinary majorities*, or majorities well above 50 percent. The presidential veto of legislation can be overridden only by a two-thirds majority in both houses of Congress. An impeached president can be convicted in the Senate only on the approval of a two-thirds majority. An amendment to the Constitution can be proposed by Congress only if there is a two-thirds majority in favor or upon the application of two-thirds of the state legislatures. To be ratified, amendments must have the approval of three-fourths of the state legislatures or conventions (depending upon which method of ratification is specified by Congress). Finally, treaties negotiated by the president can go into effect only with the approval of two-thirds of the Senate.

Such constitutional insistence on extraordinary majorities has occasionally defied the will of the majority in some important instances. Certainly the impeachment of President Andrew Johnson in 1868 would have resulted in his removal from office if a simple majority of the Senate had been permitted. (In this instance, the vote in the Senate was 35 to

19, only one vote short of the two-thirds majority required for conviction.) Another historical example was President Woodrow Wilson's unsuccessful attempt to win Senate approval for United States membership in the League of Nations in 1920. Acceptance of League membership required ratification of a treaty by a two-thirds majority in the Senate, and although a majority in the Senate approved of the League the two-thirds requirement was not attained.

Extraordinary-majority provisions have also affected the amendment process. Although amendments with substantial congressional support have usually been ratified easily, the provisions for extraordinary majorities have in fact prevented some ratifications. The controversial Bricker Amendment, for example, which would have limited the president's authority to make treaties and executive agreements, failed by only one vote to get the necessary two-thirds majority in the Senate in 1954. The requirement that three-fourths of the states must approve of amendments was a hurdle that the Equal Rights Amendment of 1972 could not overcome.

Civil Liberties and Civil Rights

Fifth, the Constitution restrains the will of the majority by creating some "hands-off" areas in which even the government is not allowed to interfere. The most notable of these are the freedoms and rights cited in the Bill of Rights. The Bill of Rights was not part of the original Constitution as drafted in 1787, but its addition was an implicit condition of ratification of the Constitution. Several states had feared that the creation of a new national government would impinge upon the rights of citizens of the states, and a bill of rights had been promised to allay the fears of delegates to the ratifying convention on this point.[15] The

Bill of Rights—the first 10 amendments to the Constitution—was originally intended to limit only actions of the *national government* that abridged the enumerated rights and freedoms of individuals. However, it became the basis for a vast expansion of civil-liberties and civil-rights protections in the twentieth century when extended, under the "due-process" clause of the Fourteenth Amendment (originally adopted in 1868), to state actions.[16] As the Supreme Court expanded the protections afforded under the Bill of Rights to include protections against state action, it was in effect acting against the will of the majority of the states, who had not seen fit to include such protections in their own constitutions or laws.

In the last few decades the Supreme Court has made many "unpopular" decisions expanding civil rights and civil liberties. Although the opposition to these decisions cannot be measured precisely, it is generally assumed that the Supreme Court often was not in agreement with a large segment of the American people. Even though the Court is now proceeding more slowly in the advancement of civil rights, there is no doubt that it is committed to protecting the freedoms described in the Bill of Rights. This line of interpretation has favored minorities generally and has run counter to the will of a large portion of the populace.

Besides the Bill of Rights, the Constitution contains other specific prohibitions on governmental exercise of power over individuals. These limit the power of majorities, regardless of how firm a hold they may have on the machinery of government. Most of the prohibitions have to do with criminal law. For ex-

---

[15]The addition of a separate bill of rights to the Constitution was by no means universally accepted. Alexander Hamilton, in paper No. 84 of *The Federalist*, argued vigorously that the Constitution of 1787 contained sufficient

safeguards against governmental intrusion upon the rights of citizens, and that an additional bill of rights would be not only gratuitous but also dangerous, because it would imply that the national government had inherent powers to abridge the rights of citizens if protections against such intrusion were not explicitly enumerated.

[16]For a discussion of the "nationalization" of the Bill of Rights, see Chapter 4, pp. 76–87.

ample, Congress is not permitted, except in the case of rebellion or invasion, to suspend an individual's right to a *writ of habeas corpus*. This right directs that any official must show the reason for detaining or holding a person in custody. In addition, neither Congress nor a state government can pass a *bill of attainder*— that is, condemn and punish a person without a trial. The Constitution also prohibits the passage of an *ex post facto* law, which makes an act a crime after it has been committed. These provisions are clearly intended to prevent the insistence by a majority on measures that might cost an individual his or her freedom.

CONSTITUTIONAL EXPANSION OF NATIONAL POWER

Although many features of the Constitution were originally intended to limit the power of the national government, the document has been the foundation for the expansion of national government as well. The Constitution lists all the powers that each branch of the government is to possess. Even though this listing may have been thought of originally as limiting the power of each branch, it has, in fact, allowed the branches to expand in certain areas. (For example, the Framers never imagined that giving Congress the power to tax would eventually allow the legislature to establish a social security tax on salaries and wages.)

The Powers of Congress in Article I

Article I of the Constitution, which defines the powers of Congress, is the most extensive prescription of authority contained in the Constitution. As such, it reflects the all-important emphasis placed on legislative power by the Framers of the Constitution. At the same time, the careful *enumeration of the powers* delegated to Congress points to the Founding Fathers' suspicion that the legislature itself might try to encroach on the rights of other branches. They believed that if the rights of Congress were carefully prescribed, there would be no such expansion of authority.

Article I states that Congress has the following powers:

To lay and collect Taxes, Duties, Imposts, and Excises, to pay the Debts and provide for the common Defense and general Welfare of the United States . . .;

To borrow Money on the credit of the United States;

To regulate Commerce with foreign Nations, and among the several States, and with the Indian tribes;

To establish a uniform Rule of Naturalization . . .;

To coin Money, regulate the Value thereof, and of foreign Coin . . .;

To provide for the punishment of counterfeiting . . .;

To establish Post Offices and post Roads;

To promote the Progress of Science and useful Arts . . .;

To constitute Tribunals inferior to the supreme Court;

To define and punish Piracies and Felonies committed on the high Seas, and Offenses against the Law of Nations;

To declare War . . .;

To raise and support Armies . . .;

To provide and maintain a Navy;

To make Rules for the Government and Regulation of the land and naval Forces;

To provide for calling forth the Militia to execute the Laws of the Union, suppress Insurrections and repel Invasions;

To provide for organizing, arming, and disciplining the Militia, and for governing such Part of them as may be employed in the Service of the United States . . .;

To exercise exclusive Legislation . . . over such district . . . as may . . . become the Seat of the Government of the United States . . .;

To make all Laws which shall be necessary and proper for carrying into execution the foregoing Powers, and all other Powers vested by this Constitution in the Government of the United States, or in any Department or office thereof.

The problem of interpretation. There are two ways of looking at the powers enumerated in the Constitution. First, they can be seen as giving Congress the authority to accomplish certain things. Second, they can be regarded as restraining legislative action within definite boundaries. Because the language employed to express them is general, the expansion or contraction of these congressional powers depends on the way in which they are interpreted.

Commerce clause as an example. The *commerce clause* of Article I (the third in the list above) offers a prime example of how constitutional interpretation has worked. When the Framers stated that Congress could regulate commerce "among the several States," there was no general agreement as to what this re-

ally implied. It could be interpreted narrowly to mean commerce when it crossed a state's borders, or it could be construed broadly to include commerce conducted within a state that eventually affected interstate commerce.

Chief Justice John Marshall, in the famous case *Gibbon v. Ogden* (1824), chose the latter interpretation. In his opinion Marshall concluded that "the power of Congress . . . comprehends navigation within the limits of every state in the Union, so far as that navigation may be, in any manner, connected with 'commerce with foreign nations, or among the several States, or with the Indian tribes.'" Thus, through broad interpretation the commerce clause has become an important stone in the edifice of national power. It has generally been cited as an example of how the authority of the national government has been increased at the expense of the states.

In general, Article I has proved flexible enough to permit Congress to increase its own power within the government. There are instances, however, when some of the provisions of Article I have been used to limit the national authority of Congress. During the New Deal period of the 1930s, some of the major legislation passed by Congress was ruled unconstitutional when the Supreme Court reasoned that the former had exceeded its enumerated powers. Congress has fared well in this respect though, and usually a broad interpretation of its powers prevails.

The Nature of the Presidency

Article II of the Constitution, which details the president's duties and powers, also furnishes several important elements that add to the strength of the central government and to the executive branch in particular. Certainly it was intended by the Framers that executive power should be concentrated in the hands of one person rather than being divided among the members of a group. Early in the

(Le Pelley; reprinted by permission from *The Christian Science Monitor.* © 1970 The Christian Science Publishing Society. All rights reserved.)

"What it says isn't always what it means."
Even though Congress has certain stipulated powers, the Supreme Court can still reinterpret them.

(Rollin Kirby. Reprinted from the *New York Post.*)

"—Thrice presented him a kingly crown, which he did thrice refuse"—Julius Caesar
The refusal of a third term by a president was virtually a foregone conclusion until 1940.

proceedings of the Constitutional Convention, an attempt by Virginia to create a plural executive was quickly outmaneuvered by the proponents of strong executive leadership.

A fixed term. In addition to unifying the presidency in one person, the Constitution strengthened the office by denoting a fixed term of four years. During this term the president can only be removed through impeachment and conviction, a cumbersome procedure that has never been accomplished. President Andrew Johnson was impeached by the Radical Republicans of the House of Representatives in 1868, but his conviction was not voted by the Senate, which failed by a single vote to achieve the two-thirds majority necessary to remove him.

Not only was the president given a fixed term, but he was able to repeat his tenure in office as often as he liked. There were proposals at the Constitutional Convention to limit the president to one term, but, like proposals for the creation of a plural executive, they did not succeed. Although no constitutional limit was set for the number of terms a president could serve, until 1940 there was an unwritten tradition that a president would occupy no more than two terms. This tradition was broken by Franklin D. Roosevelt under the extraordinary circumstances of World War II. In March 1951, the states ratified the Twenty-second Amendment, which provides that

No person shall be elected to the office of the President more than twice, and no person who has held the office of President, or acted as President, for more than two years of a term to which some other person was elected President shall be elected to the office of the President more than once.

Election of the president. Having placed the executive power in the hands of one man, and having given him a fixed term that could be repeated, the Constitutional Convention went on to develop a separate means of selecting the president—through a system of electors. Each state was allowed the same number of electors as it had members of Congress, the method of appointing these electors being left to the individual state legislatures. By discarding the proposals of both the Virginia and New Jersey Plans to have the president elected by the Congress, the Founding Fathers completed the work of making the president independent of the national legislature.

Over the years proposals have been made to alter the electoral college or to abolish it altogether. Suggested reforms have been to apportion electoral college votes according to the percentage of the popular vote received by presidential candidates in each state or to have the president elected directly by the people.

Effect of separating the president and Congress. By assigning the election of the president to electors rather than to Congress, the Framers gave the president an independent constituency. They thereby increased the president's ability to muster political support and further augmented his political power. (See Figure 3.2.)

If, instead, Congress had been empowered to select the president, the United States probably would have developed some form of parliamentary government. In the latter sys-

tem, the legislature dominates by selecting the prime minister and he or she is nearly always a member of the party that is in control of the parliament. This is effective in a country that has a disciplined two-party government, where either one party or the other dominates the legislature. Great Britain, for example, has a powerful legislature whose power is reflected in the executive. (See Figure 3.3.) However, if a country is composed of diverse economic, political, and regional interests, these in turn may be mirrored in the national legislature by a number of political parties. Such a variety of interests weakens the legislature due to perpetual and often irreconcilable conflict. If a legislature is thus fragmented, and if it chooses the executive, the executive will be weak, because he or she will have to respond to a number of parties that control the legislature. There may even be frequent changes in the executive. This was the situation in France until the Fifth Republic, when the selection of the premier was placed in the hands of the president.

The president's legal authority. Besides fixing his term and giving him a separate constituency, the Constitution also listed special powers that the president would have. He is the commander in chief of the armed forces. He is chief executive, and in this regard he "may require the opinion, in writing, of the principal officer in each of the executive departments, upon any subject relating to the duties of their respective office. . . ." Moreover, Section 3 of Article II provides that he is to give to the Congress

information of the state of the Union, and recommend to their consideration such measures as he shall judge necessary and expedient; he may, on extraordinary occasions, convene both Houses, or either of them, and in case of disagreement between them with respect to the time of adjournment, he may adjourn them to such time as he shall think proper; he shall receive ambassadors and other public ministers; he shall take care that the laws be faithfully executed, and shall commission all the officers of the United States.

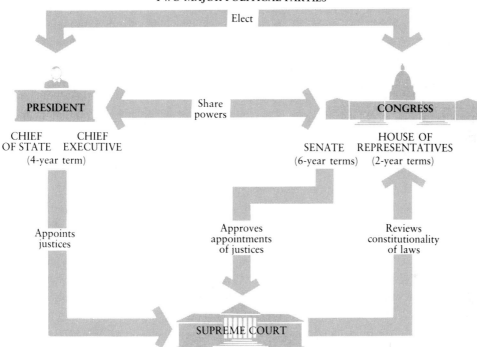

FIGURE 3.2

Although the president has never used his power to adjourn Congress, all the other provisions of Article II, vesting him with extensive and independent legal authority, have been employed at one time or another to bolster executive power. Most of the constitutional provisions for this authority are now generally accepted and continuously used by the president to maintain and increase the political power of his office.

The Power of the Judiciary

The evolution of a dynamic Supreme Court has been the most unexpected expansion of our government's power. Although there is some evidence to suggest that the Framers feared the power of the legislature more than that of any other branch of the national government, they probably did not foresee the strength that the Supreme Court would eventually acquire.

B. GREAT BRITAIN

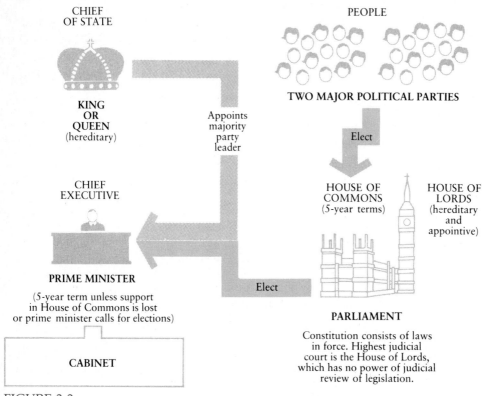

FIGURE 3.3

Article III of the Constitution contributed in its own way—and, to a considerable extent, unintentionally—to the development of judicial authority. It instituted one Supreme Court whose members were to be chosen by the president, "with the advice and consent" of the Senate. Furthermore, the judges "both of the supreme and inferior Courts, shall hold their Offices during good Behaviour, and shall, at stated Times, receive for their Services, a Compensation, which shall not be diminished during their Continuance in Office."

Beyond the simple establishment of a Supreme Court, however, Article III did not, in fact, provide explicitly for some of the more significant powers the Court soon assumed. In particular, it did not expressly give to the Court the power of judicial review. Due to the vagueness of Article III, it has been necessary for the Supreme Court itself to interpret the precise meaning of such terms as "judicial power," "cases," and "controversies." This is another instance of the continued need for interpreting the Constitution. In *Marbury v. Madison* (1803) Chief Justice John Marshall held that the "judicial power" included the power of judicial review, which could nullify those laws considered not in keeping with the Constitution. Certainly this power could not be inferred merely from the language of Article III, and Marshall had to rely on logic and historical evidence to support his conclusion.

Moreover, the Court has often had to redefine what is meant by "cases" and "controversies." It has decided it will not hear cases set up to test the Court's opinions but will hear only cases in which there are adversaries with adequate interests at stake. All the Court's many rules pertaining to the definitions of cases and controversies have been formulated through judicial interpretations.

Judicial restraint. It might be asked: If the Court is so free to interpret as it wishes, why has it not become the real force in the country? History has shown that judicial self-restraint is as common as judicial excess. Still, there have been periods when the Court seized the initiative and acted in opposition to the desires of Congress and the president. During the New Deal period of the 1930s, the Supreme Court boldly turned down programs supported by both President Franklin D. Roosevelt and Congress.

After 1937 the New Deal Court retreated from its interventionist stance, and a period of judicial self-restraint ensued. However, beginning in 1954 Chief Justice Earl Warren presided over a Court that boldly innovated in civil liberties and civil-rights cases, applying the national standards of the Bill of Rights to the states. The Warren Court also struck down segregation laws in the South and developed strict standards of equal protection under law to end other forms of discrimination (for example, discrimination based upon gender). When Richard M. Nixon came to the presidency in 1968, he promised to change the liberal direction of the Court. To this end he proceeded to appoint conservative justices, including Chief Justice Warren Burger. However, the Burger Court remained an active protector of civil liberties and civil rights, in 1973 rendering one of its most controversial decisions of all in *Roe v. Wade* and thereby overturning state laws prohibiting abortions. As the decade of the 1980s began, conservatives, such as North Carolina Republican Jesse Helms, renewed their attacks on what they considered to be an overly interventionist Supreme Court. Legislation was even introduced in Congress to curb the Court's authority to rule on controversial abortion, busing, and school-prayer cases.

During his two terms President Ronald Reagan attempted to shift the Supreme Court in the direction of judicial self-restraint through his appointments of Sandra Day O'Connor, Antonin Scalia, and Anthony Kennedy, all conservatives who opposed judicial activism. Reagan's most controversial nomination, of Circuit Court Judge Robert Bork, a leading conservative and spokesperson for judicial self-restraint, failed in the Senate after acrimonious hearings and debate. Nevertheless Reagan, who appointed Chief Justice William J. Rehnquist to replace Warren Burger, who stepped down in 1986, succeeded in moving the Court towards judicial self-restraint, primarily with regard to the scope of judicial review over state legislation. President George Bush promised to continue the Reagan philosophy should he have the opportunity to appoint Supreme Court Justices.

In cases where the president or Congress makes an unpopular decision that transcends the bounds of constitutionality, the courts have been an important check. For example, President Harry S. Truman stretched the powers of the presidency when he ordered the seizure of the steel mills in 1952 to avert a strike that he felt would cripple the Korean War effort. He did not have strong political backing for his action, and the Supreme Court, in *Youngstown Sheet and Tube Co. v. Sawyer* (1952), struck down his decision on the basis that it exceeded his constitutional powers. And in 1974, in *United States v. Richard M. Nixon,* the Court held that the president had gone beyond his power in refusing to yield tape recordings and other materials subpoenaed by District Court Judge John Sirica in the criminal trial of presidential subordinates charged with obstructing justice by concealing the Watergate break-in.

While the Court has exercised judicial self-restraint throughout history, it has not retreated from making politically difficult decisions that have shaped the Constitution and, ultimately, the way in which government rules. The justices of the Supreme Court are well aware that they must function in what is often a highly charged political arena, and in general they have acted boldly and with foresight to defend the Constitution.

The Principle of Judicial Review

Judicial review simply refers to the authority of the courts to consider the actions of other governmental branches and bodies in order to determine whether or not they conform to constitutional or statutory requirements. Judicial review as exercised by the federal courts in the United States extends to presidential, congressional, administrative, and state actions. It is the broadest form of review to be found in any government because it covers legislative acts.

The silence of Article III of the Constitution on the important issue of judicial review was clarified first by Alexander Hamilton's interpretation of judicial authority in *The Federalist*, No. 78, and then by the actions and opinions of the Supreme Court itself. In explicitly stating that the federal judiciary would have the power to overturn congressional laws that were repugnant to the Constitution, Hamilton clearly expressed the view of the majority of the delegates at the Constitutional Convention. More importantly, the Supreme Court, from its inception, had assumed the authority to declare congressional acts unconstitutional. As early as 1792 the justices of the Court had refused to accept what they considered to be nonjudicial responsibilities delegated to them by Congress on the ground that the law violated Article III (In Re Hayburn's Case, Dallas 409).

In 1803, the Supreme Court, under the great Federalist, Chief Justice John Marshall, unequivocally stated the power of judicial review over congressional laws in *Marbury v. Madison*. Republican President Thomas Jefferson had refused to deliver a justiceship-of-the-peace commission to Marbury, who had been appointed to that position by outgoing Federalist President John Adams. Marbury sought an original writ of mandamus from the Supreme Court to compel Secretary of State James Madison to give him his commission.[17] (The Judiciary Act of 1789 had granted the Supreme Court the authority, in its original jurisdiction, to issue writs of mandamus.) Chief Justice Marshall thus had to decide whether or not Article III of the Constitution allowed the Court to mandamus executive officials when it exercised its original jurisdiction to hear cases "affecting ambassadors, other public ministers, and consuls, and those in which a state shall be [a] party."[18]

Marbury v. Madison

Mr. Chief Justice Marshall delivered the opinion of the Court, saying in part:

. . .The authority, therefore, given to the Supreme Court by the [Judiciary Act of 1789] . . .establishing the judicial courts of the United States, to issue writs of mandamus to public officers, appears not to be warranted by the Constitution [because it adds to the original jurisdiction of the Court delineated by the framers of the Constitution in Article III; had they wished this power to be conferred upon the Court it would be so stated, in the same manner

1 Cranch 137 (1803). Early Supreme Court cases were collected annually under the name of the Court's reporter.

[17] A *writ of mandamus* is a judicial order that compels officials to perform their duties under the law.

[18] There was also the question potentially before the Court as to whether or not it could rule on this case at all because neither Marbury, the plaintiff, nor Madison, the defendant, were parties that came within the Court's original jurisdiction. The term "public ministers" in Article III refers to *foreign* public ministers, not to a public minister such as Madison was, the Secretary of State. However, for political reasons, Marshall did not want to decline jurisdiction at the outset because he both wanted to lecture President Jefferson on the proper performance of his duties and state the principle of judicial review. Marshall finally disposed of the case by declaring that the Court could not issue an original writ of mandamus because the Constitution did not grant it that power.

that the other parts of the Court's original jurisdiction are stated] . . .it becomes necessary to inquire whether a jurisdiction so conferred can be exercised.

The question whether an act repugnant to the Constitution can become the law of the land, is a question deeply interesting to the United States; but, happily, not of an intricacy proportioned to its interest. It seems only necessary to recognize certain principles supposed to have been long and well established, to decide it.

That the people have an original right to establish, for their future government, such principles as, in their opinion, shall most conduce to their own happiness, is the basis on which the whole American fabric has been erected. The exercise of this original right is a very great exertion; nor can it nor ought it to be frequently repeated. The principles, therefore, so established, are deemed fundamental. And as the authority from which they proceed is supreme, and can seldom act, they are designed to be permanent.

This original and supreme will organizes the government, and assigns to different departments their respective powers. It may either stop here, or establish certain limits not to be transcended by those departments.

The government of the United States is of the latter description. The powers of the legislature are defined and limited; and that those limits may not be mistaken, or forgotten, the Constitution is written. To what purpose are powers limited, and to what purpose is that limitation committed to writing, if these limits may, at any time, be passed by those intended to be restrained? The distinction between a government with limited and unlimited powers is abolished, if those limits do not confine the persons on whom they are imposed, and if acts prohibited and acts allowed, are of equal obligation. It is a proposition too plain to be contested, that the Constitution controls any legislative act repugnant to it: or, that the legislature may alter the Constitution by an ordinary act.

Between these alternatives there is no middle ground. The Constitution is either a superior paramount law, unchangeable by ordinary means, or it is on a level with ordinary legislative acts, and, like other acts, is alterable when the legislature shall please to alter it.

If the former part of the alternative be true, then a legislative act contrary to the Constitution, is not law; if the latter part be true, then written constitutions are absurd attempts, on the part of the people, to limit a power in its own nature illimitable.

Certainly all those who have framed written constitutions contemplate them as forming the fundamental and paramount law of the nation, and, consequently, the theory of every such government must be, that an act of the legislature, repugnant to the constitution, is void.

This theory is essentially attached to a written constitution, and is consequently to be considered, by this court, as one of the fundamental principles of our society. It is not, therefore, to be lost sight of in the further consideration of this subject.

If an act of the legislature, repugnant to the Constitution, is void, does it, notwithstanding its invalidity, bind the courts, and oblige them to give it effect? Or, in other words, though it be not law, does it constitute a rule as operative as if it was a law? This would be to overthrow in fact what was established in theory; and would seem, at first view, an absurdity too gross to be insisted on. It shall, however, receive a more attentive consideration.

It is emphatically the province and duty of the judicial department to say what the law is. Those who apply the rule to particular cases, must of necessity expound and interpret that rule. If two laws conflict with each other, the courts must decide on the operation of each.

So if the law be in opposition to the Constitution; if both the law and the Constitution apply to a particular case, so that the court must either decide that case conformably to the law, disregarding the Constitution, or conformably to the Constitution, disregarding the law, the court must determine which of these conflicting rules governs the case. This is of the very essence of judicial duty.

If, then, the courts are to regard the Constitution, and the Constitution is superior to any ordinary act of the legislature, the Constitution, and not such ordinary act, must govern the case to which they both apply.

Those, then, who controvert the principle that the constitution is to be considered, in court, as a paramount law, are reduced to the necessity of maintaining that courts must close their eyes on the Constitution, and see only the law.

This doctrine would subvert the very foundation of all written constitutions. It would declare that an act which, according to the principles and theory of our government, is entirely void, is yet, in practice, completely obligatory. It would declare that if the legislature shall do what is expressly forbidden, such act, notwithstanding the express prohibition, is in reality effectual. It would be giving to the legislature a practical and real omnipotence, with the same breath which professes to restrict their powers within narrow limits. It is prescribing limits, and declaring that those limits may be passed at pleasure.

That it thus reduces to nothing what we have deemed the greatest improvement on political institutions, a written constitution, would of itself be sufficient, in America, where written constitutions have been viewed with so much reverence, for rejecting the construction. But the peculiar expressions of the Constitution of the United States furnish additional arguments in favor of its rejection.

The judicial power of the United States is extended to all cases arising under the Constitution.

Could it be the intention of those who gave this power, to say that in using it the Constitution should not be looked into? That a case arising under the Constitution should be decided without examining the instrument under which it arises?

This is too extravagant to be maintained.

In some cases, then, the Constitution must be looked into by the judges. And if they can open it at all, what part of it are they forbidden to read or to obey?

There are many other parts of the Constitution which serve to illustrate this subject.

It is declared that "no tax or duty shall be laid on articles exported from any State." Suppose a duty on the export of cotton, of tobacco, or of flour; and a suit instituted to recover it. Ought judgment to be rendered in such a case? Ought the judges to close their eyes on the Constitution, and only see the law?

The Constitution declares "that no bill of attainder or ex post facto law shall be passed."

If, however, such a bill should be passed, and a person should be prosecuted under it, must the court condemn to death those victims whom the Constitution endeavors to preserve?

"No person," says the Constitution, "shall be convicted of treason unless on the testimony of two witnesses to the same overt act, or on confession in open court."

Here the language of the Constitution is addressed especially to the courts. It prescribes, directly for them, a rule of evidence not to be departed from. If the legislature should change that rule, and declare one witness, or a confession out of court, sufficient for conviction, must the constitutional principle yield to the legislative act?

From these, and many other selections which might be made, it is apparent that the framers of the Constitution contemplated that instrument as a rule for the government of courts, as well as of the legislature.

Why otherwise does it direct the judges to take an oath to support it? This oath certainly applies in an especial manner to this conduct in their official character. How immoral to impose it on them, if they were to be used as the instruments, and the knowing instruments, for violating what they swear to support!

The oath of office, too, imposed by the legislature, is completely demonstrative of the legislative opinion on this subject. It is in these words: "I do solemnly swear that I will administer justice without respect to persons, and do equal right to the poor and to the rich; and that I will faithfully and impartially discharge all the duties incumbent on me as———, according to the best of my abilities and understanding, agreeably to the Constitution and laws of the United States."

Why does a judge swear to discharge his duties agreeably to the Constitution of the United States, if that Constitution forms no rule for his government—if it is closed upon him, and cannot be inspected by him?

If such be the real state of things, this is worse than solemn mockery. To prescribe, or to take this oath, becomes equally a crime.

It is also not entirely unworthy of observation, that in declaring what shall be the supreme law of the land, the Constitution itself is first mentioned; and not the laws of the United States generally, but those only which shall be made in pursuance of the Constitution, have that rank. Thus, the particular phraseology of the Constitution of the United States confirms and strengthens the principle, supposed to be essential to all written constitutions, that a law repugnant to the Constitution is void; and that courts, as well as other departments, are bound by that instrument.

The rule must be discharged.

The Rights of Citizens: Civil Liberties and Civil Rights

The policies of our government in the area of civil liberties and civil rights are oriented to the protection of the individual, but at the same time such policies must take into account the public interest, whether national, state, or local. The essential issue in all discussions of civil-liberties and civil-rights policies is how best to balance individual rights and public needs. Neither the individual nor the community, as represented by government, has an absolute claim to superiority in the system. Nevertheless, constitutional democracy is predicated upon a belief in the sanctity of the individual and requires the protection of individual rights against governmental encroachments.

For a democracy to be worthy of the name, it must preserve the rights and freedoms of the individuals who constitute its very reason for existence. In the United States these rights and freedoms cover an extremely broad area. They include the freedoms to speak, write, and worship as one pleases, the civil rights guaranteeing equal opportunities for education and employment, and such specific rights as the right of the accused to refuse to speak until he or she has received legal advice from an attorney. All these individual freedoms and rights touch the very core of democracy.

Since the founding of the republic, the importance of protecting civil liberties and civil rights has been a major constitutional principle. After their experiences under the Articles of Confederation, the states in 1789 were very concerned with limiting the national government so that it would neither overwhelm their own authority nor usurp the freedoms of their inhabitants. For this reason many of the states insisted on adding the first 10 amendments to the Constitution as a condition of ratification.

The Bill of Rights, as these amendments were called, continued to be a restraint only upon the national government even after the adoption of the Fourteenth Amendment in 1868, an amendment whose language could even then, as it was to be over a hundred years later, have been interpreted as extending the protections of the Bill of Rights to state actions. During the nineteenth century and for over half of the twentieth, the Supreme Court respected what it considered to be the needs of the states for flexibility in governing their own affairs and exercised judicial self-restraint in extending the Bill of Rights to the sphere of state action. It was not just a changing judicial philosophy that made the Court more active in gradually nationalizing the Bill of

Rights by applying most of its provisions to the states, but also increasing political pressures for such action on the national government itself.

The most important branch of government in setting national policy with respect to civil liberties and civil rights has been the Supreme Court. Because of this, the most effective demands for change have come from such groups as the American Civil Liberties Union (ACLU) and the National Association for the Advancement of Colored People (NAACP), which have taken specific cases to the courts. Through the efforts of such groups, the Supreme Court has reinterpreted the Fourteenth Amendment in a number of cases, extending the restraints of the Bill of Rights to state and local governments. The voting rights guaranteed by the Fifteenth Amendment also have been applied by the Court to overrule state actions.

The lead taken by the Supreme Court in extending civil-liberties and civil-rights protections to citizens, particularly during the era of the Warren Court in the 1950s and 1960s, has never been fully matched by the president or Congress.

Over the years, neither the chief executive nor the legislature has been concerned with defending First Amendment freedoms of expression. Both the president and Congress have more often than not decried Supreme Court decisions that have upheld individual freedoms under the First Amendment. For example, in 1989 the Supreme Court, in *Texas v. Johnson*, overturned a Texas law, mirrored by statutes in forty-eight states, that made the burning of the American flag a criminal act. The Court held that the law violated First Amendment freedoms of expression. Members of both parties on Capitol Hill responded by passing a law that for the first time explicitly made flag burning a national crime, and the president immediately signed it with much fanfare. It did not take long for the law to be challenged in a federal district court, and on February 21, 1990, a federal district court

judge in Seattle struck down the new law, declaring that the four defendants who had burned flags were exercising their First Amendment rights of freedom of expression. The judge concluded, "In order for the flag to endure as a symbol of freedom in this nation, we must protect with equal vigor the right to destroy it and the right to wave it."[1] The decision in this case was upheld by the United States Supreme Court in 1990. Flag burning is understandably not acceptable to a majority of Americans who, like the president and members of Congress, do not agree with the Supreme Court that it is a protected form of political expression. Presidents and legislators, elected by the people, express popular, not abstract, views on how far First Amendment protections should extend.

The president and Congress have expanded civil rights in response to popular pressures. The broad civil-rights movement of the 1960s, led by Martin Luther King, Jr., spurred President Lyndon B. Johnson and Congress to pass the historic Civil Rights Act of 1964, which banned discrimination in public accommodations and employment. Political demands also led to congressional passage of the 1965 Voting Rights Act that gave the Justice Department new authority to protect minority voting rights.

THE NATURE OF CIVIL LIBERTIES AND CIVIL RIGHTS

The terms *civil liberties* and *civil rights* are often used interchangeably, but they identify two different concepts of a government's relationship to individual citizens. The concept of *civil liberties* is based on the idea that government must be *restrained* from interfering with or encroaching upon the freedom of in-

---

[1]*Congressional Quarterly Weekly Report*, February 24, 1990, p. 602.

dividuals to do certain things. Thus the First Amendment freedoms of speech, press, assembly, petition, and religion are appropriately called "civil liberties."

A *civil right* is more in the nature of a specific interest possessed by an individual, based on a constitutional or statutory grant, which the individual can claim in court and which the government must actively protect against intrusion by government itself or by private individuals. For example, the Bill of Rights establishes the right to a jury trial, the right to bear arms, the right to protection against unreasonable searches and seizures, and the right against being compelled to be a witness against oneself. Rights may also be created by statute, as in the case of the Civil Rights Act of 1964, which protects individuals against job discrimination on the basis of sex.

In the area of civil liberties, the government restrains itself from intruding upon individual liberties, with the important caveat that these freedoms can be limited in the public interest. In the sector of civil rights, individuals can make statutory or constitutional claims upon the government that, if legitimate, the latter must actively support. While *rights* are more in the nature of absolutes than *liberties*, in both areas the government, and finally the courts, must balance individual rights against the needs of the government in arriving at a definition of the scope of liberties and the degree of rights that will be granted to individuals.

Individual Liberties and Rights in the Constitution

The constitutional basis for any judicial determination of civil liberties and civil rights is found in the Bill of Rights and in subsequent amendments, particularly the Fourteenth and Fifteenth. The Bill of Rights guarantees liberties and protects rights, and the Fourteenth Amendment has been used to extend most of the Bill of Rights to the states.

Civil liberties and rights in the Bill of Rights. The most significant limitations on government in the first 10 amendments have been those that prohibit infringement upon specific liberties and rights of individuals. Liberties such as the freedoms of religion, speech, and press; the right to peaceful assembly; and the right to petition the government for the redress of grievances are considered basic to personal freedom. The First Amendment prohibits Congress from passing any law that interferes with these liberties.

Other important elements in the Bill of Rights guarantee certain legal procedures and protections to all citizens. These are *procedural rights* and are identified in the Fourth through Eighth Amendments. Procedural rights are given the most extensive treatment in the Bill of Rights and have been the subject of many cases before the courts. The Fourth Amendment protects people and their property against "unreasonable searches and seizures" by government and provides that search war-

(© Donald Reilly. 1968, *Saturday Review*.)

"I'm so proud of you—imagine having your hair defended by the American Civil Liberties Union!"

Standards of dress and hair length imposed by public institutions have sometimes been challenged in court.

Freedom of expression extends to unpopular as well as popular speech.

rants can be issued only upon "probable cause." The Fifth and Sixth Amendments ensure important rights in criminal proceedings. The Fifth Amendment guarantees that no person shall be held for a capital crime without indictment by a grand jury nor be compelled to act as a witness against himself or herself (self-incrimination) in a criminal case. The Fifth Amendment also specifies that no individual can be deprived of "life, liberty, or property, without due process of law." A person accused of a crime is guaranteed "the right to a speedy and public trial by an impartial jury" and to legal counsel and witnesses for defense by the Sixth Amendment. The Seventh Amendment guarantees a person the right to a jury trial in most civil cases. Excessive bails and fines as well as cruel and unusual punishment are forbidden by the Eighth Amendment.

In addition to protecting and guaranteeing such liberties and rights, the Bill of Rights includes other guarantees against arbitrary actions by the federal government. The right of the states to keep militias, the right of people to "keep and bear arms," and the prohibition against the quartering of soldiers in private homes, although mostly anachronistic today, were felt to be important defenses against authoritarian and military government at the end of the eighteenth century. (The right to bear arms is still considered vital by many persons.)

Although the Bill of Rights made civil liberties an inviolable part of constitutional government, the imprecise language of some of its clauses has permitted variations in application to different situations. No one can dispute the right of a person to a trial by jury, established in the Sixth Amendment. There *can*, however, be a difference of opinion as to whether a trial is "speedy," a jury "impartial," or a bail "excessive." The meaning of these and other terms, such as "probable cause" and "due process of law," have had to be defined by the courts over the years as cases have been brought before them.

Civil liberties and rights in the Fourteenth Amendment. By the end of the Civil War, it was apparent that the federal government had to extend the Bill of Rights so that former slaves would not be denied their civil liberties and other rights as citizens. Three amendments, known as the "Civil War

(Drawing by Handelsman; ©1989 The New Yorker Magazine; Inc.)

"How very exciting! I have never before met a Second *Amendment lawyer."*
The Second Amendment, granting the right to bear arms, has often been cited by opponents of gun control but has rarely been raised in the courts.

Amendments," were therefore added to the Constitution. The Thirteenth Amendment prohibits slavery. The Fifteenth Amendment guarantees every citizen the right to vote.

The Fourteenth Amendment, however, is less clear-cut than either of the former. It provides, first, that

all persons born or naturalized in the United States, and subject to the jurisdiction thereof, are citizens of the United States and of the state wherein they reside. No State shall make or enforce any law which shall abridge the privileges or immunities of citizens of the United States.

Second, the Fourteenth Amendment provides that no state may "deprive any person of life, liberty, or property, without due process of law." Finally, no state may "deny to any persons within its jurisdiction the equal protection of the laws." The amendment then authorizes Congress to enforce its provisions by appropriate legislation.

Like the Bill of Rights, the Fourteenth Amendment has required clarification by the courts. Just what did the authors of the amendment mean by "privileges or immunities of citizens of the United States"? The meaning of "due process of law" is no clearer in the Fourteenth Amendment than it is in the Fifth. What exactly is "equal protection of the laws"? The Supreme Court's interpretations of "due process of law" and "equal protection of the laws" in the Fourteenth Amendment have been most important to the evolution of federal policies concerning civil

liberties and civil rights. No precise meaning has been given to either clause, but both have been interpreted by the Court to negate state laws and actions that it has considered unreasonable. The same is true of the Court's definition of "due process of law" in the Fifth Amendment, which has been used to prevent what were considered to be unreasonable federal actions.

Like the decisions of other governmental bodies, the interpretations of the Supreme Court have often changed with the prevailing attitudes and demands of the times. In *Near v. Minnesota* (1931) the Court began to negate, by means of the "due process" clause of the Fourteenth Amendment, state laws that abridged civil liberties and rights guaranteed in the Bill of Rights. The equal-protection clause of the Fourteenth Amendment has also been interpreted to broaden the obligations of state governments to protect the rights and opportunities of citizens for equal education and equality in voting.

Constitutional Dilemmas

In addition to being subject to reinterpretation due to changing attitudes, judicial principles involving civil liberties and civil rights may often come into conflict with other constitutional requirements. Thus, in formulating its interpretations and decisions, the Supreme Court has had to determine the proper balance among conflicting principles.

Individual rights versus community needs. Because civil liberties and rights are fundamental to democracy, it is often assumed that personal freedoms cannot be limited in such a system. However, when individuals exercise their freedoms in ways that are harmful to others or to the society as a whole, there is conflict between the rights of the person and the needs of the community. For this reason, the freedom of individuals, like the power of government, must have limits.

For example, the rights of all citizens to

"At least I'll be some company."
The Supreme Court's reading of the Fourteenth Amendment has helped blacks in their fight for equality.

the freedoms of speech, press, and assembly are guaranteed by the First Amendment. Thus people can organize themselves in order to achieve common purposes and to express personal opinions without these rights being abridged. However, freedom of assembly does not extend to those who meet for the purpose of conspiring to bomb a department store any more than freedom of the press prevents a newspaper from being sued for printing libelous statements. As Justice Oliver Wendell Holmes declared, "The most stringent protection of free speech would not protect a man falsely shouting 'Fire!' in a theatre and causing a panic." Thus the freedoms of each individual, although guaranteed by the Constitution, must be limited to some extent if public order and the rights of others are to be preserved.

There are times, however, when the boundaries between First Amendment rights and community rights are not clear-cut. This is particularly true when the exercise of free speech and press conflict with the taste and standards of the community. A novel that is considered a masterpiece in literary circles may be deemed "obscene literature" by the general community. What, then, is the meaning of "obscenity"? What are the community's standards? How can the effects of such literature on the community be measured? Obviously, questions like these are not easily answered by the courts.

The procedural rights of suspected or accused criminals can also conflict with the welfare of the community. For example, the Constitution protects every person against unreasonable searches and seizures, against self-incrimination, and against being detained without a *writ of habeas corpus*—an order issued by a court to show cause for such a detention. The decisions of the Warren Court (1953–1969) supported stringent adherence to these procedural rights, and many law-enforcement officials and public groups maintained that such protection of suspected criminals inhibited the control of crime and threatened the safety of the community.

The Burger Court (1969–1986) made a series of rulings granting the police more discretion than previously allowed by the Warren Court, giving prosecutors the right to rely on evidence obtained without search warrants in questioning witnesses before grand juries. Moreover, it "watered down" the Fourth Amendment's protection against unreasonable searches and seizures by permitting police to search a driver arrested for a traffic violation and to use the evidence to convict the same individual of an entirely unrelated offense. (For example, a Washington, D.C., resident found driving without a license was searched, and the police discovered a packet of heroin in his shirt pocket. The driver was subsequently convicted for possession of heroin.[2]) The Rehnquist Court continued the tone of judicial self-restraint with regard to the review of state legislation concerning law enforcement. Generally the Court upheld "reasonable" state practices and, unlike the Warren Court of the 1960s, gave greater weight to the interests of law enforcement authorities than to the rights of criminal defendants.

This conflict of individual and community interests has been at issue in recent years with respect to suspected drug pushers. The distribution of hard drugs in this country and abroad has serious and harmful consequences for society. Yet constitutional protections such as the prohibition of unreasonable searches and seizures have often prevented officials from apprehending those suspected of dealing in drugs. On the one hand, groups concerned with the preservation of civil liberties argue that the denial of constitutional rights, even to suspected criminals, will ultimately lead to the infringement of the rights of law-abiding citizens. On the other hand, groups concerned with the problem of crime believe

---

[2]*United States v. Robinson*, 414 U.S. 218 (1973).

"Hey! I just killed 24 people—and you got that confession without advising me of my rights!"
The Supreme Court's insistence on protecting a suspect's rights has sometimes complicated law enforcement.

that the protection of society is more important than the rights of suspected criminals. Such arguments must certainly be weighed and considered by the courts when constitutional questions are at stake.

The courts also have had to find the proper balance between community welfare and individual civil rights in regard to equal public education. Although the Supreme Court declared that racial segregation in public schools denies "equal protection of the laws," it has had to allow the lower courts discretion in determining the appropriate rate of desegregation necessary to preserve public order.

Free press and fair trial. The Supreme Court has also taken community interests into account in confronting the difficult problem of balancing the First Amendment's guarantee of freedom of the press with the Sixth Amendment's provision that any accused person "shall enjoy the right to a speedy and public trial, by an impartial jury of the state and district wherein the crime shall have been committed." The problem arises when a trial court, either at the initiative of its judge or on the motion of the accused's attorney, closes the trial proceedings or a portion thereof to the press and the public in order to prevent or restrict news accounts that might be prejudicial to the accused. Sensational media coverage of *pretrial* proceedings may create an atmosphere of prejudice in the community that makes it all but impossible to select an impartial jury. And even during the trial itself the media may create an inflammatory atmosphere against the defendant. Obviously it is difficult to completely isolate a jury from a prejudicial environment both within and without the courtroom.[3] Moreover, witnesses as well as jurors may easily be influenced by the media.

The trial court in *Nebraska Press Association v. Stuart* (1976) attempted to deal with prejudicial publicity surrounding the trial of the defendant for a particularly brutal murder of six members of a family by censoring press accounts of the pretrial proceedings. The court's decision was appealed to the state supreme court, which issued a restrictive order detailing what the press could report about the pretrial hearing. This order was in turn appealed to the United States Supreme Court, which skirted the constitutional issue of freedom of the press by holding that since the pretrial proceeding had not originally been completely closed to the press (a procedure authorized by state law) there could be no censorship of what was reported. Chief Justice Warren Burger's opinion for the Supreme Court in *Nebraska Press Association v. Stuart* seemed to imply that if a decision had been made at the outset, pretrial proceedings could then have been closed to the press and the public if there were reasonable grounds to conclude such was necessary to prevent adverse publicity.[4]

The Supreme Court finally upheld the closure of pretrial proceedings in another case, *Gannett Company v. de Pasquale* (1979). A majority of justices concluded that, although open trials are in fact presumed a norm, the right to a public trial does not guarantee open proceedings under all circumstances, and that there is no unconditional constitutional guarantee to open *pretrial* proceedings. Justice Lewis Powell wrote, in a concurring opinion, that the First and Fourteenth Amendments create a legitimate press interest in attending

pretrial hearings, but that the right of access to courtroom proceedings is not absolute. The trial court, Powell concluded, thus acted properly in weighing the right of access against the requirements of a fair trial in arriving at its closure order. He emphasized that excluding all members of the press from the courtroom in *Gannett Company v. de Pasquale* differed substantially from the "gag order," or prior restraint, in *Nebraska Press Association v. Stuart*. Three of the five justices who voted with the majority in the Gannett case wrote concurring opinions, which led to confusion regarding the exact meaning of the decision. Justice William Rehnquist, for example, stated that "The trial court is not required by the Sixth Amendment to advance any reason whatsoever for declining to open a pretrial hearing or *trial* to the public." However, Chief Justice Burger emphasized in his opinion that the ruling applied only to *pretrial* proceedings.[5]

The Supreme Court finally clarified the question of press and public access to criminal trials in *Richmond Newspapers v. Virginia* (1980). The case involved an appeal from the decision of a Virginia judge to close a murder trial to all parties except the witnesses when they testified. The judge was acting under a Virginia statute providing in the trial of all criminal cases that "the court may, in its discretion, exclude from the trial any persons whose presence would impair the conduct of a fair trial, provided that the right of the accused to a public trial shall not be violated." The Supreme Court held decisively, by a vote of seven to one, that the closure violated the First Amendment, which had been made applicable to the states through the Fourteenth Amendment's due process clause. "We hold," wrote Chief Justice Burger for a plurality of the Court, "that the right to attend criminal trials is implicit in the guarantees of the First Amendment; without the freedom to attend

---

[3]In *Sheppard v. Maxwell*, 384 U.S. 333 (1966), the Supreme Court overturned the murder conviction of Dr. Sam Sheppard due to blatantly prejudicial media publicity and activities within the courtroom. In many controversial cases, juries are sequestered and are not permitted to see, hear, or read media accounts of the trial.

[4]427 U.S. 539 (1976).

[5]443 U.S. 368 (1979). Emphasis added.

such trials, which people have exercised for centuries, important aspects of freedom of speech and of the press could be eviscerated." In a concurring opinion, Justice Brennan stressed that the First Amendment supports the right of both the public and the press to information, limited only by compelling governmental interests in security or confidentiality. The Virginia statute, concluded Brennan, is clearly unconstitutional because it "authorizes trial closures at the unfettered discretion of the judge and parties." The statute thus violated the presumption that trials are customarily open. However, Justice Burger pointed out in a concluding footnote:

[O]ur holding today does not mean that the First Amendment rights of the public and representatives of the press are absolute. Just as a government may impose reasonable time, place, and manner restrictions upon the use of its streets in the interest of such objectives as the free flow of traffic, . . .so may a trial judge, in the interests of the fair administration of justice impose reasonable limitations on access to a trial."[6]

All of the majority justices stressed that in the case at bar the Virginia judge had given no reason for his closure order.

Freedom of the press may conflict with the right to a fair trial, not only because of publicity adverse to the defendant, but also when reporters claim constitutional immunity from subpoenas requiring them to testify and reveal the sources of their information. Reporters often promise confidentiality in return for information, a process that many consider essential to a vibrant and free press. However, the "confidential information" acquired may be essential to the fair disposition of a criminal trial, or of a civil trial as well (for example in a libel suit against a newspaper). The Supreme Court has therefore refused to grant media and newspaper reporters the constitutional immunity that would prevent the rev-

"One more time—are you ready to reveal your news sources?"
Freedom of the press was limited by a 1972 Court ruling that required newspeople to reveal their sources of information.

elation of their confidential sources.[7] Thus on more than one occasion reporters have been jailed for contempt due to their refusal to testify in court. Although members of the press have not been granted immunity by the courts, they have won their battle to protect confidential sources of information in more than one-half of the state legislatures, which have passed "shield laws" that in varying degrees grant reporters protection from forced testimony. However, shield laws yield to court orders, and in extenuating circumstances the courts have shown no hesitation in citing for contempt reporters who have refused to testify.

NATIONALIZING THE BILL OF RIGHTS

Constitutional law is constantly changing because the Supreme Court's interpretations of the Constitution tend to reflect the changing attitudes of the national community. Such change has taken place in the twentieth cen-

---

[6]448 U.S. 555 (1980).

[7]*Brandburg v. Haynes,* 408 U.S. 665 (1972).

tury with regard to civil liberties. The protection of personal freedoms, once thought to be exclusively the duty of the states, is now regarded as the national government's responsibility as well.

Early Interpretations of the Bill of Rights

The Bill of Rights was added to the Constitution in 1791 to safeguard individual rights against encroachment by the federal government. However, the question of whether its provisions also applied to the states remained unsettled for more than 40 years. When the issue was finally brought before the Supreme Court in 1833, the Court determined that the Bill of Rights applied to the federal government alone. For almost a century thereafter, individuals had to rely on their own state governments to safeguard civil liberties against state infringements.

Barron v. Baltimore. The first decision on this question was handed down in 1833 by Chief Justice John Marshall. Barron was the owner of a wharf in Baltimore. The city had diverted several streams while paving streets, and the diverted streams deposited dirt near Barron's wharf, making it too shallow for some boats. Barron claimed that his wharf had been rendered useless and that he had thus been deprived of property without compensation and in violation of the Fifth Amendment. Although the initial verdict of the state trial court was in Barron's favor, the decision was later reversed by the state court of appeals, whereupon Barron took his case to the Supreme Court.

The Supreme Court, however, decided that Barron's suit was not a federal matter and dismissed it. In his opinion Marshall established that the Fifth Amendment pertained only to cases brought against the national government. State and local governments could therefore not be sued for violations of the Fifth Amendment: "Each state established a con-

stitution for itself, and, in that constitution, provided such limitations and restrictions on the powers of its particular government as its judgment dictated." Marshall concluded further that "these amendments [the Bill of Rights] demanded security against the apprehended encroachments of the general [national] government—not against those of the local governments."[8]

The Fourteenth Amendment and the *Slaughter-House* **cases**. In keeping with the *Barron v. Baltimore* decision, individuals had to rely almost exclusively on their state constitutions or state legislation for protection of civil liberties and rights. But after the Civil War, with the adoption of the Fourteenth Amendment parties to civil liberties cases began to invoke that amendment for protection of various freedoms against state encroachment. The first case argued under the Fourteenth Amendment concerned the constitutionality of a Louisiana law that created a slaughterhouse monopoly and kept other companies from competing in that state. The independent butchers of New Orleans protested the statute on the grounds that it violated their "privileges and immunities" and their right to "due process of law" and "equal protection of the laws" guaranteed by the Fourteenth Amendment.

In the *Slaughter-House* cases of 1873, the Supreme Court gave a very narrow interpretation to the Fourteenth Amendment so that it would not interfere with the laws of the states. The Court answered the plaintiffs' first argument by distinguishing between United States citizenship and state citizenship.

Not only may a man be a citizen of the United States without being a citizen of a state, but an important element is necessary to convert the former into the latter. He must reside within the state to make him a citizen of it, but it is only

---

[8]7 Peters 243 (1833).

necessary that he should be born or naturalized in the United States to be a citizen of the Union.

On the basis of this distinction the Court distinguished further between the privileges and immunities of the citizens of the United States and those of the citizens of a state. Since the Fourteenth Amendment expressly prohibits only the violation of the "privileges and immunities of the citizens of the United States," the Court explained, it is in no way a limitation on the states and their jurisdiction over state citizenship. Thus the right to do business within a state—which was at issue in the *Slaughter-House* cases—was a privilege of state citizenship and as such was "left to the state governments for security and protection."[9] The Court also dismissed the other arguments of the plaintiffs in the case. In the opinion of the Court, the Louisiana law did not violate due process of law. And, finally, the Court contended that since the equal-protection clause of the Fourteenth Amendment had been written only to apply to emancipated blacks, it was not applicable to the parties in the *Slaughter-House* cases.

The Supreme Court's verdict in the *Slaughter-House* cases reflected the dominant importance that was still given to the concept of state sovereignty in the late nineteenth century. The Court thus maintained essentially the same views regarding the Fourteenth Amendment that it had expounded earlier with respect to the Bill of Rights in *Barron v. Baltimore*. It left the responsibility for protecting individual liberties and rights against state encroachment entirely within the jurisdiction of the states and outside the national government's constitutional powers.

Extension of the Bill of Rights to the States

A gradual change in the Supreme Court's interpretations of civil liberties began in 1925.

Since that time, in making decisions in specific cases and controversies the Court has included more and more provisions of the Bill of Rights within the meaning of the due process clause of the Fourteenth Amendment. By 1970 these later decisions provided a constitutional basis by which the national government could force states to uphold most of the individual freedoms guaranteed by the Bill of Rights. This included not only the generalized freedoms in the First Amendment but also the procedural rights specified in the Fourth, Fifth, Sixth, Seventh, and Eighth Amendments.

Including the Bill of Rights in due process. The first time that the Supreme Court included part of the Bill of Rights in its interpretation of the Fourteenth Amendment was in the historic case *Gitlow v. New York* in 1925. Benjamin Gitlow had been convicted in New York under the state's Criminal Anarchy Act for distributing a publication that advocated the violent overthrow of government. Gitlow challenged the conviction on the grounds that the New York law violated his right to due process of law guaranteed by the Fourteenth Amendment.

The Supreme Court upheld the constitutionality of the New York law and Gitlow's conviction as well. However, the majority opinion handed down by the Court included a new definition of the meaning of the Fourteenth Amendment's due process clause. The Court said:

We may and do assume that freedom of speech and of the press—which are protected by the First Amendment from abridgment by Congress—are among the fundamental personal rights and "liberties" protected by the due process clause of the Fourteenth Amendment from impairment by the states.[10]

This was the first time the Court formally recognized that the due process clause pre-

---

[9]16 Wallace 36 (1873).

[10]268 U.S. 652 (1925).

vented a *state* from encroaching on the freedoms of speech and press guaranteed by the First Amendment. An important implication of the *Gitlow* decision was that the states as well as the federal government could be restrained from violating other liberties guaranteed by the Bill of Rights.

By nullifying a state law in a subsequent decision, the Court went a step further and gave the federal government a new role of *protecting* individual civil liberties against actual state violations. The first time that the Supreme Court declared a state law unconstitutional under the due process clause of the Fourteenth Amendment was in 1931 in *Near v. Minnesota*. The law in question, known as the "Minnesota gag law," permitted the suppression of newspapers that had published malicious, defamatory, or obscene materials. The law provided that injunctions on such publications could be lifted only if the publishers could first prove that they would print no such materials in the future.

Although the Supreme Court's opinion noted that any publisher must take the consequences for issuing what is "improper, mischievous or illegal" after it was published, freedom of the press—which was guaranteed specifically by the First Amendment and through the due process clause of the Fourteenth Amendment extended to the states—meant freedom from "prior restraint." Thus a newspaper could not be sued for what it intended to publish, but only if the questionable material had appeared in print and was offered for sale. The Minnesota law was therefore declared to be an unconstitutional restraint on freedom of the press.

Once the Court had set a precedent for including civil liberties within the meaning of the due-process clause, it was not long before all the First Amendment provisions were "interpreted into" the Fourteenth Amendment. By 1947 the Court had decided through various cases that many of the rights in the Bill of Rights—including the freedoms of religion,

petition, and assembly, as well as freedoms of speech and of the press—were all individual rights that could not be abridged by the states.

Including procedural rights in due process. The interpretation of the due-process clause to include the procedural rights of those accused of criminal acts has taken longer than the nationalization of First Amendment rights. This has been due in part to the reluctance of the Supreme Court to interfere with specific court procedures of the individual states. Since World War II, however, the Court has gradually interpreted the criminal procedural rights of the Bill of Rights into the meaning of the Fourteenth Amendment and has used such interpretations to limit certain procedures of the state courts.

In 1949, in the case *Wolf v. Colorado*, the Court declared that the "core" of the Fourth Amendment's restriction against unreasonable searches and seizures was binding on the states through the Fourteenth Amendment. The federal "exclusionary rule," however, was *not* applied to the states; the Court held that evidence gathered through an unreasonable search and seizure could be admitted in a state court. Eleven years later the Court decided that evidence acquired by state officials through any unreasonable searches and seizures could not be introduced against a defendant in a federal criminal trial. In 1961, in another decision, the same restriction was made applicable to state court trials.

During the 1960s other constitutional procedural rights were made binding on state criminal proceedings. Among these were the Sixth Amendment guarantees of legal counsel and jury trials to all defendants in criminal prosecutions and the Fifth Amendment guarantee against self-incrimination.

The right to privacy. A development of great importance in the 1960s and 1970s was the extension of the due process clause of the Fourteenth Amendment to include the right to privacy. In *Griswold v. Connecticut* (1965) Jus-

(Courtesy of Handelsman and *Saturday Review*.
Copyright © 1967 by Saturday Review, Inc.)

"If that click on the extension is you, Mother, remember that wiretap evidence is inadmissible."
Legalizing the use of wiretaps has to be weighed against its potential threat to civil liberties.

tice William O. Douglas, writing for the Court's majority, found the right to privacy implied in several parts of the Bill of Rights, including the First, Third, Fourth, Fifth, and Ninth Amendments. He held the right to privacy to be fundamental and therefore incorporated under the due process clause of the Fourteenth Amendment. In the *Griswold* case the Court overturned the Connecticut birth-control statute forbidding the use of contraceptives because it violated the right to privacy of married couples. In *Roe v. Wade* (1973) the Court overturned the Texas criminal abortion laws that prohibited procuring or attempting abortion (except for the purpose of saving the life of the mother) on the basis that they violated a woman's right to privacy. The

Roe case did not, however, grant an absolute right to abortion except during the first three months of pregnancy, when the fetus is not viable (capable of living outside the mother's womb).

At the time the Court decided *Roe v. Wade*, many states had already liberalized their abortion statutes, making abortion no longer a criminal offense and permitting abortions under a wide variety of circumstances. Changes in abortion laws had proceeded quietly and largely without controversy. However, the Supreme Court's dramatic *Roe* decision suddenly called national attention to the abortion issue and made it the center of a growing political controversy between "right-to-life" and "pro-choice" groups. Abortion politics focused not only on the federal courts but also on the presidency, Congress, and state legislatures. The right-to-life movement's goal was to have the Supreme Court overturn its *Roe* decision. Right-to-life groups became active in presidential politics, seeking a candidate who would nominate antiabortion justices to the Supreme Court. At the same time, in the wake of the *Roe* decision—which had the effect, once litigation was completed, of overturning all state criminal abortion statutes—the right-to-life movement pressured state legislatures to reenact strict controls over abortion. The new statutes would provide test cases for the federal courts to determine how much leeway they would grant state legislatures to control abortion.

Litigation over the abortion issue continued throughout the decade of the 1980s, and in 1989 the Supreme Court held in *Webster v. Reproductive Health Services* that the states could prohibit the use of public funds for abortion and ban doctors working for the state from performing abortions. The *Webster* decision, made by a Court that had become increasingly conservative as the result of President Ronald Reagan's three successful nominations—Sandra Day O'Connor, Antonin Scalia, and Anthony Kennedy—while not overruling *Roe*, appeared to be an important step in widening the authority of state legislatures to regulate abortion. Ironically, the *Webster* decision galvanized pro-choice forces, reactivating a movement that had lost much of its intensity and effect after the *Roe* decision. Public opinion polls indicated that a majority of the electorate supported the pro-choice position, making it highly unlikely that most state legislatures would use their newly found au-

thority after the *Webster* decision to enact strict abortion statutes.

State extensions of civil rights. The process of nationalizing the Bill of Rights has involved the imposition of national standards upon the states, many of which had not in their own constitutions or laws gone as far as the national government in protecting individual liberties and rights. However, in the 1970s and 1980s activist state courts defined and ap-

(Gary Brookins, 1989, Richmond *Times-Dispatch*)

The Supreme Court appeared to return the abortion issue to the states in a series of decisions in 1989 and 1990.

plied new constitutional rights that in fact go beyond the federal Constitution and its interpretation by the Supreme Court. Justice Douglas of the New Hampshire Supreme Court expressed the emerging view of many state judges: "Why should we always be the tail being wagged by the federal dog? As a federalist, I feel that it's safer in the long run to have an independent state judiciary. No matter what happens 200 years from now in Washington maybe some things can be presented at the state level."[11] The state courts, often led by the California high court, have extended the right to counsel (Alaska, California, Michigan, New York, Pennsylvania, Utah, and West Virginia), expanded jury trial requirements (Alaska, Alabama, North Carolina), strengthened free-speech guarantees (Arizona, Connecticut, New Jersey, Ohio, Oregon, Pennsylvania, Washington, and West Virginia), bolstered the right to privacy (Alaska, California, Connecticut, Massachusetts, and New Jersey), upheld the right to an education (Arkansas, California, Colorado, Connecticut, Maryland, and New Jersey), fortified self-incrimination protections (California, Hawaii, Pennsylvania), and tightened search and seizure rules (Alaska, California, Florida, Hawaii, Michigan, Montana, Rhode Island, and South Dakota).

While many states are taking the lead in extending civil liberties and civil rights, only the United States Supreme Court has the authority to establish uniform national standards. The importance of those standards was recognized by the nation's 50 chief justices, who unanimously voted in February 1982 to oppose congressional efforts to strip the federal judiciary of jurisdiction over abortion, school desegregation, busing, and school-prayer cases. United States Supreme Court Justice William Brennan, who had served on

the New Jersey high court, applauded the vote, declaring,

Even the premise that state courts can be trusted to safeguard individual rights cannot justify either the Court or Congress in limiting the role of the federal judiciary. For to do so overlooks one of the strengths of our federal system—that it provides a double source of protection for the rights of our citizens. Federalism is not served when the federal half of that protection is crippled.[12]

Religious freedom and the "Wall" of Separation

Unlike other civil liberties, the First Amendment restriction on the government with respect to religion is twofold: "Congress shall make no law respecting the establishment of religion, or prohibiting the free exercise thereof." This means that Congress is prevented not only from interfering with an individual's freedom to worship according to his or her own beliefs but also from establishing an official state religion. The latter restriction was of particular concern to Americans in the eighteenth century because the diverse religious groups that had settled here sought to prevent the kinds of persecution they had experienced abroad in countries with "established" religions.

By 1947 the First Amendment provisions on religion were nationalized when the Supreme Court included them within the meaning of the due process clause of the Fourteenth Amendment. As with other constitutional liberties, the exact meanings of these First Amendment restrictions have had to be interpreted by the Court. With respect to the "free exercise" of religion, Court decisions have generally involved defining the proper balance between individual and community rights. The issue of the establishment clause has been more complex. And the precise meaning of

---

[11]David Margolick, "State Judiciaries Are Shaping Law That Goes Beyond the Supreme Court," *New York Times*, May 19, 1982, p. B8.

[12]Ibid.

BOX 4.1

An Abrupt Change on Abortion: A Survey of College Freshmen Finds Increased Support / *Kenneth J. Cooper*

The number of college freshmen who want to keep abortion legal rose significantly after last July's Supreme Court decision giving states increased powers to regulate abortion, according to an extensive survey of students.

The survey, administered to 216,382 freshmen on 403 campuses last year, found 64.7 percent agreed when asked whether "abortion should be legalized," up from 57 percent in 1988. Support had stayed between 53 percent and 59 percent since the annual survey first posed the abortion question in those words in 1977. About 1.6 million students entered college last fall.

"An abrupt change in student attitudes of this magnitude in just one year is most unusual. . . .I think that's the single largest increase we've seen on any question," says Alexander M. Astin, an education professor at UCLA and director of the survey, first conducted in 1966.

Astin attributes the relatively large jump in student support for legalized abortion to the impact of public protests following the Supreme Court's decision in *Webster v. Reproductive Health Services.*

"Until the Webster decision, a lot of the younger people tended to look at this as an abstract, moral question that didn't have any practical impact on their lives," Astin says. "This Webster decision alerted them to the fact that this is a right that might be taken away."

The survey also found students leaning toward liberal positions on the environment, gun control and health care.

But the students also took some conservative positions. Those agreeing that "employers should be allowed to require drug testing of employees and job applicants" increased from 71 percent in 1988 to 77.8 percent. About 67 percent favored mandatory testing to control the spread of AIDS. Support for legalizing marijuana dropped to an all-time low of 16.7 percent.

Asked which political party ought to be more pleased with the survey results, Astin replies: "If I were a conservative Republican, I'd be more distressed about it. The students want more governmental action on things like the environment and health care."

But a spokeswoman for the Republican National Committee doubts that the survey's findings foreshadow a reversal of a recent trend among younger voters of supporting the party's candidates in national elections.

"I don't think that shows anything troublesome," says Leslie Goodman, the RNC spokeswoman. "The Webster case was not about legalization."

Goodman suggests that the survey reflects the greater public attention paid to the abortion issue in the aftermath of the Webster decision. Astin says most of the surveys were completed between late August and early October although a small number were done earlier in the summer. But he says he doubts that the jump in support will prove ephemeral. It would be unprecedented in the survey's history to see such an increase in support disappear the next year.

"separation of church and state" is still open-ended and has been evolving as specific government activities concerning religion have been challenged through the judicial system.

The free exercise of religion. Individuals are free to worship as they please as long as the religious doctrines they uphold and the rituals they practice do not result in injury to accepted community standards of public safety, morals, or health. In an 1878 case the Supreme Court upheld the conviction of a Mormon who had been practicing polygamy by ruling that polygamy could be punished as a crime even though sanctioned by the Mormon religion. Religious freedom, like all freedoms, is not absolute.

In other cases the Court has nullified various laws that placed what it considered to be unconstitutional restraints on religious freedom. In 1943, for example, it was determined that a state could not tax the distribution of religious material by a religious group. In the same year, overturning an earlier decision, the Court held that a state could not compel the members of a religious group to salute the flag when such an expression was contrary to the group's religious doctrines. In this instance the Court noted that the religious belief presented no "clear and present danger" to the interests of the state.

The free-exercise questions that have confronted the Court over the last several decades have primarily concerned conflicts between religious practices and state laws that require Sunday closing of business and compulsory school attendance. Is the free exercise of religion "burdened" through state legislation requiring businesses to shut down on Sundays, a day that members of the Jewish faith, for example, do not observe as the sabbath? In the 1961 case *Braunfeld v. Brown*, members of the Orthodox Jewish faith challenged closing laws in Pennsylvania, claiming that their religion required them to observe the sabbath on Saturday, not Sunday, and that because they could not keep their business open on Sunday they suffered unfair commercial com-

petition. (Other businesses, open on Saturday, were able to operate for one full day of the week more than they could.) In its decision the Court noted the following:

Certain aspects of religious exercise cannot, in any way, be restricted or burdened by either federal or state legislation. Compulsion by law of the acceptance of any creed or the practice of any form of worship is strictly forbidden. The freedom to hold religious beliefs and opinions is absolute. But this is not the case at bar; the statute before us does not make criminal the holding of any religious belief or opinion, nor does it force anyone to embrace any religious belief or to say or believe anything in conflict with his religious tenet.

It was thus concluded that states do have the power to provide weekly respites from labor and can set aside one day of the week for this purpose. The *Braunfeld* decision was not unanimous, however. Justices Brennan and Stewart dissented, holding that the Pennsylvania statute did in fact interfere with the free exercise of religion.

In 1963, in *Sherbert v. Verner* the Court held that a state could not deny unemployment benefits to a person who refused to accept Saturday work due to religious beliefs. And whether Saturday work could be compelled by a private company became an issue in *Trans World Airlines v. Hardison* in 1977; an employee claimed that TWA's dismissal of him because he refused for religious reasons to work on Saturday violated Title VI of the 1964 Civil Rights Act (which prohibits discrimination on the basis of religion). The majority of the Court found that TWA, which had unsuccessfully sought to find the plaintiff a non-Saturday shift, was not discriminating religiously under the 1964 act.

Compulsory school attendance posed a problem to the free exercise of religion in *Wisconsin v. Yoder*, decided by the Supreme Court in 1972. Amish parents had been convicted and fined five dollars each for failing to send their children to school after the eighth grade in accordance with Amish beliefs against formal high school education beyond that point. The Wisconsin Supreme Court had overturned the conviction, and the U.S. Supreme Court affirmed, holding that the state law constituted an undue interference with the Amish religion. The Court cited the deep religious convictions of the Amish and the fact that they live apart from the community at large. Implied, but not explicitly stated, in the opinion was the Court's recognition of the lack of a compelling state interest in compulsory school attendance for Amish children beyond the eighth grade, since most Amish live the entirety of their lives within the separate boundaries of their own community.

Questions concerning the free exercise of religion continued to confront the Court from time to time. An interesting case arose in 1986, *Goldman v. Weinberger*, involving Air Force captain Goldman, an orthodox Jew and an ordained rabbi, who brought suit against Defense Secretary Weinberger claiming that an Air Force regulation which banned him from wearing a yarmulke (skull cap) indoors infringed his First Amendment freedom to exercise his religious belief. The Supreme Court ruled that the regulation was constitutional. Justice Rehnquist's opinion noted: "Our review of military regulations challenged on First Amendment grounds is far more deferential than constitutional review of similar laws or regulations designed for civilian society." He concluded, "The desirability of dress regulations in the military is decided by the appropriate military officials and they are under no constitutional mandate to abandon their considered professional judgment." The decision caused such a stir that Congress passed legislation in 1987 reversing it. The new law permitted the Secretary of Defense to prohibit the wearing of religious apparel only if it interfered with the performance of military duties, which clearly allowed the wearing of a yarmulke.

Separation of church and state. In defining the establishment clause of the First Amendment, the Supreme Court has held that there must be a "wall" of separation between church and state. That is, the government must not actively aid, support, or encourage any church or religious activity.

The majority of cases dealing with this issue have concerned the role of church and state with regard to education. In these instances the Court has had to decide whether certain governmental activities—such as the financing of transportation and textbooks for students in parochial schools, the use of public school time and facilities for religious instruction, and the sanctioning of official prayer—constitute governmental "establishment of religion."

In the case *Everson v. Board of Education* (1947) the Supreme Court considered the issue regarding local governmental aid to Catholic parochial schools. The state of New Jersey had authorized local school boards to reimburse parents for bus transportation, whether their children attended public or private schools. The New Jersey law was challenged by some taxpayers as a violation of the separation of church and state. In its opinion the Court reasoned that New Jersey was not contributing money or supporting religious schools but was only providing a public service to all schoolchildren. In the words of Justice Hugo Black, the law did "no more than provide a general program to help parents get their children, regardless of their religions, safely and expeditiously to and from accredited schools."[13] In another case, however, the Court held that a board of education could not use tax-supported property for religious instruction. The case, *McCollum v. Board of Education* (1948), involved an Illinois program where students attended classes in religious instruction on public school property.

The distinction between what is and what is not considered an aid to religion was even more closely defined in *Zorach v. Clauson* (1952). The case established a precedent re-

---

[13]330 U.S. 1 (1947).

garding the question of whether state or local governments could authorize public schools to give students time off for religious instruction. New York City had a program that released students to receive such instruction outside the schools but during school hours. The students had to have parental permission, and the churches made reports to the schools of those who attended. In its decision the Court retreated from its previous stand and held that the New York City program did not violate the First Amendment. (In the *McCollum* case the Court had said that the public school was actually used to *promote* religious instruction, whereas in *Zorach* it maintained that "the public schools do no more than accommodate their schedules to a program of outside religious instruction.")[14]

The Supreme Court's most controversial decision regarding the religious question and the establishment clause was rendered in *Engel v. Vitale* (1962). In this case it was held that the recitation of prayers in a public school clearly violated the First Amendment. New York State had adopted a program of daily classroom prayers that were not linked to any particular religion. The state's Board of Regents had recommended that all the schools use the prayers. The parents of 10 students in New Hyde Park, New York, challenged the prayer program in the state court of appeals, which upheld the prayer as long as no student was compelled to join in the recitation. The Supreme Court, however, reversed this decision, declaring that a "program of daily classroom invocation of God's blessing . . . is a religious activity." The Court concluded that such an activity "officially establishes the religious beliefs embodied in the Regent's prayer," and that even though the prayer was "denominationally neutral" it nevertheless violated the establishment clause.[15]

The decision in the *Engel* case caused a furor during which the Court was accused of "driving God out of the schools" and of "abolishing God." Some people have seen the Court's interpretation as interfering with the moral standards taught in the state educational system. On the other hand, some laypeople and religious leaders have considered the Court's stand admirable because it upholds the doctrine of governmental neutrality regarding religion.

The controversy the *Engel v. Vitale* case stirred up over school prayer continued in the decades following the decision. Proponents of school prayer and their congressional allies proposed the adoption of a constitutional amendment to overrule the Court's decision; however, while public opinion polls revealed that well over 80 percent of the American people supported prayer in public schools, the constitutional amendment got nowhere in Congress, due in part to the strong opposition of the chairman of the House Judiciary Subcommittee on the Constitution that had jurisdiction over the matter.

On another front, "Bible Belt" states in particular passed legislation to circumvent the decision. For example, in 1978 Alabama passed a law that authorized its public schools to adopt a one-minute period of silence "for meditation." Another Alabama law, passed in 1981, authorized public schools to have periods of silence "for meditation or voluntary prayer," while yet another law passed the following year authorized school teachers to lead "willing students" in a prayer to "Almighty God . . . the Creator and Supreme Judge of the World." The law was challenged, using the *Engel* precedent, as a violation of the constitutional requirement for the separation of church and state.

The *Engel* case did not phase the federal district court judge who held that new historical evidence supported the authority of states to establish religions! The court of appeals overturned the district court, and in *Wallace*

---

[14]343 U.S. 306 (1952).

[15]370 U.S. 421 (1962).

v. Jaffree (1985) the case reached the Supreme Court. Finding that the intent of the Alabama laws was to put religion back into the public schools, the Court overturned the Alabama legislation. However, several justices left open the question of whether or not "moment-of-silence" statutes would be constitutional in the absence of a religious intent. In another case, *Edwards v. Aguillard* (1987), the Supreme Court overturned a Louisiana Creationism Act which forbade the teaching of the theory of evolution in public schools unless "creation science" was also taught. The law, stated the Court's majority, violated the First Amendment's establishment clause because its purpose was to advance "a religious doctrine by requiring either the banishment of the theory of evolution from public school classrooms or the presentation of a religious viewpoint that rejects evolution in its entirety."

Interpretation of the "wall-of-separation" doctrine is still somewhat ambiguous. Some decisions show a rigid use of the doctrine, while others illustrate a liberal approach. The Supreme Court has held that a religious oath for office requiring an expressed belief in God is unconstitutional. Yet it has held that Sunday closing laws are not unconstitutional, for even though they may once have had religious connotations, today they achieve the secular goals of providing a day of rest and amusement and a time for families to be together.

The most recent decisions of the Court suggest that it will continue to take a firm stand on the separation of church and state. Probably the most difficult problem it will have to face is whether extensive federal aid to education should be granted to religious and nonreligious private schools. Token aid by state and local governments has been upheld. The Court held in 1971, in *Tilton v. Richardson,* that Congress could give aid to sectarian colleges and universities to be used for secular purposes, although in companion cases it barred similar state aid to elementary and secondary parochial schools. In later cases

(From *Straight Herblock* [Simon & Schuster, 1964])

"Every schoolchild should be made to pray against government interference with private lives."

There was much antagonism toward the Court after its decision forbidding prayers in the public schools.

the Court continued to strictly forbid any but the most minor state aid for parochial schools (for example, state loans for textbooks for children in nonpublic elementary and secondary schools).

EQUAL PROTECTION OF THE LAWS

The equal protection clause of the Fourteenth Amendment provides that "no state shall . . .deny to any person in its jurisdiction the equal protection of the laws." The purpose of this clause, which applied only to state action, was to protect the newly freed blacks in the South from discriminatory laws following the Civil War. The Thirteenth and Fifteenth Amendments, also adopted after the Civil War, respectively prohibit slavery and forbid the government to deny citizens of the United States the right to vote on account of race, creed, color, or previous condition of servitude. These amendments uphold equal protection by preventing government discrimination against classes of persons.

Other parts of the Constitution in addition to the Civil War amendments have been interpreted to include equal protection requirements. The Supreme Court has used the due process clause of the Fifth Amendment to apply equal protection standards to the national government.[16] The Court also interpreted Article I, Section 2, of the Constitution—which provides that representatives be chosen "by the people of the several states"— to mean that "as nearly as is practicable, one man's vote in a congressional election is to be worth as much as another's."[17] Finally, at the state level, the privileges and immunities clause of Article IV, Section 2, requires that states grant equal treatment under their laws to citizens of other states.

The meaning of the term "equal protection of the laws" is of course subject to interpretation, and the courts have applied different equal protection standards from one era to another. When laws treat groups or *classes* of persons differently, a potential problem of equal protection arises. Hence race, gender, wealth, and age classifications have appeared in many national and state laws and regulations. For example, the Regents of the University of California promulgated regulations that provided for racial quotas for the admission of students to its medical schools. The Supreme Court overturned the use of strict racial quotas, however, finding them to be in violation of equal protection requirements.[18] Other classifications have also been found constitutionally deficient. For example, the Court struck down provisions of the Social Security Act, which granted survivors' benefits to widows but not to widowers, holding that equal protection standards were not met.[19]

Legislative and administrative classifications that treat people differently are not per se unconstitutional. However, the Supreme Court during the Warren era essentially held that *racial* classifications are inherently unconstitutional. Moreover, the Court required Congress and the state legislatures to demonstrate important, if not compelling, circumstances to justify gender and other classifications, such as alienage and illegitimacy. The evolution and eventual demise of the separate but equal doctrine that once sustained racial classifications to allow the legal segregation of the races illustrates one area in which the Supreme Court dramatically changed its interpretation of equal protection of the laws.

"Separate but Equal"

Despite the Fourteenth Amendment provision that no state may "deny to any person within its jurisdiction the equal protection of the laws," racial segregation has been a fact of life in many parts of the United States. After the Reconstruction era, some states began to pass laws that required racial separation in public facilities, including transportation and recreational facilities, residential areas, and public institutions such as schools. Although "separate," these facilities had to be "equal" in order to avoid violation of the Fourteenth Amendment's equal protection clause.

Plessy v. Ferguson. The separate but equal doctrine was first articulated by the Supreme Court in *Plessy v. Ferguson* (1896). A

---

[16]*Bolling v. Sharpe*, 347 U.S. 497 (1954).

[17]*Wesberry v. Sanders*, 376 U.S. 1 (1964).

[18]*Regents of the University of California v. Bakke*, 438 U.S. 265 (1978).

[19]*Weinberger v. Wiesenfeld*, 420 U.S. 636 (1975).

Louisiana statute required that all railroad companies "carrying passengers...in this state shall provide equal but separate accommodations for the white and colored races." The Supreme Court upheld the statute, saying that the Fourteenth Amendment could not possibly have been intended

to abolish distinctions based upon color, or to enforce social, as distinguished from political, equality, or a commingling of the two races upon terms unsatisfactory to either. Laws permitting, and even requiring their separation in places where they are liable to be brought into contact do not necessarily imply the inferiority of either race to the other, and have been generally, if not universally, recognized as within the competency of the State legislatures in the exercise of their police power.[20]

Thus state laws requiring the separation of the races, the Court said, were perfectly legal. The *Plessy* decision implied that social prejudices could not be overcome by legislation and that blacks should not attempt to obtain equality by commingling with whites. In its formal opinion the Court considered that a state law had forced segregation in railroad cars, but that separate facilities were not "unequal" and that therefore the state law did not violate the equal protection clause of the Fourteenth Amendment. The Court added that the Louisiana law was "reasonable" because it reflected the dominant interests and traditions of its citizens. In upholding the validity of separate but equal facilities in 1896, the Supreme Court itself merely reflected the customs and traditions of the time.

However, the prevailing mores did not prevent Justice John Marshall Harlan, a Kentuckian, from writing a vigorous and impassioned dissenting opinion. To Harlan, the separate but equal doctrine was clearly a violation of constitutional rights. Accommodations that were supposedly "equal" were really not, and state segregation laws implied the inferiority of blacks. In Harlan's opinion:

The destinies of the two races in this country are indissolubly linked together and the interests of both require that the common government of all shall not permit the seeds of race hate to be planted under the sanction of law. What can more certainly arouse race hate, what more certainly create and perpetuate a feeling of distrust between these races, than state enactments which in fact proceed on the ground that colored citizens are so inferior and degraded that they cannot be allowed to sit in public coaches occupied by white citizens?[21]

Implications of "separate but equal." It is, of course, impossible to speculate what the consequences would have been if the Supreme Court had handed down a different decision in *Plessy v. Ferguson*. Since the nation was still recovering from the Civil War, it is quite possible that state segregation might have yielded. Racial separation had not yet become firmly entrenched by a century of tradition. To say this is not to overlook the difficulties that would have existed in overcoming the prevailing social attitudes. But it cannot be said that the *Plessy* decision was the only decision possible in the late nineteenth century. (The very fact that there was a vigorous dissent in the *Plessy* case indicates that another result might have been possible.)

Following the decision in *Plessy v. Ferguson*, many states took advantage of the Court's approval of separate but equal and passed new laws providing for racial segregation. In the first decade of the twentieth century the Court was extremely lenient and permitted the state segregation of the races regardless of whether facilities were in fact equal. In one case it went so far as to say that a school district did not have to provide a high

---

[20]163 U.S. 537 (1896).

[21]163 U.S. 537 (1896) (dissenting opinion).

(Fitzpatrick in the St. Louis *Post-Dispatch*)

Carrying on the "Separate but Equal" Theory
Separate but equal Supreme Courts could only result in the inadequacy of one of the paired institutions.

school at all for black children, even though it had one for whites.

The inequalities of state segregation that were pointed out by Justice Harlan in 1896 soon became evident, however, to an increasing number of people. As time passed, the Court became more and more insistent that the states provide equal facilities, at least in physical properties.

End of "Separate but Equal"

By the time the Supreme Court held segregation of public education to be unconstitutional, in 1954, precedents already had been established that weakened the separate but equal tradition. As early as 1938 the Court held, in *Missouri ex rel. Gaines v. Canada*, that the refusal of a state to admit an applicant to

its state law school solely on the basis of the applicant's race was a denial of equal protection of the laws. The state of Missouri, which had no separate law school for blacks, in order to maintain racial segregation had devised a plan whereby black law students would be granted tuition if they went out of state for their legal education. On the basis of this plan, Lloyd Gaines, a black citizen of Missouri, had been denied admission to the University of Missouri Law School. Gaines took his case to the Supreme Court. In its decision the Court said that the Missouri plan did not release that state from its responsibility to provide equal educational facilities for blacks and whites *within its borders*. Gaines was thus "entitled to be admitted to the law school of the state university in the absence of other and proper provision for his legal training within the state."[22]

Ten years later the Court reaffirmed its 1938 decision and held in *Sipuel v. University of Oklahoma* that a black student could not be denied admission to the University of Oklahoma Law School if whites were permitted to attend. And in *McLaurin v. Oklahoma State Regents* (1950) the Court decided that blacks attending the University of Oklahoma Law School had to be accorded facilities the same as and not just "equal to" those of whites.

Relevant to the *Gaines*, *Sipuel*, and *McLaurin* cases, since Missouri and Oklahoma had provided legal education for whites without making any provision whatsoever for blacks, the Court could justify its decision that such action was a denial of equal protection of the laws. But if the states made provisions for separate law schools for blacks, would not the Court then hold such action to be in conformity with the separate but equal doctrine?

Sweatt v. Painter. In an actual case the Supreme Court decided that separate law

---

[22]305 U.S. 337 (1938).

schools could not in fact be equal. The decision in *Sweatt v. Painter* (1950) set the stage for the final blow to the separate but equal doctrine.

In 1946, at a time when no Texas law school admitted blacks, Sweatt applied for admission to the University of Texas Law School. Because his application was turned down due to his race, he appealed to a state court for a writ of mandamus, which would compel university officials to admit him. As a result of a delay in state court action, Texas gained six months in which to provide equal law school facilities for blacks. During the course of the appeal, a law school for blacks was opened in Texas, and the state courts found that the new law school offered Sweatt the same "privileges, advantages, and opportunity for the study of law" as those given to whites.

Sweatt then took his case to the Supreme Court, which found that the facilities offered by Texas to blacks and whites were clearly unequal. In reaching a decision, the Court considered first whether the separate facilities in Texas for legal education were equal. It found that the new law school for blacks had no independent faculty or library. Four members of the University of Texas Law School faculty taught courses in both institutions. Although the library of the new school was supposed to have 10,000 volumes, virtually no books had arrived. There was also no provision for a full-time librarian. As a result of these defects, the new school had not been accredited. By comparison, the University of Texas Law School—with a student body of close to 900, a library of over 65,000 volumes, a law review, moot court facilities, scholarship funds, an active alumni with access to numerous state legal positions, and full accreditation—was obviously superior. The Supreme Court in fact found that the University of Texas Law School "may properly be considered one of the nation's ranking law schools." Most important, the Court decided after its investigation that

no separate schooling could ever be equal in legal education:

> Few students and no one who has practiced law would choose to study in [a] . . . vacuum, removed from the interplay of ideas and the exchange of views with which the law is concerned. The law school to which Texas is willing to admit petitioner [Sweatt] excludes from its student body members of the racial groups [whites] which number 85 percent of the population of the state and include most of the lawyers, witnesses, jurors, judges and other officials with whom petitioner will inevitably be dealing when he becomes a member of the Texas bar. With such a substantial and significant segment of society excluded, we cannot conclude that the education offered petitioner is substantially equal to that which he would receive if admitted to the University of Texas Law School.[23]

Brown v. Board of Education of Topeka.
In 1954, in one of the most far-reaching decisions in the history of the Supreme Court, the principle that separate was *not* equal was extended to all public education. The decision actually involved four separate cases in which black students were seeking admission to all-white public schools in the states of Kansas, South Carolina, Virginia, and Delaware. Because the four separate cases involved a single legal question, the Court determined that they should be heard and decided together.

The significance of the *Brown* case prompted the filing of amici curiae briefs by a number of groups interested in civil rights. The cases on behalf of the students were argued by a legal team led by Thurgood Marshall of the NAACP.

The decision of the Court was unanimous in finding that the school districts in the case had separate schools for blacks that were relatively equal with regard to "buildings, curricula, qualifications and salaries of teachers,

---

[23]339 U.S. 629 (1950).

and other 'tangible' factors." But tangible factors were not enough. The Court went on to say: "We must look instead to the effect of segregation itself on public education."

Education, the Court said, is the very keystone of individual success in all endeavors today. It is "a principal instrument in awakening the child to cultural values, in preparing him for later professional training and in helping him to adjust normally to this environment." Even though the tangible properties may be equal among segregated schools, this does not mean that they will have an equal impact on children. The Court concluded that "separate educational facilities are inherently unequal" and that such segregation "is a denial of the equal protection of the laws."[24]

Since the Court was aware that its decision would not be easily implemented, it refrained from dealing with implementation until the following year. In its 1955 decision the Court said that desegregation was to be carried out with "all deliberate speed," but it permitted the district courts to determine the proper rate for desegregation. Taking into account the impact its decision would have, the Court did not force immediate integration on states with a tradition of segregation. Consequently, the progress of school integration has been slow. By 1969 most of the black students in 17 Southern states, including the District of Columbia, were attending integrated schools. By the mid-1970s all Southern school districts had begun to end dual systems. However, many black students were still attending schools that were predominantly black, not only in the South but throughout the country. Thus racial separation in public schools is as great, if not greater, in the North as in the South. The doctrine of equal education for all has been clearly established by the judiciary, but the courts alone cannot enforce their decisions.

---

[24]347 U.S. 483 (1954).

Enforcement problems after *Brown*. Although 35 years have passed since the decision of the Court in *Brown v. Board of Education*, the fact remains that meaningful school integration has not occurred in either the South or the North. The percentage of black students attending all-black schools decreased dramatically in the decade from the early 1960s to the early 1970s. However, in the schools of most communities this did not produce in the succeeding decade a balance corresponding to the representation of the races in those communities.

One problem, of course, is how to define what constitutes a "community" for the purposes of public education. Should cities and the suburbs that surround them be considered one large public school district within which integration is required? Or should urban and suburban schools be permitted to maintain their racial patterns?

Residential segregation leads to school segregation. When students are assigned to schools on the basis of the neighborhoods in which they live, patterns of racial segregation in the schools go largely undisturbed. In the early 1970s the courts began to require the busing of students within large metropolitan areas in both the North and South to achieve ratios within the schools that approximated the racial balance existing within the larger communities. In *Swann v. Charlotte-Mecklenburg County Board of Education* (1971) the Supreme Court held that in Southern states where there had been a history of legally enforced segregation, the district courts had broad authority to order the integration of school systems by requiring the reassignment of pupils and teachers so as to reflect a racial balance similar to that within the communities. This meant the courts could order the busing of students for this purpose, and the *Swann* decision established a precedent for court-ordered busing that affected a number of Southern communities, including Charlotte-Mecklenburg, North Carolina, and Richmond,

Virginia. The busing of pupils in those communities to achieve integration produced a sometimes violent backlash from parents and other supporters of neighborhood schools. In general there was, and still is, widespread reaction against busing both from whites and from many members of minority groups in both the South and North. One response to court-ordered busing in Southern and Northern cities, by whites who can afford it, has been a growing exodus to the suburbs.

This "white flight," as it has been called, has created predominantly white suburban school districts. During the 1970s the courts interpreted the equal protection clause to require racial balance not only within school districts but also in some cases *between* city school districts and the surrounding but legally separate suburban school districts. In such cases the busing of pupils across district lines was ordered to achieve racial balance.

Although the *Swann* decision ordered busing, it did not involve busing *between* districts, because Charlotte already includes the surrounding county in its city school district. But only 18 of the 100 largest city school districts are like Charlotte in this respect. Thus in many cities integration would require interdistrict busing, and to achieve racial balance in largely black inner-city schools in cities that are predominantly black, civil rights activists have pressed for the enactment of this measure.

Civil rights activists received a severe setback to this goal in 1974, when the Supreme Court in *Milliken v. Bradley* abruptly halted court-ordered interdistrict busing. In the *Milliken* case the Court held that the equal protection clause only requires racial balance *within* school districts, not between them. Residents of Detroit had successfully sought from the lower federal courts an order to integrate the Detroit school system with 53 outlying school districts. In overturning the lower court's decision, the Supreme Court stated:

Disparate treatment of white and Negro students occurred within the Detroit school system and not elsewhere, and on the record the remedy must be limited to that system.

The *Milliken* case left untouched court orders for busing within such city school districts as Boston and San Francisco. (The federal court abandoned its busing plan in San Francisco in 1977 when it found it to be unfeasible.)

Extending the Equal Protection Clause to New Areas

The potential controversy over judicial interpretation of the equal protection clause as it applied to the delivery of public services threatened to be as great or even greater than that caused by *Brown v. Board of Education* (1954) and the busing decisions of the early 1970s.

Discrimination against the poor. Both federal and state courts began to hold that the equal protection clause required equality in the financing of public education. The pioneer decision in this extension of the equal protection clause was that of the California Supreme Court in *Serrano v. Priest*, initially rendered in 1971 and affirmed in 1976. Citing the state as well as the federal Constitution, the decision invalidated the local property tax as a basis for financing public education, because it discriminated against poor communities. The reasoning was that the per-pupil expenditures for education in wealthy communities greatly exceeded those in poor ones if the property tax was used to finance education. The *Serrano* decision was followed by a number of others of a similar nature in both state and federal courts.

The Supreme Court, however, in *San Antonio v. Rodriguez* (1973) essentially overruled that part of the *Serrano* decision and related decisions which had applied the Fourteenth Amendment equal protection clause to require equality in state financing of education. In

Rodriguez the Court held that the equal protection clause of the Fourteenth Amendment does not require equality in the financing of education. In a complicated decision the Court found that "poor people" do not constitute a class of persons that can be identified as such for the purposes of determining discrimination. Moreover, the Court held that there is no "fundamental" right to education under the Constitution. The Court found, too, that judicial self-restraint should be exercised in cases of this kind involving local control over education—namely, that it should defer to the judgment of state and local communities regarding the financing of their educational systems. (This philosophy was in line with the more conservative approach of the Burger Court in intergovernmental relations.)

Another extension of the equal protection clause came in 1972, when the Supreme Court used this clause to overrule the imposition of the death penalty. In *Furman v. Georgia* (1972) the Court held in a five-to-four decision that the death penalty as imposed "in these cases" violated the Eighth and Fourteenth Amendments. Neither the majority nor the dissenting justices could agree on a basis for the decision, and nine separate opinions were written. The implication that can be drawn from the opinions of the justices in the majority is that the death penalty is unconstitutional because it is not imposed consistently and tends to fall heavily on the "poor, young, and ignorant." A number of states attempted to meet the objections of the Court by passing laws in which the death sentence was mandated, thereby ensuring equal treatment to all those convicted of capital crimes.

Although the *Furman* case was a successful challenge to the death penalty, subsequent cases modified the ruling, and the death penalty was restored and carried out long after the *Furman* case. In the late 1970s a new tack was taken by those challenging capital punishment, who alleged that it violated the constitutional prohibition upon cruel and unusual punishment in the Eighth Amendment. The Supreme Court, however, did not accept the argument and held, in *Gardner v. Florida* (1977) and in other cases, that the death penalty is not, per se, a violation of the Eighth Amendment. But before the death sentence can be imposed the judge or jury must take into account a defendant's record and extenuating circumstances. Mandatory death sentences, a way in which the states attempted to get around the *Furman* decision because such sentences by definition could not be unequally imposed for the same crime, are cruel and unusual punishment under the Eighth Amendment and are therefore unconstitutional.

Gender discrimination. The Warren Court continued to amplify the equal protection clause in its treatment of sex-discrimination cases. The failure of a majority of states to ratify the proposed Equal Rights Amendment (ERA) makes the Court's decisions preventing discrimination on the basis of sex particularly important.

A potential issue of sex or gender discrimination arises when a federal, state, or local law classifies women or men of the same status as their opposite-sex counterparts for differential treatment. For example, federal laws, until they were declared unconstitutional on equal protection grounds, denied the same benefits to the male spouses of female members of the armed forces as were granted to the female spouses of male members. Under the Social Security system, federal laws also granted survivors' benefits to widowers and widows on a different basis.[25]

At the state and local level, gender classifications designed to "protect" women and more importantly to preserve the traditional view of the male-dominated family have been commonplace. In 1873 the Court, upholding a state law that prohibited the practice of law by women, wrote that "man is, or should be,

---

[25]These two laws were respectively declared unconstitutional in *Frontiero v. Richardson*, 411 U.S. 677 (1973) and in *Weinberger v. Wiesenfeld*, 420 U.S. 636 (1975). See also *Califano v. Goldfarb*, 430 U.S. 199 (1977).

woman's protector and defender" and that the "paramount destiny and mission of women are to fulfill the noble and benign offices of wife and mother. This is the law of the Creator."[26] The Court sustained state laws based upon the stereotypical view of women as weaker than men (and therefore needing protection for their own good) in upholding state statutes that (1) limited the working hours of women,[27] (2) prohibited the licensing of women as bartenders unless they were wives or daughters of the male owners of bars,[28] and (3) exempted women from jury duty unless they volunteered, while requiring men to serve on juries.[29] As late as 1974 the Court upheld a Florida law that granted a property tax exemption to widows but not to widowers. Justice William O. Douglas wrote the Court's opinion, arguing that the state statute was "reasonably designed to further the state policy of cushioning the financial impact of spousal loss upon the sex for which that loss imposes a disproportionately heavy burden."[30] And in 1975 the Court sustained a law granting female naval officers more time to qualify for promotions than their male counterparts. The Court pointed to the "demonstrable fact that male and female line officers in the navy are *not* similarly situated with respect to opportunities for professional service" and concluded that Congress reasonably could treat women more favorably in order to rectify patterns of past career discrimination.[31]

Although the Court continues to allow gender classifications under certain circumstances, in the 1970s it began to strike down classifications based on stereotyped distinctions between the sexes. The key case was

Frontiero v. Richardson (1973), which overturned the law that treated the spouses of female and male members of the armed services differently. The Court unapprovingly recalled the history of sex discrimination:

There can be no doubt that our nation has had a long and unfortunate history of sex discrimination. Traditionally, such discrimination was rationalized by an attitude of "romantic paternalism," which, in practical effect, put women, not only on a pedestal, but in a cage. . . .

. . .[O]ur statute books gradually became laden with gross, stereotyped distinctions between the sexes, and indeed, throughout much of the nineteenth century the position of women in our society was, in many respects, comparable to that of blacks, under the pre-Civil War slave codes. Neither slaves nor women could hold office, serve on juries, or bring suit in their own names, and married women traditionally were denied the legal capacity to hold or convey property or serve as legal guardians of their own children. And although blacks were guaranteed the right to vote in 1870, women were denied even that right . . .until adoption of the nineteenth amendment half a century later.

It is true, of course, that the position of women in America has improved markedly in recent decades. Nevertheless, it can hardly be doubted that, in part because of the high visibility of the sex characteristic, women still face pervasive, although at times more subtle, discrimination in our educational institutions, in the job market, and, perhaps most conspicuously, in the public arena.[32]

Among the cases reflecting the new judicial attitude and the strict scrutiny of gender classifications is *Orr v. Orr* (1979), which declared unconstitutional Alabama's alimony statutes that placed the obligation of alimony upon husbands but not upon wives. The statute was designed to benefit needy wives, but the Court pointed out that the same objective could be obtained without a gender classification that excluded needy males. The Court

---

[26]*Bradwell v. State,* 83 U.S. 130, 141 (1873).

[27]*Muller v. Oregon,* 208 U.S. 412 (1908).

[28]*Goesaert v. Cleary,* 335 U.S. 464 (1948).

[29]*Hoyt v. Florida,* 368 U.S. 57 (1961).

[30]*Kahn v. Shevin,* 416 U.S. 351 (1974).

[31]*Schlesinger v. Ballard,* 419 U.S. 498 (1975). Emphasis added.

[32]411 U.S. 677 (1973).

emphasized that "even statutes purportedly designed to compensate for and ameliorate the effects of past discrimination must be carefully tailored. Whereas here, the state's compensatory and ameliorative purposes are as well served by a gender-neutral classification as one that gender-classifies and therefore carries with it the baggage of sexual stereotypes, the state cannot be permitted to classify on the basis of sex."[33]

Gender classifications continue to exist in law but are now carefully analyzed by the courts to make certain they are not based upon sexual stereotypes and are justified on the basis of a demonstrably important governmental interest. The Equal Rights Amendment, which died in 1982, would have ended all gender classifications, even those designed to remedy the effects of past discrimination against women.

Judicial policy on affirmative action programs—the *Defunis* and *Bakke* cases. The 1970s witnessed not only attempts to expand the equal protection clause to provide equality in public service delivery but also an effort to extend the equal protection clause to prohibit "reverse discrimination"—the "affirmative action" programs under which educational institutions admitted members of racial minorities on a preferential treatment basis. In the case of *Defunis v. Odegard* (1974) the Supreme Court was asked to decide whether or not an affirmative action program used by the University of Washington Law School violated the equal protection clause of the Fourteenth Amendment. The rules of the University of Washington Law School provided that special consideration could be given to black, Hispanic, American Indian, and Filipino applicants. Defunis, who was white and had been denied admission to the school, claimed he was being discriminated against since his qualifications were superior to those of some minority students who had been given special consideration.

A Washington state trial court agreed with Defunis and ordered his admission to the University of Washington Law School in 1971. The Washington Supreme Court overturned the trial court's decision, but Justice Douglas of the United States Supreme Court issued a stay that suspended the application of the decision of the Supreme Court of Washington until the Court could resolve the issue. This meant that the trial court's decision stood, and Defunis was admitted to the University of Washington Law School.

In a classic decision illustrating judicial self-restraint the Supreme Court voted five to four in 1974 to refuse to decide the *Defunis* case, essentially holding that since Defunis was going to graduate at the end of the 1974 spring term, there was no longer a live case and controversy.

While the issue of reverse discrimination temporarily died with the *Defunis* case, it was brought up again in the case of *Regents of the University of California v. Bakke* in 1977. Allan Bakke, a white, 36-year-old engineer, decided that he wanted to become a doctor and applied twice (in 1973 and 1974) for admission to the University of California Medical School at Davis. Each time he was turned down, the reason being given by the school that there were too many qualified applicants, which resulted in only one out of twenty-six applicants being accepted in 1973, and one out of thirty-seven in 1974. Sixteen of the one hundred openings in the Davis Medical School were set aside for "minority" applicants. Bakke's "objective" qualifications, such as his Medical College Admission Test scores and his undergraduate grades, were better than those of some of the minority applicants accepted during the years when he was rejected. He therefore alleged reverse discrimination, charging that the Davis program violated the equal protection clause of the Fourteenth Amendment.

In holding that the Davis program was not unconstitutional on its face, the California Supreme Court ruled that since the university

---

[33]440 U.S. 268 (1979).

had not attempted to realize its stated goals of providing better medical care for minority communities through nonracial quotas or other means, there could be no demonstration of a "compelling state interest" justifying the quota program. Therefore the university had violated the equal protection clause of the Fourteenth Amendment. In issuing a writ of certiorari[34] to the California Supreme Court to review the decision, the U.S. Supreme Court squarely faced the issue of reverse discrimination once again. Simply upholding the California Supreme Court's decision would not mean the death of minority recruiting programs in professional schools, colleges, and universities but would require that nonracial means be tried in recruiting and admitting applicants to serve minority or disadvantaged communities. The controversy over the decision was illustrated by the filing of 60 briefs on the case with the Supreme Court, representing the views of more than 150 individuals and groups. Minority groups made this the key issue of 1977, proclaiming that the abolition of racial quotas for admission to medical and professional schools would be a disastrous and unfair blow to the progress of integration in higher education.

Over eight months after the Bakke case was argued, a split Supreme Court ruled that Bakke should be admitted to medical school. A majority on two issues in the five-to-four decision held that the racial quota system at the Davis Medical School was not an acceptable means for deciding who should be admitted. The majority justices favoring admission and a ban on quotas were Powell, Burger, Stevens, Rehnquist, and Stewart. Brennan, White, Marshall, and Blackmun dissented on these issues, arguing that "Davis's special admissions program cannot be said to violate the Constitution simply because it has set aside a predetermined number of places for qualified minority applicants. . . ."

Justice Louis F. Powell, who was in the majority favoring admission and a ban on quotas, joined with the four dissenters to form a majority that held an applicant's race can be considered in deciding who should be admitted to a university program. The California court had rejected not only quotas, but also had enjoined the university from ever considering race as a factor in its admissions program. In response to this, Justice Powell, announcing the judgment of the Court in the *Bakke* case, said: "In enjoining petitioner [University of California] from ever considering the race of any applicant, however, the courts below failed to recognize that the state has a substantial interest that legitimately may be served by a properly devised admissions program involving the competitive consideration of race and ethnic origin. For this reason, so much of the California court's judgment as enjoins petitioner from any consideration of the race of any applicant must be reversed."

The effect of the Bakke decision was limited in that it extended only to the denial of the use of strict racial quotas in admissions programs. Presumably such quotas would also be considered unconstitutional in other affirmative action programs. Neither universities nor other institutions, however, were precluded from giving favorable treatment in admissions or employment to racial minorities. "Flexible" affirmative action programs throughout the nation remained intact after the decision, and several rulings following *Bakke* seemed to affirm the Court's lenient attitude toward affirmative action. The Court declined to review a lower court decision that had upheld a program of the American Telephone and Telegraph Company, which established employment and promotion goals for women, blacks, and minority groups. It also directed the Court of Appeals for the fourth circuit to reconsider its decision striking down the University of North Carolina's rules of the student government, under which two seats

---

[34]The Supreme Court issues a *writ of certiorari* to lower courts to have them certify the accuracy of their record of the case and submit it to the Court for review.

on the student legislature were set aside for black representatives, whether they had been elected or not. The Supreme Court referred the Appeals Court to its *Bakke* decision, which would allow race to be taken into account in student government rules, while at the same time prohibiting strict racial quotas from being established.

A divided Supreme Court during the Reagan years in the decade of the 1980s alternately supported and rejected affirmative action plans. Critical to the Court's decisions was a determination of whether or not organizations charged with violating the affirmative action provisions of the 1964 Civil Rights Act and subsequent executive orders demonstrated an *intent* to exclude minorities and women. For example, in *United States v. Paradise* (1987), the Court, on a five-to-four vote, upheld lower court orders directing the Alabama state troopers to step up their appointment and promotion of blacks to the force under an affirmative action plan. The prior year, in *Firefighters v. Cleveland* (1986), the city admitted to past racial discrimination, and the Supreme Court, by a vote of six to three, upheld a dissent decree establishing a quota for minority promotions. But, in *Wygant v. Jackson Board of Education* (1986), the Court overturned a contract between a union and a school board that gave probationary blacks preference over tenured whites when layoffs occurred. No past discrimination on the part of the school board was found, and the Court's majority held that discrimination by society in general in the past was insufficient to uphold preferential treatment for minorities.

In the future, affirmative action will continue to be debated in the political arena and litigated in the courts. An increasingly conservative Supreme Court, due largely to President Reagan's appointments in the 1980s, will very likely require a solid demonstration of specific past discrimination on the part of organizations before the Court will uphold affirmative action decisions.

CIVIL RIGHTS LEGISLATION

Since the report of President Harry S. Truman's Committee on Civil Rights in 1947, occupants of the White House have been urging Congress to pass various types of civil rights legislation. The 1954 *Brown* decision of the Supreme Court provided additional impetus for Congress to take positive action. Finally, in 1957 Congress passed its first civil rights legislation in 82 years. Civil rights legislation passed since 1957 has dealt with the safeguarding of voting rights and federal protection against discrimination in public accommodations, jobs, and housing.

Protecting the Right to Vote

The 1957 civil rights legislation pertained to voting rights. Essentially, the Civil Rights Act of 1957 empowered the Civil Rights Commission to investigate any situation where the denial of suffrage due to race or color was suspected. Before 1957, a black who had been denied the right to vote had to take his case into the courts. This was a costly and time-consuming procedure, and few people took advantage of it. The 1957 act gave the attorney general of the United States the authority to file a suit against any state official who denied a person the right to vote.

Three years later, in 1960, Congress strengthened this legislation with another Civil Rights Act that gave the Justice Department the authorization to send voting referees to areas where a "pattern or practice" of discrimination in voting had become evident. The voting referees were supposed to encourage the registration of black voters.

The Voting Rights Act of 1965 augmented the referee concept by barring all discriminatory "tests and devices" wherever less than 50 percent of the eligible voters had been registered in 1964. Examiners were appointed by the Justice Department to register qualified voters in these areas.

The sweeping Civil Rights Act of 1964 was

THE WHITE MALES OUT FRONT ARE A NICE TOUCH, REHNQUIST...

(Washington Post National Weekly Edition, July 24–30, 1989, p. 14; by Ohman for the *Oregonian*, Portland)

The Supreme Court, under Chief Justice William H. Rehnquist, retreated from affirmative action.

the first major piece of civil rights legislation since Reconstruction. It was passed only after much debate and a lengthy Senate filibuster. The 1964 act first fortified the voting rights acts of 1957 and 1960. The act made it illegal for any local or state voter-registration procedure to be applied in a discriminatory way and prohibited the voiding of registrations on the basis of minor errors on registration forms. The 1964 act also required that all literacy texts be given in written form unless the attorney general, in agreement with state and local authorities, allowed oral tests. The act further provided that any adult person with a sixth-grade education had to be considered literate.

Public Accommodations

The 1964 act also established national criteria for ending discrimination in public accommodations. In setting these standards, the 1964 legislation preempted any state laws or actions supporting discrimination if the lodgings in question were used to house transient guests or interstate travelers or if the goods sold or entertainment provided moved in interstate commerce. Under this provision restaurants, movie houses, theaters, hotels, and other "public" establishments were directed to permit access to their facilities without regard to the race, color, or national origin of customers. The scope of the 1964 act also extended to nondiscrimination in federally assisted programs. It outlawed some discriminatory employment practices, such as the classification of employees into particular jobs due to race, the exclusion of such employees from labor unions, and discrimination against minorities in apprenticeship or job-training programs.

Policies of nondiscrimination in housing have emerged from both the executive and legislative branches. In 1962 President John F. Kennedy signed an executive order forbidding discrimination in all housing built with federal assistance. This included not only public housing constructed with federal funds but also private homes whose mortgages were guaranteed by the Federal Housing Administration or the Veterans Administration.

In 1966 President Lyndon Johnson began asking Congress to pass more extensive openhousing legislation. Measures were included in the Civil Rights Act of 1968 by which discrimination in sale or rental became illegal for approximately 80 percent of all housing. The Department of Housing and Urban Development (HUD) was authorized to investigate violations, and the attorney general was empowered to sue whenever there was any evidence of continued discrimination.

A Continuing Struggle

The Johnson era marked the culmination of direct governmental efforts to protect civil rights through legislation and executive action. The President had unilaterally taken dramatic and far-reaching action when he signed an executive order requiring the federal bureaucracy and all private recipients of federal funds to establish affirmative action programs. The civil rights thrust of the Johnson administration was to protect classes of persons—minorities and women—who had suffered past discrimination from being denied equal opportunities in the future. Under affirmative action programs, the government encouraged

"reverse discrimination," *in favor of* racial minorities and women in order to remedy the effects of past discrimination. The proponents of affirmative action argued that the government and institutions in the private sector owed favored treatment to those who had formerly suffered discriminatory treatment.

The decade of the 1960s was the zenith of the civil rights movement, a time of vigorous government action to reinforce the Warren Court's new emphasis upon the importance of equal protection of the laws. The constitutional definition of civil rights was extended, and in some cases supplanted, by political outcomes. While the politics of the 1960s supported new legislation to protect civil rights, the politics of the 1970s and 1980s have reflected a rising conservative tide that views skeptically—and often antagonistically—the efforts of the federal government to expand the civil rights of minorities and women.

As the civil rights movement receded along with the turbulent 1960s, a new conservatism began slowly to take hold. The *Bakke* decision had been an important milestone that modified affirmative action programs. The conservative Nixon appointees to the Supreme Court made the difference in its shift against affirmative action, although Justice William O. Douglas, one of the Court's staunchest liberals, had originally opposed the concept in the *Defunis* case.[35]

President Ronald Reagan's 1980 victory, as well as the installation of a Republican Senate for the first time in 28 years, marked significant changes in the politics of civil rights. Perhaps the Republican chairman of the Senate Labor and Human Resources Committee, Orrin Hatch of Utah, best expressed the attitude embodied in the new conservatism:

I believe affirmative action is an assault upon America, conceived in lies and fostered with an

---

[35]The *Defunis* and *Bakke* cases have been discussed previously in this chapter.

when a Japanese attack was considered by large numbers of people within and outside the government, including military leaders, to be an imminent possibility on the West Coast. An even more likely probability was considered to be sabotage and subversion by Japanese infiltrators and fifth column agents from within. These fears eventually led to the establishment of concentration camps for Japanese Americans, largely based upon an executive order of President Roosevelt, a decision that was upheld by the Supreme Court against constitutional challenges in *Korematsu v. United States* in 1944. Writing for the majority of the Court, Justice Hugo Black said that during wartime, military necessity justified the order that excluded Japanese Americans from the West Coast because, after all, "hardships are a part of war and war is an aggregation of hardships." Did the exclusionary order constitute racial discrimination? No, said the Court, for although only the Japanese Americans were excluded, the reason was not race but military necessity. The *Korematsu* case was an extreme one, but it illustrates the degree to which civil rights have been denied on the basis of the public interest.

In drawing the line between public interest and individual freedom, the Supreme Court has relied upon the "balancing test," which attempts to weigh the needs of government against the rights of individuals to determine the proper balance between permissible government restraints and individual freedom. One of the most important spheres of civil liberties where the balancing test has been applied is with regard to the civil liberties and rights enumerated in the First Amendment, particularly the liberties of speech, press, and, primarily at the local level, the right of assembly. In addition to the balancing test, the "clear and present danger" test is particularly used in determining the permissible scope of political speech, press, and assembly. In this political sphere the clear and present danger test is used to judge the extent to which Congress or the state legislatures may regulate and control the expression of political ideas.

"Clear and Present Danger"

The most rigid policies against internal threats are usually initiated during times of war. At such times foreign powers could undermine the nation's fighting capability by encouraging espionage, sabotage, or the circulation of subversive propaganda. During wartime, the people are usually primed by the government to be suspicious of the enemy—looking for enemy agents even among loyal citizens—and to be ready to counteract any potential threat. At the same time they are less likely to resist the sacrifice of their own individual freedoms when this would aid a war effort.

An example of this attitude occurred in the United States during World War I. Even before the country joined its allies in the fighting, there was a great deal of pressure on Congress to pass legislation that would curtail certain activities by disloyal individuals. In June 1917, two months after the United States entered the war, the Espionage Act was passed. Under this law anyone circulating false statements that might interfere with military success, obstruct recruiting efforts, or encourage disloyalty in the armed forces was liable to punishment. To some individuals this act seemed in direct conflict with the freedoms of speech and press protected by the First Amendment.

The *Schenck* case. The first opportunity the Supreme Court had to rule on the constitutionality of the Espionage Act came two years later in *Schenck v. United States* (1919). Schenck and his associates had circulated a pamphlet among draftees that was allegedly intended to cause insubordination and to obstruct recruitment.

The pamphlet argued that the military draft violated the Thirteenth Amendment prohibition against involuntary servitude and suggested that the draft was a despotic, monstrous wrong against humanity committed in the interests of Wall Street. The pamphlet urged new recruits to assert their rights and oppose conscription. Although this appeal was couched in rather strong language, for the most part the form of resistance suggested by the pamphlet was not violent. After Schenck was convicted in a federal district court for violating the Espionage Act, he appealed to the Supreme Court on the grounds that his First Amendment freedoms of speech and press had been unconstitutionally abridged.

The Supreme Court upheld Schenck's conviction. In delivering the majority opinion of the Court, Justice Oliver Wendell Holmes enumerated for the first time the clear and present danger test that has guided decisions in similar cases ever since. Said Holmes:

In many places and in ordinary times the defendants in saying all that was said in the circular would have been within their constitutional rights. But the character of every act depends upon the circumstances in which it is done. . . .The question in every case is whether the words used are used in such circumstances and are of such a nature as to create a *clear and present danger* that they will bring about the substantive evils that Congress has a right to prevent. . . .When a nation is at war, many things that might be said in time of peace are such a hindrance to its effort that their utterance will not be endured so long as men fight, and that no court could regard them as protected by any constitutional right [emphasis added].[37]

Thus Schenck's First Amendment freedoms of speech and press did not extend to the distribution of a pamphlet that constituted a clear and present danger by obstructing military recruitment during wartime. Congress had the "right" (authority and responsibility) to prevent obstructions to military recruitment during times of war, and if individuals through speech or press presented a clear and present danger that they would bring about

the "substantive evil" of obstruction, their First Amendment rights could be curtailed. The Espionage Act was constitutional, and Schenck's conviction was upheld because the purpose and tendency of his actions was to violate the act by obstructing military recruitment.

On the basis of the *Schenck* case, it became clear that the Supreme Court would limit the freedom of speech if such freedom resulted in a clear and present danger to national security. But just what constituted a clear and present danger was obviously a matter for further interpretation. As with other constitutional interpretations, the definition has varied from case to case, depending upon the times and the circumstances.

The Smith Act and the *Dennis* case. After the Supreme Court's decision in the *Schenck* case, many subsequent controversies were decided that further clarified the clear and present danger doctrine. One of the most famous of these involved the constitutionality of the Smith Act, which was passed in 1940 prior to the entrance of the United States into World War II. The Smith Act made it unlawful for any person "to knowingly or willfully advocate . . .overthrowing or destroying any government in the United States by force or violence" or to belong to any organization that so advocated. The Smith Act raised many serious questions concerning the freedoms of speech and press, the main issue being the extent to which the government could properly curtail these basic freedoms in the interest of national security.

The issue was squarely faced in the case of *Dennis v. United States*, which was decided by the Supreme Court in 1951. On the basis of provisions of the Smith Act, the 11 top leaders of the American Communist party had been indicted for conspiring to teach and advocate the overthrow of the government by force and violence. The initial trial was held in a federal district court in New York before a jury that brought in a verdict of guilty for

---

[37]249 U.S. 47 (1919).

all 11 party members. After the court of appeals affirmed the conviction, the defendants petitioned the Supreme Court for a review of the case, and the Court granted the petition because the case raised several questions about the constitutionality of the Smith Act.

The authority of Congress to pass laws to prevent the violent overthrow of the government was not questioned by the Court. Of primary constitutional importance to the Court was the issue of whether the Smith Act provision in making it a crime to *advocate* violent overthrow of the government was an abridgment of freedom of speech.

In answering this question the Court found a significant difference between *advocacy* of an illegal activity and the *discussion* of such ideas, which was protected by the First Amendment right to freedom of speech. Advocacy was considered to involve the *intent* to perform such activity, whereas the discussion of ideas did not. Therefore, according to the Court, the Smith Act restriction on advocacy did not abridge freedom of speech:

Congress did not intend to eradicate the free discussion of political theories, to destroy the traditional rights of Americans to discuss and evaluate ideas without fear of government sanction.

The Court therefore reasoned that the restriction against advocacy in the Smith Act was directed against *intentions* to overthrow the government, which by their nature constitute clear and present danger to the system. Congress clearly had the authority to protect the government against intentions that constituted such danger.

The majority opinion of the Supreme Court further pointed out that the district court judge at the original trial had made the distinction between advocacy and discussion very clear to the jury that had convicted the defendants in the *Dennis* case:

[T]he trial judge properly charged the jury that they could not convict if they found that

petitioners did "no more than pursue peaceful studies and discussions or teaching . . . in the realm of ideas."[38]

Although it is difficult to prove conclusively that any group intends to overthrow the government, there had been no doubt in the minds of the jury at the *Dennis* trial that the members of the American Communist party had had such an intention. The Supreme Court therefore upheld both the constitutionality of the Smith Act and the conviction in the case.

In upholding the constitutionality of the Smith Act in the *Dennis* case, the Supreme Court introduced a new dimension to the clear and present danger test, namely that the more grave the evil that was intended to be brought about by political advocacy, the less immediate or present had to be the danger in order to uphold government suppression of individual freedom. Since it had been the intent of the Communist party to overthrow the government by force and violence, the gravity of this evil was indeed extreme; therefore political advocacy in this direction could be suppressed without a demonstration that governmental overthrow was imminent, a demonstration that presumably would be required under a strict application of the clear and present danger test of Justice Holmes.

The *Yates* case. As a result of the decision in *Dennis v. United States*, the federal government proceeded to indict and convict close to 100 individuals who were connected with the Communist party. The reasoning behind these convictions was that the party was a conspiracy organized for the purpose of overthrowing the government and that anyone connected with the party obviously intended to be part of such a movement.

However, in 1957, in *Yates v. United States*, the Supreme Court overturned the conviction of 14 Communist party members and further

---

[38]341 U.S. 494 (1951).

clarified the meaning of "advocacy" as it related to clear and present danger. The Court said that the advocacy of the forcible overthrow of government as an *abstract principle* could not in itself be prohibited. Only if such a belief was extended to the actual "incitement to action" would clear and present danger be involved. To violate the Smith Act, the Court asserted, "those to whom advocacy is addressed must be urged to *do* something now or in the future, rather than merely to *believe* in something."[39] As a result of the *Yates* decision, belief in a doctrine such as communism—which advocates violent overthrow of government in principle—is protected by the First Amendment as long as no specific action for carrying out such a belief is contemplated.

The effects of the *Yates* case. The issues raised in the *Dennis* and *Yates* cases, which concern the extent to which the government can go in regulating any form of political expression that it considers to be a clear and present danger to the foundations of the state, became less acute and immediately pressing as the decade of the 1950s came to an end. That decade had begun with the Cold War between the United States and the Soviet Union firmly entrenched and the communist threat considered to be very real. President Harry S. Truman had established the first loyalty program for federal employees, which for the first time in United States history required loyalty oaths and enabled the government to fire any employee even suspected of subversive activities. The Eisenhower administration had continued and strengthened the loyalty oaths and had seen the rise of Senator Joseph McCarthy of Wisconsin, who made Communism the major governmental and social issue of the early 1950s.

By the time of the *Yates* case, the political environment had calmed somewhat, which enabled the Court to interpret the clear and present danger doctrine in a way that would

prevent government witch-hunts against suspected subversives and protect political expression that did not constitute a real threat. The *Yates* decision heightened the standards of proof required to demonstrate subversive activity under the Smith Act; and the Supreme Court applied the standards of the *Yates* opinion in later cases. For example, in *Scales v. United States* (1961), the Court upheld the conviction of a Communist party member who had full knowledge of the revolutionary intent of the party. The Court found that the trial court had properly construed the law by requiring the demonstration, not merely of "nominal" membership, but of active membership in the party and of specific intent to overthrow the government. Revolutionary organizations, the Court concluded, are not to be protected under the First Amendment.

***Communist Party v. Subversive Activities Control Board* (1961).** The Smith Act of 1940 was strengthened by two later laws, the Internal Security Act of 1950, Title I of which was known as the Subversive Activities Control Act, and the Communist Control Act of 1954. These laws required Communists and members of other organizations designated as subversive to register with the government and imposed stiff penalties on them. For example, no member of a subversive organization could hold federal office, secure a passport, or become an official or employee of a labor union; and individuals associated with subversive organizations could not work in any defense plant specified by the secretary of defense. The Subversive Activities Control Board administered these laws.

The Communist party challenged the registration requirements of the Subversive Activities Control Act on the grounds that they violated the First Amendment protection of freedom of expression. Justice Felix Frankfurter, expressing the views of the five justices who voted to uphold the law, held that it was not unconstitutional under the First Amendment and that the judgment made by Congress was supported by the fact that the World

---

[39]354 U.S. 298 (1957). Emphasis added.

Communist Movement and its satellite organizations were a threat to the nation. Deference must be given to congressional judgment "when existing government is menaced by a world-wide integrated movement...to destroy the government itself," wrote Frankfurter. He concluded: "The legislative judgment as to how that threat may best be met consistently with the safeguarding of personal freedom is not to be set aside merely because the judgment of judges would, in the first instant, have chosen other methods." Frankfurter stressed the fact that the law applied "only to foreign-dominated organizations which work primarily to advance the objectives of a world movement controlled by the government of a foreign country."

Four justices, led by Chief Justice Earl Warren, dissented on various views expressed in Frankfurter's opinion. All agreed that the registration provisions of the law violated the privilege against self-incrimination protected by the Fifth Amendment. Justice Warren also dissented on the grounds that the requirement in *Yates* for the demonstration of efficacy had not been met. Justice Black expressed the strongest views in support of the First Amendment protections of freedom of expression:

I do not believe that it can be too often repeated that the freedoms of speech, press, petition and assembly guaranteed by the First Amendment must be accorded to the ideas we hate or sooner or later they will be denied to the ideas we cherish. The first banning of an association because it advocates hated ideas—whether that association be called a political party or not—marks a fateful moment in the history of a free country. That moment seems to have arrived for this country.[40]

While upholding the Subversive Activities Control Board, the Court in *Aptheker v. Secretary of State* (1964) held that the 1950 act could not deny passports to members of Communist organizations. The State Department had revoked the passports of two party leaders, but the Court overturned this action on the grounds that the law under which it was taken "too broadly and indiscriminately restricts the right to travel and thereby abridges the liberty guaranteed by the Fifth Amendment."[41]

Constitutional trends. The government continued to focus upon control of subversive activities in the 1960s, and particularly during the administration of Richard M. Nixon from 1969 to 1974. Congress granted new authority to the government to curb subversives in Title III of the Omnibus Crime Control and Safe Streets Act of 1968. This law provided that the president's constitutional power to protect against the overthrow of the government or against "any other clear and present danger to the structure or existence of the government" is not limited by any law. President Nixon's "hit" squad (called "the White House Plumbers") presumably believed they were operating under this provision when they broke into the office of Daniel Ellsberg's psychiatrist in Beverly Hills, California. The government had accused Ellsberg of leaking Top Secret security documents ("the Pentagon Papers") to the press in violation of national security statutes. (Ellsberg, after two trials, was not convicted.) While the president broadly interpreted his authority to act directly and unilaterally to protect national security, the courts did not go so far. In *United States v. United States District Court* (1972), the Supreme Court held that the Fourth Amendment shields private speech from unreasonable "searches and seizures"—namely, electronic surveillance—without prior judicial approval. (The case applied only to United States citizens, not to the activities or agents of foreign powers.)[42]

The dilemma of how to balance national security interests with individual rights and

---

[40]*Communist Party v. Subversive Activities Control Board*, 367 U.S. 1 (1961).

[41]*Aptheker v. Secretary of State*, 378 U.S. 500 (1964).

[42]*United States v. United States District Court for Eastern Michigan*, 403 U.S. 930 (1972).

the freedom of expression protected by the First Amendment will continue to confront all branches of the government in the future. The circumstances of the times, and particularly general perceptions as to the gravity of the threat, will affect government action and the willingness of the courts to permit or disallow invasions of fundamental rights and freedoms. And at least in times of relative calm, judges will perhaps echo the opinion of District Judge Warren J. Ferguson in a 1971 wiretap case:

National security cannot be invoked to abridge basic rights . . .To guarantee political freedom, our forefathers agreed to take certain risks which are inherent in a free democracy. It is unthinkable that we should now be required to sacrifice those freedoms in order to defend them.[43]

MAINTAINING PUBLIC ORDER AND COMMUNITY STANDARDS

Controversy is essential to the democratic process. It is vital that new ideas be introduced and tested through debate. The election of members of Congress, for example, would be inconceivable without the rounds of heated argument that the candidates engage in prior to the actual balloting. Recognizing the importance of open debate, the Framers made the freedoms of speech and press basic individual liberties in the Bill of Rights. These were also the first freedoms to be nationalized by the Supreme Court's interpretation of "due process of law" in the Fourteenth Amendment.

Yet the Supreme Court has permitted limitations on the freedoms of speech and the press when the security of the nation seemed to take precedence. Moreover, there has also

been a tendency to limit individual freedoms when it has been considered necessary to maintain public order and the standards of the general community.

Protection of Public Order

The maintenance of public peace and order is a requirement in any community so that people can conduct their daily lives without fear of physical harm or the destruction and loss of their property. The need to maintain public order is a major reason for establishing government, and it remains one of government's major responsibilities.

The guardians of public order. In the United States there is no single national police force. Many federal administrative agencies, however, do maintain special agents to enforce particular laws. Both the Food and Drug Administration and the Public Health Service, for example, have inspectors who make sure that the regulations established by these agencies are followed. The Internal Revenue Service has agents who apprehend tax evaders. Customs Bureau agents engage in activities to prevent the smuggling of goods into the country. The agents of the Bureau of Narcotics and the Office of Drug Abuse Law Enforcement have an even more difficult job, that of stopping illegal drug traffic. Enforcement officials in these and other federal agencies together constitute a large force of agents who guard and preserve public order.

There are also two federal law enforcement agencies: the United States Secret Service and the Federal Bureau of Investigation (FBI). The United States Secret Service was created in 1860 within the Treasury Department to track down counterfeiters. Its concerns have been expanded to include detection of the forgeries of United States securities and other financial documents as well as foreign money. "T-men," or Treasury agents, also protect the president and his family and maintain uniformed police units at the White

---

[43]*United States v. Smith*, 321 F. supp. 424 (1971).

House and the Treasury Department buildings.

Set up in 1908 within the Department of Justice, the FBI has responsibility for investigating violations of all federal laws not assigned to other agencies. There are about 170 types of felonies that the FBI can investigate. Among these are espionage; treason; kidnapping; extortion; bank robbery; thefts of government property; interstate transportation of stolen goods; fraud against the government; civil rights matters; and the assault or assassination of a president or other federal officer.

Another force for protecting the public order is the National Guard, which is an auxiliary force of the army made up of the militias of the separate states. Whereas Congress provides for the organizing and arming of the National Guard, the governor of each state is the commander in chief of his state's militia and may call upon it to deal with riots or such natural disasters as floods and earthquakes. During wars and other national emergencies the federal government may call the state militias into federal service; at such times, the National Guard comes under federal instead of state jurisdiction.

Apart from these national and quasi-national enforcement groups, the maintenance of public order is usually the responsibility of state and local agencies and officials. Exceptions to this practice occur when a problem is of such magnitude that it is necessary to call in the National Guard or federal agents.

Public order versus individual freedoms. A primary dilemma to be solved by those trying to maintain public order is how to do so without usurping individual freedoms. Just as the federal government has statutes that limit political expression where there is a clear and present danger to the very existence of government itself, state and local governments have their own laws and ordinances to preserve order and protect public institutions. State sedition statutes are common, regardless of the ruling by the Supreme

"I'm not going to marry either one of you."
To preserve both civil liberties and public order, government has to avoid any course that is too extreme.

Court in *Pennsylvania v. Nelson* in 1956 that held that the federal government preempted this field.[44] (However, charges of sedition at the state level have not been made since the *Nelson* case.) The commonly used state laws are breach of the peace statutes and ordinances. For example, the Chicago ordinance declared unconstitutional in the *Terminiello* case discussed below provided that "all persons who shall make, aid, countenance, or assist in making any improper noise, riot, disturbance, breach of the peace, or diversion tending to a breach of the peace, within the limits of the city . . .shall be deemed guilty of disorderly conduct." While that particular ordinance was declared unconstitutional, most state and local breach of the peace statutes

[44]*Pennsylvania v. Nelson,* 350 U.S. 497 (1956).

have been upheld, although often construed narrowly by the courts to prevent excessive abridgments of the freedoms of speech and association.

The courts face a dilemma when reviewing attempted government suppression of First Amendment freedoms of expression. How far should the government be permitted to go to protect its interests? Generally, two approaches have been taken to the solution of the problem. First, the Court applies a "balancing test" that weighs the interests of the government against the freedoms of the individuals or groups involved. Second, a clear and present danger test is often used, allowing the government to limit expression only when it is clearly necessary for self-preservation or the protection of public order. The Supreme Court has confronted the issue of how far state and local governments may go in suppressing expression in several historic cases. Two of the most important were *Terminiello v. Chicago* (1949) and *Feiner v. New York* (1951).

Terminiello was charged and found guilty of breaching the peace when he made an inflammatory, racist speech in Chicago that incited a protest crowd of about one thousand persons to riot. When the case reached the Supreme Court, it was decided that the local ordinance, as interpreted by the trial judge, was unconstitutional because it permitted undue abridgment of the freedom of speech. Justice William O. Douglas concluded the *Terminiello* opinion by stating that

the function of free speech under our system of government is to invite dispute. It may indeed best serve its high purpose when it induces a condition of unrest, creates dissatisfaction with conditions as they are, and even stirs people to anger.[45]

Thus the *Terminiello* decision held that freedom of speech had priority over the Chicago ordinance for maintaining public order.

Two years later, in the *Feiner* case, the Supreme Court delivered what appears to be an almost contrary opinion. Feiner was arrested and convicted of disorderly conduct while addressing a meeting of about eighty persons on a street corner in Syracuse, New York. Two policemen who were witnesses to the incident testified that the crowd listening to Feiner had been "pushing, shoving, and milling around." As a result the policemen, fearing that the situation would become uncontrollable, urged Feiner to ask the crowd to disband. Feiner was arrested when he refused to comply with this request. In this case the Supreme Court upheld the conviction. The majority of the Court pointed out that when the speaker "passes the bounds of argument or persuasion and undertakes incitement to riot," the police must not be powerless to prevent public disorder.[46]

Although these two cases appear similar, there is an important distinction between the factors reviewed by the Supreme Court in producing the two decisions. In the *Terminiello* case, the appeal was based on the fact that the original trial judge had interpreted the Chicago ordinance as putting excessive limits on the freedom of speech. In the *Feiner* appeal, on the other hand, only an isolated police action was in question. Thus the *Feiner* decision established a precedent for upholding limitations on freedom of speech in public places when there was a clear and present danger that a riot would occur.

How far can government go in using the clear and present danger standard to abridge civil liberties and civil rights? Clearly, courts differ in their interpretation of the clear and present danger standard, depending upon the different orientations of justices at different times in history. During wartime the Court tends to allow the government more leeway in restricting individual freedoms than at other times; and it may be similarly swayed at times

---

[45]337 U.S. 1 (1949).

[46]340 U.S. 315 (1951).

when the government is facing other types of extreme emergencies. But judicial philosophy and approaches to public policy always differ among individual justices. And it is the philosophy of the justices that in large part shapes their broad orientation to the cases and controversies coming before them.

The Warren Court, for example, took a stricter view of the limitations imposed upon government by the Bill of Rights than had previous Courts. It was particularly sensitive to the Civil Rights movement of the 1960s, reversing state breach of the peace convictions of black sit-in demonstrators throughout the South. Essentially the Court looked behind the cases, coming to the unofficial conclusion that racial prejudice was behind the convictions. The first sit-in case was *Edwards v. South Carolina* (1963), in which the Court reviewed a breach of the peace conviction of 187 black civil rights demonstrators who had walked in small groups to the South Carolina State House to protest what they considered to be discriminatory treatment under state laws. The demonstrators loudly sung "The Star-Spangled Banner," clapped their hands, stamped their feet, and refused to move when told they would be arrested if they did not disperse within 15 minutes. The Court, citing the *Terminiello* case, overruled the conviction of the demonstrators on the ground that "the courts of South Carolina have defined a criminal offense to permit conviction of the petitioners if their speech 'stirred people to anger, invited public dispute, or brought about a condition of unrest.' A conviction resting on any of those grounds may not stand."[47]

Several years after the *Edwards* decision the Court again struck down convictions of civil rights demonstrators in *Cox v. Louisiana* (1965). The first *Cox* case involved a breach of the peace conviction under Louisiana law for picketing segregated lunch counters in Baton Rouge. The Louisiana Supreme Court upheld the conviction of the demonstrators, defining a breach of the peace as any activity designed "to agitate, to arouse from a state of repose, to molest, to interrupt, to hinder, to disquiet." The United States Supreme Court reversed, holding that the Louisiana court's definition of a breach of the peace "would allow persons to be punished merely for peacefully expressing unpopular views."[48] The second *Cox* case reviewed the convictions of the demonstrators for violating a Louisiana law that proscribed picketing or parading near a courthouse with the intent to interfere with the administration of justice or to influence a judge, juror, witness, or court officer. The Supreme Court upheld the statute but voided the conviction of the civil rights demonstrators under it on the ground that the record "clearly shows that the officials present gave permission for the demonstration to take place across the street from the courthouse."[49]

The *Edwards* and *Cox* cases reflected a desire on the part of the Supreme Court to protect civil rights protestors against discriminatory treatment.[50] The Court applied an implicit balancing test to the cases and found no compelling state interest to justify the suppression of First Amendment freedoms. Moreover, although the judicial standard of clear and present danger was not raised in the civil rights demonstration cases, implicitly the Court found no clear and present danger to the maintenance of public institutions and order in the activities of the demonstrators.

The clear and present danger standard was, however, applied in a case unrelated to the Civil Rights movement to protect the activities of the Ku Klux Klan in Ohio. The Court found, in *Brandenburg v. Ohio* (1969), that the application of the Ohio criminal syndicalism

---

[47]*Edwards v. South Carolina*, 372 U.S. 229 (1963).

[48]379 U.S. 536 (1965).

[49]379 U.S. 559 (1965).

[50]See also *Brown v. Louisiana*, 383 U.S. 131 (1966).

statute to prevent an assembly of Klan members was unconstitutional. The law could not be sustained because it criminally punishes "mere advocacy not distinguished from incitement to imminent lawless action."[51] Mere advocacy, the Court concluded, does not meet the conditions of a clear and present danger to the state or public order as required to sustain government limits upon freedom of expression.

Maintenance of Community Standards

States and, more commonly, local communities not only may curtail freedoms of expression in order to maintain public order but also may impose the moral views of the majority upon a minority. State and local governments throughout history have passed stringent laws regulating sexual conduct, obscenity, alcohol, and drugs. The federal government too has been involved in protecting public morals (for example by regulating legal drugs and by prohibiting trafficking in illicit drugs), but state and local communities have the most pervasive laws regulating moral conduct.

The rise of the Moral Majority and other evangelical movements that sought to turn their views of morality into public policy increased pressures upon government at all levels to curtail the freedoms of expression, including the right to privacy. The demands of the evangelical Christians reflected a reaction to a liberal Supreme Court that in *Roe v. Wade* (1973) culminated its drive to maximize individual rights and liberties.

In general, the Supreme Court has used a balancing test, weighing public interests against individual liberties and rights to determine how far a community can go in enforcing the moral codes of the majority upon minorities. Except in the area of political expression, the Court for the most part did not disturb state and local statutes regulating public morality until the late 1960s. Censorship has been the approach commonly used by communities to limit what their majority considered undesirable expression.

Censorship of magazines and newspapers. In a democracy where freedom of speech and press are so highly regarded that they are guaranteed in the Constitution, it is almost ironic to think that censorship exists at all. Nevertheless, it does. Although prepublication censorship is forbidden (see the discussion of *Near v. Minnesota* in this chapter), the censorship of published material has been permissible when the moral standards of the community seem to be threatened. Obscene material is not protected, then, by the First Amendment. But what is "obscene" is often a matter of taste. This poses another basic question: If the community's moral standards are not stipulated in the Constitution, what *are* these standards, and who should decide what they are?

Ordinarily, it has been the responsibility of the states to establish the standards of their respective communities and to prosecute those who publish or sell materials that offend these standards. However, the national government has also been able to control the circulation of certain materials through its regulation of imports and of the postal service. The Warren Court provided a counterbalance to any overzealous government action that infringed on basic freedoms in the name of upholding moral standards.

The Warren Court adopted a three-part measure for determining whether an item is obscene: (1) if it appeals to prurient, or lustful, interest; (2) if it offends community standards in relating representations of sexual matters; and (3) if it is utterly devoid of any social value. In addition, the Warren Court decided who may purchase materials that fall into these categories. In *Butler v. Michigan* (1957) it ruled that adults cannot be deprived of access to printed material that might be offensive to children. A later case, *Smith v. Cal-*

---

[51]395 U.S. 444 (1969).

ifornia (1959), upset a lower court decision that had convicted a bookseller of selling obscene material. The Supreme Court held that there could be no conviction unless it was first proved that the bookseller had sold the item with an intent to distribute obscene material. Since the bookseller could not be expected to be familiar with every item on his shelves, he had to be cleared of the charge. In the case of material openly advertised and sold as obscene or pornographic, however, even the Warren Court was more rigid. In *Ginzburg v. United States* (1966) the Court upheld the conviction of a New York publisher for mailing obscene material that had been advertised as such.

The Burger Court, although not explicitly overruling any of the prior decisions concerning obscenity, changed two of the tests that were formerly used to determine whether material can be declared obscene. In *Miller v. California* (1973) the Court held that the former test, which required that obscene material must be "utterly without redeeming social value," need not be applied. By eliminating the word *utterly* from the test for obscenity the Court made it far easier to make a determination that material is obscene. In the same case the Court held, moreover, that the local community's standards may be used by a jury in determining what appeals to "prurient interest." In rejecting the use of a national standard for determining obscenity the Burger Court gave local communities much more leeway in banning obscene material, whether books, magazines, or motion pictures.

The Rehnquist Court grappled with the obscenity issue in *Hustler Magazine v. Falwell* (1988). Moral Majority leader Jerry Falwell, a crusader against obscenity and pornography who had frequently attacked *Hustler,* sued the magazine for libel when it published a parody of an advertisement depicting him as a drunk who engaged in obscene acts. The jury, finding that the parody was not believable, rejected the libel claim but awarded damages to Falwell for emotional distress. After the Circuit Court affirmed the District Court's judg-

ment, the case was appealed to the Supreme Court. Chief Justice William H. Rehnquist wrote the majority opinion, holding that "public figures [such as Falwell] and public officials may not recover for the tort of intentional infliction of emotional distress by reason of publication such as the one here at issue without showing in addition that the publication contains a false statement of fact which was made with 'actual malice,' i.e., with knowledge that the statement was false or with reckless disregard as to whether or not it was true." In the course of his opinion Rehnquist pointed out that political cartoons, often of a vicious and outrageous nature, have always been protected by the First Amendment. He admitted that the "caricature of respondent and his mother published in *Hustler* is at best a distant cousin of [past] political cartoons." But the Court, concluded Rehnquist, cannot refuse First Amendment protections to "outrageous" cartoons and caricatures because "'outrageousness' in the area of political and social discourse has an inherent subjectiveness about it which would allow a jury to impose liability on the basis of the jurors' taste or views, or perhaps on the basis of their dislike of a particular expression. An 'outrageous' standard thus runs afoul of our longstanding refusal to allow damages to be awarded because the speech in question may have an adverse emotional impact on the audience."

Censorship of movies. In contrast to the printed media, the film industry is a relatively recent development. And only in the past few decades has the motion picture attained status as a means of communication as well as of entertainment. Since there were no provisions for motion pictures in the Constitution, the Supreme Court has had to decide whether freedoms guaranteed in the First Amendment can be applied to the production of films as well as to the other media. If films were not so protected, they would be subject to the jurisdiction and censorship of both the states and the national government.

In one of the early motion picture cases,

Mutual Film Corporation v. Industrial Commission of Ohio (1915), the Court held that films were not part of "the press of the country" but rather a form of entertainment. At issue was an Ohio statute that required the prior approval of a board of censors before a motion picture could be shown in the state. Motion pictures had to be "of a moral, educational, or amusing and harmless character" to be approved by the Ohio board. In its opinion the Supreme Court said that

the exhibition of moving pictures is a business, pure and simple, originated and conducted for profit, like other spectacles, not to be regarded . . .as part of the press of the country, or as organs of public opinion.[52]

The Ohio statute, according to the Court, therefore did not violate the First Amendment. Following this ruling, many states and local communities established film censorship procedures.

It was not until the *Miracle* case in 1952 that this interpretation was challenged. *The Miracle*, an Italian film, was initially licensed and shown in New York City. The plot of the movie involved a poor goatherd who was seduced by a stranger whom she later believed to be a saint. The film offended some people and was attacked vigorously by the Roman Catholic Church. The outcry caused the New York State Board of Regents, which was authorized to censor motion pictures under state law, to reconsider its original consent to the exhibiting of the picture. The film was subsequently found to be "sacrilegious" under a provision of the New York censorship statute that declared a film could not be licensed if it was "obscene, indecent, immoral, inhuman, sacrilegious, or . . .of such character that its exhibition would tend to corrupt morals or incite to crime."

When the New York censorship board's decision was appealed, the Supreme Court held first that films were part of the press and therefore entitled to protection under the First and Fourteenth Amendments. As such, the Court said, a film cannot be banned by a state on the basis of a censor's conclusion that it is "sacrilegious." The Court claimed that this term is so vague that it would give over all power to the censor. Although the Court's decision in the *Miracle* case did not consider whether movies could be banned under the other provisions of the New York law, the Court continued to upset New York bans on other films in later cases.

Both the Warren and Burger Courts adhered to a very strict rule that precludes prior censorship of motion pictures. One isolated case that was decided in 1961, *Times Film Corporation v. City of Chicago*, did seem to contradict this rule by providing that a city ordinance requiring the submission of films to a censor was not necessarily a violation of the freedoms of speech and press. In that case, in a five-to-four decision, the Supreme Court majority held that a municipality can protect its people against obscenity and that prior censorship in these cases can sometimes be justified. However, the *Times Film Corporation* case has never been used as a precedent for upholding prior censorship in other cases. In fact, throughout the 1960s and 1970s the Supreme Court overturned actions of local governments that attempted to suppress films without giving the defendants due process of law. Only after a film has been shown can it be legally seized, and then only on the basis of adequate evidence presented to a judge, justice of the peace, or magistrate and upon the issuance of a proper warrant for the seizure.[53]

Constitutional trends. Government censorship has always been a particularly thorny constitutional problem, and the Supreme Court has been notably uncompromising in protecting political expression. Only the most

---

[52]236 U.S. 230 (1915).

[53]See *Roaden v. Commonwealth of Kentucky,* 413 U.S. 496 (1973).

(From *Straight Herblock* [Simon and Schuster, 1964])

"I enjoyed censoring the movie so much, one of these days I'd like to censor the book."

The matter of censorship poses a problem as to *who* should decide what the community's standards are.

compelling governmental needs justify prior censorship of the press, such as the interest of the government in protecting military secrets during wartime.[54]

The Court also protects absolutely literary and artistic expression, provided they are not obscene. While the Supreme Court seemed to grant local communities open discretion in determining suppressible obscene publications and motion pictures in *Miller v. California* in 1973, a year later in *Jenkins v. Georgia* (1974) the Court reduced local discretion. Georgia had interpreted the "community standards" criteria of the Miller case to mean the prevail-

ing local view on obscenity, and on that basis the film *Carnal Knowledge* had been declared obscene by a Georgia jury. However, the Supreme Court held in the *Jenkins* case that local juries did not have complete discretion to determine questions of fact in obscenity cases. The justices viewed the film and concluded that it "could not be found under the Miller standards to depict sexual conduct in a patently offensive way." The Court went on to state:

While the subject matter is, in a broader sense, sex, and there are scenes in which sexual conduct including "ultimate sexual acts" is to be understood to be taking place, the camera does not focus on the bodies of the actors at such times. There is no exhibition whatever of the actors' genitals, lewd or otherwise, during these scenes. There are occasional scenes of nudity, but nudity alone is not enough to make material legally obscene under the Miller standards.[55]

The *Jenkins* case reflected a Supreme Court dilemma. As hard as the justices had tried, they simply had been unable to define obscenity in previous cases with sufficient clarity to guide local authorities. The *Jenkins* case was a return to an ad hoc court process of determining obscenity. It had tried to develop objective standards, but ended up by subjectively defining obscenity. Justice Brennan, calling attention to the difficulty of Supreme Court judgment on a case-by-case basis to determine obscenity, dissented in the *Jenkins* case. He argued that the Court should hold that the First and Fourteenth Amendments prohibit state and federal governments from suppressing sexually oriented materials unless they are distributed to juveniles or unless there is "obtrusive exposure to unconsenting adults." The Court continues to grapple with the issue of censorship of obscenity on a case-by-case basis. The majority of justices oppose criminal prosecutions for obscenity, although local dis-

---

[54]*Near v. Minnesota*, 283 U.S. 697 (1931); *New York Times Co. v. United States*, 403 U.S. 713 (1971).

[55]418 U.S. 153 (1974).

trict attorneys occasionally continue to embark upon such prosecutions.

Censorship by the bureaucracy. Although most censorship is carried out in accordance with state regulations, some federal administrative agencies also have censorship powers granted to them by Congress. Customs officials, for example, have been given authority to stop material they deem harmful to the public interest from entering the country. This authority has been couched in such vague terms that officials have a great deal of discretion. Not only may they ban what they consider to be obscene material, but they may also exclude foreign political propaganda.

Under the old postal system the postmaster general had the authority to revoke the second-class mailing privileges of publications he considered obscene, fraudulent, or subversive. On several occasions the courts had to curb the postmaster's authority. When D. H. Lawrence's *Lady Chatterley's Lover* was first published in this country, the Post Office Department threatened to exclude it from the mails but was finally prevented from doing so by the courts.

Unlike postal officials, customs officials may seize obscene material. However, such action must be promptly reviewed by the courts, and judicial proceedings must begin within 14 days of any seizure and conclude within 60 days.

Control of television and radio. The federal Communications Commission (FCC) has been granted responsibility by Congress for regulating the radio and television industries. Within very broad limits the FCC sets the standards that govern the industry. It can license television and radio stations and can revoke the license of a station that has committed a serious violation of the law. But the FCC must also heed the interests of the broadcasting industry, which is one of the most powerful in the country. When the FCC threatens action that would affect the financial position of the industry, it is subjected to intense crit-

icism from the networks. Naturally the networks have access to members of Congress and officials in other branches of the government. Thus, although the FCC has broad authority for setting standards that affect the major broadcasting groups, its power is counterbalanced by the political influence of these groups. On the other hand, when the FCC applies sanctions against the smaller and less powerful broadcasters, its sanctions are less likely to be challenged.

The Supreme Court has ruled that the First Amendment does not protect broadcasting in the same way that it protects other forms of political expression. In *Red Lion Broadcasting Co. v. Federal Communications Commission* (1969), the Court held:

There is no "unabridgable" First Amendment right to broadcast comparable to the right of every individual to speak, write, or publish. . . .This is not to say that the First Amendment is irrelevant . . .to broadcasting. . . .But it is the right of viewers and listeners, not the right of the broadcasters, which is paramount.

However, when Congress passed a law that prohibited educational broadcasting stations that received grants from the Corporation for Public Broadcasting from editorializing, the Supreme Court overturned the ban in *FCC v. League of Women Voters of California* (1984). Justice Brennan, writing for the Court's majority of five, held that the law violates the First Amendment because it "singles out noncommercial broadcasters and denies them the right to address their chosen audience on matters of public importance." The Court observed that in the past the scarcity of broadcasting channels justified regulation, but that new broadcasting technology, such as cable television, that supports a vast expansion of channels may require the government to reexamine past regulatory policies with a view toward more deregulation. A footnote in the opinion observed that, for example, if the "fairness doctrine" that the FCC had established, requiring broadcast stations to give equal access to opposing opinions, restricted rather than enhanced freedom of speech, the Court would be forced to reconsider earlier opinions supporting the doctrine.

Private Censorship

Ordinarily, censorship, when used, is imposed by the government. Government censorship, though, can be counteracted by the courts when individual freedoms are unduly threatened. However, there is another kind of censorship that neither the government nor the courts are capable of stopping—private censorship.

If a sponsor of a television program, for example, disagrees with the message the program is communicating, financial support may be withdrawn and the program will be dropped. Or if a network itself decides that a program does not maintain the moral standards of the community, the contracts of the people working on the program will not be renewed. For radio and television, the specter of private censorship is very real indeed, and the Constitution offers no redress against it.

As with all other policy decisions within the political system, civil rights policies must be reached through compromise. A balance must be struck between demands made to keep public order and uphold community standards and the need to protect individual liberties. If this balance is not kept, the result could be anarchy or dictatorship.

Freedom of Expression and the American Flag

Nothing stirs patriotic emotions more than the American flag. The chief justice of the Supreme Court, William H. Rehnquist, expressed the views of the vast majority of citizens when he wrote the following in his dissenting opinion in the 1989 flag-burning case *Texas v. Johnson*: "The flag is not simply another 'idea' or 'point of view' competing for recognition in the marketplace of ideas. Millions and millions of Americans regard [the flag] with an almost mythical reverence regardless of what sort of social, political, or philosophical beliefs they may have." Justice John Paul Stevens, dissenting in the same case, observed that the flag, in addition to being a symbol of nationhood and national unity, "is a symbol of freedom, of equal opportunity, of religious tolerance, and of goodwill for other peoples who share our aspirations. The symbol carries its message to dissidents both at home and abroad who may have no interest at all in our national unity or survival."

Both federal and state laws prevent desecration of the flag. Historically, state laws have always regulated how the flag is to be treated, including prescriptions concerning its display and its disposal when it wears out. In 1942 Congress passed the first United States flag code prescribing how the flag is to be displayed. Many countries have similar flag codes. Generally, the laws prescribe how the flag is to be hung both indoors and outdoors; how it is to be raised, lowered, carried, saluted, and cared for; and what are its permitted and prohibited uses. A vast majority of citizens strongly support federal and state flag-desecration laws, and virtually no one opposes laws against flag burning, which the federal government and 48 states have made a crime.

Because the flag is such an important national symbol, flag desecration is considered by everyone, including those who do it, to be an attack upon the nation and its political institutions. Burning the flag is the ultimate form of desecration, but there are many other ways to show disrespect for the flag and what it represents—for example, by hanging it upside down.

The Supreme Court has on more than one occasion confronted the difficult constitutional issue of whether or not flag burning and other forms of desecration are protected political expressions under the First Amendment which restrains both federal and, under the due process laws of the Fourteenth Amendment, state action that limits freedom of expression, particularly in the political realm. For example, in *Street v. New York* (1969), the Court considered the case of a black appellant who had publicly burned the flag on a street corner in Brooklyn to protest the murder of civil rights leader James Meredith. Street was arrested and convicted under a New York law which made it a misdemeanor "publicly [to] mutilate, deface, defile or defy, trample upon, or cast contempt upon either by words or act [a flag of the United States]." While he was burning the flag Street uttered, "We don't need no damn flag," and he told a passing police officer, "Yes, that is my flag; I burned it. If they let that happen to Meredith, we don't need an American flag. The Supreme Court's majority sidestepped the issue of whether or not the New York law was constitutional and overturned Street's conviction on the grounds that it was based upon his *words*, not his act in burning the flag. The first Amendment protected Street's political expression because it did not constitute a clear and present danger to civil peace and order which the state had the authority to protect. Chief Justice Earl Warren, along with Justices Black and Fortas, strongly dissented in the *Street* case, arguing that state laws forbidding flag burning were clearly constitutional and that Street's conviction should have been upheld because it was based not upon his words, which could be considered political expression, but upon his act, which was not political expression.

Several years after the *Street* case the Supreme Court confronted the issue of the constitutionality of a flag-desecration statute, this time in the state of Washington. *Spence v. Washington* (1974) involved the case of a college student who had hung the United States flag upside down outside of his apartment window in Seattle, attaching to it a peace symbol. His *act* violated an "improper use" state law which provided that no person could publicly display a United States flag that had been painted or marked in any way. The Supreme Court this time held that Spence's act was protected political expression under the First Amendment.

The Supreme Court finally confronted the highly emotional and politically sensitive issue of the constitutionality of laws banning flag burning in the 1989 case of *Texas v. Johnson*, printed below. At issue was a Texas flag-desecration law that made flag burning a crime, under which Johnson had been charged, convicted, and sentenced to a one-year prison term and fined $2,000. Johnson's act occurred while the Republican National Convention was taking place in Dallas in 1984. He publicly and provocatively burned the American flag in front of the Dallas City Hall to protest the policies of the Reagan administration. While the flag burned, he and other protestors chanted, "America, the red, white and blue, we spit on you." Was Johnson's act, or his words, protected political expression under the First Amendment? Read on.

Texas v. Johnson (1989)—Is Flag Burning Protected Political Expression?

Justice William J. Brennan, Jr., joined by Justices Thurgood Marshall, Harry A. Blackmun, Antonin Scalia, and Anthony M. Kennedy, wrote the majority opinion, saying in part:

After publicly burning an American flag as a means of political protest, Gregory Lee Johnson was convicted of desecrating a flag in violation of Texas law. This case presents the question whether his conviction is consistent with the First Amendment. We hold that it is not.

I

While the Republican National Convention was taking place in Dallas in 1984, respondent Johnson participated in a political demonstration dubbed the "Republican War Chest Tour." As explained in literature distributed by the demonstrators and in speeches made by them, the purpose of this event was to protest the policies of the Reagan administration and of certain Dallas-based corporations. The demonstrators marched through the Dallas streets, chanting political slogans and stopping at several corporate locations to stage "die-ins" intended to dramatize the consequences of nuclear war. On several occasions they spray-painted the walls of buildings and overturned potted plants, but Johnson himself took no part in such activities. He did, however, accept an American flag handed to him by a fellow protestor who had taken it from a flagpole outside one of the targeted buildings.

The demonstration ended in front of Dallas City Hall, where Johnson unfurled the American flag, doused it with kerosene and set it on fire. While the flag burned, the protestors chanted, "America, the red, white and blue, we spit on you." After the demonstrators dispersed, a witness to the flag burning collected the flag's remains and buried them in his backyard. No one was physically injured or threatened with injury, though several witnesses testified that they had been seriously offended by the flag burning.

Of the approximately 100 demonstrators, Johnson alone was charged with a crime. The only criminal offense with which he was charged was the desecration of a venerated object in violation of Texas Penal Code Ann. § 42.09(a)(3)(1989). After a trial, he was convicted, sentenced to one year in prison, and fined $2,000. . . .

. . .

Johnson was convicted of flag desecration for burning the flag rather than for uttering insulting words. This fact somewhat complicates our consideration of his conviction under the First Amendment. We must first determine whether Johnson's burning of the flag constituted expressive conduct, permitting him to invoke the First Amendment in challenging his conviction. . . .

The First Amendment literally forbids the abridgement only of "speech," but we have long recognized that its protection does not end at the spoken or written word. . . .

In deciding whether particular conduct possesses sufficient communicative elements to bring the First Amendment into play, we have asked whether "[a]n intent to convey a particularized message was present, and [whether] the likelihood was great that the message would be understood by those who viewed it." . . . Hence, we have recognized the expressive nature of students' wearing of black armbands to protest American military involvement in Vietnam; . . . of a sit-in by blacks in a "whites only" area to protest segregation, . . . of the wearing of American military uniforms in a dramatic presentation criticizing American involvement in Vietnam, . . . and of picketing about a wide variety of causes. . . .

Especially pertinent to this case are our decisions recognizing the communicative nature of conduct relating to flags. Attaching a peace sign to the flag, . . . saluting the flag, and displaying a red flag, we have held, all may find shelter under the First Amendment. . . . That we have had little difficulty identifying an expressive element in conduct relating to flags should not be surprising. The very purpose of a national flag is to serve as a symbol of our country; it is, one might say, "the one visible manifestation of two hundred years of nationhood." . . . Pregnant with expressive content, the flag as readily signifies this Nation as does the combination of letters found in "America." . . .

. . .

Texas claims that its interest in preventing breaches of the peace justifies Johnson's conviction for flag desecration. However, no disturbance of the peace actually occurred or threatened to occur because of Johnson's burning of the flag. . . .

The State's position, therefore, amounts to a claim that an audience that takes serious offense at particular expression is necessarily likely to disturb the peace and that the expression may be prohibited on this basis. Our precedents do not countenance such a presumption. On the contrary, they recognize that a principal "function of free speech under our system of government is to invite dispute. It may indeed best serve its high purpose when it induces a condition of unrest, creates dissatisfaction with conditions as they are, or even stirs people to anger." . . .

Nor does Johnson's expressive conduct fall within that small class of "fighting words" that are "likely to provoke the average person to retaliation, and thereby cause a breach of the peace." . . . No reasonable onlooker would have regarded Johnson's generalized expression of dissatisfaction with the policies of the Federal Government as a direct personal insult or an invitation to exchange fisticuffs. . . .

We thus conclude that the State's interest in maintaining order is not implicated on these facts. The State need not worry that our holding will disable it from preserving the peace. We do not suggest that the First Amendment forbids a State to prevent "imminent lawless action." . . . And in fact, Texas already has a statute specifically prohibiting breaches of the peace, Texas Penal Code Ann. § 42.01 (1989), which tends to confirm that Texas need not punish this flag desecration in order to keep the peace. . . .

. . .

It remains to consider whether the State's interest in preserving the flag as a symbol of nationhood and national unity justifies Johnson's conviction. . . .

Johnson's political expression was restricted because of the content of the message he conveyed. We must therefore subject the State's asserted interest in preserving the special symbolic character of the flag to "the most exacting scrutiny." . . .

Texas argues that its interest in preserving the flag as a symbol of nationhood and national unity survives this close analysis. Quoting extensively from the writings of this Court chronicling the flag's historic and symbolic role in our society, the State emphasizes the "'special place'" reserved for the flag in our Nation. . . . According to Texas, if one physically treats the flag in a way that would tend to cast doubt on either the idea that nationhood and national unity are the flag's referents or that national unity actually exists, the message conveyed thereby is a harmful one and therefore may be prohibited.

If there is a bedrock principle underlying the First Amendment, it is that the Government may not prohibit the expression of an idea simply because society finds the idea itself offensive or disagreeable. . . .

We have not recognized an exception to this principle even where our flag has been involved. . . .

. . . If we were to hold that a State may forbid flag burning wherever it is likely to endanger the flag's symbolic role, but allow it wherever burning a flag promotes that role—as where, for example, a person ceremoniously burns a dirty flag—we would be saying that when it comes to impairing the flag's physical integrity, the flag itself may be used as a symbol—as a substitute for the written or spoken word or a "short cut from mind to mind"—only in one direction. We would be permitting a State to "prescribe what shall be orthodox" by saying that one may burn the flag to convey one's attitude toward it and its referents only if one does not endanger the flag's representation of nationhood and national unity.

We never before have held that the Government may ensure that a symbol be used to express only one view of that symbol or its referents. . . .

. . . To conclude that the Government may permit designated symbols to be used to communicate only a limited set of messages would be to enter territory having no discernible or defensible boundaries. Could the Government, on this theory, prohibit the burning of state flags? Of copies of the Presidential seal? Of the Constitution? In evaluating these choices under the First Amendment, how would we decide which symbols were sufficiently special to warrant this unique status? To do so, we would be forced to consult our own political preferences, and impose them on the citizenry, in the very way that the First Amendment forbids us to do. . . .

There is, moreover, no indication—either in the text of the Constitution or in our cases interpreting it—that a separate juridical category exists for the American flag alone. Indeed, we would not be surprised to learn that the persons who framed our Constitution and wrote the Amendment that we now construe were not known for their reverence for the Union Jack. The First Amendment does not guarantee that other concepts virtually sacred to our Nation as a whole—such as the principle that discrimination on the basis of race is odious and destructive—will go unquestioned in the marketplace of ideas. . . . We decline, therefore, to create for the flag an exception to the joust of principles protected by the First Amendment. . . .

We are fortified in today's conclusion by our conviction that forbidding criminal punishment for conduct such as Johnson's will not endanger the special role played by our flag or the feelings it inspires. To paraphrase Justice Holmes, we submit that nobody can suppose that this one gesture of an unknown man will change our Nation's attitude towards its flag. . . .

We are tempted to say, in fact, that the flag's deservedly cherished place in our community will be strengthened, not weakened, by our holding today. Our decision is a reaffirmation of the principles of freedom and inclusiveness that the flag best reflects, and of the conviction that our toleration of criticism such as Johnson's is a sign and source of our strength. Indeed, one of the proudest images of our flag, the one immortalized in our national anthem, is of the bombardment it survived at Fort McHenry. It is the Nation's resilience, not its rigidity, that Texas sees reflected in the flag—and it is that resilience that we assert today.

The way to preserve the flag's special role is not to punish those who feel differently about these matters. It is to persuade them that they are wrong. "To courageous, self-reliant men, with confidence in the power of free and fearless reasoning applied through the process of popular government, no danger flowing from speech can be deemed clear and present, unless the incidence of the evil apprehended is so imminent that it may befall before there is opportunity for full discussion. If there be time to expose through discussion the falsehood and fallacies, to avert the evil by the processes of education, the remedy to be applied is more speech, not enforced silence." . . .And, precisely because it is our flag that is involved, one's response to the flag-burner may exploit the uniquely persuasive power of the flag itself. We can imagine no more appropriate response to burning a flag than waving one's own, no better way to counter a flag-burner's message than by saluting the flag that burns, no surer means of preserving the dignity even of the flag that burned than by—as one witness here did—according its remains a respectful burial. We do not consecrate the flag by punishing its desecration, for in doing so we dilute the freedom that this cherished emblem represents.

V

Johnson was convicted for engaging in expressive conduct. The State's interest in preventing breaches of the peace does not support his conviction because Johnson's conduct did not threaten to dis-

turb the peace. Nor does the State's interest in preserving the flag as a symbol of nationhood and national unity justify his criminal conviction for engaging in political expression. The judgment of the Texas Court of Criminal Appeals is therefore affirmed.

Justice Anthony M. Kennedy, concurring:

I write not to qualify the words Justice Brennan chooses so well, for he says with power all that is necessary to explain our ruling. I join his opinion without reservation, but with a keen sense that this case, like others before us from time to time, exacts its personal toll. This prompts me to add to our pages these few remarks.

The case before us illustrates better than most that the judicial power is often difficult in its exercise. We cannot here ask another branch to share responsibility, as when the argument is made that a statute is flawed or incomplete. For we are presented with a clear and simple statute to be judged against a pure command of the Constitution. The outcome can be laid at no door but ours.

The hard fact is that sometimes we must make decisions we do not like. We make them because they are right, right in the sense that the law and the Constitution, as we see them, compel the result. And so great is our commitment to the process that, except in the rare case, we do not pause to express distaste for the result, perhaps for fear of undermining a valued principle that dictates the decision. This is one of those rare cases.

Our colleagues in dissent advance powerful arguments why respondent may be convicted for his expression, reminding us that among those who will be dismayed by our holding will be some who have had the singular honor of carrying the flag in battle. And I agree that the flag holds a lonely place of honor in an age when absolutes are distrusted and simple truths are burdened by unneeded apologetics.

With all respect to those views, I do not believe the Constitution gives us the right to rule as the dissenting members of the court urge, however painful this judgment is to announce. Though symbols often are what we ourselves make of them, the flag is constant in expressing beliefs Americans share, beliefs in law and peace and that freedom which sustains the human spirit. The case here today forces recognition of the costs to which those beliefs commit us. It is poignant but fundamental that the flag protects those who hold it in contempt.

For all the record shows, this respondent was not a philosopher and perhaps did not even possess the ability to comprehend how repellant his statements must be to the Republic itself. But whether or not he could appreciate the enormity of the offense he gave, the fact remains that his acts were speech, in both the technical and the fundamental meaning of the Constitution. So I agree with the court that he must go free.

Chief Justice Rehnquist joined by Justices Byron R. White and Sandra Day O'Connor, dissenting:

In holding this Texas statute unconstitutional, the Court ignores Justice Holmes' familiar aphorism that "a page of history is worth a volume of logic." . . .For more than 200 years, the American flag has occupied a unique position as the symbol of our Nation, a uniqueness that justifies a governmental prohibition against flag-burning in the way respondent Johnson did here. . . .

The flag symbolizes the Nation in peace as well as in war. It signifies our national presence on battleships, airplanes, military installations, and public buildings from the United States Capitol to the thousands of county courthouses and city halls throughout the country. Two flags are prominently placed in our courtroom. Countless flags are placed by the graves of loved ones each year on what was first called Decoration Day, and is now called Memorial Day. The flag is traditionally placed on the casket of deceased members of the armed forces, and is later given to the deceased's family. . . . Congress has provided that the flag be flown at half-staff upon the death of the President, Vice President, and other government officials "as a mark of respect to their memory." . . .The flag identifies United States merchant ships, 22 U.S.C. § 454, and "[t]he laws of the Union protect our commerce wherever the flag of the country may float." . . .

No other American symbol has been as universally honored as the flag. In 1931, Congress declared "The Star Spangled Banner" to be our national anthem. In 1949, Congress declared June 14th to be Flag Day. In 1987, John Philip Sousa's "The Stars and Stripes Forever" was designated as the national march. . . .Congress has also established "The Pledge of Allegiance to the Flag" and the manner of its deliverance. . . .The flag has appeared as the principal symbol on approximately 33 United States postal stamps and in the design of at least 43 more, more times than any other symbol. . . .

Both Congress and the States have enacted numerous laws regulating misuse of the American flag. Until 1967, Congress left the regulation of misuse of the flag up to the States. Now, however, Title 18 U.S.C. § 700(a), provides that: "Whoever knowingly casts contempt upon any flag of the United States by publicly mutilating, defacing, defiling, burning, or trampling upon it shall be fined not more than $1,000 or imprisoned for not more than one year, or both." . . .

The American flag, then, throughout more than 200 years of our history, has come to be the visible symbol embodying our Nation. It does not represent the views of any particular political party, and it does not represent any particular political philosophy. The flag is not simply another "idea" or "point of view" competing for recognition in the marketplace of ideas. Millions and millions of Americans regard it with an almost mythical reverence regardless of what sort of social, political, or philosophical beliefs they may have. I cannot agree that the First Amendment invalidates the Act of Congress, and the laws of 48 of the 50 States, which make criminal the public burning of the flag.

. . .[T]he public burning of the American flag by Johnson was no essential part of any exposition of ideas, and at the same time it had a tendency to incite a breach of the peace. Johnson was free to make any verbal denunciation of the flag that he wished; indeed, he was free to burn the flag in private. He could publicly burn other symbols of the government or effigies of political leaders. He did lead a march through the streets of Dallas, and conducted a rally in front of the Dallas City Hall. He engaged in a "die-in" to protest nuclear weapons. He shouted out various slogans during the march, including: "Reagan, Mondale which will it be? Either one means World War III"; and "Ronald Reagan, killer of the hour, Perfect example of U.S. power"; and "red white and blue, we spit on you, you stand for plunder, you will go under." . . .For none of these acts was he arrested or prosecuted; it was only when he proceeded to burn publicly an American flag stolen from its rightful owner that he violated the Texas statute.

. . .As with "fighting words," so with flag burning, for purposes of the First Amendment: It is "no essential part of any exposition of ideas, and [is] of such slight social value as a step to truth that any benefit that may be derived from [it] is clearly outweighed" by the public interest in avoiding a probable breach of the peace. The highest courts of several States have upheld state statutes prohibiting the public burning of the flag on the grounds that it is so inherently inflammatory that it may cause a breach of public order. . . .

. . .The Texas statute deprived Johnson of only one rather inarticulate symbolic form of protest—a form of protest that was profoundly offensive to many—and left him with a full panoply of other symbols and every conceivable form of verbal expression to express his deep disapproval of national policy. Thus, in no way can it be said that Texas is punishing him because his hearers—or any other group of people—were profoundly opposed to the message that he sought to convey. Such opposition is no proper basis for restricting speech or expression under the First Amendment. It was Johnson's use of this particular symbol, and not the idea that he sought to convey by it or by his many other expressions, for which he was punished.

. . .The uniquely deep awe and respect for our flag felt by virtually all of us are bundled off under the rubric of "designated symbols," . . .that the First Amendment prohibits the government from "establishing." But the government has not "established" this feeling; 200 years of history have done that. The government is simply recognizing as a fact the profound regard for the American flag created by that history when it enacts statutes prohibiting the disrespectful public burning of the flag.

The Court concludes its opinion with a regrettably patronizing civics lecture, presumably addressed to the Members of both Houses of Congress, the members of the 48 state legislatures that enacted prohibitions against flag burning, and the troops fighting under that flag in Vietnam who objected to its being burned: "The way to preserve the flag's special role is not to punish those who feel differently about these matters. It is to persuade them that they are wrong." . . .The court's role as the final expositor of the Constitution is well established, but its role as a platonic guardian admonishing those responsible to public opinion as if they were truant school children had no similar place in our system of government. The cry of "no taxation without representation" animated those who revolted against the English Crown to found our Nation—the idea that those who submitted to government should have some say as to what kind of

laws would be passed. Surely one of the high purposes of a democratic society is to legislate against conduct that is regarded as evil and profoundly offensive to the majority of people—whether it be murder, embezzlement, pollution, or flag burning.

Our Constitution wisely places limits on powers of legislative majorities to act, but the declaration of such limits by this Court "is, at all times, a question of much delicacy, which ought seldom, if ever, to be decided in the affirmative, in a doubtful case." . . .Uncritical extension of constitutional protection to the burning of the flag risks the frustration of the very purpose for which organized governments are instituted. The Court decides that the American flag is just another symbol, about which not only must opinions pro and con be tolerated, but for which the most minimal public respect may not be enjoined. The government may conscript men into the Armed Forces where they must fight and perhaps die for the flag, but the government may not prohibit the public burning of the banner under which they fight. I would uphold the Texas statute as applied in this case.

Justice Stevens, dissenting:

As the court analyzes this case, it presents the question whether the State of Texas, or indeed the Federal Government, has the power to prohibit the public desecration of the American flag. The question is unique. In my judgment, rules that apply to a host of other symbols, such as state flags, armbands, or various privately promoted emblems of political or commercial identity, are not necessarily controlling. Even if flag burning could be considered just another species of symbolic speech under the logical application of the rules that the Court has developed in its interpretation of the First Amendment in other contexts, this case has an intangible dimension that makes those rules inapplicable.

A country's flag is a symbol of more than "nationhood and national unity." . . .It also signifies the ideas that characterize the society that has chosen that emblem as well as the special history that has animated the growth and power of those ideas. The fleurs-de-lis and the tricolor both symbolized "nationhood and national unity," but they had vastly different meanings. The message conveyed by some flags—the swastika, for example—may survive long after it has outlived its usefulness as a symbol of regimented unity in a particular nation.

CASE STUDY 3

So it is with the American flag. It is more than a proud symbol of the courage, the determination, and the gifts of nature that transformed 13 fledgling Colonies into a world power. It is a symbol of freedom, of equal opportunity, of religious tolerance, and of goodwill for other peoples who share our aspirations. The symbol carries its message to dissidents both at home and abroad who may have no interest at all in our national unity or survival.

The value of the flag as a symbol cannot be measured. . . .

The ideas of liberty and equality have been an irresistible force in motivating leaders like Patrick Henry, Susan B. Anthony, and Abraham Lincoln, schoolteachers like Nathan Hale and Booker T. Washington, the Philippine Scouts who fought at Bataan, and the soldiers who scaled the bluff at Omaha Beach. If those ideas are worth fighting for—and our history demonstrates that they are—it cannot be true that the flag that uniquely symbolizes their power is not itself worthy of protection from unnecessary desecration.

I respectfully dissent.

SHOE   by Jeff MacNelly

Politicians like to wrap themselves in the flag.

CHAPTER FIVE

The Structure of Federalism

The political situation that existed in the American colonies, and for a short time in post-Revolutionary America, virtually cried out for the creation of some form of centralized government. This was not recognized in 1781 by those who set up the Articles of Confederation—the first attempt at self-government by the new American states—and the loose organization of sovereign states, which had relinquished little real power to the central government, was not successful.

Even at the Constitutional Convention in 1787, it would have been almost unthinkable, given the state of political affairs in America, to establish a really centralized system. The states had enjoyed a great deal of autonomy under the Articles and were unwilling to give up their hard-earned sovereignty. Thus a federal form of government was the only solution that would permit the states to maintain some autonomy and would also allow the establishment of a stronger, more effective central government. Like many other fundamentals of the new republic, the structure of federalism was not necessarily adopted because of its theoretical merits but rather due to its political suitability to the situation that existed at that particular time.

THE THEORY OF AMERICAN FEDERALISM

Once it had been accepted that the new federal government would be composed of two parts—the national, or central, government and the state governments—other questions had to be resolved. What was to be the relationship between this new central government and the states that had joined to create it? What authority would the states yield to the national government? What authority would be retained by the states? On what matters would the authority of the states and the national government overlap? The structure of American federalism was forged as the delegates to the Constitutional Convention responded to these questions.

Characteristics of Federalism

Unlike a unitary centralized system in which some power is delegated by the central government to regions, *federalism* is a method of governmental organization in which authority is divided between the central government and the constituent governments. Historically, federalism has been a recognized form of government since the leagues of ancient Greece. Switzerland, Mexico, Canada, and Australia are all nations that have modern federal systems.

One characteristic of federalism is that the constituent governments usually are endowed with more than a trivial amount of authority. Naturally, the amount of power held by the constituent governments depends on how strong they are at the time of union. A second characteristic of federalism is the equal distribution of power among the constituents. Constituent governments usually possess equal authority on their own levels and yield 125 equal amounts of authority to the central government. In the United States authority is divided between the national government and the 50 states that now comprise the federation.

Since the Constitution does not specifically mention federalism, the system is implied rather than stipulated. Some scholars, therefore, have suggested that because federalism is not outlined in the Constitution, perhaps the Framers intended to set up a stronger central government than actually exists. (There is in fact little in the Constitution that would prohibit the federal government from vastly expanding its powers over the states.) Nevertheless, whether as an afterthought or not, the Tenth Amendment to the Constitution, ratified in 1791, does clarify the issue. The amendment states that "the powers not delegated to the United States by the Constitution, nor prohibited by it to the States, are reserved to the States respectively, or to the people." And it certainly seems obvious, both from the debates of the Constitutional Convention and from the later arguments of James Madison and Alexander Hamilton in *The Fed-*

(Drawing by Richter; ©1989 The New Yorker Magazine, Inc.)

"They have very strict anti-pollution laws in this state."
Contrasting laws from state to state is an important characteristic of federalism.

eralist, that it was the clear intent of the Framers of the Constitution to limit the scope of authority of the national government over the states. Federalism, as a device, was an instrument of national power—the furthest point to which the nationalists at the Constitutional Convention felt they could go in the direction of establishing an independent national government.

INITIAL ARGUMENTS FOR A STRONGER CENTRAL GOVERNMENT

Discussions today about the merits and deficiencies of the federal system are not unlike those that took place in 1787. Such discussions have focused on the encroachments of the national government on the power of the states. Supporters of a stronger national government in the eighteenth and nineteenth centuries, however, did not advocate a complete unitary form of government, as today's supporters often do. Rather, in choosing federalism they felt that they had a vigorous enough national government to overcome the problems of the loose confederation they had already tried.

At the time when the Constitution was being drafted, the states were the dominant powers. Thus, when Alexander Hamilton discussed the merits of a federal government over a confederacy he was arguing against a background of overwhelming state power. Because the states were concerned with maintaining their sovereignty in 1787, Hamilton had to convince the states that a federal government would not usurp state power. This was not an easy task, and it was to be expected that the states would zealously guard their powers to raise militias, levy taxes, and regulate commerce.

In *The Federalist*, No. 16, Hamilton carefully explained that the central government would possess only limited powers under the Constitution and that it would be foolhardy to imagine it could ever completely dominate the states. Since power continued to be lodged in the states, Hamilton reasoned, the only way the central government could ever control the states would be through the recruitment and maintenance of a large and powerful national army. But Hamilton felt this was unlikely because the states would certainly continue to exert a great deal of authority. In any case, Hamilton wrote:

> The resources of the Union would not be equal to the maintenance of an army considerable enough to confine the larger States within the limits of their duty; nor would the means ever be furnished of forming such an army in the first instance. Whoever considers the populousness and strength of these States singly at the present juncture, and looks forward to what they will become, even at the distance of half a century, will at once dismiss as idle and visionary any scheme which aims at regulating their movements by law. . . .

Hamilton's argument was not intended to convince those who supported the Constitution and a stronger central government. It was to gain support from those who wanted state power and who were worried about real domination by the national government. Another element of discontent among the political factions of 1787 was expressed by those who favored a very strong central government and were unable to recognize the document's potential for establishing a dominant national government.

In *The Federalist*, No. 16, Hamilton went on to defend the strengthening of the central government. He pointed out that the weakness of the central government under the Articles of Confederation had led to the chaos that had made necessary a new Constitution. Some form of central government capable of regulating the mutual concerns of the states was definitely needed. Hamilton felt that in order to fill this need, the central government would have to be able to enforce its legisla-

(Courtesy of the American Antiquarian Society)

This cartoon of the federal chariot being drawn by 13 states appeared on the cover of a 1788 almanac.

tion without any "intermediate legislation." In other words, it "must itself be empowered to employ the arm of the ordinary magistrate [law officer] to execute its own resolutions." The courts and other means of enforcing national authority, Hamilton thought, should be entrusted to the national government rather than to the state governments.

Penalties of Nullification

Hamilton also argued that the states should not be allowed to evade federal laws. If that were the case, he said, there would be no point in having a central government. However, the doctrine of *nullification*, whereby states could invalidate federal laws within their own jurisdictions, was accepted practice during the early republic. The Kentucky and Virginia Resolutions of 1798 and 1799 even stated that "nullification" was the "rightful

remedy" for the states to follow whenever they felt the central government had overstepped its bounds. Hamilton hoped to end this practice and explained that in the proposed Constitution the authority of the national government would be superior to that of the states. According to Hamilton, nullification of federal law by individual states could not take place "without an open and violent exertion of unconstitutional powers." It would thus constitute an act of rebellion. Hamilton's predictions were borne out by the Civil War.

National Versus State Power

Although Hamilton argued in *The Federalist*, No. 16, that the national government probably would not be able to maintain an army strong enough to keep the states in line, he also believed that the states would find it difficult to go beyond the boundaries of their own jurisdictions. But this presented another problem. If restraints were placed on the states, would that not allow the national government to take over the authority that resided with the states?

In *The Federalist*, No. 17, Hamilton made the distinction between national and local matters. He argued that politicians controlling government at the national level would have sufficient ways to exert their authority over diverse objectives and interests without having to turn to the local sphere. Hamilton concluded this argument by stating that "it will always be far more easy for the State governments to encroach upon the national authorities, than for the national government to encroach upon the State authorities." He was confident that as long as the states acted with "uprightness and prudence" in their relations with the people, they would enjoy greater influence than the national government.

When Hamilton suggested that the states had nothing to fear from the constitutional authority granted to the national government, in the opinion of his contemporaries he was making a logical point. He was emphasizing that regardless of the constitutional division of authority between the national and state governments, other factors, such as the attachment of the individual to his home locale, would prevent the national government from completely dominating the political system. As long as so many interests remained local, people would turn to their state and local governments for redress of grievances and would give these governments their support.

Of course it was not realized then that with the growth of the national economy interests that in the eighteenth century were regarded as purely local would eventually expand into the sector of the federal government. As this extension of nationalization occurred, federalism as the protector of local interests was undermined. When the focus of political interests changed from the local to the national scene, the balance of governmental power also shifted in the same direction.

In *The Federalist* James Madison described the intricacies of the new federal system in a way designed to alleviate the fears of the proponents of states' rights that the new federal Constitution would inevitably result in the domination of national power over legitimate state interests. In the thirty-ninth paper of *The Federalist*, Madison wrote that in form and operation the new federal government was both national and federal, reflecting national interests in assigning national power where the common concerns of the nation were involved, and at the same time providing for the representation of state interests and the retention of state power over matters of purely state and local interest. Ratification of the Consti-

(From *The Herblock Book* [Beacon Press, 1952])

"In two words, yes and no."
States want federal aid without strings attached.

tution in the first place, argued Madison, was a federal and not a national act, because ratification required the approval of at least nine of the thirteen independent states by state ratifying conventions. Thus in effect the principle of individual state sovereignty was retained in the ratification process because the states were treated as individual units and not as part of a collective whole. The ratification of the Constitution, Madison wrote, "is to be given by the people, not as individuals composing one entire nation, but as composing the distinct and independent states to which they respectively belong."

After noting that the ratification process was essentially federal in character, Madison went on to list the national attributes of the Constitution on the one hand and its federal aspects on the other. He wrote that the House of Representatives was essentially national in character because it represented the people of the United States collectively, apportionment being on the basis of population of the individual states. The states would not have representatives in the House simply as states, as was the case in the Senate, but solely on the basis of the number of people residing within each separate state. This in effect meant that the people were to be directly represented in the House. On the other hand, the Senate was also an important federal attribute of the Constitution, argued Madison, because of its equal representation of the states regardless of their individual populations. The presidency was both federal and national in character, said Madison: Voting by the electoral college reflected the separate powers of individual states, but representation in the electoral college was apportioned, as in the House, according to population within the states.

Madison's argument essentially was that where the states were represented in the national government without regard to the size of their population the federal principle was being maintained, but where the people were directly represented in government the na-

tional principle was being supported. And because the powers of the national government were specifically enumerated by the Constitution, the states had nothing to fear from unauthorized national incursions into their domains.

THE TWILIGHT ZONE BETWEEN NATIONAL AND STATE POWER

The Framers of the Constitution devoted considerable attention to how much strength should be given the central government. And the Constitution did provide for a fairly strong national government as well as for a division of authority between the federal government and the states. Still, many practical issues could not be anticipated by the Founding Fathers and had to be resolved as they emerged after the federal system had begun to operate.

Judicial Expansion of National Authority

One of the early landmarks in resolving the nature and limits of national authority was the famous Supreme Court case *McCulloch v. Maryland* (1819). It was in this decision that Chief Justice John Marshall stated the doctrine of national supremacy. Two extremely important constitutional questions were raised in this case. First, should the Constitution be interpreted broadly or narrowly? Second, in areas where the two shared authority, was the national government supreme over the states?

McCulloch v. Maryland arose from a dispute between a bank incorporated under a congressional law and the state of Maryland, which wished to tax a Baltimore branch of the bank. McCulloch, a cashier of the Baltimore branch of the Second Bank of the United States, had refused to pay the state tax, justifying his action on the assumption that an instrumentality of the national government could not be taxed by a state. The state of Maryland contended, on the other hand, that Congress had no authority to incorporate a bank. Where was this explicitly stated in the Constitution? Certainly, Maryland argued, even if Congress did have this power, a sovereign state would be able to tax a branch of a national bank within the state's own boundaries.

The Supreme Court thus had to decide whether the Constitution was to be construed broadly enough to permit Congress to charter a bank. The Court also had to decide whether the national government or the state governments had priority in a conflict where both levels of government had some jurisdiction. Chief Justice Marshall's opinion emphatically decided these issues in favor of the national government.

Implied powers. First, Marshall held that even though the enumerated powers of Congress did not explicitly grant it authority to charter a national bank, such authority was *implied* by the powers listed in Article I. The Chief Justice argued that

although, among the enumerated powers of government, we do not find the word "bank," or "incorporation," we find the great powers to lay and collect taxes; to borrow money; to regulate commerce; to declare and conduct a war; and to raise and support armies and navies. The sword and the purse, all the external relations, and no inconsiderable portion of the industry of the nation, are entrusted to its government. . . .It may, with great reason, be contended, that a government, entrusted with such ample powers, on the due execution of which the happiness and prosperity of the nation so vitally depends, must also be entrusted with ample means for their execution.[1]

The Constitution, Marshall went on to note, "does not profess to enumerate the means by which the powers it confers may be

executed; nor does it prohibit the creation of a corporation, if the existence of such a being be essential to the beneficial exercise of those powers." Stating the theory of implied powers, Marshall concluded that if the result were "legitimate," then any means of achieving that result—as long as it was not prohibited by the Constitution but was "consistent with the letter and spirit of the Constitution"—was constitutional. The Chief Justice had thus decided that the Congress could charter a bank on the basis of its general enumerated powers. Even though this power was not specifically stated in the Constitution, it was *implied* by the powers Congress did have to regulate commerce and to borrow money.

National supremacy. Having determined that the national government could incorporate a bank, Marshall then dealt with the question of whether the state of Maryland could tax a branch of the bank within its own boundaries. Speaking first of the general supremacy of the national government, the Chief Justice stated, "If any one proposition could command the universal assent of mankind, we might expect it to be this: that *the government of the Union*, then, though limited in its powers, *is supreme within its sphere of action*." [Italics added.] The Constitution, because it is the basis for the national government is, then, the "supreme law of the land."

Building on this principle of national supremacy, Marshall considered the legitimacy of a state tax on a national bank. "The power to tax," Marshall said, "involves the power to destroy," and cannot be used by the states against a legitimate agency of national authority. The Court's opinion concluded that "the states have no power, by taxation or otherwise, to retard, impede, burden, or in any manner control, the operation of the constitutional laws enacted by Congress to carry into execution the powers vested in the general government."

The *McCulloch v. Maryland* decision of the Supreme Court under its Federalist chief jus-

---

[1] Wheaton 316 (1819).

tice, John Marshall, who presided from 1801 until 1835, was only one important decision in a long series of cases that affirmed national supremacy and the flexibility of the Constitution in its delegation of authority to the national government to legislate in the national interest. The doctrine of the supremacy of the Constitution, federal law, and decisions of the federal judiciary over the states had begun even before John Marshall became Chief Justice. Supreme Court justices in the 1790s, acting primarily as circuit court judges,[2] had in several cases overturned state actions that they considered to be in conflict with the Constitution. There was little doubt by the time of *McCulloch v. Maryland* that the intent of the Federalist judiciary was clearly to affirm broad national power and dominance over the states. In 1824, five years after *McCulloch v. Maryland*, *Gibbons v. Ogden* was decided. It reaffirmed the broad authority of Congress to legislate, in this case under the commerce clause, and the supremacy of national law.[3]

The onward march of the Federalist doctrine of national supremacy, so dear to the hearts of such prominent Federalists as Alexander Hamilton and John Marshall in the late eighteenth and early nineteenth centuries, was, as might be expected, highly controversial. After all, this was a time when states' rights doctrines were firmly embedded in all states, particularly in the South and the West. As obvious as it may seem today that national supremacy and the expansion of national powers were inevitable, it was not until the guns were silent after the Civil War, with the North victorious, that national supremacy was firmly established. Even after the Civil War and long into the twentieth century, states resisted national encroachments upon what they considered to be their reserved powers.

The early resistance to doctrines of national supremacy was both a reflection of the past sovereignty of the states and a precursor of what was to come in the seemingly never-ending battle over the proper parameters of national authority over the states. Above all, the mere announcement of its formal decisions by the Supreme Court has never brought about automatic acquiescence on the part of the states, either in the nineteenth century or in the twentieth century.

Early political resistance to Supreme Court decisions establishing national supremacy can be observed in the reaction to John Marshall's decision in *McCulloch v. Maryland*. In the southern and western states in particular, Republican opposition to the Marshall doctrine was stated in colorful terms. In Virginia, Thomas Jefferson and James Madison led the opposition, and Thomas Ritchie, editor of the *Richmond Inquirer*, attacked the decision as presaging the demise of states' rights:

If such a spirit as breathes in this opinion is forever to preside over the judiciary then indeed it is high time for the states to tremble . . .all their great rights may be swept away one by one. . . .If Congress can select any means which they consider "convenient," "useful," "conducive to," the execution of the specified and granted powers; if the word "necessary" is thus to be frittered away, then we may bid adieu to the sovereignty of the states; they sink into contemptible corporations; the gulf of consolidation yawns to receive them. This doctrine is as alarming, if not more so, than any which ever came from Mr. A. Hamilton on this question of a bank or any other question under the Constitution. . . .The people should not pass it over in silence; otherwise this opinion might prove the knell of our most important states' rights. This opinion must be controverted and exposed.[4]

---

[2]Circuit court judges "rode circuit," which meant that they participated in the decisions of the federal circuit courts along with judges of the lower courts, a system that lasted well into the nineteenth century.

[3]See *Gibbons v. Ogden*, 9 Wheaton 1, 1824.

---

[4]Charles A. Warren, *The Supreme Court in United States History* (Boston: Little, Brown, 1922), Vol. 1, p. 516.

Newspapers in Mississippi, Tennessee, Georgia, Kentucky, and South Carolina, among other states, charged that Marshall's opinion obliterated states' rights entirely. In a typical criticism of that part of Marshall's opinion which stated the doctrine of implied powers, a Democratic newspaper in New Jersey wrote:

If Congress may incorporate banking companies, notwithstanding the want of specific constitutional authority, and in defiance of the general constitutional prohibition, we scarcely know what they may not do![5]

A Philadelphia newspaper criticized Marshall for general incompetence as a judge. When Chief Justice Marshall reaffirmed the McCulloch decision in *Gibbons v. Ogden* in 1824, the opposition was again as widespread, vociferous, and, sometimes, scurrilous as after the *McCulloch* decision.

The opposition to such decisions as *McCulloch* and *Gibbons* did not prevent the implied powers and national supremacy doctrines from prevailing, and their later use by Congress in the expansion of national authority over the states realized the worst fears of the early opponents of the Marshall court's decisions in this area. By using these two doctrines—implied powers and national supremacy—the national government has vastly expanded its authority over the states. The most important enumerated powers used by Congress for this purpose are its authority to regulate commerce among the several states, to tax, and to provide for the general welfare. At certain times Congress's war-making powers have also been used to justify significant extensions of national power.

Concurrent Powers

The sphere of national supremacy is sometimes more difficult to determine than it was in *McCulloch v. Maryland*. In that case there was a clear conflict of issues between federal and state law, but in other cases the lines are not so clearly drawn.

There are many areas in which both the states and the national government have jurisdiction within their own spheres—that is, they have *concurrent power.* For example, both the states and the national government have the power to regulate commerce. The states have jurisdiction over intrastate commerce, and the federal government regulates interstate commerce. The police power to protect the health, morals, and safety of the community is also a concurrent power of the states and the federal government. Treasury agents and agents of the FBI are representatives of the national government, while state police are responsible for law enforcement within the states.

Many parts of the Constitution do clearly designate exclusive power to the national government in certain areas—naturalization, the regulation of commerce with foreign nations, the setting of the value of money, and so forth. In those areas, however, where there is no clear designation of authority to the national government by the Constitution, the power to legislate is concurrently shared between the national government and the states. In cases where the division of power is not clearly drawn the limits of concurrent powers must be determined by the Supreme Court. (See Figure 5.1.)

National preemption. Generally, when cases involving concurrent jurisdiction are brought before the Supreme Court, the Court holds that congressional action takes precedence, or *preempts*, in the area. This was exemplified by the Court's ruling in the case *Pennsylvania v. Nelson* in 1956. A Pennsylvania court had convicted Steve Nelson, an acknowledged member of the Communist party, of violating a Pennsylvania statute by threatening to overthrow violently the federal government.

When the case was appealed to the state supreme court, it was ruled that Nelson could

---

[5]Ibid., pp. 521–522.

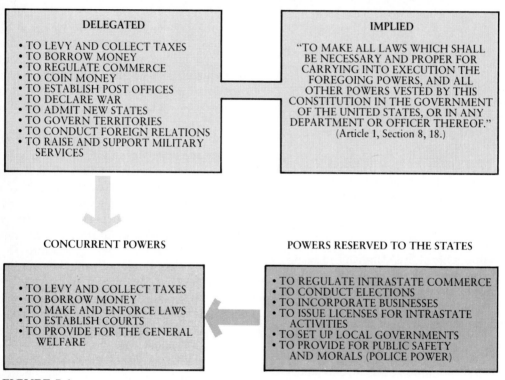

THE AMERICAN FEDERAL SYSTEM
Division of Powers Between the National Government
and the State Governments

POWERS DELEGATED TO THE NATIONAL GOVERNMENT

DELEGATED

- TO LEVY AND COLLECT TAXES
- TO BORROW MONEY
- TO REGULATE COMMERCE
- TO COIN MONEY
- TO ESTABLISH POST OFFICES
- TO DECLARE WAR
- TO ADMIT NEW STATES
- TO GOVERN TERRITORIES
- TO CONDUCT FOREIGN RELATIONS
- TO RAISE AND SUPPORT MILITARY
  SERVICES

IMPLIED

"TO MAKE ALL LAWS WHICH SHALL
BE NECESSARY AND PROPER FOR
CARRYING INTO EXECUTION THE
FOREGOING POWERS, AND ALL
OTHER POWERS VESTED BY THIS
CONSTITUTION IN THE GOVERNMENT
OF THE UNITED STATES, OR IN ANY
DEPARTMENT OR OFFICER THEREOF."
(Article 1, Section 8, 18.)

CONCURRENT POWERS

- TO LEVY AND COLLECT TAXES
- TO BORROW MONEY
- TO MAKE AND ENFORCE LAWS
- TO ESTABLISH COURTS
- TO PROVIDE FOR THE GENERAL
  WELFARE

POWERS RESERVED TO THE STATES

- TO REGULATE INTRASTATE COMMERCE
- TO CONDUCT ELECTIONS
- TO INCORPORATE BUSINESSES
- TO ISSUE LICENSES FOR INTRASTATE
  ACTIVITIES
- TO SET UP LOCAL GOVERNMENTS
- TO PROVIDE FOR PUBLIC SAFETY
  AND MORALS (POLICE POWER)

FIGURE 5.1

not be convicted under the state statute because Congress had already preempted the field with the Smith Act of 1940. Like the Pennsylvania law, the Smith Act made it a crime to advocate the violent overthrow of the United States government. The Pennsylvania Supreme Court inferred that if the threat had been made against the government of Pennsylvania it probably would have been proper for the state to prosecute. The state then appealed, but the Supreme Court held that the Smith Act, together with other federal subversive control statutes (the Internal Security Act of 1950 and the Communist Control Act of 1954), outlawed advocacy of violent overthrow of any government, whether federal, state, or local. On the basis of all the federal statutes in the sedition field, the Court concluded that

Congress has intended to occupy the field of sedition. Taken as a whole, they [the statutes] evince a congressional plan which makes it

(From *Herblock's Special for Today* [Simon & Schuster, 1958])

"Pardon me, but I think that's my hat."
The Supreme Court's decision in 1956 concerning the Pennsylvania state sedition law evoked this cartoon.

reasonable to determine that no room has been left for the States to supplement it. Therefore, a state sedition statute is superseded regardless of whether it purports to supplement the federal law. . . .[6]

The Pennsylvania law, along with the sedition acts of other states, was therefore void.

THE BALANCE OF NATIONAL AND STATE POWERS

Both the constitutional law and the political forces of this country have shaped the balance of power between the national government and the states. The nationalist Supreme Court

[6]350 U.S. 497 (1956).

under Chief Justice Marshall, which consistently buttressed national power in relation to the states, was replaced in the 1830s by a Court under Roger Taney (chief justice from 1836 to 1864) that had a majority which was far more sympathetic to the proponents of states' rights. The Supreme Court, of course, ultimately reflects the underlying balance of political power in the community. And the Court particularly tends to mirror the views of political elites. Generally, from the end of the Civil War until the beginning of President Franklin D. Roosevelt's second term in 1937, Supreme Court opinions favored state power and private property interests.

The National Government Ascendant

Political and economic forces that surfaced during the Great Depression of the 1930s altered the balance of national and state power. A conservative Supreme Court at first clung to the doctrines of the past, striking down many key pieces of Franklin D. Roosevelt's New Deal legislation primarily on the grounds that Congress had exceeded its constitutional authority in enacting them. (A key example of the defeated legislation was the National Industrial Recovery Act of 1933, the showpiece law of the Roosevelt administration, which was overturned by a unanimous Court decision led by Chief Justice Charles Evans Hughes.)

Roosevelt's response to the Great Depression was to strengthen greatly the powers of the national government in relation to the states and the business community. The states simply did not have the resources to cope with the rising unemployment, falling industrial production, business failures, bank panics, and other economic dislocations that characterized the national and worldwide depression of the 1930s. Nor could the states accommodate the growing number of extremist political movements on the right and the left that threatened to undermine the very foundations of the political system. National action was called for and expected. It was both econommically and politically essential for the national government to take the lead in putting the economy and the ship of state back on an even keel.

The Supreme Court could not resist for long the political tide that demanded national action. The structure of federalism was fundamentally altered when the Court, in Roosevelt's second term, adapted its interpretation of the Constitution to allow the expansion of national power both over the states and corporate interests. The New Deal was the beginning of a trend toward centralization of power in the hands of the national government that reached its height during the administration of Lyndon B. Johnson in the 1960s.

The growth in federal programs begun during the Roosevelt administration continued unabated and peaked in the Johnson era. The "Great Society" of Lyndon Johnson carried the New Deal to an extreme and spurred vast new government programs to cure the economic and social ills of society. Although there remained a few voices, mostly Republican, in the wilderness proclaiming states' rights, there seemed to be no political or constitutional obstacles in the path of the growing power of the federal government. The Supreme Court itself, under Chief Justice Earl Warren, had taken a highly interventionist stance in applying national standards of civil liberties and civil rights to the states. Moreover the Court applied in the area of electoral reapportionment even stricter standards to the states than the Constitution required of the federal government. Under the "one-person-one-vote" rule that emerged from *Baker v. Carr* in 1962 and *Reynolds v. Sims* in 1964, both branches of state legislatures were required to create electoral districts with equal populations.

With the president, Congress, and the Supreme Court all fully supporting the expansion of national power during the 1960s, any attempt to challenge the growing power of the federal government under the charge that it was exceeding its constitutional authority—for

example, under the commerce clause or due to the invasion of the reserved powers of the states—was bound to fail.

The futility of constitutional challenges to federal power during the Johnson years was illustrated in the case *Heart of Atlanta Motel, Inc. v. United States* in 1964. Congress had used the commerce clause as the basis of its authority for Title II of the Civil Rights Act of 1964, which prohibited discrimination in public accommodations, including inns, hotels, motels, restaurants, and motion picture theaters. The Heart of Atlanta Motel challenged the act on constitutional grounds, claiming that the commerce clause could not be applied to motels in requiring them to desegregate. The plaintiff maintained that "persons and people are not part of trade or commerce. Persons and people are not the objects, the means nor the end of trade or commerce. People conduct commerce and engage in trade, but people are not part of commerce and trade."[7] The attorneys for the Heart of Atlanta Motel predicted dire consequences if the law was upheld:

The theory advanced in the trial court by the government . . .was that Congress in passing the Civil Rights Act of 1964 was simply exercising its full power under the commerce clause. If that is the theory of our government now, then Congress can do no wrong and can legislate on any and all matters affecting people on the grounds that they are part of interstate commerce. . . .The next act of Congress . . .would include your home—and then we shall have arrived at the full and complete socialistic state that the framers of the Constitution despised, dreaded and detested.[8]

The Heart of Atlanta Motel lost its case before the Supreme Court by a unanimous vote of the justices. Justice Tom Clark, a Texan and

---

[7]Philip P. Kurland and Gerhard Casper, eds., *Landmark Briefs and Arguments of the Supreme Court of the United States* (Arlington, Va.: University Publications of America, 1975), 60:362.

[8]Ibid., pp. 326–327, 330.

Truman appointee, wrote the majority opinion. Citing *Gibbons v. Ogden*, he declared that "the power of Congress to promote interstate commerce also includes the power to regulate the local incidents thereof, including local activities in both the states of origin and destination which might have a substantial and harmful effect upon that commerce."[9] Discrimination, Clark concluded, has a clear and adverse effect upon commerce.

State sovereignty as a limit on national power. By the end of the Johnson administration state sovereignty seemed to be an anachronism. However, the election of Richard M. Nixon brought a change, although admittedly slight, in federal-state relations. Nixon's "New Federalism" and revenue-sharing programs, under which federal revenues were transferred directly to the states and local communities with no strings attached, was designed to give state and local governments a more independent role, allowing them to make and support public policies without always having to heed the wishes of the federal government.

Nixon also indirectly contributed to a change in the formal doctrine of federalism that had come to accept unlimited national power, by appointing conservatives to the Supreme Court. By the time Richard Nixon resigned the presidency on August 9, 1974, he had named four of the nine justices. Chief Justice Warren Burger and Justices Lewis Powell, William Rehnquist, and Harry Blackmun (who was slightly less conservative than the others) voted together along with Dwight D. Eisenhower's appointee, Potter Stewart, to uphold a claim of state sovereignty against federal action in *National League of Cities v. Usery* in 1976.

The *National League of Cities* case concerned a constitutional challenge to 1974 amendments to the Fair Labor Standards Act that extended minimum-wage and maximum-hour provisions to the employees of states and their political subdivisions. Congress had again used its commerce power as the source of its authority for the law, which had previously governed only private employers. The Court held that the application of the law to state and local employees unconstitutionally impinged upon state sovereignty. Justice William Rehnquist's plurality opinion for the court supported the plenary authority of Congress under the commerce clause, *but* declared that "there are limits upon the power of Congress to override states' sovereignty even when exercising its otherwise plenary powers to tax or to regulate commerce which are conferred by Article I of the Constitution." Thus the authority to determine the wages paid to state and local employees is part of the sovereign authority of the states into which Congress cannot intrude.

The dissenting justices in the case viewed Rehnquist's opinion as a startling departure from the constitutional principle of national supremacy over the states. Justice William Brennan, joined in dissent by Justices White and Marshall, declared (1) that Congress alone should determine the reach of federal authority over the states under the commerce clause, (2) that the authority of Congress was plenary, and (3) that it should not be subject to judicial limitation. It was ironic and surprising, wrote Brennan, that

my Brethren should choose this bicentennial year of our independence to repudiate principles governing judicial interpretation of our Constitution settled since the time of Mr. Chief Justice John Marshall, discarding his postulate that the Constitution contemplates that restraints upon exercise by Congress of its plenary commerce power lie in the political process and not in the judicial process. For 152 years ago Mr. Chief Justice Marshall enunciated that principle to which, until today, his successors on this Court have been faithful.[10]

---

[9]379 U.S. 241 (1964).

[10]426 U.S. 833 (1976).

The resurrection of the Tenth Amendment in the *National League of Cities* case to limit federal power over the states did not herald a return to states' rights, however. For example, the Court in 1981 unanimously voted to turn down a challenge to the Surface Mining Control and Reclamation Act of 1977 that had been made in part on the basis that the law violated the Tenth Amendment by invading the reserved powers of the states. Justice Rehnquist nevertheless warned, in a concurring opinion, that

one of the greatest "fictions" of our federal system is that the Congress exercises only those powers delegated to it, while the remainder are reserved to the states or to the people. The manner in which this court has construed the commerce clause amply illustrates the extent of this fiction. Although it is clear that the people, through the states, *delegated* authority to Congress to "regulate commerce . . .among the several states" . . .one could easily get the sense from this Court's opinion that the federal system exists only at the sufferance of Congress."[11]

Rehnquist then reiterated his view that there are limits upon the authority of Congress over the states, and that in order to justify intrusions upon traditional realms of state power Congress must demonstrate that the activities regulated have a *substantial* effect upon interstate commerce.

ADVANTAGES AND DISADVANTAGES OF FEDERALISM

Just as the constitutional system of federalism was the result of political compromises at the Convention of 1787, the evolution of the federal system has been shaped not only by its formal attributes but also by informal political and social forces. The flexibility of the constitutional system, indeed the fact that federalism as such was not even mentioned explicitly in any of the terms of the original Constitution, largely left the definition of federalism and the resolution of conflict over the proper extent of national authority in relation to the states, as well as issues concerning the general political role of the national government in relation to the states, to the courts and the other branches of the national government.[12] And the decisions of government, as is always the case, reflected input from interest groups, political parties, and the community in general.

How well has federalism worked in the United States? While initially federalism had clear nationalistic implications and was designed to create an effective national government in contrast to the weak Articles of Confederation, the political, social, and economic forces underlying state sovereignty remained and produced the Civil War—which itself was a clear indication of the failure of federalism by itself to reconcile national and state interests. The Supreme Court could and did announce doctrines of national supremacy over the states, but this did not prevent divisive forces from tearing the nation apart over economic issues, slavery, and states' rights. Alexis de Tocqueville was too optimistic about the future of federalism in his famous treatise *Democracy in America*, first published in 1835 in Paris, after his famous sojourn in the United States.[13] Tocqueville admired the federal system, feeling that it combined the advantages of large and small nations by permitting the preservation of local interests while at the same time establishing a national government

---

[11]*Hodel v. Virginia Surface Mining and Reclamation Association*, 452 U.S. 264 (1981).

[12]The Tenth Amendment, ratified after the original Constitution, also did not mention federalism, but it did explicitly provide for a division of authority between the national government and the states.

[13]One readily available and excellent edition of this work is Alexis de Tocqueville, *Democracy in America*, 2 vols. (New York: Vintage Books, 1954).

to deal with common national concerns. But, characteristically, Tocqueville pointed out that the preservation of the federal system did not depend upon formal constitutional provisions, provisions that indeed were vague and ambiguous at best, but upon the ability and willingness of the American people to understand and accept federalism. In the larger sense, Tocqueville felt that the inherent weaknesses of federalism, and particularly the lack of a strong national government, would be overcome by general acquiescence in the system as well as political astuteness about how the system was to work. Tocqueville expressed these and other thoughts on federalism when he wrote:

In examining the constitution of the United States, which is the most perfect federal constitution that ever existed, one is startled at the variety of information and the amount of discernment that it presupposes in the people whom it is meant to govern. The government of the union depends almost entirely upon legal fictions; the union is an ideal nation, which exists, so to speak, only in the mind, and whose limits and extent can only be discerned by the understanding [of the people]. . . .I have never been more struck by the good sense and the practical judgment of the Americans than in the manner in which they elude the numberless difficulties resulting from their federal constitution. I scarcely ever met with a plain American citizen who could not distinguish with surprising facility the obligations created by the laws of Congress from those created by the laws of his own state, and who, after having discriminated between the matters which come under the cognizance of the Union and those which the local legislature is competent to regulate, could not point out the exact limit of the separate jurisdictions of the federal courts and the tribunals of the state.[14]

What Tocqueville failed to point out—and apparently failed to see—was that the under-

standing of federalism shown by American citizens did not reflect agreement on the proper boundaries of national and state authority.

Tocqueville was prescient in his analysis of the requisites for federalism. Federalism not only required understanding and agreement among the diverse interests of the United States but also could only exist, he said, in a nation unthreatened by foreign wars and internal crises, a nation in general able to afford the luxury of a weak central government and administration. The growth in the power and responsibilities of the national government in relation to the states that has taken place in the twentieth century has been largely due to wars and domestic crises.

It is interesting to view the twentieth-century debates and political struggles over federalism from the vantage point not only of Tocqueville but also of an even more thorough and insightful nineteenth-century analyst, James Bryce, who discussed the advantages and disadvantages of federalism from a post-Civil War and an English perspective in his classes treatise *The American Commonwealth*, first published in 1888. Bryce's outline of the merits and limitations of American federalism provides an excellent frame of reference for the discussion of contemporary federalism.

Advantages According to Bryce

Bryce noted eight advantages of the federal form of government.

One nation with state identities. The first advantage of federalism, according to Bryce, is that it "furnishes the means of uniting the commonwealth into one nation under one national government without extinguishing . . . separate administrations, legislatures, and local patriotisms."[15] Thus, without destroying the identity of the states, the federal form of

---

[14]Ibid., Vol. 1, pp. 172–173.

[15]This and all subsequent quotes in this section are taken from James Bryce, *The American Commonwealth* (London: The Macmillan Co., 1888).

government permitted America to become one nation.

Internal flexibility. A second advantage of federalism, according to Bryce, is that it allows the flexibility required to answer a variety of needs that naturally arise in a nation rapidly expanding its territory. "Thus the special needs of a new region are met by the inhabitants in a way they find best: its special evils are cured by special remedies. . . ." This argument by Bryce in favor of federalism is still valid today. Although American federalism is essentially based on state units, there are few frontiers that do not conform to the state boundaries. The whole realm of regional associations opens up vistas for a new type of federalism.

Prevention of despotism. Third, Bryce maintained that federalism "prevents the rise of despotic central government, absorbing other powers, and menacing the private liberties of the citizen. . . ." This argument is not completely valid, for nonfederal governments are not necessarily despotic. France, the Netherlands, Norway, Sweden, Denmark, and Japan, for example, all have unitary forms of government rather than a federal system, but none of these countries could be described as despotic. The underlying forces of a government tend to shape the character of the system as much if not more than constitutional arrangements. From a formal point of view, the Soviet Union is a federal system, but its central government was for most of the twentieth century a totalitarian dictatorship. Soviet leader Gorbachev began to change the fundamental character of Soviet government and politics as the decade of the 1990s began, promising more political competition and decentralization. As the Soviet Union before Gorbachev demonstrated, without the accompaniment of a wide range of social, political, and economic conditions that support freedom and democracy, federalism by itself does not prevent despotic government. How far Gorbachev can move the cumbersome Soviet

bureaucracy and party apparatus in the direction of decentralization and greater freedom remains a question that only the future will answer.

The necessary conditions of democracy can be met equally by a unitary form of government and by the federal system. Nor can it be argued that the federal system will be a greater protector of individual liberties than centralized governments. Actually, the reverse is somewhat true in the United States. When the history of the struggle for civil liberties and civil rights in America is examined, it becomes clear that the state governments tend to curtail these rights far more than the national government. By permitting a state to adopt whatever policies conform to the wishes of the majority dominant within its boundaries, federalism sometimes condones government action that would not be tolerated by a national majority.

Interest in local government. A fourth advantage, Bryce noted, is that "self-government stimulates the interest of people in the affairs of their neighborhood. . . ." Bryce's point here was probably more valid in the nineteenth century than it is today. Although people's awareness of local conditions may be desirable, it is not necessary to have a federal system in order to have local self-government. Moreover, public interest can be activated by many things, such as the effect of legislative action on the individual citizen or the attention paid to governmental affairs in the news media. As a result citizens often become more interested in the national government than in their local community. Interest in government is not a function of formal constitutional provisions but rather is based upon a wide range of informal forces.

Better local government. The fifth argument advanced by Bryce in favor of federalism is that through federalism, "self-government secures the good administration of local affairs by giving the inhabitants of each locality due means of overseeing the conduct of their business. . . ." Here again Bryce's argument can be countered somewhat by the reality of present-day situations. There is no guarantee that citizens are able to participate more directly and effectively in local than in national affairs. Conditions have changed radically since the framing of the Constitution. Where it still exists, the town meeting is often a sparsely attended function, and local elections rarely attract as many voters as national ones do.

Political experimentation. A sixth advantage of federalism noted by Bryce is that it

> enables a people to try experiments in legislation and administration which could not be safely tried in a large centralized country. A comparatively small commonwealth like an American state easily makes and unmakes its laws; mistakes are not serious, for they are soon corrected; other states profit by the experiences of a law or a method which has worked well or ill in the state that has tried it.

Here Bryce was advancing an argument that has been used frequently in favor of federalism and of greater decentralization of power among the states in general.

Bryce was speaking from the vantage point of the nineteenth century. The history of federalism reveals the cyclical nature of governmental experimentations at both the state and the national levels. The New Deal period witnessed the eclipse of the states as the administration of President Franklin D. Roosevelt embarked upon such new governmental experiments as the Tennessee Valley Authority, social security, fiscal and monetary controls, and expanded regulatory programs. Federal grant-in-aid programs provided money to the states for welfare and many other programs, but only on the terms set by the federal government.

The era of the 1970s marked a resurgence of state experimentation in governmental policies in such areas as abortion, divorce, automobile insurance, urban development, and

(From *Herblock's Special for Today* [Simon & Schuster, 1958])

"The mean old federal courts are trying to impose their will on others."
State governments have complained about federal court intrusions on their powers, but often they give little leeway to local government.

environmental protection (as in control over nuclear plants and requirements regarding disposable containers).

Experimentation by state courts in the development of new constitutional law was an important aspect of the federalism of the 1980s. The California Supreme Court, for example, has extended the protection of civil liberties and civil rights beyond the guarantees of the federal Constitution. Other state courts as well, sometimes following California's lead, have established new constitutional rights for their citizens. The right to an education, for example, first established in California, has been upheld in Arkansas, Colorado, Connecticut, Maryland, and New Jersey. By contrast, the United States Supreme Court has declared that there is no fundamental right to an education.[16]

Political stability. The seventh advantage that Bryce pointed out was that although federalism may diminish the collective force of the nation, it also reduces

the risks to which its size and the diversities of its parts expose it. A nation so divided is like a ship built with watertight compartments. When a leak is sprung in one compartment, the cargo stowed away there may be damaged, but the other compartments remain dry and keep the ship afloat. So if social discord or an economic crisis has produced disorders or foolish legislation in one member of the federal body, the mischief may stop at the state frontier instead of spreading through and tainting the nation at large.

There is much validity in this argument. However, the problem is that a nation with a federal system is not composed entirely of "watertight compartments." The compartments may "leak" and thus actually expose the nation as a whole to greater danger than would be the case if the national government could marshal the nation's resources to plug up the leaks as soon as they are discovered.

Bryce himself was writing during the period when Populism, an extreme political movement for the time, was gaining enthusiastic adherents to its policies of free silver, nationalization of transportation and of telephone and telegraph lines, income tax, direct election of United States senators, the secret ballot, and limitations on immigration. Although most of these reforms sound mild by today's standards, they were considered quite radical at the end of the nineteenth century. Dominant in the Rocky Mountain states, the Dakotas, Kansas, and Nebraska, as well as in the rural South, the Populists had a broad enough base in the election of 1892 to win 22 electoral votes; but by 1896 they were forced

to align with the Democrats. Although such radical movements do "leak" from one state to another, the size, diversity, and various levels of government have tended to dilute them.

Efficient government. The eighth advantage that Bryce claimed was that federalism, "by creating many local legislatures with wide powers, relieves the national legislature of a part of that large mass of functions which might otherwise prove too heavy for it. Thus business is more promptly dispatched, and the great central council of the nation has time to deliberate on those questions which most nearly touch the whole country. . . ." This is probably Bryce's most valid point. It is impossible to imagine the national government handling the innumerable concerns, such as marriage and divorce laws, traffic regulations, motor vehicle inspection, liquor licenses, and so forth, that face state and local governments. It is a job beyond the capabilities of the central government.

The Disadvantages of Federalism

From the arguments that have been set forth to underline the advantages of federalism, it is obvious that there should be counterarguments that would demonstrate its disadvantages. James Bryce found that there were six weaknesses generally attributed to American federalism that would not exist under a unified system. He listed these as follows:

1. Weakness in the conduct of foreign affairs;
2. Weakness in home government through a lack of authority over the states and individual citizens;
3. Threat of secessions or rebellion of states;
4. Threat of division into groups and factions by the formation of separate alliances among the states;
5. Lack of uniformity among the states in legislation and administration;
6. Trouble, expense, and delay due to the

---

[16]*San Antonio v. Rodriguez*, 411 U.S. 1 (1973). Compare *Serrano v. Priest*, 5 Cal. 3d 584 (1974).

complexity of a double system of legislation and administration.

Bryce noted that in any federal system the first four weaknesses could be the result of one cause: the sapping of the central government by various local centers of force (the states). These centers, Bryce said, are more effective in directing opposition to the national government than individuals would be because each has "a government, and revenue, a militia [the state police or the National Guard], a local patriotism to unite them."

Weakness in foreign affairs. Bryce's argument that federalism makes a nation ineffective in foreign affairs has not been borne out by the facts of American history. Although the states do have conflicting interests among themselves and with the national government with respect to trade policies, they do not have such conflicts in general foreign policies. In any case the Constitution avoided any intergovernmental rivalry in this area by clearly stating that the national government is supreme in foreign affairs.

The Constitution provided that states cannot enter into treaties, alliances, or confederations; nor can they lay any imposts or duties on imports or exports unless absolutely necessary to execute inspection laws. Moreover, states cannot, without the consent of Congress, "lay any duty of Tonnage, keep Troops, or Ships of War in time of Peace, enter into any Agreement or Compact with another State, unless actually invaded, or in such imminent Danger as will not admit of delay." (Article I, Section 10.) These prohibitions on the states in the area of foreign affairs have strengthened rather than weakened the federal government's conduct of foreign affairs in the United States.

Weakness in home government. Certainly it could be argued that even in a unitary system there is some significant opposition by local communities against national power. Such opposition might not be as frequent and as vigorous as in a federal system. A unitary form of government would require a stronger central administration and would create a more centralized system of patronage (appointments to government jobs), thereby strengthening the hold of the dominant political party on the national level.

Political patronage would surely encourage the loyalty of local officials, who would actively support the dominant party to guarantee their own jobs. Government funds would also be allocated in accordance with the amount of support given to government programs by the local politicians. Although political patronage now exists to some extent in the national government, it is not too effective because the states can control substantial patronage within their own boundaries and thus create their own sources of loyalty and support.

Threat of rebellion. This weakness is somewhat linked with Bryce's disadvantage above. The Civil War bears out Bryce's contention that secession and rebellion are threats to the federal structure. Although the secession movement failed, the states as units of government still have the potential to resist national policy. Both Presidents Eisenhower and Kennedy had to call out the National Guard to quell violent Southern opposition to school integration. As Bryce would have said, these states were legal entities, with their own governments, revenues, and local patriotisms, and this enabled and even encouraged them to resist national power. Ordinarily, though, in these clashes between national and state power, national power emerges victorious.

Threat of division into groups and alliances. Again, the Civil War serves as an illustration of Bryce's point. The Confederacy, however, lost in its attempt to establish a separate alliance of states, and there has been no subsequent attempt by American states to follow its example.

Lack of uniformity in legislation and administration. The lack of uniformity in policy and administration among the states, which was noted by Bryce, is a fact of American federalism. Whether this is desirable or not is largely a matter of opinion, but there is little doubt that it is often troublesome. When traveling from state to state or changing state residences, individuals are confronted with different laws governing such matters as motor vehicle registration and operation, divorce, education, taxation, civil rights, civil liberties, and so forth. In some of these matters it would be highly desirable to have some kind of national uniformity, or at least some consistency among the states.

Double system of legislation. Although in some federal systems two sets of legislative subsystems might lead to conflict, this has not happened in the United States. Authority over most matters has been carefully divided, so that although there is some overlapping of governmental functions, it has not disrupted the system too much.

On the whole it appears that in the case of the United States, the advantages of federalism have outweighed its disadvantages. The system has its noticeable flaws, but, in general, compromises have been reached in those areas where the problems of the two levels of government seemed insoluble.

CONTEMPORARY FEDERALISM

This chapter has dealt with the *structure* of federalism—that is, its formal definition. This definition fundamentally comes from the Constitution and its division of authority between the national government and the states. James Bryce's analysis of the advantages and disadvantages of federalism arises out of what he considered to be the consequences of this formal division of authority. In a broader sense, Bryce was discussing the merits of centralization versus decentralization of government, a debate that continues today.

The twentieth century has witnessed crosscurrents of centralization and decentralization of the federal system. The New Deal under Franklin D. Roosevelt saw a vast expansion of the powers and responsibilities of the national government, which increasingly has seemed to take over areas that previously were considered the special domain of state authority. The crisis of the Depression highlighted the fact that the states were simply unable to cope with the economic, social, and political problems arising from a major economic recession. What had once been state and local problems now became national problems. The failure of the states to sustain what had become an interdependent national economy produced demands for national action to guarantee economic stability, employment, and social security. The "watertight compartments" that Bryce felt the states represented in a federal form of government were no longer able to contain and isolate crises. State problems had essentially become national problems. While the politics of the New Deal did not alter the fundamental constitutional division of national and state authority, it did produce dramatic changes, through legislation, in the structure of federalism. And these changes were toward centralization of authority in the hands of the national government.

The major structural device of the New Deal to deal with federalism was the grant-in-aid program through which Congress set conditions upon the receipt of federal funds by state and local governments. The burgeoning of federal grant-in-aid programs by the thousands meant the intrusion of the national government into state and local affairs; and equally it meant centralization of control in Washington over many activities that had once been accepted as being within the jurisdiction of the states. Today, federal grant-in-aid programs exist in such areas as welfare, housing, highways, air and water pollution programs, and numerous other areas of economic development and social need. A major feature of the design of such programs is the creation of separate bureaucracies within the states to carry them out, bypassing state governors, state legislatures, and, often, regular state bureaucracies. This phenomenon was described by one member of a state planning agency in the following terms:

It would be difficult to argue that the system of grants-in-aid that has developed in the United States has not had an adverse effect on the chief executive offices in state and local governments. The educational establishment, the agricultural establishment, the housing establishment, the welfare establishment, and many other "establishments" in state and local government all owe their independence and freedom from central control [within the states] to immense amounts of federal dollars and technical assistance that has supported them over the years. Even within the executive sphere of responsibility, in the personnel system, federal support has managed to create an independence from executive control that now stifles creative personnel management by perpetuating competition, rather than cooperation, with executive offices.[17]

Thus while the formal aspects of federal grant-in-aid programs would seem to result in centralization of authority in the hands of the national government, these programs have in reality fragmented the political system beyond what it was before they were put into effect. What grant-in-aid programs have increased, then, is *not* the general authority of the national government but rather the power of newly created separate bureaucracies within both the national and state governments. The dispersion of power and the "local patriotism" of the traditional federal system were replaced, under grant-in-aid programs, by a new dispersion of power and new "patriotisms" centered around specific bureaucra-

cies and the policies under their control. All of this was taking place at the same time that the rhetoric of the New Deal proclaimed the need for the national government to expand its authority over the states and assume responsibilities for better coordination and planning of government activity, particularly in the economic sphere.

The grant-in-aid approach—spawned by the New Deal and still largely intact in the 1990s—was the beginning of a series of experiments in federalism designed to solve state and local problems while balancing national and local interests. In contrast to the traditional federalism of the nineteenth century, the twentieth century has seen the demise of the states as the principal intergovernmental unit in the federal system. Just as the grant-in-aid program created new federal-state bureaucracies that often replaced the traditional functions carried out by the states and added new functions of their own, so were there experiments at other levels of government. At the local level, experiments were undertaken that linked suburbs with central cities under one unified government to deal with common metropolitan problems. The "metropolitan approach," once considered a panacea for the solution of urban problems, never succeeded in gaining widespread acceptance. Moreover, its unified structural approach was directly contradicted by a more pervasive device—the special district government—that arose throughout the United States, usually in urban areas, to deal with such problems as transportation and schools. Special district governments are essentially separate local units with their own taxing authority and separate administrations that administer public policy in specialized spheres. (The Port Authority of New York is one example of a special district government.)

The New Deal approach to federalism accepted at least rhetorically the desirability of a greater national role in state and local problems. However, the centrifugal forces of fed-

---

[17]Leigh E. Grosenick, "Institutional Change to Improve State and Local Competencies," in *The Administration of the New Federalism: Objectives and Issues* (Washington, D.C.: American Society for Public Administration, 1973), p. 95.

More than 25 years ago, President Eisenhower and the nation's governors made a concerted effort to reallocate functions and programs among the federal, state and local governments. The results were disappointing: after months of negotiation, only two small program areas and one minor federal tax resource were approved for transfer to the states.

Now, thanks to President Reagan's "New Federalism" initiative, another attempt is being made to end the confusion over the proper roles and responsibilities of the various levels of government. Unfortunately, Congress and the news media seem to be overlooking the deeper significance of the president's initiative. I am concerned that unless we begin to focus our attention on the basic issues, President Reagan's efforts will suffer the same fate as the attempted realignment of the 1950s.

Although most people think of Washington when they hear the word "government," the fact is that our government *is* federalism. As the United States has practiced it, federalism is a system of shared authorities and responsibilities. We are a nation of governments —not a one-government nation—and the current debate over federalism is really about how we want our government to be organized and where we want its responsibilities to reside.

Yet this fundamental point is being ignored by many of the participants in the debate. "New Federalism" is much more than a breezy game of Program Poker, in which the players bid on handfuls of program swaps and revenue turnbacks. We are dealing with a system of government which has grown too big, too complex, too expensive and too distant from the citizens. As things now stand, no one knows for certain who is responsible for what programs. After more than 200 years of haphazard evolution, it is time to establish a clear set of principles for federalism which will realign and define the functions to be carried out by the various levels of government.

I think we should begin by agreeing on a set of principles which can be used as guidelines for reallocating programs and responsibilities. Here are a few of the factors that should be considered:

1. Whenever possible, public functions should be carried out by the level of government closest to the affected community. Many categorical grants, for example, serve no major national purpose. Instead, they simply substitute the judgment of federal officials for that of state and local officials, who are much more aware of the needs of the people being served.

2. Where a problem has large and uncontrollable spillover effects across many states— for example, environmental pollution—we should strongly consider retaining an active federal role.

---

eralism were persistent and produced during the 1960s and 1970s a "new federalism" that emphasized the need to decentralize as much as possible the administration of federal programs and encouraged local autonomy over matters of local concern, even though federal funds might be sued to support local endeavors. The era of Lyndon Johnson saw widespread bypassing of the states in programs that gave direct aid to the cities as well as giving discretion to local communities in administering federal funds. The late 1960s and the decade of the 1970s saw the rise of yet another panacea for state and local problems, namely, "revenue sharing." Under the revenue-sharing formula plans were developed to disburse federal funds to the states and to local communities to be spent largely at the discretion of the state and local recipients. Revenue sharing was a response to widespread fears of federal domination of state and local affairs.

Ronald Reagan's New Federalism. In 1982 President Ronald Reagan called upon Congress for yet another "New Federalism"

3. National action or involvement by the federal government should be reserved for functions which are beyond the capabilities of state and local governments, and for continuing responsibilities that only the federal government can undertake, such as national defense, foreign policy and interstate economic matters.

4. All the functions that citizens can comfortably perform without government involvement should be left to private initiative. If government is performing a function in competition with the private sector, or is providing a service which could just as easily be left to individuals or businesses, then we should consider eliminating the government's role.

5. The strengths and weaknesses of each level of government must be taken into account. The federal government has a broad revenue base, but it cannot adapt well to widely varying conditions or needs across the country. The states' resources are limited, but they can more readily gauge local needs and tailor programs to meet them. The states can also act more quickly to address new problems.

6. We must recognize that we are dealing with programs that affect people's lives. There are no easy answers to the problems of the poor, the elderly and the handicapped. Our solutions must serve those who are in

need, and not be used as a pretext to shift burdens from one level of government to another.

7. Finally, whatever federalism reform ultimately emerges from this process must result in a government that is more comprehensible to our citizens, better able to deliver services to the public, and most of all, more accountable to the American people for its actions, both good and bad.

The president has served the nation well by pushing the federalism question to center stage. His plan takes a long-term look at reform and contains the basics for a constructive debate on how we want to govern ourselves.

It remains for us in Congress, along with the governors and other state and local officials, to work with that plan, discuss it, change it where appropriate, and then move quickly to implement it. Unless we act soon, I fear that one Democratic governor is right when he warns that we will be forced to confront this problem in a Constitutional Convention.

(Reprinted with permission from *National Journal*, June 26, 1982.)

Senator William Roth (R., Del.) argues that the central issue of federalism is whether the centralized national government or the decentralized state governments can perform more democratically, efficiently, and effectively.

---

program in his State of the Union message to Congress. The role of the federal government in solving state problems should be reduced, he said, and he targeted many grant-in-aid programs for elimination. He pointed out, "In 1960, the federal government had 132 categorical grant programs, costing $7 billion. When I took office, there were approximately 500, costing nearly $100 billion—13 programs for energy conservation, 36 for pollution control, 66 for social services, 90 for education. And here, in the Congress, it takes at least 166 com-

mittees just to try to keep track of them."[18] Such committees, of course, have a vested interest in continuing the programs under their jurisdiction. The committee chairmen and the overseeing members gain political advantage by being able to claim credit for the federal benefits that flow to their states and districts. Moreover, having federal bureaucracies under their control gives legislators power and sta-

---

[18]*Congressional Quarterly Weekly Report*, Vol. 40, No. 5 (January 30, 1982), p. 178.

tus on Capitol Hill and increases the importance of their casework responsibilities with constituents—all of which are beneficial in the electoral process.

As Reagan saw it, the structure of federalism that he inherited undermined the democratic system. He noted that a "maze of interlocking jurisdictions and levels of government confronts average citizens in trying to solve even the simplest of problems. They do not know where to turn for answers, who to hold accountable, who to praise, who to blame, who to vote for or against." To the applause of Congress, Reagan referred to the comments of one Democratic governor who said that the national government should be worrying about "arms controls, not potholes."[19] He recommended returning over 40 federal grant programs to the states, with full responsibility for financing them after a transitional period. The Republicans and a scattering of Democrats applauded the President's address on the New Federalism. However, whether or not it would be politically possible to transfer wide-ranging federal programs to the states was another matter. State and local political leaders, particularly large-city mayors, began to organize opposition to

this decentralization of power, for they foresaw impossible financial burdens being placed upon their governments. The forces of centralization in the political system remained potent, and while the conservatism of the Reagan administration might have temporarily halted the assumption by the federal government of additional state and local responsibilities, it seemed unlikely that there would be a lasting decentralization of such authority.

When the Bush administration came into power in 1989 it inherited huge budget deficits from the Reagan administration which pushed federalism issues aside as the White House and Congress attempted to grapple with the budget. State and local governments continued to cry for more federal aid, but their pleas fell on deaf ears.

The structural arrangements for federalism in the future will continue to reflect forces both for centralization and for decentralization and will continue to produce a variety of governmental forms both at the national and state and local levels. Whatever else may be said about the evolution of federalism, it will almost certainly continue to buttress the pluralism of the political system. The philosophy and structure of the original constitutional system seem relatively simple in comparison with what federalism has become today—and what it is likely to become in the future.

---

[19]Ibid.

FEDERALISM IN THE 1990s

Both the rhetoric and the reality of federalism in the 1990s draws upon the past but also reflects new political and economic trends. The centralization of power in the hands of the national government, which characterized President Franklin D. Roosevelt's New Deal in the 1930s and which reached its pinnacle in President Lyndon B. Johnson's Great Society programs in the 1960s, permanently changed the balance of national and state power. The states had been unable to cope with the massive economic problems and dislocations caused by the Great Depression. The New Deal began what was to become a long-term expansion of federal grant-in-aid programs to the states to alleviate economic problems such as unemployment and to

---

From *Governing*, November 1989, pp. 21–26. Reprinted by permission. *Governing* Magazine. Copyright, 1989.

help the states meet social welfare needs. The federal government was soon to become a major force, however, in many other spheres as it expanded grant-in-aid programs to such areas as education, transportation and highways, housing, health care, and law enforcement.

The expansion of federal programs from the New Deal to the Great Society threatened to eclipse state and local governments. However, while the states received large amounts of federal aid with strings attached, they still remained viable, important, and independent entities in their own right. After President Lyndon B. Johnson stepped down in 1968, the election of Republican President Richard M. Nixon marked the beginning of a "new federalism" characterized by a loosening of federal controls over the states with the introduction of revenue sharing and block grants to both state and local governments without strings attached. Federal grant-in-aid programs remained important and even expanded, but the states now had additional sources of federal money which they could spend as they wished.

While Nixon's New Federalism recognized state and local dependency upon the federal government, the election of President Ronald Reagan in 1980 led to a gradual return of responsibility for many important public policies to the states as federal aid for many programs was reduced and sometimes eliminated. State and local officials of both parties strongly criticized Reagan's New Federalism, for they had become dependent upon federal aid, which many of them viewed as a legal entitlement. After Reagan called for a roll-back in federal programs, New York City Mayor Ed Koch stated, "[The Reagan plan is] a con job, a snare and a delusion, a steal by the Feds. . . .I don't think he understands the impact of what he is doing."[20] Because state and local politicians viewed federal aid as an entitlement, they did not have any problem in labeling Reagan's cutbacks as "stealing" from the states and local governments. When they confronted political problems at home because of the failure of their governments to undertake popular programs, governors and mayors did not hesitate to blame the federal government.

The federal system in the 1990s continued to reflect a delicate balance of national and state power. President George Bush's administration, confronting large budget deficits, a legacy of Reagan's sweeping tax cuts, and the failure of Congress to reduce federal expenditures, had very little flexibility in dealing with national policies toward the states. While the White House and Congress concentrated on the solution to the budget deficit, governors and mayors continued to lobby the federal government for more financial aid and programs to solve their problems. How the politicians back home pressured Congress to solve one of their most pressing problems—air pollution—is the subject of this case study.

The Governors Lobby Washington for Cleaner Air / *William Fulton*

At dinner time on Wednesday, June 15, 1988, the air-pollution monitoring station on Isle au Haut, in Maine's Acadia National Park, registered a reading that startled the state environmental officials who later analyzed the data. It was 0.202 parts per million of ozone—far above the federal clean air standard of 0.12 ppm and the highest ozone reading ever recorded in Maine.

The reading was surprising because ozone, the main ingredient of what most people call "smog,"

usually appears in automobile-intensive metropolitan areas on hot, still days. It is manufactured in the air after hydrocarbons and other pollutants emitted from tailpipes in the morning have "cooked" under the sun all day. In short, 0.202 parts per million is the kind of reading that would be expected in a Los Angeles suburb on a broiling summer afternoon, not on an island off Penobscot Bay, some 90 miles from Portland and 200 miles from Boston, the nearest big city.

The ozone that arrived on Isle au Haut was part of one of the worst air pollution episodes ever experienced on the Eastern Seaboard. An air mass,

[20]*Time*, June 22, 1981, p. 15.

blocked from moving out to sea by a high-pressure system, had pushed its way up the coast, picking up ozone as it went, from Baltimore, Philadelphia, New York, Boston and other parts of the Northeastern megalopolis until it finally reached Maine.

Thirteen months later, in an event not entirely unconnected to the first one, the governors of eight Northeastern states announced a dramatic agreement to get tough on ozone. The eight states, stretching from New Jersey to Maine, agreed to jump ahead of the federal government and adopt California's tough emissions standard for new cars.

In reaching that decision, the Northeastern governors were informing Washington that, because of incidents like the Isle au Haut pollution episode, the politics of clean air was changing and they intended to exploit that change in the impending debate over a new federal Clean Air Act.

They were warning Congress, though never stated in so many words, that residents of the Northeast were demanding cleaner air and a new Clean Air Act without tighter emissions standards for new cars and trucks would cause political trouble not only for the governors but perhaps for Congress as well. The tailpipe emission standards proposed by President Bush just three weeks earlier as part of his clean air legislation were inadequate, the governors were saying. Those proposed standards were not only weaker than California's, but, according to most environmentalists, potentially weaker than the existing federal standards.

The political problem the Northeastern governors had identified results from the way the Clean Air Act works. The federal government sets the standard for new-car emissions, and the states are responsible for regulating factories, other stationary sources of pollution and older vehicles. Yet states bear the full responsibility for meeting federal clean air standards.

The Northeastern governors knew that even with their regional compact in place, ozone and other pollutants could blow in from far away, forcing them to get tougher on small, local pollution sources, such as print shops, dry cleaners, bakeries and house painters and, perhaps most important, on emissions from older cars. Such steps would plainly be difficult politically for the governors and legislatures—unpopular and possibly inadequate as well. And some of that unpopularity could spill over onto the members of Congress.

"We're sending a message to the U.S. Congress and to the Northeast congressional delegation that the president's [proposed] Clean Air Act doesn't go far enough, and this is where they should take it," John DeVillars, the Massachusetts environmental secretary, said in announcing the Northeastern policy.

As the Clean Air Act debate heated up in Congress, the Northeastern states' action, and the public mood it reflected, put pressure on Michigan Democrat John D. Dingell, the powerful and stubborn chairman of the House Energy and Commerce Committee and the auto manufacturers' leading ally in Congress.

Dingell had succeeded throughout the 1980s in killing attempts to toughen auto emissions standards by bottling up the legislation in his committee. With mayors, governors and state legislators now joining the usual complement of bureaucrats and environmentalists in lobbying for tougher national standards, Dingell, to the astonishment of official Washington, the auto industry and environmentalists alike, folded. In early October, he struck a deal with his main congressional adversary, environmentalist Henry A. Waxman, the California Democrat who chairs the key subcommittee of Dingell's own committee. Under the deal, Dingell has agreed to incorporate the California standards in the new Clean Air Act, while Waxman has agreed to support a slower timetable for phasing them in nationally.

It is no surprise that the states stepped so aggressively onto the ozone battlefield. The prospects for clean air in America today depend much more on what spills out of the end of a tailpipe than on what spews out of the top of a smokestack. . . .

PART TWO

The Political Process

"Why should I vote for him? What's he done for me?" "Taxes, taxes—they go higher and higher!" "Democrats, Republicans, they're all alike! Just a bunch of politicians!" "I think I'll write my congressman. They're not going to get away with this!" All these comments are about the way the government is working, and all of them or similar ones are heard every day in American homes and streets. The people making these comments are concerned about government and what it is doing and is not doing for them. It is natural for citizens to make these comments. It is part of the constitutional democratic system. But what can these citizens really do? How can they make their complaints or their support for the actions of their representatives known to the government?

In the complex American political system direct participation is often more limited than it might be in smaller or less populated democracies, where the structures of government tend to be less complicated and where people may have more direct contact with government officials. Everyone, of course, cannot participate in government all the time. The voter does not sit in the legislature but elects a delegate who does. This allows the government to function more efficiently.

One way in which citizens can register their support of, or discontent with, governmental policy is through the ballot box—by retaining or rejecting the representatives who speak for them in the government. But voting is only one means of linking the people with their government. Participation in government can take place in many other ways as well.

Democratic societies have developed several vehicles for achieving participation in government. Among these are the political parties and interest groups that serve as liaisons between the main body of the electorate and the officials of government. In Part Two the formation of political attitudes in general, as well as the nature and role of political parties and interest groups, will be explored.

Political Attitudes

Democratic government is predicated upon a belief in an active and rational electorate that has not only the capability but also the interest to participate in government. The mechanisms of participation include free elections, political parties, and interest groups. Ideally, people can express their political opinions through their selection of leaders. In turn, elections are given meaning through political parties, which provide a bridge between citizens and their government, developing issues for the consideration of the electorate and helping to implement public policy based upon electoral choice. Interest groups as well help to organize public opinion by channeling the views of specialized publics to government.

While *public opinion* is often discussed in general terms, in fact on most issues of public policy there are no general public views. Segments of the public will always have views on particular issues, but attempting to assess the collective wishes of the nation at large is virtually impossible. Such pollsters as George Gallup and Louis Harris nevertheless attempt to measure "public opinion" on selected issues of public policy and government performance. Their carefully selected publics and issues are designed to reflect accurately the broader picture of public opinion.

A careful analysis of public opinion polls, however, soon reveals that the issues presented for the solicitation of opinion are couched in the broadest possible terms and are in areas of concern that touch a wide range of people. This kind of public opinion is important to government decision makers only in a very limited sense because it does not usually reveal concrete responses on the part of the public to specific issues confronting policy makers. For example, nationwide public opinion on such broad national policy issues as welfare, economic growth and inflation, defense expenditures, and energy does not come to grips with the realities of government decision making in these areas. Citizen opinion may be "for" more defense expenditures or "against" welfare and inflation, but such generalized viewpoints are not of much utility to the government that must deal with these matters in concrete terms.

It is best to think of public opinion in terms of the views of particular segments of the public, particularly political parties and interest groups, and, even more important, their leaders. Since political parties tend to represent a broad range of interests, it is even difficult to speak with authority about the collective views of the two major parties. Interest groups, being specialized, tend to reflect more cohesive opinion on particular issues of public policy. However, even interest groups do not reflect a united opinion on many issues. The *leaders*, both of parties and of interest groups, have far more sharply defined views on public policy and political issues generally than do party or interest-group memberships.

The ambiguity of public opinion makes it very difficult to link it with government. Perhaps more important than the actual expression of public opinion is the perspective of political leaders about what the public is thinking, a perspective that, though sometimes inaccurate, may nevertheless guide the actions of elected politicians, especially in election years. Remember, however, that a vast range of governmental decision making is outside the arena of direct electoral politics and occurs in the bureaucracy and the courts. There, it is the opinions of specialized publics, expressed largely through interest groups, that link the public with government.

EVANSVILLE CONN.
POP. 186
YES   NO   DON'T KNOW
94   70   22

bond

(Courtesy of Simon Bond)

Public opinion polling is a favorite sport.

THE MEASUREMENT OF PUBLIC OPINION

Public opinion, whether general or specific, must somehow be measured and transmitted to the government. This is both a requirement and a condition of democracy. In order to determine whether it is functioning in cooperation with or counter to the will of the people, a democratic government must depend on public opinion. If public opinion is to affect the governmental process, the government must be made aware of the broad issues of concern to the public.

Measuring Opinion on Broad Policy Issues

Opinion surveys. Americans are bombarded with public opinion polls on virtually every issue imaginable. The major network news anchors report the results of the ABC/ *Washington Post*, CBS/*New York Times*, and NBC/*Associated Press* polls on major issues confronting the electorate, such as the deficit, military spending, social security and Medicare, and social issues such as abortion and school prayer. The major polling organizations— Gallup, Roper, and Harris—that periodically conduct their own polls, measuring political

"It's very difficult making predictions, especially about the future." Casey Stengel said it and political science professor Lee Maringoff of Marist College repeated it last week at an important meeting of the New York chapter of the American Association for Public Opinion Research.

The session was devoted to a wide-ranging technical discussion of what really went wrong with last month's pre-election and exit polls in the New York City mayoral and the Virginia gubernatorial elections. Those surveys consistently overstated the lead of the black candidate over his white opponent.

Included on the program was Larry Hugick of the Gallup Organization. Gallup had interviewed 3,000 voters the weekend before the New York election and found Democrat David Dinkins holding a commanding 14-point lead over his Republican rival Rudolph W. Giuliani. Dinkins won by a margin of 2 percentage points.

Since then, Hugick and his colleagues at Gallup have been picking through that huge data base in an attempt to explain what may have gone wrong. Their preliminary answers, reported at the meeting, have implications far beyond New York and Virginia, particularly as more high-profile political races across the country feature strong black and white candidates.

Gallup's analysis-in-progress suggests that race played a critical factor in the gap between pre-election survey results and the vote on Election Day, but not exactly in the way most people immediately suspected.

"Perhaps we should have paid more attention to the track record of pre-election polls in other contests featuring black candidates," Hugick says. "Had we done so, we would have found strong evidence that pre-election polls in mayoral general elections featuring a black Democrat and a white Republican pretty consistently underestimate the white Republican's vote-getting ability."

Here's the evidence, as collected in recent weeks by Gallup researchers:

• A Gallup poll taken two weeks before the April 1983 Chicago mayoral election showed Harold Washington leading his white Republican opponent by 14 percentage points. Washington won by 4 percentage points.
• A Philadelphia Daily News poll taken two weeks before that city's 1983 mayoral election showed Wilson Goode leading his white Republican opponent by 30 percentage points. Goode won by 18 percentage points.
• In the 1987 race, Goode led Frank Rizzo by 11 points in Gallup's final survey before the vote. He won by 2 points.

The effect probably isn't just limited to mayoral races. In Virginia, a Washington Post poll completed the Thursday before the election showed Democrat L. Douglas Wilder with an 11-point lead; a survey by the Richmond Times-Dispatch published the Sunday before the election showed Wilder with a 9-point advantage. He won by less than a percentage point.

And four years ago, a Post pre-election poll showed Wilder with a 19-point lead over his Republican challenger in the lieutenant governor's race; Wilder won by only 3 points.

Gallup researchers have developed a working hypothesis to explain why these differences occur that they are now refining. Simply stated, it is that the discrepancies are the result of the contradictory tugs of party and race.

"In these kinds of elections, race and party clash," Hugick says. "The plurality of voters are white and Democratic. Race seems to pull them one way while party tugs in the other direction. Many continue to say they are undecided when polled down to the final days before the election. But in the end, race seems to win out over party."

Hugick notes that Gallup's New York City polls showed the undecideds to be disproportionately white and Democratic. In Virginia, the most striking characteristic of the undecideds was that they were disproportionately white, disproportionately female and generally older than the likely electorate. In both contests, the polls had the black candidate's share of the vote about right, but underestimated the white loser's support.

Hugick notes, as does ABC's research associate John Brennan, that the apparent shift in the undecided candidate "doesn't seem to occur with regularity in biracial primary elections." In fact, Brennan notes that ABC's final tracking poll in the New York Democratic primary slightly overstated Mayor Ed Koch's support in his race against Dinkins.

Those results suggest that race alone isn't causing the problem. Rather, the Gallup hypothesis is that race and party are both factors.

"It would seem that this conflict between race and party is not limited to white Democrats," Hugick says. "Earlier this year in Chicago, Richard Daley won the Democratic nomination and faced black Democrat Timothy Evans in the general election where Evans was running as an Independent. This time, black voters faced a conflict between party and race. In this election, the late undecided vote was disproportionately black. And the final pre-election poll results proved to be an underestimation of the vote Evans ended up receiving."

Hugick says he and his colleagues are now attempting to answer one key question: Is there a true "shift" at the very end of the campaign caused by genuinely undecided and cross-pressured voters moving en masse to one candidate? Or is there just the false perception of movement because whites who have made up their minds to support the white candidate choose to tell survey interviewers they are still undecided? This question awaits a definitive answer, which Hugick says may be available in time for the national conference of the opinion research association in May.

If their initial suspicions are confirmed, Hugick's proposed response has little to do with the way surveys are done and everything to do with the way they are reported in the media.

He argues, perhaps with tongue slightly in cheek, that stories about polls conducted in elections featuring strong black and white candidates come with this consumer's warning:

"Other polls in biracial contests of this type have consistently underestimated the white candidate's support."

(*Washington Post National Weekly Edition*, December 11–17, 1989, p. 37. © The Washington Post.)

attitudes on a wide variety of issues, also do polling for the networks, newspapers, and other organizations.

The pollsters seek all kinds of opinions from the public. During presidential campaigns, for example, they ask potential voters how much attention they pay to the campaign, how they follow it, and whether or not they engage directly in political activities themselves. Examples of some questions asked on the eve of the presidential campaign of 1988 include:

1. How important are the activities at the party conventions to your decision on voting for president?
2. How long before [past presidential elections] did you decide that you were going to vote the way you did?
3. How much influence do you feel news organizations have on which candidates become presidential nominees?

Polling results should not be taken as gospel (see Box 6.1). The Gallup polling organization has never lived down its 1948 prediction that New York Governor Thomas E. Dewey would resoundingly defeat President Harry S Truman. And before the 1988 presidential election, polling results varied so much that *Washington Post* pollster Richard Morin described the polls as the "tower of babble."[1] Some polls gave presidential nominee George Bush a lead in the race, while others taken at the same time gave his opponent, Massachusetts Governor Michael Dukakis, the lead. During the primary races in 1988 the Gallup Organization predicted that Kansas Senator Bob Dole would defeat George Bush in the New Hampshire primary, but the result was the opposite.

By their very nature, public opinion polls must count questions in broad terms on familiar subjects to elicit opinionated responses. The case study at the end of this chapter reveals public opinion on such important issues as abortion, affirmative action, drugs, and so

on. How these responses affect politics, however, remains doubtful. For example, a vast majority of the electorate favors prayer in public schools, yet the Supreme Court's ruling in *Engel v. Vitale* (1962) banning prayer in public schools remains in effect. The Supreme Court does not follow the election returns, as a wag once put it, and even the conservative Rehnquist Court has looked askance at state legislation attempting to put prayer back into public schools. On the issue of abortion, a majority of the public favors freedom of choice, yet the right-to-life movement has had a significant political impact, and many politicians have taken a pro-life stand which, in some cases, has caused their defeat at the polls.

Effect of political attitudes. Popular attitudes in areas that do not directly concern government and public policy issues may also have a profound effect on the political system. For example, constitutional democracy requires, in addition to a constitution that limits governmental power and protects civil liberties and rights, a high degree of *political tolerance*, implying the acceptance by citizens of political views that do not agree with their own (see pp. 171–175).

One important survey to measure political tolerance asked the following questions of a cross section of the population:

1. Members of the_____should be banned from being President of the United States.
2. Members of the_____should be allowed to teach in the public schools.
3. The_____should be outlawed.
4. Members of the_____should be allowed to make a speech in this city.
5. The_____should have their phones tapped by our government.
6. The_____should be allowed to hold public rallies in our city.[2]

Political and other attitudes, of course,

---

[1]*Congressional Quarterly Weekly Report*, August 19, 1989, p. 2187.

[2]John L. Sullivan et al., "The Sources of Political Tolerance: A Multivariate Analysis," *The American Political Science Review*, Vol. 75 (March 1981), p. 94.

SO, WHO DID YOU VOTE FOR IN THE ELECTION?

THAT DEPENDS... ARE YOU A POLLSTER?

(©1990 Rogers—*Pittsburgh Press*.)

Citizens may be reluctant to tell pollsters how they voted.

may change drastically over time. Moreover, new political issues constantly arise to replace previous concerns. The intense battle over the abortion issue, for example, after the Supreme Court's decision in *Roe v. Wade* in 1973, saw a previously dormant issue placed at the top of the nation's political agenda. Groups on both sides of the issue were unwilling to compromise. As the decade of the 1990s began it remained problematical whether or not the Supreme Court would once again enter the "political thicket" to affirm or overrule the *Roe* decision that granted women broad abortion rights.

On another front the decade of the 1980s witnessed some sharp changes in levels of tolerance. Table 6.1, for example, gives public responses to the question of what groups are acceptable as neighbors.

Inevitably, there are some poll respondents who feel compelled to express "opinions" on issues they know nothing about, have never heard of, or that are even fictitious. Sometimes pollsters will include a question about a nonexistent group, person, or issue in order to determine whether or not the respondents are answering the questions honestly. For example, one pollster surveyed students in eight universities and colleges around the country to determine their levels of prejudice against various ethnic groups. One of the groups included in the poll, the "Danireans," was completely fictitious. Nevertheless, the students rose to the occasion, expressing varying degrees of prejudice against the Danireans. Columbia University students were particularly prejudiced against the group, while City University of New York

(Robert Day. Copyright © 1967 Saturday Review, Inc.)

"Harry only believes in voting in the Gallup, Harris and other public opinion polls. He says the regular elections don't mean so much."
Public opinion poll results are taken seriously by both the electorate and political leaders.

business students were the least prejudiced, responding that they would accept the Danireans as classmates, neighbors, citizens, and work colleagues. In none of the colleges did the median response include acceptance of the Danireans "to my club as personal chums" or "to close kinship by marriage."[3] The median respondent in the eight colleges, however, was willing to admit Danireans to the country as "visitors only," without the right to citizenship.

Political polls can also elicit invalid responses. Voters do not want to seem unpatriotic or uninterested in politics. Thus

TABLE 6.1 GROUPS NOT WANTED AS NEIGHBORS—TREND

	1989	1987	1981
Sects, cults	62%	44%	30%
Fundamentalists	30	13	11
Unmarried couples	23	12	14
Vietnamese	18	*	17
Hispanics	16	9	18
Blacks	12	13	*
Jews	5	3	2
Protestants	5	2	1
Catholics	3	1	1

*Not asked.

Note: In the 1987 and 1981 surveys respondents were handed lists of groups and asked to name any they would not like to have as neighbors.
Source: Gallup Report, March/April 1989, p. 46.

when asked, more citizens claim to vote in congressional and presidential elections than actually cast ballots.[4] And when asked about obscure or fictitious legislation, many poll respondents instead of admitting that they have no opinion or know nothing about the issue, register a response in favor of or opposition to the legislation.

Polls are useful, however, invalid responses notwithstanding. Exit polls helped to explain why voters chose one candidate over another. For example, Table 6.2 gives the results of 1988 presidential election exit polls clearly illustrating why voters chose either George Bush or Michael Dukakis.

Poll results can determine shifts in citizen attitudes over time toward government and important issues of public policy. For example, a Gallup poll in 1988 revealed that Americans consider the biggest problems confronting them to be economic in nature, particularly the federal budget deficit, which ranked at the top of the list of concerns, far outranking inflation, unemployment, and the trade deficit.

The Harris, Gallup, and Roper organiza-

---

[3]I. A. Lewis and William Schneider, "Is the Public Lying to the Pollsters?" *Public Opinion*, Vol. 5, No. 2 (April/May 1982), p. 42. From Eugene L. Hartley, *Problems in Prejudice* (New York: King's Crown Press, 1946), pp. 4–18.

[4]Ibid., p. 43.

TABLE 6.2 **EXPLAINING THEIR VOTE**

	Percent voting for	
	Bush	*Dukakis*
Why did you vote for your candidate?		
He has more experience (34%)	97%	3%
He's more competent (27)	73	26
He seems to care about people like me (24)	25	75
It's time for a change (18)	5	92
He has a clearer vision of the future (17)	52	46
He has a better Vice President (13)	14	86
My party didn't nominate the best man (10)	50	44
He impressed me during the debates (7)	54	46
He will avoid a recession (4)	80	19
He's more likable (3)	52	46
What did you like least about his opponent?		
His views are too liberal (28%)	94%	6%
He ran a dirty campaign (28)	30	69
He has shown bad judgment (24)	46	53
He just leaves me cold (19)	55	43
He's too risky (15)	76	24
He's too close to the special interests (13)	26	72
He's too tied to the past (10)	10	88
He won't stand up for America (8)	65	33
He's too much of a wimp (7)	38	60
He isn't going to be elected (4)	63	34
Which issues were most important to your vote?		
The federal budget deficit (25%)	39%	60%
National defense (23)	84	15
Abortion (20)	63	36
Crime (18)	67	31
Ethics in government (17)	31	67
Taxes (15)	70	29
Drugs (14)	41	58
Unemployment (10)	35	64
Protecting the environment (11)	28	70
Foreign trade (5)	57	42
No issue, really (12)	52	45

Source: Cable News Network-*Los Angeles Times* exit polls.

tions are among those that have built polling into a big business. Pollsters are constantly assessing public attitudes on a wide variety of issues, and no political campaign organization is complete without its own pollster. Over the years, pollsters like Patrick Caddell, who has advised Democratic presidential candidates, and Richard Wirthlin, who served as Ronald Reagan's pollster from the time Reagan was governor of California through his two presidential administrations, have joined with media consultants to become a powerful political force in their own right.

Pollsters seek to use information about public attitudes to help their candidates win elections. Richard Wirthlin, for example, who advised Reagan's campaigns in 1980 and 1984, found that the outcome of presidential elections often hinges on which candidate projects the best leadership image, including projected competence, strength, and decisiveness. A Reagan campaign memo in 1980 reflected this view, stating that "ultimately the voters will choose the man they believe best suited to *lead* this country in the decade of the '80s."[5]

As George Bush and Michael Dukakis were wrapping up their parties' presidential nominations in 1988, a Gallup poll taken in early May revealed a public perception of greater leadership qualities in Bush than in Dukakis (see Table 6.3). That perception widened in Bush's favor as the election approached.

While pollsters can offer sound advice to their candidates, polling is often a precarious undertaking. Public opinion is not always well-formed, making the pollster's job difficult and predictions chancy at best. Richard Wirthlin, who mistakenly predicted in the 1988 presidential primary campaign that Kansas Republican Senator Robert Dole would win the New Hampshire primary, jokes about the uncertainty of polling. "It's one of the things that makes what we do a little exciting," he remarked. "That's why I call polling the ABC science—the science of Almost Being Certain."[6]

THE DETERMINANTS OF POLITICAL ATTITUDES

A wide variety of influences help to shape political attitudes, which encompass one's view of the role of government and one's stand on issues such as abortion, school prayer, busing, welfare, and taxes. Ronald Reagan and his followers, for example, had very definite political attitudes supporting cutbacks in federal programs, increases in defense expenditures, and tax cuts to fulfill the "supply side"

---

[5]Richard Wirthlin, Vincent Breglio, and Richard Beal, "Campaign Chronicle," *Public Opinion*, February/March 1981, p. 44.

[6]*National Journal*, July 30, 1988, p. 1976.

TABLE 6.3 CANDIDATE QUALITIES

Question: Please look down this list and tell me which items you think apply to George Bush.... And what about Michael Dukakis?

	George Bush	Michael Dukakis
Has the record and experience for the job of president	51%	17%
Well informed	44	33
Steady and dependable	33	26
Can get things done	29	29
Honest and ethical	28	34
Thoughtful	25	28
Concerned about the needs of people like me	19	35
Can bring about the changes the country needs	19	31
Strong and forceful	18	22
Too extreme on issues	13	12
Has a fresh approach	9	35
Excites and inspires people	9	21

Source: Public Opinion, July/August 1988, p. 11. Reprinted with the permission of the American Enterprise Institute for Public Policy Research.

economic view that prosperity depends upon increasing the disposable income of individuals. The conservative political attitudes of the Reagan camp were opposed by liberals like Edward Kennedy and Walter Mondale, who supported an important role for the federal government in many spheres—especially in economic affairs—to spur growth and foster equality.

Family background, education, income level, occupation, religious affiliation, and ethnic and racial characteristics are all important determinants of political attitudes.

The Family

Just as the family has perceptible influence on a person's attitudes about religion or racial tolerance, it is also often the basis for shaping a person's attitude about where he or she stands politically. This is because the family itself adopts general attitudes about occupations, education, and economic issues that in turn affect the individual's political attitudes.

It has been shown by some political scientists that there is a direct correlation between the occupation of parents and the attitudes of their children concerning labor, business, governmental participation in the economy, and world affairs. Children most frequently reflect their parents' thinking on these matters. The degree to which children are influenced in their political attitudes by their parents depends largely on the amount of similarity between the interests and attitudes of the parents. If the parents support the same political party and agree about policies, their offspring will probably follow in their footsteps.

Taking this conclusion one step further, it has also been suggested that the family, as a basic source of political attitudes, determines the intensity of *party loyalty*—the individual's attachment to a particular political party. Political scientists have found that voters who support the party favored by their families develop firmer and more consistent habits of party allegiance than those who renounce the family preference. Since an individual is likely to acquire friends and select a spouse from the same social environment and with the same life style as his or her own, party loyalties acquired from the family are likely to be strengthened later in life. The family, then, is a force for political stability.

Definite correlations can also be drawn between the degree of interest expressed by parents in politics and the political involvement of their children. There are notable examples of this in politically active families, such as the Roosevelts, Lodges, Tafts, and Kennedys, who have had a substantial effect on national politics. Moreover, on all levels of politics the family has an important impact in determining which citizens become active or remain inactive politically.

Education, Income Level, and Occupation

Political activity and behavior can also be determined by education, which in turn is largely predicted by the parents' occupation

and level of income. A majority of Americans exhibited upward occupational and educational mobility from 1972 to 1980, with the greatest upsurge occurring in the professional/ technical and managerial/administrative occupational areas.[7] Although only 16 percent of the members of the former and 10 percent of the latter occupations had fathers in the same field, blue-collar workers and farmers followed the occupations of their fathers in far greater numbers. (Particularly striking is the fact that from 1972 to 1980 86 percent of the farmers followed their families' occupation.)

Educational as well as occupational mobility characterizes American society. In the population as a whole, 14 percent are college graduates, 17 percent have had some college, 34 percent have finished high school, and 35 percent are less than high school graduates. However, of the college graduates, 36 percent had fathers who had not finished high school and only 25 percent had fathers who had completed college.

Income level, occupation, and education level are closely linked. They affect political behavior and have important political consequences. (See Table 6.4.) Generally, the higher up the scale in these categories persons are, the greater their involvement in politics and their concerns about important issues of public policy. The percentage of citizens who vote is always the largest in upper-income areas, where most people have a college education and are in the professional, managerial, or well-paid technical occupations (for example, engineering or computer science). While the interrelations of education, income, and occupation make it difficult to determine the influence of each, political scientists Raymond Wolfinger and Steven Rosenstone have concluded that close examination "confirms the very strong effect of education and shows that

---

[7]The statistics on education, income level, and occupation in this section are drawn from *Public Opinion*, June/ July 1982, pp. 21–40.

TABLE 6.4 **VOTING PATTERNS ACCORDING TO EDUCATION LEVEL, OCCUPATION TYPE, AND UNION INVOLVEMENT—1972 TO 1988**

	1972		1976			1980		
	McGovern	*Nixon*	*Carter*	*Ford*	*McCarthy*	*Carter*	*Reagan*	*Anderson*
EDUCATION								
College	37	63	42	55	2	35	53	10
High School	34	66	54	46	*	43	51	5
Grade school	49	51	58	41	1	54	42	3
OCCUPATION								
Prof. & business	31	69	42	56	1	33	55	10
White collar	36	64	50	48	2	40	51	9
Manual	43	57	58	41	1	48	48	5
LABOR UNION								
Union Families	46	54	63	36	1	50	43	5

	1984		1988	
	Mondale	*Reagan*	*Dukakis*	*Bush*
EDUCATION				
College	39	61	42	58
High School	43	57	46	54
Grade school	51	49	55	45
OCCUPATION				
Prof. & business	34	66	NA	NA
White collar	47	53		
Manual	46	54		
LABOR UNION				
Union Families	52	48	63	37

*Less than one percent

Note: From 1976 onwards, results do not include vote for minor party candidates.
Source: Gallup Poll, November 1988, pp. 6–7.

the effect of income is modest and limited."[8] The authors point out that

At every level of income, increases in education raise the probability that a person will go to the polls. Increases in education through high school graduation have the same effect in all income categories. Finishing grammar school raises turnout by 8 percent, irrespective of income. Getting a high school diploma increases the probability of voting by 22 percent across the board. The effect of a college education, however, varies inversely with income. Going to college has the most impact on the poorest people and somewhat less on those in the higher income brackets. A college degree produces a 42 percent increase in turnout for people earning less than $2,000. This is an exotic combination, and we are unsure what kinds of people populate the category. As income rises, the effect of college attendance diminishes somewhat, to the point where it increases turnout by 'only' 34 percent for those earning more than $25,000.[9]

[8]Raymond Wolfinger and Steven Rosenstone, *Who Votes* (New Haven: Yale University Press, 1980), p. 23.

[9]Ibid., pp. 24–25.

Education is also far more important than occupation as a determinant of who votes. Education has "the greatest effect on the probability that those in the lowest status categories will vote."[10] Little variation exists in voting turnout from one occupation to another. For example, "Upper middle-class occupations are not strongly related to turnout. When other demographic variables are controlled, the marginal effect of being a professional is small and that of being a manager is almost nonexistent."[11]

Wolfinger and Rosenstone give three reasons for the overriding importance of education in determining who votes. First, education

(Courtesy of Frank Interlandi)

"Glad to give you my opinion. I'm for disarmament, the Common Market, foreign aid, federal aid to education, Medicare, the UN—Oh, yes, and aid to teachers who get fired for expressing their opinions!"

Personal matters are still of primary concern, no matter how political attitudes have been formed.

increases cognitive skills, which facilitates learning about politics. Schooling increases one's capacity for understanding and working with complex, abstract, and intangible subjects such as politics. This heightens one's ability to pay attention to politics, to understand politics, and to gather the information necessary for making political choices. Thus, education is a resource that reduces the costs of voting by giving people the skills necessary for processing political information and for making political decisions.[12]

Second, "better-educated people are likely to get more gratification from political participation. They are more likely to have a strong sense of citizen duty, to feel moral pressure to participate, and to receive expressive benefits from voting."[13] Finally, citizens who have education can more readily understand registration requirements and other bureaucratic hurdles to voting.

Income, education, and occupation also determine political preferences. Higher-income groups tend to vote Republican in far greater numbers than blue-collar or unskilled

workers. (See Table 6.4.) Labor union members are mostly Democrats.

For example, a 1982 Roper survey of notions of rights and privileges revealed, not surprisingly, that the level of household income is an important determinant of attitudes. The lower a person's income, the more support was given to the notion that citizens have a right to an adequate provision for retirement, a reasonable standard of living, and a raise in wages or salary each year. Lower-income persons also supported in greater numbers the right to a college education.[14] These responses translate into greater support among lower-

---

[10]Ibid., p. 25.

[11]Ibid., p. 28.

[12]Ibid., pp. 35–36.

[13]Ibid., p. 36.

---

[14]*Public Opinion*, June/July, 1982, p. 27.

income citizens of governmental benefit programs.

Just as income correlates with attitudes toward many important issues of public policy, a person's level of education often exerts an important influence on political views. The better educated a citizen is, for example, the more strongly he or she supports United States membership in the United Nations.[15] Better-educated citizens also, understandably, have a more optimistic view of the future and of the chances for achieving "the good life."[16] Virtually all Americans, however, regardless of the level of education attained, are proud of their country and strongly support the free-enterprise system.[17]

Religious Influences

As with other predictors of political behavior, it is difficult to measure the exact effect of religious influences. Nevertheless, from an analysis of election data it is possible to detect distinct *voting patterns,* or party preferences in elections, among specific religious groups. Table 6.5 illustrates the tendencies in recent presidential elections.

Conclusions about the general relationship between religion and political behavior are difficult to draw from these election statistics, yet they do show definite voting patterns based on religion. The Jewish vote, which is concentrated in urban areas, and the Catholic vote, which is heavily working class, tend to be largely Democratic. A greater proportion of Protestants—who tend to be more suburban or rural and often in higher income brackets—support the Republican party. Thus, to some extent, religious voting patterns are tied to economic and social factors and cannot be isolated from them.

The biggest problem in an evaluation of

the religious factor is that voters are often influenced profoundly by the personal characteristics of the candidates. For example, in the elections of 1952 and 1956 there was a general shift away from the Democratic party, due largely to the personal popularity of the Republican candidate, Dwight D. Eisenhower. Thus the shift of the Catholic vote in 1952 and 1956, which had tended to be Democratic in other years, is easier to explain in terms of the candidate than in terms of the religious factor.

Religion can, however, overshadow all other issues in an election, and when this is the case the effect of religious voting patterns is dramatic. In the presidential elections of 1928 and 1960, voting patterns did not reflect concern over public issues as much as the fact that one of the candidates was a Catholic. The defeat of Al Smith in 1928 was essentially due to his Roman Catholicism, many Protestants having voted against him. Likewise, in the election of 1960 John F. Kennedy's Catholicism was a widely publicized issue that cost him some Protestant votes. A relatively heavy Catholic vote, though, allowed him to squeak through with a narrow victory. The Jewish vote, too, was more heavily Democratic in 1960 than usual. However, this was in all likelihood due to Jewish support of Kennedy's policies. Although Kennedy's Catholicism cost him votes, his victory indicated that the minority religious affiliation of a presidential candidate was no longer an insurmountable barrier. In congressional, state, and local elections, too, the religious affiliation of candidates does not by itself often determine who wins, although a candidate's religion can be a distinct benefit when it represents the majority of voters in an electoral district.

Ethnic and Racial Influences

In present-day America, ethnic identity, like religion, tends to have less and less in-

---

[15]Ibid., pp. 35–36.

[16]Ibid., p. 24.

[17]*Public Opinion,* June/July, 1981, pp. 24–31.

TABLE 6.5 RELIGIOUS FACTORS IN VOTING 167

Election Year	Religion	Voted Democratic	Voted Republican	Voted Other	
		(Truman)	(Dewey)	(Thurmond)	(H. Wallace)
	Protestant	47%	48%	3.0%	.8%
1948	Catholic	70	26	1.3	2.2
	Jewish	60	20	1.6	18.0
		(Stevenson)	(Eisenhower)		
	Protestant	37%	63%		
1952	Catholic	56	44		
	Jewish	77	23		
		(Stevenson)	(Eisenhower)		
	Protestant	37%	63%		
1956	Catholic	51	49		
	Jewish	75	25		
		(Kennedy)	(Nixon)		
	Protestant	38%	62%		
1960	Catholic	78	22		
	Jewish	81	19		
		(Johnson)	(Goldwater)		
	Protestant	60%	36.7%		
1964	Catholic	79.8	17.1		
	Jewish	91.3	4.6		
		(Humphrey)	(Nixon)	(G. Wallace)	
	Protestant	32.6%	50.1%	13.5%	
1968	Catholic	50.3	36.2	8.4	
	Jewish	81.3	11.6	(Not available)	
		(McGovern)	(Nixon)		
	Protestant	27.7%	66.9%		
1972	Catholic	41.1	51.8		
	Jewish	57.1	42.8		
		(Carter)	(Ford)		
	Protestant	46%	54%		
1976	Catholic	55	45		
	Jewish	68	32		
		(Carter)	(Reagan)	(Anderson)	
	Protestant	31%	64%	5%	
1980	Catholic	41	53	6	
	Jewish	46	40	14	
		(Mondale)	(Reagan)		
	Protestant	39%	61%		
1984	Catholic	39	61		
	Jewish	67	31		
		(Dukakis)	(Bush)		
	Protestant	42%	58%		
1988	Catholic	51	49		
	Jewish	64	35		

Source: Ivan Hinderaker, ed., *American Government Annual 1961–1962* (New York: Holt, Rinehart and Winston, 1961), p. 74; releases of the American Institute of Public Opinion (Gallup Poll); and the Roper Survey. Data for 1976 and 1980 are from the CBS Almanac; data for 1984 and 1988 are from Gallup polls.

fluence on political attitudes. As immigrants become absorbed into the broader society, their separate group identity as a factor swaying the way they vote recedes into the background, although not completely. Members of an ethnic group will gradually vote and think more like members of other groups with similar educational, income, and occupational levels. Many black Americans, however, have not followed this trend due to the difficulties they encounter in making educational, social, and economic gains.

Patterns of black voting have shifted over the years. During the post-Civil War period many blacks supported the Republican party because it was the party of "freedom." But since the New Deal in the 1930s blacks have given substantial voter support to the Democratic party. This is due somewhat to a migration of blacks into urban areas and a new identification of the black voters with the Democratic party already well-established in most urban centers. Table 6.6 gives a breakdown by race of the vote for each party in recent presidential elections.

While a vast majority of blacks affiliate

TABLE 6.6 RACIAL VOTING PATTERNS

Election Year	Race	Voted Democratic	Voted Republican	Voted Other
1948	White	53%	47%	—*
	Black	81	19	—
1952	White	43	57	
	Black	79	21	
1956	White	41	59	
	Black	61	39	
1960	White	49	51	
	Black	68	32	
1964	White	59	41	
	Black	94	6	
1968	White	38	47	15%**
	Black	85	12	3
1972	White	32	68	
	Black	87	13	
1976	White	49	51	
	Black	83	17	
1980	White	36	56	7
	Black	86	10	2
1984	White	34	66	
	Black	87	13	
1988	White	41	59	
	Black	82	18	

*Percentages for the candidates of the States' Rights and Progressive parties were not tabulated.

**Percentages are for the American Independent party.

Source: Ivan Hinderaker, ed., *American Government Annual 1961–1962* (New York: Holt, Rinehart and Winston, 1961), p. 74; CBS Almanac; and releases of the American Institute of Public Opinion (Gallup Poll).

with and give support to the Democratic party, racial patterns do not clearly emerge as important determinants of attitudes on most public policy issues. Blacks understandably support affirmative action and civil rights programs more than whites do, as the case study at the end of this chapter illustrates, because such programs have been designed to alleviate racial discrimination. But on other public policy issues, such as government welfare programs, for which racial patterns may appear to be significant, black support for increased government spending is not because of *race* but rather is because of the economic position of many blacks who stand to benefit from such programs. Surveys of racial groups should take into account economic, religious, and gender influences to help determine the extent to which race by itself shapes opinions.

Gender Influences

There are no discernible differences in *voting turnout* between men and women that can be explained on the basis of sex. Men and women vote at the same rates until approximately age 40, after which slightly more men than women turn out to vote. By age 60 the turnout gap is approximately 2 percent, widening to 3.5 percent between the ages of 70 and 78 and to 4.5 percent for voters over the age of 78. However, "nearly all the differences in turnout between older men and women are accounted for by differences in other demographic variables."[18]

Political attitudes based on gender. Before 1976 there were very few discernible differences between the political attitudes of men and women. The only meaningful difference between the sexes was that women had less political information and therefore fewer political views. Women also were more reluctant than men to advocate the use of force to solve international or domestic problems. They opposed war and the death penalty and

supported gun control in greater numbers than did men. On one politically moot issue, prohibition, women differed sharply from men. A 1948 survey found that 44 percent of the women but only 27 percent of the men supported a national prohibition law.

Men's and women's political attitudes began to diverge more sharply as the decade of the 1980s began. More significant and sustained variations between the sexes became evident in their attitudes toward the role of government in fostering full employment, reducing the gap between rich and poor, improving the condition of blacks, and spending for social security. Significantly more women than men favored a greater role for the government in these areas. More women than men were often in favor of strong government regulation over the environment. Past differences between the sexes over the use of force in international and domestic affairs remained, with more women than men continuing to oppose war, the military draft, and increases in defense expenditures. As in the past, women more strongly supported gun control and opposed the death penalty. Generally women exhibited less confidence than men in the future of the system. On the "women's issues" of abortion, sex discrimination, and the Equal Rights Amendment, attitudes between the sexes did not sharply diverge. In fact, slightly more men than women supported the right to abortion and the Equal Rights Amendment in the late 1970s and early 1980s.[19]

It is difficult to determine how the differing political attitudes of men and women affect politics. The accompanying data illustrate that in their choices of presidential candidates, a small but not necessarily insignificant percentage of men and women voted differently (see Table 6.7). Women, for example, voted more heavily for Jimmy Carter than they did

---

[18]Wolfinger and Rosenstone, pp. 42–43.

[19]See *Public Opinion,* April/May 1982, pp. 21–32, for the data used in the preceding discussion concerning differences in the political attitudes of men and women.

TABLE 6.7 VOTE BY GENDER IN PRESIDENTIAL ELECTIONS SINCE 1952

| | *1952* | | *1956* | | *1960* | | *1964* | |
	Stevenson	*Ike*	*Stevenson*	*Ike*	*JFK*	*Nixon*	*LBJ*	*Goldwater*
National	44.6%	55.4%	42.2%	57.8%	50.1%	49.9%	61.3%	38.7%
Male	47	53	45	55	52	48	60	40
Female	42	58	39	61	49	51	62	38

| | *1968* | | | *1972* | | *1976* | | |
	HHH	*Nixon*	*Wallace*	*McGovern*	*Nixon*	*Carter*	*Ford*	*McCarthy*
National	43.0%	43.4%	13.6%	38%	62%	50%	48%	1%
Male	41	43	16	37	63	53	45	1
Female	45	43	12	38	62	48	51	*

| | *1980* | | | *1984* | | *1988* | |
	Carter	*Reagan*	*Anderson*	*Mondale*	*Reagan*	*Dukakis*	*Bush*
National	41%	51%	7%	41%	59%	46%	54%
Male	38	53	7	36	64	44	56
Female	44	49	6	45	55	48	52

*Less than 1 percent.
Note: 1976 and 1980 results do not include vote for minor party candidates.
Source: The Gallup Opinion Index, December 1980, Report No. 183; Gallup Report, November 1988, pp. 6–7.

for Ronald Reagan, while men in far greater numbers than women chose Reagan. Perhaps the results reflect the higher "compassion" index of women and their greater support of a more active governmental role in curbing unemployment and protecting minorities, positions more strongly supported by the Democrats than the Republicans. The differences between men and women on these issues have emerged since 1976, which might explain why women did not vote as heavily for Carter when he first ran. While women by a slight edge voted more for the Democratic than the Republican candidates in the 1984 and 1988 presidential elections, how women will vote in the future cannot be predicted.

Age Influences

Major public policy issues, as well as changes in the age structure of the American population, have focused attention on age categories in public opinion and voting. In 1990

one of every eight Americans—about 32 million persons—was 65 years of age or older. The U.S. Bureau of the Census projects that by the year 2030, when the post–World War II "baby boom" reaches old age, one in every five Americans—nearly 60 million persons—may be aged 65 or older.[20]

For over a decade, more than a quarter of the federal budget has been expended on benefits to the aged. And the absolute dollar amount has kept growing to the point that about $300 billion is spent on such benefits annually by our national government. As early as 1980 one alarmed analyst projected that the proportion of the budget spent on

[20]Gregory Spencer, U.S. Bureau of the Census, "Projections of the Population of the United States, by Age, Sex, and Race: 1988 to 2080," *Current Population Reports*, Series P-25, no. 1018, U.S. Government Printing Office, Washington, D.C., 1988.

old age could reach 60 percent by the year 2025.[21]

Against the background of these dramatic figures, specific contemporary issues have raised the specter of intergenerational political conflict. In the 1990s, for example, this type of conflict has emerged in relation to Medicare, the federal program that provides health insurance to persons aged 65 and over, which is financed largely through the social security payroll tax paid by current workers. Within the present climate of concern about America's rapidly escalating health care costs, in general, and in anticipation of the increasing older population, financing the health care of the elderly population is perceived by many as an unsustainable burden, or, as one observer puts it, "a great fiscal black hole."[22] Some political leaders and so-called biomedical ethicists have even proposed that older persons should be denied lifesaving health care as a way to reduce Medicare expenditures. At the same time, interest groups representing older persons are pressing Congress to expand Medicare so that it will insure them against the expenses of long-term care in a nursing home, or at home, for chronic disabling diseases and conditions. Issues such as these have led many observers of American politics to perceive a "politics of age," with different age groups in conflict with respect to political attitudes and behavior.

Despite these images of intergenerational conflict, the factor of age by itself has little impact on political attitudes and behavior. Numerous recent polls of political attitudes still support the general conclusion stated by political scientist Angus Campbell some two decades ago that

because each age cohort includes people who differ profoundly in many important conditions

of life it is not likely that any group will be very homogeneous in its attitudes. The evidence which national surveys provide us does in fact demonstrate that attitudinal differences between age groups are far less impressive than those within age groups.[23]

Older Americans constitute a large block of participating voters, comprising from 17 to 21 percent of those who actually voted in recent national elections.[24] However, older persons appear to be no more likely to vote in a monolithic bloc than are middle-aged or younger persons. And while aging-based organizations, like various other interest groups, can play a role in framing or reacting to the agenda of public policy, they have not demonstrated a capacity to swing the votes of older persons, even on the rare occasions when they have tried to do so. For example, although the leaders of a number of major age-based organizations endorsed President Jimmy Carter in his 1980 presidential campaign, there was no apparent impact in the distribution of votes cast by persons 60 years of age and older, as compared with those 45 to 59 years old and those 30 to 44 years old. In fact, throughout the presidential campaigns of the 1980s (see Table 6.8) no significant differences were apparent among these age groups in the distribution of their votes among candidates. Only among voters under the age of 30 have there been some indications of an age-related difference.

Political Tolerance

Ethnic, racial, religious, economic, and social class differences create a pluralistic mix that requires a high level of political tolerance—acceptance of the contrasting political views and opinions of others—in order to

---

[21]U.S. Senate Special Committee on Aging, *Emerging Options for Work and Retirement,* U.S. Government Printing Office, Washington, D.C., 1980, p. 45.

[22]Daniel Callahan, *Setting Limits: Medical Goals in an Aging Society,* Simon and Schuster, New York, 1987.

[23]Angus Campbell, "Politics through the Life Cycle," *The Gerontologist,* Vol. 2 (1971), pp. 112–117.

[24]U.S. Senate Special Committee on Aging, *Developments in Aging,* U.S. Government Printing Office, Washington, D.C., 1988, p. 11.

TABLE 6.8 NATIONWIDE VOTE DISTRIBUTION BY AGE GROUPS AND SEX IN RECENT ELECTIONS FOR U.S. PRESIDENT

	1980			*1984*		*1988*	
	Reagan	*Carter*	*Anderson*	*Reagan*	*Mondale*	*Bush*	*Dukakis*
All Voters	51%	41%	7%	59%	41%	53%	45%
Men							
All ages	55	36	7	62	37	57	41
18–29 years old	47	39	11	61	37	55	43
30–44 years old	59	31	4	62	37	58	40
44–59 years old	60	34	5	63	36	62	36
60 years or older	56	40	3	62	37	53	46
Women							
All ages	47	45	7	56	44	50	49
18–29 years old	39	49	10	55	45	49	50
30–44 years old	50	41	8	54	46	50	49
45–59 years old	50	44	5	58	41	52	48
60 years or older	52	43	4	64	35	48	52
All adults							
18–29 years old	43	44	11	58	41	52	47
30–44 years old	54	36	8	58	42	54	45
45–59 years old	55	39	5	60	39	57	42
60 years or older	54	41	4	63	36	50	49

Sources: Data from 1980, 1984, and 1988 nationwide exit polls conducted by the *New York Times*/CBS News Poll, published in *The New York Times*, Nov. 9, 1980, p. 28; Nov. 8, 1984, p. A-19; and Nov. 10, 1988, p. 18-Y. Copyright ©1980, 1984, 1988 by The New York Times Company. Reprinted by Permission.

make constitutional democracy work. The Constitution guarantees all citizens freedom of expression and equal access to the political process. And legislation and executive action supplement these constitutional rights.

In the past, the American public and its political leaders have been extremely intolerant of Communists, Bolsheviks, anarchists, syndicalists, and any other left-wing groups that they felt posed a threat to the government and the free-enterprise system. National and state laws are geared to the suppression of subversive political expression, and states have consistently prosecuted persons advocating violence as the means to political and economic change. A unanimous Supreme Court, for example, upheld the California conviction of a woman who had assisted in organizing the Communist Labor party for the avowed purpose of criminal *syndicalism*, which seeks to bring the government and industry under the control of labor unions by radical means, including sabotage. The Court held that a state may punish mere membership in a radical organization and, furthermore, may punish the expression of radical views if it finds such acts to constitute a clear and present danger to the public peace and security of the state.[25] From 1917 to 1920, 20 states adopted criminal syndicalism laws. Espionage acts at the national level were also passed during the same period and were used to punish radical opponents of World War I.

The nation has never tolerated what the majority of citizens consider to be dangerous political views. The advocacy of communism and joining a Communist organization were made criminal offenses by the Smith Act of 1940 and by the Subversive Activities Control

---

[25]*Whitney v. California*, 247 US 357 (1927).

Act of 1950. President Harry S. Truman vetoed the 1950 law, but Congress passed the bill over his veto within 24 hours. Later, in his memoirs Truman wrote:

I believed that [the 1950 law] would give government officials vast powers to harass all of our citizens in the exercise of their right of free speech. Government stifling of the free expression of opinion is a long step toward totalitarianism. There is no more fundamental axiom of American freedom than the familiar statement: In a free country, we punish men for the crimes they commit but never for the opinions they have.[26]

The wave of anti-Communist hysteria, fueled in the early 1950s by Senator Joseph McCarthy of Wisconsin, led to widespread intolerance not only of Communist views but also of opinions that in any way could be considered left-wing, subversive, or unpatriotic. Although President Truman had vetoed the 1950 Subversive Activities Control Act, he ordered the establishment of a federal loyalty and security program to screen federal employees. His successor, Dwight D. Eisenhower, strengthened the program, suspecting widespread disloyalty within the federal establishment. In his 1954 State of the Union message Eisenhower proudly announced that he had rid the government of 2,200 security risks. The renowned physicist J. Robert Oppenheimer was one of those labeled a security risk and suspended from his job with the Atomic Energy Commission. The chairman of the Loyalty Review Board that heard Oppenheimer's case announced in advance that the hearings "present the almost unrelinquishable opportunity for a demonstration against communism."[27] The board's attorney revealed the secret proceedings to radio commentator Fulton Lewis, Jr., who broadcast

them on his "I Caught a Communist" program.

Political tolerance ebbs and flows with the times. Extreme political views are always suspect and are rarely tolerated. The vast majority of Americans consider the Communists on the left, and the Ku Klux Klan and the Nazi party on the right, to be outside the mainstream of acceptable politics and opinions.

While degrees of political intolerance always exist, one important study concludes that "the overwhelming proportion of the American public supports the principles of minority rights, majority rule, equality under the law, and free speech when these principles are posed in an *abstract* form."[28]

The determinants of political tolerance. Various studies have suggested that a wide range of factors, such as religious preference, education, and age, affect levels of political tolerance. However, John Sullivan and his colleagues conducted a study of political tolerance and concluded that the psychological makeup of individuals is the best indicator of their political tolerance.[29] Persons with a high sense of self-esteem, trust in others, and low levels of dogmatism—all of which indicate psychological security—support the democratic system and are generally tolerant of different political views.

Aside from personality, social status—particularly a person's level of income—affects political tolerance. This may be because persons at higher income levels tend to be more psychologically secure, enabling them to be tolerant of the political views differing from their own. Sullivan's study further concluded that religious affiliation and secular detachment, education, and age "have a very small indirect impact on political tolerance."[30] The Sullivan study examined levels of political tol-

[26]Harry S. Truman, *Memoirs*, vol. 2, *Years of Trial and Hope* (Garden City, N.Y.: Doubleday, 1956), p. 284.

[27]William O. Douglas, *The Court Years, 1939–1975* (New York: Random House, 1980), p. 73.

[28]John L. Sullivan et al., "The Sources of Political Tolerance: A Multivariate Analysis," *The American Political Science Review*, Vol. 75 (March 1981), p. 97. Emphasis added.

[29]Ibid., p. 101.

[30]Ibid., p. 104.

TABLE 6.9 TOLERANCE INDICES

	Jan. 24–26, 1989 (telephone)			
	Would welcome all groups	*All groups except: Religious cults or sects*	*All groups except: Religious cults or sects, fundamentalists*	*Number of interviews*
NATIONAL	18%	32%	45%	1001
SEX				
Men	21	35	47	502
Women	16	29	44	499
AGE				
18–29 years	21	35	49	240
30–49 years	21	38	52	399
50 & older	13	25	36	354
REGION				
East	20	36	51	235
Midwest	17	30	45	279
South	15	27	35	327
West	21	37	53	160
RACE				
Whites	17	32	45	873
Non-whites	24	31	45	126
Blacks	23	30	42	80
EDUCATION				
College graduates	22	47	63	260
College incomplete	22	34	50	252
High school graduates	15	28	42	363
Not high school graduates	15	21	27	121
POLITICS				
Republicans	16	28	38	348
Democrats	16	31	49	326
Independents	22	38	50	312
HOUSEHOLD INCOME				
$40,000 & over	23	42	54	275
$25,000–$39,999	18	34	50	272
$15,000–$24,999	13	26	38	187
Under $15,000	17	27	37	191
RELIGION				
Protestants	16	29	40	603
Catholics	20	31	53	245
EVANGELICALS				
Evangelicals	16	29	37	392
Non-evangelicals	20	35	52	576

Source: Gallup Poll, March/April 1989.

erance among Protestant, Catholic, Jewish, and nonreligious persons. The researchers concluded, "We found almost no difference among Protestants, Catholics and Jews in their levels of political tolerance, although we did find some large differences in percentages selecting left-wing groups as least-liked targets."[31]

The fact that factors such as "sex, region, race, and size of city, which previous research has suggested are strongly related to political tolerance, do not correlate with political tolerance,"[32] is perhaps important to an understanding of why democracy can work so well in a country of such great ethnic, racial, and regional diversity.

---

[31]Ibid., p. 101, fn. 3.

[32]Ibid., p. 104.

POLITICAL ISSUES AND ATTITUDES IN THE 1990s

This chapter has analyzed the way in which a number of factors, such as sex, age, race, education, and religion, affect political attitudes. The following case study lines up these and other categories with major national issues to determine how these variables shape political attitudes in areas of particular public concern in the 1990s. What patterns emerge from an examination of the data? Can you discern important attitude differences based upon gender, age, race, education, party affiliation, and religion?

Not Much of an Impact

The abortion issue may have little bearing on the results of next year's House election, a new survey shows.

To figure out how attitudes toward abortion might affect voting behavior, the Wirthlin Group, a Republican polling firm in McLean, Va., asked 1,000 people from July 17–19, "If the 1990 congressional elections were to be held today, would you be voting for the Republican candidate or Democratic candidate from your district?"

The poll then posed this hypothetical question: "Now just suppose that the Republican candidate for Congress from your district took a position on the issue of abortion that would be considered pro-life, that is, restricting abortion in certain circumstances, such as cases involving rape, incest or endangerment of the mother's life, while the Democratic candidate took a position that would be considered pro-choice, that is, allowing a woman to have an abortion without restrictions. Now knowing this, how would you vote?"

Questions such as these are far removed from the real world because voters would know more about the candidates than just their parties and their stands on abortion. "Whenever you use brand 'X' and brand 'Y,' it exaggerates the movement" of voters from one candidate to another, Neil S. Newhouse, a senior vice president at the Wirthlin Group said. But, he added, the poll "shows how powerful the abortion issue can be in realigning voters' decisions in the 1990 elections."

Though the poll shows that there can be significant swings within many voter subgroups, it found over all only a very small net gain for the Democrats on the abortion issue. When respondents were asked how they would vote for a House candidate on the basis of partisanship alone, they went Republican, 39–38 per cent, with the rest undecided. After they were told of the candidates' stands on abortion (the Republican on the pro-life side; the Democrat, pro-choice), they voted Democratic, 46–45 per cent. According to Newhouse's analysis, "36 per cent of the generic GOP congressional voters leave their party's candidate to vote for a Democratic pro-choice candidate, [and] 34 per cent of generic Democratic congressional voters leave their party's candidate to vote for a Republican pro-life candidate."

In the table, the numbers in the Republican (R), Democratic (D) and undecided (U) columns show the percentage of respondents who selected the hypothetical candidate after being told of the candidates' positions. The numbers in the other columns are the percentage point change in respondents before the subject of abortion was introduced.

	R	Change	D	Change	U	Change
(Party/age)						
R 18–34	57%	−28	38%	+35	4%	−7
R 35–54	62	−8	33	+21	3	−15
R 55+	56	−19	35	+28	9	−9
D 18–34	36	+26	61	−23	3	−3
D 35–54	36	+30	56	−20	5	−14
D 55+	34	+30	52	−27	12	−6
(Sex/age)						
Men 18–34	47	−3	46	+12	5	−9
Men 35–54	47	+10	42	+8	6	−21
Men 55+	49	+9	38	−3	11	−14
Women 18–34	44	0	50	+14	6	−12
Women 35–54	48	+17	48	+1	3	−17
Women 55+	39	+7	49	+6	10	−14
(Education)						
Some high school	43	+12	43	0	14	−12
High school grad	50	+8	42	+4	4	−14
Some college	44	0	50	+15	5	−14
College grad	43	0	52	+16	3	−15
Grad school	30	+5	63	+28	4	−25

Poll Discovers Opinions on Issue Are Deep-seated

One thing is clear from the USA TODAY Poll on abortion—almost everyone has an opinion.

Asked for their stand on abortion, 3 percent of the 662 adults polled said they had no opinion.

That's an unusually low figure, says pollster Robert Hurd of Gordon S. Black Corp., which conducted the poll. Ten percent is more standard, and some issues produce as high as 20 percent. On abortion, Hurd says, "Everyone has an opinion. It's bipartisan, it's not divided by men and women. It really cuts across the board."

Fifty-seven percent felt strongly about the issue one way or the other—a startling number for such a poll, he says. Interest in the issue was spread across the spectrum, spanning differences in age, sex, party affiliation and region.

Nine percent had no opinion of Monday's Supreme Court ruling. In an earlier *Los Angeles Times* poll: 13 percent.

Respondents also were more careful in answering than expected. Hurd said the poll was expected to take five minutes to complete. Most respondents took seven minutes.

Court abortion ruling divides nation

A USA TODAY poll shows half the nation opposes the Supreme Court's decision Monday to let states set limits on abortion. The telephone poll of 662 people nationwide was conducted by the Gordon S. Black Corp. Sampling error is plus or minus 4 percent.

Half oppose Supreme Court ruling. . .

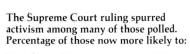

Support	40%
Oppose	50%

. . .and an unusually large percentage feel strongly. . .

Strong opinion	57%
Moderate opinion	33%

. . .and strongest feelings are in Great Lakes region

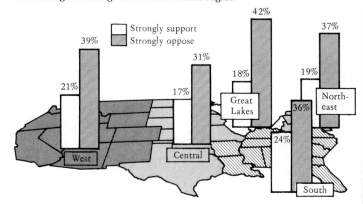

Strongly support
Strongly oppose

39% 21% 31% 17% 42% 18% 37% 19% 36% 24%

Great Lakes   North-east   West   Central   South

The Supreme Court ruling spurred activism among many of those polled. Percentage of those now more likely to:

Work for candidate to promote own views	46%
Participate in a march	22%
Give money to sympathetic group	41%
Write a letter to a legislator	46%

What we would choose

Most would allow some abortions. . .

Should never allow	8%
Allow with severe restrictions	33%
Woman's decision, first 3 months	17%
Always woman's decision	39%
Don't know	3%

. . .and oppose a ban of abortion on demand in public hospitals.

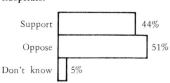

Support	44%
Oppose	51%
Don't know	5%

Most back law saying parents must be notified before an abortion is performed on girl under age 18. . .

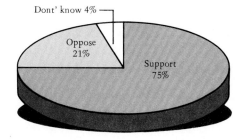

Dont' know 4%
Oppose 21%
Support 75%

. . .but fewer would back law requiring notification of a husband or partner.

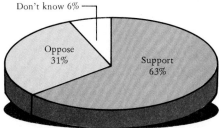

Don't know 6%
Oppose 31%
Support 63%

TABLE 6.10 **AFFIRMATIVE ACTION RULING (BASED ON REGISTERED VOTERS)**

Question: *The U.S. Supreme Court has ruled that employers may sometimes favor women and members of minorities over better qualified men and whites in hiring and promotion, to achieve better balance in their work force. Do you approve or disapprove of this decision?*

June 24–26, 1988 (Telephone)

	Approve	Dis- approve	No opinion	Number of inter- views
NATIONAL	25%	69%	6%	1,210
SEX				
Men	26	71	3	605
Women	25	67	8	605
AGE				
18–29 years	26	72	2	204
30–49 years	26	70	4	468
50 & older	24	68	8	519
65 & older	26	64	10	248
REGION				
East	27	68	5	299
Midwest	24	70	6	357
South	28	66	6	356
West	23	73	4	198
RACE				
Whites	22	74	4	1,042
Blacks	45	42	13	94
EDUCATION				
College graduates	22	75	3	373
College incomplete	22	75	3	232
High school graduates	23	73	4	443
Not high school graduates	38	51	11	151
POLITICS				
Republicans	21	75	4	396
Democrats	31	62	7	408
Independents	23	71	6	406
HOUSEHOLD INCOME				
$50,000 and over	18	80	2	206
$30,000–$49,999	21	77	2	306
$15,000–$29,000	27	69	4	328
Under $15,000	34	59	7	235
RELIGION				
White Protestants	21	75	4	618
White Catholics	23	74	3	280
LABOR UNION				
Labor-union families	25	70	5	204
Non-union families	25	69	6	1,006

Source: Gallup Report, July 1988, p. 17.

AFFIRMATIVE ACTION RULING

(Based on registered voters)

	Approve	Dis- approve	No opinion
1988			
June	25%	69%	6%
1987			
April*	29	63	8

*Question read "recently ruled."

TABLE 6.11 **LEGALIZATION OF DRUGS**   179

CASE STUDY 5

QUESTION: *Some people feel that current drug laws haven't worked, and that drugs like marijuana, cocaine, and heroin should be legalized and subject to government taxation and regulation like alcohol and tobacco. Supporters of this idea say it would take drug profits away from criminals and possibly reduce violence. Others oppose drug legalization, feeling that it might lead to greater drug use in society and only make things worse. Which position comes closer to your view?*

	Favor legalization	*Oppose legalization*	*Favor legalizing only certain drugs (vol.)*	*No opinion*	*Number of interviews*
			July 1–7, 1988 (Telephone)		
NATIONAL	16%	74%	4%	6%	1,000
SEX					
Men	18	74	5	3	495
Women	13	75	3	9	505
AGE					
18–29 years	15	77	5	3	248
30–49 years	15	76	4	5	399
50 & older	17	71	4	8	349
REGION					
East	17	75	4	4	229
Midwest	14	75	3	8	271
South	14	78	3	5	323
West	19	67	6	8	176
RACE					
Whites	16	73	5	6	911
Non-whites	17	80	*	3	86
EDUCATION					
College graduates	18	73	4	5	286
College incomplete	16	73	7	4	257
High school graduates	17	76	3	4	342
Not high school graduates	10	73	3	14	111
POLITICS					
Republicans	14	78	4	4	333
Democrats	16	73	3	8	340
Independents	18	72	5	5	294
HOUSEHOLD INCOME					
$40,000 & over	21	72	5	2	270
$25,000–$39,999	15	76	4	5	285
$15,000–$24,999	15	78	5	2	190
Under $15,000	12	72	4	12	194
RELIGION					
Protestants	13	78	2	7	587
Catholics	17	73	6	4	266

*Less than one percent.
Source: Gallup Report, September 1988, p. 25.

QUESTION: *Would you favor or oppose:*
  a) The registration of all firearms?
  b) A law requiring that any person who carries a gun outside his home must have a license to do so?
  c) A national law requiring a 7-day waiting period before a handgun could be purchased, in order to determine whether the prospective buyer has been convicted of a felony or is mentally ill?

| | *September 25–October 1, 1988 (Telephone)* | | | | | | |
| | *a) Registration* | | *b) Licensing* | | *c) Waiting period* | | |
	Favor	*Oppose*	*Favor*	*Oppose*	*Favor*	*Oppose*	*Number of interviews*
NATIONAL	67%	30%	84%	15%	91%	8%	1001
SEX							
Men	60	37	77	22	87	12	501
Women	73	22	89	9	94	5	500
AGE							
18–29 years	70	27	86	12	90	10	226
30–49 years	63	34	83	16	93	7	416
50 & older	68	27	83	15	88	8	346
REGION							
East	77	22	93	6	92	7	238
Midwest	65	29	83	15	92	7	255
South	64	31	80	18	88	9	295
West	60	38	78	20	90	9	213
RACE							
Whites	68	28	83	15	91	7	866
Non-whites	59	38	86	11	86	13	127
Blacks	59	37	86	13	86	13	83
EDUCATION							
College graduates	71	28	85	14	89	9	288
College incomplete	66	30	79	19	95	4	228
High school graduates	66	30	86	12	90	9	355
Not high school graduates	66	30	85	14	90	7	122
POLITICS							
Republicans	66	30	79	18	93	6	343
Democrats	69	28	86	12	91	8	344
Independents	68	30	86	14	91	8	276
HOUSEHOLD INCOME							
$40,000 & over	71	27	82	18	92	8	238
$25,000–$39,999	63	33	81	17	95	4	227
$15,000–$24,999	65	31	85	13	91	8	196
Under $15,000	68	28	88	11	86	12	213
RELIGION							
Protestants	64	32	80	18	89	10	562
Catholics	74	23	90	8	94	5	247
GUN OWNERSHIP							
Gun owners	58	38	84	15	90	9	501
Non-owners	75	21	94	5	92	7	500

Note: "No opinion" omitted.
Source: Gallup Report, January 1989, p. 26.

TABLE 6.13 PRAYER IN PUBLIC SCHOOLS (BASED ON REGISTERED VOTERS)

Question: *Do you generally favor or oppose prayer in public schools?*

	June 24–26, 1988 (Telephone)			
	Favor	*Oppose*	*No opinion*	*Number of interviews*
NATIONAL	70%	21%	9%	1,210
SEX				
Men	65	24	11	605
Women	74	19	7	605
AGE				
18–29 years	59	30	11	204
30–49 years	71	22	7	468
50 & older	75	15	10	519
65 & older	77	13	10	248
REGION				
East	67	22	11	299
Midwest	71	19	10	357
South	80	13	7	356
West	57	34	9	198
RACE				
Whites	68	23	9	1,042
Blacks	82	11	7	94
EDUCATION				
College graduates	57	34	9	373
College incomplete	64	23	13	232
High school graduates	77	15	8	443
Not high school graduates	77	16	7	151
POLITICS				
Republicans	72	20	8	396
Democrats	75	19	6	408
Independents	00	00	00	406
HOUSEHOLD INCOME				
$50,000 & over	59	30	11	206
$30,000–$49,999	67	25	8	306
$15,000–$29,999	71	22	7	328
Under $15,000	76	14	10	235
RELIGION				
White Protestants	74	18	8	618
White Catholics	68	23	9	280
LABOR UNION				
Labor-union families	71	21	8	204
Non-union families	69	21	10	1,006

PRAYER IN PUBLIC SCHOOLS

	1988	1984
Favor	70%	69%
Oppose	21	28
No opinion	9	3

Source: Gallup Report, July 1988, p. 16.

CHAPTER SEVEN

The Organization and Functions of American Political Parties

American political parties are alive and thriving in the 1990s, regardless of the commonly heard rhetoric that the party system is on the decline. Political parties are invaluable channels of popular participation in government, each major party reflecting a wide variety of group interests that help party leaders develop major political issues for electoral choice. Political leaders are not merely reflections of group interests, however, but also bring their own styles and views to their parties and government.

American parties are, to be sure, "umbrella" organizations that welcome a wide variety of groups. National parties are loose confederations of state and local political organizations as well as interest groups. The Democratic and Republican National Committees are representative bodies of their party leaders throughout the nation.

Ronald Reagan's victories in 1980 and 1984 and the subsequent sharp change in the direction of national policy illustrated the importance of parties. Reagan was elected not only because of his popular style and policy proposals, but also because the Republicans had developed an effective national party organization that helped deliver the votes for their presidential and congressional candidates.

That organization helped George Bush win a decisive victory over Michael Dukakis in 1988.

Clearly parties and party organizations can make a real difference in national as well as state and local politics. Parties are not the cohesive force in American politics that they are in nations such as Great Britain that have highly disciplined parties that effectively aggregate diverse political interests under party labels. Party diversity in the United States reflects our pluralistic political system that defies easy generalization either in ideological or practical terms.

THE ROLE OF POLITICAL PARTIES

The primary role of the political party is to bridge the gap between the people and their government. In a democracy the performance of this role means that the party should aid in transmitting public opinion to government and in transforming that opinion into governmental action.

Edmund Burke defined a political party as "a body of men united for promoting by their joint endeavors the national interest, upon some particular principle in which they are all agreed." This definition comes from an idealistic school of thought that holds that parties must operate in the national interest and not according to individual or local demands.

Max Weber, the German sociologist and political economist of the late nineteenth century, was less idealistic when he defined a party. As interpreted by Robert Michels, Weber described a party as

a spontaneous society of propaganda and of agitation seeking to acquire power, . . .for the realization either of objective aims or of personal advantages, or of both. Consequently, the general orientation of the political party, whether in its personal or impersonal aspect is that of *machtstreben* [striving for power].[1]

Weber's definition is much more cynical than Burke's. Weber recognized that political parties may be used either for high moral ends or merely for personal gain.

Whether political parties are idealistic or not, their immediate objective is gaining and maintaining political power. Practically, then, *political parties* are groups of people who unite for the purpose of achieving a general political objective. They do this by organizing to elect officials who will carry out their demands.

Political parties have developed in all political systems that grant voting and other citizenship rights to large numbers of people. In Great Britain, for example, the development of democracy in the nineteenth century was closely associated with the rise of political parties. Democracy expands as more people gain the right to vote, and the political party serves as a vehicle by which people can make this right meaningful. Parties state issues of public concern and outline programs of governmental action. They try to gain the power to carry out their aims by nominating candidates for public office and then campaigning for

their election. Through the processes of nomination, campaign, and election, millions of voters are provided with opportunities to focus and unite the demands they make upon government. Meaningful popular participation in democratic government depends in large measure on the effectiveness with which political parties perform these various functions.

Just as there are contrasting ideas about the nature of political parties, there are many different types of parties. Some are based on strict ideologies or philosophical principles, whereas others are more loosely defined and are organized only for the practical purpose of gaining specific objectives.

Contrast with European Parties

American parties are usually far less disciplined than their British counterparts and far less ideological than parties on the European continent. Although British parties usually arrive at their programs through political compromise, once the compromise is accepted, the party ranks close behind the decision. Political parties in America also depend on compromise to establish programs, but their members are not obligated to support these programs.

Many European parties adhere to narrow ideological interests based on some "absolute truth." The Socialist parties, for example, that developed in Italy, France, Sweden, and other European nations prior to World War II accepted rigid programs based on ideological doctrines. These parties do not change their programs for practical reasons if such changes mean a divergence from ideology.

American political parties, however, are far more pragmatic than those in Europe. At the state and local levels of politics, parties are organized to secure the election of their candidates rather than to espouse particular ideological viewpoints. Nor is there any overriding ideological divergence between Repub-

---

[1]Robert Michels, *First Lectures in Political Society*, trans. Alfred de Grazia (Minneapolis: University of Minnesota Press, 1949), p. 134.

licans and Democrats at the national level, although there are significant program differences in different electoral periods. Since the New Deal of the 1930s, Republicans have generally been fairly consistent in espousing a reduced role for the federal government and a balanced budget. The Democrats have tended to believe more in positive government and in the ability of the national government to rectify social injustice and bring about economic prosperity. However, these programmatic differences are not dogmatic ideologies, as is reflected in the fact, for example, that in the 1980s the Democrats shifted away from a blind faith in the social and economic engineering of the New Deal and the Great Society.

Early American Concern About Parties

Although no formal organization of parties existed in eighteenth-century America, an informal political system did operate. A passage from the diary of John Adams reveals that by 1793 the concept of political organization was already part of the American political tradition:

This day I learned that the Caucus Club meets at certain times in the garret of Tom Dawes, the Adjutant of the Boston Regiment. He has a large house, and he has a movable partition in his garret, which he takes down, and the whole club meets in one room. There they smoke tobacco till you cannot see from one end of the room to the other. There they drink flip, I suppose, and there they choose a moderator who puts questions to the vote regularly; and selectmen, assessors, collectors, firewards, and representatives are regularly chosen before they are chosen in the town.[2]

Some traces of this informal system can still be seen today. In many cities (Cincinnati,

for instance), parties are prohibited by law from participating in city elections. In cases like these, certain groups, such as civic organizations or groups of influential citizens behind the scenes, function as if they were parties. These informal parties recruit and endorse candidates whose names are then placed on ballots by means of nonpartisan nominating procedures.

The Constitutional Context of Parties

Initially, the American national government was to be a system of indirect election. State legislators would choose senators for Congress, and electors chosen by each state according to its own formula were to select the "best man" for president.

Provision for national political parties was not included in the original constitutional framework, because it was thought that in an indirect election parties would not be needed to select candidates or to convince the voters of who deserved election. The public was voting indirectly through the representatives in the state legislatures and through the electoral college. Despite this, however, political parties did develop, and they became a vital feature of the American constitutional system.

America's Two-Party System

In the development of political parties a variety of social, economic, cultural, and constitutional factors can exert influence. Although most of America's political traditions originated in Great Britain, the political parties of the two nations are different in character. France, like the United States, has had strong and diverse economic, regional, and social interests. With the institution of the French Republic following the revolution in 1789, a *multiparty* system developed in France to represent each of these various and diverse interests.

---

[2]Cited in V. O. Key, Jr., *Politics, Parties, and Pressure Groups*, 3d ed. (New York: Crowell, 1952), pp. 217–218.

The United States, on the other hand, has only two major political parties. This development can be attributed to three major factors: (1) the election system, (2) the centralizing influence of the presidency, and (3) the general division of interests into two camps. This does not mean, however, that multiple interests are not represented politically. It means that the two American parties must be broader in scope than the French parties in order to include the diverse interests within the electorate.

The election system. Whether a nation's political party structure consists of two or many parties will depend, in part, on the election system. Election systems are usually based either on the *single-member district* or on *proportional representation*. Whatever form the election system takes, the political parties must be able to get candidates elected and must be organized so that they function well for this purpose.

Single-member district. Under a single-member-district system, no matter what size an election district is, whether it be a congressional district, a state, or the nation, it elects only one individual at a time—a representative, senator, or president. This is the method used in the United States.

To win an election in a single-member district, a candidate needs a mere *plurality*, or just more votes than any other candidate, to be elected. For example, if A, B, and C are running for office and, out of 1,000 votes cast, A has 450 ballots, B has 300, and C has 250, A wins because he has a plurality. Thus he does not need a majority, or more than half the votes, to win.

A candidate for representative, senator, or president (except in rare instances) thus needs only a plurality of votes to win, and only one candidate is elected. There is only one president for the entire nation, only one senator at a time up for election from a state, and only one representative from a congressional district. Thus there is a tendency for some groups

within a district to form coalitions, or to combine forces, so that together they can elect that official. This tightens the development of political organization. As more coalitions are formed, there are fewer parties.

This is not to suggest that the single-member-district system always produces only two parties. There have been some exceptions. But the single-member district does in fact produce a favorable situation for the development of two opposing parties rather than many parties.

Proportional representation. Unlike the election system of the United States, which is based on single-member districts, under the proportional-representation method a district may elect several representatives in a single election. Under such a system, legislative seats for each district are divided according to the percentage of total votes given to each political party. For example, let's say that in a certain district there are 20 delegates to be elected to a local council. The Blue party wins 40 percent of the vote and gets 8 of the 20 seats; the White party wins 30 percent of the vote and gets 6 seats; the Green party wins 25 percent of the vote and gets 5 seats; and the Red party wins 5 percent of the vote and gets 1 seat. Such an election procedure encourages a multiparty system because all parties have a chance to gain at least some representation.

In a proportional-representation system, coalitions of diverse interests and parties occur not before but after an election, when policies are formulated. For example, once on the council, the Green party members have to form a coalition with the White party or the Blue party to enact specific legislation. By joining forces, the Green and White parties can control the council even if the Blue and Red parties, which are at the extremes of the political poles, decide to discard their ideological differences and vote together on a proposal.

The effect of the presidency. A second important reason for the evolution of the two-

"Oh, Washington himself is all right. It's the men around him like Jefferson and Adams and . . ."
The public often judges the president by the caliber of his advisers.

party system in the United States is the centralizing influence of the office of the presidency. To elect a presidential candidate, the political party tries to band together as many different groups as possible. This requires a vast coalition of interests throughout the country. Those interests that oppose the groups in one party flock to the opposing party. The nation, which is the single-member district that elects the president, thus tends to split into two major parties. The objective of both parties is to win a simple majority of the nation's total electoral-college vote.

The presidency is such an important office that it is a catalyst for coalition among interests that would normally be at loggerheads.

It has succeeded, for example, in unifying southern conservatives and northern liberals in the Democratic party. The Republican party, composed of eastern moderates and midwestern and western conservatives, as well as some southern conservatives, also seems able to close ranks behind a presidential nominee. Through such coalitions, interests (or potential parties) that are too small ever to elect a president of their own selection can influence the selection of a candidate who may be successful in obtaining a majority. A president elected with coalition support is somewhat responsive to the demands of each interest within the coalition.

Division of interests. A third reason for

our two-party system is that in this country there tends to be a polarization of interests on any problem. Some people will be for a proposition and some people will be against it. Different sets of interests in conflict normally gravitate to one of two opposite political parties. Even prior to the adoption of the Constitution in 1787, there was a natural polarization of the country into two camps along economic and political lines.

After 1787 there was a division over the nature of constitutional government itself, and this formed the basis for the Federalist and Antifederalist parties. A similar division also developed between the agricultural interests and the mercantile and financial groups. By the end of George Washington's administration in 1796, agricultural interests were represented largely by Jefferson's Democratic-Republicans, who, like the Antifederalists, desired a weaker federal government. Financial and commercial interests, on the other hand, were represented by Hamilton's Federalists, who advocated a powerful central government.

With the passage of years, these original separations assumed new forms. The Civil War established different patterns and at the same time reinforced some old ones. Added to the original industrial-agricultural division, there developed a hatred-charged schism between North and South that resulted in the Civil War. As a reaction to the Republican North's victory, the South became the bastion of the Democratic party, and even today traces of the sharp conflict between Democrats and Republicans can be attributed to this nineteenth-century regional division.

The widening division between the North and the South in the 1850s, principally over the issue of slavery, had also been reflected in political party changes. The Whig party, founded during the Jacksonian era to become the Democrats' primary opposition, split over the slavery issue at its Baltimore convention in June 1852. The focal issue was the Com-

promise Act of 1850, known as the Fugitive Slave Law, which required runaway slaves to be returned to their owners. The law was opposed by northern Whigs but was supported by party members from the South. The convention failed to nominate its incumbent president, Millard D. Fillmore, who supported the South, and instead chose Winfield Scott, who was ambivalent toward the Fugitive Slave Law and who was supported by delegates from the North and the West. This split in the Whig party was a major factor in the election of the Democrat Franklin Pierce to the presidency in 1852, and in the eventual demise of the Whigs.

The new Republican party was born in 1854, filling the vacuum left by the disarray of the Whigs. The party opposed the extension of slavery in its first platform, adopted by its first convention in Philadelphia in 1856. Four years later the party nominated as its presidential candidate Abraham Lincoln, who ran on a platform that at once opposed the extension of slavery but rejected radical abolitionism by espousing states' rights. The Republican party of the twentieth century—the "Grand Old Party"—is the party of Abraham Lincoln. President Andrew Jackson had founded the Democratic party, which went through a variety of changes and regrouped after the Civil War, counting upon the solid South as its major political base. The Republicans, in their 1876 platform, noted "with deep solicitude that the Democratic party counts, as its chief hope of success, upon the electoral vote of a united South, secured through the efforts of those who were recently arrayed against the nation; and we invoke the earnest attention of the country to the grave truth, that a success thus achieved would reopen sectional strife and imperil national honor and human rights."[3]

In the twentieth century the division of

---

[3]*Guide to U.S. Elections* (Washington, D.C.: Congressional Quarterly, 1976), p. 45.

political and economic interests in the United States has continued. With the growth of urban areas, the old agricultural-industrial division has been replaced increasingly by a division along labor-management lines. Labor unions ordinarily support the Democratic party, which formerly was rooted in the rural agricultural sections, especially in the South. Business interests, on the other hand, tend to support the Republicans.

Of course, each party attracts some followers who would normally be categorized as belonging to the opposing party. Thus some businesspeople are Democrats, while some labor-union members vote Republican. Issues of a local or specialized nature often cause individuals to abandon their usual party loyalties to support the candidate of another party who promises solutions for some immediate problem. A workingman who agrees generally with the Democratic party's position may vote for a "safety in the streets" Republican conservative. Nevertheless, the overall division of interests definitely seems to contribute to the maintenance of the two-party system.

Geographic distribution of party strength. During the last century, the economic and political differences between the two parties have been complicated by an uneven geographical distribution of party strength. Until recently, the Democratic South was counterbalanced by heavily Republican areas in northern New England and certain parts of the Midwest. Curiously enough, these *one-party regions* allow the minority party, even in a landslide election, to retain some representation in Congress.

The two-party system would not function so effectively if political strength were evenly distributed geographically over the whole nation. In the latter case it might then be possible for one party to receive 51 percent of the vote and capture all the representatives in government, legislative as well as executive. The party obtaining 49 percent of the popular vote would have no representation at all. This has in fact happened in certain state elections. However, in national elections a sufficient number of dedicated Democratic or Republican areas, despite campaign issues or trends stemming from social and economic change, will consistently return traditional party choices to the legislature.

In the United States, political, economic, and geographic influences are relatively weak, whereas the spirit of compromise is strong. The country does not have strong political divisions based on principle and ideology. Consequently, a variety of interests have been able to work together within the framework of just two political parties.

Third-Party Dilemma

Because two major political parties have always dominated the political system, peripheral parties are referred to as "third parties." The language of politics uses the term "third party" to refer to all minor or splinter parties, regardless of how many there are. "Third parties," wrote Richard Hofstadter, "are like bees; once they have stung, they die."[4]

Third parties reflect more extreme views than the traditional middle-of-the-road political philosophies of the two major parties. Vice President Henry Wallace, who ran for president in 1948 on the Progressive party ticket, gave the rationale of third parties: "When the old parties rot, the people have a right to be heard through a new party."[5] In the same year that Henry Wallace ran, Governor Strom Thurmond of South Carolina headed another states' rights party that espoused racial segregation. In 1968 Alabama Governor George C. Wallace's Independent party, which received 13.5 percent of the popular vote, also advocated states' rights and segregation.

---

[4]Cited in William Safire, *Safire's Political Dictionary* (New York: Random House, 1978), p. 722.

[5]Ibid., p. 723.

Wallace's campaign had a strong antigovernment tone, opposing the Johnson administration's policies on Vietnam, national defense, the Middle East, crime, and the economy. He urged the nation to "send a message" to Washington by voting for him. Wallace's national political career came to an abrupt halt in 1972 when an unsuccessful assassination attempt left him paralyzed, although he reentered state politics and became governor of Alabama again in 1983.

Of the several dozen third parties in American political history, perhaps the most successful were the Populists (1892–1908) and the Progressive–Bull Moose party (1912). Although the Populists did not achieve electoral success, they forced the Democrats to adopt some of their programs supporting freer credit than would otherwise have been the case. The Bull Moose party, led by the irrepressible Theodore Roosevelt, received 27.4 percent of the popular vote in 1912, splitting the Republican electorate and thereby helping Democrat Woodrow Wilson win the White House.

The 1980 presidential election once again saw a number of third parties competing, the most important of which was former Illinois Congressman John Anderson's Independent party. Other third parties in the contest were the Libertarians and the Citizens' party, headed respectively by Ed Clarke and the environmentalist Barry Commoner. Anderson, who achieved the considerable feat, for a third party candidate, of being listed on the ballots of all 50 states, won 7 percent of the nationwide vote. Originally an unsuccessful Republican candidate for the presidency, Anderson adopted a program that was liberal on social issues and conservative on fiscal matters. Although the major candidates tried not to take Anderson seriously, incumbent President Jimmy Carter, in particular, was worried that Anderson might be a spoiler, drawing away enough votes to defeat him. However, Anderson's candidacy had little effect upon the final electoral results in 1980.

Third parties will continue, from time to time, to offer voters a chance to send a message to Washington expressing their discontent with the governing establishment. And for their part, Republican and Democratic candidates will warn voters not to waste their votes on third parties, which have no chance of victory. The American political system will remain a major obstacle to third-party success because virtually all politically popular issues find a home in one of the major parties, and sometimes in both. The generally more extreme views of third parties are never representative of the mainstream of American political opinion.

Moreover, changes in federal election laws have further buttressed the two-party system. The candidates of the two major parties are automatically financed by federal funds if they choose to accept them, whereas third-party candidates must struggle to obtain federal financing. To qualify for public funding, a third party must have received at least 5 percent of the popular vote in the last election. For example, the Federal Election Commission, which administers the financing laws, ruled in 1980 that John Anderson could receive a share of federal funds only if he achieved 5 percent of the vote. In the meantime, Anderson was unable to persuade various banks to lend him money on the chance of a good showing in the fall. Also, political action committees, which have been spurred by the election laws, rarely "waste" their money on minor candidates. Even getting the necessary signatures and meeting other conditions to appear on state ballots is difficult for third-party candidates.

Given these difficulties, why do third parties persist? The answer goes to the heart of politics, a game participants often play against virtually insurmountable odds and with little chance of winning. Running for the presidency is an "ego trip" for all candidates, regardless of whether they represent major or minor parties. Quests for the presidency are often quixotic, but modern-day politicians, like the fictional hero Don Quixote, tend to believe in their heroic destiny. Power seekers often tilt at windmills in the course of seeking higher office. In presidential politics, for example, they do not have to capture the ultimate prize to enjoy success in the race. Power can be found within party organizations, and the Jesse Jacksons of the political world who know that they have only a slim chance of capturing the White House nevertheless can reveal their power through victories in party caucuses and primaries, and by influencing party platforms and rules. Also, candidates with an ideological bent find fulfillment in spreading the message and in leading a political cult, even if it is of minor importance. But third parties, some led by committed ideologues, others primarily by power seekers, and the majority by a mixture of both, have taken their place in our political history. The Free Soil, Greenback, Anti-Monopoly, Equal Rights, Prohibition, Socialist-Labor, Progressive, Single-Tax, Farmer-Labor, Vegetarian, Peace and Freedom, People's, and Libertarian parties are all among the "lost causes" in presidential politics, but together they have added a powerful footnote to American political history.

AMERICAN PARTY ORGANIZATION

There are literally hundreds of separate party organizations throughout the country that are labeled either Democratic or Republican. As such, party labels would not meet even the most minimum government standards regarding truthful packaging. Each party organization has different candidates and programs to appeal to the "street" (local) constituencies they represent. Thus voters cannot simply use party shibboleths as a shorthand way to predict the policies that candidates support. How-

ever, each of the two major parties, particularly at the national level, has done an amazing job of developing a common denominator of policy preferences among their members on major issues. The electorate can therefore accurately conclude that *in general* the Republicans favor less government intervention in the economy and in the social affairs of citizens, while the Democrats favor more government intervention.

The major purposes of party organizations are, first, to supply candidates for office and to win elections and, second, to provide enough cohesiveness to govern once an electoral choice has been made. For example, at the national level the parties seek to capture the White House and Congress, after which they strive to maintain sufficient support among their members to enact their programs. The New Deal, Fair Deal, and Great Society programs of Presidents Franklin D. Roosevelt, Harry S. Truman, and Lyndon B. Johnson, respectively, could not have been enacted without strong Democratic support on Capitol Hill. Similarly, President Ronald Reagan counted on the Republican majority in the Senate and on cohesiveness among House Republicans to pass his tax and spending proposals. With the help of the conservative coalition on Capitol Hill Reagan succeeded in his first administration in getting his budgetary proposals passed, but a solidly Democratic Congress in his second administration seized the initiative and forced the president to compromise on his tax and spending proposals. President George Bush also faced Democratic majorities in both the House and the Senate which resoundingly defeated in his first year his major proposal to reduce the tax on capital gains that the president had placed at the top of his legislative agenda.

While parties exhibit considerably more unity at the national level than is attributed to them generally, their organizations are necessarily pluralistic, containing many divergent groups. The state and local parties themselves are an important centrifugal force within each national party organization. In addition, hundreds of interest groups of every stripe also seek a home in one or both of the major parties. The cacophonous sounds of the national party conventions symbolize the confederate nature of the parties.

The Effect of Federalism

The decentralization of the party system is buttressed by federalism, which provides for state governments that are independent of the national government. Moreover, the United States is not only a community of separate state governments, each of which has hundreds of elected offices to fill, but also of local governments with separate elective offices. Thus state and local political parties throughout the nation are constantly busy supplying candidates for and contesting offices.

The separate authority of state and local governments under the federal system supports independent, decentralized parties. State and local party organizations are committed primarily to their own objectives. They form loose coalitions every four years to elect the president, a prize that yields important political payoffs at the state and local levels in the form of patronage appointments. The national party organizations are in turn confederations of state and local party interests. Accordingly, the Democratic and Republican National Committees are representative bodies made up of state and local party leaders. The parties are built and controlled from the bottom up, not from the top down.

Traditionally, candidates for the presidential nomination have sought the support of state and local party leaders before making their run. In the past, the big-city party bosses, such as the late Mayor Richard Daley of Chicago, were Democratic kingmakers. They controlled the blocs of votes that often could swing their large electoral-vote states to the candidate of their choice. Urban-machine

politics were less characteristic of the Republican party, especially after the long Republican era ended in 1933. Nevertheless, Republican candidates as well have had to gain the backing of powerful governors and other important state and local Republican leaders in order to achieve the presidential nomination. Richard M. Nixon carefully cultivated Republican leaders throughout the nation to secure his 1968 nomination. Ronald Reagan, too, built a solid political base in state and local politics. State and local party leaders also have a strong impact upon the choice of congressional candidates. Those selected by urban political machines are virtually guaranteed election. Powerful state organizations—such as the Long machine in Louisiana—can often elect the congressmen of their choice.

Formal and Informal Party Organization

In spite of their loose formation and lack of national leadership, American political parties do conform to a definite formal pattern in their structure. Each party is composed of the following:

1. A national committee, with a national chairman who heads the party
2. National congressional and senatorial campaign committees, chosen independently of the national committee
3. State Committees
4. County and city committees
5. Sometimes, ward committees, including precinct and block captains

Formal organization charts, however, rarely reveal who does or does not have power within the organization. In the past, party bosses, particularly those who controlled urban political machines, were able to dominate politics at the local level and exert a great deal of influence upon the national party organization because they could deliver votes to national candidates.

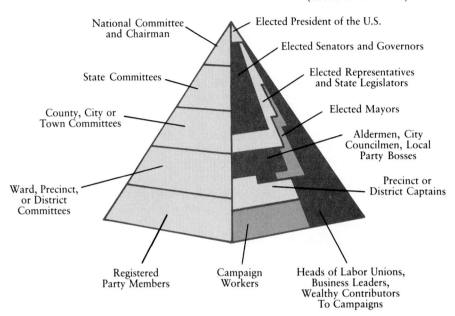

MAKEUP OF FORMAL AND
INFORMAL PARTY ORGANIZATIONS

FORMAL PARTY ORGANIZATION

INFORMAL PARTY ORGANIZATION
(Levels of Influence)

National Committee
and Chairman

State Committees

County, City or
Town Committees

Ward, Precinct,
or District
Committees

Registered
Party Members

Campaign
Workers

Elected President of the U.S.

Elected Senators and Governors

Elected Representatives
and State Legislators

Elected Mayors

Aldermen, City
Councilmen, Local
Party Bosses

Precinct or
District Captains

Heads of Labor Unions,
Business Leaders,
Wealthy Contributors
To Campaigns

FIGURE 7.1

While virtually all political candidates label themselves either Democrat or Republican, there is no national organization for either party that controls candidates' platforms or actions. National, state, and local party candidates essentially form their own personal organizations and decide which policies they will advocate. The national parties are loosely knit organizations at best, their biggest draw being the presidential contest every four years during which diverse party interests have an incentive to join together to win the presidency. Party loyalty, at least on the surface, increases during presidential elections but is far from assured. Presidential primary contests may leave leading party politicians bitter, causing them to give only lukewarm support to their party's nominee.

Party unity exists only when political incentives support it. The president, for exam-

ple, is always the titular leader of his party, but his ability to persuade members of his party to go along with him depends, as Richard Neustadt has pointed out, upon a merging of their interests with his.[6] Congressional leaders of the president's party and powerful congressional committee chairmen will go along with the president if they feel that by doing so they will enhance their reelection prospects or, more likely, their power on Capitol Hill.

At least, at the national level, the party of the presidency has a titular leader. The "out" party is always in a quandary without a president to give it identity. Congressional leaders often step in to speak for the "opposition party," but they can represent the party

[6]See Richard E. Neustadt, *Presidential Power* (New York: Wiley, 1960), p. 32.

(Drawing by Mulligan; © 1982 The New Yorker Magazine, Inc.)

*"Reagan started out as a Democrat and ended up a Republican. I
started out as a Republican and ended up a bum."*
Political party labels are important to some, but not to all.

only weakly. The situation in the out party is somewhat akin to an anarchistic state in which feuding warlords roam the countryside trying to solidify and expand their powers. The political "warlords" of the out party are constantly contending for the position of the party's principal spokesperson. Congressional party leaders vie with state and local politicians to represent the party. Many claim the title, but in reality no one possesses it.

Party Leaders and Followers

Ultimately, political parties in a democracy should give the electorate a meaningful choice of alternative policy proposals. The way in which parties are organized profoundly affects their capacity to connect the people with government. The "umbrella" nature of the two major parties makes them broadly represen-

tative of a wide variety of interests, and party platforms reflect the eclectic character of party organizations.

The pluralistic base of each major party makes it difficult to identify precisely what programs "the party" supports. The most representative group of party leaders is each party's national committee, which speaks for the party on a number of important matters. The committee formulates policies, votes on the delegate-selection formulas for the national conventions, and runs training programs to teach the candidates how to win elections and raise money. The national committees have become increasingly important party fund raisers and candidate seekers, all of which has helped the national parties to become more cohesive.

Party leaders and activists, who include at the national level members of Congress and at state and local levels governors, mayors, and other elected officials, as well as those who are elected to party positions and take an active role in party affairs, define the party. In party councils and in their elected offices they take stands on public policy issues and positions on the proper direction of government. Their views are more "extreme" than those of party followers—voters who simply identify with one party or the other but who do not actively participate in the party.

Party Contrasts

As the decade of the 1990s began, the Republicans were in the fortunate position of having occupied the White House for the previous decade under a president who clearly defined the party's direction. President Ronald Reagan put his conservative stamp upon his party, which represented a victory for the party's conservative wing. For much of the twentieth century, with the exceptions of Arizona Republican Barry Goldwater's candidacy in 1964 and Richard M. Nixon's presidency

from 1969 to 1974, conservative Republicans were unable to capture their party's presidential nomination. Goldwater won the nomination but was soundly defeated in the 1964 election. Nixon had the opportunity to make a strong imprint upon the party and leave a conservative legacy, but his resignation and disgrace over the Watergate affair and his distraction during it essentially aborted his presidency.

The Reagan legacy. President Ronald Reagan was the Franklin D. Roosevelt of his party. FDR and his New Deal gave the Democrats an identity that lasted for almost half a century. FDR shaped not only the party's policies but also its organization, forming the famous Roosevelt coalition that included farmers, union members and workers, academics and intellectuals, and conservative Southern Democrats.

While Ronald Reagan's party legacy is likely to be less dramatic and lasting than that of FDR, his impact on the Republican party will nevertheless be felt for years to come, in part because the Republicans gained with the electorate in the 1980s (see Table 7.1). However, as Paul Allen Beck has pointed out, "the prospects for an emerging Republican majority depend on the ability of Reagan's successors to hold together their party's presidential coalition and then to accomplish what eluded even Reagan—the extension of that coalition to other offices or its institutionalization in GOP party loyalties."[7]

The Democrats. The Reagan era and the election of George Bush in 1988 did not bode well for the presidential wing of the Democratic party. The party searched for a new identity as the 1990s began. "Happy Times are Here Again," which was FDR's theme song, was as outdated as the Roosevelt coalition and

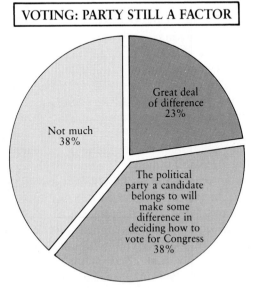

VOTING: PARTY STILL A FACTOR

Great deal of difference 23%

Not much 38%

The political party a candidate belongs to will make some difference in deciding how to vote for Congress 38%

(Source: Survey by CBS News/*New York Times*, September 13–18, 1982. © by The New York Times Company. Reprinted by permission.)

FIGURE 7.2

[7]Paul Allen Beck, "Incomplete Realignment: The Reagan Legacy for Parties and Elections," in Charles O. Jones (ed.), *The Reagan Legacy: Promise and Performance* (Chatham, N.J.: Chatham House Publishers, Inc., 1988), p. 169.

TABLE 7.1 POLITICAL PARTY AFFILIATION GALLUP TREND

In politics, as of today, do you consider yourself a Republican, a Democrat, or an Independent?

	Republican	*Democrat*	*Independent*
1989			
2nd Quarter	45%	38%	28%
1st Quarter	33	42	25
1988	30	42	28
1987	30	41	29
1986	32	39	29
1985	33	38	29
1984	31	40	29
1983	25	44	31
1982	26	45	29
1981	28	42	30
1980	24	46	30
1979	22	45	33
1976	23	47	30
1975	22	45	33
1972	28	43	29
1968	27	46	27
1964	25	53	22
1960	30	47	23
1954	34	46	20
1950	33	45	22
1946	40	39	21
1937	34	50	16

NOTE: This table excludes persons who say they belong to other parties or have no party allegiance.
Source: Gallup Report, August 1989.

the New Deal–Fair Deal–Great Society policies. Party differences and distinctions of the early 1980s (see Tables 7.2 to 7.4) began to fade in the 1990s as the country moved toward the political center.

THE ROLE OF PARTIES IN GOVERNMENT

Party organizations outside of government, such as the national committees, conventions, and the host of state and local party groups, develop programs and supply candidates for office, but they do not control their elected party members. The chairman of the Democratic and Republican National Committees, for example, cannot dictate to a president of their own party or to party members on Capitol Hill. Parties organize *within* government to carry out their programs and—perhaps more importantly in the American party system—to optimize the power of their members in relation to the opposition party. The members of the majority party of each branch of Congress must organize and vote together on questions of congressional organization, procedure, and leadership in order to control committee chairmanships and other perquisites of power. Party balances in the House and Senate have fluctuated over the years as the popular vote has shifted.

TABLE 7.2   OPINIONS OF PARTY LEADERS AND FOLLOWERS ON PUBLIC POLICY ISSUES

	Republicans		*Democrats*	
	Republican National Committee	*Rank-And-File*	*Democratic National Committee*	*Rank-And-File*
GOVERNMENT SPENDING ON . . .				
MILITARY/DEFENSE				
Increase	89%	60%	22%	48%
Decrease	1	5	18	13
Keep same	7	31	51	36
FOOD STAMPS				
Increase	2	9	16	16
Decrease	71	63	14	40
Keep same	19	24	64	37
AID TO THE ARTS				
Increase	3	6	17	7
Decrease	65	41	17	33
Keep same	26	47	58	52
JOB PROGRAMS/CETA				
Increase	3	19	39	46
Decrease	66	39	13	17
Keep same	22	39	44	31
REAGAN'S TAX CUT				
Approve	97	44	17	26
Disapprove	—	5	73	14
Not sure	3	51	10	60
REAGAN'S BUDGET				
Approve	99	48	10	23
Disapprove	—	3	80	22
Not sure	1	49	10	55
PRAYER AMENDMENT				
Favor	46	81	19	79
Oppose	41	15	65	16
E.R.A.				
Favor	29	46	92	62
Oppose	58	44	4	29
TOO MUCH GOVERNMENT REGULATION OF BUSINESS				
Agree	98	72	35	59
Disagree	1	22	49	30
ALLOW ABORTIONS WITH DOCTOR'S CONSENT				
Should	52	55	80	64
Should not	13	30	8	26
Depends	23	11	8	7

Source: Adapted from *Public Opinion*, October/November 1981, p. 49. Reprinted with the permission of the American Enterprise Institute for Public Policy Research.

TABLE 7.3 **DEMOCRATIC LEADERS AND FOLLOWERS ON THE POLITICAL SPECTRUM**

	Rank-and-File Democrats	Democratic National Committee Members	1980 Democratic National Convention Delegates
Liberal	24%	36%	46%
Moderate	42	51	42
Conservative	29	4	6

Source: Public Opinion, October/November 1981, p. 47. Reprinted with the permission of the American Enterprise Institute for Public Policy Research.

TABLE 7.4 **REPUBLICAN LEADERS AND FOLLOWERS ON THE POLITICAL SPECTRUM**

	Rank-and-File Republicans	Republican National Committee Members	1980 Republican National Convention Delegates
Liberal	11%	1%	2%
Moderate	33	31	36
Conservative	51	63	58

Source: Public Opinion, October/November 1981, p. 48. Reprinted with the permission of the American Enterprise Institute for Public Policy Research.

Limits on Party Policy Making

Political programs, such as the platforms of the national party conventions, developed outside the government are not readily translated into public policy. And parties within and without government are not representative of the same interests, nor, more importantly, are they controlled by the same leadership. The party forces that dictate the policies of the national convention are separate and distinct from those that control Congress. Nor are the members of the national committees representative of the same interests that prevail on Capitol Hill.

An understanding of the internal political world of Congress is essential in order to comprehend why it cannot be dominated by party forces from the outside. First, the members of Congress of the same party are only loosely organized and therefore are not unified, disciplined, or responsive to the wishes of their leaders. Each member has his or her own constituency and a personal organization that is largely independent of the national party. While junior members certainly find the support of prominent legislators of their own party useful for fund raising, and need the support of their party's national and congressional campaign committees to provide some of their campaign funds, as they become more senior they are generally able to create independent political organizations that are sufficient to achieve reelection.

The most important attribute of Congress that reduces party control from any source is the fragmentation of power into hundreds of committees, the chairmen of which continue to be in many respects, in the words of Woodrow Wilson, "feudal barons." Thus even if the congressional party leadership were connected directly to outside party forces, it could not control the power of the committees. Party policy making is also limited due to the constitutional separation of powers and the bicameral structure of Congress. The president need not be of the same party as the majority members of Congress. Nor is the House necessarily controlled by the same party as the Senate. President Reagan, for example, was fortunate to have his party control the Senate, but still had to deal with a Democratic House.

Divisions within parties. Party loyalties are often split, too, over certain party proposals. Even when the same party controls both the White House and Capitol Hill, there may be splits within the party over particular legislation. Some party leaders and followers will support the president, whereas others will support Congress. Thus although the party may be considered the primary means of making demands on the government, often its power is fragmented when it comes to making policy.

At several times in the nation's history, a party in the government has attained enough cohesion to implement dramatic new government policies. The New Deal was an illustration of this. Most of the Democratic party as well as some Republicans supported President Franklin D. Roosevelt to enact a domestic policy designed to solve the dilemmas of economic depression. Another example of strong party leadership resulting in cooperation among Democrats within the executive and the legislative branches occurred during the early days of President Lyndon Johnson's administration. The Democratic party acted in unison to enact major domestic programs such as Medicare, increased aid to education, and antipoverty programs. Nevertheless, congressional parties do not display anything like the "discipline" that characterizes many parties in other democratic countries. Party disunity more than unity prevails on Capitol Hill. (See Table 7.5.)

Divisions between parties. Party splits between the president and Congress, however, have characterized national politics in the closing decades of the twentieth century. With the exceptions of the Carter administration (1977 to 1980) and Ronald Reagan's first term, during which his Republican party controlled the Senate, Republican presidents have faced solidly Democratic Congresses. The Democrats have a particularly iron grip on the House of Representatives because they were the majority party when the "incumbency effect" began to take hold and virtually guarantee the reelection of House incumbents. (See Chapter 8.)

Other limits on party policy making. Divisions within and between parties and the general decentralization and dispersion of party power complements other factors limiting party influence on policy making. Other constraints on the ability of parties to make policy include the following:

1. The size and complexity of both the national and state governments

2. The complexity of public issues
3. The power of interest groups
4. The role of administrative agencies in policy formulation

The pluralistic and fragmented character of American politics and constitutional structure that emphasizes the division rather than the unification of governmental power undermine effective national political parties. However, through all the political haze political parties do act as umbrella organizations and bring together interests as well as can be expected.

Other Functions of Parties

Whether or not parties successfully implement policy, they do perform other functions vital to the political system.

Reconciliation of interests. First, the fact that there are only two major parties demonstrates the ability of these parties to reconcile highly diversified interests within society. The parties have organized the politics of a huge nation and have expressed in somewhat meaningful terms the population's divergent points of view.

The parties provide the channels of reconciliation and compromise by binding the different political interests together for the purpose of gaining the political rewards of office, power, and prestige. In so doing, they have prevented the fabric of the democracy from being torn apart by the opposing interests within the society.

The loyal opposition. In a democracy one key function that the party system must perform is that of providing *loyal opposition* to the party in power. This consists of criticizing the program of the party in power without advocating a radical change in the system—that is, without taking over the government by force (*coup d'état*) or by initiating revolution.

The party in power should be subject to constructive criticism by various members of the opposition on an almost continuing basis. Unfortunately, such criticism tends to be spo-

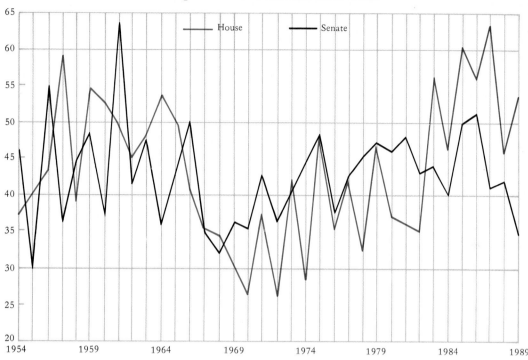

Proportion of Partisan Roll Calls

(Source: Congressional Quarterly Weekly Report, December 30, 1989, p. 3546. Reprinted with permission from Congressional Quarterly, Inc.)

FIGURE 7.3

radic because the opposition will criticize only when it is well organized and feels strongly about a matter. Sometimes criticism is initiated for reasons other than party interest or the merits of an issue. The motivation, in some cases, may be personal advancement or publicity seeking rather than party interest. For example, a senator may criticize the president's labor policy not because his party feels strongly about it, but because through such opposition he may further his own career by securing union backing and campaign support in the next election. Despite its self-interested side, party criticism is a valuable attribute of the party system. In the United States the opposition is constantly testing, debating, and challenging the party in power.

Supply of candidates for office. Political parties also supply the personnel needed to fill the elected offices of government at all lev-els—national, state, and local. The parties are, in effect, government personnel agencies, in an organized manner providing the candidates from among whom the electorate can select the people to do the job of governing. Naturally, government could not continue if such a supply of candidates was not available.

In addition, parties channel personnel into appointive offices. Senators, officials in the president's administration, and other party leaders frequently suggest people for posts as ambassadors or judges. These patronage jobs permit each political party to have an additional but indirect voice in the making of public policy. By making suggestions for appointments, political leaders try to choose men and women who agree with their policies and at the same time are suited for the job.

Political socialization. Through public debating, campaigning for candidates, and formulating policy proposals, the political parties aid in the general political socialization of the public. They help to educate the public on political issues, but it must be kept in mind that this is always within the party framework. With the help of television coverage and other mass media, national party conventions and the presidential campaigns bring the major problems confronting government home to the people and help them to make judgments. The political party is directly responsible for initiating most of this information.

Evaluation of America's Two-Party System

The American party system has been heavily criticized by some political scientists for a long time. These critics of the system contend that it is weak and generally ineffective, that leadership is not strong and deliberate, that there is not enough difference between the parties, and that the parties do not accurately reflect public sentiment on policy issues. These criticisms are healthy but sometimes exaggerated.

Political parties should be judged in terms of the characteristics of the system in which they function. If American parties are evaluated by this standard, they perform reasonably well. The American political system is characterized by pluralism and fragmentation of the governmental policy-making structure. It is not realistic to expect the party structure in such a system to be unified. When the nature of the system in which American parties operate is taken into account, they are more cohesive and effective than might be expected. Criticisms of American political parties are really criticisms of the American political scene as a whole.

Reform of the Party System

Even though the American political party is adequate for the system in which it operates, there is room for reform. Ways to produce a more vigorous and disciplined national party system have been suggested. As yet none of these reforms has been pursued energetically, largely because they would require basic changes in the Constitution and might even upset the present system of the separation of powers.

Coinciding terms of office. As one possibility, the election terms for the House of Representatives, the Senate, and the president might be made to coincide. Or, at least, the terms of representatives could be increased from two years to four years, and the terms of senators could be reduced from six to four years. With this arrangement, a president and Congress of the same party might be elected at the same time and for a long enough period to carry out a party program. At the same time, credit for the success or failure of the program could be fixed on the particular party in power without passing on the rewards or reproaches to a succeeding presidential administration of the other party.

On the other hand, meshing of election periods might produce serious problems. Even if the terms of office for the president and the Congress were made to coincide, there still would be no guarantee that the White House would be occupied by the same party that provided the majority in Congress. Nor could it be assured that the House of Representatives would be controlled by the same party as the Senate. Thus the net result of having the terms of the executive and legislators coincide might be a stalemate in government for longer periods than is the case with staggered terms of office. Or it might allow one party to become so entrenched that the opposition would never be able to replace it.

Repeating terms of the president. Another feasible constitutional reform that would strengthen party government would be repeal of the Twenty-second Amendment. This amendment, which limits any presidency to two terms, tends to diminish the president's authority during his second term of office. By prohibiting a third term of office, the Twenty-second Amendment reduces the president's potential for party leadership and decreases the meaningfulness of party responsibility at the national level. Toward the end of a president's second term, interest shifts from the incumbent to the personalities and programs of potential candidates who may take his place.

Evaluation of parties. Although the American party system certainly has its imperfections and pitfalls, over the years it has managed to formulate issues and funnel public opinion into government. Even though not originally specified by the Framers of the Constitution, the political parties have been able to develop and have become an important wheel in the machinery of government. They are a practical answer to the necessity for selecting candidates and for providing a channel for dissent.

The major premise of this chapter is that disciplined political parties are desirable to organize the disparate politics of democracy. People cannot participate in government, nor can political leaders govern, without the aid of strong party organizations. American parties have never been as disciplined as their European counterparts. This is not entirely undesirable because many European parties are inflexibly ideological in their approaches and unwilling to compromise—and compromise is essential to achieve effective democracy. Nevertheless, American parties have claim to the allegiance, however loose, of most voters, even though their organizations are essentially confederations of separate state and local party units.

In the United States, political parties are built from the bottom up and not from the top down. Their organization and their ability to function reflect their underlying support, which will be revealed in our next chapter.

PARTY ALIGNMENTS IN THE 1990s

CASE STUDY 6

Pluralism and complexity continue to characterize political parties in the 1990s. What Ronald Reagan's 1980's legacy was for political parties continues to be debated. Apparent popular shifts toward Republican presidents may reflect a long-term shift in party identification at the *presidential* level, but continuing Democratic party successes in Congress, state legislatures, and local politics make it difficult, if not impossible, to generalize about party alignments. In the following case study, the author sums up the politics of the 1980s and suggests that their effect, reflected in the 1988 elections, is a new phenomenon which he labels "party de-alignment."

The Legacy of the 1988 Elections: Party De-alignment* / *Michael Nelson*

The results of the elections of 1988 were singular in some ways. Never before has a president been elected (by a landslide, no less) while the other party gained ground in the House, the Senate, the state legislature, and the state governorships. Never before have voters given a newly elected president fewer fellow partisans in Congress than they gave Bush. Never has the Constitution's federal system—separate levels of government and separate branches within each level—been characterized by such partisan segmentation.

But 1988's singularities are best understood as extreme manifestations of the underlying pattern that has characterized American politics for two decades: Republican domination of the White House, Democratic ascendancy almost everywhere else.

Source: Michael Nelson, ed., *The Elections of 1988* (Washington, D.C.: Congressional Quarterly Press), pp. 195–201. Reprinted with permission of Congressional Quarterly, Inc.

Republicans have won five of the last six presidential elections: Nixon in 1968 and 1972, Reagan in 1980 and 1984, and Bush in 1988. The last four Republican victories have been by landslides; in contrast, the Democrats' single victory (Carter in 1976, two years after the Watergate crisis drove Nixon from office in disgrace) was narrowly fought. From 1968 to 1988 Republican presidential candidates led their Democratic opponents in popular votes by 264 million to 215 million, by 2,501 to 679 in electoral votes, and by 251 to 54 in states (including the solidly Democratic District of Columbia). Indeed, Dukakis's 46 percent of the popular vote was easily the second best showing by a Democrat in recent presidential elections. (Compare 43 percent for Humphrey in 1968, 38 percent for McGovern in 1972, 50 percent for Carter in 1976, 41 percent for Carter in 1980, and 41 percent for Mondale in 1984.) Dukakis's 111 electoral votes almost doubled the Democratic tally in the two preceding elections combined (49 in 1980, 13 in 1984).

The Democrats, for their part, have dominated Congress and the states. The House has been a Democratic preserve since 1954; in 1988 the Democrats gained three seats to increase their majority over the Republicans to 260 to 175. The Democrats added one to their ranks in the Senate, a body they have controlled for all but six years since 1954. (The Democratic majority, after the 1988 elections, was fifty-five to forty-five.) At the state level, Democrats also maintained their longstanding hold on a majority of the governors' mansions, adding one in 1988 for a total of twenty-eight (of fifty). Their increase of 14 seats in the state legislatures gave them approximately 4,500 to the Republicans' 2,900. The Democrats control both legislative houses in twenty-eight states, the Republicans eight.

Changing Patterns of Party Alignment

No historical precedent exists for the current political situation. Since 1968 different parties have controlled the presidency and Congress more often than not—twelve of twenty-two years—and in all cases, the president was Republican and Congress Democratic. The party that did not occupy the White House controlled one house of Congress for another six years (the first six years of the Reagan administration, when Democrats had a majority in the House). Same-party control of the presidency and Congress prevailed just 18 percent of

the time, during the four years that Carter, a Democrat, was president. In contrast, same-party control existed 79 percent of the time from 1900 to 1968.

Scholars and political analysts have offered a number of explanations of what has been happening recently in the political system. The most common theories—realignment and dealignment—seem less persuasive than a third: split-level realignment.

Realignment? The normal historical situation in American politics has involved more than just same-party control of the presidency and Congress. For long periods of time, one party usually has exercised such control: in this century, the Republicans until the 1930s, then the Democrats. The Democratic majority came about through a party realignment that was led by Franklin Roosevelt in 1932 and solidified by his New Deal policies. The Roosevelt realignment was not unlike those that had occurred regularly (every thirty years or so) before then, around 1800, 1828, 1860, and 1896. Classic realignments such as these are marked by "a significant and enduring change in the party coalitions—that is, in the partisan loyalties of the electorate." New voters typically gravitate to the rising party during a classic realignment; some older voters change parties. Political participation rises. Above all, classic realignments are top-to-bottom affairs: gains for the new majority party occur at all levels and in all the elected branches of the federal system.

The elections of 1980 seemed to some to augur a full-scale Republican realignment. Reagan's landslide was accompanied by substantial gains for his party, including 34 seats in the House, 12 in the Senate, 302 in the state legislatures, and 5 in the governors' mansions. Growing numbers of voters, especially the young, identified themselves as Republicans in national surveys.

But Republican hopes were diminished when the party lost seats in the 1982 and 1986 midterm elections and, perhaps most important, when it gained little ground from the Reagan reelection landslide in 1984. Young voters proved to be inconsistent, not reliably Republican; they voted Democratic in 1982 and 1986 and were Bush's weakest age group in 1988. Participation in elections declined, rather than increasing, as it had in previous realignments. The voter turnout rate in 1988 was 50 percent, the lowest since 1924.

Dealignment?   The elections of 1980 were not the first recent elections to prompt premature thoughts of realignment. The elections of 1968, coming as they did thirty-six years after the Roosevelt realignment and marked by substantial Democratic defections to third party candidate George Wallace, were described in one book as heralding the "emerging Republican majority." But the 1970s witnessed not Republican gains among the voters, but losses for both parties. Fewer people identified themselves as either Republicans or Democrats, and those who did, when voting, were more inclined than ever to abandon their parties or to split their tickets. The theory arose that the American political system was dealigning: voters, with more years of education than in the past, were said to be relying less on partisan labels than on their own appraisals, derived largely from the now omnipresent mass media, of the candidates and issues in each election.

But the dealignment theory was as surely undermined by political developments in the 1980s as the classic realignment theory. Dealignment implies a virtual randomness of partisan election outcomes over time—a dealigned electorate presumably would swing back and forth erratically between Republican and Democratic candidates. Instead, voters have settled into a discernible partisan pattern: Republican presidents, Democratic Congresses and state governments. What is more, the direction of change in the main statistical indicator of dealignments has been reversed: more voters, not fewer, recently have been identifying themselves as party loyalists.

A New Kind of Alignment.   Because neither realignment nor dealignment describes the modern political situation, a new term has to be employed: split-level realignment. Presidential politics, for its part, clearly bears some of the hallmarks of a classic realignment. The New Deal coalition of blue-collar ethnics, liberals, Catholics, Jews, blacks, and southern whites crumbled when blacks made civil rights and minority progress central issues of American politics during the 1960s, thereby antagonizing many southern whites and, eventually, northern ethnic workers. By 1988 Democrats no longer could win the presidency by, as Dukakis

did, better than any Democratic nominee in the history of polling, uniting the party's base of voters; the base simply had become too small. Republicans not only have added many disaffected Democratic voters to their coalition in presidential elections, they also have taken command of the rhetorical high ground in policy debates. Like Republicans in the 1940s and 1950s, when the Democratic New Deal coalition was dominant, modern Democrats have become the "me-too" party, accepting Republican definitions of most foreign and economic policies and promising mainly to pursue them more fairly and efficiently. Their current political posture confines Democratic presidential candidates almost entirely to winning elections that are marked by special circumstances, such as a scandal or a severe economic recession during a Republican administration.

But the realignment in presidential politics has not carried over into other arenas of political competition, in the top-to-bottom manner of past party realignments. Democratic control of Congress is as solid as ever. Some of the Democrats' success in congressional elections can be attributed to partisan redistricting by Democratically controlled state legislatures, but not much, as Jacobson notes in chapter 6. As Jacobson also argues, although incumbency is a powerful inertial force in congressional elections, the power of incumbents to maintain their positions in the House and, to a lesser but still impressive degree, in the Senate, does not explain why Republicans have not done better at winning open seats. Nor does incumbency account for either the Republicans' success in capturing the Senate in 1980 or their loss of it to the Democrats in 1986.

The Basis of Split-Level Realignment

A number of theories have been advanced to uncover the basis of split-level realignment. Some voters may prefer to reinforce the constitutional checks and balances between Congress and the presidency by placing different parties in charge of each branch. Others may regard Democratic control of Congress as the best safeguard of their desire for an active federal government and a Republican president as insurance against their corresponding fear of high taxes. But, more than in either of these explanations, split-level realignment is grounded in the voters' expectations of presidents and of individual members of Congress and in the nature of the Republican and Democratic parties.

Voters' Expectations. Other than the vice president, the president is the only nationally elected official in the United States. Not surprisingly, most voters have national criteria in mind when they decide whom to support in presidential elections; that is why "peace and prosperity" is the standard formula for victory for the presidential candidate whose party can make the best case that it will provide them.

If Congress were a nationally elected branch of government, voters might well employ national criteria in choosing it as well. But Congress is a locally elected branch. Each member represents one state or congressional district; correspondingly, each voter has a say in the selection of just 1 of 435 representatives and, over a period of six years, two of one hundred senators. Predictably, most voters base their choices in congressional elections less on the consequences for the nation (neither they nor the few members of Congress they each help to elect is likely to have much leverage over national policy) than on the consequences for their own state or district. Not national, but local prosperity forms voters' standard of judgment in congressional elections; not the federal budget, but the share of the budget that is spent on them; not national defense, but the local defense installations and contracts that generate jobs and income for their communities.

Different expectations of presidents and individual members of Congress help to explain the modern pattern of divided partisan control of the two branches. In recent years, voters usually have regarded Republican presidential candidates—more confident of their political ideology, more nationalistic in their view of foreign affairs, and less associated in the public mind with the "special interests" stereotype—as their best guarantors of national well-being. But, because most voters have their states and districts in mind when judging candidates for Congress, it is pragmatism, not ideology, they look for; localism, not nationalism, that preoccupies them; and their particular special interests, not special interests in general, that are at stake. The Democratic party, with its more sympathetic view of government, comes out ahead on all counts according to most voters' criteria for con-

gressional elections. The Democrats enjoy the same advantage, and for the same reasons, in other state and local elections, whether for governor or state legislature.

The Nature of the Parties. The nature of the Republican and Democratic parties also helps to explain their varying success in congressional and presidential elections. The Republicans, despite some differences between their evangelical "moralist" and economically motivated "enterpriser" wings on social issues like school prayer and abortion, are a fairly homogeneous party—white, middle-class or higher, Protestant, and conservative. The Democrats, in contrast, are raucously diverse—white, black, and Hispanic; liberal and conservative; Catholic, Protestant, and Jewish; uneducated and professionally educated.

In fielding candidates for Congress, the Democrats' diversity is politically beneficial. It corresponds well to the nation's geographic diversity. Depending on the character of each state or congressional district, the Democrats usually have little trouble fielding a candidate who is ideologically, ethnically, and personally suitable. In elections to Congress or to other state and local offices, the Democratic party is, in one place or another, virtually all things to all people: liberal in the North, conservative in the South; pro-gun control in the city, anti-gun control in the country; environmentalist in most parts of the nation, development-oriented in the industrial areas; and so on. The candidates of the more homogeneous Republican party, not surprisingly, seem almost everywhere to have been cast in similar molds.

But heterogeneity haunts the Democrats in presidential elections. Ideologically and otherwise, the Republicans do not have to worry about defining their party's identity when writing their platform or choosing the candidate who will represent them to the nation. They have little problem projecting a confident, united front at their presidential nominating conventions. The 1988 Republican convention put Bush into the lead against Dukakis for the first time, a lead Bush never relinquished. In contrast, the Democrats, who thrive on being many different parties in local elections, face the challenge of deciding which one party they will be in nominating a candidate for president. Almost invariably, either the decision is contentious, producing unhappy losers and a divided party and projecting to the voters an image of vacillation and incompetence, or, as in the last two elections, the presidential nominee achieves temporary unity by making such sweeping concessions to the most vocal constituencies in the party (the vice-presidential nomination to feminists in 1984, a remarkable share of the spotlight for Jesse Jackson to blacks in 1988) as to alienate substantial numbers of voters.

The Consequences of Split-Level Realignment

For many years students of American politics have remarked upon the persistence of conflict between the president and Congress. In 1940 Edward S. Corwin traced the main source of contention to the Constitution, which designed the two branches in such a way as to create "an invitation to struggle." A quarter-century later, James MacGregor Burns argued that internal divisions in the Republican and Democratic parties created a "deadlock of democracy" by limiting the parties' ability to bridge the constitutional gulf between White House and Capitol. Yet neither constitutional design nor intraparty divisions seem nearly as potent a force for interbranch conflict as the split-level realignment that now typically places the presidency in Republican hands and Congress under the control of the Democrats.

The period of split-level realignment—1968 to the present—already has been marked not just by differences between the president and Congress over policy, but by each branch's efforts to weaken the other. As Benjamin Ginsberg and Martin Shefter note, through unilateral military actions, efforts to reduce spending on federal grant programs to states and congressional districts, and other assertions of presidential authority, "Republicans have reacted to their inability to win control of Congress . . .by seeking to enhance the powers of the executive branch and to circumvent legislative restrictions on presidential conduct. The Democrats, in turn, have responded to the Republican presidential advantage through legislative investigations . . .as well as through the imposition of statutory limits on executive power," including the War Powers Resolution, the Budget and Impoundment Control Act, and the Ethics in Government Act.

In one area of constitutional responsibility, split-level realignment seems especially likely to heighten conflict between the president and Congress: appointments to the third branch of government, the federal judiciary.

CHAPTER EIGHT

Nominations, Campaigns, and Elections

Jodi Golinsky has been nominated by the Democratic party to run for Congress from Colorado. How was she selected as a candidate for the position? What credentials does she have that qualify her for the office? And, now that she has been chosen, what forces will shape her electoral campaign? Who will decide what principles and demands she will advocate—in other words, what her *platform* will be? Will she rely upon her personality to get elected, or will she emphasize issues? If elected, will she support the president if he is a member of her own party, or, if there is divergency on an issue, will she follow the Democratic leadership of the House? Will her most important constituency be the local, the presidential, or the congressional party? Or will she be able to take an independent stand, even though she was nominated as a Democrat?

SELECTION OF CANDIDATES

One of the most important functions performed by the political parties is the *nomination* of candidates for political offices. In the United States there are tens of thousands of electoral offices that must be filled, as well as thousands of offices that are filled by political appointments. A major task of political parties is supplying candidates for these offices. This is one of the most important potential ways in which parties can control government decision making. To the extent that party candidates reflect collective party views on important issues of public policy, their placement in key government positions helps to guarantee the passage and implementation of party programs. Moreover, if the nominating process were centralized within the major parties, their respective leaderships could exert a great deal of control over public policy by carefully selecting candidates who agree with official party positions. The decentralization of the nominating process in the American party structure reinforces the confederate nature of party organization, diminishing effective national control over the party apparatus. The large number of elective offices to be filled and the lack of party control over the nominating and electoral processes has encouraged a large number of "self-starters" to run for political office—individuals who may have party identification but who have not risen up through the ranks of the party organization.

The Nominating Procedure

Early in the history of the republic there was no provision for the nomination, or selection, of candidates to run for office. But then, the Framers did not intend that political parties would form a central core of the election system, and a nominating procedure was even further from their thoughts. The philosophy of the Framers was echoed by James Madison in *The Federalist*, No. 10, in which he defined political parties, or as he termed them, "factions," as being against the national interest, requiring strict control through formal constitutional divisions of governmental authority (see p. 34). The Constitution now provides for the election of senators and representatives by the people, but it does not outline how candidates are to be chosen. The election of the president is stipulated in the paragraphs on the electoral college, but there is no mention in the Constitution of nominating procedures for the presidency. These procedures have, instead, evolved over the years along with the evolution of political parties and the gradual democratization of the political system.

Caucuses, Conventions, and Primaries

Prior to the 1830s all party candidates were chosen by small groups of party leaders, called *caucuses*. Presidential candidates were nominated by caucuses of influential party members in Congress, and congressional candidates were selected by similar caucuses in state legislatures. Because it was too exclusive, this method was felt to be undemocratic. By 1832 all major-party candidates for the presidency were nominated by national *conventions*, or meetings of party members. The state parties also developed convention systems for nominating candidates for Congress and statewide offices. Gradually, the state convention systems as well were taken over by local party bosses and the elites of the political parties within the states. As a result, conventions for the selection of congressional and state offices have been largely, though not completely, replaced by *primary* elections. However, conventions are still held on a national scale for the nomination of presidential candidates and are also widely used on the state level for the selection of party delegates to the national conventions.

Party primaries have grown in popularity as the convention system has declined. Primaries allow the rank-and-file members of a political party to vote more directly for the candidates they wish to support in an election. First held in New York and California in 1866, primaries quickly took on one of two forms: (1) direct selection of candidates by party members or (2) selection of candidates indirectly by party members, who chose delegates to nominating conventions. The *direct primary* soon became the selection device most recommended by reform groups throughout the country to circumvent the "smoke-filled rooms," or private gatherings of the party elite, where candidates were traditionally chosen. By the turn of the century, two-thirds of the states had passed primary laws, and by 1927 almost all states held statewide primaries for the selection of candidates for all federal and many state offices.

Control over Nominating Procedures

Since the election process is such an integral part of democracy, as well as a key means of providing inputs for the political system, the procedures that parties use to nominate candidates are not determined solely by the parties themselves. Nominating procedures and the qualifications for voters in primaries are generally regulated by state laws.

The endorsement of candidates by conventions held prior to primaries, however, is generally left to the discretion of the parties. In Colorado and Massachusetts the holding of conventions to endorse candidates is required by law, after which primaries are held. But in every other state where nominating conventions are held, the latter are conducted according to the rules set up by the parties rather than by the state.

Reprinted by permission of United Features Syndicate, Inc.

Contemporary presidential candidates often do not appear to compare favorably to past presidents.

Types of primaries. In most states the procedures for selecting delegates to state party conventions, and for running the conventions, are within the discretion of the parties. Primaries, whether for the selection of delegates to national presidential nominating conventions or for the nomination of candidates for such political offices as representative and senator, are regulated by state law. The parties are free to determine the qualifications for delegates to national nominating conventions and can turn down slates of delegates elected under state laws that conflict with party requirements. The Supreme Court upheld the right of the parties to determine their own selection procedures, which, it ruled, is protected under the First Amendment freedom of association clause.[1]

State laws regulating primaries generally have established two types—closed and open. One or the other of these types of primaries is used in all states for the nomination of senators, representatives, and governors. "Blanket" primaries, in which voters can choose candidates of more than one party, are held in Alaska, Louisiana, and Washington. In 1988, 35 states, the District of Columbia, and Puerto Rico used primaries for the selection of delegates to the national presidential nominating conventions of the two major parties. (See Table 8.1.)

In *closed primaries,* used by 17 of the states, a voter must be a member of a party to participate in its primary, and registration in that party must have occurred several months in advance of the primary date. In *semiclosed primaries,* used by seven of the states, voters are asked to indicate their party preference at the time of voting. *Open primaries* (also called *crossover primaries*) are permitted by only six states; in these states there is no requirement for party registration and therefore no way to determine officially a voter's party identification. Semiclosed and open primaries both permit voters to participate in the party primary of their choice, and if large numbers of nonparty members choose to vote in the primary, they may skew, or distort, the result in such a way that the candidate selected will not be the one most favored by the regular party voters. In this way primaries can be "raided" by opposition-party voters, who enter the opposing party's primary to vote for candidates they

[1]*Cousins v. Wigoda,* 419 U.S. 477 (1975) and *O'Brien v. Brown,* 409 U.S. 1 (1972).

TABLE 8.1 PRESIDENTIAL PRIMARY STATES, 1988

State (date)

New Hampshire (2/16)
South Dakota (2/23)
Vermont (3/1)
Alabama (3/8)
Arkansas (3/8)
Florida (3/8)
Georgia (3/8)
Kentucky (3/8)
Louisiana (3/8)
Maryland (3/8)
Massachusetts (3/8)
Mississippi (3/8)
Missouri (3/8)
North Carolina (3/8)
Oklahoma (3/8)
Rhode Island (3/8)
Tennessee (3/8)
Texas (3/8)
Virginia (3/8)
Illinois (3/15)
Puerto Rico (3/20)
Connecticut (3/29)
Wisconsin (4/5)
New York (4/19)
Pennsylvania (4/26)
District of Columbia (5/3)
Indiana (5/3)
Ohio (5/3)
Nebraska (5/10)
West Virginia (5/10)
Oregon (5/17)
Idaho (5/24)
California (6/7)
Montana (6/7)
New Jersey (6/7)
New Mexico (6/7)
North Dakota (6/14)
  Total 37

Source: Adapted from Harold W. Stanley and Richard G. Niemi, *Vital Statistics on American Politics*, 2d ed. (Washington, D.C.: Congressional Quarterly Press, 1990), p. 84. Reprinted with permission of Congressional Quarterly, Inc.

feel will be least effective in winning votes in the general election. Closed primaries, on the other hand, encourage party voting and responsibility by attempting to limit access to the nominating procedures to party members.

NATIONAL NOMINATING CONVENTIONS

Political party nominating conventions in the United States have been so colorful and disorganized in the past that one European observer has called the convention a "colossal travesty of popular institutions," and the platform a "collection of hollow, vague phrases."[2] Although the conventions may not be august assemblages, they have performed the vital function in the political system of naming candidates to run for the offices of president and vice-president.

The "smoke-filled rooms" of past conventions, where party bosses met to choose the candidates most likely to reflect a balance between their interests and voter appeal, were replaced in the 1970s by more open and democratic convention procedures. The burgeoning of the number of states holding presidential primaries, from six in 1960 to thirty-five states plus the District of Columbia and Puerto Rico respectively in the Republican and Democratic parties in 1988 reflected a dramatic shift toward the grass-roots selection of presidential candidates. Since 1972 it has become possible in both parties to win the nomination through the primary process. And the conventions are no longer controlled by the bosses at the top but by party voters spread throughout the country.

The national nominating conventions were developed to fill a serious gap in the constitutional structure. It was originally antici-

[2]Moisei Ostrogorski, *Democracy and the Organization of Political Parties*, abridged by Seymour M. Lipset (New York: Anchor Books, 1964).

pated that the electoral-college procedure would suffice for selecting a president. Ideally, electors in each state would assemble, debate, and deliberate solemnly and judiciously to arrive at their selection for president. The early development of political parties, however, required a broader nominating process that included all elements within a party.

At first the congressional party caucuses acted as nominating bodies. For a time these caucuses worked because members of Congress were in fact the most important party leaders from each state. Thus a congressional-caucus decision about who was to run for president was sufficiently representative of a party's interests. But when the Federalists lost control of Congress in 1804, the Federalists remaining in Congress no longer represented the party as a whole. A new method had to be devised to select candidates with support outside Congress as well as within it; otherwise, defeat at the polls was certain.

In 1808 Federalist party leaders met secretly in New York in the first American nominating convention and selected candidates for the presidency and vice-presidency. By 1831 the popular base of the existing parties had greatly expanded, and the rank-and-file party members wanted more voice in the selection of candidates. Before the 1832 election all three political parties—the National Republican, Anti-Mason, and Democratic—held full-fledged national presidential nominating conventions, which enabled many party followers to participate in the selection of a presidential candidate.

Allocation of Delegates

Naturally, the national presidential nominating conventions would be too cumbersome if all party members attended. Therefore, some means of allocating the number of delegates from the various states, as well as methods of selecting the delegates, had to be devised.

The formulas by which the parties allocate convention delegates change from time to time. They are determined by the national leadership of each party and are based on the strength of the party within the respective states. (The states that show the strongest party affiliation have the largest number of delegates.)

During the first half of the twentieth century the Democrats had party strength in virtually every state, which made it easy for them to use a simple formula for the allocation of delegates that treated each state in much the same way. The Republicans, however, had a serious problem in the South because, although skeleton Republican party organizations existed there, they could not deliver anywhere near the number of votes required to put the states in the Republican camp in a presidential election.

The National Republican party did not want to give the minority Republicans in the South strong representation at party conventions because presumably their views would not be representative of areas of Republican strength throughout the nation, which ultimately elected Republican candidates. The Republicans therefore decided to reward those regions, states, and districts that had supported previous Republican candidates by giving them "bonus" delegates at national party conventions.

Regardless of allocation formulas that award bonus delegates on the basis of party strength, both the Republican and Democratic national conventions are dominated by large-state delegations. California, Illinois, New York, and Pennsylvania have the greatest weight in both parties. However, the power of party leaders in those and other relatively large states has been significantly reduced in recent years by the expansion of presidential-preference primaries in both parties and by delegate-selection rules that have returned the control of national party conventions largely to the grass-roots contingents. Beginning with the Democratic convention of 1972 and last-

TABLE 8.2 **SIZE OF NATIONAL PARTY CONVENTIONS, 1932–1988**

Year	Delegate votes	
	Democrats	*Republicans*
1932	1,154	1,154
1936	1,100	1,003
1940	1,100	1,000
1944	1,176	1,056
1948	1,234	1,094
1952	1,230	1,206
1956	1,372	1,323
1960	1,521	1,331
1964	2,316	1,308
1968	2,622	1,333
1972	3,016	1,348
1976	3,008	2,259
1980	3,331	1,994
1984	3,933	2,235
1988	4,161	2,277

Note: The number of delegates (persons attending) may be larger because of fractional votes.

Sources: Democrats, 1932, 1940–1984: *Congressional Quarterly's Guide to U.S. Elections,* 115, 198–221 (Reprinted with permission from Congressional Quarterly, Inc.); Democrats 1936, 1988: Democratic National Committee; Republicans (all years): Republican National Committee.

ing through the conventions of both parties in 1988, most state delegations were committed in advance to one presidential candidate or another for up to three ballots, and the "proportional representation" rules of the Democrats allowed state delegations to be split among candidates receiving more than 15 percent of the primary vote. The influence of convention "power brokers" of the past, the state and local party bosses who could deliver the votes of their delegation to candidates of their choice, was thus eclipsed.

Delegate-Selection Rules: From the Smoke-filled Rooms to the Grass Roots and Back

Led by the Democrats, a transformation in delegate-selection procedures for national nom-inating conventions occurred in both parties in the 1970s. The move was toward grass-roots participation in the selection of presidential nominees, giving rank-and-file party members a far greater voice than previously in party affairs.

While primaries began to be used in the nineteenth century for the selection of national, state, and local candidates, the national nominating conventions remained under the control of party leaders and bosses. The first presidential-preference primary law was passed in Florida in 1901, giving party officials the option to use primaries to select their quota of delegates to the national conventions. The Progressive Movement, which pushed for political and economic reforms in the late nineteenth and early twentieth centuries, further spurred presidential primaries, and Wisconsin passed a mandatory direct-primary law for choosing national convention delegates in 1905. The Wisconsin law did not provide for the expression of a preference for president. However, other states soon passed primary laws that did permit delegates to have the names of presidential candidates printed opposite their names on the ballot, so that they could express a presidential preference. In some states delegates became legally bound to support the winner of the preference primary on the first national convention ballot.

By 1912 there were 12 presidential-preference primary states, which expanded to 26 by 1916. Primary victories, however, did not ensure a nomination as party bosses continued to maneuver behind the scenes to ensure the selection of their nominee for president. Former President Theodore Roosevelt, for example, won 9 of the 12 primaries in 1912, defeating incumbent President William Howard Taft in Taft's home state of Ohio. Nevertheless, Roosevelt did not capture the Republican nomination, causing him to form his own Bull Moose party. Although the Progressive and other reform movements gave an impetus to presidential-preference primaries, they did not become a major factor in the selection of nominees. The grass-roots movement of the early twentieth century sputtered and died, as "brokered conventions," under the control of party elites and bosses, prevailed.

The results of brokered conventions. Franklin D. Roosevelt, Adlai Stevenson, Dwight D. Eisenhower, John F. Kennedy, Lyndon B. Johnson, Hubert Humphrey, and Richard M. Nixon are examples of the kinds of candidates chosen by politicians meeting in the proverbial "smoke-filled rooms" of national nominating conventions. Some, such as Kennedy and Nixon, used their victories in primaries to demonstrate their vote-getting abilities but in no way depended upon them for the party nominations. The party bosses were not only able to select generally good-to-excellent candidates, but—with the exception of Stevenson and Humphrey—winners.

Interest in primaries revived after World War II, and candidates unpopular in the inner circles of the parties attempted to prove their popularity with rank-and-file party members by winning a series of presidential-preference primaries. The perennial Republican candidate, Harold Stassen, governor of Minnesota from 1939 to 1943, challenged New York Governor Thomas Dewey in 1948 for the nomination by making a good showing in the party's presidential primaries. And Tennessee Senator Estes Kefauver challenged the Democratic national organization in 1952 and in 1956 by winning primary elections. The popularity of Stassen and Kefauver among regular voters nevertheless did not enable them to make much headway toward the nomination. Only war hero Dwight D. Eisenhower was able to successfully challenge the favorite of the party organization, by winning primaries in key states in 1952. Otherwise the national nominating conventions continued to be under the control of party elites until fundamental changes took place in delegate-selection procedures, beginning with the Democratic convention in 1972.

The revival of grass-roots delegate selection. The domination of presidential nominating conventions by party leaders, particularly state and local power brokers and party bosses, continued through 1968. (See Table 8.3.) In that year the issue of reform of the Democratic party became mixed with that of the Vietnam War. The powerful antiwar movement felt that it was excluded from the convention in Chicago, and the nomination of Hubert H. Humphrey was viewed as a reflection of the domination of the party by such prowar bosses as Mayor Richard J. Daley of Chicago, as well as by President Lyndon B. Johnson. Humphrey himself, as vice-president, had not been vocally opposed to the war. The situation was aggravated by the violent assault by Mayor Daley's police force on antiwar demonstrators in the streets around the convention hall. It was the force of this discord that subsequently (in 1969) produced the McGovern Commission, with its mandate to reform party procedures in a way that would ensure broader representation in the future.

The McGovern Commission recommended an expansion in the number of presidential-preference primaries, more democratic procedures for the selection of delegates, and greater representation of minorities, women, and youth. While all of the McGovern Commission recommendations were not immediately accepted by state Democratic parties, they had a strong impact on the 1972 presidential nominating process, as Table 8.3 illustrates. The Republican party as well adopted grass-roots reforms that expanded presidential primaries and resulted in a dramatic increase in the percentage of delegates selected from primary states, as Table 8.3 also illustrates.

The effects of grass-roots selection of presidential candidates—the Democrats. The Democrats turned to the grass-roots selection of their presidential candidates because many party activists had considered the results of

(Drawing by Joe Mirachi; ©1984 The New Yorker Magazine, Inc.)

"After the New Hampshire primaries! That's your answer to everything!"
The New Hampshire primary, now with the Iowa caucuses, marks the kickoff of presidential campaigns.

the 1968 convention unrepresentative of the views of a cross section of party members. Had the issue of the Vietnam War not distorted the politics of the times, Hubert Humphrey would have been considered the epitome of the Democratic party and, as the presidential candidate, could have easily garnered both the liberal and middle-of-the-road votes of the party. But that was not Humphrey's destiny, and the severe reaction to his candidacy in some quarters—even though he almost won the election— removed control over the nominating process

from the traditional Democratic power brokers. This then made possible the nominations of George McGovern and Jimmy Carter in 1972 and 1976, neither of whom represented the party's mainstream.

In their quest to make the party democratic, the McGovern proselytes sought to establish in the delegate-selection process affirmative action programs that would create quotas for the representation of minority groups, women, and youth. Moreover, they wanted to abolish the "unit rule" at all levels

TABLE 8.3 PRESIDENTIAL PRIMARIES, 1912–1988

	Democratic party			*Republican party*		
Year	*Number of primaries*	*Votes cast*	*Percentage of delegates from primary states*	*Number of primaries*	*Votes cast*	*Percentage of delegates from primary states*
1912	12	974,775	32.9	13	2,261,240	41.7
1916	20	1,187,691	53.5	20	1,923,374	58.9
1920	16	571,671	44.6	20	3,186,248	57.8
1924	14	763,858	35.5	17	3,525,185	45.3
1928	17	1,264,220	42.2	16	4,110,288	44.9
1932	16	2,952,933	40.0	14	2,346,996	37.7
1936	14	5,181,808	36.5	12	3,319,810	37.5
1940	13	4,468,631	35.8	13	3,227,875	38.8
1944	14	1,867,609	36.7	13	2,271,605	38.7
1948	14	2,151,865	36.3	12	2,635,255	36.0
1952	16	4,928,006	39.2	13	7,801,413	39.0
1956	19	5,832,592	41.3	19	5,828,272	43.5
1960	16	5,686,664	38.4	15	5,537,967	38.6
1964	16	6,247,435	41.4	17	5,935,339	45.6
1968	17	7,535,069	48.7	17	4,473,551	47.0
1972	23	15,993,965	66.5	22	6,188,281	58.2
1976	30	16,052,652	76.1	29	10,374,125	70.4
1980	35	18,747,825	81.1	36	12,690,451	78.0
1984	30	18,009,217	67.1	29	6,575,651	66.6
1988	37	23,230,525	81.4	38	12,169,003	80.7

Note: Primaries include binding and nonbinding presidential preference primaries as well as primaries selecting national convention delegates only without indication of presidential preference. Prior to 1980, votes cast in the delegate-only primaries are not included in the total votes cast.

Source: Harold W. Stanley and Richard G. Niemi, *Vital Statistics on American Politics*, 2d ed. (Washington, D.C.: Congressional Quarterly Press, 1990), p. 134. Reprinted with permission from Congressional Quarterly, Inc.

of party discussion, a rule that binds caucuses to follow the decisions of their majorities. Some form of "proportional representation" would replace the unit rule, allowing minority political views to be counted in the party's decision processes. The expansion of presidential-preference primaries was an important aspect of the emphasis upon the grass roots. But the rules were also to apply to non-primary states, where delegates were selected by caucus or convention. The primary effect of these changed procedures was to turn the presidential nominating process into a popularity contest in which the candidates vied for the votes of the party's rank-and-file members. Candidates with sufficient energy and

resources can circumvent many state and local party leaders in their quest for the nomination by going directly to the voters. George McGovern's direct-mail campaign in 1972, using lists of Democratic voters throughout the country prepared by Gary Hart, successfully circumvented state and local party elites.

The race for the presidential nomination becomes a free-for-all when the traditional power brokers can no longer control it. The candidacy of Jimmy Carter perhaps best epitomized the grass-roots nominating politics of the 1970s. As governor of Georgia, Carter had sat in his mansion looking north and dreaming of the presidency. Contemplating the candidacies of George McGovern and Richard M.

Nixon, Carter may well have thought to himself, "Why not the best? Why not me?" Virtually the morning after McGovern's defeat he decided to take a leaf from the notebook of the unsuccessful candidate for the presidency but the victor in the race for the nomination, calling in his closest advisors to help him create the organization and provide the financial backing for his long trek.

Carter became the paradigm of the grassroots candidate, traveling across the country and charming small groups of voters, many of whom seemed to feel that he was a Democratic reincarnation of Abraham Lincoln, a man of the people who would save the Union. Carter became the darling of the press, and his dark-horse candidacy was soon taken seriously. The *New York Times* political reporter R. W. ("Johnny") Apple wrote that Jimmy Carter had emerged as "a major contender for the Democratic presidential nomination" due to his "solid victory" in Iowa's precinct caucuses, and soon a bandwagon of reporters heralded Carter as the Democrats' choice. Although Carter, unlike McGovern, successfully courted party leaders throughout the country, he too had his own organization that could, if necessary, successfully circumvent regular party channels. Carter's nomination seemed to reflect a broad party consensus, but by the election of 1980 that consensus had disintegrated under the disenchantment of much of the party's leadership with his presidency. The challenge of Massachusetts Senator Edward Kennedy drew not only the support of some of the traditional power brokers of the party, such as labor union leaders, but also the backing of minority and women's groups, and the resultant party schism helped Ronald Reagan defeat Carter in 1980.

The Democrats continued to tinker with their grass-roots nominating procedures in the 1980s, giving a greater voice to the party's power brokers, but the McGovern Commission's legacy continued to make presidential-preference primaries the dominant force.

The Republican grass roots. The victory of Ronald Reagan in 1980 reflected in its turn a Republican return to the grass roots of the party, the strongly conservative element that had supported Barry Goldwater in 1964. Just as George McGovern had contrasted the Democratic grass roots with the party establishment, Republican candidates had done the same. Barry Goldwater had mobilized a constituency of rank-and-file conservative Republicans and their leaders, primarily in the South and West, to capture the presidential nomination. And he had run outside of the regular party channels, defying the party establishment, rooted in the Northeast, that had controlled the party nominating process for decades. Returning to the grass roots in the Republican party then had had a profoundly different substantive effect than did the grass-roots revolution of the Democrats. Conservative Republicans feel strongly that they are the grass roots of the party, and contrast their views with what they disparagingly call the "party establishment." Ronald Reagan had been their candidate from the late 1960s until his victory in 1980. Their opposition had been Richard Nixon, Gerald Ford, and the late Nelson Rockefeller, along with other Republicans they considered to be middle-of-the-road or even liberal.

Ironically, as the Democratic left spurred the expansion of presidential-preference primaries, which are created by state law, they helped the Republican right, which had always felt itself to be excluded from party affairs. The one exception had been the Republican Convention of 1964, stacked with Goldwater followers just as the 1972 Democratic Convention had been stacked in favor of McGovern. But Goldwater, like McGovern, had gone down in overwhelming defeat because neither had reflected important party constituencies, even while claiming to represent a majority of the party's rank-and-file members.

Ronald Reagan, like both McGovern and

Carter, built his own organization, which used the primary system to circumvent traditional party power brokers.

Republicans, unlike the Democrats, did not create affirmative action programs in their delegate-selection process to represent minorities, women, and youth, although some liberal members of the party made modest proposals in that direction during the 1970s and in the early 1980s. Nor has "proportional representation" ever been a major issue among the Republicans. Generally, the party has accepted "winner-take-all" primaries in which the candidate with a plurality of the vote receives all of a state's delegates. By contrast, the Democrats have attempted, not always successfully, to give delegate representation to candidates who have received at least 15 percent of a state's primary vote.

Delegate profiles also changed in both parties as the result of the post-1968 reforms, but less dramatically than might be expected. Table 8.4 illustrates that by 1988 delegate profiles in many respects had returned to what they had been in 1968, with a few notable exceptions. Women and blacks increased their representation in the 1980s in Democratic conventions. The percentage of delegates under the age of 30 in the 1988 Democratic convention, however, returned to its 1968 level. The same was true of the percentage of delegates attending their first convention, which dropped drastically in 1988 from levels achieved in the 1970s and early 1980s. Party professionals and power brokers again began to replace party outsiders and amateurs, who nevertheless continued to represent a majority of delegates in 1988. Finally, grass-roots

TABLE 8.4 PROFILE OF NATIONAL CONVENTION DELEGATES, 1944–1988 (PERCENT)

	1944		1968		1972		1976		1980		1984		1988	
	D	R	D	R	D	R	D	R	D	R	D	R	D	R
Women	11	9	13	16	40	29	33	31	49	29	49	44	48	33
Black	—	—	5	2	15	4	11	3	15	3	18	4	23	4
Under thirty	—	—	3	4	22	8	15	7	11	5	8	4	4	3
Lawyer	38	37	28	22	12	—	16	15	13	15	17	14	16	17
Teacher	—	—	8	2	11	—	12	4	15	4	16	6	14	5
Union member	—	—	—	—	16	—	21	3	27	4	25	4	25	3
Attending first convention	63	63	67	66	83	78	80	78	87	84	78	69	65	68
Protestant	—	—	—	—	42	—	47	73	47	72	49	71	50	69
Catholic	—	—	—	—	26	—	34	18	37	22	29	22	30	22
Jewish	—	—	—	—	9	—	9	3	8	3	8	2	7	2
Liberal	—	—	—	—	—	—	40	3	46	2	48	1	43	0
Moderate	—	—	—	—	—	—	47	45	42	36	42	35	43	35
Conservative	—	—	—	—	—	—	8	48	6	58	4	60	5	58
Median age	—	—	49	49	42	—	43	48	44	49	43	51	46	51

Note: "—" indicates not available.

Source: Harold W. Stanley and Richard G. Niemi, *Vital Statistics on American Politics*, 2d ed. (Washington, D.C.: Congressional Quarterly Press, 1990), p. 135. Reprinted with permission from Congressional Quarterly, Inc.

delegate selection appeared to reduce the influence of moderates in both parties, although lack of data before 1976 makes it impossible to judge whether Democratic and Republican national conventions have become more liberal and more conservative, respectively.

The politics of the delegate-selection process. Politics always involves individual and group struggles for power, and the politics of the delegate-selection process is no exception. Party rules reflect the balance of power within the party. And rule changes are invariably proposed to benefit some groups and individuals, to increase their power within the party. The Democratic rule changes after the 1968 convention, proposed by party outsiders who wanted to become insiders, eventually forced the traditional party elite to temporarily relinquish its control of the presidential nominating process and the national convention.

The power struggles within the Republican party between the conservative forces—led by Senator Robert Taft in 1952, Barry Goldwater in 1964, and Ronald Reagan from 1968 until his nomination in 1980—and the traditional party establishment, which was more moderate in its political views, did not revolve around rule changes but focused on the more effective use of the prevailing party processes to achieve power. The expanded primary process in the 1970s had enabled Democratic challengers to seize control of their party, and Ronald Reagan too used the primaries to come within a handful of votes of capturing the 1976 nomination and, finally, in his 1980 nomination victory. The Reagan forces did not seek the expansion of presidential-preference primaries, although the process undoubtedly benefited Reagan, whose character and political style were vastly appealing to voters. The Republican nomination had been captured by another conservative candidate, Barry Goldwater, in 1964 before primaries had a significant impact upon delegate selection. Whatever the political base of a party is, primaries tend to benefit, in this television age, charismatic and stylish leaders with strong financial backing.

While the primary-caucus process of nominating presidential candidates may increase rank-and-file participation in the selection process, it does not necessarily produce responsible and effective party organization. It is important for parties to achieve a balance between effective leadership on the one hand, and rank-and-file participation on the other. Clearly, party leaders cannot and should not control nominating procedures apart from the wishes of their own party members, but at the same time it is possible to achieve a consensus behind a nominee without resorting to such widespread grass-roots nominating procedures as are now used by both parties.

The widespread use of primaries and rank-and-file caucuses encourages "candidate parties" to develop, parties that are separate from the regular party organization and that exist to serve only the candidates. It is this personalization of the party process that is a disintegrative force, because national parties must be collective organizations that include a vast number of groups. In his successful campaign for the presidency, beginning with the primary process, Jimmy Carter circumvented the Democratic National Committee and almost lost the election at the last minute because, like George McGovern, he had alienated many national, state, and local party leaders. It was not Jimmy Carter's policies but his insufficient protocol, his failure to "touch base" and to involve regular party leaders in his organization, that caused their dissatisfaction with him. Carter was not the only unwitting victim of grass-roots politics. The grass-roots process encourages "candidate parties," organizations bearing the personal stamps of candidates and their staffs, which are not beholden to "regular" party leaders. They reflect the increasingly individualistic and entrepreneurial presidential nominating process. An effective personal organization, such as Massachusetts Governor Michael Dukakis had in

1988, can capture presidential nominations, but needs to be broadened to be successful at the polls in November.

The personalization of the campaigning process for the presidency has been an important factor contributing to the personalization of the office itself. Increasingly, presidential candidates as well as presidents are viewed as proverbial men on horseback, the white knights who will save us from ourselves, from the very politics upon which the democratic system is based. This is why candidates often take a stance that is, rhetorically, "above politics," proclaiming to be outsiders who will, once in office, change the system for the better. The expansion of primaries and caucuses may result in replacing the party with the person. Personal responsibility may replace party responsibility. A government of persons elected from their own "candidate parties" will almost certainly be a disruptive political force, for effective government needs a high degree of party unity.

The reaction against grass roots. Party unity became the theme of the Democrats after the stunning defeat of Jimmy Carter in 1980. Even before that, however, party leaders began seriously to question the grass-roots reforms of the 1970s, which they believed contributed to party disunity. Louisiana representative Gillis Long, Jr., then chairman of the House Democratic Caucus and third-ranking member of the Rules Committee, told a commission created by the Democratic National Committee (DNC) to study party reform: "Congress is not involved in the [party] platform. Congress is not involved in the convention, Congress often then is not terribly involved in the presidential election campaign. The outcome is a truncated party, that even in success, can rarely implement party platform into public policy."[3]

State party and elected officials, who had also been excluded from the Democratic

party's nominating processes since 1968, joined with members of Congress to revamp the "reforms" that they all agreed had gone too far. The party leadership, led by the DNC, decided to take action to restore some semblance of their control over the nominating process. The Rules Committee, at the 1980 Democratic Convention, had called for a review of the nominating process, and the DNC quickly seized upon the request as a mandate for change. A special Democratic Commission on Presidential Nominations was appointed, consisting of members who once would have been in charge of the party: senators, representatives, governors, mayors and other state and local leaders, and elected officials. The group set out to undo the work of the McGovern Commission by recasting the nominating process.

The DNC finally, with the support of the midterm conference of the party in 1982, adopted new rules for the presidential nominating process. Under these rules, 14 percent of the convention votes are in the hands of uncommitted party officials selected through regular party channels. Two-thirds of the Democratic members of the House and Senate, chosen by the congressional caucuses of the party, are delegates. State parties choose the official state and local delegates, including big-city mayors and state legislators. All members of the DNC are convention delegates as well.

The Democratic "superdelegates" were a powerful convention force in 1984 and 1988. It is unlikely that Walter Mondale, the 1984 Democratic presidential nominee, would have been chosen without the support of the superdelegates, most of whom voted as a block to support him. The superdelegates, particularly if they vote together, can constitute the swing vote in closely divided conventions.

Politicians with strong grass-roots support, such as Jesse Jackson, have criticized the superdelegate system. They claim that it is undemocratic because the superdelegates, unlike

---

[3]*Congressional Quarterly Weekly Report*, Vol. 39, No. 52 (December 26, 1981), p. 2565.

other delegates, do not have to run in state primaries or caucuses. Jackson and others also argue that the superdelegates can cause an undemocratic convention outcome by constituting a swing vote. However, in 1984 and 1988 the superdelegates were followers, not leaders. They fell in line behind Mondale (1984) and Dukakis (1988), the candidates who had won at the grass roots.

Unlike the Democrats, the Republicans are generally satisfied with their presidential nominating procedures. Although Republican candidates must run in as many primaries as do the Democrats, the party's leaders and elected officials have remained powerful in the presidential nominating process. Convention delegations have not been subject to affirmative action, proportional-representation requirements, and other rules that diminish the power of regular party officials. Most important of all, the party's nominating procedures selected in both 1976 and 1980 highly popular candidates among the party's leadership and rank-and-file as well. Although the party was not completely unified—for there has consistently been a division within it between the middle, represented by Gerald Ford, and the right, led by Ronald Reagan—its organization was sufficient almost to elect Ford and to give Reagan a decisive victory in 1980. The Democratic grass roots, as defined by McGovern and his followers, ultimately chose "losers" in the candidates outside of the party's mainstream, whereas the grass roots of the Republican party as defined by Ronald Reagan nominated a winner.

Overview of the grass-roots nominating procedure. Politicians, political scientists, political pundits, and journalists have, depending upon their vantage point and interests, both blamed and praised the grass-roots presidential nominating process. Most of the turmoil seems to be within the Democratic party because of its apparent failure to field candidates who can win presidential elections. The presidential nominating process seems to be a natural starting point to place the blame.

TABLE 8.5 1988 CONTEST PRIMARY-DOMINATED

Source of delegates	Delegates	Percentage of convention
Democrats		
Primaries	2,771	66.6%
Caucuses	746	17.9
Superdelegates	645	15.5
Republicans		
Primaries	1,751	76.9
Caucuses	526	23.1

Source: Michael Nelson (ed.), *The Elections of 1988* (Washington, D.C.: Congressional Quarterly Press, 1989), p. 28. Reprinted with permission from Congressional Quarterly, Inc.

Whether or not grass-roots selection of presidential candidates is good or bad—from the standpoint of the parties themselves, the candidates, the voters, and the political system as a whole—will continue to be debated. The trend which the McGovern Commission began in the early 1970s has had its setbacks, but primaries and caucuses have continued to dominate the presidential nominating process. (See Table 8.5.)

It seems doubtful that presidential primaries have produced less worthy candidates than those produced in the times of the "smoke-filled rooms" of the past, when party bosses and the most powerful elected party leaders were able to determine who would be their party's presidential candidate. Political scientist Michael Nelson has concluded that the grass-roots process strengthens the two major parties by giving the candidates a legitimacy with the public they did not have when brokered conventions prevailed. Moreover, he argues, the grass-roots reforms of the 1970s were essential to keep parties in tune with changing political currents that brought demands for broad public participation and the nominating process to the surface.[4]

---

[4] See Michael Nelson, "The Case for the Current Presidential Nominating Process," in George Grassmuck, ed., *Before Nomination: Our Primary Problems* (Washington, D.C.: The American Enterprise Institute, 1985).

However, there are more critics than defenders of the grass-roots presidential nominating system. The critics argue that the system does not nominate the best candidates, either those that are most likely to win in the general election or those that can lead the nation if they are elected. Far fewer voters participate in presidential primaries and caucuses than in the general election, and the party activists who do participate tend to represent the more extreme ideological viewpoints of the party—liberal Democrats and conservative Republicans. The early caucus and primary states—Iowa and New Hampshire—set the stage and often determine the party's choice, even though only a relatively small number of voters participate.

In 1988 the southern states joined their primaries in "Super Tuesday," which occurred on March 8, three weeks after the New Hampshire primary. Collectively far more delegates were chosen on Super Tuesday than had been selected in Iowa and New Hampshire combined, but in the end, Michael Dukakis, who won in both Iowa and New Hampshire, and George Bush, who won an upset victory in New Hampshire, captured their parties' nominations. Super Tuesday

(©Leo Abbett)

Presidential campaigns begin earlier and earlier.

seemed to confuse an already confusing picture even more by providing an opportunity for additional candidates to creditably compete for the nomination.

The grass-roots presidential nominating process seems to be here to stay. For the candidates it is a demanding, exhausting, time-consuming, and expensive ritual. For the voters who participate directly the process can be engaging and entertaining. Citizens at large, who observe the process from the outside, always have the opportunity to decide which nominee will become president, which is an important democratic check upon any flaws in grass-roots nominating politics.

Conventions in Operation

National party conventions always formally nominate candidates for the presidency and vice-presidency, although, since the grass-roots reforms of the 1970s, by the time a convention opens one presidential candidate has usually emerged from the pack with the majority or significant plurality of delegates won in party caucuses and primaries throughout the country. Conventions lack the drama that they often had in the past when party bosses and power brokers maneuvered behind the scenes to select candidates.

In 1988, for example, Massachusetts governor Michael Dukakis won 42.3 percent of the primary vote and went into the convention with 54.4 percent of the delegates (2,264). On the Republican side, George Bush won an overwhelming victory throughout the country in primaries and caucuses, going into the convention with 67.8 percent of the primary vote and 86.7 percent of the delegates (1,669). Grass-roots nominating politics does not always produce conventions with a clear winner at the outset; for example, in 1972 George McGovern had a clear plurality but not a majority of convention delegates after the primaries and caucuses and had to put together a coalition to win the nomination. In 1976 Ronald Reagan ran a strong grass-roots campaign

that almost toppled incumbent President Gerald Ford, who won his party's nomination on a close vote. Usually, however, what drama there may be over who will be the presidential nominee occurs long before the convention as candidates battle for delegates and for the label of "front-runner" in caucuses and, more importantly, in primaries.

Regardless of the extent to which the nominees have been preselected before a convention meets, national nominating conventions have always served important symbolic and organizational functions for the party. The conventions are directed solely at party members, which is one reason that without the suspense of an uncertain nomination they are boring for those outside of the party to watch. The seemingly unimportant rituals, such as the choice of the convention site, the provisions of the party platform, the rules that conventions must ratify for their future conduct—including delegate-selection and allocation processes—and the choice of the keynote speaker, are all of great symbolic and practical importance to the diverse groups within each party. State and local party organizations, interest groups, and national party functionaries want to be represented in the party processes, and the conventions provide numerous forums for representation.

The ritual of a convention begins at the preceding convention, when rules are debated and decided upon for the next convention. National party committees continue to refine the rules before they are finally set for the next national nominating conventions. These party rules are of the utmost importance to presidential contenders, who try to shape the rules to their own advantage. For example, in 1988 Jesse Jackson argued that the Democratic party rules did not permit an accurate reflection of his grass-roots support. In fact, however, Jackson received 29 percent of the primary vote, and exactly 29 percent of the delegates voted for him on the first presidential ballot. Dukakis garnered most of the superdelegates and the delegates from other candidates, winning an impressive first-ballot victory with 69 percent of the vote.

The politics of convention rules, as of other aspects of party conventions, always involve candidates and party leaders jockeying for power *within* the party organization. Candidates and party leaders who win struggles over the rules gain credibility within the party, which may be a major goal in itself. Politicians always strive for power within whatever political arena they find themselves. Presidential nominating politics offers an opportunity for candidates, party leaders, and power brokers to flex their political muscles and prove their credibility without having to achieve the final goal of being the presidential nominee or even having to be on the side of the presidential nominee. Political credibility within parties is enhanced often by small rather than large victories that demonstrate a politician's influence over matters of internal concern to the party, such as delegate-selection rules.

For example, South Dakota Senator George McGovern's ability to install many of the McGovern Commission rules for the 1972 Democratic convention boosted his credibility long before he captured the party's nomination. In 1988 Jesse Jackson demonstrated his power within the Democratic party not only by winning a large number of delegate votes through vigorous campaigning in caucuses and primaries but also by his ability to increase "proportional representation" in the delegate-selection process for the 1992 convention. The rules change benefited popular grass-roots candidates by giving them more delegates in proportion to the votes cast in primaries.

Choice of the convention site. The Democratic and Republican National Committees, long before their respective conventions open, are embroiled in controversies over the sites for the conventions. Choice of the convention site is yet another party ritual of symbolic importance to differing party interests. For example, Democratic conventions held in Chicago in the past were considered a reflection of the power of Mayor Richard J. Daley of that city, a prominent party boss whose support was considered critical for success in the November election. After the debacle of the 1968 Democratic convention, however, it would have been unthinkable to hold the 1972 convention again in Chicago. Miami represented "neutral" territory, and its choice was meant to convey the idea that the party was not controlled by any of the established political bosses located in various cities and states throughout the country.

Again, the choice of the convention site is a purely internal party matter and one that may reveal which, if any, faction has control over the party apparatus. Holding the 1976 Republican convention in the farm-belt area represented by Kansas City symbolized the conservative emphasis the party wished to project in that year, just as the final choice of New York City as the site of the Democratic convention reflected a return of the party to its traditional liberal-urban power base. The Democrats met again in New York in 1980, while the Republicans emphasized that they were not insensitive to the plight of large industrial cities by choosing Detroit for their convention. The Republicans, at the urging of President Ronald Reagan, decided to meet in Dallas in 1984, reflecting the importance of the Southwest and the Sunbelt in party politics. The 1988 Democratic and Republican national conventions met in Atlanta and New Orleans, respectively. For the Democrats the Atlanta site symbolized the party's roots in the South, and for the Republicans the choice of New Orleans represented the party's continued strength in the South at the presidential level. A national convention, then, enables the national party organization to project an *image* of the party at the very outset through its choice of the convention site.

The keynote address. The next party ritual performed in connection with the holding of a national nominating convention is the determination of who will give the keynote address or addresses. This decision is up to the person who chairs the national party committee, who, if astute, will consult the leaders of an adequate number of party groups to ensure support for the final choice. Regardless of the content of the keynote address, the person making it will represent one or more factions of the party and will be identified with certain policies.

The 1976 Republican keynoter, Senator Howard Baker of Tennessee, was chosen because of his role as a prominent member of the Senate Watergate Committee in 1973. With the party attempting to overcome the drastic adverse effects of Watergate, Baker symbolized a ranking party member of high integrity who had been unafraid to bring out the facts of Watergate. Senator Baker, who had presidential ambitions, was also widely viewed as a likely choice by President Ford to be his running mate.

Just as the choice of the keynote speaker is an internal party affair designed to symbolize the spirit of the party, the address itself is designed to "cheerlead" the party on to victory in November. The partisan excesses of almost all keynote addresses, so boring, and even outrageous, to persons outside the party, make perfect sense if this feature of the convention is viewed as a gigantic pep rally in which the members of the party team gather around the bonfire to chant their favorite party incantations.

Excerpts from keynote addresses of past conventions illustrate the general tone that has been taken. In the midst of the Great Depression in 1932, Senator Alben Barkley introduced the Democratic convention with an emotional attack on the Republican administration:

No, my countrymen, there is nothing wrong with this Republic except that it has been mismanaged, exploited, and demoralized for more than a decade by a statesmanship incapable even now in the midst of its fearful havoc of understanding the extent of its own mischief.

In 1944, even during the grave time of war, Oklahoma's Governor Walter Kerr, in delivering the Democratic keynote address, went to extraordinary lengths to inspire enthusiasm for the party in office:

Our aim is complete and speedy victory. Our goal is a just and abiding peace. Our promise to our world at peace is responsibility and cooperation. . . . To give these modern Bourbons, these Republican leaders, control of the nation for the next four years would bring about the certain return of 1932.

The keynote addresses of recent years have been equally flamboyant in their praise of the party before which they are delivered and in their denunciation of the opposition. It is difficult to imagine a broad cross section of Americans watching a televised broadcast of such an address unless they felt a strong sense of identification with the party. Actually, television coverage of the national conventions may change the style of future keynote addresses. Instead of being directed to loyal party followers, the addresses may become more sober attempts to marshal broad support for a party throughout the country.

But there was little evidence that in the 1988 conventions the keynote addresses had changed their extremely partisan and exaggerated flavor. For the Democrats, Texas treasurer Ann Richards enthralled her partisan audience with a witty speech that skewered the soon-to-be nominated Republican candidate George Bush and his party. She told the delegates:

We're not going to have the America that we want until we elect leaders who are going to tell the truth. Not most days—but every day.
Leaders who don't forget what they don't want to remember.

And, for eight straight years George Bush hasn't displayed the slightest interest in anything we care about.

And now that he is after a job that he can't get appointed to, he's like Columbus discovering America. He's found child care. He's found education.

Poor George. He can't help it—he was born with a silver foot in his mouth.

The Republican keynoter in 1988, New Jersey Governor Thomas Kean, accused the Democrats of being out of touch and of not telling the truth to the American people. Moreover, raising an issue that would become prominent in the upcoming campaign, he accused Michael Dukakis of being unpatriotic. He told the delegates:

You see this flag behind me, of red, white and blue?
  To us, that symbolizes the land of the free and the home of the brave.
  Well, you know, their media consultants in Atlanta said they didn't think those colors looked too good on television.
  So they changed that red, they changed it to pink, and they took that blue and they changed it to azure, and that white, that became eggshell.
  Well, I don't know about you, but I believe Americans, Democrat and Republican alike, have no use for pastel patriotism.

Party platforms. Although political party leaders accept the maxim that party platforms are made to run into office on, not to stand and govern on, the provisions of the platform are considered a deadly serious matter by the various groups within and without each party. Candidates struggle to have their proposals put into the platform as a symbol of their power within the party. And presidents do attempt to secure the enactment of platform planks they support. Platforms, however, are more a general statement of the philosophies of parties than a concrete guide for presidential and congressional actions.

The platform committees of the parties are conglomerates of the state and local party organizations. Prior to the conventions informal "hearings" are held, in Washington and at other locations throughout the country, to solicit the views of various party groups on proposed platform planks. In the party with an incumbent president up for reelection, the White House usually is the dominant force in shaping the overall platform.

Because each of the parties is essentially an umbrella organization—a confederation of separate and independent state and local parties and of a wide variety of interest groups—party platforms must reflect broad compromises on most issues of public policy. But platforms may at times take definite stands on issues that are controversial within the party, even causing party revolts. Because platforms reflect broad party forces, and because the parties still have different compositions and therefore in the broadest sense different ideologies in some areas—particularly in their contrasting views on the proper role of government in such spheres as regulation of the economy, economic stimulation, health insurance, and welfare programs, generally—the platforms of the two parties differ. The Republicans support private initiative; the Democrats tend to favor a larger role for the national government, reflecting in a modified form the continuation of the philosophy of Franklin D. Roosevelt's New Deal.

The Republican and Democratic party platforms in 1988 continued to differ sharply as they had in the past. The conservative wing of the Republicans wanted to boost its presidential candidates in party primaries in 1992 and 1996 by making the 1988 platform unequivocally conservative. They succeeded in replicating their platform triumphs in 1980 and 1984 through planks that continued to support tax reduction, defense spending increases, and, on the social issues, advocacy of school prayer and opposition to abortion.

The Democrats had more difficulty agreeing on their platform, especially because of internal differences between the nominee, Massachusetts Governor Michael Dukakis, and the even more liberal black leader Jesse Jackson. Several months of platform negotiations before the 1988 Democratic National Convention began yielded a compromise between the Dukakis and Jackson camps. Dukakis wanted the party to display a more conservative image than the Jackson forces would accept. Dukakis knew that he would have to appeal to the broader electorate to win in November, requiring him to be more conservative than liberal activists wanted. For Dukakis the party platform was the place to begin. But Jackson, knowing the symbolic importance of the platform for his political credibility, wanted to be able to say that he had had an important influence on it. Jackson succeeded in changing the tone of the platform to make it more liberal.

The nomination ritual. About midway through a convention the nomination ritual begins, starting with nominating and seconding speeches for the candidates. "Favorite sons," candidates popular in particular states, are often placed in nomination along with more serious candidates. While the content of all nominating speeches is essentially the same, heaping praise upon the candidate nominated, the identity of the nominator is an important symbolic gesture to the convention, a reflection of the candidate's support among certain factions of the party. And quantity counts at least as much as quality. The more nominating speeches a candidate can solicit, the more symbolic support they represent. For this reason, a varying number of seconding speeches follow the main nominating speech.

When all the nominating speeches have ended (and they often seem endless) the balloting for the presidential candidates begins. As the roll call of the states is made, the public drama of the convention, if there is to be any, begins.

The balloting ritual. The development of presidential primaries and caucus-convention systems for the selection of delegates, most of whom are then bound to vote for particular candidates, has contributed to the more routine nature of convention balloting. The drama has been removed from the convention floor to the preconvention battles over delegates. Usually, the only excitement that occurs during the balloting is over which state will "push the candidate over the top," that is, give the candidate a majority of the convention delegates. A state may "pass" when its name is called in order to be recognized at a crucial point later in the balloting (so that it can be recorded as the state whose vote gave the candidate a majority). A state may also pass during a close contest in order to increase its potential political clout for one candidate or the other at a later stage in the balloting.

While first-ballot victories are commonplace, some conventions have exhibited high drama on the convention floor during the balloting process. In the dramatic 1924 Democratic convention, it took 103 ballots over a period of nine days before John W. Davis was nominated as the Democratic candidate—only to be overwhelmingly defeated in the general election by Calvin Coolidge, who received 54 percent of the popular vote and 71 percent of the electoral vote. Since then most Democratic candidates have been nominated on the first ballot. Exceptions have been Franklin D. Roosevelt, who won the nomination of 1932 after four ballots, and Adlai Stevenson, who was nominated in 1952 on the third ballot. The one-ballot tradition has generally held for the Republicans as well, although in 1948 it took Thomas E. Dewey three ballots to secure the nomination, and in 1940 the nomination of Wendell Willkie required six ballots.

The advent of grass-roots presidential nominating processes in both parties has largely taken the drama out of the balloting ritual and pushed it back to the primary and caucus season preceding the national conventions. By the time the conventions meet, one candidate has usually emerged with a significant plurality or majority of delegate votes. The front-runner predictably captures the nomination. Early-convention delegate shifts to put the leader over the top are responsible for about the only drama left as the conventions get under way.

Selection of a vice-presidential candidate. Once the presidential candidate has been selected, a running mate, or vice-presidential candidate, must be chosen. The Constitution places an insurmountable obstacle in the path of having both the presidential and vice-presidential candidate from the same state, for it provides that under such circumstances the electoral vote from that state may not be cast for both candidates. Ordinarily, the presidential candidate merely chooses someone from another region of the country or from another political faction within the party who he feels will strengthen the ticket. Often the presidential candidate names a person who has proved to be a worthy opponent within the party and can guarantee substantial support at the ballot box. The presidential nominee's choice is rarely questioned, and the approval of the convention delegates is usually unanimous.

Examples of vice-presidential nominations to balance the ticket and strengthen it include the nomination of Lyndon B. Johnson in 1960. Johnson gained southern support for John F. Kennedy, who was not popular in the South. Hubert Humphrey in 1964 was placed on the Democratic ticket to garner liberal support. After former President Gerald Ford declined to become a vice-presidential candidate in 1980, Ronald Reagan chose George Bush as his running mate to appeal to moderate Republicans.

The relative lack of interest in the choice of a vice-presidential candidate, and the fact that the choice is entirely within the discretion of the presidential nominee, reflects the minor role of the vice-presidency in the political system. Occasionally there are stirrings over the lack of party involvement in the selection of the vice-presidential nominee, but tradition continues to prevail.

While the presidential nominee's choice of a running mate is pro forma, and usually without controversy, occasionally the choice raises party hackles. In 1988, for example, Republican nominee George Bush chose Indiana Senator Dan Quayle to be his running mate. Quayle had been a relatively effective senator, but once Quayle was in the national limelight the media dug into his background mer-

cilessly, castigating him for alleged use of family influence to avoid the draft during the Vietnam War. As the campaign got under way, Quayle's inexperience in national politics began to show, and although Bush aides carefully guided the vice-presidential candidate, his political gaffes, always front-page material, never failed to embarrass the Bush campaign. Democratic nominee Michael Dukakis, on the other hand, played traditional party politics in making his vice-presidential choice, Texas Senator Lloyd Bentsen. Bentsen, a conservative Democrat, had a distinguished career in the Senate, and Dukakis hoped, fruitlessly as it turned out, that the Texan would bring his state and possibly other southern states into the Democratic fold in November.

The Function of Conventions

Originally, conventions were developed to expand the rank-and-file participation of party members in the process of nominating candidates for the presidency. To a considerable extent, regular party members now preselect presidential candidates through the primary-caucus convention system. This has reduced the power of party bosses to choose the nominees. It has also shifted the major function of party conventions from nominating to providing a forum for the reconciliation of intraparty disputes. Not just the convention itself but all the attendant procedures and ceremonies necessary to sustain it provide important arenas in which party differences can be worked out. Conventions help to knit together the diverse strands of the party. Although now changed in form and function, conventions continue to play a vital part in maintaining the two-party system.

POLITICAL CAMPAIGNING

"Advertising," according to the journalist Joe McGinniss, "is a con game." And, he adds, "it is not surprising then that politicians and advertising men should have discovered one another, once they recognized that the citizen did not so much vote for a candidate as make a psychological purchase of him." This quote will undoubtedly impress readers as a highly cynical view of the political process. But political campaigning has become cynical and oriented to images and not to substance. Both in the marathon for the nomination and then in the final race for the presidency, campaigns are geared to the projection of a pleasing image of the personality and style of the candidate.

Issues are, of course, always included in political campaigning, but they are chosen selectively to capture votes; the more controversial issues are played down and even avoided, if possible, by the candidates.

Political campaigning, especially at the presidential level, is a physically grueling and very expensive undertaking. Walter Mondale withdrew from the pre-1976 convention primary campaign with the statement that he was not willing to go to the ultimate extreme to prove himself a worthy candidate. However, he indicated his support for the process—the mental and physical obstacle course of the primary campaign (and presumably of general election campaigns as well): "Basically, I found that I do not have the overwhelming desire to be President, which is essential for the type of campaign that is required. I don't think anyone should be President who is not willing to go through fire."[5] In 1984 Mondale decided that he was ready to go through the fire, and he won the Democratic party presidential nomination but lost resoundingly in the fall election to Ronald Reagan.

The extraordinary physical and emotional strains of political campaigning, particularly presidential campaigning, make it virtually impossible for candidates to concentrate on substantive issues of public policy, even if they had been inclined to do so before they

(Copyright © Walt Kelly Estate. Reprinted by permission.)

Ghost to Ghost Network
Is it possible for a candidate's image to be entirely molded by public relations techniques in a campaign?

entered the race. At the presidential level, and even below it, political campaigning can be equivalent to a drug experience—a constant high in which the ego of the candidate is continuously being stimulated, producing a sense of exhilaration that becomes an end in itself. As Elizabeth Drew has pointed out:

Running for the presidency appears to have an impact on the ego that is unlike that of any other endeavor. Homo candidatus might be said to undergo a unique human experience. . . .They feel an extraordinary exhilaration in making the race—a great lift, an unparalleled expansion of self-esteem. It is as if the limits on ambition and ego were removed.[6]

Because running for the presidency is an ego trip without any parallel in politics, many candidates show up to enter the race even though they rationally know they have little

[5]*Congressional Quarterly Weekly Report*, Vol. 34, No. 5 (January 31, 1976), p. 225.

[6]Elizabeth Drew, "Running," *The New Yorker*, December 1, 1975, p. 54.

chance of winning it. A credible showing in presidential primaries and caucuses, however, always enhances a candidate's position in the party, which is an important goal in itself.

The Lure of Political Campaigning

Despite the physical exhaustion and emotional stresses of political campaigning, both candidates and their staffs seem to enjoy the process immensely. Presidential campaigns in particular are exciting for all concerned.

The *campaign staffs* of political candidates are an integral and important part of the campaigning process. These staffs congregate around candidates that they feel will be successful, the candidate's success being their success. At all levels of politics, and particularly at the presidential level, the campaign staffs consist of public relations advisers, press aides, advance forces who prepare the way for the candidate's speaking engagements and public appearances (making hotel and plane bookings and generally making certain that the candidate is where he is supposed to be at any particular time), schedulers, and a host of other assistants.

For each day of the campaign the candidate's staff prepares a schedule that outlines how the candidate is to spend every minute of time from morning until late at night. Often the candidate seems to be little more than the puppet of those on the campaign staff, a vehicle for and an extension of their egos and ideas. They program the candidate at least as much as he or she influences them. Everything is done for the candidate, including the writing of speeches. The leadership potential of candidates can be projected to some extent by judging the caliber of the persons who congregate around them, for inevitably the campaign staffs of candidates follow them into office.

Traditionally, democratic theory has posited that the purpose of political campaigning is to present contrasting party positions to the electorate so that a meaningful choice can be made between alternative policies. We have already seen that the widespread use of television, and the growth of a public relations industry, have made the image of the candidate as important if not more so than the issues he or she presents. But quite apart from the issues, political campaigning can serve as a valuable test of the ability of the candidates themselves to meet and deal with a variety of intense pressures—pressures that will follow them into office. Campaigns, then, in addition to presenting policy choices to the electorate, can reveal character traits that may be very important to effective leadership.

How accurately do modern political campaigns disclose relevant character traits of politicians? Do successful campaigns demand the same qualities as successful political leadership? At the presidential level there are similarities between effective leadership in the White House and successful campaigning, but the constituencies of the president and those of a presidential candidate differ. Effective presidential leadership requires good relations with Congress and an understanding of the bureaucracy, the balance of power in international relations, and, in particular, the limits of power. As Richard Neustadt has pointed out, the power of the president is "the power to persuade."[7]

Presidents must learn to use the reputation for power in the White House to persuade congressional leaders to follow them, bureaucrats to implement their proposals, and foreign nations to follow their lead. The real question is not so much whether the president can exercise effective leadership in the White House, but whether the president's staff has the political sophistication to deal with the highly complex Washington and international power relationships. Campaigns tend to prepare presidents and their staffs more for the public relations and image-building dimensions of political leadership than for the more

---

[7]Richard E. Neustadt, *Presidential Power* (New York: Wiley, 1960), p. 32.

subtle problems of persuasion that arise in confrontation with the established centers of power in the government.

The expansion of the campaigning process has its most serious consequences in reference to the presidency. The problems that arise in campaigning at the lower levels of politics are a microcosm of those that exist in presidential politics. As the presidential campaigning process has been vastly expanded to include the lengthy and strenuous preconvention primary-caucus phase, the campaign mentality has become ever more firmly embedded in candidates and their staffs.

When Jimmy Carter reached the White House in 1977, neither he nor his staff was able to make the sharp transition from campaigning to leadership. Not only did the entirely new constituencies in government, as well as in the international arena, with which Carter had to deal take him by surprise, but his approaches to them reflected his prior emphasis upon image building and appeals to the public rather than upon serious negotiations involving power trade-offs. Once in the White House, his campaign staff was soon to learn that while it had been easy enough to make superficial promises during the election campaign, changing the policies and practices of entrenched Washington interests was another matter entirely.

President Ronald Reagan made the transition from campaign to Washington politics far more smoothly and astutely than Carter. The new President recognized the intricacies and often arcane ways of Washington politics. He courted Capitol Hill, the city's power establishment, interest groups, and even the Supreme Court. "Hail the conquering hero," was the title of a *Newsweek* story describing Reagan's first visit to the capital after his election. The President-elect made it clear that he was going to work with Capitol Hill, not against it, in attempting to change the face of the federal government and its responsibilities. Like all presidents, however, he did not hesitate to go to the people over the heads of

Congress when he felt that the legislature was undermining his program. His campaign style continued to be an important part of his political arsenal in coping with the Washington political establishment.

President George Bush also made a smooth transition from political campaigning to presidential governance. He had years of Washington experience even before he assumed the vice-president's office in 1981. He kept not only experienced members of his own vice-presidential staff but also many of the most experienced members of the Reagan team, including in particular former Chief of Staff and Treasury Secretary James Baker, whom Bush made secretary of state. Bush did, however, choose a Washington outsider, former New Hampshire Governor John Sununu, to be his White House chief of staff.

Campaigning and Governance

The expansion of the primary-caucus process in the nomination of presidential candidates means that political campaigning ability is emphasized over other attributes of political leadership in the selection of candidates. In 1952 Adlai Stevenson was a handpicked candidate of the party leaders and was backed by President Truman. Although doubts were expressed as to his ability to win, he nevertheless was viewed as a proven political leader of high quality (among other offices he held was the governorship of Illinois). A person such as Stevenson would probably never be picked through the current presidential selection process, nor would he be likely to choose to "go through fire" to win the presidential nomination. The extraordinary physical requirements of present-day political campaigning might also have eliminated from the presidency a person such as Franklin D. Roosevelt, who was confined to a wheelchair. This is conjecture, but it is used illustratively to raise the question of whether an expansion of the grass-roots campaigning process at all levels is really desirable in terms of the ultimate objective—which is not just democratic responsiveness but effective governmental leadership.

Campaign Expenditures

Political campaigning has become increasingly expensive over the years. Campaign costs have inflated to a point where direct and indirect expenditures in a presidential campaign are in the hundreds of millions of dollars. Nor are Senate and House campaigns cheap: Senate candidates commonly spend anywhere from $2 to $10 million, while candidates running for the House not infrequently incur costs approaching $1 million. Political consultants, high-priced staffers, and the high cost of media advertising, particularly on television, are major contributors to the high costs of campaigning.

In 1971 Congress passed the Federal Election Campaign Practices Act, which was designed to tighten the reporting requirements for contributors and to control expenditures for political campaigns. The law went into effect on April 7, 1972, and replaced the Corrupt Practices Act of 1925. Congress amended and strengthened the 1971 election law in 1974 and 1976, placing stricter reporting requirements and limits on candidates and contributors alike. The 1974 amendments were passed in direct response to revelations during the Watergate era that the Republican Committee to Reelect the President had not so subtly demanded contributions from a wide range of corporations, sometimes threatening governmental retribution if the funds were not forthcoming. Conservative and liberal politicians, including New York Senator James Buckley and Daniel Patrick Moynihan, who captured Buckley's seat in 1976, challenged the legislation as an unconstitutional interference in elections in the case of *Buckley v. Valeo* in 1976.[8] The Court upheld the following pro-

visions of the law: those that set limits on how much individuals and political committees might contribute to candidates, those that provided for the public financing of presidential-primary and general-election campaigns, and those that required disclosure of campaign contributions of more than $100 and expenditures of more than $10.

However, the 1974 law's *spending* limits on individuals and groups, including limits on the use of personal funds by political candidates, were ruled an unconstitutional violation of the First Amendment right of free expression and association. The Court also held that the Federal Election Commission, which Congress had created to administer the law, was a violation of the principle of separation of powers because four of its six members were appointed by Congress. The appointment power is an executive function, the Court maintained. The statute being ruled in part unconstitutional on the very eve of the 1976 presidential primary campaigns produced a quandary that Congress resolved by passing a revised law on May 3 to meet the Court's objections to the 1974 act. Funds continued to be held up, however, until President Gerald Ford finally agreed to sign the new campaign finance law on May 11, 1976.

The 1976 campaign finance law amended the 1974 statute by making the Federal Election Commission a six-member body appointed by the president and confirmed by the Senate. The new law also removed the spending limits that had been placed upon House, Senate, and presidential campaigns as well as on party nominating conventions, although it did retain spending limits for presidential candidates who accepted public funds.

The rise of political action committees (PACs). Ironically, the same campaign finance laws that were passed in 1971, 1974, and 1976 to restrict the influence of money in politics actually encouraged the creation of thousands of political action committees (PACs) by corporations, professional groups, citizens' orga-

---

[8]424 U.S. 1 (1976).

nizations, labor unions, agricultural groups, and every interest group that sought to influence the political process. The campaign finance legislation, while controlling and limiting campaign contributions, made PACs a legitimate conduit to channel voluntary contributions to political candidates from corporate employees, labor union members, professionals, and others. Moreover, no limitations were placed upon the "indirect" expenditures of political action committees in behalf of candidates.

In the 1987–1988 election season, for example, presidential, Senate, and House candidates received many millions of dollars in independent contributions. (See Figure 8.1.) Direct PAC contributions to candidates, however, are far greater than indirect PAC spending in behalf of candidates. (See Table 8.6.)

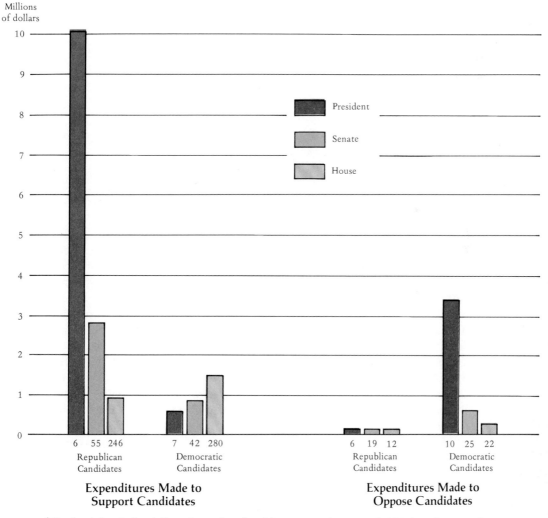

INDEPENDENT EXPENDITURES IN 1987-88 *

Millions of dollars

President
Senate
House

6   55   246   7   42   280   6   19   12   10   25   22
Republican   Democratic   Republican   Democratic
Candidates   Candidates   Candidates   Candidates

Expenditures Made to   Expenditures Made to
Support Candidates   Oppose Candidates

* Numbers below the bars indicate the number of candidates supported or opposed with independent expenditures.

(Federal Election Commission, *Record*, Vol. 16, No. 8, August 1989)

FIGURE 8.1

TABLE 8.6 CONTRIBUTIONS AND INDEPENDENT EXPENDITURES BY TYPE OF PAC, 1987–1988

Type of PAC	Number[a]	Receipts[b]	Contributed to candidates[c]		Independent expenditures[d]	
			Amount	Percentage	Amount	Percentage
Corporate	1,613	$ 96,429,934	$ 56,254,449	58	$ 54,368	0.1
Labor	253	75,966,281	35,546,980	47	188,544	0.2
Trade/member-ship/health	626	86,406,330	41,210,121	48	3,893,403	5
Cooperative	51	4,632,632	2,740,732	59	4,550	0.1
Corporations without stock	121	8,634,276	3,316,674	38	288,450	3
Nonconnected	623	97,433,295	20,338,460	21	15,783,956	16
Total	3,287	369,502,748	159,407,416	43	20,213,271	5

[a]As of December 31, 1988. The numbers shown are those PACs that actually made contributions.

[b]Adjusted for money transferred between affiliated committees.

[c]Figures include contributions to all federal candidates, including those who did not run for office during 1987–1988.

[d]Independent expenditures include money spent on behalf of candidates and against candidates. Some independent expenditures made in 1987 pertained to candidates for previous elections.

Source: Harold W. Stanley and Richard G. Niemi, *Vital Statistics on American Politics,* 2d ed. (Washington, D.C.: Congressional Quarterly Press, 1990), p. 164. Reprinted with permission from Congressional Quarterly, Inc.

While PACs became fashionable in the 1970s, they had not been unknown in the past. Labor unions formed the first PACs, the most famous of which was the Committee on Political Education (COPE) of the AFL-CIO, founded in 1965. COPE received voluntary funds from union members, donating them to the candidates it favored. Corporations did not see the need to create separate PACs, for those that were politically active gave money secretly to political campaigns, often in violation of the Corrupt Practices Act of 1925, as in the corporate contributions made to Richard M. Nixon's 1968 and 1972 campaigns. When the Watergate revelations threatened to prevent even voluntary contributions from corporations and labor unions, the AFL-CIO lobbied vigorously to have political action committees like its own preserved in the new campaign laws of the 1970s. The labor unions enlisted corporate support for their position, only to find later that once PACs had been authorized to make campaign contributions the corporations far outdistanced the unions in establishing new PACs.

Political action committee contributions to congressional candidates have greatly increased over the years. (See Tables 8.7 and 8.8.) Donations have expanded from $22.6 million in 1976 to over $349 million in 1988. Although any PAC is limited under the law to $10,000 in direct contributions to any one candidate for primary ($5,000) and general election ($5,000) campaigns, the cumulative effect of PAC contributions can be profound. For example, each corporate PAC may give only $5,000 to a candidate, and while one such contribution by itself might not sway the legislator's vote, a score of such business contributions will undoubtedly have an impact on

TABLE 8.7   PACs: RECEIPTS, EXPENDITURES, CONTRIBUTIONS, 1975–1988

Election cycle[a]	Adjusted receipts[b] (millions)	Adjusted expenditures[b] (millions)	Contributions to congressional candidates (millions)	Percentage contributed to congressional candidates
1975–1976	$ 54.0	$ 52.9	$ 22.6	42
1977–1978	80.0	77.4	34.1	43
1979–1980	137.7	131.2	55.2	40
1981–1982	199.5	190.2	83.6	42
1983–1984	288.7	266.8	105.3	36
1985–1986	353.4	340.0	132.7	38
1987–1988	369.5	349.6	151.3	41

[a]Data cover January 1 of the odd-numbered year to December 31 of the even-numbered year.

[b]Adjusted receipts and expenditures exclude funds transferred between affiliated committees.

the representative's behavior. The same can be said for concentrated labor union contributions. Because PACs want to get the most for their dollars, they generally donate to incumbents, especially in the House, rather than taking a risk on challengers. Key committee chairmen are singled out for special attention. The protection of congressional incumbents is in fact a major result of the growing financial strength of PACs.

While business and other interest groups, such as the National Rifle Association and the National Association of Realtors, outspend labor unions in making direct contributions to candidates, the unions outspend business in using money from their treasuries to sway their members politically. Money spent for "communications" between employer and employees and between union leaders and union members, for or against political can-

TABLE 8.8   SPENDING BY TYPE OF PAC, 1977–1988 (MILLIONS)

Election cycle	Corporate	Labor	Trade/ membership/ health	Non-connected	Other connected[a]	Total
1977–1978	$15.2	$18.6	$23.8	$ 17.4	$ 2.4	$ 77.4
1979–1980	31.4	25.1	32.0	38.6	4.0	131.2
1981–1982	43.3	34.8	41.9	64.3	5.8	190.2
1983–1984	59.2	47.5	54.0	97.4	8.7	266.8
1985–1986	79.3	57.9	73.3	118.4	11.1	340.0
1987–1988	89.0	70.4	81.6	97.0	11.6	349.6

Note: Adjusted expenditures exclude transfers of funds between affiliated committees. Detail may not add to totals because of rounding.

[a]This category combines the FEC categories of cooperatives and corporations without stock.

Source: Harold W. Stanley and Richard G. Niemi, *Vital Statistics on American Politics,* 2d ed. (Washington, D.C.: Congressional Quarterly Press, 1990), p. 163. Reprinted with permission from Congressional Quarterly, Inc.

Ever since 1974 amendments to the Federal Election Campaign Act enabled corporations to form Political Action Committees, a chorus of critics has moaned that PACs are the instrument of wicked businessmen out to buy legislators and even presidents. This chorus reached a crescendo just before the recent Congressional election.

One legislator has said PACs give rise to "the politics of intimidation." And a prominent newscaster told his TV listeners that PACs "can make politicians and break them...As the PACs know, the politicians may not have a price, but the office does."

What's most striking about all this furor is that it arose only after business corporations were permitted to form PACs. Never mind that the first Political Action Committee was formed in 1943 by organized labor's CIO, and that PACs organized by a large number of unions are among the largest political contributors today. Never mind also that environmentalists—often industry's most vocal critics—can and do contribute to, say, the Friends of the Earth PAC, or the Environmental Political Action Committee of Southern California.

The basic complaint against corporate PACs—that they enable big business to sway elections and legislation with big money—is patently spurious. It ignores two simple facts:

• Corporations are not by law permitted to fund PACs—*employees do, voluntarily.* Just as voluntarily, we might add, as union members give money to labor PACs; or farmers, physicians, and dentists to PACs of their own. They do so because they have a mutual point of view and want to help elect public officials who share that viewpoint. They see nothing wrong in such participation in the democratic process, and neither do we.

• No PAC—company or otherwise—may by federal law contribute more than $5,000 to any one Congressional candidate in a single election. That's hardly enough in these days of costly campaigns to "buy" 30 seconds on TV, let alone an election.

Now that election furor has died down, we think it's time to consider these additional facts about PACs:

• In broadest terms, an attack on the principle of Political Action Committees is really an attack on the First Amendment guarantee of free expression. PACs, after all, are simply a way in which individuals may participate more effectively in the political arena than they could on their own.

• While PACs organized by business firms have increased numerically, not one of

didates, is not limited by the campaign laws. Such expenditures are in the "indirect" category, and although they must be reported they are not restricted.

The debate over campaign financing continues. (See Box 8.1.) A major argument of Common Cause and other groups supporting the public financing of elections is that it removes the influence of contributors, particularly large contributors, in politics. Common Cause seemed to imply that offices can be bought, and that those who make large con-

tributions to political candidates will have undue influence over them. While Congress was willing in 1974 to support public financing of presidential elections, it has never been able to agree on the financing of its own campaigns. This may seem incongruous, but congressional incumbents usually have a tremendous advantage over challengers in raising campaign funds, an advantage they do not wish to relinquish through a public financing system that would allocate money equally to them and to legitimate challengers.

them is on the Federal Election Commission's list of the 10 largest donors during the 1981–82 campaign cycle. In fact, their total share of disbursements to candidates in the 1980 election was only 23.6 percent of campaign contributions by all PACs combined.

• During 18 months leading up to the 1982 election, total corporate PAC contributions of $23.1 million were surpassed by the $39 million spent by unaffiliated PACs and the $23.2 million disbursed by trade/health/membership PACs. Labor PACs contributed $17.7 million.

• Far from being worrisome, PACs are actually among the most effective ways in which the man or woman on the street—union member, company employee or whoever—can play a more active role of citizenship. The alternative to such voluntary group participation, usually proposed by PAC critics, calls on the government to finance election campaigns out of federal tax revenues. But such funding would impose an additional burden on taxpayers and, at the same time, deprive them of much say in how the funds would be apportioned among candidates. (Contributors to PACs, by contrast, can indicate which candidates should get their money.) We feel strongly that President Reagan is right to op-

pose further government financing of campaigns.

When you cut through all the anti-PAC rhetoric, it becomes obvious that PAC opponents really don't want the voices of average citizens to be amplified. Their motive is to keep the reins of power in the hands of politicians who think they know what's best for the great mass and wish to brook as little interference as possible.

Frankly, we're not only bored with such elitism, but outraged by the false characterization of business-organized Political Action Committees as spenders of shareholders' money to exert undue pressure on the workings of democratic government. The money, as we've said, is volunteered by individual employees, and no PAC, business or otherwise, has the clout to exert undue influence on any official.

Ask yourself this: what's wrong with American citizens organizing to make their choices better known in Washington? The answer, obviously, is nothing.

Corporations are sensitive to criticisms of the growing influence of their political action committees.

TYPES OF ELECTIONS

Once the voter enters the voting booth, the *campaign* is over and the *election* has begun. It is the election process that can give real meaning to democracy, because it is through the election that people can express their political hopes and dissatisfactions to government. Without the opportunity to choose among real alternatives, however, such expressions have little meaning. There is certainly a more mean-

ingful choice in a multiparty ballot, as in the elections of France, the United States, or Japan, than in the one-party ballot that has always existed in the Soviet Union, although Gorbachev promised to make the party system more competitive as the decade of the 1990s began. It is the element of choice in elections that makes for one of the important differences between a constitutional democracy on the one hand and an authoritarian form of government on the other. In the United States, of course, voters do not have to show

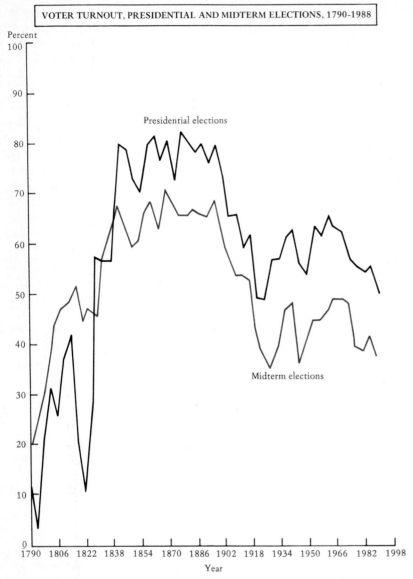

VOTER TURNOUT, PRESIDENTIAL AND MIDTERM ELECTIONS, 1790-1988

FIGURE 8.2
(From Harold W. Stanley and Richard G. Niemi, *Vital Statistics on American Politics*, 2d ed. [Washington, D.C.:
Congressional Quarterly Press, 1990], p. 78. Reprinted with permission from Congressional Quarterly, Inc.)

up on election day. Voter turnout reached its peak in the nineteenth century and began to decline after 1886 with only a few short-lived upturns. (See Figure 8.2.) Presidential elections have drawn the greatest turnout, and voting in midterm congressional elections has been dismal in the twentieth century. (See Fig-

ure 8.2.) Whether or not a low voter turnout reflects a healthy or unhealthy polity is a matter of debate. Some argue that the political apathy that low turnout suggests reflects nothing more than satisfaction with government. Others, however, believe that broad failure to vote means that a large portion of the electorate is alienated and a potential time bomb.

Effect of the Ballot

Two types of ballots are used in the United States—*single-choice* and *multiple-choice*. The states individually decide which form of ballot they prefer. Both types are marked in secret by the voters, and the votes are then placed in ballot boxes or are tabulated by voting machines.

Single-choice ballots. On a single-choice ballot each party's candidates for various offices are listed in a column, or party "ticket." Voters have the option of voting for all the party's candidates, from president to county clerk, usually by simply pulling a lever under the party's symbol.

Multiple-choice ballots. Multiple-choice ballots require a greater effort from the voter than single-choice ballots. Each candidate is listed on the ballot with other candidates for the same office. Although each candidate's party is indicated, the voter must search for this information and then vote for each separately. This form of ballot is more flexible but is often thought to be more confusing. On the other hand, it encourages the voter to switch from one party to another as he or she votes.

Whether the ballot is single-choice or multiple-choice, the party must gear its campaign to take this into account. Where the single-choice ballot is used, the campaigner will try to identify more closely with the party. Because a strong candidate will sometimes "carry" the rest of the slate, or ticket, with him, the party is likely to concentrate the campaign on popular candidates. Where a multiple-choice ballot is used, each candidate must stand on his or her own campaign and impress the voters with his or her own abilities. The voter, in this case, is more likely to vote on familiarity with the names and records of candidates than solely for the party.

Essentially, the results of elections reflect popular attitudes toward governmental policies, personalities, and parties. Changes in the electorate's attitudes should produce changes in the outcomes of elections. Each election is different from every other. For example, the Democratic party landslide in the 1932 presidential election was profoundly different from the Democratic party's victory in 1960, when John Kennedy "squeaked" into the White House with less than a 1 percent margin over his opponent in the popular vote. The issues were different, the electorate was different, and the elections were therefore different.

Classification of Elections

Members of the Center for Political Studies at the University of Michigan, as well as the late political scientist V. O. Key, Jr., developed a classification of elections that is useful in analyzing how the electoral system works and what the long-range results are. These researchers feel that presidential elections not only have the immediate effect of electing a president for four years but also show trends and may indicate changes in the electorate's thinking about politics in general. On the basis of such indications, researchers have divided elections into four categories: (1) maintaining elections, (2) critical, or realigning, elections, (3) deviating elections, and (4) reinstating elections.

Maintaining elections. The type of election that occurs most frequently is the *maintaining election*. In this type the electorate, voting according to previously established voting patterns, retains the party already in power. As a result the balance of the parties in government remains about the same as it was before the election.

The fact that most American elections have fallen into this category has produced a pattern of political continuity. A series of maintaining elections over a few decades would indicate a lack of drastic changes within the electorate and the government. Maintaining elections mean that most voters accept the status quo and go along with the political party in power.

There have been several eras of maintain

ing elections—one immediately following the Civil War, one at the turn of the century, and another during the 1920s—during which Republican control was virtually uninterrupted. Similarly, after 1932 the Democratic victories of 1936, 1940, 1944, and 1948 can all be categorized as maintaining elections.

Critical or realigning elections. When voters diverge from their ordinary partisan loyalties, elections become more crucial. This is true whether the party in office retains its power or not. *Critical elections* are those in which there are lasting shifts in the fundamental political thinking of a large portion of the voting public.

By examining a few trend-setting districts in New England, V. O. Key, Jr., concluded that the elections of 1896 and 1928 were critical because new permanent partisan alignments were formed. In these years the voting in the sample New England districts forecasted what was going to happen in the rest of the country in subsequent elections.

In 1896 there was a decided shift of New England voters, dissatisfied with Democratic President Grover Cleveland, to the Republican William McKinley. This shift, which became nationwide, solidified behind a succession of Republican presidents and lasted until 1932, broken only by Woodrow Wilson's two terms, which began in 1913. Although most people consider the 1932 election critical because it changed the party in power, regrouping of party alignments had actually begun to take place in New England by 1928. Working-class and urban voters had switched to the Democratic party four years before the first Roosevelt campaign. Whether 1928 or 1932 is taken as the turning point, there is no doubt that the election of Franklin D. Roosevelt in 1932 reflected a realignment among voters in favor of the Democrats. As it turned out, that realignment was a long-term one that has lasted into the 1980s as far more registered voters continue to identify with the Democratic than the Republican party. (See Figure 8.3.)

Deviating elections. Unlike a critical election, a *deviating election* is one in which temporary shifts take place in the electorate as a result of temporary issues. The deviation in voting is not the result of a fundamental change in political thinking. A deviating election is most likely to occur when a popular figure is running for the presidency.

The Center for Political Studies has established that the Eisenhower victories of 1952 and 1956 fall into the deviating category. The personality of Dwight D. Eisenhower was a powerful factor in swaying voters to vote Republican. In addition, the voters had been dissatisfied with the Democratic party's performance during the second Truman administration. The issue of corruption in the federal government was raised, and the Korean War had become increasingly unpopular. Eisenhower's promise to end the hostilities won him many votes.

All these issues, it should be noted, were temporary, and no permanent political realignment was established. This was evidenced by the fact that although the president was a Republican, Congress returned to the control of a Democratic majority in 1954 after Eisenhower's first two years in office. The voters did not change their basic partisan loyalties in state or congressional elections.

Ronald Reagan's victory in 1980 raised considerable discussion concerning whether or not the election was critical or deviating. Opinion seemed to be divided about whether or not the Republican party now had a sufficiently solid base to win the presidency and congressional elections on a fairly consistent basis in the future. Democrats, however, remained in a clear majority among registered voters, and in the population as a whole they held a 43-to-27 percent lead over the Republicans even after Reagan became president. In 1980 voters split their tickets, voting for candidates of different parties on 60 percent of the ballots cast. Twenty-two percent of the voters choosing Reagan did so because they

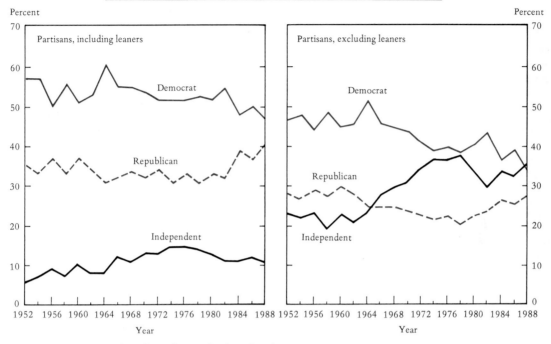

PARTISAN IDENTIFICATION, NATIONAL ELECTION STUDIES, 1952-1988

Note: "Leaners" are independents who consider themselves closer to one party.

(From Harold W. Stanley and Richard G. Niemi, *Vital Statistics on American Politics*, 2d ed. [Washington, D.C.: Congressional Quarterly Press, 1990], p. 145. Reprinted with permission from Congressional Quarterly, Inc.)

FIGURE 8.3

were dissatisfied with Jimmy Carter, and 21 percent of the Reagan voters simply felt it was time for a change. Only 12 percent of Reagan's majority voted for him because they thought he would make a better leader.[9] The "Reagan phenomenon" seemed to be based more on the candidate's personality and style than on a long-term shift by the majority of the electorate to the Republican party. Nevertheless, since 1968 at the *presidential* level only one Democrat has been elected, Jimmy Carter in 1976. While Democrats are soul-searching to find the cause, perhaps there is an emerging

Republican majority in presidential elections, but ticket-splitting and strong Democratic majorities on Capitol Hill and in many state legislatures make it impossible to pinpoint a "critical election" from 1968–1988. Widespread ticket-splitting, which reflects a decline of the importance of parties in the minds of voters, has made it increasingly difficult since 1968 to identify elections reflecting long-term shifts in party allegiance.

Reinstating elections. A *reinstating election* occurs when the electorate returns to normal voting patterns. Reinstating elections take place after deviating elections, when the temporary forces that caused the transitory shift in partisan loyalty are no longer operative.

---

[9]*George Gallup Report,* Vol. 174–184 (1980–1981), pp. 29–30.

TABLE 8.9   SPLIT DISTRICT OUTCOMES: PRESIDENTIAL AND HOUSE VOTING, 1900–1988

Year	Total number of districts[a]	Number of districts with split results[b]	Percentage of total
1900	295	10	3.4
1904	310	5	1.6
1908	314	21	6.7
1912	333	84	25.2
1916	333	35	10.5
1920	344	11	3.2
1924	356	42	11.8
1928	359	68	18.9
1932	355	50	14.1
1936	361	51	14.1
1940	362	53	14.6
1944	367	41	11.2
1948	422	90	21.3
1952	435	84	19.3
1956	435	130	29.9
1960	437	114	26.1
1964	435	145	33.3
1968	435	139	32.0
1972	435	192	44.1
1976	435	124	28.5
1980	435	143	32.8
1984	435	196	45.0
1988	435	148	34.0

[a]Before 1952 complete data are not available on every congressional district.

[b]Congressional districts carried by a presidential candidate of one party and a House candidate of another party.

Source: Harold W. Stanley and Richard G. Niemi, *Vital Statistics on American Politics*, 2d ed. (Washington, D.C.: Congressional Quarterly Press, 1990), p. 133. Reprinted with permission from Congressional Quarterly, Inc.

The election of 1960 can be classified as a reinstating election. Even John F. Kennedy's loss of a large number of votes due to his Catholicism did not keep the electorate from reinstating the Democrats after the Eisenhower years. The Center for Political Studies team concluded that

the eight-year Eisenhower period ended with no basic change in the proportions of the public who identify themselves as Republican, Democrat, or Independent. If there had been an opportunity in 1952 for the Republican Party to rewin the majority status it held prior to 1932, it failed to capitalize on it. The Democratic Party

remained the majority party, and in the 1960 election returned to the Presidency.[10]

In 1960 the Center for Political Studies estimated that the Democratic majority within the electorate was 53 to 54 percent. As long as this majority was maintained, reinstating and maintaining elections would continue to return the Democratic party to control of the government. Even Richard Nixon's victories in 1968 and 1972 did not contradict this pat-

[10]Philip E. Converse et al., "Stability and Change in 1960: A Reinstating Election," *American Political Science Review*, 55 (June 1961), p. 280.

tern; for although Nixon won the presidency, he failed to carry many Republican candidates into the Congress.

Elections and party choice. The voting habits of citizens often make it difficult to evaluate the true meaning of elections in terms of party choice. There is a clear-cut apportionment of the registered electorate among the two major parties. However, party divisions are not always reflected in electoral results because voters split their tickets, electing, for example, the president from one party and rep-

resentatives or senators from the other. Such politically eclectic voting habits make it difficult to label elections critical, deviating, or reinstating because such terms imply an underlying consistency of voting along party lines against which elections are evaluated.

Increasingly, party choice reflects a candidate's popularity and his or her personality and style rather than the views of voters on important issues of public policy. The leaders of the two major parties in this country differ fairly sharply on many important issues, but

1988 Electoral Votes by State

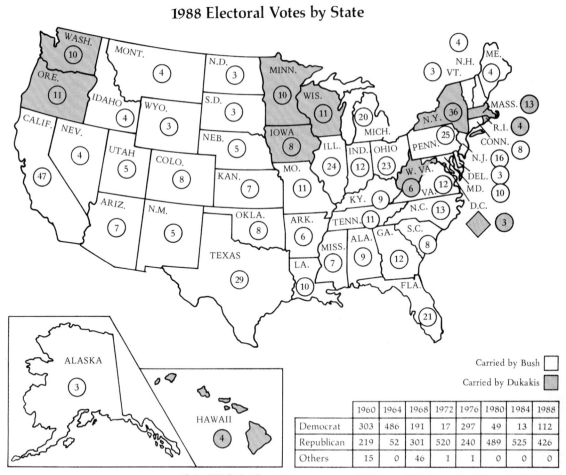

	1960	1964	1968	1972	1976	1980	1984	1988
Democrat	303	486	191	17	297	49	13	112
Republican	219	52	301	520	240	489	525	426
Others	15	0	46	1	1	0	0	0

(*Spring 1989 Guide to Current American Government* [Washington, D.C.: Congressional Quarterly, 1989], p. 94. Reprinted with permission from Congressional Quarterly, Inc.)

FIGURE 8.4

rank-and-file Republicans and Democrats do not diverge widely from one another in their views on many important public policy concerns.

Evaluation of Elections

The pluralism of American politics is reflected in several ways in the electoral system. There is a seemingly endless number of elections at periodic intervals at national, state, and local levels of government. The pluralistic character of the parties makes it virtually impossible to draw profound conclusions about political trends from electoral results. Nevertheless, political commentators and pundits of all kinds foster political speculation through their writings and columns—which is their job.

In democratic theory, elections are supposed to transmit the will of the majority to government through political parties that present meaningful policy choices to the electorate. Regardless of the effectiveness or ineffectiveness of political parties in providing an overarching rationale to explain electoral choices, elections remain essential to the vitality of the political system. Their frequent occurrence constantly engages in politics the 50 percent of the electorate that votes. And in times of crisis, critical elections provide the "safety valve" that preserves the system by making the realignment of government possible through the party system.

CHOOSING A PRESIDENT

Debate over how we choose our presidential candidates has existed from the earliest days of the republic. The Constitution makes no provision for *nominating* presidential candidates, and, as Chapter 8 has pointed out, as the presidential nominating process has evolved, procedures have changed. As parties expanded, congressional caucuses, which had originally nominated candidates, were dropped in favor of national party conventions. The beginning of the Jacksonian era (1828) marked the emergence of the presidency as a full-fledged democratic institution.

The twentieth century witnessed the injection of presidential-preference primaries into the delegate-selection process, but it was not until after 1968 that grass-roots presidential nominating politics really took root. Chapter 8 has analyzed the grass roots and described reactions to it in the decade of the 1980s, particularly the Democrats' attempt to roll back the process somewhat by injecting superdelegates into national party conventions. The article in this case study was written looking forward to the 1992 presidential election. The article presents the continuing debate over how we should nominate our presidential candidates.

Is This Any Way to Nominate a President? / *Rhodes Cook*

The 1988 presidential nominating process may not be over quite yet, but it is clear already that it has not been the disaster many people feared it would be.

Each presidential campaign is a trek into the unknown, but no recent campaign has started out looking as thoroughly unpredictable as this year's—with more than half the country, including the en-

tire South, voting in rapid-fire fashion within a few weeks of the early February Iowa caucuses.

Some feared the possibility of early momentum meeting Super Tuesday so quickly; they warned that a little-known dark-horse candidate could vault from the back of the pack to the verge of his party's nomination without coming under sustained public scrutiny.

From the *Congressional Quarterly Weekly Report*, June 11, 1988, pp. 1575–1577. Reprinted with permission from Congressional Quarterly, Inc. Dave Kaplan also contributed to this report.

Others feared that the glut of early events would produce a totally different result—a hopelessly muddled race that would only be resolved after bitter party infighting.

But neither of those possibilities occurred. By the time the primaries and caucuses had run their course, they had yielded two clear winners—Republican Vice President George Bush and Democratic Gov. Michael S. Dukakis of Massachusetts—who had begun the primary season at or near the top of their parties' public opinion polls.

The 1988 process also offered something to those who dreaded a front-runners' cakewalk devoid of suspense. Despite their strong organizations and ample campaign coffers, both Bush and Dukakis had at least one scare thrown into them before they got a grip on their nominations.

Satisfaction with the 1988 process, however, does not extend to all quarters. Some states felt overlooked this time around, and the Rev. Jesse Jackson still maintains, as he did in 1984, that aspects of the Democratic Party rules are unfair to him. For these and other reasons, it seems safe to predict that the nominating campaign four years from now will be different from the one now winding down.

A Few New Wrinkles

Basic elements of the 1988 nominating calendar likely will remain the same for 1992, with Iowa and New Hampshire retaining their lead-off spots before the contest turns to larger-state battles in the South and the industrial Frost Belt.

But candidates in 1992 probably will face some different strategic considerations. If they want, for instance, they may be able to devise a strategy that does not lead through Des Moines. "It seems like Iowa was a bust this year," says Rep. Al Swift, D-Wash., chairman of the House Administration Elections Subcommittee.

Although candidates of both parties devoted an unprecedented amount of campaign time to the state, the winners—Democratic Rep. Richard A. Gephardt of Missouri and Republican Sen. Robert Dole of Kansas—got virtually no payoff. Both lost the next week in New Hampshire, were routed on Super Tuesday (March 8) and were out of the race by the end of March.

The Iowa caucuses are in no danger of becoming irrelevant in 1992. Many still agree with veteran Republican consultant Eddie Mahe, who says,

"A single-state start-up makes a lot of sense for the press and the voters. Someone has to screen these candidates." And Iowa, he believes, is an "excellent place to start."

But there is no doubt that the failure of the Dole and Gephardt campaigns has diminished Iowa's reputation as a launching pad for presidential contenders.

Another likely change in the process four years from now will be in the scope of Super Tuesday, which this year was a 20-state votefest that included virtually the entire South and border South. "A lot of states will move away from Super Tuesday," predicts Democratic National Committeeman Mark Siegel of Maryland. "My state will move out; we were ignored. Many people thought Super Tuesday was a Texas-Florida primary."

The Urge to Tinker Ebbs

Any significant changes in the nominating process are likely to be made by the major players who have significantly influenced its evolution over the last 20 years—the national Democratic Party, the states and the U.S. Congress.

Since the Democrats' tumultuous convention in Chicago in 1968, the national party has been the most consistent instigator of change, routinely writing and rewriting its nominating rules after each presidential election. In the 1970s, changes were made to open the process to increased grass-roots participation, implicitly stirring a dramatic increase in the number of presidential primaries.

In recent years, the emphasis has been on restoring party leaders to a prominent place in the nominating process—an effort highlighted in 1984 by the creation of automatic delegate slots for party and elected officials ("superdelegates").

At this point, most party leaders would just as soon keep things as they are. "We've taken great pains to achieve balance between the two [grass-roots participation and input from party leaders]," says Michigan Democratic Chairman Rick Wiener, a co-chairman of the party's post-1984 rules commission. "There is no such thing as a perfect nominating system."

But Democratic leaders may have trouble maintaining the status quo, particularly if Jackson chooses to make a fight at the convention over superdelegates and bonus primaries. Jackson has argued for one-man, one-vote in the allocation of delegates, complaining that superdelegates and bonus systems of awarding delegates are undemocratic, as well as unfair to him.

A Grievance Revisited

In the 1984 nominating season, Jackson opposed both superdelegates and bonus systems, but he agreed to let the party's post-election rules commission handle his complaints. That commission, however, was dominated by party insiders, and the Jackson forces were hardly satisfied with the results. "We got one-quarter of a loaf," says Ron Walters, a Howard University political scientist and long-time Jackson adviser.

The commission lowered the threshold that a candidate needed to reach to win delegates from 20 percent to 15 percent of the vote, but it did not eliminate thresholds, as Jackson wanted, nor did it abolish superdelegates or bonus-allocation systems.

The direct-election, district winner-take-all form of primary that Illinois, New Jersey and Pennsylvania employ has been particularly onerous to Jackson. In those states' contests this year, Jackson swept the delegates from the handful of districts with black majorities, but was virtually shut out elsewhere.

The result is that while Jackson won 31 percent of the popular vote in Illinois, he won only 21 percent of the delegates; while he won 28 percent of the popular vote in Pennsylvania, he took only 8 percent of the delegates; and while he drew 33 percent of the popular vote in New Jersey, he garnered only 8 percent of the delegates.

Direct-election primaries "are a travesty," says Steve Cobble, Jackson's delegate-selection coordinator. "They distort the system against outsider candidates and against blacks. When you get a Jesse Jackson, who is both, you get a double distortion."

Risky Business

Based on his earlier experience with a rules commission, Jackson may figure that his best chance to force change is under the klieg lights in Atlanta, where he will have more than one-quarter of the delegates and a Democratic leadership eager to present an image of party harmony.

But the key question for Jackson is how hard to push. Even Walters has acknowledged that his candidate has won a more equitable share of the delegates this year than he did in 1984. Four years ago, Jackson drew 18 percent of the nationwide primary vote but only 12 percent of the delegates; this year, he won 29 percent of the Democratic primary ballots and finished the primary season with 27 percent of the delegates.

Also, Jackson must weigh how an assault on party rules would affect his future in the Democratic Party. "He may do it," says Thomas E. Mann, the director of governmental studies at the Brookings Institution, "but it would detract from his credibility and his moral high ground."

If Jackson decides to push for abolition of superdelegates or direct-election primaries, then the question for Dukakis becomes how hard to resist. "It will be Dukakis' political call," says Siegel.

It could be a tough call. Dukakis may feel he has no compelling personal reason to care much about the 1992 rules: Either he would be the incumbent president in 1992—and therefore a likely favorite for renomination regardless of the party rules—or he would be a defeated former presidential nominee who would likely be on the political sidelines.

Still, the superdelegates and bonus primary systems are important to many party insiders, who do not want a final decision on them made in the volatile environment of the convention or its rules panel, which will meet in Washington, D.C., on June 25–26. "The [convention] rules committee is not a particularly good place to make decisions for 1992," says Siegel. "It's driven by candidate interests rather than party interests."

Dates Are Affairs of State

Whatever the Democratic Party ultimately decides for 1992, it is up to each state to decide how to select its delegates—through a primary or a caucus—and to determine when the event will be held. Since 1980, national Democratic rules have required states to schedule their delegate-selection primary or first-round caucus within a three-month "window" period, extending from the second Tuesday in March to the second Tuesday in June, with Iowa, New Hampshire and a handful of other states granted exemptions to go earlier.

Still, the Democrats' "window" has not slowed the creation of more and more primaries on earlier and earlier dates. Of the 17 primaries held in 1968, only one took place before the end of March. At a similar point of the 1988 primary season, 23 of the year's 38 primaries had already been held.

But the nominating process may not be so

"front-loaded" in 1992. A number of Super Tuesday states felt lost in the shuffle this year, and a few, such as Maryland, are likely to return to their traditional late-spring primary date.

Yet while Super Tuesday may be unraveling, political leaders in other parts of the country continue to talk of forming regional events. Discussions have been going on for several years in the Rocky Mountain states, which traditionally have exerted little influence on the nominating process by voting individually. Meanwhile, Minnesota Democrats have expressed interest in finding a common date to hold a delegate-selection event with their Midwestern neighbors.

The Primary-Caucus Debate

One of the major uncertainties about the shape of the nominating process in 1992 is the primary-caucus mix. The balance can shift dramatically from one election to another. In 1984, there were roughly an equal number of primary and caucus states. This year, with the attraction of Super Tuesday encouraging many Southern states to shift from a caucus to a presidential primary, the number of primaries was at an all-time high.

Regional interests can be a major force in determining which system a state uses. So can candidate interests. Much of the early activity these days revolves around Republican response to religious broadcaster Pat Robertson.

In Southern primary states such as Texas, where Robertson forces have made inroads in the party apparatus, there could be efforts by his people to abolish the Republican primary and return in 1992 to the caucus process, where his organized cadre of supporters would be more effective.

But in non-Southern caucus states such as Michigan and Washington, where Robertson showed unexpected strength this year, there is already sentiment among members of the GOP establishment to switch to a primary.

Some Noise, Little Movement

From time to time over the years, Congress has seemed poised to become involved in shaping the nominating process. Bills to mandate regional primaries have been a popular item of discussion, and on June 7 the Senate Rules and Administration Committee held the latest round of hearings on proposals for regional primaries.

At the June 7 hearing, former Vice President Walter F. Mondale, the Democratic presidential nominee in 1984, testified in favor of a bill (S 1786), introduced by Alan J. Dixon, D-Ill., that would establish six regional primaries, to be held every other week beginning the last Tuesday of March. The Federal Election Commission (FEC) would determine by lot the order in which to hold the events.

Sen. Bob Packwood, R-Ore., has proposed a bill (S 2319) that would create a system of 10 regional primaries. Under his measure, the lottery to determine the order would be held only 70 days before each event. Packwood has longstanding ties to election-reform legislation: He and then-Sen. Mondale sponsored bills in the early and mid-1970s to establish regional primaries.

Still, while Mondale's presence at the hearing drew a large crowd of reporters, the next-day coverage of the event was sparse, and regional-primary legislation is not expected to make much headway in Congress this year.

The House Administration Subcommittee on Elections held hearings of its own in 1986. Chairman Swift and his colleagues listened to concerns about the possible effects of "front-loading" on this year's nominating process, but the committee decided to wait and see how the process worked this year before determining how to proceed.

At present, Swift sees little need for congressional involvement. "Anyone can think up a system that's more orderly," he says. "But I don't see that this system was unfair to anyone."

And, says Swift, he does not hear his colleagues clamoring for congressional action. "I don't hear the grumbling that would provide the impetus for major reform," he says. "If they're not grumbling about it now, they certainly won't be grumbling about it next February."

Swift indicated that he may try to gauge congressional sentiment for legislation that would establish a fixed starting date for primaries and caucuses that no state, including Iowa or New Hampshire, could violate.

But it is more likely in the next year or two that Congress will focus on the one part of the presidential nominating process that it has played a major role in shaping—campaign finance. Swift foresees discussions to eliminate the state-by-state spending limits, a facet of the public-financing system that has been particularly bothersome to candidates in budgeting for the early high-stakes events in Iowa and New Hampshire.

CHAPTER NINE

Interest Groups and Their Demands

"Right-To-Life Movement Pushes for Abortion Ban"; "Pro-Choice Marchers Demonstrate in Front of State Capitols"; "Special Interests Jeopardize Tax Reform"; "Environmentalists Propose Stricter Regulation"; "Senior Citizens Oppose Cuts in Medicare." Such headlines illustrate that a variety of special interests make demands upon government. However, the ways in which groups make their demands known vary from one group to another.

Interest groups arise from common bonds among people who share special economic, political, and social concerns. They include corporations, labor unions, and such professional groups as the American Medical Association and the American Bar Association; they also include "public interest" groups, such as Common Cause, the Ralph Nader organization, and such environmental groups as the Sierra Club and the Audubon Society. They take in groups representing political ideologies and causes, such as the National Conservative Political Action Committee, the Moral Majority, the Right to Life, Freedom of Choice, and the National Rifle Association.

In a pluralistic democracy, interest groups, also called "pressure groups," complement political parties as a vehicle used by citizens to express their wants and complaints to government. Whereas political parties are umbrella organizations within which a multiplicity of often conflicting interests congregate, interest groups directly reflect specialized concerns. Often interest groups seek to influence both of the major parties. They stand outside the electoral process, putting

pressure upon the government regardless of which political party is in the White House or dominates Congress. Administrative agencies and courts are major access points for pressure groups in making demands upon government. Unlike political parties, however, interest groups do not directly nominate and run candidates for public offices; but they do influence the choice of candidates.

INTEREST-GROUP DEMANDS ON GOVERNMENT

James Madison's concern over "factions" in *The Federalist*, No. 10, covered interest groups as well as political parties (see pp. 33–35). Both interest groups and political parties, as factions, were considered by Madison to be intrinsically opposed to the "national interest." But just as political parties were forming at the very time that Madison wrote *The Federalist* in 1787 and 1788, there were also a wide variety of interest groups. In particular, the states themselves could be considered as major interest groups at the time of the framing of the Constitution. Groups in manufacturing and agriculture were also developing to push for the protection of their divergent interests—the manufacturing groups demanding a protective tariff on imports, the agricultural groups free trade to benefit the exporting agricultural sector located largely in the South.

The system that Madison felt would control the evil effects of factions (at no time did he propose their abolition, for as he said, only by abolishing liberty could factions be eliminated, the remedy being therefore worse than the disease) did not seem to inhibit their growth in any way. In fact, one of the facts that struck Alexis de Tocqueville as most remarkable when he visited the United States in 1831 was the large variety of interest groups, reflecting a highly pluralistic society. Madison felt that the large geographical area encompassed by the United States would confine the influence of interest groups largely to the individual states, toward which their energies would be directed and by which they would be absorbed. Madison felt the dangers of national factions, whether in the form of parties or interest groups, would be remote under the new Constitution. However, the system of separation of powers and checks and balances, by producing a government in which each branch has an important say over public policy, actually buttressed the access points that interest groups could use to influence government policy. Protected by First Amendment rights of association and the right to petition government for a redress of grievances, interest groups can for the most part operate freely to persuade executives, legislators, judges, and bureaucrats to their point of view. Although their influence on government is more negative than positive, it nevertheless constitutes an important control over public policy.

The degree to which interest groups should have a veto over the public policies affecting them is a matter of debate. An important strand of political thought, beginning with nineteenth-century South Carolina statesman John C. Calhoun's famous work *A Disquisition on Government* (written in the 1840s but published posthumously in 1853) and extending to what is called modern "group theory," represented by David Truman's *The Governmental Process* (published in 1951) holds that interest groups not only are legitimate but

should have a dominant say over the public policy affecting them. Pressure groups, say the group theorists, collectively represent the will of the people and individually stand for legitimate interests that government must take into account. The primary job of government, according to these theorists, is to reconcile competing group interests in particular spheres of public policy. Opponents of this view of government, however, suggest that there is a national interest that is above the individual interests of separate groups and that government, in formulating public policy, should strive to rise above "brokerage politics," that is, politics based upon the simple compromising of group interests.[1]

Major Categories of Interest Groups

Interest groups can be divided into two major categories—*private* and *governmental*. Groups in both categories try to influence the policies and decisions made by various parts of the government in order to obtain the results they desire.

Private interest groups. There are private interest groups outside government that represent almost every facet of society—economic, religious, professional, and so forth. Private groups place pressure on all the branches of national government—the legislature, the president, administrative agencies, and the courts.

The judiciary and the bureaucracy are particularly accessible to direct influence from private interest groups. For example, interest groups can bring cases directly to the courts or can make complaints directly to the administrative agencies. Because of their highly specialized functions, administrative agencies

[1]See David Truman, *The Governmental Process* (New York: Knopf, 1951). For a criticism of group theory, see Theodore J. Lowi, *The End of Liberalism* (New York: Norton, 1969).

(Mike Keefe, *The Denver Post*)

Political action committees have increased interest-group power.

tend to rely on the support of those interest-group constituents who maintain close relationships with the agencies. Since the president and Congress have broader constituencies supporting them, the private pressure groups find it harder to influence the decisions of these two branches.

Governmental interest groups. The second major category of interest groups is found within the government itself. Agencies, departments, congressional subcommittees, and executive offices of government sometimes act as pressure groups when they have an interest in policies being handled by other parts of the government. After all, the constitutional

system of separation of powers and checks and balances was itself built around creating each branch of the government as a separate interest; and the contrasting interests of the three branches were to be guaranteed by differing constituencies and independent powers. The fact that the White House must act as an interest group in pressuring Congress to support its policies stems directly from the Constitution, as does Congress's inevitable opposition to the president in its desire to protect its independence and interests against presidential intrusion. The Supreme Court too is an interest group, checking both Congress and the president.

· The growth of the bureaucracy, however, has added to governmental pluralism an important dimension that expands governmental interest groups far beyond the vision of the Framers of the Constitution. Administrative agencies have become major governmental pressure groups, constantly seeking to buttress their power through the mobilization of support within their constituencies. Agency is often pitted against agency in fights over policy jurisdiction, which is an important ingredient of administrative power. For example, for years the Environmental Protection Agency (EPA) has fought the Occupational Health and Safety Administration (OSHA) for jurisdiction over the regulation of noise. EPA had dragged its heels in regulating this area, over which it can claim jurisdiction under its statutory mandate, whereupon OSHA aggressively entered the field and proposed to promulgate noise control standards in the mid-1970s. EPA joined battle with OSHA, claiming that the latter's standards were inadequate, and succeeded in delaying action by OSHA for years. Such intra-agency conflict reflects the different parts of the bureaucracy acting essentially as independent interest groups.

Administrative agencies and departments also act as interest groups in pressuring Congress for legislation and appropriations. The Defense Department, for example, maintains a staff of over 150 officers to lobby the House and Senate Armed Services committees and the Defense Appropriations subcommittees in the House and in the Senate. Virtually every major administrative agency has a "legislative liaison" office employing large numbers of civil servants whose sole task it is to deal with Capitol Hill, protecting the agency's interests.

The power of administrative agencies and their role as governmental pressure groups is affected directly by their private constituencies. The agencies draw important political support from groups they regulate and over which they have jurisdiction. The Department of Agriculture, for example, draws support from farm organizations, the Labor Department from labor organizations, the Defense Department from the armaments industry, the Department of Housing and Urban Development from the housing and banking industry, and the independent regulatory commissions from the groups they regulate, such as the airlines, the railroads, labor organizations, securities, banking, utilities, and numerous others. Administrative agencies, then, are an important channel through which private demands are made upon government.

Interaction of Interest Groups

Specialization of interest and expertise is a major characteristic of our society. Such specialization has affected both government and the private sector. Although there are overlapping memberships among many interest groups—for example, a doctor may be a member of the American Medical Association and of the Veterans of Foreign Wars at the same time—pressure groups tend to be run by elites and their policies oriented toward specialized concerns that may not greatly affect a broad spectrum of interests. This means that American politics is divided into arenas of power in which a relatively small number of private interest groups interact with particular administrative agencies and congressional committees to formulate public policy. For example, the Defense Department, the Armed Services and Appropriations Committees of Congress, and the armaments industry together constitute a powerful alliance in shaping armaments policy. The White House is, of course, involved in this important sphere, but it often finds that it is standing outside a relatively closed circle of special interests, which makes it very difficult for the president to achieve his objectives if they differ from those of the Department of Defense and its allies within and without government.

Most regulatory policy is of specialized concern only to the regulatory agencies and the groups they regulate, not to the general public. And the same limitation on the relevancy of interests in different policy spheres prevails throughout government. The policies that are enacted by the spheres of special interests do affect a broader public, but they are usually not perceived by that public as being of special concern to it. General public apathy about special issues that are of concern primarily to a relatively narrow sphere of pressure groups increases the power not only of the private groups but also of specialized governmental interests in the policy process. Private interest groups can roughly be divided into the following categories: (1) economic, (2) political and "public interest," and (3) professional. The concerns, methods, and goals of the interest groups in each of these categories tend to differ as they affect public policy.

Economic Interest Groups

Private economic interest groups can be divided into broad categories, corresponding to the three major sectors of the economy—business, labor, and agriculture. The interests of private groups in each of these economic sectors are in turn reflected in administrative agencies and congressional committees that have jurisdiction over them. Business interests are represented by the Department of Commerce, labor interests by the Department of Labor, and agricultural interests by the Department of Agriculture. In turn, each of these departments operates in conjunction with separate committees on Capitol Hill.

Business groups. The business community includes people who earn their living in profit-making enterprises in such industries as manufacturing, insurance, banking, and so forth. Business is represented by several private pressure-group organizations, including the National Association of Manufacturers, the Chamber of Commerce of the United States, and the National Small Business Association. The Department of Commerce aids all of these organizations. The Business Round Table, a group of chief executives of over 40 major business corporations, was formally created in 1974 to influence government policy, and it has become a leading spokesman for business interests in Washington. Corporations such as General Motors, IBM, AT&T, General Electric, DuPont, Exxon, and United States Steel are among those represented by the Round Table. The principal focus of the Round Table is Capitol Hill.

Although the interests of a particular industry may be served by one government department, frequently groups within the industry deal with different government agencies. For example, although the overall interests of the transportation industry are served by the Department of Transportation, the industry includes specialized interests—such as railroads, airlines, and trucking—that are in competition with one another in a limited number of activities. A strong trend toward deregulation of industries was implemented during President Reagan's administration. Yet some agencies still cope with conflicting pressures of serving a particular industry while promoting the public interest. The Federal Aviation Agency (FAA), for example, is responsive to the needs of the airline industry, but is still responsible for regulating safety. This conflict is reflected in an ongoing controversy over whether the FAA should require the airlines to install, at great expense to them, safer passenger seats in each of the airplanes currently being used, or only require such seats in new aircraft.

At the same time that agency policies influence business activities, interests within the business community also affect agency policies. The influence of business on policy making is accomplished primarily by pressure groups that have direct access to the administrative agencies with which they trade specialized information. Subtler business pressures are applied to politicians and legislators when interest groups contribute to political campaigns or give publicity to government officials.

Labor groups. During the first third of the twentieth century, America experienced the rise of a powerful labor movement. As conflict developed between the interests of labor and management before and during the New Deal era of the 1930s, labor succeeded in securing governmental agencies to represent its interests. There had been a separate cabinet-level Department of Labor since 1913, and in 1935 the National Labor Relations Board (NLRB), an independent agency, was established to handle disputes between business and labor. Both the Labor Department and the NLRB were responsive to the demands of labor groups such as the American Federation of Labor (AFL), the Congress of Industrial Organizations (CIO), which includes the International Brotherhood of Teamsters, and other unions. At first the NLRB favored the interests of labor groups over those of business groups in cases of unfair labor practices and union representation. The Taft-Hartley Act of 1947 attempted to restore a balance between labor and business. More recently, however, the NLRB has ceased to rely so strongly on labor groups for political support and has begun to render decisions that reflect the influence of business as well as labor.

The major labor organization in the United States is the AFL-CIO. It includes two giant unions that merged in 1955: the AFL, a federation of unions organized according to trades or crafts, such as plumbers, carpenters, or bricklayers; and the CIO, a federation of unions organized by industry, such as steelworkers or automobile workers. Today the combined membership of the AFL-CIO is approximately 12 million workers. The list of affiliated unions is extensive, and each has a membership of from 100,000 to 200,000 workers. Together, these affiliated unions represent almost all the craft, trade, and industrial workers in the nation.

As labor-union membership grew, it was feared that labor groups would be able to gain control over the electoral process by dictating

(Charles G. Werner, *The Indianapolis Star*)

"Hey, Jimmy!"
The AFL-CIO considers Democratic presidents to be on their side.

how their members should vote. Since union members represent 10 percent of the total population, they, together with their families and other sympathizers, could thus become a significant political force. They could even form a separate political party or gain control of an existing one. So far, however, control of the election system by labor groups has never been realized because the interests of union members are almost as diverse as those of other groups in society.

Agricultural groups. Special interest groups, both public and private, also represent the agricultural segment of the economy. In the private sphere there are three major farm organizations that exercise great influence over farm legislation in Congress and thus help to shape the policies of the Department of Agriculture. The American Farm Bureau Federation, the most important of the three, was founded in 1920 and now contains over 1.5 million farm families as its members.

It is particularly strong in the Midwest. The National Grange, founded in 1867, lists about 860,000 dues-paying members. It is strong in New England, the Northwest, and Ohio. The National Farmers Union was founded in 1902 and numbers about 250,000 farm families. It is influential in the Plains states and in the Great Lakes region.

In addition to these three large farm organizations, the agricultural community includes special groups interested in particular commodities. These include the National Milk Producers Federation, which represents dairy-farmer cooperatives and federations, the National Livestock Feeders Association, the American Meat Institute, the National Wool Growers Association, and others. At the government level the demands of these groups are focused on the House Agricultural Committee, which is divided into commodity subcommittees. Representatives on each of these subcommittees are generally from districts where the particular commodity is farmed extensively. Thus they are primarily interested in supporting legislation that will benefit their constituents. The Senate Agriculture Committee, too, although not divided into commodity subcommittees, generally supports agricultural interests. The Department of Agriculture represents the agricultural sector in the bureaucracy.

All these private groups, large and small, are concerned about federal agricultural programs relating to their particular commodity areas and special interests. As in the areas of business and labor, the scope and complexity of federal agricultural legislation is truly staggering. It involves farm price supports, acreage allotments, land diversion, soil conservation, and other programs. Such legislation is of great concern not only to the agricultural community in this country, but also to other countries that import farm produce or that depend on United States agricultural surpluses to help them avoid mass famine.

Due to the pluralism within the agricultural community, there are some basic disagreements among the major farm pressure groups about public policy goals. The Farm Bureau Federation favors a reduction in the role of the federal government, whereas the National Farmers Union has stepped up its backing of federal price-support and commodity-control programs. The interests of the smaller specialized groups are highly varied, too, and often come into conflict, although there is a general effort among them to secure federal protection for all commodity areas.

Political and Public Interest Groups

Most pressure groups are "political" in the sense that they strive to advance their own interests via the governmental process. On another level, there are special groups that are based entirely on advancing a particular political philosophy.

Some political or "ideological" groups have been around for a long time. For example, the Americans for Democratic Action (ADA) was founded in 1947 to pressure government for the adoption of liberal programs and for the protection of civil liberties at home and human rights abroad. In 1952 the AFL-CIO created its Committee on Political Education (COPE), which sought to advance liberal causes in the economic sphere and supported a liberal philosophy in other areas as well. Yet another liberal group is the National Association for the Advancement of Colored People (NAACP), which for most of the twentieth century has supported black causes and, like the American Civil Liberties Union (ACLU), has effectively used the courts. The NAACP was single-handedly responsible for *Brown v. Board of Education* (1954), which with companion and subsequent cases resulted in overturning legal segregation of public education in 17 southern and border states, as well as in the District of Columbia. There are many other ideological groups with long histories. The ACLU has used the judicial process effectively to protect civil liberties, often adopting controversial stands in defense of free political expression for unpopular groups. In the 1980s the National Conservative Political Action Committee (NCPAC) and the Moral Majority raised large sums of money to promote conservative candidates for public offices. The American Conservative Union (ACU), founded in 1971, promotes its conservative philosophy in government, focusing on foreign, social, and budgetary policies.

Many political groups keep tabs on members of Congress, following their voting records closely and publishing the results. Such groups give members of Congress liberal and conservative scores to discourage voters of similar persuasion from supporting representatives or senators with high scores in the opposition camp. Well-known liberals, such as Massachusetts Senator Edward Kennedy, and prominent conservatives, such as Utah Senator Orrin Hatch, consistently receive high liberal and conservative scores, respectively, which is hardly a surprise to voters. Political interest groups independently rate office holders, but their scores seem to balance out nicely as, for example, in the case of Senator Robert Bird (D., W. Va.), who at a given time received from the ADA a 70 percent liberal rating and from the ACU a 30 percent rating.

Citizens' groups. A recognition of the importance of organized groups in politics is reflected in the rise of citizens' groups or what are sometimes called—usually by the groups themselves—"public interest pressure groups." Under this rubric, interest groups of all kinds have organized to represent the views of particular publics, such as consumers, conservationists, food stamp recipients, gun owners, hunters, women, Indians, taxpayers, students, and National Public Radio.

Ralph Nader, the consumers' "Lone Ranger" of the 1960s, began seriously to organize consumers at the grass-roots level as the decade came to a close. Nader's groups

continue to represent consumers and to pressure government in the 1990s, and Nader himself appears before congressional committees and in other forums to support his causes. Nader founded or helped to establish over one hundred consumer organizations, including public interest research groups on college campuses throughout the country. Public Citizen is an umbrella organization for Nader's Washington-based groups, including Congress Watch, Litigation Group, Health Research Group, and Tax Reform Research Group. Although Nader has been actively involved in attempting to influence legislation on Capitol Hill, and has been instrumental in the passage of major consumer-protection laws, he does not consider himself to be a lobbyist in the traditional sense and has refused to register as one under the Federal Regulation of Lobbying Act of 1946.

Another major citizens' group, founded in the 1970s, is Common Cause. John Gardner, an upper-class Californian who had served as Secretary of Health, Education, and Welfare under President Johnson, founded and was president of Common Cause during its formative years. The underlying premise of the organization is that democracy can work effectively only if there is a concerned citizenry actively following and participating in government. Common Cause leaders feel they are the citizens' "David" leading the charge against the "Goliath" of special interests. Common Cause focuses primarily on Congress, hoping to reduce special interest influence on Capitol Hill. Common Cause declared "war" on political action committees (PACs) as they grew in influence in the 1980s, and it has put the reduction or elimination of PAC influence at the top of its political agenda.

The Nader organization, Common Cause, and environmental groups such as the Sierra Club are broad-based citizens' groups that define the public interest in terms of the needs of consumers and the wider public. The term

National Audubon Society (founded 1905)
Members: 516,220
Budget: $32,852,672
Staff: 337
Offices: 16

Defenders of Wildlife (founded 1947)
Members: 80,000
Budget: $4.5 million
Staff: 30
Offices: 4

Environmental Action (founded 1970)
Members: 20,000
Budget: $1.2 million
Staff: 24
Offices: Washington only

Environmental Defense Fund (founded 1967)
Members: 125,000
Budget: $12.9 million
Staff: 100
Offices: 6

Friends of the Earth (founded 1969)
Members: 50,000
Budget: $2.5 million
Staff: 35
Offices: 2

Greenpeace (founded 1971)
Members: 1.4 million
Budget: $33.9 million
Staff: 1,200
Offices: 30

Izaak Walton League of America (founded 1922)
Members: 50,000
Budget: $1.8 million
Staff: 26
Offices: Washington and St. Paul, Minn.

League of Conservation Voters (founded 1970)
Members: 15,000
Budget: $500,000
Staff: 40
Offices: 3

National Clean Air Coalition (founded 1974)
(Coalition group, made up of 35 other groups)

National Parks and Conservation Association
  (founded 1919)
Members: 100,000
Budget: $3.8 million
Staff: 30
Offices: 4

National Wildlife Federation (founded 1936)
Members: 5.6 million members and supporters
Budget: $85 million
Staff: 700
Offices: 12

Natural Resources Defense Council (founded 1970)
Members: 125,000
Budget: $13 million
Staff: 125 (40 lawyers)
Offices: 5

Sierra Club (founded 1892)
Members: 553,246
Budget: $28 million
Staff: 185
Offices: 16, plus 57 chapters divided into 355 groups

The Wilderness Society (founded 1935)
Members: 330,000
Budget: $20 million
Staff: 130 staff
Offices: 15

Source: Congressional Quarterly Report, January 20, 1990, p.
146. By Robert Clayton. Reprinted with permission from Congressional Quarterly, Inc.

Environmental interest groups are a major political force.

"public interest," however, is subject to many interpretations, depending on the objectives of the individual or group defining it. Citizens' groups frequently do not agree on the public interest. Common Cause, for example, supported stricter registration requirements for lobbyists when Congress was considering strengthening the Federal Regulation of Lobbying Act in 1975. The Common Cause stand was strongly opposed by both the Sierra Club leaders and Ralph Nader, who felt that their organizations would be forced to meet burdensome red tape and registration requirements that they had avoided in the past.

Definitions of "public interest" also sharply differ between the two citizens' groups concerned with gun control. The National Rifle Association of America, with one of the most broadly based memberships of any citizens' group, strongly opposes gun control in any form. The other side of the issue is taken by Handgun Control, Inc., a far smaller organization, that supports gun control.

Other public interest groups include the National Organization for Women (NOW), which lobbies against restrictions on abortions and in behalf of equal rights for women. The National Abortion Rights Action Committee has joined NOW in its fight for abortion rights, as have the Planned Parenthood Association, the NAACP, and other groups. The right-to-life movement has organized and led nationwide demonstrations against abortion, picketing abortion clinics and pressuring Congress and state legislatures to take a stand against abortion. The Supreme Court's decision in *Webster v. Reproductive Health Services* (1989), upholding a Missouri statute that restricted public funding and the use of public employees for abortion, increased their lobbying for and against abortion in state capitals throughout the nation.

Citizens' groups differ from most pressure groups in that they do not have economic interests at stake. Their policy proposals will not increase their profits. Ralph Nader, Common Cause, and the conservationist groups do not hesitate to attack special interests, and generally are viewed as having an antibusiness bias.

"Public Interest" law firms. The Nader organizations and other citizens' groups have effectively used litigation to achieve their policy objectives. Litigation has been brought in the interests of consumers, minorities, and the poor, not only by citizens' groups but also by attorneys working in free legal clinics generally attached to law schools, and by civil rights activists practicing pro bono (for the public good) law.

Conservative "public interest" law firms began to emerge in the late 1970s and became firmly established in Washington in the early 1980s. The pro bono work of these firms, however, was in support of business interests. The Capital Legal Foundation, headed by Dan Burt, sided with corporations fighting government regulations and worked for less restrictive regulatory policies. At the same time, Burt attacked Ralph Nader in a book entitled *Abuse of Trust,* which portrayed the Nader organization as a secretive lobbying group that failed to conform to legal-reporting requirements. Nader responded: "The function of these right-wing foundations is to do for their corporate backers and benefactors what the corporations would be too ashamed or sensitive to do directly."[2] Conservative foundations and large corporations, such as General Electric, Chase Manhattan Bank, and Exxon support the Capital Legal Foundation with contributions of over $5 million a year. But, contends its president, the Capital Legal Foundation remains independent and has on more than one occasion opposed government subsidies for business.

Professional Interest Groups

Professional groups also play a considerable role in the development of public policy. The American Medical Association (AMA), the American Bar Association (ABA), and the

---

[2]Stuart Taylor, Jr., "Conservative 'Public Interest' Firms Emerge," *New York Times,* April 22, 1982, p. B10.

National Education Association (NEA) have influenced legislation affecting their respective fields. Although the American Medical Association could not defeat Medicare legislation in 1965, it was able to shape various proposals relating to it, and undoubtedly, the AMA's continuing interaction with government officials who administer Medicare will affect future public policy. The American Bar Association affects policy development in all branches of the government but most particularly within the judiciary and in the Department of Justice. Primarily, the ABA has been concerned with the education of lawyers, the methods of selecting judges, and the clarification of laws. The National Education Association has been working to improve conditions for teachers by demanding more federal funds for education. The NEA achieved its greatest success when President Jimmy Carter, in response to its demand and support of him in the 1976 election, created with congressional backing a new cabinet-level Department of Education in 1977. President Reagan promised to abolish the new department; however, its political support on Capitol Hill sidetracked Reagan's recommendation.

Some special interest groups, such as those that represent veterans, have managed to work through several government agencies to obtain their objectives. They have secured financial bonuses, civil service preference, and a separate health care system. Major veterans lobbies include the American Legion, the Veterans of Foreign Wars, and the Disabled Veterans. The U.S. Department of Veterans Affairs, a cabinet agency, provides American veterans with nearly $20 billion in benefits each year.

CHARACTERISTICS OF INTEREST GROUPS

For a *lobby* (another term for "pressure group") to be effective, it must be fairly well organized so that the goals desired by the membership can be related to the policy-making structures in the government. Any pressure group must solve the problem of setting goals that will truly represent the views of the people it claims as members. Once the general goals of a pressure group have been determined, its leaders must decide which of the techniques available is best for getting the results it wants.

Pressure-Group Organization

Despite the variety of pressure groups and their interests, all share some common organizational characteristics. Most pressure groups include (1) elite members, who lead the organizations and formulate the policies and tactics to be used; (2) lobbyists, who work for these elites and bring policy demands to the attention of either the people or government; and (3) the members, who provide the basis of and reason for the establishment of the interest group in the first place.

Reasons for joining a pressure group. People do not necessarily belong to an interest group because they agree with its political objectives. It is true that members of some interest groups, such as the Daughters of the American Revolution (DAR) or the NAACP, join because they agree with the particular philosophy or general goals of the group. But people often join interest groups, particularly those representing economic and professional interests, due to practical or financial considerations. For example, a carpenter may find he has to join the United Brotherhood of Carpenters and Joiners of America to get a construction job on a building site in his home city. A policeman may find that by joining the Policemen's Benevolent Association, he adds his voice to those of others striving for the same benefits; and a teacher will discover that by joining the NEA, he or she acquires group support. In none of these in-

TABLE 9.1 UNION AND NONUNION OPINION ON TAFT-HARTLEY ISSUE

Opinion	White Collar		Blue Collar	
	Union	Nonunion	Union	Nonunion
Repeal or change to prolabor	23%	12%	29%	10%
Leave as is or change to promanagement	20	20	12	9
Change, no attitude how	22	25	18	9
No opinion	35	43	41	72

Source: V. O. Key, Jr., *Public Opinion and American Democracy* (New York: Knopf, 1964), p. 509. Copyright © 1961 by V. O. Key, Jr.

stances does the member have to accept the group's political goals.

Differences between elites and members. Just as there are significant gaps between the attitudes of political party leaders and followers, similar divisions exist between the leaders and members of pressure groups. Sometimes the leadership of a pressure group cannot even obtain support for those policies that clearly seem to be in the group's interest.

For example, after 1947 union leadership was very much in favor of repealing the Taft-Hartley Act. The act limits the power of the unions somewhat by outlawing the *closed shop* (an industrial plant where a person has to be a union member before he can be hired) and providing for a *cooling-off period* before a threatened strike may occur. A survey of union and nonunion workers taken in 1952, however, revealed that although union members favored repeal of the act more often than nonunion workers, the majority of union members either did not favor repeal or had no opinion at all on the issue. In fact, the highest percentages of both union and nonunion workers had no opinion (see Table 9.1). About 40 percent of the union members, both blue collar and white collar, registered no opinion on the Taft-Hartley issue, and another 20 percent felt the act should be changed but had no opinion about the nature of the changes needed. Such data indicate that leadership attitudes and intensive group propaganda do not necessarily have an impact on the political opinions of members.

Overlapping memberships. The limited impact of organized interest groups on their members is due in part to the overlapping group memberships of some individuals. An individual who is a member of one interest group may have many concerns and thus belong to several other groups as well. For example, a member of a labor union or professional organization may also belong to a conservationist group, an athletic association, or a political club—all of which compete for his loyalty and support. Add to this the influence of family, friends, neighbors, and other informal groups on political attitudes, and it becomes almost impossible for any one interest group to win the complete adherence of all its members to its political goals. This phenomenon has been called by one political scientist "the law of the imperfect mobilization of political interests."[3]

An example of conflicting loyalties. Obviously the goals of different interest groups do not always coincide. Therefore, a person is bound to develop conflicting loyalties for the various groups to which he or she belongs.

For several decades, sharp differences of opinion have been expressed by the American Medical Association (AMA) and the Department of Veterans Affairs (VA) over the is-

---

[3]E. E. Schattschneider, *Party Government* (Holt, Rinehart and Winston, 1942).

sues of socialized medicine, health insurance, and, particularly, the free medical care provided for veterans by the VA. Yet doctors who work for the VA are at the same time members of the AMA. As members of two groups that are diametrically opposed on important issues of public policy, these doctors are pulled in several directions at once. They are confronted with the dilemma of deciding whether to go along with the AMA or to support the VA.

Although there is no conclusive evidence on this question, there are indications that VA doctors oppose the AMA on these conflicting issues. It is only natural that a doctor's first loyalty is going to be with the group that employs him. Thus the VA has more direct influence on the views of its doctor-employees than the AMA does on its VA members. The VA doctor may have only indirect contact with the political pronouncements of the AMA through its professional journal or through television and other news media.

While overlapping group memberships make it difficult for any one group to claim the complete loyalty of its members on all of the policy objectives sought by group leaders, *single-issue* groups in the 1980s and 1990s have had increasing success in mobilizing their memberships behind single causes. For example, the National Rifle Association members oppose gun control. Those who join anti-abortion groups oppose abortion. Members of single-issue groups have other groups with which they identify; however, the intensity and focused nature of single-issue politics can claim their loyalties and cause them to vote for the candidates and more easily support the single cause endorsed by the group.

The Mechanics of Putting on Pressure

Due to fragmentation by differences between leaders and members, overlapping memberships, and conflicting loyalties, it would seem that interest groups might have little real influence on government policy making. Actually, though, some groups are quite powerful not only because of their lobbying activities but also because they command the attention of certain segments of the population by means of their lobbying, public relations, and electioneering methods. Pressure-group activity, then, is a two-way street. Group leaders engage in making demands known to the government, and they gain support from the general public as well as their own members for the policies they are advocating.

Objectives of lobbying. Although lobbyists are drawn from many professions, many are lawyers, former congressmen, congressional aides, or officials of the executive branch, including Cabinet secretaries. A lobbyist who is a member of the congressional fraternity in Washington has special access to former colleagues and political credibility that can get results for clients. The techniques used by lobbyists are highly varied, depending on the individuals involved and on the public policy issues at stake.

No matter who they are or how they operate, lobbyists have two principal goals: (1) to influence legislation and (2) to gain entry into administrative agencies so as to acquire information about how policies affect supporters. Probably the most important function of the lobbyist today is that of obtaining information about matters pertaining to the group's interests. In turn, the lobbyist supplies information to government officials.

Public relations. Much pressure-group activity today is directed at developing a favorable public image of the institutions the groups represent, in the hope that this may have some influence on the policy-making process. Public relations techniques are thus a primary tool of the interest groups.

Articles may be written for the newspapers showing how a particular industry is joining in the fight against pollution. Or posters in subways and buses may inform the riders of how the International Ladies Garment Workers Union has carried on the fight for better working conditions or why people should "look for the union label" before they purchase clothes.

In addition, public relations techniques are sometimes used by pressure groups to win public support for their viewpoint on an important issue. There may be a concerted effort by a labor union, for example, to educate the public as to why the union favors a countermeasure to the Taft-Hartley Act.

If all the pressure-group expenditures for advertising on television, in magazines, newspapers, and other media were totaled, the amount would be staggering. It is estimated that millions of dollars were spent in advertising by the AMA to defeat compulsory health insurance when it was proposed by the Truman administration in the late 1940s.

Electioneering. A third method used by pressure groups to influence the public and get policy goals accepted by the government is to help elect people to public office. The elected official, it is hoped, will in turn support the objectives of the pressure group. A pressure group may help a sympathetic candidate's election by contributing to his or her campaign or by entering directly into the campaign with its own public relations staff. It may also try to influence the platform committee of a party to adopt a plank that will benefit the pressure group.

The electioneering activities of interest groups have intensified with the tremendous growth in the number of political action committees (PACs) since 1975. In the 1987–1988 election cycle, 4,828 PACs raised and spent over $350 million in direct and indirect campaign expenditures.

Administrative Lobbying and Propaganda

Technically, lobbying is a function of private interest groups, but administrative agencies themselves perform a similar function within the government. Administrative agencies are essentially interest groups with definite policy goals they would like to see achieved. The suggestion that governmental agencies are involved in lobbying activities would be surprising to many people, but the agencies often become major spokesmen for specific policies. As experts in their particular fields, agency representatives are called before congressional committees and consulted in other ways. In addition, their viewpoints are far more likely to be heeded by members of Congress than those put forward by lobbyists of private pressure groups.

Due to their access to Congress, administrative agencies have an inside track on the formulation of legislation. Since they are staffed by specialists who have continuous contact with the subject matter under their jurisdiction, the administrative agencies are often asked to submit ideas about legislation. The passage of legislation without the approval of dominant administrative agencies is virtually impossible today.

Like private pressure groups, agencies employ many public relations techniques to press their viewpoints in Congress. Although an agency cannot set up a publicity department, which would be in violation of congressional statutes, many administrative agencies do have extensive public relations staffs. Another major function of such a staff is to provide the news media with press releases that are favorable to the particular agency. Therefore, an important part of the staff's activity is to maintain good relations with the press. This activity increases in proportion to the administrative agency's strength and its involvement in the process of policy making.

INTEREST GROUPS IN A DEMOCRACY

Despite their use of the "hard sell" approach through lobbying and public relations techniques, the pressure groups and their spokespersons in the government serve a vital function in the overall panorama of a democratic state. Collectively, they are the voice of a large segment of the nation's people.

On the other hand, some people feel that to keep pressure groups within democratic bounds, such groups must not be allowed to gain so much power that they could direct the policy-making process entirely. For this reason, controls over lobbying activities have been a concern of government since early in the twentieth century.

Role of Interest Groups in a Democracy

Undoubtedly, the development of interest groups, both private and public, has altered the mechanics of the constitutional system. Government can no longer be limited only through such constitutional devices as the separation of powers and built-in checks and balances. Government today is large and complex, and many demands for policy that formerly came directly into the legislative arena from the people now arrive via the interest groups.

In some cases it appears that interest-group activity does not conform to what would be expected in a constitutional democracy. The leaders of interest groups occasionally develop policies that do not conform to the attitudes of the members. The elites may also make decisions about which the memberships have no opinions at all.

If interest groups do not always reflect the opinions of their members, does this mean that interest groups do not function democratically? Can interest-group participation in the governmental process be called popular participation? Democracy does not *demand* the participation of the entire electorate, nor is everyone required to have opinions on all matters of public policy. On the contrary, the democratic process should permit people to participate in any area they feel concerned about. Interest groups provide a means by which informed and politically active members and other interested citizens can participate in the political process.

(From *The Herblock Gallery* [Simon & Schuster, 1968])

"There's getting to be a lot of dangerous talk about the public interest."

Interest groups naturally fear confrontation with any broad consensus that would oppose their goals.

The Power of Interest Groups

The fact that there are conflicts among pressure groups over goals would indicate that no single interest group could ever dominate the government. Still, interest groups do operate in coalitions, thereby increasing their strength. In each of the government's policy-making spheres—defense, budget, transportation, agriculture, securities regulation, labor, health, education, welfare, natural resources, urban housing, and so on—there are coalitions of interest groups that are extremely powerful.

In addition, the general fragmentation of the policy-making process between legislative, executive, and administrative branches, plus the increasing delegation of legislative and judicial power to the administrative agencies, means that final decision-making power often rests with a few people who could easily be swayed by strong coalitions of interest groups. If such groups can gain control of the policy-making apparatus through the administrative agencies, how is the interest of the general public protected?

Formal Control over Lobbies

A major concern of American legislators and political commentators has been the power and actions of lobbies. As with other segments of the democratic society, interest groups are limited legally so that they do not gain too much power. Because of the vast amounts of money spent by pressure groups each year on lobbying and public relations activities, the government has taken measures to limit these activities to some extent.

Such limitation has seemed necessary for several reasons. It has been felt that lobbies, acting in the name of groups of people and being financed by these people, must be prevented not only from exerting excessive and improper pressure on the government but also from acting against the interests of their own memberships. In addition, lobbies are often pictured as an evil influence on government because their past activities have ranged from furnishing propaganda in order to influence the legislative process to outright bribery, fraud, deceit, and chicanery.

Early attempts to control pressure-group activities. Since the start of the twentieth century, Congress has tried to set up legislative restrictions on some interest-group activities. Early attempts at such legislation were directed at eliminating the pressures exerted both on political parties and on individual members of Congress. In 1907 Congress passed a law prohibiting corporations from making political campaign contributions in federal elections. A statute passed in 1909 made it a crime to attempt to bribe a member of Congress or to accept such a bribe.

Attempts were made later to legislate controls on expenditures rather than to eliminate lobbying activities outright. In 1919 the Internal Revenue Service held that lobbying expenditures were not deductible from federal income taxes by businesses or individuals. The Corrupt Practices Act of 1925, which has now been replaced by the stricter Campaign Practices Act of 1972 and 1974 (see Chapter 8), required political candidates to report campaign receipts and expenditures so that it would be easier to determine who had paid for their

(Copyright © 1962 *The Chicago Sun-Times*. Reproduced by courtesy of Wil-Jo Associates, Inc. and Bill Mauldin.)

"Thanks, sport—and here's a little something for you."
Such abuses by some lobbies have resulted in congressional legislation to curb pressure-group activities.

campaigns. But loopholes in the law have made it possible to avoid full disclosure.

There were also numerous statutes enacted to regulate corporation and labor-union contributions to political parties. In 1943 the War Labor Disputes Act barred political campaign contributions by labor unions in federal elections for the duration of the World War II emergency. In addition to these statutes, Congress has passed a number of bills designed to halt the use of federal funds by administrative agencies for public relations purposes, thereby prohibiting the agencies from pressuring Congress.

An attempt was made to control lobbyist activities in 1936 when the House passed a registration bill for lobbyists, but the bill was never enacted into law. It was not until after World War II that such a measure was finally passed.

The Federal Regulation of Lobbying Act of 1946. At the war's end Congress engaged in an extensive investigation of legislative procedures. The purpose was to re-tailor the legislature to meet the needs of an increasingly complex society. The extent of lobbying was also included in these investigations. As a result of congressional hearings, a section of the Legislative Reorganization Act of 1946 dealt with the regulation of lobbying. The major provisions of this act required lobbyists to register with the clerk of the House of Representatives and the secretary of the Senate, divulging their names, addresses, and employers, and to submit quarterly reports of income and expenditures.

The penalty for violation of the registration requirements was set at a fine of not more than $5,000, imprisonment for not more than 12 months, or both. Moreover, any person convicted of violating the act was prohibited for a period of three years from attempting to influence directly or indirectly the passage or defeat of any proposed legislation before Congress. Violation of this section carried a fine of not more than $10,000, imprisonment for not more than five years, or both.

Constitutionality of the Lobbying Act. The Lobbying Act of 1946 was challenged before the Supreme Court in 1954. Two years after the bill was enacted, the government had charged several individuals with supposed violations of the registration and reporting sections of the act. A lower federal court had ruled in 1953 that the lobbying law was vague and unconstitutional on the grounds that it violated the due process clause of the Fifth Amendment. Furthermore, the lower court had found that the registration, reporting, and penalty provisions of the Lobbying Act abused First Amendment freedoms of speech, assembly, and the right to petition government for a redress of grievances.

In *United States v. Harriss* the Supreme Court, in a five-to-three decision, upheld the constitutionality of the Lobbying Act, stating that the Congress

wants only to know who is being hired, who is putting up the money, and how. . . .Under these circumstances, we believe that Congress, at least within the bounds of the Act as we have construed it, is not constitutionally forbidden to require the disclosure of lobbying activities. To do so would be to deny Congress in large measure the power of self-protection.[4]

At the same time the Court gave a narrow interpretation of the act. Chief Justice Earl Warren made it clear that the act applied only to direct lobbying. *Direct lobbying* was defined as activities dealing with legislation pending before Congress and contributions that "in substantial part" are used to influence such legislation.

Vigorous dissents were registered to the opinion of the Court in the *Harriss* case by three Court justices. Justice Robert H. Jackson contended that the Court had gone too far and was, in effect, "rewriting" the act. He felt that an act of Congress could not be rewritten by the Court in order to be upheld, and he opted

---

[4]*United States v. Harriss*, 347 U.S. 612 (1954).

.eturning the act to Congress for restudy. Justices William O. Douglas and Hugo L. Black claimed that if the act were construed as originally intended by Congress, it would be unconstitutional, because virtually anyone could be ensnared in a violation. Black and Douglas further contended that even as "re-written," the act was unconstitutional.

Registrants under the act. The 1954 Supreme Court decision did little to clarify the provisions of the Lobbying Act of 1946, and today there is a great deal of ambiguity about who is supposed to register. The exact meaning of a "direct" attempt to affect legislation before Congress is still undetermined.

For example, the National Association of Home Builders registered a lobbyist in Washington who also had a number of other responsibilities. When asked to identify the particular legislation before Congress that interested him, the lobbyist answered, "I am interested in all legislation affecting the home-building industry and its members." Which part of his compensation was devoted to directly influencing legislation before Congress? He could not say, but he observed that "my annual rate of total compensation is $35,000, of which quarterly reports will detail the amount which might be considered to be allocable to legislative interests." The lobbyist could not relate his expenses in any greater detail.

Since lobbyists are required to report only those sums that are billed to legislation actually before the Congress, total amounts expended by them are difficult to determine. The money spent to influence administrative agencies or in general propaganda is not reported. Periodically Congress grapples with the issue of whether or not stricter controls should be placed upon the activities of lobbyists, especially in response to revelations or accusations of improper influence on Capitol Hill. Massachusetts Senator Edward Kennedy, who supports a stricter lobbying law, has cynically remarked that "the Congress is the best

that money can buy." In the early 1990s legislation was introduced to put a limit on the total sum a candidate could receive from PAC contributions, but this proposal was put on the "back burner" as Congress grappled with difficult budgetary and tax questions.

Pressure Groups and the Public Interest

The First Amendment freedoms of the Constitution that have the effect of guaranteeing the rights of people to organize and petition government reflect a formal recognition of the importance of the free expression of ideas, whether by interest groups or individuals, in the political process. Any attempt to exercise formal controls over lobbying raises potential constitutional issues, as was the case with the 1946 Lobbying Act. There is a fine line between permissible government regulation of interest groups and the maintenance of constitutional freedoms of expression and petition. In *Buckley v. Valeo,* in 1976, the Supreme Court held unconstitutional the Campaign Finance Law limitations that have been placed upon expenditures that could be made by political candidates. The Court found such restrictions to be a violation of the First Amendment.

While the "public interest" is certainly not automatically promoted by compromising the interests of the diverse pressure groups in particular spheres of public policy, these groups do perform an important democratic function in providing the government with information and expertise on matters of concern to them. Of course some pressure groups are more powerful than others in terms of money, membership, access, and expertise, but the imbalance of power that exists does not warrant the denial of the right of pressure groups to present their points of view to all branches of the government and to use the rules of the game of the political system to affect public policy. The various campaign practices acts that have placed controls over contributions in political campaigns have attempted to remove the unfair advantage of large contributors and large concentrations of money in the political process. But, even these laws have raised constitutional questions and have had to be narrowed in order to meet constitutional standards established by the Supreme Court.

The rise of public-interest groups to counterbalance the previously dominant business and corporation lobbyists is a demonstration that in a free political process open access can provide the means to express legitimate political concerns and help to offset the influence of opposing interests. The Ralph Nader organizations, conservationist groups, and Common Cause have collectively exerted a major influence upon government decision making in the name of "public interest." Regardless of whether one fully agrees with the views of the public-interest pressure groups, they have provided a healthy spirit of competition in the pluralistic political world that has made both government and powerful economic interests think twice before pursuing courses of action that in the past were taken for granted as being acceptable.

Pluralistic conflict among differing interest groups is an inevitable and desirable feature of the democratic process. While it is true that interest-group conflict often makes it very difficult for the government to act and produces "pluralistic stagnation," the aim of democracy is as much representation of interests as it is efficiency.

The checks and balances that exist among the diverse pluralistic interests of society and government help to control the arbitrary exercise of political power, which was one of the principal purposes of the original constitutional system of separation of powers and checks and balances. However, the Framers of the Constitution recognized that government not only must be controlled and checked but also must be capable of taking effective action to formulate and implement public policy in the national interest.

The lack of disciplined political parties and the proliferation of interest groups has buttressed limited government, but it has not increased the capabilities of government to take positive action. If any institutions are to be faulted in this regard it should be the political parties and not the interest groups. It was an independent and powerful presidency that was to be the principal constitutional institution for effective government; but in the absence of strong political parties capable of binding the president and Congress together on many important issues, the White House often stands alone, incapable of taking action to meet pressing public needs and, in particular, to overcome the disintegrative force of a multiplicity of groups all pressuring for the protection of their own interests.

It is important to turn now to a consideration of the major institutions of government—Congress, the president, the bureaucracy, and the judiciary—to assess how they have responded to public opinion, political parties, and interest groups.

THE EMERGENCE OF PROFESSIONAL INTEREST-GROUP POLITICS

Interest groups have always been part of the political landscape, often giving a colorful and controversial dimension to politics. Advocates of political pluralism proclaim that the give-and-take of interest-group politics represents democracy at its best. Special interests, these advocates of pluralism argue, collectively reflect the nation as a whole and separately represent constituencies that deserve to be heard in Washington's corridors of power. While group theorists defend freewheeling interest-group politics, a far more common rhetorical theme attacks special interests for their pursuit of "selfish" goals that they define to be contrary to the national interest. This case study analyzes not only the growing power of interest groups but also the emergence of professional managers who have turned group politics into a big business that does not always keep in touch with political consumers.

The New World of Interest Politics / *Norman J. Ornstein and Mark Schmitt*

When Congress put together the Medicare Catastrophic Coverage Act of 1988, it trusted the endorsement of the most powerful and established of Washington lobbies for the elderly, the American Association of Retired Persons (AARP). With 31 million members from the most politically active segment of the population, and with a legion of lobbyists among a total staff of 1,300 located in a gleaming office building in the heart of the nation's capital, the AARP has everything an interest group needs—prestige, money, constituents, and a noble mission. Its imprimatur gave Congress everything it needed, too, to pass this landmark piece of legislation.

Less than a year later, when Congress frantically backpedaled on the Medicare Catastrophic Coverage Act, AARP looked less like the diligent advocate for the elderly and more like a hidebound, out-of-touch bureaucracy making its constituents' golden years more burdensome. Angry senior citizens quickly decried the higher Medicare premiums and other levies as the "AARP tax." The grassroots reaction to the rise in Medicare premiums "was not anticipated because it had AARP's blessing," Senator Bob Packwood said in retrospect.

What is going on here? This hardly fits our textbook understanding of how interest groups and lobbies work in Washington. "The interests are always awake while the country slumbers and sleeps," warned the late British statesman William Gladstone—but here is a case of an interest in an apparent extended reverie that turned into a nightmare. For decades, we have argued about whether interests are insidious, whether they push their narrower needs over the national interest, or whether they possess unfair advantages because of their money and access. But we have always assumed that interests will represent—at the very least—their interests.

Our misgivings about their influence remains the same, but the world in which Washington interest groups operate has transformed itself in the past two decades from a closed-door marketplace of political influence by a few established interests to something like a Moroccan *Casbah*, with thousands of groups clamoring for the attention of government as well as potential members and donors. The old divisions, such as business versus labor, are there, but with many new twists—it is just as often business versus business, or business and labor versus domestic or foreign competitors.

These days, groups with similar interests compete with each other (the National Organization for Women and the National Women's Political Caucus, for example, or the Sierra Club and the Audubon Society, or the Conservative Caucus and the National Conservative Political Action Committee), and groups with divergent interests squabble fiercely where their territories intersect. Groups now build layers of professional staff, lawyers, professional fund-raisers, and "grass-roots consultants." They often employ former members and staffers of Congress, most of whom have developed their professional careers in Washington and have little direct connection with the constituencies they now represent. These well-paid staffs look for immediate results, emphasizing short-term tactics over the long-term goals of the groups' members. As a consequence, they are gradually losing touch with their own memberships and slipping out of sync with today's political climate.

Organizations as different as the National Rifle Association and the National Organization for Women today face problems juggling the agendas of their leaders, staff, and members. We can no longer assume that an interest group has reached an understanding or a consensus on what constitutes its interest.

And that's not all. At the same time that AARP went on its walkabout, another phenomenon of

Source: The American Enterprise, pp. 47-51, January/February 1990. Reprinted with permission from *The American Enterprise*. Copyright ©1990 American Enterprise Institute for Public Policy Research, Washington, D.C. 20036.

modern interest politics emerged: an apparently irrational internecine warfare among groups, reflecting a strange new tension about who is responsible for what in the interest-group community. *The Washington Post*'s David Ignatius recently chronicled the plight of a consortium of environmental groups that endorsed a "Blueprint for the Environment," a wide-ranging document comprising 511 recommendations, including one that urged the United States to resume participation in global population-control efforts that had been curtailed during the Reagan administration.

Whether the environmental groups that signed the document read all 511 recommendations, much less endorsed each and every one, is open to question. Nevertheless, the anti-abortion lobby mobilized for total war. The National Right to Life Committee, for example, alerted its members that the Audubon Society "is now a pro-abortion organization" and unleashed torrents of letters to the other groups in the consortium labeling them "babykillers." The head of a group called Trout Unlimited was furious: "We don't have a position on abortion. We never will. We deal only with trout!"

The time and effort expended on these inside-the-Beltway catfights are certainly one reason these groups are drifting apart from their constituents. Groups spend more time looking over their shoulders to ensure that no other groups encroach on their well-crafted niches in the political ecosystem of Washington than they spend pursuing their stated objectives. Douglas Johnson, National Right to Life director, was particularly blunt about why his group was so exercised by the environmentalists: "Environmental groups . . .should stay out of our bailiwick, and we'll stay out of theirs."

Even fiercer competition these days occurs among groups trying to fill the same niche—the same constituents, the same agenda, the same sources of funding. This is a partial explanation for the AARP's debacle: over the past few years a new and ruthless challenger began breathing down AARP's neck—James Roosevelt's National Committee to Preserve Social Security and Medicare. The Roosevelt group is first and foremost a fund-raising operation, shameless in making its direct mail look like time-sensitive official correspondence from the Social Security Administration.

With a minimal presence and a miserable reputation in the nation's capital—it didn't help to be named one of the "worst interest groups" by the *Washington Monthly*—the Roosevelt group could accomplish very little on Capitol Hill. But by tapping into AARP's funding base and encouraging the elderly to accept nothing less than a comprehensive home-care program, the Roosevelt group forced AARP to demonstrate some kind of legislative progress. In a year of sharp fiscal constraints, the result was the Medicare Catastrophic Coverage Act, a law that turned out to be catastrophic for the AARP.

Although this interest-group turmoil is recent, it represents the culmination of changes in the world of Washington interest groups since World War II. When nineteenth-century reformers gave the word "interests" a bad name, they had in mind a tiny sector of commercial enterprises that could afford a presence in Washington. To be sure, unlike Gladstone's Britain, America always had many and varied mass-based organizations—a phenomenon that particularly struck de Tocqueville—but few other than organized labor could be considered political "interest groups" engaged daily in the task of influencing policy.

In the past few decades, though, interest groups have proliferated and changed. Mass-based membership organizations have become an integral part of interest politics and lobbying. The National Organization for Women, the AARP, and the Sierra Club have obvious differences, yet all three, and scores of others, seek to represent the loose, often noneconomic interests of diverse populations, each reached by the creative use of computerized direct mail.

Unlike an earlier time, none of these organizations stands alone. For each, there is at least one group trying to do the same thing. The postwar widening of Washington interests brought our democracy very close to the sort of pluralism envisioned by James Madison in *Federalist 10*. Interests could pose no threat if every conceivable interest—economic or noneconomic—was adequately represented. But instead of lively pluralism, today's interest groups are remarkably bland. Each peddles the same lowest common denominator of fear, funding appeals, and minor legislative progress, trying to captivate the same core of charitably inclined or ideologically active donors. The flow of activity in interest groups is not from the bottom up—from the grass roots to the leaders—but from the top down. One prime objective for all groups is to keep other groups from encroaching on their market share; another is to keep those checks and letters coming in. It is no wonder, then, that the public sees Washington as isolated and out of touch with the country. Legislators bear most of this criticism, but as the AARP incident shows, the groups that claim to intervene on behalf of constituents may be more out of touch than the lawmakers.

The founders of most mass-based interest groups, at least until very recently, were citizens who came to Washington to make their voices heard. Those founders, though, have long since turned over the reins to a new class of professional interest-group managers with degrees in such fields as nonprofit management, experience solely in Washington, and membership in groups such as the American Society of Association Executives. The AARP was founded in 1958 by a retired school principal from California who had trouble getting insurance. When it launched its lobbying effort on the Medicare Catastrophic Coverage Act, AARP hired a new director whose resumé included stints at the National Association of Realtors and the U.S. Chamber of Commerce. With lobbying for the public interest thus reduced to a set of interchangeable techniques, it's no surprise that all the groups' letters, ads, and lobbying appeals look and sound alike—and no surprise that their constituents are growing cynical and restless.

Interest groups, of course, need professional staffs because they have increasingly become commercialized. These groups are more than collections of people with the same affinities, affiliations, or interests; they are businesses with bottom lines of their own. Many are quite explicit about it: the AARP, with an estimated $10 million annual cash flow from magazines, discount pharmaceuticals, and other commercial services, would be one of the largest corporations in the Washington, D.C., area if it went public. The Roosevelt group produces millions of dollars in profits—about 70 percent of its revenues—for associated firms specializing in direct mail. The internal conflicts of interest posed here, apparent or real, are legion. The AARP, relying heavily on its pharmaceutical business, lobbied hard for a generous prescription-drug provision in the Medicare Catastrophic Coverage Act. The Roosevelt group needs to use increasingly hysterical appeals to contributors to keep its direct-mail

business running—whether a real crisis exists or not.

Even less well-heeled groups are businesses in a sense, each with two sometimes-conflicting clients. Each group must sell itself to its members as their most effective advocate in Washington. And each group must sell itself to legislators as the legitimate proxy for those voters. If a group succeeds at one and not the other, the result is trouble for the group and for the political system. In the case of the elderly, the Roosevelt group sold itself best to its constituents, and the AARP sold itself to the legislators. We have seen the results.

The National Rifle Association (NRA) still claims the loyalty of the voters it represents through its membership, but it may have paid a steep price in its credibility in Washington and elsewhere. As the organization fought laws that would control undetectable plastic handguns, armor-piercing bullets, and assault weapons, it turned to a lavish mass-media campaign featuring Charlton Heston on television, and a full-page ad in newspapers suggesting that if the Chinese students in Tiananmen Square had had the benefit of our own Second Amendment, they would have been armed and therefore able to fight back against China's soldiers.

These ads indicate that the organization is playing a risky game of ever-increasing stakes to hold on to both its voters and its legislators, purveying ever more apocalyptic images to convince members that the NRA's legislative agenda is in their best interests—and that they need the NRA to pursue it. The organization has already lost the support of many law-enforcement officials and groups around the country and has gone through a messy internal shakeup. Still, even though observers periodically declare that the NRA has "gone too far" and predict that it will fade as a political force, the organization has so far avoided this fate, and no serious competitor has appeared to challenge them for the anti-gun-control niche.

Party Politics

That the disaffection of interest groups from their constituents has grave consequences for the political system should be apparent to anyone who has observed the perils of the Democratic Party in the 1980s. Ironically, the first mass-based interest group, organized labor, was also the first group to lose the unshakable political loyalty of its members. The Democratic Party, which trusted labor as the proxy for middle-class workers, paid the price. In 1984, the party went out of its way to cultivate the support of the AFL-CIO and other unions, winning the backing of all except the Teamsters, but a majority of white union voters backed Ronald Reagan. Similarly, Walter Mondale satisfied the demands of the National Organization for Women when he put a woman on his ticket. But women backed Reagan by 54 to 46 percent.

So far, the Republican Party has escaped major damage from the interest groups with which it is allied, but this may change. Before the Supreme Court's decision in the *Webster* case, the GOP's alliance with the pro-life groups did not threaten the party's base among affluent, educated voters who tend to favor abortion rights, but now that the issue is less abstract, some believe the GOP will suffer. But here, too, Democrats may be hurt by the uncompromising stance of pro-choice interest groups.

After World War II, as interest groups proliferated, political party organizations began to decline. The Democrats in particular compensated for the breakdown of local political machines by relying on emerging interest groups—labor, civil rights groups, environmental coalitions—to perform some of the machine's duties and to secure the allegiance of voters. The party paid a price for this change, becoming known as the "party of special interests," but the price would have been worth paying if those interests had delivered the political loyalties of their members.

Voters need some kind of structure to mediate between their day-to-day interests and the federal government; if interest groups can't do it, perhaps political parties will have to reassemble as modern versions of their older selves. In a sense, this dilemma lies at the heart of all the Democratic Party's navel-gazing this year.

Unfortunately, this is a difficult time to ask the national parties to reclaim their role as mediators between citizens and government. Neither party is a complete national party, reaching from the grass-roots level to the White House. Republicans seem to have a lock on the upper tier of national politics, but in many states the GOP barely exists at the community level. Democrats monopolize local offices, but they have trouble bringing voters' concerns together at the national level. If revitalized parties cannot take the place of weakened interest groups, the best solution may be for interest groups to become more democratic, less dominated by staff, more sensitive to their own internal conflicts, and more willing to accept compromise even if it cuts down on direct-mail revenues.

Before we lose too much sleep over the dissension and turmoil embroiling interest groups, we should note that the problem is an inevitable result of what is best in American politics today: that we live in a time of comfortable consensus, when the vast majority of Americans agree on our goals as a society but differ only on the specific policies to achieve them. We are not going to significantly expand or contract domestic spending, taxation, civil liberties, or social services this year or the next. Nearly everyone can accept this except the staffs of interest groups, who are paid well to demonstrate short-term progress. The torpor of today's politics compels these staffs to embrace the kind of policy progress that might be worse than no action at all (*a la* catastrophic care) or to paint apocalyptic images of the clock being turned back on our freedoms (NRA, pro-choice groups). These interest groups have trouble seeing that policy is neither moving in their favor nor moving against them—it is standing still. For many such groups, the politics of consensus presents far more confusion than did the sharp divisions that nearly split American society in the 1960s. For most of the rest of us, it's fortunate that we're not asking much of Washington today, since it's not clear who would represent our interests there if we were.

PART THREE

The National Government in Action

"President Announces New Budget Cuts, and Calls for Decreased Defense Expenditures"; "Congress Grapples with Plan to Bail Out Savings and Loans"; "Supreme Court Reviews Abortion Cases"; "Environmental Protection Agency Refuses to Delay Clean-Air Standards." These headlines illustrate the government in action. Behind the headlines various political forces are vying to advance their own interests.

Each branch of the national government—the presidency, Congress, the Supreme Court, and the bureaucracy—has independent power and its own base of political support. The presidency and the Supreme Court are relatively unified institutions, acting as units; but Congress and the bureaucracy are highly fragmented. Both must be viewed in terms of the separate committees and agencies that make up these branches and whose interests often conflict with one another.

The Constitution's simple formula—whereby Congress would make the law and the president would execute it—has been altered and complicated by the course of events since 1789, when George Washington took office. Today the president and the bureaucracy are primary sources of the legislative proposals enacted by Congress. The Supreme Court, too, has become more prominent in government than was foreseen by the Framers.

The change in the relative power of the three branches in some areas has challenged traditional standards of constitutional responsibility. In foreign-policy making and engaging the nation in war, twentieth-century presidents have often failed to consult Congress. For example, since World War II the congressional power to declare war has been replaced by "police actions" initiated by the president in Korea, Vietnam, and other parts of the world. In the domestic arena, too, before Watergate, a general acceptance of the growth of presidential prerogatives supported an "imperial presidency." Watergate caused a sharp reaction on Capitol Hill to a dominant presidency, and Congress asserted its independence of the White House for the remainder of the decade of the 1970s. President Ronald Reagan's strong leadership once again shifted the initiative to the White House.

The system devised in 1787 will undoubtedly continue to face challenges in the future. But will the fragmented mechanism of government remain adequate for the needs of a highly technological, complex, and interdependent society? The solutions to many questions of public policy may require greater coordination among the branches of government.

Congress: Its Framework and Members

By congressional decree, no building in the city of Washington may be built to stand higher than the Capitol dome. In this way the dominance of Congress over the other branches of the government was to be symbolized—a dominance clearly foreseen by the Framers of the American Constitution.

The role of Congress has changed considerably over the past 200 years. Although at times overshadowed by an "imperial presidency," Congress has valiantly attempted to control the reins of power in Washington. By any measure it is a critical part of the Washington power establishment, perhaps more important than the presidency in its continuous ability to shape policy—both its development and its implementation by the bureaucracy. Congress has more permanency and more expertise than the president and his personal staff, who are compelled by the Twenty-second Amendment's two-term limitation to leave their jobs just as they reach the threshold of understanding the complexities as well as the important limits of presidential power.

To understand Congress—the changes that have occurred in that body, and their significance—it is necessary to examine the role this branch of government was intended to play in the original constitutional scheme.

CONSTITUTIONAL BACKGROUND

While the constitutional system of separation of powers and checks and balances was based upon some sharing of legislative, executive, and judicial powers among the three branches of the government, each branch was to retain primary control over the sphere of power assigned to it. Congress was to be the primary legislative body, checked only by the presidential veto (which could be overruled by a two-thirds majority vote) and by judicial review of the constitutionality of its acts.[1] Congressional dominance of policy making by the national government was considered a logical extension of the principle of parliamentary supremacy embodied in the Anglo-American political tradition.

Parliamentary or legislative supremacy assumes that sovereignty resides with the people and their elected representatives. The House of Representatives was to be the only body of the national government directly

---

[1]Although not explicitly delegated to the Supreme Court by the Constitution, judicial review was considered by most of the Framers of the Constitution to be an implicit judicial power. For a discussion of judicial review, see pp. 64–66.

elected by the people, both the Senate and the president being indirectly selected. Congress was to be the people's body, with the sole authority to make laws. The president, in addition to veto power, was also given the responsibility to recommend legislation to Congress from time to time, and this reflected an original conception of a presidency that was not strictly limited to the exercise of executive functions. The legislative responsibilities of the president, however, in no way detracted from the principle of congressional supremacy in the law-making sphere.

While Congress was to be the supreme legislative body, its powers were limited to those enumerated in Article I of the Constitution. Originally these Article I powers—such as the power to tax and provide for the general welfare, regulate commerce among the states, declare war, and raise and support armies—represented the very core of the authority of the national government. Virtually nothing could be done by the other branches of the government without congressional approval. Indeed, without congressional support, in the form of appropriations and legislation establishing executive departments and courts below the Supreme Court, both the executive and the judiciary would be virtually powerless. Although Congress was of course limited by its enumerated powers, they nevertheless constituted the most extensive list of prerogatives delegated by the Constitution to any branch of the national government.

The constitutional powers of Congress not only gave it the edge over coordinate branches of the national level but also gave it potentially vast authority over the states. The scope of national authority over the states depended upon how the enumerated powers were interpreted; with the "loose interpretation" of Chief Justice John Marshall in such cases as *McCulloch v. Maryland* and *Gibbons v. Ogden* in 1819 and 1824, respectively, the basis was laid for a vast expansion of national (congressional) authority over the states.

The Bicameral Framework

As intended by the Framers, the House was to be the forum of popular representatives, dealing with matters of local concern, whereas the Senate was to be the forum of state governments, concerned with the matters of wider national interest. The *bicameral*, or two-chamber, structure was deliberately designed to accommodate federalism by giving each state the same number of senators, regardless of its population. At the same time this structure helped prevent the arbitrary exercise of power by Congress by establishing checks and balances between the House and the Senate.

Members and functions. The original constitutional formula for selecting members of Congress, and the particular functions designated to each house, were based on the constituency and purpose that each house was to serve. Thus the Framers provided that members of the House of Representatives would be elected directly by the people every two years. The frequent election of representatives, it was felt, would ensure that these legislators would always be responsive to the constituents of their local districts.

Although the popular election of senators was eventually guaranteed by ratification of the Seventeenth Amendment, the Constitution as originally written left the selection of senators to the state legislatures. In 1787 this seemed a logical arrangement, for at that time it was assumed that the primary responsibility of the upper house would be to represent the interests of the states as sovereign entities.

Although all appropriations bills must be approved by both houses, the lower house—because it alone was to represent the people—was given the authority to originate money bills, which would be funded through taxes paid by the people. In addition, the House was also granted the power to impeach high government officials. The Senate, on the other hand, was given exclusive authority to ap-

(Misha Richter. Copyright © 1967 Saturday Review, Inc.)

"Did you ever have one of those days when you didn't know whether to advise or consent?"
The Senate has the authority to give advice and consent on treaties and presidential appointments.

prove treaties, to confirm certain presidential appointments, and to conduct trials of officials who had been impeached.

The character of the two houses. When they designed the bicameral legislature, the Framers expected that the two houses would check each other. It was thought that the older members of the Senate would act with wisdom and moderation, offsetting the more enthusiastic approach to legislation that might come from the popularly elected House. *The Federalist*, No. 62, describes "the nature of the senatorial trust" as that which, "requiring greater extent of information and stability of character, requires at the same time that the senator should have reached a period of life most likely to supply these advantages."

Thus the Framers provided that senators

should be at least 30 years old, as opposed to representatives, who could be elected at the age of 25. Senators had to have been citizens for at least nine years, two years longer than the time required for representatives. Furthermore, by providing senators with six-year terms, by leaving their selection to the state legislatures, and by requiring that only one-third of the Senate could be chosen every two years, the Framers intended to isolate the Senate from direct popular control and from being swayed by popular pressures. Thus any rash or unreasonable legislation proposed by the lower house in response to popular whim would be modified or rejected by the more conservative upper house.

Today, however, political forces, more than constitutional prescriptions, dictate the character of the Senate. Senators, like representatives, are elected and must respond to constituent demands. And senators are much more likely to be challenged politically than are members of the House, where incumbency is an almost certain guarantee of reelection. The Senate no longer occupies its exalted constitutional perch, which was to be above day-to-day political pressures.

Size of the Legislature

The Constitution provides that each state shall have two senators; the number of representatives allotted to each state depends on the size of its population, with each state having at least one representative. The Framers assumed that each of the houses of Congress would be small enough for all members to participate directly in the enactment of legislation.

The author of *The Federalist*, No. 58, warned that under no circumstances should the size of the House of Representatives be indiscriminately increased, because "in all legislative assemblies, the greater the number composing them may be, the fewer will be the men who will in fact direct their proceedings." Little did the author of *The Federalist*, No. 58, realize that the United States would grow to have a population of well over 200 million, spanning the North American continent and including the noncontiguous states Alaska and Hawaii.

During the early years of the republic, the House and Senate were small bodies in comparison to their present size. The first Senate, which had 26 members, was not much larger than legislative committees are today. Each state subsequently admitted to the Union added two more senators to the upper house so that today there are now 100 senators representing the 50 states.

The Constitution provides that a census is to be taken every 10 years in order that the number of representatives can be properly apportioned. The House of Representatives in the first session of Congress was allotted 65 members. For more than a century, with Congress reapportioning representatives after each census, the membership of the House grew as the population of the country increased. By 1810 the total number of seats had risen to 186,

and a century later, in 1910, there were 435 representatives (see Figure 10.1).

After the 1920 census it became evident that the House would grow to such a size that debate and business would become more and more difficult to conduct. So in 1929 a reapportionment act was passed that permanently fixed the number of representatives at 435. The result has been that since 1929 the number of citizens represented by each member has increased as the population has increased. Thus in 1990 each representative spoke for about 500,000 people.

The "one-man, one-vote" rule that applies to the House keeps its districts equally representative within each state. This rule, combined with overall reapportionment every 10 years, assures democratic representation in the House (see Figure 10.2). However, no such rules apply to the Senate, which is increasingly becoming an unrepresentative institution. Each state has two Senators regardless of its population, but states may and do

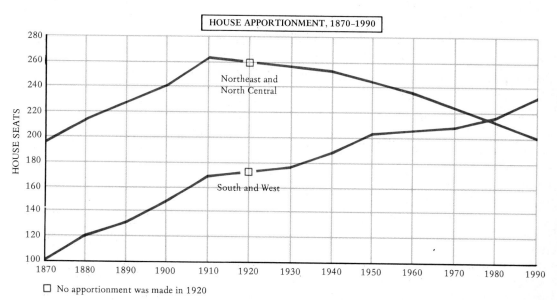

HOUSE APPORTIONMENT, 1870–1990

Northeast and North Central

South and West

HOUSE SEATS

□ No apportionment was made in 1920

(Source: *The New York Times*, January 23, 1976, p. 20. Copyright © 1976 by the New York Times Company. Reprinted by permission. Data for 1980 are from U.S. Bureau of the Census.)

FIGURE 10.1

1990 Reapportionment: Projected Gainers and Losers

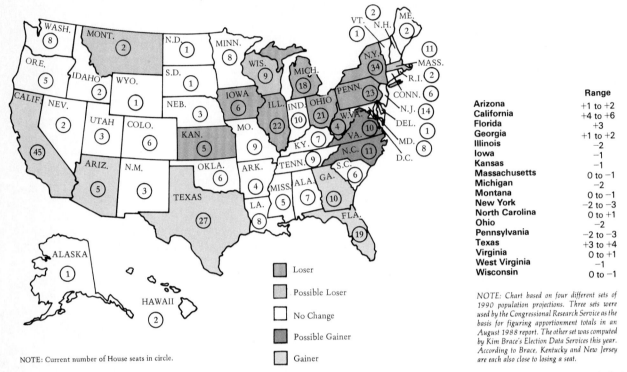

	Range
Arizona	+1 to +2
California	+4 to +6
Florida	+3
Georgia	+1 to +2
Illinois	−2
Iowa	−1
Kansas	−1
Massachusetts	0 to −1
Michigan	−2
Montana	0 to −1
New York	−2 to −3
North Carolina	0 to +1
Ohio	−2
Pennsylvania	−2 to −3
Texas	+3 to +4
Virginia	0 to +1
West Virginia	−1
Wisconsin	0 to −1

- ■ Loser
- ▨ Possible Loser
- □ No Change
- ▨ Possible Gainer
- ▨ Gainer

NOTE: Current number of House seats in circle.

NOTE: *Chart based on four different sets of 1990 population projections. Three sets were used by the Congressional Research Service as the basis for figuring apportionment totals in an August 1988 report. The other set was computed by Kim Brace's Election Data Services this year. According to Brace, Kentucky and New Jersey are each also close to losing a seat.*

(Source: *Congressional Quarterly Weekly Report*, August 12, 1989, p. 2139. Reprinted with permission from Congressional Quarterly, Inc.)

FIGURE 10.2

have only one representative if they have small populations (Alaska, Delaware, North and South Dakota, Vermont, Wyoming).

Officers of Congress

The Framers were aware that certain presiding officers would be needed by the Congress to direct the legislative proceedings. Article I of the Constitution provides that "the House of Representatives shall choose their Speaker and other Officers. . . ." Several paragraphs later it is stipulated that the vice-president of the United States is to be president of the Senate and that the members of the Senate "shall choose their other Officers, and also a President pro tempore, in the ab-

sence of the Vice President, or when he shall exercise the Office of President of the United States." As the political parties grew in importance, these posts became the rewards of the dominant party in each house of the legislature (see Figure 10.3).

Speaker of the House. A very influential individual, the Speaker of the House presides over the chamber. The Speaker recognizes members who wish to speak and appoints members to select and special committees. Moreover, since the Speaker is selected by the majority party in the House, he or she is also able to use the position to encourage the passage of his or her party's political programs.

Various Speakers in the past have wielded much power. From the 1820s until 1850,

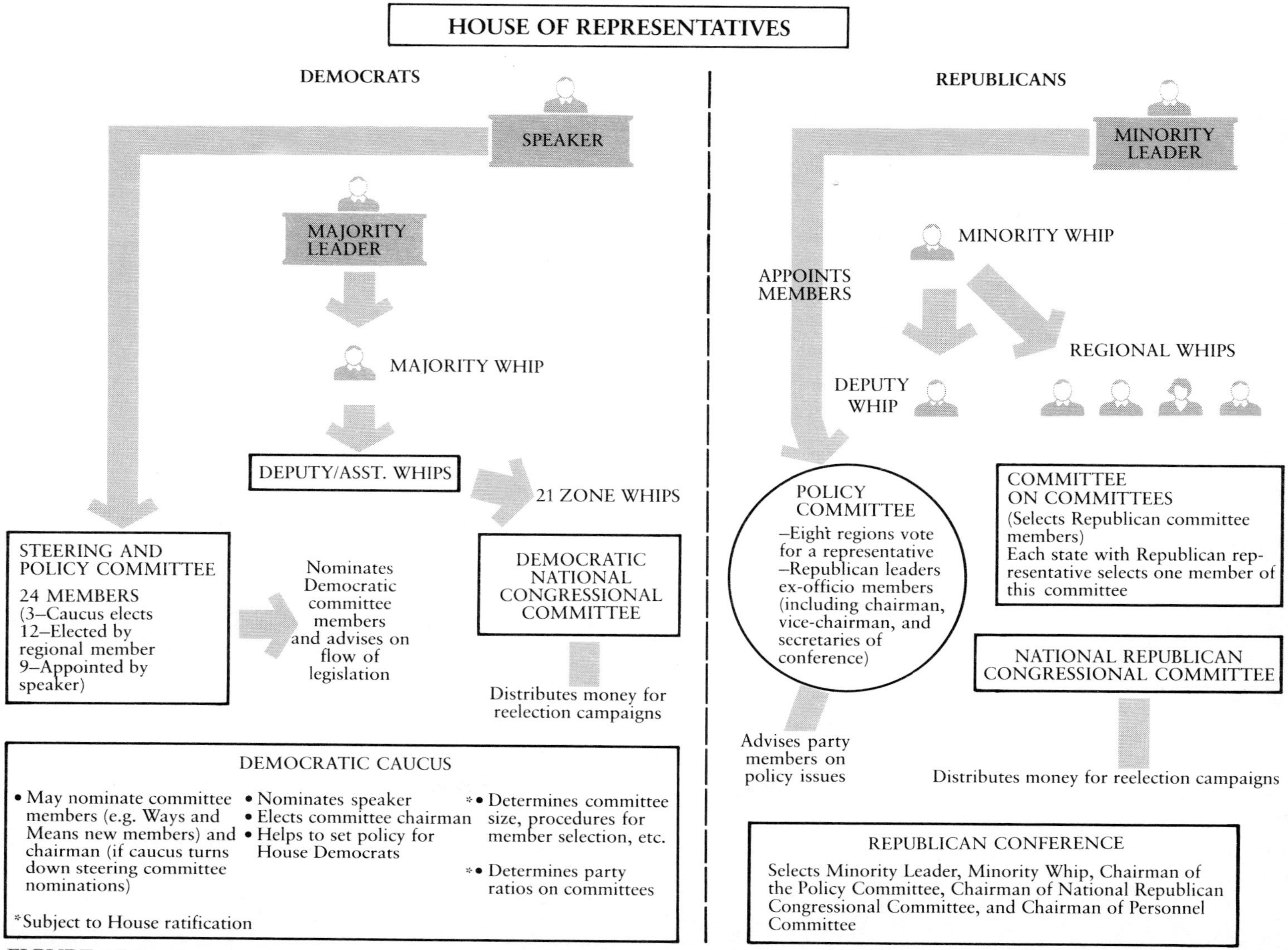

HOUSE OF REPRESENTATIVES

DEMOCRATS

SPEAKER

MAJORITY LEADER

MAJORITY WHIP

DEPUTY/ASST. WHIPS

21 ZONE WHIPS

Nominates Democratic committee members and advises on flow of legislation

DEMOCRATIC NATIONAL CONGRESSIONAL COMMITTEE

Distributes money for reelection campaigns

STEERING AND POLICY COMMITTEE

24 MEMBERS
(3—Caucus elects Ways and Means new members) and 12—Elected by regional member chairman (if caucus turns 9—Appointed by down steering committee speaker) nominations)

*Subject to House ratification

DEMOCRATIC CAUCUS

- May nominate committee members (e.g. Ways and Means new members) and chairman (if caucus turns down steering committee nominations)
- Nominates speaker
- Elects committee chairman
- Helps to set policy for House Democrats
- * Determines committee size, procedures for member selection, etc.
- * Determines party ratios on committees

REPUBLICANS

MINORITY LEADER

MINORITY WHIP

DEPUTY WHIP

REGIONAL WHIPS

APPOINTS MEMBERS

POLICY COMMITTEE
—Eight regions vote for a representative
—Republican leaders ex-officio members (including chairman, vice-chairman, and secretaries of conference)

Advises party members on policy issues

COMMITTEE ON COMMITTEES
(Selects Republican committee members)
Each state with Republican representative selects one member of this committee

NATIONAL REPUBLICAN CONGRESSIONAL COMMITTEE

Distributes money for reelection campaigns

REPUBLICAN CONFERENCE

Selects Minority Leader, Minority Whip, Chairman of the Policy Committee, Chairman of National Republican Congressional Committee, and Chairman of Personnel Committee

FIGURE 10.3

Henry Clay was able to engineer compromises that held North and South together. In his classic 1885 work *Congressional Government* (written when he was a graduate student in history and political philosophy at Johns Hopkins University), Woodrow Wilson noted:

The most esteemed writers upon our Constitution have failed to observe, not only that the standing committees are the most essential machinery of our governmental system, but also that the Speaker of the House of Representatives is the most powerful functionary of that system. So sovereign is he within the range of his influence that one could wish for accurate knowledge as to the actual extent of his power. But Mr. Speaker's powers cannot be known accurately, because they vary with the character of Mr. Speaker.[2]

Wilson was describing a Congress in which the Speaker had the potential to dominate the legislative business of the House through control over the Rules Committee (of which the Speaker had been ex officio chairman since 1858) and by dominating floor proceedings through rulings on parliamentary procedure. This power became particularly important in 1890 when, under the speakership of Thomas B. Reed of Maine, the House formally adopted rules that gave the Speaker almost dictatorial authority to control the proceedings on the House floor, particularly by ruling out of order "dilatory motions."

The power of the Speaker to direct floor proceedings was complemented by his authority to appoint both the chairmen and the members of all the standing committees of the House. At the time of Wilson's writing, seniority was the customary criterion in bestowing committee chairmanships; however, powerful speakers, such as Thomas Reed (1889–1891, 1895–1899) and Joseph Cannon (1903–1911), unhesitatingly manipulated both

parliamentary procedures and their power to appoint committee chairmen to rule the House with an iron hand. The "1910 revolt" against the excessive power of the Speaker, particularly against his authority to appoint the members of committees and his domination of the Rules Committee, succeeded in greatly reducing the influence of this position.

Since the House reforms of 1910–1915, which decentralized authority to the committees and reduced the Speaker's power to the control of floor proceedings, Speakers have had to rely on their informal powers of persuasion to exercise influence over the House. Twentieth-century Speakers have not, however, been without power, as is illustrated by the large measure of control over the House during the speakership of Sam Rayburn of Texas (1940–1947; 1949–1953; and 1955–1961) and, beginning in the Ninety-fifth Congress in 1977, by the dominant force of Speaker Thomas ("Tip") O'Neill, Jr., of Massachusetts. O'Neill announced his retirement in 1985. When he left Congress after his term expired in 1986, the House elected Texas Democrat Jim Wright, who had been majority leader under O'Neill, to the speakership. Wright promised to continue the House tradition of forceful Speakers, but he resigned in June 1989 in the face of Republican-initiated charges that he had violated House gift and outside-income rules. The House then elected the mild-mannered and low-key Majority Leader Thomas Foley (D., Wash.) to be Speaker. Missouri Democrat and former presidential candidate Richard Gephardt replaced Foley in the majority leader's slot. Foley and Gephardt, however, did not get off to a good start. Foley seemed weak and ineffective, and Gephardt appeared more to be running for president in 1992 than paying attention to House politics.

Behind the scenes the Speaker retains extraordinary power over the scheduling of legislation on the floor and over committee

---

[2]Woodrow Wilson, *Congressional Government* (New York: Meridian Books, 1956), p. 83.

legislative activity in which he or she is particularly interested. With the approval of the majority caucus, the Speaker now appoints the majority members of the House Rules Committee, a move that strengthens the control of the majority party over a committee that had too frequently, in the views of the 1975 Democratic caucus that voted the action, exercised independent power to stall legislation.

President of the Senate. The constitutional provision that the vice-president is to serve as president of the Senate makes this leadership position ineffective, particularly compared to that of the Speaker of the House. The vice-president is not a member of the Senate and can vote only in case of a tie. If individual power exists in the Senate, it is exercised through the position of the majority leader, who is elected by and is directly under the control of the majority party's members in the body. In effect, the majority leader directs the presiding officer—whether the vice-president, the president *pro tempore* (for a limited time) or a senator presiding on a pro tempore basis—in his disposition of parliamentary matters. John Adams was the first president of the Senate, and although a Federalist in a Senate controlled by the Federalists, he nevertheless did not attempt to direct Senate proceedings, setting a precedent for the future. Adams was succeeded by Thomas Jefferson, a Republican, who had no influence whatsoever over the Federalist-controlled body.

The president pro tempore. Whenever the vice-president is unable to attend Senate meetings, a president pro tempore or, as is usually the case, one of the senators taking over the chair on a rotating basis, acts as the presiding officer. Although the presidency pro tempore of the Senate is elective, like the speakership of the House, it is a *pro forma* office without any inherent power. Although a member of the body, the president pro tempore has not traditionally been given any

independent power to direct the floor proceedings of the Senate.

The lack of a powerful presiding officer in the Senate is due not only to the constitutional assignment of the vice-president as the chief presiding officer but also to the nature of the Senate itself. While from time to time party leadership has reared its head in the upper body, for the most part each senator has been and continues to be treated as a sovereign power within the body. Since the president pro tempore of the Senate is elected by the members, the majority party invariably controls this position, which by custom is awarded to the most senior senator of the majority.

Informal organization of the House and the Senate. The Constitution provides only the most sketchy outlines of House and Senate organization. Over the two centuries since the adoption of the Constitution, the House and the Senate have undergone a variety of organizational and procedural changes that have shaped their character in ways entirely unforeseen by the Framers of the Constitution. The rise of committee government in both bodies of Congress has been a major development, overshadowing in the twentieth century the power of partisan influences in Congress to control the legislative proceedings. In the House, in particular, committee rule has largely replaced the powers that the Speaker possessed in the nineteenth century; and in combination with the weak party apparatus in the House, this has meant a dispersion of power. In comparison to the House, the Senate has been an institution dominated more by individuals than by its leadership or by its party organization. Party organization in Congress—majority and minority leaders, whips, party committees, and caucuses—was not foreseen by the Constitution. (See Chapter 11 for further discussion of the development of leadership and party organization in the House and the Senate.)

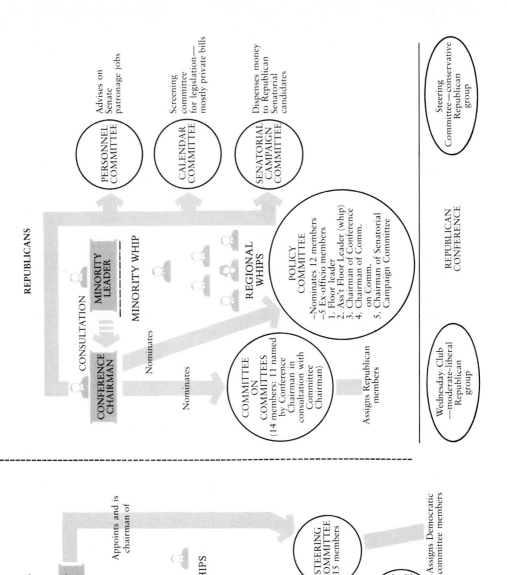

THE SENATE

REPUBLICANS

PERSONNEL COMMITTEE — Advises on Senate patronage jobs

CALENDAR COMMITTEE — Screening committee for legislation—mostly private bills

SENATORIAL CAMPAIGN COMMITTEE — Dispenses money to Republican Senatorial candidates

CONSULTATION

MINORITY LEADER

MINORITY WHIP

CONFERENCE CHAIRMAN

Nominates

Nominates

REGIONAL WHIPS

POLICY COMMITTEE
—Nominates 12 members
—5 Ex-officio members
1. Floor leader
2. Ass't Floor Leader (whip)
3. Chairman of Conference
4. Chairman of Comm. on Comm.
5. Chairman of Senatorial Campaign Committee

COMMITTEE ON COMMITTEES
(14 members; 11 named by Conference Chairman in consultation with Committee Chairman)

Assigns Republican members

Wednesday Club —moderate–liberal Republican group

REPUBLICAN CONFERENCE

Steering Committee—conservative Republican group

DEMOCRATS

MAJORITY LEADER

WHIP

Appoints and is chairman of

Appoints and is chairman of

REGIONAL WHIPS

STEERING COMMITTEE 15 members

Appoints and is chairman of

Assigns Democratic committee members

SENATORIAL CAMPAIGN COMMITTEE

—POLICY COMMITTEE * (7 members)
—LEGISLATIVE REVIEW COMMITTEE (4 members also whips)

COMBINED

* Reviews legislative proposals and agenda for the party.

FIGURE 10.4

FUNCTIONS OF REPRESENTATIVES AND SENATORS

The Constitutional stipulation that Congress was to be the principal lawmaking body clearly established the legislative responsibility of Congress, and placed legislation at the top of the list of its functions. Lawmaking has always been considered of paramount importance on Capitol Hill, and the ever-increasing length of congressional sessions is in large part attributable to increased legislative activity. This activity, however, does not involve simply the passage of laws but also the seemingly endless hearings, reports, "markup" sessions of committees (in which bills are taken up item by item and amendments are made and voted upon by the committee), investigations, and the informal meetings and machinations of all sorts that inevitably surround the performance of legislative functions.

Perhaps the most important fact about Congress is its institutionalization as a body, which provides rewarding and often profitable careers for its members. As members gain tenure on Capitol Hill, they are more inclined to view Congress as an end in itself. They tend to seek above all to increase their personal power and status within the institution—first through assignment to powerful and prestigious committees, and second, in the House of Representatives, through achieving positions of leadership. (In the Senate, leadership positions are relatively far less important than in the House in terms of power and status.)

For almost the first one hundred years of its existence, Congress was essentially an amateur body composed of citizen-legislators who rarely stayed in Washington for more than two terms of office. The House was particularly prone to turnover from the very beginning, but the Senate, too, was not a place for political careers until the latter part of the nineteenth century. Some of the Framers of

(Drawing by Stan Hunt; © 1977 The New Yorker Magazine, Inc.)

"There are days, Hank, when I don't know who's President, what state I'm from, or even if I'm a Democrat or a Republican, but, by God, I still know how to bottle up a piece of legislation in committee."

Congress tends to be dominated by its committees.

the Constitution had feared that senators might entrench themselves for life, but this was hardly borne out by the activities of senators in the first decades of the republic. Between 1789 and 1801, 33 of the 94 senators had resigned before their terms were up, 6 doing so to take other federal offices. Between 1801 and 1813, 35 senators resigned. Such resignations reflected the low esteem in which the Senate was held as a place to advance political careers. Added to voluntary resignations, there was an extremely low rate of reelection in both the House and the Senate until well after the Civil War.

The emergence of Congress as an institution that provided an arena for the development of political careers began in the 1870s, as is illustrated in part by the decreasing rate of turnover in Congress in the latter decades of the nineteenth century. This rate has continued to decrease steadily in the twentieth century. (The reason for the high turnover in the Congresses of the pre-Civil War period was an unwillingness on the part of incumbents to run for reelection, not an unusual capriciousness among the electorate.) The trend toward greater congressional stability at the end of the nineteenth century is illustrated in the House, where 50 percent of representatives were freshmen in the 1870s and only 30 percent were freshmen in 1899. In Congress as a whole, close to 60 percent were freshmen in the 1870s, and between 30 and 40 percent were freshmen in the 1880s; by the 1890s the number of freshmen had been reduced to be-

tween 20 and 30 percent—a range that has continued with downward variations since then.

The institutionalization of Congress has had important consequences for the role of the legislature. Essentially, it has meant that Congress is viewed very differently from the inside than from the outside. The strivings of members to advance their political careers on Capitol Hill may or may not advance the broader constitutional purposes of Congress or the interests of the citizens whom the legislators are elected to represent.

Freshmen representatives and senators usually arrive in Washington full of optimism, and even idealism, about how they are going to help the country. They soon find that they are in the center of a whirlpool; they lose their sense of direction and feeling for what they can accomplish. New members of the House make reelection their first objective because they know they must serve for at least three or four terms before they can be seriously involved in congressional decision making as subcommittee chairmen, ranking minority party members of subcommittees, or in party leadership posts. Senators can achieve power far earlier on Capitol Hill than representatives

Congressmen always look out for their districts' interests.

because the Senate is far smaller, collegial, and more a body of equals than the House. Freshmen senators in the majority party generally receive subcommittee chairmanships and, unlike in the past, begin early to participate fully in Senate proceedings.

Congress today is composed of 435 representatives and 100 senators. This is a rather unwieldy body that nonetheless is expected to work efficiently in a disunited and complex political system. Congress is so large and fragmented that most important decisions are made in congressional committees or through informal consultations between members of Congress and bureaucrats. Since Congress is the principal lawmaking body in the country, its members naturally consider the lawmaking function to be their primary responsibility. However, as representatives of the people and as lawmakers in a complex political system, they must respond to many constituent demands, and perform numerous functions that are only indirectly related, or even unrelated, to making laws.

As Representatives

As elected representatives of the people, members of Congress are expected to make laws that reflect the will of the electorate. But the relationship between legislators and their constituents is a complex one extending far beyond that of a simple transmission belt conveying demands from the voters to their representatives. Political scientist David Mayhew, in a study of the House of Representatives, found that members seek reelection not only by adopting positions they believe will be supported by their constituents but, more importantly, through advertising and "creditclaiming."[3] House members make every effort to present a favorable *image* to their constituents and to avoid going "out on a limb" on controversial issues.

Position taking. Mayhew defines *position taking* as "the public enunciation of a judgmental statement on anything likely to be of interest to political actors [voters]."[4] Legislators have many forums in which they can take positions, including committee hearings and roll-call voting on Capitol Hill, radio and television appearances, speeches before their constituents, press releases, newsletters, and ghost-written books and articles.

Position taking can be informative, giving voters knowledge of their representatives' views on major public policy issues. Legislators would prefer not to have to take stands on emotionally charged and controversial issues, such as abortion, school prayer, busing of schoolchildren to achieve racial balances, and social security tax increases and benefit reductions. However, these and many other controversial issues are frequently raised in legislation and floor amendments to bills introduced by members with strong views who want to see government action taken one way or the other.

Position taking may be particularly dangerous to senatorial incumbents who are more likely to be challenged than representatives, and who, due to the size of their constituencies, have less opportunity to build the solid constituent relationships often based on personal contacts that have consistently helped to ensure the reelection of the overwhelming majority of House incumbents. The visibility and exalted status of senatorial office make senators prime electoral targets.

The hazards of position taking were illustrated in the 1980 elections, when at least four prominent Senate incumbents were successfully attacked and unseated because of their liberal views on a variety of issues. For example, Idaho Senator Frank Church, chairman of the Senate Foreign Relations Committee, incurred electoral disfavor for supporting the Panama Canal treaties that returned the Ca-

---

[3]David Mayhew, *Congress: The Electoral Connection* (New Haven: Yale University Press, 1974).

[4]Ibid., p. 61.

(Drawing by Dana Fradon; © 1980 The New Yorker Magazine, Inc.)

"Senator, according to this report, you've been marked for defeat by the A.D.A., the National Rifle Association, the A.F.L.-C.I.O., the N.A.M., the Sierra Club, Planned Parenthood, the World Student Christian Federation, the Clamshell Alliance . . ."

Senators are vulnerable to electoral challenges because of their high visibility.

nal to Panama. Church, elected in 1956, had had to wait until 1978 to become chairman of the prestigious Foreign Relations Committee. He had served his constituency well over the years, taking positions on domestic issues that were in agreement with the opinions of the majority of voters in Idaho. He had opposed gun control and voted for an end to the constitutional ban on prayer in public schools. He also had opposed publicly funded abortions and supported a constitutional amendment to give the states authority to legislate abortion

policy. Nevertheless, Church's electoral opponent, Congressman Stephen Symms, called attention to the positions Church had taken in foreign affairs, accusing him of giving away the Panama Canal and crippling the Central Intelligence Agency when he had been the chairman of a Select Intelligence Committee investigating the agency. Church had also voted against the neutron bomb and had supported legislation to pardon draft resistors who had opposed the Vietnam War—positions that Symms did not fail to call to the attention of the conservative Idaho constituency. Symms finally defeated Church by a handful of votes (4,262) in one of the closest Senate races in the nation.

House members must also take positions that may make them electorally vulnerable. A wide variety of liberal and conservative interest groups, such as Americans for Democratic Action, Consumer Federation of America, National Rifle Association, and Americans for Constitutional Action, rate members of Congress on the basis of the positions they have taken on issues that are of concern to these groups. And interest group leaders work diligently to defeat legislators who have consistently opposed them.

Representatives, however, are less likely than Senators to be held politically accountable by their constituents for the positions they take. Congressmen cultivate close ties with their constituents through casework—helping to solve the grievances voters have with government. They build their images through advertising. Senators do the same, but for most of them the large numbers of voters in their states make it difficult to develop the kinds of contacts with influential individuals and groups that characterize House members' relationships with their constituents. Congressmen are thus far more likely to be supported *in spite of* their positions than senators. Constituents know "their" congressmen are working for them, and an unpopular position or two will not undermine the ongoing good relationship between members of the House and their electorates.

House members also find it easier than senators to equivocate on the positions they take. The media, both back home and in Washington, scrutinize the votes and the legislative activities of senators closely. A senator's stand is generally considered to be relatively more important than that of a House member. For example, the foreign policy views of members of the Senate Foreign Relations Committee can make headlines, but the activities of the House Foreign Affairs Committee and its members are more often than not forgotten. For the most part, the local press supports representatives, dwelling less on their positions than on their activities on behalf of constituents.

Senators cannot get away with the kind of position-taking ambiguity engaged in by California Democrat Edward Roybal, who told an interviewer how he had approached the highly controversial issue of American involvement in Vietnam:

You may find this difficult to understand, but sometimes I wind up making a patriotic speech one afternoon and later on that same day an antiwar speech. In the patriotic speech I speak of past wars, but I also speak of a need to prevent more wars. My positions are not inconsistent; I just approach different people differently.

The interviewer noted,

Roybal went on to depict the diversity of crowds he speaks to: One afternoon he is surrounded by balding men wearing Veterans' caps and holding American flags; a few hours later he speaks to a crowd of Chicano youths, angry over American involvement in Vietnam. Such a diverse constituency, Roybal believes, calls for different methods of expressing one's convictions.[5]

David Mayhew concludes that "The best position-taking strategy for most congressmen at most times is to be conservative—to cling to their own positions of the past where possible and to reach for new ones with great caution where necessary." Mayhew also suggests that "marginal" members of the House, those in danger of electoral defeat, often innovate in position taking to broaden their appeal to the voters. Congressional marginals may "fulfill an important function here as issue pioneers—experimenters who test out new issues and thereby show other politicians which ones are usable."[6]

Credit claiming. While position taking

---

[5]William Lazarus, "Nader Profile on Edward Roybal (D., Cal.)," cited in Mayhew, op. cit., pp. 64–65.

[6]Mayhew, op. cit., pp. 67, 68.

may be electorally hazardous, claiming credit for the concrete benefits of government that flow directly to a legislator's district can only serve to enhance a member's popularity. David Mayhew defines *credit claiming* "as acting so as to generate a belief in [voters] that one is *personally* responsible for causing the government, or some unit thereof, to do something that the [voter] considers desirable."[7] Legislators claim credit for particularized benefits bestowed on districts, such as the many "pork barrel" projects, including dams, bridges, defense contracts and military bases, grants to local communities, colleges, and schools, government funds for disaster relief, and federal buildings. Members also claim credit for casework that benefits individual constituents (see pp. 289–290).

Credit claiming affects the representative role of legislators in several ways. First, members can use effective credit claiming to build almost impenetrable legislative bases in their respective districts. The overwhelming incumbency advantage of members of the House is in fact largely based upon their credit-claiming activities. Senators claim credit too, but the generally large sizes of their constituencies and their greater vulnerability in position taking makes it impossible for them to rely upon credit claiming for electoral support. Second, because House members can rely to such a large extent upon credit claiming for reelection, they do not have to depend upon electoral appeals based upon policy positions. Their representative role becomes one of channeling particular benefits to constituents rather than of representing the policy preferences of voters.

Advertising. Congressmen advertise to sell themselves to constituents. David Mayhew defines *advertising* as "any effort to disseminate one's name among constituents in such a fashion as to create a favorable image, but in messages having *little or no issue content*. A successful congressman builds what amounts to a brand name, which may have a generalized electoral value for other politicians in the same family."[8]

Advertising is carried out through newsletters, opinion columns in newspapers, radio and television broadcasts (which are often conveniently recorded in Capitol Hill studios at public expense), and by engaging in newsworthy activities. Incumbents have considerable advantages over challengers in advertising because they not only have the staff, facilities, and expenses to engage in advertising, but also because the media of their own accord are far more likely to publicize incumbents than challengers.

Effective advertising, like credit claiming, tends to ensure the reelection of House incumbents, and it benefits Senate incumbents as well. Challengers find it difficult if not impossible to unseat incumbents by waging a campaign based on issues. They know that before even beginning to deal with issues they must attract attention to themselves to gain recognition among voters. The "campaign walk" is a favored advertising technique for challengers. Democratic Senator Lawton Chiles of Florida, an obscure state senator in 1970, won his seat by walking over five hundred miles between Pensacola in the northern panhandle of the state to the offshore island of Key West in the south. "The Walking Senator" became Chiles's "brand name," and Chiles kept his original walking boots propped up behind his Senate desk as a constant reminder to visitors of his feat.

"Homestyle." Political scientist Richard Fenno has pointed out that a legislator's career in Washington and his or her constituency career are often separated. Representatives are rarely reelected solely because of what they accomplish on Capitol Hill. A mem-

---

[7]Ibid., pp. 52–53. Emphasis added.

[8]Ibid., p. 49. Emphasis added.

"The first time I ran, I came back to the office one day and everybody who was working for my campaign was arrayed, sitting across the desk and in chairs on either side, like this [arms folded]. They said, 'We have something to tell you. *You* are the candidate. *We* are the campaign staff. If *you* don't stop acting like the campaign manager, we quit!'

"I was running the campaign. I'd *always* run the campaign. I like to campaign. I ran my husband's campaigns, and I've also run several national campaigns within the Democratic Party.

"The nitty-gritty of politics is as essential to the success of the campaign as all of the media hype. The real challenge is to put together enough of the small organizations so you feel you have the entire district covered. I've always been good at that. I put them together for Hale.

"[For example], in 1984 the district was made into a majority black district by court order, and I had a real campaign challenge from Judge Israel Augustine. A group of 100 ladies was very concerned about that and upset that someone of his stature and longtime friendship with the Baptists would run against me, so they incorporated themselves as 100 Black Ladies for Lindy. I think they have about 268 members. When it's time to activate the campaign, they are there.

"I also have experts in many different fields. Depending on the size of the threat, we activate as much as we need to. Then we have all these little organizations who endorse you and who have their own staffs. The coordination of all of that becomes your campaign superstructure.

"You have to play to the organizations. There isn't a phase of your campaign that isn't in some way affected by the desires of the groups who are supporting you.

"The expense primarily is in media coverage. The mail production also has gone up. It's incredible.

"The tools of the trade have changed a great deal. I think the name-calling and the negative campaigning are horrid. You have standards for advertising any other kind of product, and if you're going to market politicians as you market goods, you should have to abide by some standards.

"Unfortunately, I think that some of the old-time campaigning with volunteers is almost looked down upon by the people who do the campaign for money. But there's no way you can really combat a well-organized grassroots campaign without having one of your own. The only danger I think that incumbents really encounter is when they forget that the grassroots are out there. I never stop."

Lindy Boggs succeeded her husband, House Majority Leader Hale Boggs, after his plane disappeared over Alaska in 1972. She has represented Louisiana's 2nd Congressional District for nine consecutive terms.

Source: Reprinted by permission of *Campaigns & Elections Magazine*, 1835 K St., NW, #403, Washington, D.C. 20006, 202-331-3222. December 1989, p. 39.

ber's goal is to build a district organization and personal image—a "homestyle"—that will ensure reelection. (See Box 10.1.) Representatives want to be free to pursue their congressional careers, to build power as committee chairmen or party leaders, and to gain recognition *within* Congress for their policy achievements.

Junior members of Congress spend much of their time building their constituency careers. One member, near the end of his second term, described the position of the junior member: "I haven't been a congressman yet. The first two years, I spent all of my time getting myself reelected. That last two years,

(Yardley—Courtesy of *Baltimore Sun.*)

"I love to sample these grass roots."
The opinion samplings that lawmakers receive tend to come from only small segments of their constituencies.

I spent getting myself a district so that I could get reelected. So I won't be a congressman until next year."[9]

While representatives must account for their Capitol Hill activities, they have the initiative in what they tell voters. One congressman pointed out that constituents "don't know much about my votes. Most of what they know is what I tell them." He described the result of effective constituency relations:

It's a weird thing how you get a district to a point where you can vote the way you want to without getting scalped for doing it. I guess you do it in two ways. You come back here [to the district] a lot and let people see you, so they get a feel for you. And, secondly, I go out of my way to disagree with people on specific issues. That way, they know you aren't trying to snow them. And when you vote against their

views, they'll say, "Well, he's got his reasons." They'll trust you. I think that's it. If they trust you, you can vote the way you want, and it won't hurt.[10]

An overwhelming majority of voters agree that "their" representatives are doing a good job. Political scientist Gary Jacobson's study of the 1978 and 1980 elections found that

reactions to incumbents, both general and specific, are overwhelmingly favorable. More than 70 percent of the voters . . .rated the incumbent's performance in office as good or very good in 1978; 88 percent approved mildly or strongly of his performance in 1980. About 90 percent in each year's sample thought he would be helpful or very helpful if they brought him a problem. Satisfaction with the incumbent's response to voter requests runs very high indeed; a large majority were "very satisfied" as were friends who had made similar requests. Nearly three-quarters of those reporting generally agree with the incumbent's votes; 69 percent of them agree with his vote on a specific bill they recall. From 75 to 80 percent think he would do a better job dealing with what they perceive to be the most important problem facing the nation.[11]

Jacobson concludes that effective position taking, credit claiming, and advertising, which taken together constitute a member's homestyle, account for the overwhelming success of House incumbents in their reelection bids. (From 1946–1988, over 80 percent of House incumbents who have chosen to run have been reelected. In a majority of election years over 90 percent of the House incumbents win their reelection bids.) Moreover, Jacobson points out: "It is also apparent that the electoral strategy of discouraging opposition before the campaign begins is both effective and effectively pursued. Most incumbent House members face obscure, politically in-

---

[9]Richard Fenno, *Homestyle* (Boston: Little, Brown, 1978), p. 215.

[10]Ibid., pp. 153, 154.

[11]Gary Jacobson, *The Politics of Congressional Elections* (Boston: Little, Brown, 1983), p. 110.

experienced opponents, whose resources fall far short of what it takes to mount a serious campaign."[12] (See Box 10.2.)

Effective *casework,* a form of credit claiming, is one of the most important ways in which incumbents buttress their reelection chances. (Casework is explained in more detail in the next section.)

As Buffers between Government and People

Given the scope and nature of present-day governmental activity, some agent must act for the people in their day-to-day affairs with government. Congress is the ideal choice for this task. Legislators are close to the people and should understand their concerns and problems. Whatever the extent to which the viewpoints of legislators influence the choices of voters, their ability to service the requests of their constituents is at least of equal importance. Members of Congress cannot afford to ignore these requests. Their public images are determined as much by their handling of these nonlegislative functions as by their prowess in the lawmaking arena.

The relationship between a member of Congress and his or her individual constituents is often based on representation of the latter in counteractions to adverse decisions by administrative agencies. The grievances of constituents usually involve complaints or challenges to measures taken by administrators as a result of legislation already passed. For example, a group of suburbanites may challenge the Defense Department's construction of a missile site near a residential area. In handling such grievances of their constituents against the government, members of Congress have earned the designation by some cynics of "errand boys."

Political scientist Morris Fiorina has observed:

As the years have passed, more and more citizens and groups have found themselves dealing with the federal bureaucracy. They may be seeking positive actions—eligibility for various benefits and awards of government grants. Or they may be seeking relief from the costs imposed by bureaucratic regulations—on working conditions, racial and sexual quotas, market restrictions, and numerous other subjects. While not malevolent, bureaucracies make mistakes, both of commission and omission, and normal attempts at redress often meet with unresponsiveness and inflexibility and sometimes seeming incorrigibility. Whatever the problem, the citizen's congressman is a source of succor. The greater the scope of government activity, the greater the demand for his services.[13]

Casework. Members of Congress refer to the bulk of their work load pertaining to administrative action as *casework.* As a convenience to legislators, many administrative departments maintain liaison groups within the House of Representatives for the sole purpose of answering congressional inquiries about decisions the agencies have made. For example, Congress members receive so many inquiries about actions of the military regarding servicemen and their families that the Pentagon maintains a special office in the House Office Building to deal with these matters.

The Department of Agriculture has estimated that in a typical year it spends about 31,000 hours answering requests relating to congressional casework. In one year alone the department received 13,477 letters and 43,201 telephone calls. During the same period the Treasury Department liaison staff received close to 22,000 requests for congressional information, and the Post Office Department handled about 30,000 requests. This list could be expanded at length. Obviously the volume of representative business handled by Con-

---

[12]Ibid., p. 114.

[13]Morris Fiorina, *Congress: Keystone of the Washington Establishment* (New Haven: Yale University Press, 1977), pp. 46–47.

By any measure, Representative Dan Rosten-kowski, chairman of the House Ways and Means Committee, had a tumultuous year in 1989.

The Chicago Democrat was in the thick of the fight over tax policy. He clashed bitterly with many elderly people over the Medicare program to protect the aged from the cost of extended illnesses. It was the kind of year that might have made enemies. But when the filing deadline passed not long ago, not a single person, Democrat or Republican, had filed to run against Mr. Rostenkowski in 1990.

He is perhaps the ultimate safe incumbent, with a heavily Democratic district, a still powerful party organization and a campaign war chest of more than $1 million, enough to daunt the most optimistic challenger.

His ward-based political strength harks back to an earlier era. But in other respects, his circumstance underscores the nature of House elections in the late 1980s. They were very, very good to incumbents.

In 1986 and 1988, 98 percent of House members who sought re-election were returned to office. Most had some competition on the ballot, but still won comfortably. More than 85 percent were elected with at least 60 percent of the vote. Many people in both parties predict that the House elections of 1990 will run about the same, with only the slightest of shifts.

These statistics are at the heart of many political debates in Washington these days, from the effort to rewrite laws governing campaign finance to the first jousting over Congressional redistricting that will occur in 1991.

To some, the basic question is: Has the political system stifled competition and stacked the deck in favor of incumbents? Those who raise that question cite factors ranging from the laws on fund raising to the perquisites that come with Congressional office to the way Congressional district lines are drawn.

"The issue is whether we have any kind of real, competitive electoral process, particularly in the House of Representatives," said Fred Wertheimer, head of Common Cause, the Washington advocacy group.

Republicans, who last held a majority in the House in 1954, have argued that the current system has created a permanent Congress, and by extension a well-nigh perma-

gress that is unrelated to pending or proposed legislation is very great indeed.

Morris Fiorina has argued persuasively that the programmatic, or policy-oriented, activities of congressmen "are dangerous (controversial) on the one hand, and programmatic accomplishments are difficult to claim credit for, on the other. While less exciting, casework and pork barreling are both safe and profitable. For a reelection-oriented congressman the choice is obvious."[14] Fiorina goes on to point out that the rise of a permanent Washington establish-

ment—with Congress at the apex, linked to administrative agencies and interest groups to form an "iron triangle" of power—has been largely the result of a growing continuity of power on Capitol Hill due to the easy reelection of incumbents. The reelection of the latter has, in turn, been facilitated by the growth of the federal bureaucracy, which places congressmen in a necessary intermediary role between the citizen and the government.

As Investigators

In addition to personal grievances expressed to individual members, major appeals

---

[14]Ibid., p. 46.

nent Democratic majority. Democrats counter that incumbents have always had high re-election rates. Thomas S. Foley, the Speaker of the House, has noted that 100 percent of the 45 incumbents seeking re-election in 1792 were successful.

Thomas Mann, director of governmental studies at the Brookings Institution, a Washington research group, says the last few election cycles have been unusually comfortable for incumbents. The re-election rates for 1980 and 1982 were about 90 percent, considerably lower than in recent years. But Mr. Mann argues that the rise in re-election rates largely reflects the temper of the late 1980's. "The national times were good and there was little sentiment for throw the rascals out," he said.

Still, many advocates of new campaign financing laws argue that, at a time when money is looming ever larger in the electoral process, the current fund-raising system gives unfair advantage to incumbents.

"You've got incumbents sloshing around in huge amounts of money, most of which they don't need, while challengers are starving," Mr. Wertheimer said. For example, Common Cause said, political action commit-tees gave $82 million to incumbents and $9 million to challengers in the 1988 House races.

The threat of a permanent Congress has become a rallying cry for many Republicans this year as they take to the political trenches, hoping to expand their power in governors' offices and state legislatures, which will help draw the lines in the 1991 redistricting.

"Ninety-eight percent!" Lee Atwater, the national Republican chairman, declared not long ago, referring to the re-election rates. "For the Democrats, those odds aren't good enough. They want to draw district boundaries even tighter to protect themselves."

Both parties, meanwhile, agree there will be a large turnover in the House in 1992, because of redistricting and a large number of expected retirements. In the meantime, a drive to limit terms in Congress is making some noise. A fund-raising solicitation for one such effort was recently mailed to LaVerne Rostenkowski, the wife of the Ways and Means chairman who came to Congress in 1958.

Source: *New York Times*, February 7, 1990.

to Congress as a whole often occur after an unpopular administrative decision has been made. Here larger interests are at stake. The Food and Drug Administration (FDA), for example, may have ordered the removal of a potentially dangerous drug from the market. Both the pharmaceutical corporations that have done extensive research on the drug and the users who have been relieved by it will demand to know why it has been removed. In 1977 when the FDA ordered a ban on the artificial sweetener saccharin because it had been found to cause cancer in laboratory animals, a nationwide outcry was heard from both consumers and producers, and particularly from soft drink manufacturers whose diet products used the chemical. As a result Congress legislated an 18-month suspension of the FDA saccharin ban.

When members of Congress receive an unusually large number of complaints about a particular governmental action, or when a civil wrong or the improper administration of government policy is brought to their attention, members often react by calling for investigations. Such in-depth studies of particular problems are most often conducted by congressional subcommittees. Through such in-

(Drawing by Richter; © 1982 The New Yorker Magazine, Inc.)

"Fellow-incumbents!"
Congressional incumbents view themselves as a club in relation to the outside world.

vestigations, Congress publicizes major issues of public policy, thus helping to inform and interest the public as well as the other branches of the government.

In addition to helping to mold public opinion, congressional investigations increase the public's acceptance of future legislative and administrative changes. For example, widely publicized investigations of crime, labor racketeering, monopoly practices by manufacturers, and so on, may build public sympathy for government policies relating to such problems. In addition, the investigations provide legislators with information on which to base new legislation. In turn, information and insights gained by Congress are employed by the president, the administrative agencies, and even the judiciary in making decisions.

As Researchers

The congressional committee system is one means of coping with the specialized knowledge needed to make or reshape laws. But the subjects handled by these special committees—for example, defense policy or taxation—are often so broad that committee members, with their many other responsibilities, cannot hope to match the knowledge of the administrators who deal with the same subjects every day.

Thus when confronted with these special matters, members of Congress must obtain their information from those who have it—primarily from the administrative agencies and their client groups. The views of legislators on policy matters are formed by the kinds of information supplied by these outside groups.

Congressional staffs. Members of Congress, however, are not wholly dependent on the administrative agencies for their information. Their own staffs also supply them with information necessary for legislation. The Legislative Reorganization Act of 1946 increased the staffs of legislators and congressional committees so that they would no longer have to depend on the administrative agencies for all their research.

However, the congressional staff members must rely to a considerable extent on outside sources of information anyway. Because the operating agencies of government are the most available repositories of specialized information, members of Congress and their staffs still rely on these agencies and on private interest groups for a considerable amount of the information they need.

While congressional staffs frequently rely upon outside sources of information, this does not detract from the increasing power of staff aides within Congress. The budget for congressional operations (excluding the Library of Congress, the General Accounting Office, and the Government Printing Office—all of which are directly accountable to Congress) is over one-half billion dollars yearly. This represents an eightfold increase over expenses for congressional operations during the 1950s.

"Senator William J. Billworth and his team!"
Senators are usually accompanied by one or more of their aides.

Much of this expenditure is accounted for by an increase in the personal and committee staffs of the House and Senate, from 4,489 in 1957 to over 13,000 in 1983.[15] Each committee has its special staff on the committee payroll, and all representatives and senators have their own personal staff aides, paid out of their office budgets.

Congressional staffs develop legislative proposals and often guide them through the intricate maze of the legislative process in Congress. It is these staffs who write most of the speeches given by representatives and senators—including many of their statements in the *Congressional Record* (usually inserted into the record even though not given verbally on the floor of the House or the Senate)—and

---

[15]For more background information, see Harrison Fox, Jr., and Susan Webb Hammond, *Congressional Staffs* (New York: Free Press, 1977), p. 171. This work provides an excellent discussion of the history of congressional staffs and an evaluation of their contemporary role. The staffs of Congress were originally called "clerks," and they were then available only to committees. Staffs for sena-

tors were first authorized in 1885 and for members of the House in 1893. It was not until after the passage of the Legislative Reorganization Act of 1946, however, that the professional staffs of Congress began to expand in earnest.

[Harley] Dirks is in many ways a legendary man on Capitol Hill. Rumor has it that he was once a shoe salesman in Othello, Washington, a drowsy little farm town in the dry Columbia Basin. A more likely version is that Dirks *owned* a shoe store in Othello, and if he occasionally fitted the customers himself, it was not because he lacked grander dreams. Othello is miles from anywhere, an oasis of sorts in prairielike Eastern Washington, and its isolation—even from Seattle—cannot be adequately expressed in a mileage number on a road map. Othello was so slow, and Dirks so fast, that soon he found himself owning a host of its businesses and one of its banks—or so the story goes—despite the fact that he spent much of his time catching trout, shooting pheasant, and siring offspring. For whatever reason, Dirks eventually felt the urge to move on, and to a man of his imagination that did not mean bundling up the family and heading for Walla Walla. Instead, he worked for Senator Magnuson in the 1962 campaign and then followed him back to Washington, D.C.

Dirks became a "clerk" on the Appropri-

ations Committee at a time when Magnuson handled the funds of HUD, NASA, and the many independent agencies and regulatory commissions. When Magnuson switched to the HEW Appropriations post, Dirks went with him, simply moving his pipe rack to a new office and confronting a new set of figures. At first, his nominal superior was the "Chief Clerk" of the Subcommittee, an irascible Southerner who had served under chairmen now almost forgotten on Capitol Hill. Before long, however, Dirks moved in behind the Chief Clerk's desk (his own had become an unworkable mountain of papers), and within a few months the Chief Clerk stopped coming to work altogether. Dirks redecorated the staid office with oils he had painted, and as a quiet joke he arrayed on his new desk such "authoritative" academic works as *The Power of the Purse* and *The Politics of the Budgetary Process.* He had neither the time nor the need to read books about appropriations; he ran a Subcommittee that appropriated nearly $40 billion each year (an amount second only to the Defense Department's).*

who generally provide senators and representatives with positions on particular pieces of legislation or legislative proposals. To a far greater extent than is generally known, members of Congress, and more particularly senators, are directed by their staffs. In a very real sense staff aides operating behind the scenes often act as surrogate members of Congress (see Box 10.3). To a considerable extent congressional staffs are becoming an "invisible government" operating out of the offices, committee rooms, and corridors of Capitol Hill, just as there is an "invisible presidency" in the staff operating out of the White House.

Institutional staff aids. Apart from the staffs of individual members and committees, there are other institutions that aid Congress with research, such as the Library of Congress and its Congressional Research Service (CRS). The Library of Congress, the original core of which was provided by Thomas Jefferson's donation of his own library while he was president, now contains nearly all books and periodicals published in the United States as well as many publications printed in foreign countries. It also has available historical items, including personal papers, opera librettos, original manuscripts,

Like other Appropriations Committee clerks, Dirks is unknown to the public and to much of the Washington press corps. Tourists do not call at his office (although Senators and Secretaries do), and at appropriations hearings members of the audience sometimes whisper, "Who is that man sitting next to the Chairman?" That Dirks carries his power so judiciously says much about his fierce loyalty to Senator Magnuson, his sole constituent. Magnuson relies on Dirks heavily, not simply because he is loyal, or because a chairman has little choice, but also because Dirks is thorough, alert, and discreet. The only outsider, in fact, who has ever sensed Dirks's true influence was an academic researcher who interviewed him in connection with a study attempting to correlate appropriations figures with Senators' backgrounds; amused, Dirks simply jotted down for his visitor his own prediction of dollar amounts, by program, in an appropriations bill the Senators themselves had not yet even discussed. When the bill finally passed, Dirks's projections corresponded uncannily with the approved figures.

Dirks's anonymity does not extend to the Department of Health, Education and Welfare. Bergman and I witnessed a revealing, if somewhat comic, demonstration of this as we walked with Harley down HEW's long corridors on our way to discuss the earmarking strategy with Dr. Egeberg. From one doorway after another, men and women emerged to intone respectfully, "Good morning, Mr. Dirks," or "Hello, Harley!" and so on down the list of ingratiating pleasantries. Bergman and I felt obscure and incidental, as if we were Secret Service escorts; Dirks, for his part, smiled and waved like a Presidential candidate. It was hard to imagine him ever going back to Othello.

*When trust fund expenditures are included, the HEW appropriation totals some $80 billion, an amount in excess of the regular Defense Department appropriation.

(Source: *The Dance of Legislation*, pp. 44–46. Copyright © 1973 by Eric Redman. Reprinted by permission of Simon & Schuster, Inc.)

This extract illustrates how the strategic location and expertise of one Senate staffer enabled him to wield significant power on Capitol Hill.

motion pictures, and prints. The CRS answers congressional requests for information of all kinds. These queries may or may not relate to legislation. Over 30 percent of all congressional requests to the CRS come originally from constituents, and Congress members simply transfer these constituent requests to the service for an answer.

The Congressional Budget Office, created by the Budget and Impoundment Control Act of 1974, is a major institutional staff aid of Congress, employing hundreds of professionals (mostly economists) involved in assessing the budgetary impact of legislation and mak-

ing economic projections. The Office of Technology Assessment, too, was originally conceived as a general staff aid of Congress, although it has been for the most part under the control of Senator Edward Kennedy. (See Chapter 11 for further discussion of these agencies.)

As Speakers, Correspondents, and Guides

Members of Congress must spend a great deal of time performing other, nonlegislative jobs for the citizens whom they represent. These duties, added to their functions in dealing with a vast bureaucracy, make the Congress member's job seem endless.

Senators and representatives are present at ground-breaking ceremonies, college and high school commencements, and parades; they appear on local television programs and attend meetings of all types in their home districts. They may make policy speeches on some of these occasions, but more often they simply attend because their constituents expect it of them.

A considerable amount of time is spent by members of Congress and their staff aides in maintaining direct contact with individual constituents. In addition to general mailings that inform all constituents of a representative's activities, letters of a more personal nature often must be written. Sometimes these letters explain legislation, but in most cases they are written to congratulate new mothers, to extend holiday greetings, or to offer sympathy to the bereaved. Even if the majority of these letters are composed by aides, the representative still has to establish the general tone of this correspondence, keep abreast of how extensive it is, and know what subjects are being discussed.

When constituents visit the capital, members of Congress act as hosts and arrange tours of Washington. They also must respond to constituent requests for jobs and appoint children of their electorate to the service academies at West Point, Annapolis, and Colorado Springs. And they must make suggestions for administrative and other executive appointments as well.

OTHER INFLUENCES ON CONGRESS

The electorate is not the only group that makes demands on the congressional structure through its senators and representatives. Members of Congress must also respond to the president, the administrative branch, and private pressure groups.

The President

Probably the most important and concentrated source of demands on Congress in matters of major public policy is the president. The president's program of legislation is outlined every year in his State of the Union message and in subsequent budgetary proposals and special messages. Many proposals that come from the president also reflect administrative demands. In any case, administrative requests for legislation must be formally channeled through the White House via the Office of Management and Budget.

There are great variations in presidential success in getting legislative proposals from the White House passed by Congress (see Figure 10.4). Both the president's political skill and the relative strength of his party in Congress play a significant part. When the president faces an opposition majority in Congress, his legislative proposals usually have greater difficulty getting through Congress than when the body is dominated by his own party.

This point is illustrated by the Eisenhower years. During 1954 there was a slim majority of Republicans in Congress, and almost 65 percent of President Dwight D. Eisenhower's legislative proposals were passed. But after the congressional elections in November of that year, both houses of Congress shifted to slim Democratic majorities. During the remainder of Eisenhower's terms, the strength of the Democratic party increased in Congress with each succeeding congressional election. By 1960 Eisenhower was successful in gaining congressional approval for only 30 percent of his legislative requests. Republican Presidents Nixon and Ford also faced Democratic Congresses. Although at times they were successful in getting their legislation passed, their success rate on Capitol Hill was generally low (see Figure 10.4).

On the other hand, presidential success with the legislature is not always assured when the president and the majority in Congress are from the same party. From 1961 to 1963 President John F. Kennedy had only moderate success with Congress, even though the Democratic party had a majority in both houses of the legislature during this period. In contrast, President Lyndon Johnson's record in 1965 was extraordinary. Compared to both Eisenhower and Kennedy, Johnson was able to have his proposals passed by Congress with relative ease during all the years of his administration. President Jimmy Carter's low success rate with Congress illustrates once again the fact that even with heavy majorities of his own party on Capitol Hill, the inevitable conflict between Congress and the president makes for rough sledding for presidential proposals.

President Ronald Reagan had unusual success with Congress at the beginning of his administration. His "honeymoon" with Capitol Hill lasted for almost an entire year, during which his sweeping proposals for reductions in taxes and government spending were enacted. Even at the end of his second year Reagan was able to garner enough support in Congress to pass a major tax increase, much to the chagrin of his conservative supporters. The President's initial success was partly attributable to the crisis atmosphere that resulted from the deepest recession since World War II and the historic rise in interest rates that threatened to bring depression to all sectors of the economy. There was no doubt, however, that Reagan's understanding of the politics of Capitol Hill, and his ability to persuade both corporate leaders and the general electorate of the rightness of his cause, also helped to launch his programs. Reagan's early success on Capitol Hill, however, soon deteriorated, as Figure 10.5 illustrates. His problems with Congress did not differ from those of many previous presidents, who found their respective honeymoons with Capitol Hill all too brief. President George Bush tried to cultivate Congress at the outset of his administration in 1989; however, although Bush was a highly popular president and had adopted a conciliatory tone with Congress, he could not overcome entrenched Democratic majorities on both sides of Capitol Hill. In the first year of his administration, Congress handed

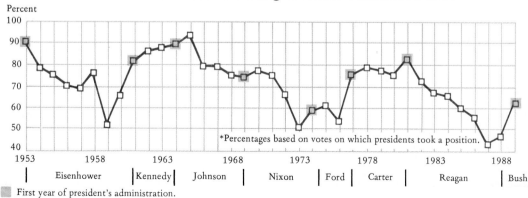

Presidential Success on Congressional Votes, 1953-1989*

*Percentages based on votes on which presidents took a position.

First year of president's administration.

(Source: *Congressional Quarterly Weekly Report*, December 30, 1989, p. 3544. Reprinted with permission from Congressional Quarterly, Inc.)

FIGURE 10.5

him a stunning defeat on his capital gains proposal, which he had placed at the top of his political agenda.

Although presidents have far greater success with their own party in Congress when they take strong stands on policy issues, the loose organization of parties is not able to provide a bridge between the president and Congress that will guarantee the success of legislative proposals coming from the White House. The presidential wings of the parties are loosely knit organizations that come together every four years to nominate and elect their candidates. The rise of candidate parties in presidential elections has further disintegrated party organization (see Chapters 7 and 8). Congressional parties are also not cohesive organizations, and are entirely separate from the loose confederation of interests that form the basis of presidential parties. Congressional parties have their own organizations and policies that reflect not only narrower constituencies than the broad national constituency of the presidency but also the adversary position of Congress in relation to the president under the constitutional system of separation of powers and checks and balances.

The responsibilities of the president in the legislative process derive not only from the Constitution but from the fact that the president (along with the vice-president) is the only official nationally elected. The White House is therefore the focus of popular expectations about the proper role of the government, and people expect the president to take the lead in formulating public policy. He is the symbolic leader of his own political party, and his program is supposed to reflect party views, however vaguely and ambiguously they may have been previously stated in party conventions and platforms. The White House can act with greater dispatch and unity in developing legislative proposals than can Capitol Hill. The president not only has at his command a potentially vast range of information flowing to his office from the bureaucracy (which also provides Congress with information) and that developed by his own staff, but he also can make direct appeals to the people for the support of his programs. However, presidents cannot rule by fiat. Thus, insofar as legislation is concerned, the White House is more the seat of frustration than of achievement.

Administrative Agencies

When Congress formulates legislation on a particular matter, it tends to rely substantially on the experience of those who deal directly with the area concerned rather than on its own sources of data. The staff of the Congressional Research Service (CRS) of the Library of Congress can reply only to factual questions. It cannot advise legislators on general questions of policy, such as: Which changes should be made in the weapons system to ensure proper balance of offensive and defensive capabilities? Which changes should be made in the securities laws to protect the public against fraud and unnecessary stock market fluctuations? Which kind of fiscal policy will promote employment, reduce inflation, and spur expansion of the economy? Which type of labor legislation is needed to reduce employer-employee conflict? Should agricultural supports be expanded or modified in any way? Information relevant to such questions is generally in the hands of the administrative agencies and the private pressure groups concerned, and they pass it on to legislators.

Besides obtaining information from administrators, members of Congress depend on the agencies for an honest appraisal of what is in the public interest. After all, one of the primary reasons that Congress creates an agency is to deal with the public's needs and interests in a particular subject area.

There is a common bond of purpose between Congress and the administrative branch. Many administrative agencies, particularly the independent regulatory commissions, are agents of Congress. Among other things, they are supposed to recommend legislation to Congress when there is a need for it. It is highly unlikely that any regulatory legislation will pass Congress without the approval of the agency that has jurisdiction over the area. Congress may veto legislative proposals from the commissions, but it rarely supports regulatory legislation that has not been cleared by the commission concerned.

Liaison between Congress and the bureaucracy. The exchange of information between Congress and the bureaucracy takes place on several levels. Formal channels via the Executive Office are used for official communications. The president's Office of Management and Budget (OMB), acting as the chief clearinghouse for legislative proposals from administrative agencies, seeks to bring them into line with presidential policy.

Budgetary proposals coming from the bureaucracy also must be approved by the OMB. If the OMB approves such a proposal without any major changes, it is evident to the Congress that the president agrees with the purpose and performance of the agency initiating the proposal. Official communications of this sort from the executive branch reflect the policy stand of the party in the White House.

The primary formal way in which agency heads make their views and those of the administration known to Capitol Hill is through testimony called for by congressional committees. The president's political appointees, particularly cabinet secretaries and undersecretaries, present the administration's viewpoint in written statements that must first be cleared by the OMB, which makes certain that the opinions presented are in line with presidential policies. Committee members do, of course, question administration witnesses in person after reading their formal written testimony, and sometimes, but not frequently, elicit views that do not agree with those of the White House. However, political appointees who wish to survive for very long try to make their public pronouncements in accord with the wishes of the president.

Informal channels. Often, however, it is through informal channels of communication with the bureaucracy that Congress acquires the most revealing information on legislative matters. Whereas political appointees who support the administration are heard at such formal occasions as committee hearings, career civil servants may not have the same opportunity to make their views heard. And Congress is interested in the opinions of both.

In their informal contacts with members of Congress—by telephone and at parties, luncheons, and the like—subordinate administrative officials may express opinions on legislation or even provide aid on the actual drafting of bills. Even though the president may wish to prevent such informal contacts, it is almost impossible for him to do so.

Members of Congress who oppose a presidential program that is being supported with vigor will find it difficult to acquire information from the bureaucracy, however. Formal testimony before congressional committees, whether given by cabinet appointees or lower-level career bureaucrats, must be cleared in advance by the OMB. While informal channels of communication can circumvent the censorship of OMB, lower-level officials in particular are taking risks if they go behind the president's back to Congress. Some administrators will defend presidential policy, whether they personally like it or not. For example, members of Congress have found it difficult to get information from the armed forces, even when the military has opposed the policies of the president and the secretary of defense. Military officials are usually reluctant to testify in open committee hearings, where their views and plans may be aired before the public. The feelings of the military chiefs regarding defense policy are usually conveyed, if at all, through informal channels.

Generals and admirals, of course, have a status that most bureaucrats below the cabi-

(The Commercial Appeal 1977. Reproduced by permission.)

Congress is often pictured as the captive of outside interests.

net level do not possess. They can sometimes act without fear of losing their positions, whereas civilian bureaucrats cannot. Subordinate administrators have to be cautious when they supply Congress with information that opposes a program of the president or contradicts the views of their department or agency heads.

Pressure Groups

Lobbyists also play an important role in making demands on members of Congress and supplying information to them. The amount of attention a legislator pays to the views of a particular interest group is often based on the influence that group might have in future elections. If the group has considerable strength in the constituency, the senator or representative may be more than normally attentive to its wishes.

Many pressure groups—especially the larger ones, such as the Farm Bureau Federation, the AFL-CIO, and the National Association of Manufacturers—maintain research staffs that are available to members of Congress. Lawmakers can call on such organizations to provide information regarding legislative proposals. Congressional use of such facilities is by no means universal; many members of Congress rely only slightly, if at all, on information supplied by private pressure groups—which would seem to indicate that these groups do not have a profound impact on Congress.

Many pressure groups maintain ratings on representatives and senators, giving the percentage of times the legislators have voted "correctly" (that is, in support of the group's position) on particular legislative issues. Prominent in the ratings game are such pressure groups as the Americans for Democratic Action (ADA), the Committee on Political Education of the AFL-CIO (COPE), Public Citizen (founded by Ralph Nader in 1971), the Ripon Society of the Republican party (a liberal Republican group), the National Farmers' Union, the Consumer Federation of America, and the Americans for Constitutional Action (a conservative group).

The evangelical movement joined the ratings game when it decided to become politically involved. The Moral Majority and other evangelical groups rated congressional candidates, giving high scores to those who opposed the Equal Rights Amendment, abortion, busing to achieve racial balance, sex education in schools, and penalties for segregation in private education. Candidates were also given points if they supported a balanced budget and prayer in public schools. One evangelical group, Christian Voice, even added foreign policy issues to its ratings, applauding legislators who defended Taiwan.

Predictably, the more conservative members of Congress received high ratings by conservative groups such as the Americans for Constitutional Action (ACA), the American Conservative Union (ACU), which is close to the New Right, and the National Taxpayers Union (NTU), which lobbies for reduction in taxes and federal expenditures. Liberal legislators, by contrast, always receive high ratings from the Americans for Democratic Action (ADA) and COPE, the AFL-CIO's Committee on Political Education.

The ratings by interest groups are supposed to be guides to the group's membership in voting for members of Congress; however, it is doubtful that low or high ratings by any particular group have ever had a significant impact upon the electoral process.

Sometimes private pressure groups influence congressional committees and individual members of Congress indirectly through the administrative agencies. Private groups are important supporters of such agencies, and some of their demands are transferred to Congress by the agencies through legislative proposals. In this way agencies may support the cause of private interest groups. The Defense Department, for example, wins support from the armaments industry when it obtains money from Congress for developing a new tank, fighter airplane, or other weapons system.

Congress in Crisis

The American people hold Congress, as an institution, in low esteem. They question the ethics and efficiency of Congress, feeling that most members of Congress (but not their own representatives) are self-serving and out to enrich themselves and their friends at the expense of the public. The president, the media, and even members of Congress themselves fortify this popular distrust of Congress. Presidents accuse Congress of acting selfishly and against the national interest when Capitol Hill fulfills its constitutional responsibility of checking the White House. The media often overplay congressional scandals, sometimes even accusing members of improprieties before there is evidence to support the accusations. Finally, and most ironically, members of Congress "run against" Congress itself in their reelection campaigns, separating themselves from the institution and accusing it of inefficiency, neglect of duty, and even malfeasance. They know all too well the popularity of the anti-Congress theme.

Criticism of Congress is not a new phenomenon, and congressional reform is a perennial issue. *Within* Congress reform is always tied to the issue of the distribution of power on Capitol Hill. Congressional party leaders and more junior members try to "reform" Congress to increase their personal power—for example, by reducing the traditional power of senior committee chairpersons. Also, members sometimes seek to "reform" Congress to increase its strength in relation to a dominant presidency. *Beyond* Capitol Hill the reform issue takes on a different tone as reformers seek to reduce the influence of special interests and improve congressional ethics. The following article represents a typical citizen's view of what should be done to improve Congress.

So You Want to Reform Congress? / *Fred Barnes*

Everybody's got it wrong about campaign spending in Senate and House races, incumbent power, and political action committees. The real problem isn't money, though there's too much of it floating around. It isn't PACs—they're only part of the problem. Eliminating them is a step in the right direction but no more than that. And the problem isn't one-party rule in Congress either. True, 34-plus years of Democratic control of the House haven't been good for America. But had Republicans ruled the House, there'd still be lots to complain about.

The problem is Washington. Something awful happens to our elected officials when they get to Washington. The longer they stay, the worse it gets. They get swallowed up by the political culture of the city. It's almost like *Invasion of the Body Snatchers* come true, except there's no need to put big pods by their beds at night. They absorb Washington's ways by osmosis.

This means they become skillful Washington politicians. Even the duds figure out what it takes to get along in Washington—and stay, year after year. They love the life-style in Washington. The city isn't a backwater anymore. Life is pretty luxurious. There are plays, art galleries, fancy foreign restaurants, pleasant suburbs, good schools for their kids (outside of Marion Barry's District of Columbia, that is). Washington is a wonderful compromise between New York and the boondocks.

Too wonderful, it turns out. Many members of Congress cease representing their states or districts in Washington beyond the grubby pursuit of narrow special interests (retaining an Air Force base, getting a HUD grant, and so on). After a year or two on Capitol Hill, they become representatives of Washington to the folks back home. A few decades ago, they'd have been voted out of office if they put on Washington airs. Now they've rigged elections so they can't lose unless they're caught in a scandal.

In Washington, senators and House members quickly fall in with the permanent establishment of bureaucrats, lobbyists, political consultants, journalists, lawyers, flacks, and representatives of businesses, unions, trade associations, and other special interests. It's not an iron triangle they join; it's an iron octagon.

The result is that real change occurs only fleetingly—when the voters register their desire for it in seismic terms, as they did in 1980 with the Reagan landslide. The momentum from that election soon dissipated. After mid-1981, things were back to normal. Virtually every social program, no matter how wasteful or redundant, survived. So did every Pentagon weapons system, regardless of cost-effectiveness. And why not? In both cases, the programs had permanent friends in Congress.

I think strong campaign reforms are needed. The trick is deciding which ones and getting Congress to pass them. There's not much incentive now for Congress to act, since the current system serves incumbents so handsomely. It may take an election in which congressional ethics, perks, and money-grubbing—Washington ills—are a major issue. And I mean an issue that actually defeats some incumbents. That may occur in 1990, though I'm not getting my hopes up.

In judging proposed reforms, the standard should not be simply whether they curb PACs or reduce spending. The standard should be whether they make elections for the Senate and House more competitive, and keep members from adhering to the inside-the-Beltway playbook. Does a reform create incentives for them to reflect the broad interests of their constituents (the parochial interests will take care of themselves)? Does it make them more responsive to their constituents, less to organized interests in Washington? That's the test. Now, Washington provides powerful disincentives.

President Bush's reform package is good, as far as it goes. He would eliminate business, trade, and union PACs, and he'd restrict ideological PACs to donations of $1,000 per candidate per election, not $5,000. He'd force the disclosure of "soft money," which supposedly goes for party-building, but in 1988 was devoted to bolstering the parties' presidential campaigns. He'd prohibit incumbents from carrying over campaign funds from election to election, and he'd bar unsolicited mass mailings that members of Congress send out under the frank—at no expense to them, naturally.

Bush is correct in rejecting public financing of congressional campaigns and spending limits. "If anything," Bush said in June, public financing "would strengthen the status quo." It would make incumbents all the more unbeatable, since their challengers couldn't outspend them or match their exploitation of incumbency. Spending limits, Bush said, will only keep people from participating in campaigns. "The answer is reform," he said. "We need reforms that curtail the role of special interests, enhance the role of the individual and strengthen the parties."

Eliminating PACs is good for starters, but let's be clear about what it will achieve. PACs do not buy the votes of senators and House members by giving them campaign money. As chairman of the Democratic Congressional Campaign Committee, Rep. Tony Coelho realized this in the early 1980s. Liberal Democrats could take money from business PACs, vote as antibusiness as they wished, and then go back in the next election cycle for more PAC money. PACs pony up the money every time, thinking that at the very least they're purchasing access.

In truth, businesses, unions, and trade associations can get all the access they want on Capitol Hill just for the asking. I'm amazed the people who run PACs haven't caught on. Or maybe they have, and just don't want to give competing special interests even the slightest edge. Giving $5,000 to Tom Foley every two years probably makes PAC managers feel more secure. But they're not buying anything. They'd find this out if they stopped paying. If a few PACs did, then they might all feel that it's safe to stop, and PAC-banning legislation wouldn't be needed. I'm not holding my breath.

PACs, which are concentrated in Washington, pull members of Congress away from the folks at home. Every night in Washington, members hold fundraising receptions to which PAC officials flock with their checks. This is an easy way for incumbents to raise money, and spares them the agony of traveling to their state or district to drum up funds. The more they rely on PACs to finance their campaigns, the more Washingtonized they become. In 1988, Democratic candidates for Congress got 47 percent of their campaign funds from PACs. Republicans got 31 percent.

PACs of all ideological and partisan stripes must be happy with the status quo. Why else would they try so hard to maintain it? Until the Coelho revolution, Republican challengers had a good shot at getting money from business PACs. This made races against Democratic incumbents more competitive, and it forced incumbents in Washington to tune the voters in. Democratic challengers got campaign funds from labor PACs, which made contests with Republican incumbents more competitive. Now the situation is different. Business PACs give their money to incumbents, period. Challengers need not apply. Union PACs, however, still fund Democratic challengers.

The advantage for incumbents is potent, even for Republicans. GOP incumbents get a lot more money from business PACs than their challengers get from labor PACs. In 1988, "PACs gave four times as much money to incumbent senators as they gave to challengers, and contributed more to sitting congressmen as against challengers by an 8 to 1 margin," said Democratic Senator David Boren of Oklahoma, who has proposed a modest package of campaign reforms. "With a virtually unlimited supply of PAC contributions available in Washington, is it any wonder that 98 percent to 99 percent of House members are reelected time and again?" Nope.

Michael Malbin, an aide to Defense Secretary Dick Cheney and co-author of *Vital Statistics on Congress, 1989–1990,* says it takes at least $200,000 for a challenger to run a credible campaign for the House. The average spent by Republican challengers was $99,383, compared to an average of $358,212 for Democratic incumbents. Republican incumbents spent $408,000, compared to $143,000 for Democratic challengers.

Once PACs, which handed out $156 million in 1988, are killed, money for campaigns will have to come from somewhere else. But where? Bush would allow the parties to more than double the amount they contribute to congressional candidates in "coordinated expenses." Fine. That would enhance the two parties. Another overdue reform is a hike in the $1,000 limit on individual contributions. It ought to be raised to $5,000, or higher, or better yet, eliminated altogether.

Of course that would create another problem: fat cats. No one wants a member of Congress beholden to a fat cat who contributed $500,000. There's a way around this—and around the entire issue of money in political campaigns. In most races, the bulk of campaign spending is for one thing: advertising. The money goes for TV or radio ads, or for direct mail. Since TV and radio stations are a public trust, they should be compelled to provide free air-time for congressional candidates, some of it in prime viewing hours. The candidates could divide the time as they wish, some for 30-second spots, some for five-minute speeches, some for 30-minute biographical sketches, and so on.

Don't raise the objection that this won't work in House races, where TV and radio aren't cost-effective and thus aren't used. I've accommodated for that. For obvious reasons, buying time on Los Angeles television doesn't make sense for Henry Waxman, the Democratic House member from west Los Angeles, a small sliver of the L.A. television market. He relies heavily on direct mail, paid and franked. The franking privilege lets a member of Congress send newsletters, announcements, and other thinly disguised propaganda to constituents with no postage. Bush would bar unsolicited mass mailings by members of Congress. House Republicans would trim the number from twelve to three, with only one in an election year. I'd go with the

House Republicans, and also give challengers in districts like Waxman's the franking privilege to match the mailings of the incumbent.

For the time being, Congress is unlikely in the extreme to legislate free TV time for candidates. Incumbents don't need free television. With the dough they get from PACs, they can buy all they want. But the odds are better on killing or curbing PACs. If that occurs, incumbents will be desperate to get on TV. So they might compel TV and radio stations to provide free airtime. And they'd have to give free time to challengers too. The public's thirst for fairness would force them to.

One of the biggest impediments to contested congressional elections is the money that incumbents collect and hold. As the law now stands, House members in office in 1980 can convert that money to personal use when they retire. Nearly every reform plan, including Boren's would take away this privilege.

Big deal. That's not attacking what's really wrong. These bloated campaign funds are chiefly used by incumbents to scare off challengers. They reduce competition. This, in turn, allows incumbents to ignore their constituents. Who would want to run against Democrat Dan Rostenkowski, the chairman of the House Ways and Means Committee, when he's got $1,034,438 stashed in a campaign fund? Nobody in his right mind, that's for sure. Or Democrat Stephen Solarz of New York, who's saved up $1,158,484? Or Republican Larry Hopkins of Kentucky, whose permanent campaign treasury has $608,792? In all, 190 House members are hoarding leftover campaign funds. They should be required to spend the money in their next campaign, or lose it.

What members of Congress do with their personal finances is also important. Coelho resigned from the House in June after it was revealed he'd purchased a junk bond from Drexel Burnham under questionable circumstances. Coelho wasn't the only one. Conflicts of interest abound. Jim Wright got favored treatment on loans and investments. I could go on. There's a solution, one I first heard from Robert Novak, the columnist and conservative folk hero. He says House or Senate members should be required to put their personal holdings in a blind trust that's truly blind. I agree, and I'll bet Coelho would too, now.

I've saved the most radical proposal for last. It's one I've come to reluctantly: a limitation on congressional terms to twelve years. In fact, I'd add to that by letting senators and House members serve as committee chairmen and in leadership posts such as Speaker and majority leader for only four years. I didn't pluck these reforms out of thin air. There are precedents for both. The Twenty-second Amendment limits Presidents to two consecutive terms, and that's worked fairly well. I'm sure I'd have voted for Reagan if he'd run for a third term in 1988. He'd have won. But in hindsight, I think we're better off with Reagan, at 78, in Santa Barbara and Bush in the White House. The Twenty-second Amendment saved us from ourselves.

As for Congress, the chairmen of the intelligence and budget committees are switched every four years. It's worked well. After four years, the budget chairmen grow weary of advocating spending cuts and tax hikes. This isn't what members of Congress like to do. They love to spend, not cut. Not that the budget chairmen propose sweeping cuts. They don't. But at least they propose some cuts. Imagine how they'd act if they lingered past four years as chairmen. They'd want no cuts.

I concede that Senate and House members aren't suicidal. So it'll be awfully hard to get a 12-year limit through Congress. But there's a way. Don't penalize incumbents for their years in Congress. Let them start at zero, like newcomers, and stay a maximum of twelve more years. If that's still off-putting to incumbents, they could be grandfathered in their jobs. They could stay as long as they get reelected, but newly elected members could stay twelve years and no more. Under this scheme, it would take ten to twenty years to get Congress completely on the 12-year track. I'd be willing to accept this as a last resort, especially if the alternative is Congress-as-usual.

Thomas Jefferson said America needs a revolution every twenty years, or something like that. He overstated it, but he was drifting in the right direction. We don't need a revolution, but we do need more turnover in Congress. The learning curve on Capitol Hill is such that most senators and congressmen know the ropes by their second or third year in office. By then, they're capable of chairing a committee. By their fourth or fifth year, they've mingled enough with their colleagues so they've either emerged as leaders, capable of being Speaker or whip or caucus chairman, or been sidetracked as followers. Steny Hoyer of Maryland, the new chairman of the House Democratic caucus, was elected in 1981, in leadership posts by 1985.

Almost by definition, members of Congress who've been in office only a few years are not entrenched. That's good. They're still worried about reelection; they keep in touch at home. After twelve years (earlier for some), they're creatures of Washington, usually safe from defeat and skeptical of sentiment outside the Beltway. Not all of them succumb—Republican Representative Henry Hyde of Illinois, first elected in 1974, hasn't—but most do. It's sad, but very, very correctable.

CHAPTER ELEVEN

Congressional Policy Making

Exactly how are the interests and demands of this nation's voters and pressure groups transformed into laws? What obstacles must legislative proposals hurdle to be enacted into statutes?

The complicated procedure by which proposals are first introduced in either house of Congress, then referred to committee for debate, re-debated by the entire chamber, and finally voted on is time-consuming and full of pitfalls. This, however, is only one half of the process. The whole cycle is repeated in the other house before a bill is finally sent to the president for his signature. Thus the impatience of members of Congress and their constituents with this slow and cumbersome procedure is understandable.

FIRST STEPS IN THE LAWMAKING PROCESS

Lawmaking is the principal business of Congress. This is now and has always been the case. As Woodrow Wilson wrote in 1885 of Capitol Hill:

. . .Once begin the dance of legislation, and you must struggle through its mazes as best you can to its breathless end,—if any end there be.

It is not surprising, therefore, that the enacting, revising, tinkering, repealing of laws should engross the attention and engage the entire energy of such a body as Congress.[1]

Legislation and legislative work are the norm respected in both the House and the Senate. And perhaps the major impetus for legislative work comes from within Congress itself, from its staff and members, constantly striving to gain the recognition of their colleagues for legislative work they have performed:

[Congress] always makes what haste it can to legislate. . . .Be the matters small or great, frivolous or grave, which busy it, its aim is to have laws always a-making. Its temper is strenuously legislative. That it cannot regulate all the questions to which its attention is weekly invited, is its misfortune, not its fault; it is due to the human limitation of its faculties, not to any narrow circumscription of its desires.[2]

The internal forces generating legislation on Capitol Hill are buttressed by pressures from the outside—from the White House, from administrative agencies, and from a wide array of private interest groups. Demands are constantly flowing to Congress for the enactment of presidential proposals, for legislation expanding and refining the powers of administrative agencies, and for laws to protect private interests of all kinds.

When internal congressional forces meet external demands, legislation is often the result. It is not that outside forces dictate to Congress the substance of legislation but that individual members and staffs on Capitol Hill reach outside of Congress whenever they can—to mobilize support behind their legis-

[1]Woodrow Wilson, *Congressional Government* (New York: Meridian Books, 1956), p. 195.

[2]Ibid., p. 193.

lation and in general to justify the legislative activity in which they engage. In order for outside interests to be served by Congress, those interests must serve the internal power incentives of members and staff, which include not only the desire for reelection (a concern principally of freshmen members and of those with little seniority) but also the desire to gain recognition on Capitol Hill itself; recognition as an effective legislator often establishes at the same time a reputation for power. In addition to incentives for reelection and power within Congress, Richard F. Fenno's interviews of congressmen suggest that "good public policy" is also an incentive of many members.[3]

Whether the incentives of members and staff on Capitol Hill are for reelection, internal power and status, or good public policy, outside interests can and do exploit each incentive in varying ways at different times to achieve their goals. The president, for example, may appeal to the "good public policy" incentive to convince Congress of the worthiness of his cause. President Jimmy Carter did this in his energy message to Congress in 1977, and in his plea for ratification of the Panama Canal treaties. And Presidents Ronald Reagan and George Bush repeatedly appealed to the "good public policy" incentives of legislators in seeking bipartisan support on Capitol Hill for their policies.

Administrative agencies will often supply the committees overseeing their activities with information and support that buttresses the committee's power within Congress. The close linkage between the Defense Department and the Armed Services committees of both the House and the Senate, for example, actually adds to the internal power and status of these committees on Capitol Hill. In addition to supplying the Armed Services committees with expert information, the Defense Department gives their members perquisites in the form of tours aboard military aircraft and naval vessels to inspect defense facilities. In turn, major portions of time are automatically set aside in Congress to ensure the passage of defense appropriations bills and other important legislation the Defense Department and the Armed Services committees consider necessary.

The reelection incentive, too, may serve outside interests as members of Congress strive to represent the concerns of their constituencies. However, constituent interests are not always instrumental in securing the final passage of legislation, as the multiplicity of constituent interests tends to cancel one another out. Thousands upon thousands of bills are *introduced*, in part to reflect the variety of interests throughout congressional constituencies, but few if any of these bills see the light of day through passage in either body of Congress, let alone through passage by both bodies. The fate of all but a handful of bills that are introduced is to die "in committee"—not in the standing committees, even, but in their subcommittees.

The first step in the legislative process, then, is not the simple introduction of a bill, which is usually nothing more than a symbolic act, but the careful marshaling of broad sponsorship within the House or the Senate for a particular piece of legislation. How is the serious legislative agenda of Congress drawn up? On the outside it is set by the president. On the inside it is set, in the House, by the leadership in conjunction with the chairmen of powerful committees and, in the Senate, primarily by members of that body with a reputation for power. The Senate Majority Leader is always at the forefront in determining what proposals will be at the top of the agenda. But the prestige of senators, because the latter are fewer in number and represent broad geographical interests and in almost all cases far larger voting constituencies than representatives, makes them more equal in power within

[3]Richard F. Fenno, Jr., *Congressmen in Committees* (Boston: Little, Brown, 1973).

the body. (Beginning in the early 1970s, freshmen senators were no longer content to stand aside while their senior colleagues controlled committee chairmanships and dominated both committee and chamber proceedings.) The greater equality of power within the Senate makes it possible for any senator, whether or not chairman of a prestigious committee, to secure the passage of legislation, provided the necessary sponsorship within the body is achieved.

Once the legislative agenda has been set, bills must follow certain routes before their final approval (see Figure 11.1), including their introduction, their referral to committees, and their placement on the legislative calendar; thereafter, in the absence of "unanimous consent," they are debated and voted upon in each body. Amendments, which must be germane to a bill's intent and subject matter in the House but not the Senate, may be attached to bills by a majority vote in either body. "Riders," which are essentially nongermane amendments, may also be attached in the Senate. (Rarely, by twisting the rules, riders may also be voted by the House.) The final stage for the resolution of conflicting House and Senate legislation is the conference committee, composed of the floor managers and members of the originating committees of the legislation in both bodies.

Introduction of Bills and Resolutions

Proposals introduced and enacted by Congress may take the form of either bills or resolutions. *Bills* are proposed laws and fall into two principal categories—public and private. *Public bills* deal with matters that apply to everyone, such as voting rights, appropriations for education, or reform of government agencies. *Private bills*, on the other hand, refer only to certain named individuals (see Box 11.1). Many private bills concern foreign citizens who are requesting dispensation from regular immigration requirements. Others concern United States citizens who are seeking damages from the federal government that they cannot obtain without the consent of Congress due to the common-law doctrine of sovereign immunity, which prohibits suits for damages against the government without its consent. While Congress has passed laws allowing suits in certain categories of cases, the sovereign immunity shield continues to require congressional action to award damages in some cases. Under the Constitution, revenue bills (tax legislation) must originate in the House. All bills must be approved by both houses before being signed into law.

Most *resolutions* are passed by either house alone and do not have the effect of law. They ordinarily deal only with the business of the chamber in which they originate. For example, either house may pass resolutions to change its rules or reorganize its committees, or to express messages of a personal nature, such as congratulations or condolences, to other members of Congress.

In addition, there are two types of resolutions that are passed jointly by both houses. *Joint resolutions* have the effect of law if they are signed by the president. Usually they concern matters requiring immediate action, such as the approval of a diplomatic move taken by the president. For example, in August of 1964, after attacks upon American vessels in the Gulf of Tonkin off Vietnam, Congress passed the "Gulf of Tonkin" resolution authorizing the president to "take all necessary measures" to prevent aggression in Southeast Asia. The resolution passed in the Senate by a vote of 82 to 2 and in the House by 414 to 0, was considered by President Lyndon Johnson at the time to be in effect a delegation to him of the power to wage war in Southeast Asia. *Concurrent resolutions* do not have the form of law and do not require the president's signature. Normally they consist of changes in rules that concern both chambers, or of ceremonial statements such as messages to other nations.

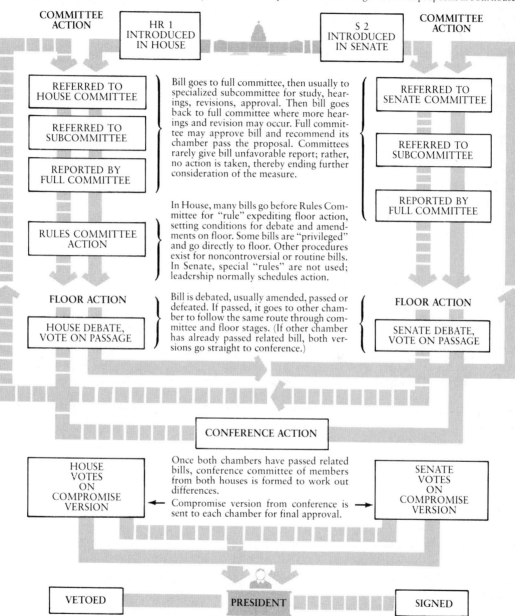

HOW A BILL BECOMES LAW

This graphic shows the most typical way in which proposed legislation is enacted into law. There are more complicated, as well as simpler, routes, and most bills never become law. The process is illustrated with two hypothetical bills, House bill No. 1 (HR 1) and Senate bill No. 2 (S 2). Bills must be passed by both houses in identical form before they can be sent to the president. The path of HR 1 is traced by a solid line, that of S 2 by a broken line. In practice most bills begin as similar proposals in both houses.

COMMITTEE ACTION

HR 1 INTRODUCED IN HOUSE

S 2 INTRODUCED IN SENATE

COMMITTEE ACTION

REFERRED TO HOUSE COMMITTEE

REFERRED TO SUBCOMMITTEE

REPORTED BY FULL COMMITTEE

Bill goes to full committee, then usually to specialized subcommittee for study, hearings, revisions, approval. Then bill goes back to full committee where more hearings and revision may occur. Full committee may approve bill and recommend its chamber pass the proposal. Committees rarely give bill unfavorable report; rather, no action is taken, thereby ending further consideration of the measure.

REFERRED TO SENATE COMMITTEE

REFERRED TO SUBCOMMITTEE

REPORTED BY FULL COMMITTEE

RULES COMMITTEE ACTION

In House, many bills go before Rules Committee for "rule" expediting floor action, setting conditions for debate and amendments on floor. Some bills are "privileged" and go directly to floor. Other procedures exist for noncontroversial or routine bills. In Senate, special "rules" are not used; leadership normally schedules action.

FLOOR ACTION

HOUSE DEBATE, VOTE ON PASSAGE

Bill is debated, usually amended, passed or defeated. If passed, it goes to other chamber to follow the same route through committee and floor stages. (If other chamber has already passed related bill, both versions go straight to conference.)

FLOOR ACTION

SENATE DEBATE, VOTE ON PASSAGE

CONFERENCE ACTION

HOUSE VOTES ON COMPROMISE VERSION

Once both chambers have passed related bills, conference committee of members from both houses is formed to work out differences.

Compromise version from conference is sent to each chamber for final approval.

SENATE VOTES ON COMPROMISE VERSION

VETOED

PRESIDENT

SIGNED

Compromise bill approved by both houses is sent to the president, who can sign it into law or veto it and return it to Congress. Congress may override veto by a two-thirds majority vote in both houses; bill then becomes law without president's signature.

(Source: *Guide to Congress*, 3d ed. [Washington, D.C.: Congressional Quarterly, 1982], p. 413. Reprinted with permission of Congressional Quarterly, Inc.)

FIGURE 11.1

The bill (H.R. 2399) for the relief of Leonard Alfred Brownrigg, was considered, ordered to a third reading, read the third time, and passed.

MR. ROBERT C. BYRD. Mr. President, I ask unanimous consent to have printed in the RECORD an excerpt from the report (No. 94–1092), explaining the purposes of the measure.

There being no objection, the excerpt was ordered to be printed in the RECORD, as follows:

Purpose of the Bill

The purpose of the bill is to waive the excluding provision of existing law relating to one who had been convicted for possession of marihuana.

Statement of Facts

The beneficiary of this bill is a 46-year-old native and citizen of Great Britain who was admitted to the United States for permanent residence in May of 1953. He was convicted in August of 1964 for possession of marihuana and placed on probation for five years. The record of conviction was expunged according to California law in March of 1965. The beneficiary is married to a citizen of the United States and resides in California where he is employed as a land surveyor.

The following information was contained in House Report 92–104 and House Report 93–491:

Deportation proceedings were instituted against the beneficiary on December 23, 1964, on the ground that he had been convicted in Superior Court of the State of California for the unlawful possession of marihuana. On June 28, 1965, he was found deportable on that charge. On August 17, 1965, his appeal was dismissed by the Board of Immigration Appeals. Deportation proceedings against him are pending before the Supreme Court on a writ of a certiorari. A mandate before the U.S. Ninth Circuit Court of Appeals has been stayed pending the action before the Supreme Court.

U.S. DEPARTMENT OF JUSTICE, IMMIGRATION AND NATURALIZATION SERVICE,
Washington, D.C., September 9, 1966

HON. EMANUEL CELLER,
Chairman, Committee on the Judiciary, House of Representatives, Washington, D.C.

Procedures for the introduction of bills and resolutions differ slightly in the House and Senate. In the House a member may introduce a bill or resolution simply by handing it to the clerk of the House or by dropping it into the box (the "hopper") at the clerk's desk. In the Senate, though, a member must be present, gain recognition from the presiding officer (the vice-president or the president pro tempore of the Senate), and announce his or her proposal orally before the other members of the chamber.

In recent years the number of bills and resolutions introduced in both houses has been extraordinary, averaging for each two-year session approximately 13,000. However, the number of bills, both public and private, that are passed is sharply below the number introduced. In a typical two-year session of Congress, less than 3,000 bills are reported from committees, and slightly more than 1,000 are passed. One-third of these are private and the other two-thirds are public. Of the approximately 700 public bills passed, many come from proposals made originally by the president and the administrative branch.

One reason for the difference between the number of legislative proposals introduced and the number passed is that many proposals made in one house are duplicated by sim-

DEAR MR. CHAIRMAN: This refers to H.R. 15337 in behalf of Leonard Alfred Brownrigg.

The beneficiary failed to file a petition with the Supreme Court of the United States for a writ of certiorari before July 16, 1966. The judgment of the Ninth Circuit Court of Appeals is now final.

Sincerely,

RAYMOND F. FARRELL,

Commissioner.

The following letter dated February 18, 1976, to the chairman of the Senate Committee on the Judiciary from the beneficiary of the bill reads as follows:

FEBRUARY 18, 1976

HON. JAMES O. EASTLAND,
Senate Office Building,
Washington, D.C.

DEAR SENATOR EASTLAND: Private Bill H. R. 2399, relieving me from deportation due to a first offense, possession of marijuana arrest in 1963, is presently before you in the Senate Judiciary Committee. This was the only time in my life I was ever arrested, and this action has been pending since 1965.

I have lived in the United States for 23 years and have been a member of the International Union of Operating Engineers for 22 years. I am presently employed by Bechtel Power Corporation in the construction of two nuclear generating stations at San Onofre, California.

My wife, Valerie, is a native-born American and it is our fondest wish to raise a family in the United States. We pray that my bill will be favorably considered by you and the Committee. If you think it would be helpful, we would be happy to fly to Washington, to meet with you and discuss this in more depth. Thank you for your time and attention.

Very truly yours,

L. A. BROWNRIGG.

The committee, after consideration of all the facts in the case, is of the opinion that the bill (H.R. 2399) should be enacted.

(Congressional Record—Senate, August 5, 1976, pp. 13637–13638)

Private bills for the relief of single grievances are an important part of Congress's legislative output.

ilar proposals in the other. Furthermore, many bills introduced do not receive strong support from powerful members—such as party leaders or committee members—or even from the legislators who have introduced them. (Members of Congress often introduce measures to please constituents even though they have no intention of working for passage.)

Referral of Bills to Committees

It would be impossible for all members of Congress to consider all the proposals introduced at every session. Thus a system of com-

mittees has been developed in each house to cope with the volume of legislation.

Types of committees. After a bill is introduced, it is given a number, prefixed by "H.R." in the House or "S." in the Senate, and gets its "first reading"—which often consists merely of having its title read aloud. It is then referred by the Speaker of the House or the president pro tempore of the Senate to the appropriate *standing committee*—a permanent committee that continues its work from one session of Congress to the next. There are 21 standing committees in the House and 16 in the Senate. In each body there are standing committees for all major subject areas, such as agriculture, foreign affairs, public works, labor, and government operations (see Figure 11.2).

In addition to these standing committees, *select committees*, also called "special commit-tees," are established from time to time by each body to deal with temporary problems or as investigatory, oversight, or advisory committees. In many cases these committees do not have the authority to draft legislation—as is the case, for example, with the Select

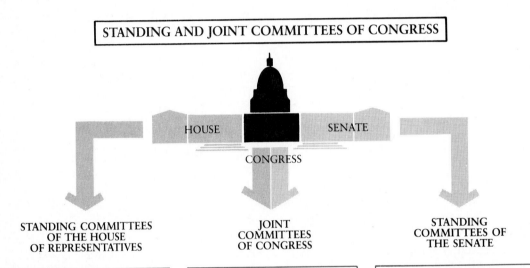

STANDING AND JOINT COMMITTEES OF CONGRESS

HOUSE   SENATE

CONGRESS

STANDING COMMITTEES OF THE HOUSE OF REPRESENTATIVES

AGRICULTURE
APPROPRIATIONS
ARMED SERVICES
BANKING, FINANCE, AND URBAN AFFAIRS
BUDGET
DISTRICT OF COLUMBIA
EDUCATION AND LABOR
ENERGY AND COMMERCE
FOREIGN AFFAIRS
GOVERNMENT OPERATIONS
HOUSE ADMINISTRATION
INTERIOR AND INSULAR AFFAIRS
JUDICIARY
MERCHANT MARINE AND FISHERIES
POST OFFICE AND CIVIL SERVICE
PUBLIC WORKS AND TRANSPORTATION
RULES
SCIENCE AND TECHNOLOGY
SMALL BUSINESS
STANDARDS OF OFFICIAL CONDUCT
VETERANS' AFFAIRS
WAYS AND MEANS

JOINT COMMITTEES OF CONGRESS

ECONOMICS
LIBRARY
PRINTING
TAXATION

STANDING COMMITTEES OF THE SENATE

AGRICULTURE, NUTRITION, AND FORESTRY
APPROPRIATIONS
ARMED SERVICES
BANKING, HOUSING, AND URBAN AFFAIRS
BUDGET
COMMERCE, SCIENCE, AND TRANSPORTATION
ENERGY AND NATURAL RESOURCES
ENVIRONMENT AND PUBLIC WORKS
FINANCE
FOREIGN RELATIONS
GOVERNMENTAL AFFAIRS
JUDICIARY
LABOR AND HUMAN RESOURCES
RULES AND ADMINISTRATION
VETERANS' AFFAIRS

FIGURE 11.2

Committee on Aging. In the House, since 1880, the Speaker has had the authority to appoint all select committees (previously the House could deprive the Speaker of the power to appoint such committees); but in the Senate, members of these committees are chosen in the same way as the members of the regular standing committees—that is, by the Steering and Policy Committee of the Democratic party and the Committee on Committees of the Republican party.

The differences between the House and the Senate in the selection of special or select committees reflect the more hierarchical organization of the House under the Speaker and the relative lack of such organization in the Senate.

Committees, whether select or standing, develop their own constituencies outside of Congress composed of groups whose interests they represent. For example, senior citizen groups feel their interests are represented by the committees on Aging in both the Senate and the House, and veterans groups by the Veterans Affairs committees in both bodies. The Senate Select Committee on Indian Affairs has a small but powerful Indian tribe constituency that prevented the Committee from being abolished in the 1970s. Agricultural interests are represented by the Agriculture committees in the House and the Senate. The internal power incentives on Capitol Hill to retain committees because of their benefits to chairmen, ranking minority members, and staff are complemented by outside power incentives to support the committees due to the special representation and access they provide interest groups.

Examples abound of the way in which committees have been used to increase the power and visibility of their chairmen. An obscure New Jersey congressman, Democrat Peter Rodino, when he was chairman of the usually low-profile House Judiciary Committee, became a national figure when his panel conducted hearings on the impeachment of Richard M. Nixon in 1974. In the Senate, Sam Ervin (D., N.C.), formerly known only to his North Carolina constituents, became a household name as he also used his Senate Government Operations Committee to conduct investigations into Nixon's alleged cover-up of his reelection committee's involvement in the Watergate break-in.[4] Senators such as Estes Kefauver (D., Tenn.), Robert Kennedy (D., N.Y.), and John McClellan (D., Ark.) became national figures as chairmen of Senate committees investigating drugs (Kefauver) and crime and racketeering (Kennedy and McClellan).

More recently, as the decade of the 1990s began, representatives John Dingell (D., Mich.) and Dan Rostenkowski (D., Ill.), chairmen of the House Energy and Commerce (Dingell) and Ways and Means (Rostenkowski) committees, not only made their mark on Capitol Hill but also used their committees to gain national publicity. As chairman of his committee's Oversight and Investigations Subcommittees, John Dingell conducted many celebrated investigations, including investigations during the Reagan years into Pentagon waste and former Reagan officials' influence peddling. During the 1980s Dan Rostenkowski was one of the authors of the tax reform bill that Reagan signed with a flourish in 1987. As a congressional "prime minister" of taxation, Ways and Means Committee chairmen will continue to use their powerful committee to influence if not dominate revenue policy.

Standing, select, and special committees are at the top of the hierarchy of committee organization in the House and the Senate, followed by subcommittees and joint committees. *Joint committees,* which are without leg-

---

[4]The Committee to Reelect the President (CREEP) had directed a covert operation of "hired guns" to break into the office of Larry O'Brien, chairman of the Democratic National Committee, to plant an eavesdropping bug so that the Nixon campaign would know its adversary's campaign plans.

islative jurisdiction, are created to study matters of special concern to both the House and the Senate.

After the committees and individual members have completed the regular legislative work of the House and the Senate, differences between the bodies must often be worked out by *conference committees* appointed by the Speaker of the House and through informal consultation between the Majority Leader and chairmen of the appropriations committees in the Senate. Although conference committees are only temporary, they often significantly rewrite legislation, becoming in effect the final powers in the legislative process. This is true even though both the House and the Senate have to ratify the compromise versions of bills agreed upon by the conference committees. Such ratification is usually pro forma due to the pressures of time at the end of legislative sessions.

Work within committees and subcommittees. Once a bill has been sent to a committee, it is placed on that committee's calendar. Many bills are pigeonholed, or disregarded, immediately because they are considered nonessential. If a bill is considered important enough for consideration, the committee chairman determines whether it will be studied by the full committee or a subcommittee, which is a smaller group chosen by and drawn from the full committee. Generally, House standing committees range from 25 to over 40 members, while their subcommittees have 15 or fewer members. Standing committees of the Senate have from 15 to 20 members, while subcommittees are generally composed of 6 or 7 senators.

The committee or subcommittee hearings studying a bill may hold *hearings* to which interested government officials, private citizens, and pressure-group spokesmen may be invited to express opinions on the measure. Most hearings are open to the public, whereas some, known as "executive sessions," are not. For some bills, both open and closed hearings

are held. In addition to hearings, committee members sometimes make field trips to a particular region to study a problem firsthand and may hold "field hearings" to gain local publicity helpful in current or future electoral campaigns.

Once committee findings or subcommittee reports on a bill have been studied, the full committee must vote on whether to *report* the bill to the chamber floor. The committee may vote to report the bill with a favorable or unfavorable recommendation or with amendments added. It may still pigeonhole the bill at this point or even substitute a completely new one—a "clean bill"—for the original. Once a bill has been reported out of committee, it is placed on a schedule, or *calendar*, for action by the entire chamber.

Committee members and chairmen. Many observers of the American political system have concluded that the committees form the backbone of the legislative system. As early as 1885 Woodrow Wilson noted that the real power in the House of Representatives resided with the committees, particularly their chairmen. Wilson likened the chairmen to feudal barons who conducted the affairs of their own territories in complete independence of one another and of any higher governing authority. As Wilson pointed out:

The chairmen of the standing committees do not constitute a cooperative body. . . .They do not consult and concur . . .there is no thought of acting in concert, each committee goes its own way at its own pace.[5]

On every standing committee, the Democratic and Republican parties are allotted the same percentage of committee members as they have of the total membership in the House (or Senate as the case may be). The Steering Committee (Democratic party) or Committee on Committees (Republican party) appoints new members to the standing com-

[5]Wilson, *Congressional Government:* pp. 58–59.

mittees (see Figure 11.3), the chairman of each being the top-ranking (usually the most senior) majority party member of the committee. Although the seniority rule was temporarily violated in the Ninety-fourth Congress, when the Democratic caucus deposed the chairmen of three powerful committees—Agriculture, Armed Services, and Small Business—this violation was essentially a symbolic act and did not in any way disturb the seniority system, which continued to be used for the selection of every other chairman of the approximately 150 committees and subcommittees in the House.

When the *seniority rule* is followed, the senior member of the majority party of each committee may choose to become its chairman. In the absence of strong party leadership in Congress the seniority rule remains the only viable alternative in the selection of chairmen. It is the only selection procedure that, regardless of rhetorical attacks upon it from time to time within Congress, has almost universal support on Capitol Hill. Outside Congress, groups such as Common Cause have attacked the seniority rule because it is thought to entrench the older and more conservative members of Congress as committee chairmen. The absence of any willingness in Congress to turn over power to the leadership, however, makes arguments against the seniority rule academic. Instead of seeking power by overturning more senior members of Congress, younger members, as they begin to gain tenure, strive to obtain their own subcommittees, thereby making themselves part of the "congressional establishment."

Power of committee chairmen. The committee system is largely controlled by individual chairmen. Generally, it is the chairmen who determine the order in which bills will be considered by their committees and the frequency of committee meetings. The Senate committees, being smaller, tend to operate on more of a consensus basis than do the much larger House committees.

It becomes immediately apparent in observing a House hearing or "markup session" (a period during which bills are considered item by item and amendments are made) that House committees are themselves rather like little legislatures; in the Senate committees an informal give-and-take atmosphere prevails. Whether in the House or the Senate, however, the tone of committee meetings is always set by the chairman.

Before 1973 an important power of a House chairman, from the members' standpoint, was the prerogative to create or to recommend the creation of subcommittees and to determine the allocation of committee funds to them. The subcommittee Bill of Rights reduced this power of chairmen and guaranteed subcommittees adequate funds.

Congressional committee organization and the seniority rule have been subject to criticism on a fairly regular basis both within and without Congress. Within Congress the House, in the Ninety-third Congress (1973–1974), and the Senate, in the Ninety-fourth (1975–1976) Congress, made internal efforts to reorganize and streamline the committee system. In the House in 1973, the Select Committee on Committees was chaired by Representative Richard Bolling (D., Mo.), and in the Senate in 1976 a committee with the same title was chaired by Senator Adlai Stevenson of Illinois. Although some of the recommendations of these committees were accepted, there was no substantial reorganization of committee jurisdictions or reduction in the number of committees in either the House or the Senate; nor were any changes made in the seniority rule.

Efforts to reform Congress often reflect a battle between the "ins" and the "outs" on Capitol Hill—between the freshmen and more junior members of both parties on the one hand, and their powerful senior colleagues who control committee chairmanships and leadership posts on the other. The failure of congressional reform efforts reflects the inabil-

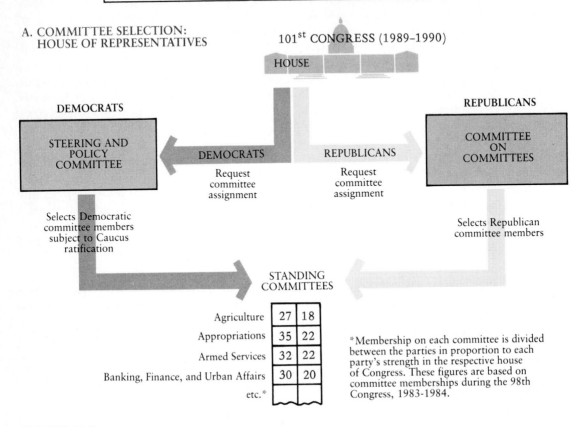

FIGURE 11.3

ity of newcomers in Congress to overturn the congressional establishment.

Reform efforts within Congress reflect a power struggle among members, whereas outside Congress committee reform is the goal of certain pressure groups that find their interests insufficiently represented by the current system. For example, Common Cause, a broad-based liberal "public interest" pressure group, has unsuccessfully sought to have Congress adopt a system in which the leadership has more effective control over committee membership and the flow of legislation on Capitol Hill. Regardless of reform efforts, the committee system continues to be the dominant feature of congressional politics. Com-

mittees continue to expand both in number and power because members find them essential to the achievement of their main objectives: reelection, influence within Congress, and "good public policy."

FROM COMMITTEE TO FLOOR ACTION IN THE HOUSE

Once a bill is reported out of committee in either house, it is listed on a calendar or schedule in the order that it will be considered by the entire chamber. The process by which a

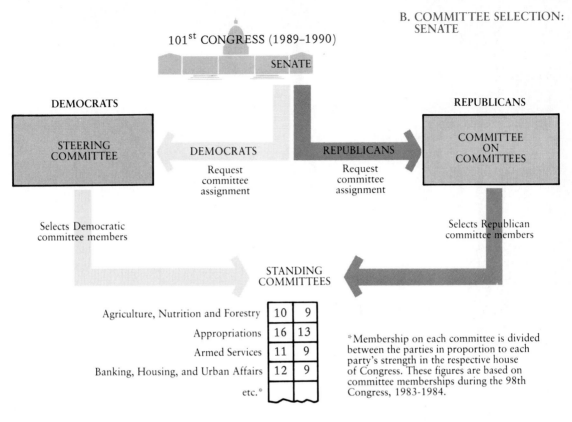

B. COMMITTEE SELECTION: SENATE

101st CONGRESS (1989–1990)

SENATE

DEMOCRATS

STEERING COMMITTEE

DEMOCRATS

Request committee assignment

Selects Democratic committee members

REPUBLICANS

COMMITTEE ON COMMITTEES

REPUBLICANS

Request committee assignment

Selects Republican committee members

STANDING COMMITTEES

Agriculture, Nutrition and Forestry	10	9
Appropriations	16	13
Armed Services	11	9
Banking, Housing, and Urban Affairs	12	9
etc.*		

*Membership on each committee is divided between the parties in proportion to each party's strength in the respective house of Congress. These figures are based on committee memberships during the 98th Congress, 1983-1984.

FIGURE 11.3 *(Continued)*

bill goes from committee to calendar and finally to *floor action* (debate and voting) is more flexible in the House than in the Senate, where the procedure is more routine. However, the former presents more obstacles.

House Calendars

Public bills dealing with appropriations and revenue are placed on the Union Calendar (the abbreviated name for the Calendar of the Committee of the Whole House on the State of the Union), whereas nonrevenue public bills are placed on the House Calendar. All private bills are listed on the Private Calendar. In addition, to speed House action on a noncontroversial public bill from the Union or House calendars that requires little debate before passage, a House member may request

that the bill be placed on the Consent Calendar. A fifth calendar, the Discharge Calendar, schedules petitions to force, or discharge, bills out of committees.

Without major objections from any member, public bills on the Consent Calendar and private bills can be passed quickly and sent on to the Senate. Bills on the Consent Calendar are "called," or considered by the floor on the first and third Mondays of each month. Ordinarily, a *quorum*, or a minimum, of 218 Representatives must be present in the House before a vote can be taken on a bill. However, bills on the Consent Calendar can be passed by a quorum of 100 members acting as a committee for the entire House. Should a bill on the Consent Calendar meet an objection the first time it is considered, it is held over until

(Ranan Lurie in *Life Magazine*.)

"They can't hear us."

The seniority system was often criticized for automatically giving senior members committee chairmanships, regardless of their responsiveness to important political trends within and without Congress.

the next time the Consent Calendar is called. If a minimum of three members object to the bill on the second call, the bill is considered controversial and is sent back to the Union Calendar or House Calendar. It cannot reappear on the Consent Calendar during that session.

Bills on the Private Calendar are called on the first Tuesday of each month; they are also called on the third Tuesday of any month if the Speaker decides it is necessary. Approval of a bill on this calendar in effect requires unanimous consent, because only two objectors are needed to have a bill sent back to a committee (usually the Judiciary Committee) for further consideration.

The Rules Committee

Before most bills reach the floor, they must pass the hurdle of a second committee, the Rules Committee, which determines how the bill will be handled in House debate. The Rules Committee provides essentially another screening action that a bill must go through before it reaches the floor. Public bills on the Consent Calendar and private bills automatically bypass the Rules Committee. A number of other bills, such as District of Columbia bills and certain categories of bills from several specific committees, also automatically bypass the Rules Committee.[6] Other bills may bypass the committee if considered under a "suspension of the rules."

The Rules Committee decides which standing rule of procedure will apply to a particular bill. Ordinarily there are two types of rules, the closed rule and the open rule. The

closed rule allows only members of the sponsoring committee to make amendments to a bill. The *open rule* permits amendments from the floor. In most cases, rules limiting debate time are also made. If no such rule is made, each member is allowed one hour of debate.

A chairman of a committee reporting a bill who wants to speed action on it may request a special rule from the Rules Committee to consider the bill out of order, to limit debate, or to declare that certain sections or none of the bill's sections may be amended. Those who oppose a special rule for one reason or another usually label it a "gag rule."

In the past, members of the House Rules Committee were able effectively to block legislation they disapproved of. Because membership on the committee was so desirable and because of the seniority system, it was usually the older, more conservative representatives who won places on the committee. In the early 1960s bills providing for federal aid to education were pigeonholed by the conservative members of the Rules Committee and thus withheld from House consideration. Civil rights legislation was similarly delayed. Often bills that were reported out of the Rules Committee had been modified to conform to the views of the conservative committee membership.

Curbing the Rules Committee. The control of the Rules Committee over the fate of legislation has long been a source of frustration to House members eager for legislative action. During this century attempts have often been made to reduce the committee's power.

Until 1910 the Speaker of the House was automatically chairman of the Rules Committee. In effect, this meant that one individual could dominate the House by combining the power of the Speakership with control over the Rules Committee. Abuses inevitably occurred. In 1903 Joseph G. "Uncle Joe" Cannon, an "Old Guard" Republican, became Speaker of the House. Over the next few years

---

[6]These bills include general appropriations bills from the Appropriations Committee, revenue bills from the Ways and Means Committee, bills governing public lands and admission of new states from the Interior and Insular Affairs Committee, bills governing rivers and harbors from the Public Works Committee, pension bills from the Veterans Affairs Committee, rules relating to the administration of the chamber from the House Administration Committee, and bills governing procedure and the order of business from the Rules Committee.

RULES TO KEEP CONGRESS FROM VOTING

DEVICES TO KEEP CITIZENS FROM VOTING

REPRESENTATIVE GOVERNMENT

©1961 HERBLOCK
THE WASHINGTON POST

(From *Straight Herblock* [Simon & Schuster, 1964])

"This is what you might call defense in depth."

In the past the Rules Committee was regarded as a major barrier to the passage of legislation.

Cannon used his power to prevent the passage of progressive legislation. Finally, in 1910 there was a peaceful revolt in the House, and a resolution was passed that thereafter excluded any Speaker from membership on the Rules Committee. The resolution also provided that members of the Rules Committee would be elected by the entire House.

Freeing the Rules Committee from the Speaker's domination, however, did not prevent conservative minorities from controlling the committee. By the time of the New Deal, the Rules Committee was again firmly controlled by a coalition of Democratic and Republican conservatives. A number of progressive New Deal measures in such areas as fair labor practices and social security met with stiff opposition from this coalition.

As the Rules Committee continued to thwart passage of legislation, new attempts were made to curb its powers. During Harry Truman's last term in office, the Rules Committee bottled up bills that provided for universal military training, amendments to social security, civil rights, and other legislation. In 1949 a 21-day rule was adopted which provided that if the Rules Committee held a bill for 21 days, the chairman of the committee originally reporting the bill could ask for House action on it. The 21-day rule was abolished in 1951, when conservatives regained a majority in the House. Again a conservative coalition on the Rules Committee began to thwart legislation counter to its views.

Liberals in the House continued to press for reform. When John F. Kennedy won the presidency in 1960, it became evident that the Rules Committee would have to be revamped if any of his progressive proposals were to pass the House. On January 31, 1961, the House, led by the Democratic Speaker Sam Rayburn, voted 217 to 212 to expand the committee by adding three new members, two Democrats and one Republican. This made it possible to force the conservatives' coalition into a minority on the committee. Conservatives on the Rules Committee experienced another setback in 1965, when the 21-day rule was restored.

The continuing struggle between liberals and conservatives over the power of the Rules Committee in the post-World War II period finally culminated, in the Ninety-fourth Congress (1975–1976), in a motion by Richard Bolling, which the House passed by a vote of 106 to 65, to give the Speaker the power to name all of the Democratic members of the Rules Committee, subject to ratification by the Democratic caucus. The Speaker at the beginning of a session has the authority to remove any incumbent members of the Rules Committee, a power that he has not chosen to exercise due to the traditional respect in the House for the rights of individual members to retain their committee assignments. By 1975 the Rules Committee was no longer the bastion of conservative House interests, acting as a conservative check upon the entire House; it was an outpost of the Speaker. Ironically, the House had come full circle since the 1910 revolt that had reduced the Speaker's powers and control over the Rules Committee. In 1975, however, the majority caucus felt that it controlled the Speaker.

Bypassing the Rules Committee. Although the Rules Committee since 1975 has become more a servant of the House and the Speaker than their master, the potential for a resurgent Rules Committee in the future remains. Dissatisfaction with the performance of the committee in the past has led the House to adopt certain procedures for bypassing it where it is acting arbitrarily and without a consensus of House members. If a bill does not belong in a category that automatically bypasses the Rules Committee, and if its advocates are unwilling to wait for its scheduling through the regular calendar, it may be forced out of the Rules Committee in one of three ways: (1) by suspension of the rules, (2) by a discharge motion, or (3) on Calendar Wednesday.

To *suspend the rules*, a member must be recognized by the Speaker and ask that the rules be ignored so that a particular bill can be considered. If two-thirds of those members present agree to suspend the rules, debate is limited to 40 minutes, and the bill is brought to a vote. No amendments, however, are allowed to be attached to a bill brought to the floor under a suspension of the rules.

A *discharge petition* requires approval of a majority of the House. This is difficult to obtain. From 1909 to 1983 only 26 discharge petitions out of 909 filed placed bills on the Discharge Calendar. Only two of these bills—the Fair Labor Standards bill of 1938 and the Federal Pay Raise bill of 1960—passed both the House and the Senate to become law after being wrested from the Rules Committee by formal discharge.

The *Calendar Wednesday* method of bypassing the Rules Committee is also difficult to use. Under this procedure, on every Wednesday of each month, as the rolls of committees are called, their chairmen can place bills that have been reported from their committees on the calendar for consideration that day. If the bill is passed on the Wednesday it is called, it becomes law without going through the Rules Committee.

Adopted in 1909, the Calendar Wednesday method has been used successfully only twice. The difficulty with this method is that opponents of a bill can easily use delaying tactics to prevent the bill's passage on the day it is considered. There is also a time limit of two hours on debate for each bill.

Due to the difficulty in using these various methods to bypass the Rules Committee, the committee still has considerable control over the passage of legislation, even though the Speaker now has greater control over the committee than at any time since 1910. There has been no serious attempt by the members of the House to abolish the committee because it does play a role necessary to the House procedure in screening out the unwanted, unsupported, and nonessential bills. And representatives can use the committee as a "whipping boy"—that is, they can publicly blame the committee for killing bills that they privately wanted to have die.

Riders. Although House rules prevent *riders,* or nongermane amendments, to most legislation, by unanimous consent or suspension of the rules by a two-thirds vote, the House has increasingly used the rider to bypass its normal legislative procedures, including the committee process. Members have become particularly fond of using riders to appropriations bills to create "Christmas tree" legislation that provides benefits to constituents and special-interest groups.

Technically, appropriations riders must be germane, but the wide scope of appropriations legislation that covers every government policy area gives members broad latitude to affect public policy through limitation riders that restrict the use of government funds for particular programs. (For example, opponents of abortion continually attach riders to appropriations legislation that would prevent the use of public funds for abortions.) The use of funding-bill riders accelerated rapidly in the latter 1970s. Committee chairmen and House leaders have understandably lamented the growth of appropriations bill riders that circumvent their power over the legislative process. Presidential power over Congress is also diminished by riders because the president does not have an item veto that would allow him to reject legislative riders and amendments without vetoing the legislation to which they are attached. Riders to important legislative proposals favored by the White House are veto-proof. The practice of attaching riders to legislation, said President Franklin D. Roosevelt in 1938, "robs the executive of legitimate and essential freedom of action in dealing with legislation."[7] When President Jimmy Carter, for example, vetoed a pay raise for Public Health Service doctors, Congress responded by incorporating the raise into a rider on a mental health service bill favored by First Lady Rosalyn Carter. The president signed the bill, which included the pay hike.

Various proposals to rein in the growing use of riders to legislate have been made by the House leadership, but to no avail. Too many members of Congress consider riders to be crucial to their power as individual legislators.

Debate in the House

When a bill finally reaches the floor of the House, it must be read for a second time, debated, and voted on. Many bills—those that

are of little concern to the majority of the members—create no opposition and are dealt with quickly. Most other legislation is first considered by the House acting as a Committee of the Whole. Tax measures and appropriations bills must be brought before a Committee of the Whole under House rules. There are two kinds of Committees of the Whole: Private bills are handled by the Committee of the Whole House, and public bills are handled by the Committee of the Whole House on the State of the Union. In both cases, the House serves as a committee of itself; the Speaker steps down and appoints a senior member who is an expert on the bill under debate to preside.

Debate under a Committee of the Whole is freer than during regular House proceedings. A quorum of only 100 members, instead of the normal 218, is required for doing business. Each member opposing or supporting amendments to a bill under discussion is given five minutes to participate in debate. Once debate is concluded and votes have been taken, the Speaker reassumes the chair and calls the House back into regular session for the final vote.

Voting Procedures in the House

Roll-call votes in the House have always been a matter of public record. But before 1971 votes in the Committee of the Whole were difficult to trace. Voting was by voice, by a "division" where members stood to be counted, and by tellers (counters who recorded the yeas and nays as members filed past them). Beginning in 1971 members were required to record their votes on signed green (yea) or red (nay) cards and put them into a ballot box in full view of the galleries. Since 1973 virtually all votes have been recorded electronically.

After the proposed amendments to a bill have been voted on, a motion may be made to recommit the bill to committee. If the motion is carried, the bill, in effect, has been

[7]*Congressional Quarterly Weekly Report*, Vol. 38, No. 44 (November 1, 1980, p. 3253.

killed. If the motion to recommit is not carried, the bill is read for a third time and the final vote is taken.

Once a bill is passed by either house of Congress, it becomes officially an act. An act passed first by the House of Representatives has reached the halfway point; it is then sent on for consideration by the Senate.

TO FLOOR ACTION IN THE SENATE

Owing to its smaller size and the longer terms of its members, the Senate is able to operate less formally than the House. A bill is introduced, given a reading and a number, and referred by the majority leadership to the appropriate committee for study and consideration. However, there is no Rules Committee in the Senate to stall legislation as there is in the House. The leader of the majority party directs the order of business under a flexible set of rules of procedure, usually conducting business by "unanimous consent."

There are only two Senate calendars. All bills reported from committees go onto the Calendar of Business, and presidential nominations and treaties go onto the Executive Calendar. Bills are scheduled for floor action by a majority vote of the Senate or by the majority party's Policy Committee in consultation with the minority leader.

Bypassing Senate Committees

When Senate committees delay action on legislation, there are a number of devices that can be used to get bills onto the floor quickly. Among these circumventing methods are the discharge rule, the rider, suspension of the rules, and the special procedures for House-passed bills.

The discharge rule. Under the *discharge rule*, a senator may introduce a motion to dis-

charge a bill or resolution from committee. Such a motion can be passed by a majority vote on the legislative day after it has been introduced.

Although this procedure seems simple, the discharge rule is almost impossible to invoke successfully. Senators opposed to a discharge motion can easily prevent its introduction by speaking on the floor during the morning hours (when such motions must be introduced according to the rules of the Senate). Moreover, the majority leader, or even a small group of influential senators who oppose the motion, can prevent the recognition of a senator who wishes to call a discharge motion introduced the previous day. Only 14 discharge motions have been made in the history of the Senate, and only 6 have passed. Only one of the passed motions resulted in a law. This one exception was a totally noncontroversial bill that permitted the federal government to make a medal for a state of Florida celebration in 1964.

Nongermane amendments. In addition to the discharge rule, senators can use *nongermane amendments* to sidestep committees. Under this procedure a proposal that is stalled in committee may be attached in the form of an amendment, or rider, to an unrelated bill that *has* been reported to the floor from committee. The use of nongermane amendments is not permitted in the House, but it is allowed in the Senate except in the case of general appropriations bills. However, senators and their aides have learned to draft amendments skillfully so that they can be attached to appropriations bills as well as to general legislation. (Republican Senator Jesse Helms of North Carolina became one of the acknowledged masters of the technique of the nongermane amendment to force the Senate to vote on controversial proposals banning the use of federal funds for abortion, prohibiting abortion itself, and for a constitutional amendment allowing prayer in public schools.) Finally, the Senate rule against nongermane amendments to appropriations bills can simply be suspended by unanimous consent or by a two-thirds vote of the members present.

Senators use riders to bypass unsympathetic committees, to facilitate the introduction of controversial legislation, and to gain Senate approval of favorite projects to benefit their constituents. When Lyndon B. Johnson was Senate Majority Leader in 1960, he called up a civil rights bill by attaching it to a minor legislative proposal to aid a school district in Missouri that, due to the presence of a military base, had more than a normal quota of local children to educate. Senate Majority Leader Robert Byrd (D., W. Va.) gained the unanimous consent of the Senate to tack on an amendment to an appropriations bill for energy and water development that authorized a $284 million flood control project in his home state. Ironically, Byrd had been a strong opponent of legislative riders to appropriations bills during his tenure as Majority Leader from 1978 to 1980. After he introduced his own rider, however, he commented, "There are times when such riders fulfill a purpose, a necessary purpose, so that I would not say that all riders under all circumstances are inappropriate or bad."[8]

Suspension of the rules. Another way to bypass Senate committees is through a *suspension of the rules*. Through this method, a procedure normally prohibited under Senate rules can be used if a two-thirds majority of senators vote to suspend the applicable rule. For example, suspension of the rules is required before a nongermane amendment can be attached to a general appropriations bill and before the amount of appropriations on such a bill can be increased. Regular Senate rules prohibit both of these procedures. Historically, suspension of the rules has been difficult to achieve in either the Senate or the House, where two-thirds of the members must also approve it. However, in recent years, both

suspension of the rules and its cousin, unanimous consent, have been used more frequently in both the Senate and the House to expedite legislative business.

House-passed bills. There is also a special Senate procedure by which House-passed bills can go directly to the Senate calendar for a floor vote without having to go through committee. This procedure is normally used to circumvent a committee that is dominated by a minority group unrepresentative of the Senate as a whole.

During the late 1950s and early 1960s, for example, when civil rights legislation was being supported vigorously by many groups, the Senate Judiciary Committee was chaired by Senator James Eastland of Mississippi. Senator Eastland represented a small minority in the Senate that wanted to block civil rights legislation at any cost. By use of the special procedure for House-passed bills, however, the civil rights bills of 1957 and 1964 succeeded in coming to the Senate floor without committee action.

The Filibuster

Unlike debate in the House, Senate debate is neither subject to rules nor limited to any time period. Senate tradition permits unlimited debate on floor motions unless three-fifths of the Senate agrees to close debate. This factor gives senators their most powerful delaying tactic, the filibuster.

A *filibuster* is employed after a bill is on the floor and open to debate, and its objective is to "talk a bill to death" in order to gain concessions or even withdrawal of the bill. Senators using this tactic talk for hours on topics that may or may not be relevant to the subject of debate. During a filibuster some senators even read aloud old issues of the *Congressional Record* or the daily newspapers to keep the process going. A filibuster continues as long as interested senators have the collective energy to go on. When one senator tires, he yields the floor to one of his col-

[8]*Congressional Quarterly Weekly Report*, Vol. 38, No. 44 (November 1, 1980), p. 3255.

leagues who has agreed to keep on with the debate. Senator Strom Thurmond of South Carolina holds the individual record for a filibuster. He talked for over 24 hours to halt the passage of a civil rights bill in 1957.

Filibusters can be stopped, however, by using the *cloture* rule (Senate Rule 22). One-sixth of the Senate (16 members) must initiate cloture action by petitioning the Senate to close the debate. The vote to limit debate by the cloture rule is automatically taken two days after the petition is submitted. The traditional requirement of two-thirds of the senators present for approval of cloture petitions was changed on March 7, 1975, to require three-fifths of the full Senate (60 votes) for cloture. Advocates of reform sought to have the three-fifths rule apply only to those present but were unable to convince the Senate of the desirability of this course of action.

Historically, most moves for cloture in the Senate have come from liberal forces seeking to end conservative filibusters. Most petitions for cloture failed until the change in the rules in 1975, after which 60 votes could break a filibuster. The success rate of the filibusters of the past has diminished sharply under the new rules, and nowadays most important legislation is finally brought before the Senate even though individual members may have attempted to filibuster it. However, the filibuster continues to be an important tactic of legislative delay that is being used increasingly by individual members and small groups of senators. Only 92 of 273 cloture votes taken since 1917 have been successful.

Adjusting House-Senate Differences

Once Senate debate on a bill has been terminated, voting on the bill is scheduled. Unlike in the House, electronic voting is not employed in the Senate, and the voting procedure is more flexible than it is in the House. Many motions and noncontroversial bills are adopted by unanimous consent. Otherwise roll-call votes are taken.

Major legislation is always represented by different bills in the House and the Senate, often requiring conference committees to work out differences between the two bodies when each has passed its own version of the bill. Usually conference committees meet in the Capitol, protocol assigning the conference room alternately to the House and Senate side of the Capitol. Conference committees are normally composed of from five to ten members.

House members of conference committees are appointed by the Speaker; in the Senate appointment is by the majority leadership in consultation with the chairman of the standing committee that reported the legislation. (There is no formal rule in the Senate regarding the appointment of conference committees as there is in the House, the procedure having developed informally.) Senate rules formally restrict the scope of the authority of Senate conferees, proscribing them from eliminating, in their report back to the Senate from the conference committee, matters that both the House and the Senate had previously passed in the legislation before the conference. There is no such formal restriction in the House rules. In reality, conference committees have a great deal of discretion in restructuring and amending the original legislation, which is always of course subject to final agreement by both the House and the Senate.

Conference committees are not established automatically. "Foot dragging" by either the Senate or the House in the appointment of conferees can stall and even defeat legislation, especially at the end of congressional sessions, after which legislation automatically dies. Nor are conference committees required on all legislation that passes Congress. Usually differences between the two bodies are resolved when the chamber initiating the bill simply accepts the second chamber's amended version. The House, for example, may pass an appropriations bill and send it to the Senate, where amendments are made. The bill is then returned to the House, which by majority vote may agree to accept the amended version of its original bill. Similarly, a bill first passed by the Senate may eventually be returned and accepted with House amendments. House-Senate differences are adjusted in this way on approximately 90 percent of all public bills passed. The version of a bill passed by the second house is usually the one that is finally accepted.

All bills passed by Congress are sent to the president for his signature or veto. Should the president decide to veto the bill, however, he must return the bill to the house of its origin within 10 days (not including Sundays) along with a veto message stating his objections. Each house may then attempt to override his veto, and if the necessary two-thirds vote can be mustered in each body, the bill becomes a law without the president's signature.

There are two other veto options that the president may choose to employ. He may merely withhold his signature without returning the bill to Congress, in which case the bill automatically becomes a law without his signature at the end of the 10-day period. (This feeble means of protest has not been used by presidents in modern times, however.) Or the president may choose to exercise a *pocket veto*. Should Congress adjourn within the 10-day period allotted for the president to sign a bill, the president may simply "pocket" the bill. He need neither sign it nor return it to Congress with a veto message, but the bill is killed. As many bills are rushed to passage in the final days of a congressional session, the president has ample opportunity to make use of this method of vetoing.

Bill signings at the White House are ceremonious occasions, often televised, with the chief sponsors of the legislation present as well as such congressional leaders as the Speaker or the majority leader of the Senate. As the several copies of the bill are signed, the president hands the pens he has used to the committee chairmen who sponsored and guided the legislation through their respective bodies.

THE ROLE OF POLITICAL PARTIES IN CONGRESS

While committee power is the outstanding feature of Congress, parties also play an important role in the legislative process.

Committee organization and procedures are importantly affected by political parties. Special party committees assign new members to congressional committees, taking into account their preferences and those of the chairmen of the committees on which they wish to serve. Party ratios in Congress determine party balances on committees. The members of committees and subcommittees organize themselves and caucus as Democrats or Republicans. Committee staffs are divided between the two parties, with the majority party receiving approximately two-thirds of the staff. During committee hearings, the rights of the minority are respected by the majority, which allocates time to minority members for the questioning of witnesses. Committee reports also may contain minority views.

Congressional parties, particularly in the House, affect the flow of legislation. Party leaders, policy committees, and caucuses of members influence the legislative agenda. The Speaker of the House and the Majority Leader of the Senate may also take party considerations into account in the assignment of bills to committees, bypassing, if possible, committees whose chairmen are unsympathetic to the views of the party leadership and a majority of its members. The Speaker of the House works hand in hand with the chairman of the Rules Committee in scheduling legislation and determining floor rules for the consideration of bills.

Political parties also shape floor debate. Majority and minority members sit on oppo-

Proportion of Partisan Roll Calls

(Source: *Congressional Quarterly Weekly Report*, December 30, 1989, p. 3546.
Reprinted with permission from Congressional Quarterly, Inc.)

FIGURE 11.4

site sides, and equal time is given to each party to debate partisan measures, those supported by one party and opposed by the other. Members overwhelmingly vote with their parties on partisan issues.

Party Influences on Voting

Party-line voting, where a majority of the members of each party vote on opposite sides, has declined sharply in the twentieth century. From the period 1887–1901, 90 percent of the members of one party opposed 90 percent of the other on more than 50 percent of the votes. However, during the period 1955–1965, only 6 percent of the votes divided the parties so sharply.[9] In recent decades party unity

patterns have been erratic. (See Figure 11.4.) The decade of the 1980s saw an increase in party unity voting in the House, while party cohesion in the Senate declined, reflecting a more individualistic Senate. Because of erratic voting patterns on both sides of Capitol Hill it is difficult to tie congressional parties to particular public policies and make accurate generalizations about where the parties on Capitol Hill stand on particular issues. Democrats on both sides of Capitol Hill have generally been more "liberal" than their Republican colleagues, supporting a more active role for the government in solving national economic problems. Congressional parties also reflect nationwide differences between Democrats and Republicans on social issues such as abortion, with Democrats being more likely than Republicans to support freedom of choice. But

[9]Charles O. Jones, *The United States Congress* (Homewood, Ill.: Dorsey, 1982), p. 234.

concrete issue differences between congressional parties, while they exist, remain elusive and difficult to identify on many issues. Members will follow their parties only when they serve their reelection, internal power, and good public policy incentives, and not because they agree with the virtually non-existent party ideologies.

The conservative coalition. The lack of party cohesion, or discipline, on Capitol Hill has spawned a powerful *conservative coalition,* which is composed of conservative Democrats who have joined with the Republicans to form a majority on many important issues. While the Democrats have controlled the House of Representatives for decades (and because of the incumbency effect promise to do so for many years into the future), conservative Democrats, mostly from the South, by form-

ing an alliance with congressional Republicans have sharply diminished the influence of the northern liberal Democrats that form the core of the party. Figure 11.5 illustrates the power the conservative coalition has wielded over the years. Historically the coalition has been particularly effective and frustrating. The presidential wing of the Democratic party, nominating and when successful electing liberal Democratic presidents, has always met stiff opposition from Democrats in the conservative coalition.

SPECIAL GROUPS IN CONGRESS

Committees and political parties are the most important groups in Congress. However, spe-

Conservative Coalition History

FIGURE 11.5

(Source: *Congressional Quarterly Weekly Report,* December 30, 1989, p. 3554. Reprinted with permission from Congressional Quarterly, Inc.)

cial caucuses and other groups play a role as well.

The Special Caucuses of Congress

A wide array of *special caucuses*, groups of members who join together to represent and advance particular interests, dot the congressional landscape. They are primarily a House phenomenon. Most groups welcome members of both parties, but some have been formed within the parties themselves to represent liberal and conservative views. Liberal Democrats formed the Democratic Study Group (DSG) in 1959 to counter the power of the conservative coalition. A Republican Study Group (RSG) arose in the 1970s to represent conservative views and give assistance to Republicans of the same persuasion. (A small number of liberal Republicans had organized the Wednesday Group in 1963.) These intraparty caucuses have offices and staffs of their own to assist their members and (as in the case of the Democratic and Republican Study Groups) to provide information and aid to all party members sympathetic to their views. Temporary and informal caucuses within parties may arise from time to time to represent the political views of a minority of party members. For example, in the Ninety-seventh Congress (1981–1982) conservative House Democrats who supported Ronald Reagan caucused under the banner of the Boll Weevils, while liberal House Republicans called themselves the Gypsy Moths.

Caucuses and causes. Besides the liberal and conservative party caucuses, legislators have joined together to form dozens of caucuses that cross party lines to represent a wide array of concerns and causes. Caucuses elect leaders to represent them and usually have staff and office space on Capitol Hill in the members' office buildings and annexes, paid for by the government. Caucuses reflect narrow, often single-issue politics. Although they are euphemistically categorized as Legislative Service Organizations (LSOs), caucuses function more as ordinary interest groups within the legislative process and furthermore have special access and facilities because they are composed of members of Congress and staff insiders. Before 1983, when Congress itself curtailed their outside fund-raising activities, caucus fund raisers were common. Beginning in 1983, LSOs that receive outside funds must give up all support from Congress.

The interests, and often the creative imagination, of members who form LSOs are reflected in the names of the special caucuses. The Black and Hispanic caucuses, respectively, represent the interests of black and Hispanic Americans. Other LSOs include the Caucus for Science and Technology, Women's Caucus, Rural Caucus, Space Caucus, Steel Caucus, Textile Caucus, Travel and Tourism Caucus, Senior Citizens Caucus, Suburban Caucus, and the Sunbelt Council. Still other caucuses are regional alliances, such as the Northeast-Midwest Congressional Coalition, New England Congressional Caucus, Great Lakes Conference, and the Sunbelt Caucus in the House. Senate regional caucuses include the Midwest Conference of Democratic Senators and the Western States' Coalition.

State Delegations

House members who represent the same state have similar concerns, regardless of their party affiliations. State delegations are informal groups that may be of importance in the legislative process. The Texas delegation, for example, has been one of the most tightly knit groups in the House over the years, exercising power in greater proportion than its numbers in capturing leadership posts, committee chairmanships, and in generally influencing legislation. Texas congressmen have felt a great sense of regional identification and pride, and, unlike most other delegations, they hold regular meetings to discuss policies and strategies.

Political scientist John Kingdon has observed that "many congressmen feel uncomfortable about voting out of step with the rest of the delegation. Newspapers all over the state regularly print delegation box scores, and it can be somewhat of an embarrassment to find oneself voting against the rest of the state's congressmen. Such occurrences can also be used against one in the next campaign." Members of Congress must vote on hundreds of issues where there is neither a definite party position to guide them nor any clear indication of the preference of the majority of their constituency. At such times legislators "cue" from fellow Congress members and, more often than not, from other members of their state delegation to determine how they will vote. Kingdon concludes that

Congressmen from large state delegations are more likely to consult within their delegation than are those from small delegations. Large delegations are more likely to have a good distribution among the committees, so that a committee member for the legislation at hand is likely to be one of the delegation. The larger delegations can also be used as blocs of votes for bargaining leverage within the House, in a way that small delegations cannot.[10]

Response to internal pressures. Parties, caucuses, and state delegations influence in varying degrees the legislative activities and voting of congressmen. Members are influenced by clear party positions, caucus interests, and state delegation pressures.

While members of Congress are subject to both internal and external pressures, perhaps the most significant fact of legislative life is the freedom of choice of members in an environment that sometimes borders on chaos. Representatives and senators heed the bells that call them to record their votes. At the end of the 1980s senators had to respond to almost 800 recorded votes *each year*, while the average number of recorded votes in the House

was 450. Members are constantly running to the floor from their committee meetings and other legislative business to vote. On a majority of these votes, congressmen receive little guidance from constituents, interest groups, and congressional parties and other internal groups.

Members themselves and their aides have described the atmosphere that so frequently prevails when votes are taken. One member commented, "I've been so busy on my committee meetings that I just went in when the bells rang, asked somebody what this was all about, cast my vote and left." Another commented, "A lot of votes come up that you know absolutely nothing about. On major issues, you will think about it beforehand. But on other things—scores of votes, really—many members rush onto the floor, seek out someone on the committee [that reported the bill] they know, have a three or four-minute talk, and make up their mind on the spot." A staffer concluded, "They may rush in from the cloakroom, look who is in the teller line, and if there are three or four people they know in the line, they'll just join it. They may not even know what they're voting on."[11]

The most important influences on congressional voting remain expressed constituent demands and clear-cut constituency interests on the outside, and fellow congressmen on the inside.

The Congress of the United States is one of the most democratic legislatures in the world. Its individual members have a profound impact upon policies that in turn affect the lives of every citizen. Criticism of Congress as an institution is a popular political sport engaged in by all segments of society and by congressmen themselves. "Running against Congress" is a tried and true campaign technique. Congress is attacked in the press, in the campaign rhetoric of members, and by

---

[10]John W. Kingdon, *Congressmen's Voting Decisions*, 2d ed. (New York: Harper & Row, 1981), pp. 89–90, 91.

[11]Ibid., p. 98.

many political scientists due to its apparent inability to function efficiently, effectively, and in some cases even fairly. Joining the chorus of criticism against Congress are public-interest groups, such as Common Cause and Ralph Nader's Congresswatch. Congressional scandals, such as Abscam—the secret FBI probe that induced a handful of representatives and senators to take planted bribes in exchange for favors and influence—are blown up by the press as representative of behavior on Capitol Hill.

For all the criticism made of it, Congress remains more an example of what is best in our political system than a reflection of weaknesses. It continues to be the most representative body of government. Moreover, Congress has never given up its power to make laws. It is still the principal debating arena for legislation. And it is one of the most powerful legislative bodies in the world, for it can and often does use its authority under the Constitution to turn down presidential and administrative requests for legislative action. It is a rare session of Congress that sees more than 50 percent of the president's legislative recommendations passed. In countries with parliamentary governments and a disciplined two-party system, such as Great Britain, the parliament is little more than a rubber stamp for the Cabinet. The Congress of the United States is anything but a rubber stamp!

Results of Fragmentation

The Framers divided Congress into two houses, partly because they hoped that such fragmentation would always provide an internal check on legislative power. The subsequent delegation and dispersal of power to the many standing committees and subcommittees expanded this initial division. The lack of disciplined political parties and the highly specialized, complex nature of policy making has made the committee system the only practical arrangement under which Congress can operate. But this system also makes it difficult for

Congress to take positive action, because agreement must be reached on so many levels.

Sometimes this fragmentation of Congress results in negative rather than positive outputs. It is relatively easy, for example, to produce vague legislation or to pigeonhole legislation in the numerous standing committees of the House and the Senate. This is true especially if there is no substantial majority support behind a proposal or if a large minority is opposed to it.

Because Congress operates largely through committees, it is almost impossible to speak of Congress as a whole. It does not act as a unit. Objectively, then, there is no collective congressional intent; there is only the intent of many individuals and groups *within* Congress.

The incentive on the part of members to cultivate their own bailiwicks in the form of committees on Capitol Hill reflects the cultivation of individualism in Congress at the expense of the whole. Indeed, members of Congress often stress their individuality and separateness from the institution in their electoral campaigns, thereby running "against" Congress. Richard Fenno has pointed out that there is an irony in a member's constant emphasis upon his or her own individuality in running for Congress and the low esteem in which Congress is generally held by the public.[12] Constituents tend to rate their own representatives higher than they do Congress as a whole. The same stress upon individuality that pervades congressional campaigns is carried over into Congress itself, reducing the effectiveness of congressional parties and supporting the members' drive for personal power. And as Congress supports the individualism of its members, it weakens itself as an institution capable of taking collective action to meet pressing public policy needs.

---

[12]See Richard F. Fenno, Jr., "If, as Ralph Nader Says, Congress is 'The Broken Branch,' How Come We Love Our Congressmen So Much?" reprinted in Peter Woll, *American Government: Readings and Cases*, 6th ed. (Boston: Little, Brown, 1978), pp. 487–495.

Congressional Reform

Congressional reform is a perennial issue. Each time it is raised the question is: Reform for what purpose and in what ways? Reform of Congress is viewed entirely differently by those on and off Capitol Hill. In Congress itself the question of reform really comes down to who is going to have power in Congress—which means not only power to control and direct the legislative process but also control over staff, legislative funds, and the perquisites of office. Beyond Congress the issue of reform is also one of power, but principally in the form of access to legislative decision making.

Since reform of Congress involves the allocation of power within and without the institution, there is virtually a constant pressure for "reform." At the end of the nineteenth century and early in the twentieth, the principal reform issue in Congress centered around the power of the Speaker of the House. Throughout the twentieth century liberals in and outside of Congress have repeatedly, but without success, attacked the seniority rule on the grounds that it helps to concentrate congressional power in the hands of senior conservative members. Liberals were also dissatisfied with the informal power of the "Senate establishment," a term used in the 1950s to describe a small group of predominantly conservative senators who, due to their seniority and closely knit collegiality, were able to dominate the institution.[13]

In the 1970s renewed efforts to change the seniority rule took place. Various pressure groups, such as Common Cause, lobbied both branches of Congress to secure a change in procedures that would result in a more democratic selection of committee chairmen. In 1973 the House Republican Conference adopted the resolution that ranking Republicans on committees (who would be chairmen if the Republicans controlled the House) would be elected by the conference in a secret ballot after being recommended by the Committee on Committees. Seniority need not then be the only criterion in selecting committee chairmen. The House Democrats also changed their rules for the selection of committee chairmen and in 1973 provided that all committee chairmen would have to be elected by a majority vote of the full party caucus of the House. Again, seniority could be used, but theoretically it did not have to be the sole criterion for the selection of chairmen. Despite the changes in procedure, in practice seniority nevertheless remained the only criterion by which the Republicans selected their ranking members on committees; and, with the exception of the action of the Democratic caucus at the beginning of the Ninety-fourth Congress in 1975 deposing three senior committee chairmen, the seniority rule continued to be followed also by the Democrats.

Efforts to change the seniority system were made in the Senate as well as in the House. In January 1973, Senator Howard Baker, Jr., of Tennessee, working with Senator Jacob K. Javits of New York, managed to secure the adoption of a plan whereby top-ranking Republicans on committees would be selected by a vote of the Republicans on each committee. Seniority was not supposed to be the sole criterion, but in practice it continued to be used as the basis for selecting the top-ranking Republican on each committee. Senate Democrats have so far made no efforts to modify the seniority practice in selecting committee chairmen.

The issue of seniority is inextricably linked with the issue of who should have power in

---

[13]While the "Senate establishment," or inner club, was mostly composed of senior southern senators who were conservatives, political philosophy did not dictate who was accepted into the group. Both Lyndon B. Johnson and Hubert Humphrey, for example, were part of the "club." The criteria for acceptance were reverence for the institution, its traditions, and its customs. This "establishment" died in the 1960s as the Senate became more democratic internally and reflected a greater turnover among its members.

RETURN MATCH

SLUGGER EXECUTIVE
= VS =
CANVASBACK CONGRESS

REFORMS

OLD
MOSSBACK
PROCEDURES

OLD
GRANDPAPPY
SENIORITY
SYSTEM

LONG
WEEKEND
CLUB

CONGRESS

© 1972 HERBLOCK

(Copyright 1972 by Herblock in *The Washington Post*.)

"Man, if you want to stay in this game, you'd better get in shape."

Many congressional reforms are designed to strengthen Congress in relation to the executive.

Congress. Substantial changes made in the House in the Ninety-third and Ninety-fourth Congresses (1973–1976) have expanded the individual power of members, which is often referred to as "democratizing" the House. In addition to giving the Democratic caucus control over the selection of committee chairmen, in 1973 House Democrats also gave to the Democratic Steering and Policy Committee the power to nominate Democratic committee members, with nominations then having to be ratified by the Democratic caucus. The Speaker's power to select Democratic members of the Rules Committee was also established in 1973. At the beginning of 1973 the House also passed a "Subcommittee Bill of Rights," which removed the power of the chairmen of standing committees to control arbitrarily the funds and staffs of subcommittees.

The "reforms" of the Ninety-third Congress, which led to the resurgent Democratic caucus at the beginning of the Ninety-fourth Congress in 1975, were heralded by certain groups outside Congress, such as Common Cause, as desirable "democratic" changes in congressional and party procedures that would break the power of conservatives on Capitol Hill. In fact, the impetus for reform was not so much to dethrone conservatives because of their political philosophy but to force members of the traditional congressional establishment, many of whom happened to be conservative, to share their power within the House. Thus the issue was not one of political philosophy but of personal power. The Subcommittee Bill of Rights was a perfect manifestation of this, for it further increased the fragmentation of the committee structure of the House. (Fragmentation does in fact guarantee that a wider range of views will be heard in the legislative process.) The greater dispersion of power in the House brought about by the reforms gave liberal Democrats relatively more power in the House than they had had prior to 1975, but it also increased the power of many members who do not fall into the "liberal" category.

The turmoil of the House in the early 1970s was not duplicated in the Senate. In 1977 the Senate did pass a resolution (S. Res. 4) that slightly reorganized its committee system, but the power status quo within the body remained unchanged. That status quo, however, reflects a far greater equality of power among senators than exists among members of the House. Most members of the Senate Democratic majority chair their own committees and subcommittees. The 1977 reforms limited the number of committees on which members may serve to three "major" (usually standing) committees and eight subcommittees, and limited the number of chairmanships any senator may hold to a total of four committees and subcommittees during the Ninety-fifth Congress and three thereafter. An attempt was also made to eliminate some committees and to transfer others to the jurisdiction of still other committees. Due to the fierce opposition within the Senate to proposed changes, there was, however, no substantial disturbance of the power and jurisdictions of most Senate committees. The failure of committee reorganization in the Senate was an almost exact duplication of the failure in the House of Richard Bolling's Select Committee on Committees to revamp the committee structure of that body in 1973.

Reform of the budget process. While the issue of congressional reform usually centers upon the way in which power is to be distributed in the House and the Senate, occasionally reforms occur within Congress to strengthen its collective capacity to deal with major problems in policy formulation and, more particularly, to increase its capacity to exercise power independently of the president. Some of the reforms of the post-Watergate "resurgent" Congress were motivated by this desire to strengthen Capitol Hill in its dealings with the White House and with the bureaucracy. A major reform in this category was the Budget and Impoundment Control Act of 1974, which created the Congressional Budget Office as well as a new Budget Committee in the House and the Senate, respectively, to coordinate the disparate appropriations and authorizations processes of Congress, which had been scattered throughout its committee system.

The 1974 legislation not only strengthened the internal budgeting procedures of Congress but also prohibited the president from permanently impounding funds appropriated by the legislature without its consent. Presidents, from Thomas Jefferson to Richard M. Nixon, had impounded funds, using their authority under Article II of the Constitution (to see that the laws are faithfully executed) and the authority derived from "anti-deficiency" and

other legislation giving the president the power to control the disbursement of money to federal agencies and programs. Presidential impoundments before the Nixon administration had often raised congressional hackles, but no serious efforts had been made to curtail the authority of the White House. However, Nixon carried the impoundment authority to extremes, refusing to release funds that Congress had appropriated for over 40 programs. The predictable response of the Democratic Congress was to curtail permanently the authority of the president to impound on his own initiative congressionally appropriated funds.

Effects of budgetary reform. The leaders of Congress sponsored the Budget Act of 1974 in the hope, not only that it would balance the budgetary power of Capitol Hill with that of the White House and the Office of Management and Budget, but also that it would increase leadership power *within* Congress. The Budget Committees were seen as leadership adjuncts, reining in the virtually autonomous appropriations and authorizations committees. However, committee chairmen in the House immediately saw the self-serving tack that the leadership was taking in backing the Budget Act and succeeded in amending it to cripple the new House Budget Committee by requiring rotating membership on it and requiring also that a controlling bloc of members on the new committee be drawn from the Appropriations and Ways and Means Committees. The Senate Budget Committee was not required to rotate its members because it was not viewed in the body as a potential threat to the powerful Appropriations Committee and Finance Committee. However, in both the House and the Senate the Budget Committees were not given unilateral authority to determine appropriations, spending authorizations, and revenue levels, all of which make up the federal budget. Instead the new committees were empowered to *recommend* budget resolutions that had to be approved by their respective bodies and then by the entire Congress. Thus the power of the new Budget Committees, like all political power, extended only as far as their ability to persuade the powerful standing committees to accept their recommendations.

The new budget process almost foundered in its initial years. The House Budget Committee was little more than an intermediary among the standing committees, which continued to control the budget as they had in the past. The Senate Budget Committee was for years virtually ignored by Louisiana Democratic Senator Russell Long, who chaired the Finance Committee, and by other powerful senators as well, who viewed the new budget process as an unnecessary intrusion into their domains of power. So often was the Budget Committee's power circumvented that Maine Democratic Senator Edmund Muskie, who had given up his post on the Foreign Relations Committee to chair the Budget Committee, seriously considered resigning his chairmanship. In the Ninety-seventh and Ninety-eighth Congresses (1981–1984) the new chairman of the Budget Committee in the Senate, Pete Domenici (R., N.M.), continued to take a back seat to Finance Committee Chairman Robert Dole (R., Kan.) and Mark Hatfield (R., Ore.), Chairman of the Appropriations Committee, in the budgetary process.

The budget process, the details of which are set forth in Tables 11.1 and 11.2, came at least temporarily into its own during the Reagan administration when government spending and tax proposals were at the top of the legislative agenda. Congressman Jim Jones (D., Okla) and Republican Senator Pete Domenici, chairmen of the Budget Committee in their respective bodies, were challenged to make the budget process work as the White House deluged Capitol Hill with proposals for drastic tax and expenditure reductions. For the first time the Budget chairmen used the *reconciliation process*, authorized by the 1974 Budget Act, under which projected entitlement expenditures that had been previously authorized by Congress could be reduced. Prior to the Ninety-seventh Congress (1981–1982), Budget Committee chairmen had been frustrated by the powerful chairmen of other panels who had refused to follow their leadership. However, the budget process began to work for the first time in the Ninety-seventh Congress largely because members felt they had been given a mandate to reduce federal taxes and expenditures, which gave them the necessary incentive to support Budget Committee proposals aimed at achieving this goal.

As the decade of the 1990s began, the congressional budgeting process continued to reflect the dispersion of power on Capitol Hill. Representatives and senators continued to pay lip service to the need to solve growing budgetary deficits, but powerful committee chairmen—particularly of the Ways and Means Committee and the Appropriations Committee in the House, as well as of the Senate Finance Committee—protected their political turfs and refused to concede power to the Budget Committees. The budget process became so paralyzed that for the first time in 1989 a provision of what was called the Gramm-Rudman-Hollings law came into effect that required the Controller General's Office to make automatic across-the-board budget cuts to meet the law's budgetary goals. The budgetary procedures Congress had put into place to bring some semblance of order out of budgetary chaos on Capitol Hill failed. Legislators' internal power incentives caused committee chairmen and their staffs to balk at giving up the power they had always had to influence the budget, and reelection incentives encouraged members to heed the cries of special interests, which demanded their "fair" share of government largesse, as well as the cries of constituents, whom legislators perceived to be strongly in opposition to an increase in taxes that might help to solve the budget crisis.

Ethics. In an entirely different vein from

TABLE 11.1 CONGRESSIONAL BUDGET TIMETABLE*

Deadline	Action to be Completed
15th day after Congress convenes	President submits his budget, along with current services estimates.†
March 15	Committees submit views and estimates to Budget Committees.
April 1	Congressional Budget Office submits report to Budget Committees.‡
April 15	Budget Committees report first concurrent resolution on the budget to their Houses.
May 15	Committees report bills authorizing new budget authority.
May 15	Congress adopts first concurrent resolution on the budget.
7th day after Labor Day	Congress completes action on bills providing budget authority and spending authority.
September 15	Congress completes actions on second required concurrent resolution on the budget.
September 25	Congress completes action on reconciliation process implementing second concurrent resolution.
October 1	Fiscal year begins.

*Congress has not always adhered to these deadlines. In recent years, Congress has fallen increasingly behind schedule.

†Current service estimates are estimates of the dollar levels that would be required next year to support the same level of services in each program as this year's budget. The Budget Act originally required submission of the current services estimates by November 10 of the previous year. Since the President was still in the midst of developing his budget proposals for the next year, Congress later agreed to permit simultaneous submission of the current services and executive budgets in January.

‡The Budget Committees and CBO have found April 1 too late in the budget process to be useful; hence CBO submits its report(s) in February, although April 1 remains the date required by law.

Source: Budget Handbook (Washington, D.C.: Congressional Quarterly, 1980), p. 4. Reprinted with permission of Congressional Quarterly, Inc.

a variety of congressional reform proposals are proposals relating to congressional ethics. At the heart of the ethics controversy is the problem of the conflict of interests between the public responsibility of members of Congress (and their aides) and the activities in which they engage—such as accepting campaign contributions that may make them beholden to private forces. The Campaign Finance Law of 1971 (amended in 1974 and 1976), which limited contributions to congressional campaigns, helped to solve a number of conflict-of-interest problems. However, many other potential conflicts remained, including the ability of legislators to use their "office accounts" in a discretionary manner, accounts that often contained funds from private contributors. In addition, the customary practice in both the House and the Senate of members increasing their income by outside speaking engagements raised possible conflicts of interest when they appeared before lobbying groups that paid them large "honoraria."

Proponents of codes of ethics within Con-

TABLE 11.2   DUTIES AND FUNCTIONS OF BUDGET PROCESS PARTICIPANTS

President	Authorizing Committees	Appropriations Committees	Revenue Committees	Budget Committees	Congressional Budget Office
Submits executive budget and current services estimates. Updates budget estimates in April and July. Signs or vetoes revenue, appropriations, and other budget-related legislation. May propose the deferral or rescission of appropriated funds.	Prepare views and estimates on programs within jurisdiction. Report authorizing legislation for the next fiscal year. Include CBO cost estimates in reports accompanying their legislation. *Limitations:* 1. Legislation providing contract or borrowing authority is effective only as provided in appropriations. 2. Entitlements cannot become effective before next fiscal year.	Report regular and supplemental appropriations bills. After adoption of a budget resolution, allocate budget authority and outlays among their subcommittees. Provide five-year projections of outlays in reports accompanying appropriations, and compare budget authority with amounts provided in latest budget resolution. Review rescission and deferrals proposals of the President. *Limitation:* After second resolution is adopted, spending cannot exceed amount set by Congress.	Submit views and estimates on budget matters in their jurisdiction. Can be directed by second resolution to report legislation changing tax laws. *Limitation:* Legislation cannot cause revenues to fall below level set in the second resolution.	Report two or more concurrent resolutions on the budget each year. Allocate new budget authority and outlays among House and Senate committees. Monitor congressional actions affecting the budget. Advise Congress on the status of the budget.	Issues reports on annual budget. Estimates cost of bills reported by House and Senate committees. Issues periodic scorekeeping reports on status of the congressional budget. Assists the budget, revenue, appropriations, and other committees. Issues five-year budget projections.

Source: Budget Handbook (Washington, D.C.: Congressional Quarterly, 1980), p. 5. Reprinted with permission of Congressional Quarterly, Inc.

gress have traditionally been seeking to elevate the image of the legislature in the minds of the public. Although there has been agitation for the creation of strict codes of ethics for Capitol Hill for decades, Congress succeeded in exempting itself from the conflict-of-interest laws pertaining to the bureaucracy without any apparent electoral backlash. It was the Watergate incident, however, that finally spurred Congress to action, the leadership of the House in particular being concerned about the low marks Congress was getting in public opinion polls. By enacting codes of ethics, both the House and the Senate could in effect assuage public opinion. And when the Wayne Hays incident gained nationwide publicity, the time for action had clearly come. Wayne Hays, the powerful chairman of the House Administration Committee, was forced to resign from Congress in 1976 when it was revealed that he kept his mistress, who never reported to work, on the payroll of his committee. The incident recalled for the public another well-known congressional figure, the powerful former chairman of the House Ways and Means Committee, Wilbur Mills, who had lavished funds (but not public money) on *his* mistress, the "Argentine Firecracker," a striptease artist in a local Washington nightclub.

The first session of the Ninety-fifth Congress in 1977 saw both the House and the Senate enact ethics codes that controlled expenditures of members from office accounts, limited outside income from speaking engagements and other sources, restricted non-monetary gifts from lobbyists, prohibited travel by lame-duck members, and prevented members from working for lobbyists immediately after leaving office. Special ethics committees were created in both bodies to develop the ethics codes and oversee their enforcement. As needed as these codes seemed to be to congressional outsiders, they were passed only after strong pressure from Speaker Tip

O'Neill in the House, and after extensive debate and controversy in the Senate, where Adlai Stevenson, chairman of the Senate Ethics Committee, worked closely with Majority Leader Robert E. Byrd to gain Senate acceptance of an ethics code. Many senators particularly objected to limits the code placed on outside income. It was not too surprising, then, when the Senate reversed itself and dropped restrictions on outside income from honoraria in December 1982.

Congressional ethics is an issue that does not die. The Abscam scandals once again focused public attention on congressional improprieties in the Ninety-seventh Congress (1981–1982) by revealing the willingness of a few representatives and one senator to take bribes in exchange for influence. In the public eye, the Abscam brush tarred the entire Congress. As the decade of the 1980s came to a close, ethics controversies again embroiled Congress. For the first time in history a House Speaker, Texas Democrat Jim Wright, had to step down from the speakership and resign from Congress in the face of allegations that he had violated House ethics rules by failing to report gifts from a Texas savings and loan executive. In the 101st Congress (1989–1990) other members of Congress as well faced increasing scrutiny about both their public and private lives.

While Congress is continually confronting questions of ethics and seeking to improve its resources to deal with the increasing responsibilities that have been placed upon it due to the expanded scope of the national government, it is the quest for personal power on Capitol Hill that will undoubtedly shape the legislative process in the future as it has in the past. The Framers of the Constitution recognized that all politics is shaped by the drive for personal power, and they sought to harness the power incentive through the separation of powers and checks and balances, to ensure that government would be limited but still capable of taking needed action to meet national problems.

Constitutional standards are not violated by the fragmentation of the legislative process, provided that process is not completely stalemated. And from the standpoint of democratic theory, the dispersion of power on Capitol Hill provides many access points for both interest groups and individuals to influence legislators. While Congress finds it difficult to take collective action rapidly, it has always attempted to meet pressing national problems with legislation, and it has fulfilled its constitutional responsibilities to be constantly vigilant against executive domination of the national government.

CASE STUDY 10

THE SENATE OF THE 1990s

From its earliest days the Senate was an institution built around its members' egos. Although the House eclipsed the Senate in prestige during the first decade of the Republic, there was little doubt that by the time of the Jacksonian era, which began in 1828, as to which was the preeminent body. In 1830 Daniel Webster described the chamber as a "senate of equals, of men of individual honor and personal character, and of absolute independence."[14]

After the "Golden Age" of the Senate, from 1829 to 1861, the character of the institution changed. The luminaries of the past were replaced by professional politicians chosen by state and local party bosses. Party leaders increasingly began to dominate the body, determining committee assignments and the legislative agenda. The individualism of the past did not entirely disappear but ebbed and flowed as the body's party leaders struggled with its powerful members for power.

The Senate's character continued to change in response to political developments and changes within and without the institution. The power political party leaders had on Capitol Hill as the nineteenth century came to a close soon ebbed to be replaced by powerful committee chairmen, "prime ministers" in their own right who controlled important public policy areas under their committees' jurisdiction. Both the House and the Senate developed their own distinctive ways of doing business, reflecting contrasting organizational patterns and procedures. The different political subcultures of the House and the Senate added to the constitutional bicameral divisions between them. Although House committee chairmen could be as powerful as their Senate counterparts, the House generally was organized in a more hierarchical way, with the Speaker and the majority leader exercising significant power. Senate traditions were different from those of the House. The Senate had always been a more collegial body than its counterpart on the other side of Capitol Hill, and by the mid-twentieth century how a member upheld Senate norms, such as hard legislative work, reverence for the institution, respect for colleagues, maintaining a low profile, avoiding "grand standing" and publicity, and—always—courtesy, determined a Senator's credibility and standing with colleagues.

The relatively sedate Senate of the 1950s and early 1960s changed dramatically in response to the changing of the guard on Capitol Hill in the 1970s. House retirements almost doubled during the period in comparison to past rates, and the rate of Senate retirements also increased. Moreover, political backlash from Vietnam and, more importantly, the Watergate affair (brought

---

[14]*Guide to Congress*, 2d ed. (Washington, D.C.: Congressional Quarterly, 1976), p. 75.

to light in 1973) caused the defeat of many incumbents, particularly Republicans. In the 1974 congressional elections only 78.9 percent of House incumbents that ran were reelected, compared to normal reelection of over 80 percent and sometimes in excess of 90 percent. Turnover in the Senate also increased, especially in the 1980 election when only 55.2 percent of those seeking reelection won.

As early as 1970 the Senate began to change. No longer were freshman senators willing to wait years before they made their "made-in-speech" on the floor, although such a waiting period had been required by Senate norms in the 1950s and 1960s. The Senate "club," the bipartisan inner corps of senators who had dominated the institution in the preceding decades, composed of senior members who had gained high marks from their colleagues because of their respect for Senate norms, began to break down along with the norms themselves. Senators began to go their own separate ways in the 1980s. Freshman senators of the majority party were given important committee assignments which they considered to be their due. Senate leaders could no longer rely upon the "establishment" to get elected or rule. They had to go to the hustings like ordinary folk to gain and hold their offices.

The Senate of the 1990s promised once again to be different from its predecessors. In the following article, a prominent congressional scholar describes the character of the 1990s Senate and the important role it continued to play in making public policy.

Tracking Changes in the U.S. Senate / *Nelson W. Polsby*

The character of the U.S. Senate has changed markedly over the last 30 years. The Senate can no longer be characterized as a well-bounded entity ruled by an "inner club" of insular grandees. Increasingly, rather, the Senate is a great forum, an echo chamber, a theater, where dramas—comedies and tragedies, soap operas and horse operas—are staged to enhance the careers of its members and to influence public policy by means of debate and public investigation.

Its special role today in the contemporary American political system is as an incubator of policy ideas and political innovations (Polsby 1984). This stands in dramatic contrast with the Senate as late as the 1950s, which was far more a body that had positioned itself as a critic and a respondent—frequently an inhospitable one—to the political innovations hatched in the executive branch and by activist presidents and forwarded to it by the House of Representatives. Thus over the last three decades the Senate has evolved from a rather negative repository of states-rights thinking, dominated by a mostly southern-led "inner club," and

hence an explicit agent of the devolved aspect of the federal system, into a predominantly nationally-oriented body.

The principal agent of this transformation has been the very great change in the life chances and therefore in the political ambitions of a large number of U.S. senators. Earlier, not so many of them entertained presidential ambitions. Today, the Senate is the main institutional source of presidential hopefuls, and for a large fraction of senators such hopes play a significant part in guiding their behavior in the Senate. Even senators with small realistic hopes of advancement to the presidency now frequently seek national recognition for their substantive legislative work, and not merely the approval of interest groups and citizens in their home states.

The major means by which senators arrange to receive national recognition, as recent research has demonstrated, are two: (1) occupying leadership positions or actually leading on significant matters of public policy within the Senate, or (2) running for president (Hess 1986). In order to do

Source: PS: Political Science and Politics, December 1989, pp. 789–792. Published by the American Political Science Association, 1527 New Hampshire, N.W., Washington, D.C. 20036. 202-483-2512.

the latter, some but not all senators do the former. Several of those who have been notably successful in presidential election politics—John Kennedy, Estes Kefauver, for example—have in fact not been notably successful in leading the Senate. The modern availability of the Senate as a platform from which—and not only an arena within which—senators might fulfill their political ambitions has changed the character of the institution.

There has been an important implication of this change in the character of the Senate for the flow of information through the institution. Whereas senators in the era of the inner club could ration their participation in public policymaking to those subjects that interested them or deeply concerned their mostly unconcerned constituents, contemporary senators must have opinions about everything. With the institution's heightened degree of public-regardingness has come the need to be a generalist. Those issues that become hot issues require senators who nurture larger ambitions to position themselves. One mechanism for meeting the formidable information needs thereby created has been the establishment of highly professional staff capabilities dedicated to the exclusive use of senators as separate and distinct from the executive branch.

Policy Incubation

It is a cliche of academic political science that in legislative matters, it is the president who initiates policy and Congress that responds, amplifying and modifying and rearranging elements that are essentially originated in the executive branch. But where do innovations in policy come from before the president "initiates" them?

Commentators have greatly underestimated the role of the Senate in gestating these ideas by providing a forum for speeches, hearings, and the introduction of bills going nowhere for the moment. This process of incubation accomplishes a number of things. It maintains a sense of community among far-flung interest groups that favor the innovation by giving them occasional opportunities to come in and testify. It provides an incentive for persons favoring the innovation to keep information up to date on its prospective benefits and technical feasibility, and it accustoms the uncommitted to a new idea. Thus the Senate has in some

respects in recent years become a crucial nerve-end of the polity. It articulates, formulates, shapes, and publicizes and can serve as a hothouse for significant policy innovation, especially in opposition to the president.

In the aftermath of World War II there was a general movement of political resources—aided and abetted by the more recent party reforms—toward Washington that has tended to divert public attention away from local and regional arenas. This has been reinforced by the growth of national news media, especially television. The impact on the presidency of this nationalization of public awareness has been frequently noted. But, to a lesser extent, the same effect can be noted for all national political institutions. The Senate has taken full advantage of its increased visibility, and senatorial names—Kefauver, McCarthy, Kennedy, Goldwater, McGovern, Sam Ervin—have become household words in the last three or four decades. In part, this reflects changes in presidential election politics. Where once a governor's control of a political "base," by virtue of his leadership of a state party organization, was the single overwhelming resource in deciding, at a national party convention, who was presidential timber, television and the nationalization of resources have on the whole eroded this gubernatorial resource. Federal programs, financed by the lucrative federal income tax, have also—at least until the partial turnaround of the Reagan era—more and more been distributed among the states in part as senatorial patronage. Governors are by no means always ignored in this process, but on the whole their influence has been much reduced.

The decline of the influence of governors and the shift of public attention to national politics and national politicians are not quite enough to explain how the modern Senate became the incubator of policies and presidential hopefuls. Historical accidents have also played a part. The first was Lyndon Johnson's majority leadership. Ambitious for the presidency and immensely skilled, Johnson sedulously perpetrated the myth of the inner club while destroying its substance. Joseph Clark, newly elected to the Senate in 1957, described a lunch Majority Leader Johnson gave for freshmen Democrats. "As we sat down . . . we found at our places copies of *Citadel* autographed 'with all good wishes' not only by its author . . .but by the majority leader as well. During the course of the lunch . . .Senator Johnson encouraged us to consider Mr. White's book as a sort of McGuffey's *Reader* from which we could learn much about the 'greatest deliberative body in the world' and how to mold ourselves into its way of life" (Clark 1964, 5).

Yet if the essence of the argument of *Citadel* was collegiality among the fellowship of the elect, the essence of Johnson's Senate operation was the progressive centralization of power in the hands of the Majority Leader. By the time Johnson left the Senate, after eight years (1953–60) as Democratic Leader, the inner club could command little of its old power. It had too long been merely a facade for Johnson's own activity, a polite explanation for the exercise of his own discretion in committee appointments, legislative priorities, and tactics. Under the looser rein of Johnson's successors, the Senate has become a collegial body whose corporate work has been pretty much determined by presidential programs and priorities. The Senate has never recaptured the sense of cohesion, community, and separateness that obtained "in the old days," before Johnson. As younger people came in, pro-administration majorities on legislation were by no means uncommon, nor were majorities for policies more liberal than those passed in the House. And the Senate has become a more public-regarding body.

New-Style Senators

The senatorial generations of the 1960s and thereafter have pursued a style of senatorial service that in their search for national constituencies and public visibility have little in common with the old Senate type. Nevertheless, these new-style senators are not regarded as mavericks. Quite to the contrary, it is the senators who do not court publicity (e.g.,

Hecht of Nevada) (Birnbaum 1988) who are regarded as deviant. The more common pattern today is for senators to seek to become national politicians, something that the mass media have made increasingly possible. These senators are following a style of service hit on by several postwar senators but most notably pioneered by Arthur Vandenberg of Michigan and, in the 1950s and 1960s, brought to full flower by Hubert Humphrey (Humphrey 1976; Solberg 1984).

Much earlier than most members of his generation, Humphrey sensed the possibilities in the Senate for long-range political education. He spent the Eisenhower era incubating ideas that in a better climate could hatch into programs. In the late 1940s and early 1950s, a flood of Humphrey bills (many of them cosponsored by other liberal senators) on all aspects of civil rights, medicare, housing, aid to farm workers, food stamps, job corps, area redevelopment, disarmament, and so on, died in the Senate. A little over a decade later, most of them were law, and Humphrey had in the meantime become a political leader of national consequence. The force of his example was not lost on younger senators.

In recent years, it has proved much easier for senators to reconcile their ambitions for large public accomplishments with accommodation to Senate norms. The Senate is now a less insular body than it was in former times, and the fortunes of senators are correspondingly less tied to the smiles and frowns of their elders within the institution. Although these changes are now widely accepted as having altered the character of the Senate, there is still in the literature no thorough account of the process by which the Senate modernized into the publicity-seeking, policy-incubating, interest group-cultivating body that it now is.

CHAPTER TWELVE

The Presidency: Its Evolution and Functions

The American presidency is unique both as an office and as an institution. Unlike a king or prime minister, the American president must perform the two functions of chief of state and chief executive at the same time. Moreover, he is directly responsible to all the people in the country. Although attempts have been made by other nations to copy the office of the United States president, no nation has completely succeeded. The nature of the American presidency is derived from traditions, history, and complexities that are peculiar to the United States.

THE EVOLUTION OF THE PRESIDENCY

In the nearly two centuries since it was established by the Framers of the Constitution, the American presidency has become more and more powerful. Like other American political institutions, the organization of the executive has undergone major changes. Although in the past the presidency was one of the weaker parts of the national system, today in certain respects it may be the strongest.

The role of the president in government has been greatly expanded. Each occupant of the White House has construed the presidency in his own way. Whereas most have not altered its strength at all, a significant

number have been adept at expanding the vaguely worded constitutional powers so as to assume more leadership in the legislative and other policy-making spheres. Strong rather than weak presidents have shaped the office. It is from presidents such as Jefferson, Jackson, Lincoln, Theodore Roosevelt, Franklin D. Roosevelt, and Harry S. Truman that the office has acquired its "imperial" character.

The unpopularity of President Lyndon B. Johnson's Vietnam War policy followed by the excesses of the Nixon presidency, which included the secret bombing of Cambodia and the Watergate break-in and cover-up, called into question the desirability of the imperial powers that had accrued to the White House. The "caretaker presidency" of Gerald R. Ford, followed by the relatively low-key Jimmy Carter presidency, helped to restore public confidence in the executive.

Ronald Reagan's presidency, which encompassed the decade of the 1980s, restored the prestige of the office that had existed in the past but had been so lacking during the Vietnam and Watergate eras. The imperial presidency that began with Franklin D. Roosevelt and ended with Richard M. Nixon had been transformed in the 1970s into the imperiled presidency. Reagan rescued the imperiled presidency, restoring in his first term the office's dignity and leadership role. During **343**

Reagan's second term the Iran-Contra controversy, involving top White House staffers who illegally diverted funds from the sale of arms to Iran to the Nicaraguan contras, sullied the president's image somewhat, although he steadfastly claimed that he did not know about the diversion of funds. In other ways the Reagan White House transformed American politics, giving it a distinctly conservative stamp by emphasizing the need to cut taxes and reduce government regulations. President George Bush inherited the Reagan legacy and carried the conservative cause into the decade of the 1990s.

Constitutional Powers

There is little in the Constitution that would have caused anyone to predict in 1789 the extent to which the powers of the presidency would be expanded. Article II states that "the executive Power shall be vested in a President" and that "the President shall be Commander in Chief of the Army and Navy of the United States, and of the Militia." Aside from providing that the president "shall take Care that the Laws be faithfully executed" and that "he may require the Opinion, in writing, of the principal Officer in each of the executive Departments," the Constitution does not specify how the "executive Power" is to be exercised. Article II does specify a few presidential powers that require the "Advice and Consent of the Senate": the powers to make treaties and to "appoint Ambassadors, other public Ministers and Consuls, Judges of the supreme Court, and all other Officers of the United States whose appointments are not . . .otherwise provided for [in the Constitution]."

Other presidential responsibilities stipulated in Article II provide for the presentation of "State of the Union" messages to Congress and the recommendation of legislation. The president can also convene either or both houses of Congress on "extraordinary Occasions." In addition, he must "receive Ambassadors and other public Ministers," see that

laws are "faithfully executed," and "Commission all Officers of the United States."

The Strengthening Factors

The Framers, of course, could not foresee all the changes that would take place in the role of the executive. They did, however, consciously provide the office with certain strengths that have enabled its power to increase to the extent that it has.

One-man office. First, the Framers rejected the idea of a plural executive and gave the executive powers to one person alone. The combination of the executive's singular office and its independent constitutional authority makes it possible for the president to act with far greater efficiency and dispatch than any other branch of the national government. In addition to being able to exercise independent constitutional prerogatives, the president has often been delegated authority by Congress that enables him to act with a great deal of discretion. (For example, Congress has given him the authority to establish tariff quotas within certain broad limits.)

Fixed four-year term. Second, because the president's term is fixed at four years, a holder of the office does not have to court popular and legislative support for every decision he makes to stay in office. This differs from a parliamentary system, in which the chief executive does not have a fixed term and must retain the confidence of the majority party or parties in the legislature to stay in power. In the United States a president can take an action that is unpopular in the short run without any immediate risk to his position. He can be voted out of office by the electorate only at the end of his four-year term. Thus the fixed term has been an important factor in permitting the power of the presidency to expand.

Separate constituency. Third, although the president is somewhat limited by the functions he must share with the other branches, his independent authority and separate constituency have provided a base from which the power of the office could expand. By granting the powers of executive and commander in chief to the president exclusively, the Constitution protects the office against encroachment by the other branches, particularly the legislature. By setting up the electoral college system, the Constitution has given the president a constituency completely free from the control of the legislature. Because the electoral college has necessarily become more and more responsive to political parties and the democratized electorate, the president has been able to broaden his power as his electoral constituency has widened.

Growth of political parties. The Founding Fathers envisioned the electoral college as a means of insulating the president from both the control of the legislature and direct participation in popular politics. The electors from each state were to be appointed according to the rules set up by the state legislatures. It was assumed that the members of the electoral college would be the more responsible people from their respective states, and that they would select the most able and respected man for president without making prior commitments to particular candidates. The man they selected for the office would, in turn, be detached from partisan influences and would fulfill his duties in the best interests of the nation.

All this was changed by the growth of the political parties. During the early 1800s, as political parties began to assume importance in the selection of presidential candidates, the electors became less independent. (Today electors are little more than puppets selected by the parties, and committed to vote in each state for the presidential ticket chosen by the majority of voters.) Each political party nominated first the candidates for president and vice-president and then the candidates for the electoral college, who were committed to elect the party's presidential choice.

As a result, potential presidential candidates and presidents seeking reelection were identified with the political parties. They had to satisfy these partisan groups in order to win nomination and the majority of the electoral college votes. After the election the political party of the successful candidate provided the president with a strong base of support.

Democratization of the election process. Another means of adding strength to the presidency was the democratization of the procedures for nominating presidential candidates and for electing presidential electors. The shift of the party nominating process from congressional caucuses to national conventions permitted greater participation by the party's rank-and-file members. But this shift was not completely successful. Although party nominating conventions reflected a broader base of party opinion than caucuses did, they were still controlled by cliques of influential politicians. The growth of presidential-preference primaries, particularly after the 1968 election, gave the rank-and-file members of both parties an important voice in the selection of presidential nominees.

Leader of the party. The president gains strength due to his role as party leader. While party discipline is far from a reality, the president can depend to a certain extent upon members of his party in Congress to follow his direction. The president's electoral strength is also buttressed by the national party organization, which represents state and local party leaders. Effective party organization is the key to winning elections.

Today the president also lends his *image* to the party he represents. The image of a party that is conveyed to the people is strongly shaped by the particular style of the White House occupant. The image of a president as a Midwestern military hero, such as Dwight D. Eisenhower, as a sophisticated Easterner, such as John F. Kennedy, or as an affable communicator, such as Ronald Reagan, has considerable appeal to certain groups of the electorate. Each president lends his own personality to the office, and each organizes the office to suit himself. People within his party or outside it identify with his particular style and consequently support him and his program.

Vagueness of constitutional language.
Lastly, the language of Article II has encouraged the growth of the president's power. Strong presidents have seized upon such vague provisions as the commander-in-chief and chief-executive clauses of Article II to justify taking the initiative in far-reaching decisions. Jefferson's Louisiana Purchase (accomplished, however, with strong congressional support); Lincoln's numerous prerogative acts during the Civil War (mobilizing troops and paying them out of the treasury without congressional appropriations, blockading the Confederacy and seizing ships that violated the blockade, and the Emancipation Proclamation); Franklin D. Roosevelt's proclamation of a bank holiday in 1933 and proclamation of a national emergency, resulting in a mobilization of national defenses and deployment of the armed forces abroad; President Truman's seizure of the steel mills (an act declared to be beyond his legal power by the Supreme Court); and the police actions taken by Presidents Johnson and Nixon—all are examples of the expansion of presidential authority based upon the commander-in-chief and chief-executive clauses of Article II and the implied authority of the president to negotiate international agreements. All these prerogative actions, with the exception of Jefferson's Louisiana Purchase, were taken without congressional authorization or specific constitutional sanction.

The presidency has never had to contend in its quest for power with the kinds of potential limitations that exist in the carefully defined powers of Congress in Article I. Although Chief Justice Marshall adopted a broad constructionist approach toward Article I, which permitted a vast expansion of congressional authority, American history has witnessed periods when congressional wings have been clipped by the Supreme Court through invocation of the limits of this article. In the early New Deal, most of the key portions of Franklin Roosevelt's program were declared unconstitutional by a conservative Supreme Court; but the Court's decision was based largely on its interpretation that Congress did not have the constitutional authority to pass the legislation Roosevelt wanted. The president's wings have not been clipped nearly so frequently, and as the Supreme Court dissenters pointed out in *Youngstown Sheet and Tube v. Sawyer* (1952), denying presidential prerogative in actions such as the seizure of the steel mills contradicted a long line of judicial precedents.

(Editorial cartoon by Don Hesse.
Copyright, *The St. Louis Globe-Democrat.*
Reprinted with permission of Los Angeles Times Syndicate.)

If executive powers strain the original concept too much, a constitutional change may be needed.

THE PRESIDENT'S DUTIES AND RESPONSIBILITIES

As the office of the presidency has been steadily strengthened, the functions and responsibilities of the president have also been increased and reshaped by changing political forces. Congress and the American people have given the president wide-ranging responsibilities that go far beyond formal constitutional prescriptions.

Chief of State

In some countries, such as Germany, Great Britain, India, and Japan, burdensome ceremonial functions are carried out by the president or the monarch acting as chief of state, whereas the prime minister handles the duties of the executive. In the United States both of these important functions fall to the president alone. The Constitution makes no provision for an independent chief of state, and the president has acquired the responsibility by default. The ceremonial functions add to his political strength. As the symbol of the American nation, he attracts a great deal of support from both within and outside the nation.

In his capacity as ceremonial chief the president receives foreign ambassadors, presides over state dinners, sponsors the arts, and meets with representatives of such groups as the Boy Scouts of America and the Urban League. He throws the switch that lights the national Christmas tree, proclaims national holidays, and throws out the first ball to open the baseball season. Moreover, he sponsors numerous charity drives, buys the first Christmas seals, supports cancer research, and so forth. (The First Lady is an indispensable aide to her spouse in carrying out many of these ceremonial functions.) As head of state the president also signs all bills, treaties, and many appointments. The mere signing of bills and executive communications can occupy an hour or more of his time every day.

Essentially, when the president acts as head of state, he represents the American people. The ceremonial functions of the nation must be performed with tact and finesse. They are vital to any nation, because a breach of standard diplomatic protocol will be noticed by other nations and may affect international relations on a wide scale.

The role of chief of state is one of the few aspects of the presidency that has not become rigid in its conduct. Each occupant of the White House has a certain amount of latitude to add his own personal touch to the performance of his ceremonial functions. The informal, hospitable style of Lyndon Johnson, who invited visiting foreign dignitaries to his Texas ranch, was replaced by the more formal manner of Richard Nixon in the late 1960s and early 1970s. Both Gerald Ford and Jimmy Carter adopted an informal style in the White House. President Ronald Reagan, along with his wife Nancy, restored glitter and glamour to the White House.

Commander in Chief

Article II, Section 2, of the Constitution provides that the president "shall be Commander in Chief of the Army and Navy of the United States, and of the Militia of the several States, when called into the actual Service of the United States." The growth of this presidential responsibility is one of the most remarkable developments in the office since the framing of the Constitution.

The president was originally given the responsibility of commander in chief for two primary reasons. First, it was clearly necessary to place this power in the branch of government that could act with the greatest cohesion and dispatch. And second, it was prudent to place the military under civilian control in order to keep its potential strength within bounds. Otherwise, the control of the government might fall into the hands of a powerful military faction.

But to prevent the president from abusing his privileges as the commander of the armed forces, the Framers balanced this presidential power by giving Congress some major responsibilities with respect to the military. Congress has the power to declare war, to raise and support armies, and generally to maintain a military establishment. As seen by the Framers, the president's duty was to direct the organization that Congress created.

Military action was to be taken only after agreement had been reached by the House of Representatives and the Senate.

Until the passage of the War Powers Resolution of 1973, limiting undeclared wars to 90 days, the role of Congress had declined as the president gained increased capability to direct military actions in undeclared wars, as in Korea and Vietnam. It would have been unthinkable to the Founding Fathers to give one man the power to declare war, just as it would be unthinkable today. Yet the commander-in-chief clause has been interpreted so as to grant the president considerable power to act in cases of armed conflict.

The significance of this presidential power was illustrated by the actions of Harry S. Truman in Korea. President Truman, acting on his own initiative, sent troops to Korea in 1950 after the North Koreans invaded South Korea. (Congress neither declared war nor participated in the initial decision to involve American troops.) Presidents Johnson and Nixon made many unilateral decisions without consulting Congress. And President Reagan did not ask Congress for permission when he decided to send the Marines to Lebanon as part of an international peacekeeping force after the Israeli invasion. Ironically, while the War Powers Resolution provides that the president must consult Congress before committing American troops to foreign engagements for more than 90 days, it implicitly recognizes the authority of the president to seize the initiative in making the first crucial decision to commit troops to a military involvement.

The Cuban missile crisis. The ability of the president to take quick and effective action in his role as commander in chief was dramatized in 1962. President John Kennedy had to react rapidly when he learned that the Soviet Union had begun to install missiles in Cuba only 90 miles from the United States mainland. Kennedy and his advisers had to review the possible consequences of any direct or indirect actions that the United States

might take. There was no time to call Congress or to consult congressional leaders. (Such consultation would not have been fruitful anyhow, because Congress lacked the necessary military and diplomatic information to give intelligent counsel.) To catch the Soviet Union off guard and enable the United States to seize the initiative, the decision to blockade Cuba and isolate the island had to be made with utmost speed and in complete secrecy. At few times since World War II had a president been confronted with a more delicate situation than the Cuban crisis.

Limits on presidential initiative. The War Powers Resolution of 1973 formally limits presidential authority to make war. But even outside this formal limitation, the president is not a completely free agent in exercising his power as commander in chief. He is limited, first, by the information and counsel of his advisers. He must also think of the political consequences of any action he takes, with respect to both international and domestic reactions.

Just as the Cuban crisis illustrated the weight of presidential responsibility, it also showed how limited the executive is in the choices he can make. The probable responses of the Soviet Union had to be carefully calculated, as well as the effect any decision would have on the United States and the rest of the world.

The Vietnam conflict. Almost all decisions pertaining to United States commitments in Indochina during recent decades have been made by the president. Actually, Congress followed a hands-off policy in Vietnam, leaving the conduct of the war entirely to the president. In August 1964, in response to a reported attack by the North Vietnamese on United States ships in the Gulf of Tonkin, Congress passed a resolution that in effect gave the president carte blanche to deal with the Vietnamese situation.

At no time since World War II has the burden of the commander in chief been as great as during the Vietnam conflict. The Cuban crisis reached a rapid climax, but the Vietnam War demanded the constant attention of two presidents. The failure of both Presidents Johnson and Nixon in peace negotiations and the continuation of this prolonged conflict prompted increasing criticism by those who opposed the war. This was an instance when the president's mantle as commander in chief was less than comfortable.

Leader of Foreign Affairs

The president's role as the leader in foreign affairs is a natural complement to his roles as ceremonial chief of state and commander in chief. In fact, all three roles merge at many points. The president often travels abroad, and when he does, he represents the American people; this is in addition to acting as a major figure in the development of American foreign policy. President Richard Nixon's trip to the People's Republic of China was a major breakthrough in opening up diplomatic and trade relations with a vast nation formerly unrecognized diplomatically. The stature of the presidency helps the occupant of the White House to deal with foreign nations, for they know that the president speaks with authority and power. A major dilemma facing the Nixon presidency in its last few years was the loss of presidential prestige due to Watergate; the result was an undermining of the ability of the president to deal with foreign nations. Secretary of State Henry Kissinger, the man in the administration least tarnished by scandal, became an even more important figure in foreign affairs after Watergate than before.

The brief presidency of Gerald Ford did not see any major involvement of the White House in new foreign policy initiatives, although Secretary of State Kissinger continued to hold the reins of foreign policy power— striving for a settlement in the Middle East and pushing for arms control and détente with the Soviet Union. Jimmy Carter took major initiatives in the Middle East during the first year of his administration, and Middle East policies continued to occupy Ronald Reagan. On another front, President Reagan initiated a stepped-up sale of arms to the government of El Salvador to prevent its overthrow by Russian- and Cuban-supplied guerrillas. Finally, the perennial problem of arms control occupied the Reagan administration, which had to deal with a growing nuclear-freeze movement in both the United States and Europe.

President George Bush was overwhelmed with foreign policy decisions and developments during his first term. Political changes swept Eastern Europe and the Soviet Union as growing demands for freedom, self-determination, and more western-style prosperity brought about the disintegration of the Soviet Bloc and caused major changes in the Soviet government itself. Bush dealt directly with Soviet leader Gorbachev and NATO leaders on wide-ranging issues from arms control to foreign policy and the nature of NATO itself. On another front, Bush had to deal with the legacy of the Reagan and other administrations on South American and Latin American issues. He ordered the invasion of Panama to capture its dictator Manuel Noriega who had been a thorn in the side of both the Reagan and Bush administrations. He restored relations with the newly elected Democratic regime in Nicaragua after the defeat of its Communist leader Ortega at the polls. As the president confronted these and many other foreign policy problems he, like his predecessors, threw down the gauntlet to Congress, asserting the president's power over foreign policy and attacking as unconstitutional congressional attempts to restrict his authority and intrude into foreign policy making.

Bush agreed with Harry S. Truman who had categorically stated, "I make foreign policy." Presidential responsibility to conduct foreign policy is derived from his constitutional powers: (1) to make treaties; (2) to nominate ambassadors, ministers, and consuls; (3) to receive foreign ambassadors; and (4) to command the military forces.

The extent to which the president becomes personally involved in the conduct of foreign policy depends on the nature of the man as well as on the times. During a major emergency, decisions will obviously require his personal attention. In most cases, though, the president can delegate his authority to subordinate officials. He relies heavily on the advice of the secretary of state, the secretary of defense, and other officials directly engaged in the nation's foreign policy.

Even when the president attempts to keep a firm hold on the reins of foreign policy power, a certain amount of delegation of decision-making authority is inevitable. Not

(Editorial cartoon by Hugh Haynie of the *Louisville Courier-Journal*. Copyright, Los Angeles Times Syndicate. Reprinted with permission.)

"But, pray! What prompts you to question my divine power . . .huh, knave?"

In foreign policy matters Congress has some powers, but the president's dominance is rarely questioned.

only the State Department, but also the Defense Department and more than 40 separate administrative agencies have been delegated authority by Congress to make decisions affecting foreign policy. It is impossible for the White House to follow everything that is done in this bureaucratic maze. Major foreign policy decisions are always made by the president and his immediate advisers, but the underlay of bureaucratic power continues to control many aspects of foreign relations.

Shared functions of the Senate. *The Federalist Papers* carefully point out that there is a need for continuity as well as for speed and wisdom in the conduct of foreign policy. The presidency, unified under one individual, is the branch most able to meet these criteria. But to check the possibility of too rash a move by a president, the Constitution also assigned certain foreign policy responsibilities to the Senate. The Framers felt that the older, and supposedly wiser, senators, with their longer terms in office, would offer more stability to the conduct of foreign affairs than would the representatives. Therefore, the Senate must approve presidential appointments of ambassadors and ministers and must ratify treaties.

A major constitutional limitation on the president's power in the conduct of foreign affairs is that he must have the consent of two-thirds of the Senate for approval of a treaty. Although the Senate has not turned down a major treaty supported by the president in many years, it did veto the treaty that provided for United States entry into the League of Nations in 1920. The Senate has vetoed only 19 treaties in its history, and only 4 since 1920. The last veto, of the Law of the Sea Convention Treaty, was in 1960.

Although the Senate rarely vetoes treaties, the possibility is always present and must be taken into account by the White House. President Carter confronted the reality of Senate power over treaties when he faced strong opposition over the treaty with Panama that granted it independent authority to run the

Panama Canal. Usually, if there is even the possibility of such a senatorial veto, the president will negotiate an *executive agreement,* an arrangement with a foreign nation that is outside the framework of a formal treaty and does not require Senate approval. The executive agreement is not mentioned in the Constitution and has been accepted only in usage. The Supreme Court, however, has declared that the authority of the president to make executive agreements is implied in his treaty-making power.

Although the Constitution recognized an important role for the Senate in foreign relations, the dominance of the president was established very early. George Washington's neutrality proclamation, issued in 1793 during a war between France and Britain, established a precedent in foreign affairs that has been carried into the twentieth century. Thomas Jefferson's agreement with France in 1803 for the purchase of the Louisiana Territory was another exercise of presidential freedom in foreign affairs, although the purchase had strong congressional backing and was not solely a presidential prerogative action. James Monroe's assertion of the Monroe Doctrine in 1823, which warned the governments of Europe against further colonization or political intervention in the Western Hemisphere, established another precedent, still in force.

The increasing involvement of the United States in foreign affairs during the twentieth century has resulted in an even greater assumption of authority by the president. On his own initiative President Franklin D. Roosevelt gave 50 destroyers to Great Britain in return for military bases more than a year before the United States entered World War II. And, given the power by Congress to grant aid to any nation whose defense was vital to the United States, Roosevelt was able to promise billions in credits to Great Britain and the Soviet Union shortly before the United States entered the war. Gradually, presidents have expanded this authority to aid and defend other nations against incursions, even ideo-

logical ones. The Truman Doctrine, which granted aid to countries in Europe for the containment of communism, and Eisenhower's extension of this doctrine to the Middle East are two examples. American involvement in Southeast Asia was brought about through the president's power to use the armed forces when he feels the interests of the United States are at stake.

The struggle between the president and the Senate over foreign policy, with power alternately flowing from one branch to the other, is a continuing political phenomenon. "Imperial" presidential powers in the making of foreign policy have been reduced somewhat since the Vietnam War, but Congress itself continues to delegate substantial discretionary power to the president in the foreign policy sphere.

The courts have generally supported the president's leadership in conducting foreign affairs. As Justice George Sutherland pointed out in his opinion in the *Curtiss-Wright* case:

In the vast external realm [foreign affairs] with its important, complicated, delicate and manifold problems, the President alone has the power to speak or listen as a representative of the nation. He *makes* treaties with the advice and consent of the Senate; but he alone negotiates. Into the field of negotiation the Senate cannot intrude; and Congress itself is powerless to invade it.[1]

Chief Executive

The role of the president as *chief executive* is clearly one of his most fundamental powers. Article II bestows on the president some authority over the bureaucracy by providing that he shall "take Care that the Laws be faithfully executed." To accomplish this task, he is given the right to "require the Opinion, in writing, of the principal Officer in each of the executive Departments, upon any subject relating to the Duties of their respective Offices."

---

[1]*United States v. Curtiss-Wright Export Corp.,* 299 U.S. 304 (1936).

Alexander Hamilton, in *The Federalist*, No. 72, recognized this duty of the president as leader of the bureaucracy. He argued that since the president would appoint those people who would be essentially responsible for carrying out his functions, they should be considered his assistants and "subject to his superintendence." Coupled with Article II, Hamilton's argument has been used to support the theory that the Framers intended the president to be leader of the bureaucracy. In line with this concept, the Report of the President's Committee on Administrative Management in 1937 recommended that the number of presidential aides be increased so that he could better deal with the bureaucracy. The report held not only that it is the constitutional responsibility of the president to be the leader of the executive branch, but also that efficiency and democracy require him to operate in this capacity. The establishment of the Executive Office of the President was a direct result of this report.

The views of the President's Committee in 1937 were echoed by the Hoover Commissions in 1949 and 1955. These two reports stated that there should be a direct line of command from the top to the bottom and from the bottom to the top within the federal bureaucracy, with the president as the leader. Later reports, such as the Landis Report on Regulatory Agencies to the president-elect in 1960, emphasized the importance of giving the president the tools for coping effectively with his responsibilities as chief executive.

President Nixon attempted to centralize power over the bureaucracy in the White House, but Watergate rendered his efforts ineffective by severely weakening the White House and allowing for a reassertion of bureaucratic power. Even without Watergate, however, Richard Nixon would never have been able to dominate the bureaucracy, which is an independent force buttressed by Congress and private-interest groups as well as by the intrinsic power gained by expertise, continuity, and specialization in particular policy spheres. The bureaucracy is an important fourth branch of the government, acting as a check on the president.

A major campaign promise of Jimmy Carter in 1976 was to reorganize the federal bureaucracy; he aimed to reduce the number of agencies from 1,900 to 200 and to generally bring the administrative branch under the control of the White House. Carter soon found, however, that White House power over the bureaucracy was minimal, and that without cooperation both from Congress and from the agencies themselves, very little could be done in the way of reorganizing and reducing administrative agencies. President Carter succeeded, after much effort, in creating new Departments of Energy and Education. Neither department, however, seriously threatened existing power relationships within the bureaucracy or among the congressional committees that consider administrative agencies to be an integral part of their network of power. Thus Carter was successful because his minimal bureaucratic reorganizations did not threaten the Washington power establishment.

President Ronald Reagan continued the tradition of his twentieth-century predecessors by proposing the reorganization of the bureaucracy at the outset of his administration. He recommended the abolition of the very departments Carter had created—Energy and Education. However, Reagan found that the legislators and special-interest groups had already coalesced around, and in support of, those departments. His recommendations were shelved on Capitol Hill as powerful committee chairmen objected to his intrusion into what they considered to be their spheres of influence. Congress considers the bureaucracy to be its "own," and vigorously opposes outside attempts to reorganize it.

Legislative Leader

The role of the president as chief legislator stems from several constitutional sources.

First, the Constitution gives him the authority to recommend legislation to Congress. Second, he is required to inform Congress about the "State of the Union" from time to time. In his annual State of the Union message the president often suggests projects or proposals for legislation.

In addition to these constitutional provisions, there are other factors from which the president derives his role as legislator. As the head of his party, he helps to shape platforms and policies that are recommended for congressional action. Furthermore, the legislative proposals coming from the administrative agencies are channeled through the Office of Management and Budget (OMB), a key White House staff agency. The president can, if he chooses, make his imprint upon these agency recommendations. Administrative agencies may also draw up proposals for legislation at the president's request.

Whenever the president involves himself in legislative activities, he can call upon the resources—the information and technological know-how—of the bureaucracy to aid him in the development of particular programs. He can also direct agencies, if they come under his authority, to take action that will have the effect of legislation. President Lyndon B. Johnson, for example, ordered the bureaucracy to implement a nationwide affirmative action program that would require all recipients of federal funds to give special attention to the hiring of minorities and women. Johnson's action extended Title VI of the 1964 Civil Rights Act, which broadly prohibited discrimination, to require "reverse discrimination" as a remedy to the effects of past discrimination against minorities and women.

President Ronald Reagan recognized his role as chief legislator. With the help of his budget director, David Stockman, Reagan dominated the legislative agenda of Congress for the first few years of his administration. The only significant congressional action in opposition to the White House was the over-

(Copyright 1982 by Herblock in *The Washington Post*.)

"So remember—whatever is wrong, blame Congress."

The president often shifts the blame to Congress for unsuccessful policies.

ride of a presidential veto of a supplemental appropriations bill permitting the government to pay its civilian and military employees. The bill contained, in addition, funding levels for student loans and other social programs that the president, on the advice of Stockman, considered unacceptable. The vast majority of legislators had originally supported the legislation, and they bristled at what they considered to be presidential attempts to interfere with the legislative process. Democratic Majority Leader Jim Wright of Texas goaded his House colleagues just before the override vote, asking them, "How many are going to let the White House lead them around with a ring

(Reprinted by permission: Tribune Media Services.)

The president is on hostile ground when he delivers his State of the Union speech.

in their nose like a prize bull at the county fair?" And Massachusetts Republican Silvio Conte abandoned partisanship to support Congress as a check upon the president. After the vote he remarked, "You just don't have 435 robots up here in Congress that are going to vote in lock step." The veto was, said Conte, "an affront to Congress. I hope [President Reagan] learned a lesson [from the override]."[2]

The congressional override of Reagan's veto was a minor victory, but a straw in the wind nevertheless. Sooner or later Congress always opposes presidential domination. Presidential "honeymoons" with Capitol Hill are

usually of brief duration, after which the White House must struggle valiantly to achieve the legislative victories that it considers important. President George Bush achieved moderate success with Capitol Hill during his first year, but his relations with Congress became increasingly acrimonious as his first term progressed.

Party Leader

The president is the titular leader of the political party to which he belongs. He appoints the chairman of the party's national committee and has a great deal of say in party affairs. However, the decentralization of parties and the dispersion of power within them severely reduces presidential influence. Congressional, state, and local parties more often

[2]*Congressional Quarterly Weekly Report*, Vol. 40, No. 37 (September 11, 1982), p. 2237.

than not go their own ways, regardless of exhortations from the president to follow his lead.

The relationship between the president and the members of his own party is one of mutual support to advance the common interests of reelection of party members and the implementation of party programs. The reelection goal is always uppermost in the minds of party candidates, who are benefited if they receive organizational and financial support from party leaders. A presidential endorsement helps candidates gain the aid of their party's national committee in their electoral campaigns, and may also help them to achieve support from the congressional campaign committees of their parties.

The president depends almost as much on the backing of party leaders and office holders as they rely upon his support. Endorsement by state and local party leaders is critical to presidential success at the polls; and the president's programs will founder on Capitol Hill unless a reasonable number of legislators of his own party support him.

The role of the president as party leader, then, both enhances and limits his power. He must accommodate the interests of his party in order to use it as a political vehicle. Strong presidents are invariably strong party leaders. This is illustrated by the administrations of several presidents over the last several decades. Franklin D. Roosevelt gave a new and vigorous image to the Democratic party in 1933. Throughout his years in office Roosevelt

(Keppler in *Puck*: Reprinted by permission of the General Research Division;
The New York Public Library; Astor, Lennox and Tilden Foundation.)

A Presidential Conjuror
One way to increase party support is to hand out favors, as President Chester A. Arthur is shown doing here.

held a firm hand on the helm of the Democratic party, and his strength in his party helped him to get New Deal legislation enacted. Dwight Eisenhower, on the other hand, was less willing to bend to all the wishes of the Republican party leaders during his two terms in office. In keeping himself somewhat aloof from party politics, Eisenhower probably limited his chances to get legislation through Congress. John Kennedy, a Democrat, followed in the footsteps of Eisenhower. Although his New Frontier policies were admired by many Democratic leaders, he was unable to gain control of his party, and this hampered his ability to have proposals passed by either house of Congress. Lyndon Johnson's term in office presents still another picture. Even before Congress had had the opportunity to examine the Great Society program, Johnson had included it in the platform of the Democratic party in the 1964 campaign. By doing this, he obtained a party commitment to his policies that many Democratic members of Congress felt they had to uphold after the election.

Modern presidents have had less than the full backing of their congressional parties, although clearly party loyalty is a highly meaningful factor in determining presidential support on Capitol Hill. Presidents Reagan and Bush received far more support on Capitol Hill from members of their own party than they did from the opposition Democrats. (See Table 12.1.)

Limits on Presidential Power

In describing the limitations of the presidency, Theodore C. Sorensen, an adviser to President Kennedy, noted: "No President is free to go as far or as fast as his advisers, his politics, and his perspective may direct him." According to Sorensen, presidential decisions must be workable, enforceable, and possible without violating constitutional or statutory law; the president is limited by money, as well as "manpower, time, credi-

TABLE 12.1 PRESIDENTIAL SUPPORT IN CONGRESS ON PARTY BASIS

Composite Presidential Support Scores for Congressional Democrats and Republicans for 1989 and 1988

	1989		1988	
	Dem.	**Rep.**	**Dem.**	**Rep.**
Support				
Senate	55%	82%	47%	68%
House	36	69	25	57
Opposition				
Senate	43%	16%	45%	25%
House	58	27	66	36

Source: From *Congressional Quarterly Weekly Report*, December 30, 1989, p. 3542. Reprinted with permission from Congressional Quarterly, Inc.

bility, patronage, and all the other tools at his command."[3]

The president is limited by the demands of his constituencies: Congress, the Supreme Court, the bureaucracy, special-interest groups, party leaders and elected officials, foreign leaders, and the public opinion of the broad presidential electorate all constrain his ability to act unilaterally. He must take into account the wide range of political interests in his constituencies, and strike a balance among them in order to be a successful leader.

A major dilemma of the modern presidency is the gap between the responsibilities that have been placed upon the White House by historical developments, popular expectations, and delegations of authority by Congress and the actual capabilities of the president to carry out these responsibilities in a satisfactory manner. The president cannot always easily accomplish what is expected of him, but the presidency remains the pillar of the political system, the beacon that the Amer-

---

[3]Theodore C. Sorensen, *Decision-Making in the White House* (New York: Columbia University Press, 1963), pp. 22–23.

ican people rely upon for guidance and leadership. And the history of the presidency has vindicated this faith.

SPECIAL PROBLEMS: SUCCESSION, DISABILITY, TRANSITION

Despite the complicated structure of the executive branch today, its key element is still only one man—the president. If he is suddenly incapacitated or dies in office, who takes his place? The Framers were aware that some provision for such a contingency was needed. Therefore, in writing Article II of the Constitution, they provided that in the case of the "Death, Resignation, or Inability to discharge the Powers and Duties" of his office, the president would be succeeded by the vice-president. But what if both the president and the vice-president become incapacitated during a single four-year term? The Constitution also authorizes Congress to enact a law providing for succession to the office if both the president and vice-president are incapable of performing the presidential duties.

Due to the expansion of both the president's functions and the executive structure since 1789, the process of transferring the presidency from one person to another has become increasingly difficult. The inadequacy of congressional statutes providing for presidential succession and disability has been only partially overcome by the ratification of the Twenty-fifth Amendment. Moreover, the burdens of the office continue to complicate even the natural transition of the presidency through the election process every four years.

Presidential Succession

The crucial problem of presidential succession was brought sharply into focus by the assassination of John F. Kennedy on November 22, 1963. Altogether, eight presidents have died or been killed in office, and one president, Richard M. Nixon, was forced to resign.[4]

Since 1789 Congress has passed three different succession laws. The first, passed in 1792, provided that the president pro tempore of the Senate and then the Speaker of the House would succeed to the presidency after the vice-president. Under this law these two congressional leaders were to be merely "Acting Presidents" and not fully empowered under the conditions of the Constitution. If both president and vice-president became incapacitated during the first two years and seven months of a term, Congress was to call for another presidential election. This succession law was never used.

The growth in size and importance of the Cabinet and of the entire executive branch during the nineteenth century dictated the need for a new succession law. A second act, passed in 1886, provided that the line of succession to the presidency, after the vice-president, would run from the secretary of state to the secretary of the treasury and on through the list of Cabinet officers in the order of each department's year of origin. No provision was made for a special election, and no man could assume the presidency unless he met the constitutional qualifications of age, citizenship, and residence.

The Succession Act of 1947. At the request of President Harry S. Truman, Congress passed another succession law in 1947. At the time, there was no vice-president, and President Truman felt it was undemocratic for him, through his power to choose the secretary of state, to name his own successor. Since the Speaker of the House and the president pro tempore of the Senate are elected officers, it seemed to Truman that they were the most natural choices to succeed the president.

---

[4]William Henry Harrison, Zachary Taylor, Warren G. Harding, and Franklin D. Roosevelt died in office; Abraham Lincoln, James Garfield, William McKinley, and John F. Kennedy were assassinated.

Following Truman's suggestions, the Succession Act of 1947 provided that the Speaker of the House and then the president pro tempore of the Senate would succeed to the presidency after the vice-president. The members of the Cabinet would then follow in the order of their department's seniority in the government.

Problems with the 1947 act. The assassination of President Kennedy revealed the weaknesses of the 1947 act. The Speaker of the House in 1963 was John McCormack, then 71 years of age, and the president pro tempore of the Senate was Carl Hayden, then 86. The country was thus faced with the prospect of a rather aged president if anything happened to Lyndon Johnson.

For a man to reach a position as the head of the House or the Senate, he must have been reelected over a period of many years. Thus both these positions would undoubtedly continue to be held by senior members of Congress who might be unable to survive the rigors of the presidency if they succeeded to the office.

Furthermore, their succession would not necessarily be more democratic than the succession of appointed government officials. Although the Speaker and the president pro tempore are chosen by their elected congressional colleagues, they do not represent the nation as a whole but only the one district or state from which they are elected. Moreover, they are likely to be from "safe" districts, which do not contain a cross-section of the national electorate.

The Twenty-fifth Amendment. One problem of presidential succession has been resolved by the Twenty-fifth Amendment to the Constitution. Ratified in 1967, this amendment provides that "whenever there is a vacancy in the office of the Vice President, the President shall nominate a Vice President who shall take office upon confirmation by a majority vote of both houses of Congress." This amendment was used for the first time in 1973, when President Nixon, after Spiro

(Cartoon by Dong. Courtesy of *Minneapolis Star Tribune*)

The Law of Succession

Agnew's resignation, nominated Representative Gerald Ford for the vice-presidency. The nomination was confirmed by Congress. Upon the resignation of Richard Nixon, Ford then became president and nominated Nelson Rockefeller as vice-president. That nomination, too, was confirmed by Congress. It was the first time in history that both the president and the vice-president were appointed officials.

Presidential Disability

Presidential succession becomes an issue not only when a president dies but also when he is disabled. Over the years the problem of presidential disability has been as crucial as the problems resulting from the death or assassination of a president. The seriousness of

(Alexander in *The Philadelphia Bulletin*)

"In which case, who'd be in charge?"
Prior to passage of the Twenty-fifth Amendment, presidential succession was a common cartoon subject.

presidential disability has been illustrated most dramatically in the twentieth century during the administrations of Woodrow Wilson and Dwight D. Eisenhower.

Wilson became incapacitated by partial paralysis in the fall of 1919 and was totally unable to cope with the responsibilities of the presidency. Wilson's paralysis was not immediately made known to the American public. In fact, an attempt was made to maintain the appearance of vitality in the White House. The possibility of his resignation was discussed but was rejected. At the suggestion of the doctors, Mrs. Wilson herself handled presidential business, and no one was given access to the pres-

ident without first going through Mrs. Wilson. The country survived the crisis, but the question remained: Will not a nation that relies so heavily on the presidency be seriously hurt when the holder of the office is actually incapable of performing his duties?

The problem arose again during the administration of President Dwight Eisenhower, who was disabled on several occasions—by a heart attack in 1955, by an ileitis attack in 1956, and by a stroke in 1957. The first two illnesses partially disabled the president for almost six months. After Eisenhower's heart attack, Presidential Assistant Sherman Adams performed most of the necessary functions for the president. Although a delegation of power to the vice-president was hinted at, it never occurred. Vice-president Nixon was placed in a difficult situation with no legal arrangement or political precedent to guide him. Under such circumstances any attempt by the vice-president to assume presidential duties while a president was living would be interpreted as something akin to a *coup d'état*.

Remedies for disability. When the death of a president occurs, someone else must, of course, take over the office. But presidential disability in many cases is almost impossible to define. Was President Eisenhower *sufficiently* disabled to require the vice-president to take over? Who should determine when a president is disabled? Who should determine when the president is sufficiently recovered to resume his duties? These are impossible questions, and it is almost impossible to reach any general agreement on the answers.

After 1957 Presidents Eisenhower, Kennedy, and Johnson made informal arrangements with their vice-presidents to provide for future presidential disability. According to these arrangements, the president himself would determine if he was disabled and would tell the vice-president when to assume his presidential functions. If the president was too disabled to communicate, the vice-president would have to assume the duties of office on his own authority after consultation with Cabinet officials and other political leaders. However, these arrangements left the solution of presidential disability to informal personal agreements reached between two men. Some constitutional or statutory authority was necessary on which the vice-president could rely to determine when he should take the reins of government.

The constitutional solution. With the ratification of the Twenty-fifth Amendment, a definite procedure by which the vice-president can assume the duties of a disabled president was established. Either the president himself or the vice-president together with "a majority of either the principal officers of the executive departments or of such other body as Congress may provide" can submit a written declaration to the Speaker of the House and the Senate president pro tempore stating that the president is unable to perform the functions of his office. In either case the vice-president would immediately become acting president. By granting the vice-president and others the authority to inform Congress of presidential disability, this amendment should provide for the filling of the office if a president is totally disabled or unconscious.

The Twenty-fifth Amendment also includes a procedure by which a formerly disabled president can resume the duties of his office. He can transmit a written declaration to the Speaker and the president pro tempore that he is no longer disabled. If the vice-president and a majority of the principal executive officers, however, believe that the president is still unable to perform his functions, they can submit a counterdeclaration to Congress. It is then up to Congress to decide within 21 days, and by a two-thirds majority of both houses, whether the vice-president should continue as acting president or the president can resume his responsibilities.

Transferral of Office

The problems of transferring the office of the presidency arise both when the president unexpectedly dies or is disabled and when there is an expected transferral of power after a presidential election. Another such situation is the resignation of the president. This has occurred only once in the country's history, with the resignation of Richard Nixon in 1974 and the transfer of power to Gerald Ford. There are certain problems that are peculiar to each situation.

Vice-president to president. When he begins his term of office, a president must decide the extent to which he wants to involve the vice-president in his administration. Usually, vice-presidents have been kept uninformed about presidential objectives, policies, and procedures. Until Franklin D. Roosevelt became president, vice-presidents did not even sit in on Cabinet meetings. Yet although Harry Truman participated in Cabinet meetings as vice-president, he was not informed about vital matters regarding foreign policy and the war then going on. (He did not even know about the development of the atomic bomb until he assumed office after Roosevelt's death.)

President Carter recognized the importance of the vice-presidency. He attempted to choose, in his own words, "the most qualified man" for the job when he added Walter Mondale to the Democratic ticket in 1976. After his election Carter immediately moved Mondale into the West Wing, breaking the long-standing precedent of the vice-president working out of his formal office in the Old Executive Office building. The close Carter-Mondale relationship was unique in presidential history.

Regardless of how close a vice-president may be to the White House, he inevitably develops his own organization and political followers. A vice-president who assumes the presidency after the death of a president in office has to decide whether he wants to keep all the Cabinet members and top administrative officials in their posts. In most instances he replaces the former president's personal advisers relatively quickly. Cabinet members, though, may remain in their posts for longer periods. When Lyndon Johnson assumed the presidency after John Kennedy's assassination, all the Cabinet members remained as the heads of their departments, and only the attorney general and the secretary of commerce were replaced before the beginning of Johnson's second administration. Whatever the particular circumstances, the transition from one man to another as head of the executive branch is bound to cause some disruptions in the administrative operation of the government.

A newly elected president. Unlike the members of Congress, who may be reelected over long periods of time, the president is certain that he will turn his office over to someone else after either four or eight years. The transfer of executive power from a president to a president-elect is a completely different situation from that created by disability or succession. There is no decision to be made as to who will succeed the president or as to how the successor will be chosen.

To ensure the smooth transferral of the office without disrupting the operation of the executive branch, a White House occupant sometimes keeps all his potential successors informed on major issues of foreign and domestic policy, even before a presidential election. Remembering the difficulty he had had when he assumed office in 1945 after Roosevelt's death, President Truman invited both presidential candidates to the White House in 1952 to inform them about world problems. Although he declined Truman's in-

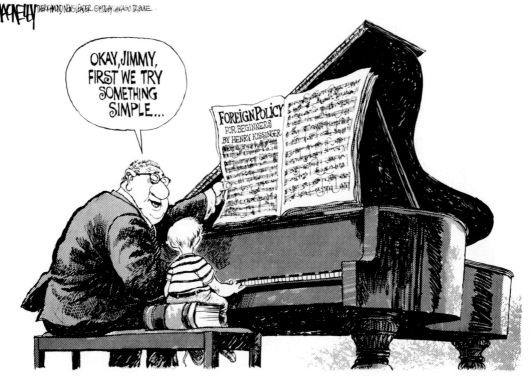

(Reprinted by permission: Tribune Media Services.)

The outgoing administration briefs the president-elect on governmental policies.

vitation, Eisenhower himself as president continued the practice for the Democratic candidate in 1956 and for both candidates in 1960. President Johnson made the same offer in 1968. Of course, transferring the presidency from a member of one political party to a member of another presents more difficulties than when the office is passed between members of the same party.

From the time of his election in November until his inauguration on the following January 20, the president-elect must bide his time. He waits under the shadow of a lame-duck administration that can still initiate some policies counter to his own goals.

Naturally, a certain period of time is needed to make the transfer from the old to the new administration. Ideally, the outgoing administration should make every effort to ease the transition by consulting with the president-elect to point out current problems and by refraining from the adoption of programs that would be embarrassing to the new administration. The position of a new president is never easy. If he is from the opposition party, he probably does not want to be identified with the outgoing administration. He may therefore withdraw from any serious attempts at consultation lest his image be tainted by such association.

Since the time of the Roosevelt administration, the most difficult transitions have occurred upon the election of Republican presidents who succeeded Democratic ones. This is because civil servants hired during the New Deal reflected the values of the Democratic rather than the Republican party. Although the bureaucracy can provide very important linkages and smooth transitions from one Democratic administration to another, it is a major obstacle to incoming Republican presidents. Nor is there any way to remedy this situation, for the concept of a neutral bureaucracy that willingly does the bidding of any president, regardless of his policy preferences, does not exist in the American system. Bu-

reaucrats have very strong policy preferences themselves. Furthermore, the bureaucracy is as much accountable to Congress as to the president. Within the boundaries of legality, agencies should follow presidential preferences. This is easily said but—ask any member of a Republican administration, past or present—almost impossible to achieve.

The Reagan administration approached the bureaucracy with typically Republican suspicions. On the one hand, it proposed cutting back federal agencies and eliminating the Departments of Energy and Education, while on the other it attempted to guarantee that its programs would be put into effect by appointing top officials sympathetic to its views. Regulatory programs, particularly those of the Environmental Protection Agency (EPA), suffered as agency heads sought to dismantle what they considered to be the overly zealous regulatory programs of the previous Democratic administration. (Political appointees at the EPA even compiled "hit lists" of employees considered to be too liberal in their regulatory orientations.)

The Carter transition of 1976–1977. "Presidential transition" became almost a household term after the election of Jimmy Carter in 1976. Carter had been preparing for the transition long in advance, appointing "issue teams" headed by experts throughout the country. They, as well as members of his campaign staff, set to compiling facts and making recommendations on a wide range of problems confronting the nation. After his election a transition team of several hundred persons ensconced themselves in an old HEW building on Independence Avenue and there set about the difficult task of channeling personnel requests to the White House and paving the way for President Carter's administration. Issues were pushed to the background as an inevitable host of job seekers and job changers sought out the transition team and submitted their resumes in the hope of bettering themselves through jobs in the new administration. The transition team, characteristically on a "high" because of its reputation for power in Washington—a bubble that burst when many team members themselves failed to get jobs in the new administration—boldly proposed everything from a plan for government reorganization to how the president should deal with Congress.[5] While the transition team was enjoying its new power, the real transition was being shaped by Carter and his headquarters staff in Georgia.

The Reagan transition: 1980–1981. The party of the presidency changed hands again after the 1980 election, requiring another major transition. Washington job seekers rushed to local bookstores to buy the "Plumb Book," published by the Committee on Post Office and Civil Service of the House of Representatives, less than two weeks after the election. (The book contains a listing of all top-level federal positions that are appointed by the president along with their salaries.)

As the job seekers scrambled for appointments, President-elect Ronald Reagan established a transition team under the direction of Edwin Meese III, who had served as Reagan's chief of staff while he was governor of California, was a top campaign adviser, and later was to become head of the White House staff. The Reagan transition team, unlike that of Jimmy Carter in 1976, was drawn from the president-elect's campaign staff. (Carter had established separate campaign and transition staffs, who often fought with each other over the choice jobs in the new administration.) President-elect Reagan also avoided another Carter mistake by including Washington insiders, persons who had had experience in prior administrations, on his transition team.

The formal transition process, which had come of age in 1976, was carried a step further by Ronald Reagan and his aides. The Reagan transition had been planned well in

(Copyright 1980 by Herblock in *The Washington Post*.)

"Wait—those aren't government regulations. They're job résumés."
Presidential transitions bring out job seekers in force.

advance of Reagan's November victory. As early as April 18, 1980, long before his nomination was certain, Reagan met in Washington with a large group of defense and foreign policy advisers to pave the way for his new administration. Richard Allen, Reagan's first national security adviser, coordinated 25 policy task forces to facilitate Reagan's takeover while the candidate was still battling for his party's nomination! An expanded transition bureaucracy was established, operating as part of an independent Reagan corporation called the "Presidential Transition Trust," eligible to receive contributions that under the Federal Election Law would not be counted as campaign gifts. (Carter had financed his transition

---

[5]See James Reston, "Carter's Amiable Computers," *New York Times*, December 17, 1976, p. A27.

from campaign funds, thereby placing financial limits upon the transition team.)

The Bush transition: 1988–1989. The transition from Reagan to Bush went particularly smoothly because the president-elect had long government experience and, as vice-president under Reagan, he had the inside knowledge and contacts to decide on the direction and personnel of his administration soon after his election. The very next day after the election Bush began to select his White House staff and cabinet, earlier than most previous presidents. Bush retained a number of Reagan people at the top levels of his administration, particularly James Baker, Bush's key appointment to be Secretary of State who had been Reagan's White House Chief of Staff and Treasury Secretary.

Preparations for presidential transitions promise to become even more elaborate in the future. Transition bureaucracies and policy task forces will help smooth the paths of incoming administrations. Future presidents, like Ronald Reagan, will want to "hit the ground running" after inauguration by being fully prepared to implement new domestic and foreign policies. Elected presidents have only eight years to serve at the most, and time is of the essence for effective leadership. Presidents know that they must establish their political credibility at the outset of their administrations in order to get the results they want from the more permanent power centers of the Capital—Congress, the bureaucracy, and the courts.

PRESIDENTIAL DECISION MAKING

Many factors influence presidential decision making, including the president's political philosophy and the advice he receives from his staff. Presidential politics, however, is perhaps the most important force on the White House. Regardless of what the presidents or their advisers may want to do, their power depends upon their political effectiveness, their ability to deal with Congress, the bureaucracy, the leaders of their political party throughout the country, special interests, the media, state and local governments, and public opinion. The interests and opinions of foreign leaders must also be taken into account in foreign policy making.

Theodore Sorensen, who learned the White House from the inside as one of John F. Kennedy's closest advisers, examines the nature of presidential politics in the following case study.

Presidential Politics / *Theodore C. Sorensen*

We can turn now to the major forces or sources of influence which shape the presidential decision itself, grouped under three frames of reference: presidential politics, presidential advisers, and the presidential perspective. (All of these classifications are arbitrary and imprecise, and another observer with equal logic and accuracy might well have listed twenty-three or indeed forty-three subdivisions.)

Some purists—if not realists—may blush at the

fact that politics heads the list. But we are discussing our prime political office and the nation's prime politician, a man who has been chosen by his party as well as the people. Some Presidents may assert that they are "above politics," yet politics, in its truest and broadest sense, still colors their every decision (including the decision to appear nonpolitical). Some issues have been traditionally deemed to be outside of politics, but considerations

From Theodore C. Sorensen, *Decision-Making in the White House* (New York: Columbia University Press, 1963), pp. 43–56. Reprinted by permission.

of public and congressional support still affect their disposition.

There is nothing dishonorable about the influence of politics on White House decisions. In a nation governed by the consent of the governed, it is both honorable and indispensable. While limitations of responsibility and accuracy should always be present, to say that we should remove such issues as Berlin or Red China from politics is to say they should be removed from public accountability and scrutiny. To charge that a President is politically motivated when he advocates a tax cut or a strong civil rights measure is simply to charge that he is doing what every elected official is elected to do.

Politics pervades the White House without seeming to prevail. It is not a role for which the President sets apart certain hours. It is rarely the sole subject of a formal presidential meeting. It is instead an ever-present influence—counterbalancing the unrealistic, checking the unreasonable, sometimes preventing the desirable, but always testing what is acceptable.

Public Opinion

But democratic government is not a popularity contest; and no President is obliged to abide by the dictates of public opinion. Our political idealism may be filled with assumptions of human virtue and wisdom, but our political history is filled with examples of human weakness and error.

Public opinion is often erratic, inconsistent, arbitrary, and unreasonable—with a "compulsion to make mistakes," as Walter Lippmann put it. It rarely considers the needs of the next generation or the history of the last. It is frequently hampered by myths and misinformation, by stereotypes and shibboleths, and by an innate resistance to innovation. It is usually slow to form, promiscuous and perfidious in its affection, and always difficult to distinguish. For it rarely speaks in one loud, clear, united voice.

A President, therefore, must remember that public opinion and the public interest do not always agree. The value to this nation of a foreign aid program, for example, is not determined by its popularity. Last year's trade expansion bill could not have awaited a spontaneous public demand. Voter enthusiasm for our space effort is high after each flight of a Soviet or American astronaut, but

in between flights new doubts and complaints will emerge. And almost any pollster in any state will find that most voters want higher federal expenditures in their areas of interest, lower expenditures elsewhere, and a balanced budget always.

No President could simply respond to these pressures. He has a responsibility to lead public opinion as well as respect it—to shape it, to inform it, to woo it, and win it. It can be his sword as well as his compass. An aroused public opinion was more effective in 1962, for example, in helping create a climate favorable to the rescission of steel prices, than any statutory tool. President Kennedy's televised explanations of his decisions on Berlin, nuclear testing, and the Cuban quarantine achieved on each occasion a new national consensus that discouraged any adversary's hopes for disunity.

But arousing public opinion is a delicate task. President Kennedy's plea for fall-out shelters in his 1961 discussion of Berlin ended the prevailing national apathy on civil defense, but it also unleashed an emotional response which grew to near-hysterical proportions (before it receded once again to near-apathy). His warnings on the presence of Soviet missiles in Cuba had to be sufficiently somber to enlist support around the world without creating panic here at home.

In 1961 he resisted the recommendation that he declare a full-scale national emergency over the threat to Berlin, recognizing that this resort to ultimate powers and public response had to be selectively used. For similar reasons, he has generally resisted urgings of disappointed partisans who would have him stir up the public against a Congress which is controlled (at least nominally) by his own party and which has consistently enacted four-fifths of his program.

In short, presidential appeals for public support must be at the right time and with the right frequency, if they are to be effective. On other occasions he may need to alienate a portion of his public support, for serving as President of all the people does not mean offending none of them. But this also cannot be done too often if he is to maintain his position, and it should not be done for meaningless or hopeless causes. President Kennedy may have struck the right balance, for he is criticized, on the one hand, for expanding the powers of his office, sending too much to the Congress, and taking on too many controversies, and, at the same time, for "hoarding" his popularity and recognizing the limitations of a largely lethargic electorate.

One important distinction should be kept in mind. In domestic affairs, a presidential decision is usually the beginning of public debate. In foreign affairs, the issues are frequently so complex, the facts so obscure, and the period for decision so short, that the American people have from the beginning—and even more so in this century—delegated to the President more discretion in this vital area; and they are usually willing to support any reasonable decision he makes.

But public opinion cannot be taken for granted. Some Presidents have tried to change it, others have rushed to catch up with it, but none has repeatedly defied it. "With public sentiment on its side," Lincoln said with some exaggeration, "everything succeeds; with public sentiment against it, nothing succeeds." Franklin D. Roosevelt wrote: "I cannot go any faster than the people will let me." And President Kennedy is acutely aware of Jefferson's dictum: "Great innovations should not be forced on slender majorities."

President Kennedy, for example, has pressed a divided Congress and a contented public to abandon century-old economic precepts and accept a sizable tax cut with a sizable deficit at a time of general prosperity, but, unwilling to be so far out in front of Congress and the country that his program would have no chance, he stretched out the proposed tax cut to avoid a peacetime deficit larger than that of his predecessor.

No President respects public opinion simply out of fear of impeachment or even solely out of a desire for reelection—for the same principle is followed in both his terms. Instead both his conscience and his common sense, both his principles and his political judgment, compel him to seek, to the extent possible, the approval of the voters who elected him and who can defeat his party, the consent of the governed who are affected by his decision and on whose consent its success may depend.

Every President must, therefore, be a keen judge of public opinion. He must be able to distinguish its petty whims, to estimate its endurance, to respond to its impatience, and to respect its po-

tential power. He must know how best and how often he can appeal to the public—and when it is better left undisturbed.

No President reaches that summit of public favor without believing he possesses (and he usually does) an extraordinary instinct for public opinion. He does not rely on the views expressed in his mail, or in public petitions, or by pickets in front of the White House, for they all too often reflect only a tiny organized group. He does not rely on opinion polls, which, outside of testing comparative candidate strengths, are still an inexact measure of the voters' views. He does not rely on the crowds that greet him on his travels, knowing they are usually a disproportionately partisan sample. Nor does he generalize from conversations with visitors, reports from his advisers, or his reading and viewing of mass media. His political intuition is in part an amalgamation of all of these—but he is likely to regard his own invisible antennae as somehow more sensitive than any. (President McKinley, according to Speaker Cannon, retained his popularity by "keeping his ear so close to the ground he got it full of grasshoppers.")

I no longer believe those who say that a poor politician could be a good President, "if he could only be appointed to the job." Without the qualities required of a successful candidate—without the ability to rally support, to understand the public, to express its aspirations—without the organizational talent, the personal charm, and the physical stamina required to survive the primaries, the convention, and the election—no man would make a great President, however wise in other ways he might be.

Pressure Groups, Congress, and the Press

Each President must also judge when to oppose or accommodate a single segment of public opinion—a region or state, an occupation or age group, an industry or profession, a pressure group or lobby. Some will have views the President respects, such as nuclear scientists on nuclear tests. Some will have influence he seeks to enlist, such as the organization of older citizens on behalf of his health bill. Some will have sufficient power to cause him concern, at least in their own sphere of influence. (The least respected and least effective lobbies in Washington, I might add, are those which rush forward to testify on every measure of every kind whether directly related or not to the interests of their members. It is doubtful, for example, that President Roosevelt was either heartened or dismayed by the 1934 resolution of a bankers' organization stating that its members would stand solidly behind the President on all emergency measures that did not infringe on their interests.)

There will always be a small but noisy group of critics intolerant of the gap between hope and possibility, complaining of a lack of leadership when long-awaited measures are not immediately enacted, while an equally small and vocal group will wail that each step forward the President takes is a gross usurpation of power.

The amount of pressure generated by those concerned over import competition must be balanced against the less active but larger number of persons benefiting from both exports and imports. The political or congressional attacks induced by a contractor whose weapons system has been discontinued must be weighed against the long-range costs of continuing an outmoded system.

The task is not always one of choosing between two interests. No President, even if he so wished, could suspend the laws in response to complaints—with respect to desegregation or antitrust, for example. But he may find it desirable to accept amendments to a tax measure, or to reach informal understandings on concessions regarding a trade bill, in order to secure the passage of those bills with the support of a diverse coalition; or he may warn his appointees against exhibiting an attitude toward business or labor that is so hostile it might dampen the economic climate.

A President's own ties with some economic or other interest group may give him additional bargaining power with that group or reduced influence with another. A President with close ties to business, for example, will meet less resistance to his anti-inflation or anti-trust efforts. On the other hand, while it should not be impossible to find an equitable constitutional formula to settle the church-school aid problem, it is difficult for that formula to be suggested by the nation's first Catholic President.

Pressure groups usually have less direct effect on the President than his relations with the Congress—a large and separate topic but a major arena of presidential politics. While this discussion is concerned primarily with White House decisions, members of the Congress will inevitably attempt to affect those decisions in much the same way as the White House attempts to affect the decisions of the Congress: i.e., legislators will privately or publicly lobby, pressure, encourage, or discourage the President and his advisers, with respect to his legislative program or budget, both before and after their passage through the Congress.

As is true of public opinion and segments thereof, the views of one or more members of Congress must sometimes be resisted, sometimes reshaped, sometimes ignored, and sometimes accepted, depending not only on the validity of those views but on the power of those who express them and the extent to which they are shared throughout the Congress. Presidents have differed in the degree of their deference to (or domination of) congressional opinion, according to their own legislative experience, their control of their party, and their party's control of the Congress, but all Presidents since Washington have noted the change in climate that occurs when Congress adjourns.

Finally, presidential politics includes attention to the American press and other media. Their selection and description of particular events—far more than their editorials—help to create or promote national issues, to shape the minds of the Congress and public, and to influence the President's agenda and timing. Ever since George Washington expressed the wish in 1777 "that our Printers were more discreet in many of their publications," our Presidents and the press have engaged in what the jargon of the Cold War would call a "contest for men's minds."

The winning side in this contest is debatable. The advent of television has given the President great resources for directly reaching the public, but even presidential corrections rarely catch up with those misstatements which now and then appear in the press. For example, the great newspaper chain which headlined a totally false scare story about Soviet planes overflying the southeastern United States has never acknowledged its error.

I have often been asked why President Kennedy, unlike his predecessor, should bother to read so many newspapers when so much of their important information and arguments—excluding overseas statements and events that occurred during the night—is at least twenty-four hours old to him. Obviously this would be even more true of weekly and monthly magazines. He reads them, I believe, partly to gain new insights for himself but primarily to know what the public and the Congress are reading, to see how his actions or choices appear to others without his access to the facts. For any President, any politician dependent on public opinion, is concerned with how that opinion is shaped, with how, to use a current phrase, the news is being "managed" in the only place it can be managed, the media editorial offices.

CHAPTER THIRTEEN

Presidential Policy Making

"President Calls for Round of Deficit Reduction Talks"; "White House Supports Plan for German Reunification"; "Bush Nominates New Hampshire Judge for Supreme Court"; "President Proposes a National 'War' on Drugs"; "President Bush Considers Veto on Civil Rights Legislation." These headlines announce presidential actions. Even though the president has wide constitutional prerogatives, especially in foreign affairs, his power in the political system extends only so far as he is able to persuade Congress, administrative departments and agencies, and state and local governments to follow him. What factors influence the policies he strives to enact and implement? What advisory and administrative apparatus does he utilize to aid him in his job? What are the sources of the dominance of the presidency?

DEMANDS ON THE PRESIDENCY

The multiple responsibilities of the president have been shaped by the Constitution, historical developments, congressional legislation, and court decisions. Congress is an important force in the constituency of the White House, constantly making demands on the presidency in its disposition of his legislative requests and in its frequent delegation of authority to the president to implement laws. Presidential actions may be subject, in addition, to judicial review by the Supreme Court, which may limit or expand the permissible scope of the president's authority. One of the most important governmental constituencies of the White House is the bureaucracy, which constantly makes demands upon the president and without whose support the enactment and implementation of presidential programs is impossible.

Outside of his governmental constituencies, the president relies on the diverse forces of his own political party and of broader public opinion to win election and to help guide his actions once he is in office. Private pressure groups also constantly seek to exert influence upon the White House. Interest groups that are important components of the president's party have more access than those that "fence sit" between the parties. For example, the leadership of the AFL-CIO has direct access to Democratic presidents due to the important role labor groups play in the politics of the Democratic party. On the Republican side, the Business Round Table, a conservative group, and many other business interests usually have special access to Republican presidents.

Before the advent of public financing for presidential campaigns in 1976, presidents were particularly beholden to party-affiliated interest groups that helped to obtain financial contributions to their campaigns. While public financing has made this aspect of pressure-group support less relevant, the efforts of pressure groups to mobilize the support of their members behind presidential candidates is considered by the candidates themselves to be an important contribution to the campaigns.[1]

To maintain the support he needs, the president must respond to the demands of his many constituencies. While setting policy, he must listen to and weigh the advice, opinions, and needs of all of them. Obviously, the president needs an enormous amount of political skill to cope with all these demands. Presidential popularity can be severely reduced in a very short time by unpopular decisions as well as by outside events.

Nongovernmental Constituencies

Presidents are always sensitive to public opinion and are constantly seeking, especially in the initial stages of their administrations, to gain widespread public support.

Electoral demands. The increasing personalization of presidential politics has caused candidates to attempt to mobilize public support outside of regular party channels even before they achieve the nomination. Although primaries are limited with few exceptions to party voters, nevertheless the kinds of grassroots appeals made by candidates to gain the support of party members are a way of "going to the people" over the heads of established state and local party leaders. The expansion of the presidential party system for the selection of delegates to national party conventions makes votes count from the very beginning of the presidential campaign process. Use of the media and of public relations advisers, coupled with the public's disenchantment with governmental and party establishments, encourages candidates to mobilize their own public, whether at the nominating, election, or governing stages.

Once in office, the president throughout

his first administration has to think about reelection. In his second administration (the Twenty-second Amendment precludes presidents from running for a third term) the president still may consider public support important to achieve programs that will enable him to take his place in history as a "great" president—a goal to which most occupants of the White House aspire.

The electoral college, originally designed to remove the presidency from the direct control of the people, continues as an important factor in presidential elections. Presidential candidates (including the incumbent) entering the electoral process must pay attention to the geographical distribution of public opinion on a state-by-state basis and concentrate upon the states with large electoral votes, which are crucial to winning the necessary majority in the electoral college. While large states are vital to winning, candidates seek the broadest support possible within each individual state they think they can carry in the final election. The electoral college system forces candidates to pay attention to small as well as large states, for a coalition of smaller electoral vote states can, with the aid of just a few of the larger states, be the winning combination.

The electoral college system, which allocates electoral votes on a state-by-state basis in accordance with a state's representation in Congress, tends to buttress the importance of state and local party organizations due to their influence in helping to "deliver" the states to the candidates. For example, in the years when Mayor Richard Daley had a stranglehold on the city of Chicago, it was necessary for any Democratic candidate for the presidency to woo him, because his organization could usually deliver Illinois by getting out the vote and running up huge Democratic majorities in the city of Chicago. Party bosses can help candidates obtain the critical margins for victory in their states. This fact has elevated the status of Democratic party bosses in particular, because Democratic presidential candi-

---

[1] In primary campaigns, financial contributions remain important to enable candidates to qualify for federal funds and to provide them with funds that the federal government will match.

dates have in the twentieth century required the support of urban voters in the large industrial states to win.

Whether Democratic or Republican, presidential candidates seek to establish a core of electoral vote support from which to launch their campaigns and achieve victory. This means that regional support is important to presidential candidates. In the past, the "solid South"—composed of Alabama, Arkansas, Georgia, South Carolina, Mississippi, and Louisiana—was important to the nomination of Democratic candidates, although the 52 electoral votes of these states have only once been necessary to elect a Democratic president (Woodrow Wilson in 1916). Even Jimmy Carter in 1976 did not need the support of the solid South, for he emerged with a margin of 56 electoral votes. While the South has traditionally supported Democratic candidates, Republicans have been able to rely with near certainty on the votes of the wheat-belt states—Kansas, Nebraska, North Dakota, and South Dakota.

The reality of presidential politics is that the urban and industrial states—such as Pennsylvania, New York, California, Michigan, and Illinois—cast a very large number of electoral votes. Urbanization and growing populations also characterize the Sunbelt states, the most important of which in presidential elections are California, Texas, and Florida. The presidential candidate who can swing all of these states will very likely win the election. And candidates must have the support of at least a few of these populous states. While trying to maintain regional support, therefore, most presidential candidates will pay more attention to party and public opinion in the larger states.

In the presidential elections of the twentieth century, there have been few variations from the rule that it is the electoral votes of the large industrial states that give candidates their winning margins. Pennsylvania and New York, for example, were more than

enough to put Jimmy Carter over the top in 1976, and he did not need California, which he lost by 1 percent of the statewide vote.

Since Democratic candidates swing the large industrial states by appeals to urban voters, they in particular must respond to the demands made upon them by their urban constituency. These include demands for improved mass transportation, welfare programs, better housing, and the cleanup of environmental (air and water) pollution.

Democratic presidents have ordinarily encouraged legislation to combat unemployment, uphold collective bargaining, increase federal aid to education, and to institute health and welfare programs such as Medicaid. The major sources of electoral strength for the Republicans have been found in the middle- and high-income areas of large and medium-sized cities and in suburban and rural areas. Only by amassing large majorities in these areas can Republican candidates hope to carry the larger electoral-vote states. Republican presidents have tended to respond to demands for fiscal responsibility, balancing of the budget, tax cuts, and less governmental control of business.

Outside of these electoral-vote-based constituencies, whose demands presidential candidates seek to satisfy, the link between the electorate and the presidency is often very weak. How, then, is the president to know the extent to which he is meeting the needs and wishes of the electorate? Public opinion polls measure support for the president in very general terms and also indicate what the public is feeling about broad issues of public policy. Presidents have "honeymoons" with the public just as they do with Congress. Public support for presidents, particularly since the late 1960s, has been highest at the outset of their administrations but rapidly declines the longer they stay in office. The public translates its hopeful expectations for a new president into support, but presidents do not have magic wands they can wave to solve economic, social, and international problems. The public blames its president for inflation, unemployment, recession, wars, and international disputes, believing that effective leadership should be able to solve all the nation's problems. Presidents eagerly review public opinion polls, hoping for indications of support. They know, however, that expressions of public support or opposition are constantly changing and cannot ultimately determine presidential decisions.

In addition to "taking the pulse" of the electorate through public opinion polls, the president can gain an understanding of the degree to which the electorate supports him by observing the results of off-year congressional elections. A strong surge in the opposition party in Congress is a clear indication of public disfavor.

In times of great unrest, mass demonstrations may reflect high levels of public discontent with government policy. During the Depression, as government action to combat massive unemployment through the New Deal was only partially successful, there were marches of the unemployed upon Washington. Martin Luther King, Jr., led the famous Poor People's March on Washington in 1963. Washington in the late 1960s was also the scene of many demonstrations against the Vietnam War. In the late 1970s and early 1980s Washington witnessed demonstrations by farmers who came from across the country in tractor cavalcades up Pennsylvania Avenue to the Capitol, protesting a reduction in federal farm price supports. Labor unions orchestrated a mass demonstration of members to protest Ronald Reagan's economic policies, which they were convinced had increased unemployment. Demonstrations are not, of course, a reflection of mass public opinion but only of particular segments of it; therefore, although demonstrators from time to time may gather in Lafayette Park or march down Pennsylvania Avenue in front of the White House, presidents cannot make the mistake of measuring public opinion by demonstrators' demands.

Even though presidents may be indebted to relatively narrow-based regional support in combination with the backing of a few of the larger states, once in office the posture is always accepted that the president represents a nationwide constituency. And presidents seek to build nationwide support, using all the prestige and public relations of the White House for this purpose. At the same time presidents are careful not to appear beholden to special segments of public opinion or particular interest groups.

Private interest groups. The presidency is not the major focus of pluralistic politics, which involves adversary group interests constantly pressuring for the enactment of policies favorable to them. Interest-group leaders do visit the White House and discuss their problems with presidential advisers and sometimes with the president himself, but the major focus of such groups is Congress, the bureaucracy, and the courts, which are more appropriate channels for the consideration of the relatively narrow viewpoints of special-interest groups. It is through the other branches of the government and through the political parties that interest groups most often gain access to the White House.

Interest groups that help elect the president will have his "ear." When the president forms his cabinet, for example, he appoints persons acceptable to dominant interests within the constituency of each cabinet-level department. Presidents usually appoint a secretary of agriculture who is supported by agricultural interests, a secretary of commerce backed by business, a secretary of labor who will represent the views of the AFL-CIO and other labor unions, and a secretary of defense who is a "hard-liner"—a necessary attribute for the backing of the defense industry.

One of the best ways to observe the indirect influence of pressure groups on the presidency is to attend the presidential-appointee confirmation hearings in the Senate committee having jurisdiction over the departments and agencies concerned in the appointment. There, interested groups will testify and present their views on the acceptability of a particular nominee. Congressional committees, administrative departments and agencies, and pressure groups often will act in unison to ensure that the president nominates an acceptable candidate before the formal confirmation process begins. The effectiveness of this behind-the-scenes clearance of nominees is one of the reasons why the Senate virtually never has to turn down a presidential appointee.

Pressure groups influence the presidency not only indirectly by channeling their demands to the White House through administrative departments and agencies and through congressional committees, but also directly by challenging presidential decisions in the courts. During the New Deal conservative business groups that sought to have New Deal legislation declared unconstitutional used this technique, and they were highly successful in the earlier part of the period. In 1952 when President Harry Truman seized the steel mills, a prerogative he based upon the war emergency and on his authority as chief executive and commander in chief of the armed forces, the steel industry successfully curbed his power by using this technique. President Richard Nixon ran into a major judicial obstacle in his attempts to impound funds for a variety of programs enacted by Congress. In the impoundment case, suits were brought by those groups that would benefit from the programs, particularly states and municipalities.

(© Pat Oliphant Washington Star/The Los Angeles Times Syndicate)

"PULL!"

The fact that the president and the leaders of Congress are of the same party does not necessarily ensure a friendly reception for the White House on Capitol Hill.

Court rulings on the legality of Nixon's impoundments ran 38 to 2 against him in late 1973. At that time Nixon began to buckle under the pressure and released funds that he had previously impounded.

Political party demands. Since the president's political party is not a unified organization under his command, his dealings with it involve relationships with all the diverse and sometimes conflicting interests within the party. Not only must the president pay special attention to the powerful private pressure groups that lend support to his party, but important party leaders on Capitol Hill and in the states and localities will have access to him as leader of the party.

Cementing relations with Capitol Hill requires the president to consult senators of his own party not only on federal appointments made by the president within their states, but also, if they are chairmen of powerful committees, on appointments to the agencies under their jurisdiction. Theoretically, senatorial courtesy extends only to those presidential appointments within the state of a senior senator of the president's party, but in practice White House consultation with the chairmen of Senate committees is expected on appointments within the senators' own spheres of influence.

Governmental Demands on the President

While private interest groups and political party leaders influence the president indirectly through the bureaucracy, the courts, and Congress, these branches of the government are powerful in their own right and are important forces in the president's constituency. The cooperation of the bureaucracy is necessary for the implementation of presidential policies, as is the assent of Congress.

Congressional forces. The president depends on the support of Congress in a number of ways. It is the members of Congress who provide or withhold support for the president by accepting or rejecting his legislative proposals, by legislating the extension or restriction of his powers, and by accepting or rejecting his governmental appointees. Thus, the president must persuade members of Congress, including those of his own party, to follow his lead by convincing them that they and the White House have mutual interests.

In a presidential election year members of the president's party and even some of the opposition party's members will fall into line behind the president if they feel he and his programs are popular. They do this to reap the rewards of his popularity. Some very popular presidents, such as Dwight D. Eisenhower, pull many congressional candidates into office on their coattails.

Presidents as popular as Eisenhower, however, are rare, and the presidential "coattail effect," as the power of the presidency to draw voters to other members of his party is called, is usually not a significant factor in congressional elections. In 1976, for example, President Gerald Ford far outdistanced most Republican senatorial and congressional candidates in their own states and districts, many of whom failed to get elected. And President Jimmy Carter, in 1980, ran *behind* many Democratic congressional candidates, who won in spite of Carter. President Ronald Reagan's coattails likewise had little impact upon the 1980 congressional election. Reagan carried only 51 percent of the nationwide vote, an insufficient victory margin to sway many House contests. In many eastern and midwestern congressional districts Reagan ran behind Republican challengers, who captured seats from the Democrats. He outpaced Republican challengers by wide margins in only a few western and southern districts. His candidacy, however, apparently did help several Republican Senate races, pushing Barry Goldwater over the top with a 1 percent victory margin in Arizona, and helping Paula Hawkins win her Florida seat by a 4 percent margin.

Legislators of the president's party on Capitol Hill do not feel compelled to support the president. It is unusual, for example, for presidents to receive the kind of support that Reagan was given by Senate Republicans during 1981, the first year of his administration, when they voted the party line 81 percent of the time. The average Republican in the House supported the party on only 74 percent of the roll-call votes. All presidents, no matter how popular they may be, must contend with pockets of opposition on Capitol Hill. Reagan, for example, was opposed on crucial budget matters by the "Gypsy Moths," a group of liberal Republicans mostly from the Northeast who felt their constituencies would be disproportionately affected by the cuts.

Whether or not a president has a party majority on Capitol Hill, he must persuade members of both parties to support him if he is to achieve legislative victories. For example, President Reagan's slim Republican majority in the Senate required him to court conservative Democrats to back his programs. In the House he confronted a Democratic majority, but he was able to count on a sufficient number of conservative Democrats to form a majority in favor of his budget and tax cuts.

Congress remains constitutionally independent of the president, and the political careers of its members do not depend upon the blessing of the president, although they may be enhanced by it. Both the powers and incentives of Congress make it a vital component of the president's constituency, often checking him and always reshaping White House programs to make them conform to the realities of congressional politics.

Administrative forces. Administrative agencies are also a vital influence on the presidency. Agencies participate in making and implementing presidential decisions. Some agencies jealously guard their independence, whereas others seek to work through the White House.

Administrative agencies relate to the president in different ways. Some agencies, such as the major executive departments, have secretaries appointed by the president, but such agencies are not necessarily controlled from the White House. Franklin Roosevelt once quipped, "When I woke up this morning the first thing I saw was a headline in the *New York Times* to the effect that our Navy was going to spend two billion dollars on a shipbuilding program. Here I am, the Commander in Chief of the Navy having to read about that for the first time in the Press."

The president is as much controlled by the agencies as he controls them. He may provide general guidelines for the agencies' policy-making activities; however, at the same time he needs the support of the agencies to implement his programs, and he depends to a great extent on the information that he receives from them when making his decisions.

If the president wants to develop and implement effective policies in such areas as defense, agriculture, environmental control, and health, education, and welfare, he must have the cooperation and support of the agencies involved. The bureaucracy is essentially a fourth branch of the government, with which the president must deal much as he deals with Congress. Agencies will support the president to the extent they feel it is in their political interest to do so. No amount of formal authority possessed by the president over the bureaucracy can overcome stubborn opposition based upon agency self-interest.

Judicial forces. In addition to congressional and administrative forces, the judicial branch, through court decisions, makes demands on and provides support for the president. For example, the Supreme Court decision in *Brown v. Board of Education* (1954) and subsequent federal court orders for school desegregation created demands on the president to uphold desegregation policies. Both Presidents Eisenhower and Kennedy responded to these demands by using federal troops to prevent the governors of Arkansas and Mississippi from defying the court orders. (The steel-seizure and executive-privilege cases discussed earlier in this chapter are further examples of judicial demands on the presidency.)

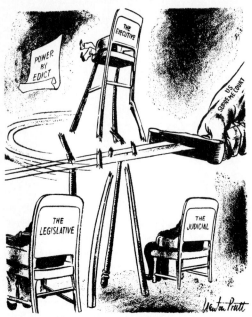

(Courtesy of The McClatchy Newspapers/Newton Pratt.)

Down to size!
Interpretation of presidential powers by the Supreme Court can weaken the executive as well as support it.

The courts also provide support for the president by upholding certain presidential actions. In a number of Supreme Court decisions, such as *United States v. Curtiss-Wright Export Corporation* (1936) and *United States v. Pink* (1942), the validity of foreign policy decisions by the president was defended against challenge (see Chapter 5).

Foreign nations. Still another constituency of the president consists of the many foreign nations whose military and economic interests must be considered when he formulates foreign policy or takes diplomatic and military action in the foreign arena. No twentieth-century president can afford to ignore these international forces, whether they be the warring nations of the Middle East, the independent nations of Africa, the developing countries of Latin America, or the conflicting communist and anticommunist forces in Europe and Asia.

Presidential words and actions in such areas as civil rights or military and economic policy all have a real impact on the image of the country as seen from abroad. The announcement of Jimmy Carter's human rights policy, for example, gave hope to oppressed people throughout the world. Wherever feasible, the president said, the United States would support the struggle for human rights—rights that no nation should deny its own people. In contrast, the Reagan administration deemphasized human rights and focused upon strong measures to contain communism.

The role of the United States as a more than equal partner among the free nations of the world shapes the responsibilities, powers, and limits of the president in foreign affairs. The dominant position of the United States among the free nations after World War II no longer exists, and the president must deal with powers, such as Japan, the European Common Market countries, and the "third world" nations of Africa and Asia, as independent bodies that may or may not wish to follow the lead of the United States. The Reagan administration, for example, was only partially successful in persuading Japan to limit automobile exports to the United States to alleviate the recession in the American automobile industry. President Reagan also failed to persuade European allies to oppose the Soviet construction of a natural gas pipeline to Europe with the help of Western technology.

THE CONTEMPORARY STRUCTURE OF THE PRESIDENCY

Obviously, it would be impossible for any one person or even a small staff directed by one individual to handle all the demands and duties with which the president is expected to deal. The structure of the presidency has expanded considerably since the early days of the office. Under the first president the structure included only four cabinet officials—the secretaries of state, treasury, and war, and an attorney general.

Originally, the president was supposed to obtain advice from the regular executive branch, and this is reflected in the constitutional provision of Article II, Section 2, which states that the president "may require the Opinion in writing, of the principal Officer in each of the executive Departments, upon any subject relating to the Duties of their respective Offices. . . ." The cabinet met to advise the president from the earliest days of the republic, beginning with the first administration of George Washington.

As the bureaucracy grew, and as cabinet departments were added and became increasingly independent, reflecting the viewpoints of their own constituencies, presidents began to find not only that the "advice" they were getting from the cabinet was self-serving but also that the bureaucracy could not be controlled through the cabinet because cabinet members represented their departments more than they reflected the views of the White House. The Executive Office of the President was designed to be independent of the regular bureaucracy, serving only the White House. The growth of the Executive Office since its establishment in 1939 reflects the ever-increasing gap between the president and the bureaucracy—not only its executive departments but its host of independent agencies. The Executive Office is not just a body of experts but a political extension of the presidency itself, a presidency that in the twentieth century is one of four branches of government (the bureaucracy having become a powerful fourth branch, exercising powers and responsibilities not foreseen by the Framers of the Constitution).

The Executive Office of the President

The Executive Office of the President— housed partly in the old War Department building adjacent to the White House and partly in a new Executive Office building facing the White House across Pennsylvania Avenue—was created by executive order in 1939. The idea for the Executive Office originated in 1937 from the President's Committee on Administrative Management, also called the Brownlow Committee after its chairman, Louis Brownlow, a firm believer in "scientific management" for government. The committee recommended an expansion of presidential staff to cope with the growing responsibilities of the White House, and particularly to aid the president in controlling the sprawling administrative branch. The premise of the Executive Office was that the president must be supreme over the bureaucracy, and the original Executive Office was supposed to give the president sufficient authority and information to establish that supremacy. In addition to controlling the bureaucracy, the Executive Office was intended to aid the president in fulfilling his other responsibilities.

The components of the Executive Office have changed during the many presidential administrations since 1939. The only formal component that has remained throughout this long period is the White House Office, consisting of the personal staff of the president— although of course the structure and functions of the White House staff have altered considerably since the original White House Office was created. The size of the Executive Office staff has remained below 2,000, going above this figure only during the administration of President Nixon.

The White House Office. The staff for the White House is chosen by the president directly. All presidents carry at least some of their campaign staff into the White House, which gives a distinct political cast to the

White House Office. The staff attribute most desired by political candidates is loyalty, and presidents know that in the combative political world of Washington they will need advisers whom they can trust.

In addition to close personal advisers drawn from his election campaign and the past political career of the president, the White House staff consists of a wide range of advisers appointed for their expertise in critical policy areas. Henry Kissinger, for example, was Richard Nixon's national security adviser, and Zbigniew Brzezinski served Jimmy Carter in the same capacity. Kissinger's wit and style made him a world-renowned figure while he was in the White House, sometimes overshadowing Nixon himself, and Nixon eventually appointed him secretary of state. President George Bush also decided to appoint his top foreign-policy expert, James Baker III, to be secretary of state. Baker's strong presidential support lessened the role of the White House staff in foreign policy making. Baker had been Reagan's chief of staff and secretary of the treasury and was regarded as one of the most skillful and powerful persons in the Reagan and Bush administrations.

The structure and operation of the White House staff are entirely up to the president. President Nixon constructed an elaborate "palace guard" with Haldeman and Ehrlichman as his political henchmen guarding the gates of the White House against expected attacks from without and even from within. Nixon believed in managerial government, and the presidential bureaucracy was to be almost a surrogate presidency, holding power over the bureaucracy and above all ensuring political loyalty to the president himself. Nixon soon found that the bureaucracy had a life of its own not amenable to control from the White House, and he even found resistance within agencies of the Executive Office to attempts by the White House staff to dominate them.

The power of the White House staff under Nixon raised questions about the "invisible presidency," as the staff is called, and the appropriate extent of its influence. White House aides often act in the name of the president, making many important decisions on their own. Since the Nixon administration, presidents have tried to keep a tighter rein on their staffs, with varying degrees of success. President Reagan, while always making the important decisions himself, nevertheless at first relied heavily on his "triumvirate"— Michael Deaver, Edwin Meese, and James Baker. Later Reagan got himself into trouble with Congress and the American people in the Iran-Contra affair when, apparently unbeknown to him, his national security adviser, John Poindexter, and Poindexter's assistant, Colonel Oliver North, secretly diverted funds from the sale of arms to Iran to the Nicaraguan Contras in violation of laws Congress had passed expressly to prevent such occurrences.

While most members of the White House staff operate behind the scenes and outside public view, the press secretary (the "flack") stands out. He must each day meet with the press in the West Wing of the White House— unless the president himself has called a press conference, in which case the meeting is in an auditorium in the old Executive Office building. Members of the White House press corps try never to forget that their relationship to government and to the president is supposed to be an adversarial one. During the daily briefings by the press secretary they do their best to embarrass him by probing behind the alleged facade that he presents. News briefings are generally held at 11 a.m. and end around noon, to give the press time to file their stories. The press secretary gives the press the president's schedule for the day and attempts to field questions from the floor (called "the pit" by one former presidential press aide). Lead stories on the front pages of daily newspapers concerning the president's position on important issues of public policy usually come from these press brief-

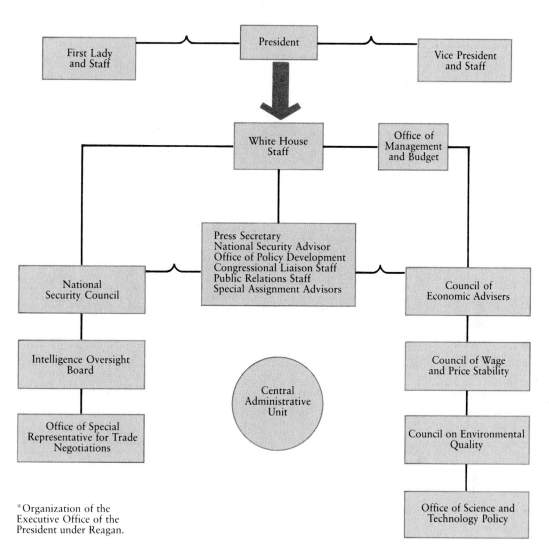

FIGURE 13.1

ings. The press secretary is an important in-formational link between the president and the press and, therefore, between the presi-dent and the public. Presidents are keenly aware of the importance of the press and the media generally, and they usually meet daily with their press secretaries.

Aside from the obvious importance of daily meetings with the press secretary and the national security advisor, the president picks and chooses the persons, places, and times of meetings with individual members of the White House staff. The atmosphere of the presidency is such that, even though the pres-

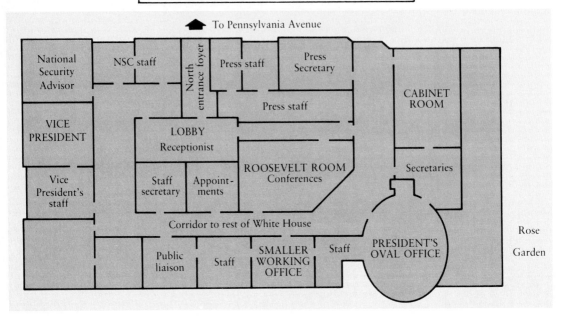

FIGURE 13.2

ident's personal staff is the group closest to him, he cannot and does not bring all its members fully into his confidence. Presidents are particularly anxious to prevent news leaks that may embarrass the administration. The Nixon White House even authorized wiretaps on the telephones of some members of the National Security Council staff who were suspected of providing inside information to the media. More commonly, presidents attempt to prevent news leaks by keeping their inner circles of advisers small.

The tone of staff operations is set by the character and style of the president himself. The staff will go as far as the president allows in exercising power in his name. The problem with the White House Office under Richard Nixon was as much in the character of the man himself as in the attributes and actions of the staff. One of the most important ways in which presidential character affects the staff is in the choice of its members in the

first place. Political staffs always tend to reflect not only the policy orientations of their candidates but, perhaps even more important, their style and approach. The White House staff is the president's most important group of advisers; ensuring that its members act with responsibility does not lie in restructuring the White House Office but in ensuring that the president is himself a person of responsible character. More than any other component of the Executive Office the White House staff is an extension of the personal attributes of the president.

The Office of Management and Budget. Aside from the White House staff, the single most important segment of the Executive Office is the Office of Management and Budget (OMB). Originated by President Nixon in his reorganization of the Executive Office in 1970, OMB replaced the Bureau of the Budget (BOB), which had been created by the Budget and Accounting Act of 1921. Under the terms of the 1921 statute, BOB, then in the Treasury Department, had performed responsibilities designated by Congress at the same time that it had directly served the president. On creation of the Executive Office in 1939, BOB was transferred into that office. By reorganizing BOB into a new Office of Management and Budget, Nixon essentially replaced a statutory agency (BOB) with an agency operating solely under the terms of executive orders (OMB). This gave him (and future presidents) greater control over OMB than he would have had over BOB and was therefore in the spirit of centralizing the presidential bureaucracy under the domination of the White House even more than in prior administrations. According to Nixon, the creation of OMB was an attempt to bring "real business management" into the executive branch.

Although OMB was supposed to be an administrative innovation in the Executive Office, in fact it essentially performs the same functions previously carried out by the Bureau of the Budget. Its principal task is to develop the executive budget, that part of the budget of the United States pertaining to the president, the Executive Office of the President, and all departments and agencies of the executive branch. The executive budget contains expenditure allocations and sources of financ-

ing for federal programs organized by the individual departments and agencies responsible for program implementation. OMB's development of the executive budget is an enormously complicated task, requiring months of work by hundreds of budget "examiners," who work in conjunction with departments and agencies in developing their budgets. No departmental or agency budget can go directly to Congress without first being cleared by OMB. OMB gives the president control over the entire budgetary process of the executive branch and enables him to put his own stamp on executive budgetary proposals presented to Capitol Hill.

OMB's control over the bureaucracy through its power to influence the executive budget is enhanced by its legislative clearance functions, that is, its authority to clear all executive branch legislative proposals before they go to Congress. The administrative branch is a major source of legislative proposals, and even the testimony of administrative officials before congressional committees on legislative matters must first be cleared by OMB.

While OMB is small in size, having less than 500 employees, its potential power is great. However, it cannot exercise arbitrary power over the departments and agencies of

Administrative departments and agencies attempt to persuade the president to increase their budget allocations each year.

the executive branch, which themselves have significant independent political bases of support in their own private constituencies and on Capitol Hill. Moreover, the technical complexities and scope of the executive budget limit the maneuvering ability of budget examiners. And while OMB is supposed to be independent of the regular bureaucracy, on more than one occasion budget examiners have essentially been "co-opted" by the agencies with which they have worked—a natural tendency of persons to become identified with those with whom they are constantly in contact. Instead of being the advocate of the president, under such circumstances OMB examiners may become the advocates of the agencies. The director of OMB, however, stands above the budget examiners and is there to see that the president's interests are protected in the budgetary and legislative clearance processes. Rarely have directors of OMB exercised the power that David Stockman did during the first few years of the Reagan administration. Stockman became the "czar" of Washington, revising the budget on his own terms and, at first, effectively persuading Congress to accept the administration's point of view. Stockman's power began to wane, however, after a widely read *Atlantic Monthly* article by a former editor of the *Washington Post* appeared, revealing that Stockman had secretly questioned the very budget figures he had presented to Capitol Hill in support of his programs.

The National Security Council. The National Security Council (NSC) was first created by the National Security Act in 1947 (the same act that merged the separate armed services into an integrated Defense Department). The NSC coordinates national security policy making within the executive branch. It is made up of the president, the vice-president, the secretary of state, and the secretary of defense. In addition to these ex officio members, council meetings are attended by other officials designated by the president. The president's national security adviser has since the administration of Richard Nixon (in which Henry Kissinger occupied this post and at the same time, during Nixon's second term, was secretary of state) become a key person at meetings of the NSC.

Since its inception the NSC has been a "hybrid" organization, seeking to find its proper place in the presidential bureaucracy. Unlike other agencies in the Executive Office of the President, the NSC has not become an important staff body on a continuous basis, primarily because its membership is ex officio and its permanent staff is small. During foreign affairs and national security crises, such as the Cuban missile crisis in 1962, presidents develop their own ad hoc advisory groups. Such an advisory group may include the members of the NSC, but other trusted advisers of the president are likely to play an even more important role.

The NSC may help to coordinate the actions of governmental departments and agencies in implementing presidential decisions in national security matters, but the same result would be as readily achieved without a formal council. Essentially, the creation of the NSC was a symbolic act clearly making "national security" a major responsibility of the president. By including the secretary of state as a member of the NSC, Congress was sending a message that national security matters were not to be solely under the control of the secretary of defense, or, even more important, of the armed services.

The Council of Economic Advisers. The Council of Economic Advisers (CEA) is composed of three economists appointed by the president with the Senate's approval. The chairmanship of the Council is a position of cabinet-level significance, although not formally a cabinet appointment. Congress has directed the CEA to keep a constant watch on the economy. Under the terms of the Employment Act of 1946, which defined its functions, the Council analyzes the national economy with a view to maintaining an adequate growth rate as well as economic stability. Each year the Council issues an economic report that forms the basis for the president's recommendations to Congress on economic matters. The establishment and continued operations of the Council indicate general acceptance of the belief that the economy can and should be stabilized through timely governmental action.

Other components of the Executive Office. As the Executive Office goes through its numerous metamorphoses, minor agencies come and go, according to the ebb and flow of presidential, congressional, and interest-group concern with the need for White House representation in particular policy spheres. The Office of Science and Technology, eliminated by President Nixon, was restored through pressure from the scientific community during the administration of Gerald Ford. The Council on Environmental Quality in the Executive Office is a reflection of presidential responsibilities in the relatively new area of environmental policy.

Presidents use the Executive Office in different ways, depending upon their styles of operation and the areas they want to stress. President Reagan, for example, relied upon Budget Director David Stockman and the Office of Management and Budget to develop and present to Capitol Hill his key budgetary proposals. Sometimes presidents create ad hoc groups within the Executive Office to deal with particular problems. For example, Jimmy Carter established a Special Executive Office Task Force on Reorganization to revamp the federal bureaucracy. President Reagan appointed his vice-president, George Bush, to head yet another task force to investigate and make recommendations concerning federal regulatory policies with a view to reducing government regulation. President George Bush appointed former Education Secretary William Bennett to be his "drug czar." Both actions kept important policy decisions close

to the president. As presidential administrations mature, inevitably more and more power is assumed by the White House staff, which is always closest to the president. The president's closest aides, with the help of OMB, are the keystone of the Executive Office.

The Cabinet

The presidential cabinet is an informal group of governmental administrators who also serve the president in an advisory capacity. Not mentioned in the Constitution, the cabinet was first formed as a four-member staff by George Washington in 1789 and gradually grew to a thirteen-member body in 1979. All but one of the present 13 members are heads of major executive departments of the federal government; these include the attorney general and the secretaries of state; treasury; defense; interior; agriculture; commerce; labor; health and human services; education; housing and urban development; transportation; and energy. The United States representative to the United Nations also has cabinet status, although he or she does not head a major department. Over the years, as Congress has expanded or consolidated the administrative departments, the size of the cabinet has changed accordingly. For example, Congress created the Department of Energy in 1977 to consolidate major federal energy programs and emphasize their importance. In 1979 a separate Department of Education was created out of the old Department of Health, Education and Welfare (HEW), and HEW was renamed the Department of Health and Human Services.

A president's nomination of cabinet secretaries must be approved by the Senate, which usually results in informal consultation in advance of the nominations between the White House and the chairmen of key Senate committees through which nominations must pass. A number of deliberations must be made by the president before making a cabinet nomination. He considers the opinions of impor-

(By permission OLD *Life*)

The Perfect Cabinet
Although a malleable cabinet of "straw men" might be desirable, it could actually damage the president's image.

tant political party leaders within Congress and in the states. The interests of private groups that come under the jurisdiction of the departments concerned also affect presidential nominations. The availability of capable candidates is another important limitation on the president's choice. In selecting his cabinet, the president must strike a balance among all these considerations. When he retires from office, the cabinet members also tender their resignations. In a few cases cabinet members have served under two presidents. Many members of Kennedy's cabinet, for example, also served Lyndon Johnson. And Henry Kissinger was secretary of state under both President Nixon and President Ford. President Reagan's secretary of state, George Schultz, had long government experience in several

prior administrations. Reagan's secretary of defense, Caspar Weinberger, had been a top official in the Nixon administration, and Bush's secretary of state, James Baker III, had served the Reagan administration.

Cabinet members aid the president in many ways. If they perform outstandingly in their jobs, they enhance the public prestige of the president. As his chief lieutenants in the bureaucracy, they provide him with assistance and advice on matters of general policy affecting their departments. They also help to represent him before Congress, where they often give long hours of testimony in defense of administration positions on controversial matters of public policy. For example, during 1966 and 1967 Dean Rusk spent many grueling hours defending President Johnson's position on Vietnam before the Senate Foreign Relations Committee. Both before and after he became secretary of energy, James Schlesinger was President Carter's key witness on Capitol Hill supporting Carter's energy program in 1977 and 1978. Because President Reagan's major programs primarily involved budgetary cuts, David Stockman, his OMB director, was his principal witness on Capitol Hill in the first year of his administration. Reagan's cabinet, however, was also involved in defending his programs before congressional committees during all hours of testimony, which was often sharply criticized by Democratic legislators. President Bush's budget director, Richard Darman, an experienced Washington hand, became the administration's point man on Capitol Hill as budgetary matters continued to occupy both the president and Congress.

Although the president and his cabinet are usually thought of as a team, cabinet members often act independently on matters concerning their own departments. The president cannot completely control the cabinet because each member is responsible not only to the president but also to the people and groups who provide support for his or her department. According to a contemporary political scientist, Richard C. Fenno, the position of cabinet members presents a paradox. In order for a cabinet member to enhance the image of the president, he needs to develop his own public image and build up his own influence within his department, sources of support within the legislature, and a following within his political party. But as a cabinet member grows in stature, he may find that while he is contributing to the prestige of the president's administration, he is also operating semi-independently—that is, outside the president's direct influence. This usually happens when he responds to political demands that do not originate in the White House. A secretary of agriculture, for example, may respond to constituents of his own department and advocate higher price supports for farmers, whereas the president may be opposed to that policy. Of course, when a cabinet member becomes too independent he or she will be replaced or asked to resign. The pluralism underlying the American democratic system is displayed on all levels, even here in the relationship between president and cabinet.

Cabinet secretaries are important sources of demands upon the president because they represent the views of special constituencies. "Advice" channeled to the White House from cabinet secretaries is anything but independent and unbiased, for it usually reflects the traditional views of their departments, which are self-serving and protecting of their own interests. Thus elevating the cabinet to the top of the advisory hierarchy of the president may make the White House a captive of the regular bureaucracy rather than dominant over it. Presidential attention to cabinet interests will boost the president's influence in the Washington power establishment but limit his policy course to traditional rather than innovative channels.

THE FUTURE OF THE PRESIDENCY

Presidential Weaknesses and Strengths

Any observer of the president cannot help but notice the aging, strain, and fatigue that the person in office often suffers. The responsibilities of the job are awesome. Even with a staff of highly competent assistants, the president is still responsible for most major decisions—some of which may determine the fate of humankind. In time of crisis the president often stands alone, separated from all but his closest advisers. And despite all his power, he is restricted in his actions by many pressures.

The effectiveness of the president's leadership is checked by several factors. First, the separation of powers provided for in the Constitution inhibits his access to congressional centers of power. He cannot always make Congress accept the legislation he wants passed. Second, the size and complexity of the federal bureaucracy also acts as a check on presidential action. The many specialized administrative agencies often operate very independently of him. Third, the undisciplined and fragmented party system in the United States places a check on presidential leadership. He cannot count on the support of his party.

Sometimes the president overcomes these limitations and draws his strength directly from his electoral constituency. Abraham Lincoln resisted the pressures of "radical" Republicans in Congress and went ahead with his plans for Reconstruction. Woodrow Wilson almost succeeded in winning approval of the League of Nations by taking the proposal to the people. Franklin Roosevelt withstood judicial and congressional attacks and took his plan for the New Deal directly to the people in his "fireside chats." President Nixon appealed to the "silent majority" for support of his Vietnam policies, and he appealed to them again for personal support in his efforts to detach himself from Watergate. He also took his economic and energy policies to the people. President Carter reintroduced "fireside chats" after assuming office, and he went over the heads of Congress to the people in appealing for support of his energy program. President Reagan was called "the Great Communicator" during the early years of his administration due to his ability to mobilize popular support for his wide-ranging programs to cut federal taxes and expenditures. Typically, after a Reagan address the switchboards of Capitol Hill were jammed with calls from around the country appealing for congressional support for the president. However, presidential leadership depends upon far more than popular backing. Presidents must be able to coordinate Congress, the bureaucracy, and the special in-

terests of the Capital in a wide array of policy spheres that are largely unaffected by broad public opinion. On the other hand, the president also finds himself in a position of espousing what he considers to be the national interest against the demands of special interests within and outside the government.

The history of the American presidency has seen an ebb and flow of popular support for the institution. Since the nature of the presidency is always shaped by the incumbent, there is never total agreement concerning the role the president plays. During the administration of Franklin Roosevelt, extraordinarily bitter dissension existed among conservative elements that opposed his efforts. Many of these groups felt that Roosevelt was betraying a sacred American trust by expanding government to regulate business. The era of the 1940s and 1950s witnessed general support for the presidency. The classic work of that period on the presidency, Clinton Rossiter's *The American Presidency*, reflected a general reverence for the institution. At the end of his book Rossiter noted:

As I look back through this book, I detect a deep note of satisfaction, although hardly complacency, with the American Presidency as it stands today. A steady theme seems to have run all through this final review of its weaknesses and problems, a theme entitled . . ."leave your Presidency alone!" . . .

It strikes a felicitous balance between power and limitations. . . .

It provides a steady focus of leadership: of administration, Congress, and people. In a constitutional system compounded of diversity and antagonism, the Presidency looms up as the countervailing force of unity and harmony. . . .

It is a priceless symbol of our continuity and destiny as a people . . .

It has been tested sternly in the crucible of time. . . .

It is, finally, an office of freedom. The Presidency is a standing reproach to those petty doctrinaires who insist that executive power is inherently undemocratic; for, to the exact contrary, it has been more responsive to the needs and dreams of giant democracy than any other office or institution in the whole mosaic of American life. It is no less a reproach to those easy generalizers who think that Lord Acton had the very last word on the corrupting effects of power; for, again to the contrary, his doctrine finds small confirmation in the history of the Presidency. The vast power of this office has not been "poison" as Henry Adams wrote in scorn; rather, it has elevated often and corrupted never, chiefly because those who held it recognized the true source of the power and were ennobled by the knowledge.[2]

In the 1960s and 1970s the presidency fell into disrepute among a broad cross-section of the population. Before Watergate, the Vietnam War helped to discredit the institution, particularly among college students. Students of the late 1960s and early 1970s who read Rossiter's book were surprised to find such a sanguine view of the institution.

Arthur Schlesinger, Jr., represented the changing position of many liberals, who had previously supported a powerful presidency. In *The Imperial Presidency* (1973) Schlesinger discussed "the problem of reining in the runaway Presidency."[3] The Watergate crisis clearly brought into question the imperial presidency—the all-powerful presidency so extolled by Clinton Rossiter. President Nixon, according to Schlesinger, carried the concept of presidential autonomy too far. He wished total centralization of power in the White House, often in disregard of express congressional wishes and even court opinions. Nixon claimed executive privilege—that, in effect, he was above the law—in his dealings with Judge John Sirica's court, which conducted a grand jury investigation of the Watergate break-in and trials of Watergate defendants, and in his

dealings with congressional committees investigating the Watergate affair. Both the court and the committees sought to subpoena all White House tape recordings of conversations dealing with Watergate that had taken place between President Nixon and his staff. However, Nixon delivered only some of the tapes, claiming that other requested tapes had been lost or accidentally erased.

President Nixon found in the end that he could not ignore the limitations upon presidential authority established in the Constitution and upheld by the Supreme Court in *United States v. Richard M. Nixon* (1974), which in effect ordered the President to deliver the tapes that had been subpoenaed by Judge Sirica. The Court recognized executive privilege, but felt that Nixon's blanket claim of privilege could not be sustained where national security was not involved and where the information contained on the tapes was possibly essential to a fair verdict in a criminal trial. Soon after the Court's decision Nixon, faced with an almost certain impeachment by the House, resigned.

The Johnson and Nixon presidencies changed, at least for a while, the imperial character of the office. Even before Nixon left office, Congress had passed the War Powers Resolution of 1973, which curtailed the president's authority to commit American troops to foreign wars. A year later, Congress passed the Budget and Impoundment Control Act, which prohibited presidential impoundments without congressional consent. In general, after the Johnson and Nixon years Congress became more alert to its constitutional responsibility to check the president.

The forces that created and sustained the imperial presidency remain and promise once again to make the institution dominant. The presidency is the focus of popular expectations, and the branch of the government most capable of giving it direction. A weakened presidency cannot meet the multiple responsibilities that Congress and the American peo-

---

[2]Clinton Rossiter, *The American Presidency*, 2d ed. (New York: Harcourt Brace Jovanovich, 1960), pp. 258–262.

[3]Arthur M. Schlesinger, Jr., *The Imperial Presidency* (Boston: Houghton Mifflin Company, 1973), p. 392.

ple have placed on the office. That Congress recognizes the importance of presidential leadership was emphasized during the first two years of the Reagan administration when the President and Congress acted together to bring about a sharp change in the course of domestic policy.

Presidents in the future, as in the past, will be expected to lead the nation, particularly during times of crisis. The independent presidency, established by the Constitution, will continue to be the beacon that guides and fulfills the political aspirations of the American people.

CASE STUDY 12

THE PRESIDENT AND THE PRESS

The president's press secretary occupies a delicate position, briefing the often obstreperous White House reporters each day on the president's activities, decisions, and plans. The president's press spokesperson has little, if any, discretion, acting merely as a conduit of information between the Oval Office and the media. However, the press secretary's style reflects and helps to determine the character of the president's relationship with the press. Presidents often attempt to "manage" the press, and, as the following case study illustrates, skillful press secretaries have become increasingly important members of the White House staff.

All the Presidents' Men / *Jonathan Alter*

Press Secretaries: Whose Image Is It, Anyway?
Ron Ziegler arranged a photo opportunity on the beach for Richard Nixon, only to find that the president showed up wearing his black business shoes. Ron Nessen tried to combat Gerald Ford's image as a klutz by avoiding pictures of the president with a Thanksgiving turkey or Mickey Mouse. The image stuck anyway. Jody Powell not only failed to prevent Jimmy Carter from being ridiculed for his encounter in a pond with a giant rabbit, it was Powell who told the press about the peculiar incident in the first place. These stories were told last week at the University of California, San Diego, during an unprecedented gathering of all living former presidential press secretaries, dating back to the Kennedy administration. Were they just the usual self-effacing anecdotes peddled on the seminar circuit? Or might the public have an exaggerated notion of just how important a presidential press secretary really is?

During their days at the podium, these 10 men were often next behind the president and vice president in recognizability. As the meeting (to be televised on PBS later this year) made plain, most are

now far from the spotlight. George Reedy, Lyndon Johnson's first spokesman, is a professor at Marquette University; George Christian, his last press secretary, is a Texas political consultant. Ziegler heads the National Association of Chain Drug Stores. Powell is a public-relations executive for Ogilvy and Mather. Jerald ter Horst, who served briefly under Ford before resigning over the Nixon pardon, now lobbies for the other Ford—the auto company. Speakes, who resigned from Merrill Lynch in 1988 after revealing in his book that he made up a quote he attributed to Ronald Reagan, has returned to Washington seeking PR clients. Only Pierre Salinger of the Kennedy White House and Bill Moyers of the Johnson administration, both broadcasters, have remained visible public figures.

Salinger, Moyers, Ziegler and Powell each had a close relationship with his boss. That made them more than mouthpieces. "You have to know how the watch is built, not just what time it is," said James Brady, who remains disabled from the 1981 attempt on Reagan's life but seemed in good spirits at the meeting. On the other hand, lack of access makes it easier to deny having told lies as press secretary. When a reporter asked in 1983 if Grenada was about to be invaded, an in-the-dark Speakes passed on a lie he heard from John Poindexter, who had told him it was "preposterous." The only one who admitted telling an intentional lie was Powell, who defended having denied plans for an Iran-hostage-rescue mission. The others confessed only to "shading" the truth.

Despite huge growth in both the press corps and the press-office staff, several conference participants defined their old role narrowly. "The press secretary must accurately reflect the president's views. Period," said Nessen. How about the image-making part of the job? That was by and large fobbed off on directors of communication (more accurately described as "directors of propaganda," said Moyers) or denied entirely. "You can make images all the way to California, and it won't matter if Mrs. Murphy's son is coming home in a box," said Reedy. "If the policy is wrong, there's ultimately no way to 'handle' it."

Like the Johnson and Nixon spokesmen, Powell learned that the hard way. He is proof of a press secretary's marginality amid the broader currents of any presidency. White House reporters viewed him as warm, cooperative and authoritative. Yet Carter got an awful press. By contrast, Speakes was viewed as distant, relatively uncooperative and unauthoritative. Yet Reagan was widely viewed as a success at press relations. Powell's explanation last week was that "American journalism punishes that which it most wants: access and openness." But he admitted afterward that even if Carter had run as closed a White House as Reagan, "it wouldn't have helped that much."

Moyers posed a related paradox: "We see more and more of our presidents and know less and less of what they do." Reagan, who held fewer press conferences than any of his modern predecessors, certainly *looked* accessible on TV. But while the White House press corps waited to be spoon-fed instructions on the best "visuals," scandals in housing programs and savings and loan regulation went unreported.

Glamour beat: There was disagreement over who is to blame for the excessive attention devoted to the White House. Reedy cited Franklin Roosevelt's leadership style. John Chancellor, the moderator, traced it back to the talents of the late James Hagerty, Dwight Eisenhower's press secretary. Hagerty understood the advantages of arranging for the president to control the news. But as Nessen told Chancellor, this development also has to do with the demands of television, which places glamour beats like the White House over real digging. "I don't remember you standing in front of the Agriculture Department," he said good-naturedly.

Of course, Nessen, a vice president of Mutual Broadcasting, is on the other side now. No administration really wants reporters snooping through the Agriculture Department or other places they can break new ground; better to have them hanging around the White House briefing room, waiting for handouts. It's this system, rather than any particular handler or press secretary, that conditions and corrodes Washington coverage. That's why it's up to reporters to redefine the concept of news so that it relies more on what they find, and less on what the president—or his press secretary—would have them believe.

CHAPTER FOURTEEN

The Bureaucracy: Organization and Power

The federal bureaucracy is the core of government. Its hundreds upon hundreds of agencies not only implement congressional laws and presidential directives but also act as major forces in shaping presidential decisions and congressional legislation.

The bureaucracy is best known through its major departments—such gigantic organizations as Defense, Labor, Commerce, and Health and Human Services. In addition to departments, powerful agencies, such as the Federal Communications Commission, Securities and Exchange Commission, and Nuclear Regulatory Commission, represent what are commonly called "independent regulatory commissions," that are in many respects formally outside the authority of the president and directly accountable to Congress. Many other bodies, such as the Environmental Protection Agency, are also largely independent.

Every president in the twentieth century has sought as a top priority to reorganize the bureaucracy and place it under the domination of the White House. And every president has failed to achieve this goal. The bureaucracy has become an independent branch in its own right, adding a dimension to the constitutional system of separation of powers and checks and balances that was entirely unforeseen by the Framers of the Constitution. While the president valiantly seeks to control the sprawling maze of administrative agencies, Congress resists presidential encroachments upon the bureaucracy; for on Capitol Hill the bureaucracy is considered to be part of the turf of Congress. The conflict between president and Congress guarantees a semiautonomous administrative branch.

CONSTITUTIONAL CONTEXT

Despite the importance of the bureaucracy today, the Framers included virtually no specific provisions in the Constitution for government administration. However, they did provide a mechanism by which an administrative structure could be created. After listing the powers of Congress, Article I, Section 8, of the Constitution states that the legislature can "make all Laws which shall be necessary and proper for carrying into Execution" the enumerated powers. It is this clause, along with the enumerated powers, that has been used to justify the legislature's creation of the administrative departments and agencies. The bureaucracy, then, is largely an extension of congressional authority.

Attempts to make the bureaucracy fit into the tripartite system of government have still not satisfied some political observers. As the bureaucracy has grown and become increas-

OVERGROWN BUREAUCRACY

(Hess in the *St. Louis Globe-Democrat.*)

The bureaucracy often seems to overshadow the government.

have the sole responsibility for administrative personnel:

The persons . . .to whose immediate management, the different [administrative] matters are committed ought to be considered as the assistants or deputies of the chief magistrate, and on this account, they ought to derive their offices from his appointment, at least from his nomination, and ought to be subject to his superintendence.

Like Hamilton, most of the Framers assumed that the president, as "chief magistrate," would supervise the individuals who would carry out the mandates of Congress. They did not make it clear, however, just where the mandates of Congress ended or where the presidential interpretation and execution of these mandates began.

Although the Constitution is vague about the powers the president can exercise over the bureaucracy, it does, without qualification, grant him the executive power, and Article II gives him the responsibility to "take Care that Laws be faithfully executed." Article II, then, points toward recognizing the president as the head of the government's administrative branch. Since the Constitution does not give the president the tools to control the bureaucracy, those who, like Hamilton, have supported presidential supremacy in this sphere have encouraged Congress to delegate more authority to him for this purpose.

Whatever the Framer's intentions may have been, the fact is that the system they constructed did permit the organization of a bureaucracy that could function independently of the president. Since the *creation* of the bureaucracy is the responsibility of Congress, which by nature competes with the president for power, the legislature has retained control over some elements of the bureaucracy instead of giving control entirely to the president.

The powers of Congress over the bureaucracy. The constitutional powers of Congress

ingly autonomous, it has been difficult to determine how the power of this administrative branch of government can be controlled.

Control of the Bureaucracy

The Constitution was not specific about who was to control the administrative branch. The president and Congress have been engaged in a continuous contest to direct the bureaucracy.

Arguments for presidential control. The intentions of the Framers as well as the language of the Constitution are cited by those who believe that the president should control the bureaucracy. In *The Federalist*, No. 72, Alexander Hamilton regarded administration as involving little more than "executive details," and he thought the president should over the bureaucracy are considerably greater than those of the president. First, Congress has virtually complete authority (should it decide to exercise it) to arrange administrative organization and determine where responsibilities shall be placed. Almost every administrative unit—whether an executive department, such as the Department of Energy, an independent agency, such as the Federal Trade Commission, or a government corporation, such as the Tennessee Valley Authority—is created by an act of Congress. It is Congress that decides whether an agency is to be part of the executive branch or outside it, and it is Congress that may or may not decide to let the president exercise various types of controls. In the case of President Carter's original plan for the Energy Department in 1977, Congress rejected a proposal that would have given the White House veto power over natural gas regulatory decisions of the department. Congress has used this power to create many independent agencies that in varying ways are beyond presidential interference.

Second, not only can Congress formally set up administrative agencies independent of the president and determine their functions and jurisdiction, it can also maintain an agency's independence. The legislature can pass laws that grant additional authority to existing agencies for implementing new programs. Congress has given the president the authority to reorganize agencies, but until recently it retained the veto power over presidential reorganization proposals. In 1983, however, the Supreme Court declared that the congressional veto of actions taken by the executive branch was a violation of the constitutional doctrine of separation of powers.

The legislative branch can also reject certain presidential appointments to the bureaucracy. Cabinet members who head executive departments, for instance, are appointed by the president but cannot take office without "the consent of the Senate." Congress may, of course, grant the president power to appoint officers to any new agencies it creates, but it may set the conditions for such appointments and for the removal of administrative officers by the president as well.

Congress also grants appropriations and is thus potentially able to exercise a great deal of power over the administrative arm. However, it is the president who has the initial say over the nature of the budgets for the various administrative agencies. Usually, appropriations measures are first recommended to Congress by the president and, when passed as amended by Congress, are returned to the chief executive for his approval or veto.

The president does play an important role in determining administrative budgets, but it is still the function of Congress to enact the laws that provide the funds. And although it is usually difficult for Congress to muster the two-thirds majority necessary to override a presidential veto, Congress does have the potential to counter the president in this way.

When the need for a larger bureaucracy developed after 1789, it was inevitable that Congress would resort to whatever constitutional powers it had in order to retain some control over the administrative structure. It has done so in part by creating many agencies in the bureaucracy that are independent of the executive branch and in part by exercising its various powers to influence the activities of all the agencies and departments it has created.

Structure of the Bureaucracy

The federal bureaucracy developed in response to realistic requirements rather than according to any set formula. Because each administrative agency was created to meet specific problems, no two agencies are exactly alike. It is therefore impossible to classify the bureaucracy as a whole according to any definite arrangement of structures or functions.

It is possible, however, to identify the general forms that different agencies have taken. The lack of agreement over who should control the bureaucracy is evident in the present structure of the administrative branch. In keeping with Hamilton's argument for presidential supervision, many government functions are assigned to executive departments whose heads are directly responsible to the chief executive. The independent regulatory commissions, on the other hand, operate outside direct presidential controls even though the president appoints the chairmen of most of these agencies and fills other vacancies whenever they occur. In addition, there are other *independent agencies,* such as the National Science Foundation and the National Aeronautics and Space Administration (NASA), that function outside the executive departments but that may or may not be subject to the president's supervision—depending on how they have been set up by Congress. *Government corporations* are yet another type of administrative unit; most of these operate as independent entities, whereas others are within the jurisdiction of executive departments.

Just as the requirements and priorities of public policy are always changing, the form of an administrative agency that performs a particular governmental function may be changed if there is sufficient need and demand. The history of the government's postal service illustrates this. Originally administered as a service outside direct executive supervision, the postal system has been reorganized twice: first into an executive department in 1872, and then as an independent agency almost a century later. But although the various subsystems of the bureaucracy are always potentially subject to reorganization, they generally take one of the forms described above.

POLICY MAKING THROUGH THE BUREAUCRACY

Administrative departments and agencies stand at the very center of the policy-making process. To say that administrators only implement public policy is a vast oversimplification. For in fact agencies have been delegated by Congress important authority to promulgate rules and regulations that are tantamount to legislation, to enforce those rules, and to adjudicate cases and controversies that arise within their jurisdiction. Each agency stands at the beginning, middle, and end of the policy-making process. Administrators help to write congressional bills, advise the president, fill in the details of vaguely worded legislation, implement laws (including their own rules), and determine through adjudication the rights and obligations of private parties under the law. Agency decisions may be subject to judicial review, but it is the agencies themselves that are the predominant implementing and adjudicating bodies in most spheres of public policy.

The fact that agencies exercise all three functions of government—executive, legislative, and judicial—makes them uniquely important in the political process. They do not exercise these functions because they have usurped them from the other branches but because they have explicitly been given the authority to do so by Congress or, as is less often the case, through delegated power by the president. Congress has provided that within each agency there must be a separation of legislative and judicial functions in order to conform broadly with constitutional norms and with traditional Anglo-American legal precepts of justice.

Regardless of which functions are exercised by administrators, they always find themselves in a highly political milieu. Administrators at the upper echelon of the bureaucracy must constantly be in touch with the chairmen of committees on Capitol Hill that exercise jurisdiction over their agencies; with other parts of the bureaucracy with which they frequently share responsibilities; with the White House, which may or may not wish to involve itself directly in agency activities; and with private pressure groups affected by agency power.

The Political Context of the Bureaucracy

Governmental bodies and private pressure groups always seek to use administrative agencies for their own purposes. Not infrequently, agencies are caught in a schizophrenic atmosphere of conflicting demands from governmental and private constituents. It is the political nature of the bureaucracy that draws it into the arena of political conflict. The president and Congress in particular look at the bureaucracy as their own. As administrators are caught in the cross fire of conflicting pressures, they seek safety by attempting to steer a course of action that will maximize their political support and minimize opposition. The degree to which the other branches of the government or private pressure groups can control administrative action depends largely upon their importance as constituents of the agencies.

Presidential influences. All modern presidents have agreed with Alexander Hamilton that they and they alone should control the executive branch, which to them means all of the regular bureaucracy. And every American president in the twentieth century has taken office pledging to reorganize the federal bureaucracy. But each has confronted the reality of agency power, based upon close links with Capitol Hill and private interests, and has had to settle for less than he wanted. The bureaucracy is interwoven with the Washington power structure, limiting not only presidential reorganization efforts but also general White House influence over the executive branch.

Regardless of the power realities that surround the bureaucracy, presidents continue to consider one of their major responsibilities to be that of "chief administrator." Presidents recognize that they need the cooperation of the administrative branch to develop and carry out their programs, as well as to provide support for the White House on Capitol Hill. Presidents know that in the long run the support of the bureaucracy is more important for getting things done in Washington than is public opinion.

The scope of the president's program sets the boundaries within which the White House tries to influence the bureaucracy. Relative to the vast number of programs carried out by the administrative branch, the number of programs proposed by the president is always small. This fact curbs presidential control over all aspects of administrative activity.

In addition to having the Office of Management and Budget (OMB) oversee the development of the executive budget and act as a clearing agency for all of the legislative proposals of administrative agencies, the president seeks to influence the bureaucracy through his appointments. Under his direct control are several thousand top-level jobs. (The exact number of patronage appointments has never been determined.) If the president and his advisers cannot directly oversee the far-flung bureaucracy, White House appointments of persons supporting the president may help to fill an important gap in direct presidential power over the administrative branch.

The use of presidential appointments to control the bureaucracy never fully succeeds, however, because the scope of these appointments is limited and, more important, because appointees more often than not are co-opted by the agencies and then take up the cudgels for the agencies' point of view in any direct conflict with the president. Moreover, appointments in the first place usually are cleared with vested congressional, administrative, and private interests, so that the persons appointed are acceptable not only to the presidential constituency but to the separate administrative constituencies as well.

The limits upon the effectiveness of presidential appointment powers in controlling the bureaucracy are seen at the highest levels in cabinet appointments. Although at first the cabinet may be part of the president's team, once cabinet secretaries are on the job they usually change sides and represent the interests of their departments.

The independent regulatory commissions constitute one major area open to presidential appointment, but the possibilities are limited by the staggered terms Congress has set for these positions, which do not simultaneously expire when a president assumes office. That is, on an agency such as the Federal Communications Commission or the

(Drawing by Stevenson; © 1982 The New Yorker Magazine, Inc.)

"It's the never-ending struggle between the State Department and the Department of Defense."
Executive departments battle each other to gain congressional support.

Federal Trade Commission, a new president may be able to appoint only one or two persons, if that, although he can designate who among those on the commission is to be the chairman. Regulatory agencies, like cabinet departments, are sensitive to private and congressional interests, and appointments to them may reflect the president's point of view even less than cabinet appointments.

While the president's appointment power is politically limited and often subject to Senate confirmation, it remains his most important tool to control the bureaucracy. Senatorial approval is more often than not a mere formality, for only under the most unusual circumstances, such as revelations that a nominee has conflicts of interest or is clearly incompetent, does the Senate turn down an appointment. Presidents name the heads of almost all independent agencies, and presidents, whether Republican or Democratic, make certain that their appointments reflect their strongly held views on the bureaucracy's proper mission. Republicans, such as Richard Nixon and Ronald Reagan, sought to cripple the bureaucracy through their appointments, while Democratic presidents generally appoint individuals who support an active and interventionist bureaucratic role.

The merit system. In addition to the political limits upon the presidential appointment power, there are statutory limits in the form of the merit system that prevails in the civil service. Civil service employees are not subject to direct presidential removal. Prior to the establishment of the Civil Service Commission in 1883, the selection of personnel for all administrative positions in government had been the reward, or *spoils*, of the victorious presidential candidate and his party. The president gave jobs to his friends and supporters, and the staffs of the various agencies changed every time the party of the White House occupant changed.

Demands for the creation of a civil service became particularly intense in 1881 after President James A. Garfield was assassinated by a man who had been turned down for a government job. Two years later Congress passed the Civil Service Act, also known as the Pendleton Act. This law set up the United States Civil Service Commission, which fixes standards for the recruitment of government employees, classifies personnel according to job categories, and oversees the competitive examinations given for various jobs. The establishment of the commission eliminated the spoils system and gave continuity and permanence to most of the bureaucracy. Employees covered by civil service regulations now retain their jobs from one presidential administration to the next. The Civil Service Commission was replaced by the Office of Personnel Management in 1977, and a separate board was created to hear appeals of civil servants who had been dismissed. The purpose of this reorganization was to separate the administrative and adjudicative functions that had formerly been combined in the Civil Service Commission. The reorganization did little to change the operation of the Civil Service System as a whole.

With the growth of the bureaucracy, federal administrative employees, except for top-ranking policy-making officials such as cabinet members, have gradually become members of the civil service. In 1983 there were nearly 3 million federal employees. The greatest concentration (about 250,000) of these employees work in the District of Columbia. The remaining federal bureaucrats are scattered throughout the 50 states or serve abroad in U.S. embassies and consulates or as civilian employees on American military bases or where economic aid programs are being carried out.

Congressional influences. The president's power over the bureaucracy is shared by Congress. Acting on the basis of its enumerated and implied powers, Congress establishes and maintains the agencies, and its authority to appropriate money is particularly

CIVIL
SERVICE

→

RE-
ORGAN-
IZATION

The Boston Globe

(Reprinted courtesy of *The Boston Globe*.)

"Go through this door, take a left, then a right, then a left, a right, a left, another left, a right. . . ."
President Carter proposed a reorganization of the civil service system to eliminate cumbersome and time-consuming procedures for the hiring and dismissal of civil servants.

important. In addition, just as Congress creates the agencies and determines how they operate, it can also alter the functions of an agency at any time by passing a law that increases or decreases the agency's independence and authority. This is probably the single most powerful stick it holds over the bureaucracy.

The administrative agencies maintain the support they need from Congress by providing Congress with information and by putting congressional policy into action. The major congressional demands on an agency come from the standing committees that determine the agency's policies and funds. Often administrative decisions are made in response to the outcomes of congressional committee hearings as well as to the demands of particularly powerful individual senators and representatives. Bills that eventually become law are formulated by these committees and are the basis of an agency's regulations and powers.

There are over 130 committees and subcommittees in the Senate, and almost 200 in the House, and most of them are tied in one way or another to different agencies in the administrative branch. Committee and especially subcommittee chairmen and their staffs seek to maintain political support within and without Congress in order to enhance their power. Agencies under the jurisdiction of these committees are considered major sources of political support, and therefore the relationship between Congress and the bureaucracy is unlike that which frequently prevails between the president and the administrative branch. While individual members of Congress may, for rhetorical and reelection purposes, attack agencies they consider vulnerable to adverse publicity, the underlying power structure of Capitol Hill backs the agencies to the hilt. The relationship between Congress and the bureaucracy, then, is not one of antagonism but of cooperation and even collusion, often in opposition to the White House. For example, presidential plans to cut defense expenditures invariably meet strong opposition from the Defense Department, the armed services committees, and the defense appropriations subcommittees. Many presidential reorganization plans meet strong Capitol Hill opposition, as President Reagan discovered when he proposed the abolition of the Departments of Education and Energy.

The relationship between agencies and congressional committees is usually informal. Staff members are sometimes exchanged between the agencies and committees, and in some cases there is continuous consultation between bureaucrats and congressional staffs. Committee chairmen who have been in office for some time usually develop informal working relationships with the administrators who report to their committees. Moreover, individ-

(©1974. Reprinted with special permission of King Features Syndicate, Inc.)

"Pointing the way to school integration . . ."
An agency must balance its independent action against guidelines imposed by the other branches of government.

ual members of Congress, acting as spokesmen for their constituents, raise a number of grievances before the agencies. In general there are a great variety of ways in which Congress communicates with bureaucratic officials and conducts its affairs with the administrative agencies.

Judicial influences. The bureaucracy's primary legal responsibilities have been stipulated in congressional statutes. Agency action must take place within the boundaries of authority established by Congress. Moreover, agency procedures cannot violate the basic constitutional safeguards found in the Bill of Rights.

By interpreting the laws under which the bureaucracy operates, the courts set limits on administrative authority. Upon review of an agency's decision, the courts may overrule the agency, denying that it acted according to the authority given it by Congress. Each time a court upholds or denies an agency's action, the agency is bound by this decision in similar cases in the future.

The courts themselves, however, are limited by the judicial process. The courts cannot initiate a case against an administrative agency but must wait until such a case is presented by outside parties.

The influence of other administrative agencies. Administrative agencies also influence each other, especially when they have related policy responsibilities. Several regulatory commissions, such as the Federal Communications Commission, the Interstate Commerce Commission, and the Securities and Exchange Commission, have jurisdiction over mergers of industries under their supervision. Because the Antitrust Division of the Justice Department also has responsibility for enforcing the antitrust laws in all areas, it may challenge the decision of a regulatory commission if it feels that the commission is not upholding antitrust statutes. But the regulatory agencies make the final judgment on a merger application, subject to judicial review.

The jurisdiction of the Environmental Protection Agency cuts across the jurisdictional lines of many other agencies. For example, the Occupational Safety and Health Administration claims jurisdiction over the regulation of noise in working places, but EPA has also staked out a claim in this area and the two agencies have fought bitterly over what standards should be adopted. The Federal Aviation Agency and the EPA disagree over the permissible noise levels for airports, with FAA claiming primary jurisdiction and the EPA arguing that it too has authority over airport noise. The confusions in the jurisdictions of agencies stem from the lack of clear delineation of administrative authority in statutes, and it is not uncommon in the fragmented structure of Congress for laws to be passed

delegating similar authority to more than one agency.

Standing above the regular bureaucracy is the Office of Management and Budget (OMB), whose demands and supports upon regular administrative agencies determine the parameters of their budgets and the substance of their legislative initiatives. While OMB represents the president, it is an important power in its own right, not only helping to shape presidential programs in the first place but also striking out on its own in that vast area where presidential programs do not exist. At the same time that OMB places limits upon the bureaucracy, it also is an important source of support in the constituencies of many administrative agencies.

Beyond OMB and other parts of the Executive Office of the President that oversee the bureaucracy, the General Services Administration (GSA) within the bureaucracy has an impact on the lives of civil servants that is scarcely noticed outside government. GSA controls the physical facilities within which the bureaucracy works, and although this does not have a policy impact upon the general public, it helps to shape an important attribute of the internal power structure of the bureaucracy—the perquisites of office in terms of space, furnishings, location, lighting, windows, and a host of other internal matters, including the types of cars in the motor pools of the agencies. (As anyone familiar with organizational politics knows, fights over office space and other physical aspects of the work environment are often considered more important than external organizational policies and operations.)

The influence of private pressure groups. Groups that fall under the jurisdiction of an administrative agency continuously make demands, both direct and indirect, for policies favorable to their own interests. *Direct* demands are expressed to administrators themselves by the spokespersons of interest groups. The demands are then reflected in agency policies and in agency advocacy of group interests before Congress. Most cabinet departments, such as Agriculture, Labor, Commerce, Health and Human Services, Transportation, and Housing and Urban Development, were created to represent a special private-sector clientele. Each of these departments tends to become an advocate for the special interests under its jurisdiction. The Defense Department, too, although not established to represent a particular clientele, has become a powerful representative of the armaments industry as part of what is known as the "military-industrial complex." Outside the major departments, many regulatory agencies, such as the Interstate Commerce Commission, National Labor Relations Board, and the Federal Communications Commis-

sion, have often seemed to act as the "captives" of the groups they regulate.

Pressure groups make demands on the bureaucracy *indirectly* whenever they bring pressure on other branches of government. When representatives of the armaments industries try to influence legislators or the president to adopt a particular weapons system, their demands indirectly affect the Defense Department and other agencies responsible for administering such programs. Private interests frequently challenge administrative decisions in court. Pressure groups also make indirect demands by attempting to influence public opinion.

Interest groups consider administrative agencies to be their representatives in government, just as they look to Congress for rep-

(Drawing by Wm. Hamilton; © 1968 The New Yorker Magazine, Inc.)

"Just because you and I don't like the interest-rate ceilings, we don't go storming the Treasury Building, do we?"
The accessibility of an agency to a particular group may determine how the group will express its demands.

resentation. Congressional committees, administrative agencies, and private groups are often linked together in different policy spheres to form "iron triangles" of power and interests.

Legislative Functions of the Bureaucracy

It is a fundamental principle of republican government that laws are to be made by a legislature, with the members elected by the people. The delegation of legislative authority by an elected legislature to other parts of the government would seem contrary to this principle. Yet as the activities of the American federal government have expanded, Congress has delegated substantial legislative authority to the bureaucracy, and the constitutionality of this process has been upheld by the Supreme Court.

The need to delegate legislative authority. It would seem contradictory that Congress should delegate its own authority to administrative agencies when it should be jealously guarding its prerogative to make laws. Yet in fact Congress is unable to determine the content of legislation on numerous subjects because it does not have sufficient knowledge. And very often members of Congress omit certain details from legislation in order to avoid taking a positive stand on a controversial issue. For both reasons, Congress often passes laws so vague that the bureaucracy must "fill in" many of the details to make the legislation workable. The decisions that the agencies make in such instances are by their nature quasi-legislative. Although not made through the regular lawmaking process, they are as enforceable as laws passed by Congress.

A perusal of congressional statutes would reveal that extraordinary delegations of legislative authority have been granted to some administrative agencies and their various divisions. The regulatory commissions, for

(Drawing by Alan Dunn; © 1968 The New Yorker Magazine, Inc.)

"Isn't it about time we issued some new guidelines for something?"
For technical and political reasons, many legislative functions are delegated by Congress to the bureaucracy.

example, are given blanket authority to make rules that are in the "public interest, convenience, and necessity." The commissions must determine what is in "the public interest" and act according to their own formulas whenever they implement new legislation.

Various divisions of the Department of Defense have also been given broad grants of authority. It is impossible for Congress to give concise guidelines to the military departments on all the technical details involved in maintaining adequate defense. Instead, Congress passes laws that state a general purpose with general guidelines, thus granting broad decision-making authority to those who have specialized military knowledge. For example, Congress has authorized the secretary of the army to:

. . .procure materials and facilities necessary to maintain and support the Army, its military organizations, and their installations and supporting and auxiliary elements, including:

(1) guided missiles;
(2) modern standard items of equipment;
(3) equipment to replace obsolete or unserviceable equipment;
(4) necessary spare equipment, materials, and parts; and
(5) such reserve supplies as is needed to enable the Army to perform its mission.[1]

On the basis of such a statute, the secretary of the army has considerable latitude for determining what missiles, equipment, and other supplies are "necessary to maintain and support" the army's operation.

In some instances Congress does pass statutes with more specific standards for administrative guidance. But these standards tend to be procedural—that is, they prescribe the *method* to be used by an agency for implementing a policy but not the details of *what* should be implemented.

Judicial Standards Governing the Delegation of Legislative Power

Since the early nineteenth century the Supreme Court has upheld the right of Congress to delegate some legislative power to the president and the bureaucracy. In a series of cases, the Court has developed the doctrine that Congress may delegate quasi-legislative authority to the agencies if, in making such delegations, Congress clearly states its intent. Furthermore, in stating its intent, Congress must establish the limitations of administrative authority.

Establishing congressional intent. The Court has realized that Congress cannot make every specific rule to be executed by the bureaucracy and thus as a practical necessity must delegate some of its authority. Theoretically, in granting such authority to the president or to administrators, Congress merely permits others to do what it would do itself if it could.

The concept of *congressional intent* has been important whenever a delegation of legislative power has been challenged in the courts. In 1922, for example, Congress passed a law permitting the president, after proper investigations by the United States Tariff Commission, to change tariffs when necessary to establish equal competition between the foreign and domestic producers of certain goods. The Constitution, however, grants Congress alone the power to set tariffs (a lawmaking function), and the law was challenged as an unconstitutional delegation of legislative power. Since the intent of Congress to permit equal competition between domestic and foreign producers was clearly stated in the law, however, the Court upheld the Tariff Act, noting that "if Congress shall lay down by legislative act an intelligible principle to which the pers n or body authorized . . .is directed to contorm, such legislative action is not a forbidden delegation of legislative power."[2]

Limitations on the agencies. Although Congress can delegate legislative authority to administrative agencies, it cannot empower agencies to do what would be unconstitutional for Congress itself to do. And just as the bureaucracy must conform to the limits of the Constitution when it exercises legislative functions, it cannot perform such functions at all except as prescribed by specific laws of Congress.

When an administrative action is challenged, the courts must determine whether the administrative agency in question has acted according to standards set by Congress. A judicial determination that an agency has acted outside of its authority is known as a determination of *ultra vires* (beyond legal power) action. Yet in order to establish that an *ultra vires* action has been committed, the courts must be able to refer to a statute that clearly indicates the limits of the agency's authority.

---

[1] 10 U.S.C. 4531; 70A Stat. 253 (1956).

[2] *J. W. Hampton, Jr. & Co. v. United States,* 276 U.S. 394 (1928).

One of the few instances in which the Supreme Court has held a delegation of legislative authority to be unconstitutional involved the failure of Congress to set such limits. The decision concerned provisions of the National Industrial Recovery Act, which Congress had passed in 1933 to deal with the economic depression. Under the act a National Recovery Administration (NRA) was set up to assist in the improvement of business and working conditions by enforcing "codes of fair competition." Under the act the codes were drawn up by representatives of various industries and became enforceable when approved by the president. The president was also authorized to impose codes on industries that failed to develop codes of their own.

When the Schechter Poultry Corporation of New York City was convicted by a federal court of violating the Live Poultry Code, the case was appealed to the Supreme Court. The Court determined that the codes were unconstitutional because they set up regulations for intrastate businesses and thus exceeded the national government's legal power to regulate only interstate commerce. The Court argued further that the act was an improper delegation of legislative power because it failed to prescribe limits to the president's authority.

Without such restrictions, the president could approve and disapprove codes completely at his own discretion and not according to any purpose intended by Congress. The Court's decision therefore narrowed its previous doctrine on the delegation of legislative power.

We have repeatedly recognized the necessity of adapting legislation to complex conditions involving a host of details with which the national Legislature cannot deal directly. . . .[T]he Recovery Act . . .sets up no standards, aside from the statement of general aims of rehabilitation, correction and expansion. . . .In view of the scope of that broad declaration, and of the nature of the few restrictions that are imposed, the discretion of the President . . .is virtually unfettered. We think that the code-making authority thus conferred is an unconstitutional delegation of legislative power. . . .[3]

Judicial flexibility. In the *Schechter* case the Supreme Court refined the doctrine of delegation of legislative authority by insisting that Congress define the limits of such a delegation to clarify its intent. Yet even during the New Deal era the Court cited other examples of vague delegations of legislative authority that were not declared unconstitutional. Since 1935 no congressional statutes have been declared to be in violation of the doctrine stated in the *Schechter* case, and the Court has always been able to find some provisions within a statute to determine the proper limits for the agency being challenged.

This does not mean that Congress always includes clearly defined restrictions on agencies when it delegates legislative authority. It seems rather that for the most part the Court has been able to rationalize congressional delegations of authority according to the needs of government. Thus during World War II, when Congress gave the Office of Price Administration almost complete discretion to set price ceilings and gave the heads of executive departments discretion to collect "excess profits" from contractors, these delegations of power were upheld in two separate challenges before the Court.

With the help of the Court's flexibility, Congress has been able to grant broad decision-making powers to the bureaucracy. The indefinite language of congressional statutes enables administrators to use considerable discretion in interpreting the intent of Congress and in setting the standards that their agencies enforce. Thus the secretary of transportation is authorized to set "reasonable, practicable, and appropriate" safety standards for motor vehicles. No doubt the secretary will have to interpret congressional intent in the light of pressures being exerted

---

[3]*Schechter Poultry Corp. v. United States,* 295 U.S. 495 (1935).

by the automobile industry. The Transportation Department—on the basis of its own determination of what is "reasonable, practicable, and appropriate"—will then issue standards that have the force of law.

Judicial and Executive Functions of the Bureaucracy

Once an agency has set standards to implement government policy, that agency usually has the responsibility of ensuring that its standards are applied and enforced. Frequently, however, questions arise as to how such standards should be applied in specific situations. The decisions necessary to settle such matters are usually made not by the courts but by the agency concerned. Such decisions are quasi-judicial because, whereas they concern specific cases and controversies and are thus judicial in nature, they are determined outside the formal judicial system.

Like legislative authority, the authority to make quasi-judicial decisions is delegated to the bureaucracy by Congress. The Constitution has placed the judicial power of the federal government in the Supreme Court and in whatever lower courts Congress chooses to create. The Supreme Court has interpreted this provision along with the implied powers of Congress as upholding the delegation of judicial authority to regulatory commissions and other agencies.

Limitations of the courts. The need for giving judicial functions to the bureaucracy is partly due to the limitations of the formal judicial system. The federal courts cannot initiate cases to force compliance with public policy because Article III of the Constitution requires that decisions of the judiciary be limited to matters brought to it. In addition the courts themselves have established rules that prevent them from making decisions on broad public policy.

The administrative agencies, on the other hand, can affect public policy directly. Thus they can initiate cases that arise from their own rules and regulations, and they can enforce the policy decisions that result from the cases they initiate.

Types of administrative judgments. Administrative agencies make different kinds of quasi-judicial decisions concerning private parties. Some administrative judgments are made to resolve controversies between private parties and an agency; other judgments are made to determine how agency policy and rules should be applied to particular individuals.

Controversies arise when an agency issues a complaint against a private party. For example, when the Internal Revenue Service (IRS) challenges a person's income tax return or when the Environmental Protection Agency charges a manufacturer with violating standards of water-pollution control, a controversy arises between the government and a specific individual or company. Usually, the same governmental agency involved in such a controversy also has the judicial authority to make a judgment settling the matter.

Agencies also make quasi-judicial decisions whenever they review applications from individuals or companies to do certain things. If a trucking company, for example, applied to the Interstate Commerce Commission (ICC) for permission to increase freight rates, the commission's judgment in the matter would be a quasi-judicial decision. Similarly, Veterans Affairs makes a judicial-type decision whenever it determines whether a particular applicant qualifies for certain benefits.

Administrative proceedings. Administrative agencies make judgments in two ways. They can come to judicial decisions informally, or they can go through formal procedures. *Informal proceedings* are highly flexible and do not follow any set procedures, whereas *formal hearings* follow many of the same procedures that are used by the courts. Almost all agencies conduct informal proceedings in an attempt to settle cases before they reach a formal stage of administrative decision.

The IRS affords a good example of how both informal and formal judgments are made. When the IRS questions an individual's income tax payment, there is a controversy between the individual and the government, and a judgment must be made. A revenue agent first meets informally with the individual to try to settle the matter. If the taxpayer is found to have been in error on his or her payments, the taxpayer usually agrees to pay the additional amount due plus an interest charge. If the IRS is found to have misjudged the individual, the matter is normally dropped.

If the matter is not settled informally, however, it may eventually reach the Tax Court. The taxpayer then becomes a defendant, must hire a lawyer, is confronted by the IRS acting as a prosecutor, and will be either convicted or acquitted.

(Drawing by Dana Fradon; © 1973 The New Yorker Magazine, Inc.)

"You'll be happy to know that nobody in government is out to get you, nobody's reported you for the finder's fee, nor have we received any anonymous tips. You're here only because we think you've been cheating on your return."

Fear of governmental reprisal often encourages individuals to settle their cases informally.

Formal hearings are usually far too time-consuming and expensive for both the agency and the individual involved. In addition, fear of governmental reprisal causes most individuals to settle informally. Informal settlements can be just as trying, however, because individuals and groups have to undergo the pressures of administrative investigation and prosecution.

Restrictions on agency actions. Administrative agencies do not have complete control over the judicial actions they take. Congressional statutes often require the agencies to hold hearings, report findings of fact, and base decisions on the records of the proceedings. Moreover, since the courts have the power of judicial review over agency decisions, they do at times require the agencies to adhere to procedures that are considered fair to all the parties involved in the proceedings. Still, the agencies do have considerable independence in determining the judicial-type procedures that they use. It is impossible for Congress, once it delegates judicial authority to the agencies, to exercise continuous supervision over their activities.

The broad judicial discretion of administrative agencies, however, has provoked some attempt to curb administrative power. For example, recommendations have been made in Congress that judicial review be expanded to permit the courts to examine agency decisions more closely. In addition laws have been proposed requiring agencies to observe legal procedures similar to those used by courts of law. In 1946 Congress passed the Administrative Procedure Act to standardize the judicial-type proceedings in various agencies so that they would more closely conform to court standards of due process of law. The act also set up a separate and independent class of hearing officers (now called administrative law judges) who listen to cases so that the same officer cannot act as both prosecutor and judge on a single matter. The Administrative Procedure Act expanded access to the courts on the part of those harmed by administrative ac-

tion and required courts to examine the administrative records more closely upon review than they had done prior to passage of the act.

Executive functions. All the functions performed by the bureaucracy outside the legislative and judicial functions are "executive." The vast programs administered by such agencies as the Departments of Agriculture, Interior, and Defense are implemented largely through the exercise of executive functions— that is, functions that do not involve general policy making or the disposition of specific cases and controversies.

New Trends in the Federal Bureaucracy

Franklin D. Roosevelt's New Deal in the 1930s marked a turning point in government as a federal service, and regulatory programs expanded along with the federal bureaucracy. The executive branch became dominant, sometimes even over the presidency itself. Lyndon B. Johnson's Great Society in the 1960s marked the height of executive *branch* power, although the presidency itself peaked in power in the Nixon administration.

Ronald Reagan's administration, like the New Deal, was a turning point at least in the short term in the role of the bureaucracy. Reagan's conservative philosophy supported a reduction in government expenditures and services, and Reagan continued the trend that began in the 1970s toward deregulation of the economy. The Reagan White House consciously set out to reduce the role and powers of the federal bureaucracy, with the exception of the Defense Department. President George Bush, although less emphatic than his predecessor, continued to stress the importance of a reduction in federal expenditures and programs, which meant less emphasis upon the important role of the federal bureaucracy in government.

The conservative philosophies of the Reagan and Bush administrations, however, inevitably confronted the reality of administrative power that is based not upon theory but upon strong and continued political support from a variety of special interests and clientele groups. Political demands had created the bureaucracy, and administrative constituencies continued to buttress bureaucratic power as the government entered the decade of the 1990s. The only major change, supported by both liberals and conservatives, was deregulation of the economy, which meant that many regulatory agencies vanished or had their powers severely curtailed.

ADMINISTRATIVE DECISION MAKING

The bureaucracy is central to the policy-making process of most governments. In many cases bureaucrats today must make decisions that formerly were made by legislators, judges, and even chief executives. Elected officials, in turn, constantly must respond to administrative initiatives and decisions.

Administrators live within a complicated political environment. They have many constituencies, including the president, the congressional committees that oversee their operations and dictate their initial policy authority, and the special interests and the segments of the public within their jurisdiction. The authors of the following case study give a fascinating inside account of the world of the bureaucracy from the viewpoint of the agency heads.

So You Want to Run an Agency / *Donald J. Devine and Jim Burnley*

The Character of Political Management

Among the most important decisions a president-elect makes are the ones that will visit him frequently in the Cabinet Room and the Oval Office: his appointments of agency heads. If the president-elect makes the right appointments, he will maximize his chances for success. If he puts the wrong person in charge of an agency, he and his White House staff will waste valuable time dealing with problems that flow from that mistake.

Most presidents-elect spend very little time making these threshold decisions. Suddenly immersed in the ceremonial and policy aspects of the office, and eager to "hit the ground running" after the long ordeal of a presidential campaign, they seldom devote adequate attention to this most fundamental of leadership tasks: choosing a team. The president's personnel choices are far more important than any comparable decisions in the private sector. The federal government is so large and complex that the chief executive must rely upon the judgment of scores of subordinates for the overwhelming number of decisions made during his tenure.

Character, Loyalty, and Competence

In considering candidates for executive departments and agencies, the president-elect need look for only three characteristics and rank them in the proper order. First, does the individual have the character, toughness, and reliability to handle this difficult assignment? The dean of presidential advisers, the late Bryce Harlow, has said that character ranks "number one to ten" in choosing a political leader. Nothing is more important, for the person will be tested, and tested again and again in Washington's trench warfare.

The second question the president should ask is, Will this individual be loyal to me and my agenda? It is impossible for the president to specify the detailed agenda for all of the complex issues in the national government. For this he must delegate responsibility to his top appointees and rely on their judgment. Even the Reagan administration—which, as David Broder correctly noted, came to office with a more complete agenda than any he had seen in his time covering Washington—set the specific agenda for relatively few policies. Loyalty is the cement that binds a team. In mak-

Source: Reprinted from the Winter 1989 issue of *Policy Review*, a publication of The Heritage Foundation, 214 Massachusetts Avenue, NE, Washington, D.C. 20002.

ing his selection, the president should examine whether the appointee knows what the president has said he wants; whether the applicant for agency head has, in general, agreed with the president's positions in the past, and whether he has a reputation for sticking by his friends.

Third, the president must ask whether the individual has the proper mix of leadership ability, management skills, and program knowledge. He must guard against falling into the trap of appointing someone who has gained program knowledge by spending many years in an industry or field with which the agency has a close relationship. Often such people are the worst appointees because they cannot subordinate loyalty to a special interest group to the loyalty they owe the president. The selection should not be based primarily on technical qualifications, but rather on who is the most qualified of those who meet the first two criteria, character and loyalty.

If the president takes the time to find the answers to these three questions for his top appointees, he will have laid the foundation on which to build a successful administration.

Know Thy Agenda

Being the head of a federal agency is among the world's toughest jobs. Presidents may have "Teflon coatings," but the "grease" will stick to the agency head who does his job. This is inevitable, since a significant part of his job is to deflect the heat from the president. And the heat will come. While the president can play the lion, the agency head must be the fox: He must not only know how to avoid trouble, but also when to confront it in order to persevere.

To perform properly as a presidential appointee, the agency head must know the president's agenda. He must study the president's speeches and writings, the party platform, and the campaign promises. This is time-consuming, but it is impossible to follow the agenda when one does not know it. Attempts will be made to foist other agendas upon the agency head—his agency's institutional prejudices, what the congressional overseers want, what the interest groups desire, what "enlightened opinion" as shaped and interpreted by the media requires. The president's agenda should always be kept in the forefront and other agendas looked upon as distractions and obstacles, never as sub-

stitutes. Then, as the agency head is buffeted by his environment, he will have the knowledge necessary to keep score. He must keep uppermost in mind: What percentage of the president's agenda have I achieved, or have I set in motion? This is the standard by which the agency head should measure his success in this once-in-a-lifetime opportunity to make a difference.

White House Clerks

The first institution that will test the agency head's mettle is the White House. In light of the priority placed on following the president's agenda and given the instinctive response of any executive to the headquarters chain of command, one would think that a loyal agency head should take direction from the White House. Yet, as with many things in the topsy-turvy world of Washington, the correct approach is counter-intuitive, for the White House staff is not always in tune with the president.

The correct relationship to pursue is the bond between the president and the agency head. The president's staff at times pursues its own interests, not necessarily the president's. That is why all good management practice emphasizes line over staff; in this case, the line is from the president to the agency head. If that works, everything else works. All that the executive office of the president can effectively do is correct errors made in the original selection of agency heads; however, this is never the optimal control device. If the agency head is loyal to the president, he should never be dictated to by the White House staff. Otherwise, every clerk in the White House will feel at liberty to call him and tell him the president wants this or that. Obviously, the wise agency head will remain open to the advice of various assistants to the president, but the final decision is his or the president's to make, not the White House bureaucracy's.

Congress's Achilles' Heel

Congress is, if anything, an even more difficult puzzle to solve. Everyone will advise the agency head of the necessity of having good relations with the members of his congressional authorizing, appropriating, and other oversight committees. The problem is that Congress typically has a different agenda from the president's. Never was it more truly said that one cannot serve two masters. Of course, the agency head must court these most critical centers of power—be nice to them, do what favors he can, answer their letters promptly, generally pay attention to their often prickly personalities. But the president is the agency head's boss and his interests will sooner or later come into conflict with theirs. Therefore, a comfortable distance should be maintained in the relationship with Congress. There must be cordiality, but there will also be inevitable confrontations.

The best defense against Congress is simple: be prepared. Congressmen have almost no time to learn the details of policy; this is their Achilles' heel. If the agency head knows the details, he can use the often-dreaded committee hearing to advance his reputation and his agenda. He should answer courteously, but never back down. The main reason many agency heads are buffeted in hearings or, even worse, choose to stay away and send cowed subordinates as surrogates, is that they are uninformed (or perhaps just cowardly). Good congressional relations, even grudging respect from the strongest opposition, can only be won by being well informed, well prepared, and having the strength of character to face the opposition.

Learning to Love the Fishbowl

Every businessman has been taught how to deal with the media. The standard advice is to keep a low profile, tend to your knitting, and stay out of trouble. While this works in the private sector, the "knitting" in the public sector is the media. Government is essentially a communication business. Ruled and ruler communicate, one nation communicates to another, interests communicate to centers of power, etc. In government, the medium is the message. Keeping a low profile as a government executive means giving up your most important asset, the opportunity to persuade. To be heard in Washington, an agency head must develop a public personality that will help him achieve his agenda. If he becomes a nonperson, Congress and even his own bureaucracy will run his agency for him.

Unfortunately, in Washington's "fishbowl," being a public personality necessarily means that the publicity will be mixed. A media story must have good and bad things to say about its characters, or it does not read well. The bad things will distress one's family, friends, and former business associates. That is why the businessman, as business executive, is correctly advised to stay out of the public's eye. A government executive, however, must swim in the sea of media or become powerless. If the agency head allows his family's and friends' concerns over this bad publicity to dissuade him from action, he might as well go home.

Aloof Respect

The textbooks advise the agency head to build a close personal relationship with the employees of his agency. Yet, they are not really his employees. They are members of a permanent bureaucracy who were there before he came and will be there after he leaves. They were selected by Civil Service examinations, not by the agency head. The head needs to befriend those who can be befriended, of course, but he must lead them, maintain a respectful distance and be somewhat aloof, if he is to motivate these independent agents of the bureaucracy into doing what he wants rather than what they want.

Many political scientists believe that the agency bureaucracies themselves are formidable lobbying groups for the interests they regulate, more so than any outside group. Since the bureaucracy has an agenda, its primary function is to win over the new agency head to its point of view. The agency head then becomes a symbolic figure, who is manipulated in the interests of the status quo. It is a test of leadership and management acumen for the agency head to get the career sector in the agency to implement his policies rather than vice versa.

Trial-by-Leak

All interest groups—the agency's bureaucracy, those regulated by the agency, potential customers and suppliers, and ideological groups—should be courted by the agency head as potential allies. He must not, however, allow himself to be drawn into their rivalries and petty conflicts, but rather remain above the fray and cast himself in the role of judge rather than player. He must reserve his limited political capital to deal with the primary issues rather than accommodating secondary concerns in building his coalitions. Moreover, interest groups are the most likely to extend perks, gifts, and other favors, which should be avoided like the plague. The agency head must behave like Caesar's wife, even if only for the practical reason that anything he does—or says, writes, or jokes about—may appear on the front page of the *Washington Post* the next morning. In the Washington game of trial-by-leak there are no secrets, no confidences. Integrity, sound judgment, and prudence call for scrupulous actions and a judicial demeanor in the face of all these environmental forces.

The agency head should pay particular attention to certain details that may seem relatively mundane when compared with policy decisions affecting millions of people or billions of dollars. Experience has shown that small matters have tripped the best-intentioned political executives, causing unnecessary embarrassment and personal hardship. Examples include using official vehicles for personal purposes, asking employees to do personal chores or errands, expensive or unnecessary refurnishing of office suites, combining personal and official travel, or misusing the perks of office leading to the appearance of personal gain. It is advisable for the agency head to set up a review and counseling session with his general counsel or designated agency ethics officer to familiarize himself and his management team on the potential pitfalls. This may be somewhat time-consuming, but in comparison to the time spent defending or explaining the appearance of wrongdoing it is a worthwhile investment. These problems can be terribly debilitating and demoralizing, and serve only to detract from the primary goal of implementing the president's agenda.

A Loyal Team

In the same way that the president must rely upon the agency head as his principal subordinate, the agency head must rely upon his political appointees. He must create a loyal team, assign accountability (through such tools as performance agreements), and then reward those who do the job well. This means that the head must personally, as does the president, select his top leaders, both political and career. He must be willing to work with the Presidential Personnel Office (PPO) to select individuals who are mutually acceptable in terms of competence, commitment, and character. But the bottom line in personnel selection is that the agency head should never accept a prospective appointee who does not meet his standards and in whom he cannot have complete confidence.

The White House has every right to monitor how well the agency team performs under the president's criteria, and the agency head should be open to high-level objections from PPO. If the subordinates are not doing their job, ultimately the White House should come after the boss—he is accountable for their performance. All of this is peripheral, however. The essential point is that the agency head should be personally involved in selecting a loyal team of subordinates who can accomplish the president's agenda.

Once the agency's team is in place it is important to create and maintain an *esprit de corps* among the team through regular meetings, briefings, and training programs. The agency head should meet with his entire political team at least once each quarter and with his personal staff at least weekly. The larger the agency and the more numerous its divisions and fiefdoms, the more important such meetings are. Policy briefings by the agency head or senior staff are effective in keeping everyone up to speed and "in the loop." Training programs aimed at improving management skills and effectiveness should be developed around generic themes such as the regulatory process, personnel management, contracts, and public affairs.

Reagan's Managerial Strength

As soon as he is selected, the agency head should begin to assimilate the president's agenda and the agency's own institutional point of view. Both must be understood if the latter is to be brought into line with the former. Here, it is wise to learn from President Reagan. Rather than trying to sort through and follow a great multiplicity of government issues, as did Jimmy Carter, Reagan focused on a few important policies. If the agency head identifies a few very important issues in his area, and uses all his resolve and every available weapon (without transgressing the law or ethical canons), he just might be as successful as President Reagan.

That there is no bottom line, however, means that the agency head must pay much more attention to detail than he did in the private sector. In the private sector, he could keep track of subordinates by looking at cost centers; in government, he must evaluate people in the context of policy (rather than profit-or-loss), and this is often made more difficult by the fact that the real policy is hidden in the minutiae of administering a program, or in the wording of a few phrases in a regulation.

While he must concentrate on relatively few issues, the agency head must know them thoroughly and, in addition, keep a watchful eye on developing policy areas that might become future problems. Public-sector management is much more difficult than private-sector management because it demands a much greater mastery of detail, provides less objective measures of success, tends to focus on a few very complicated issues rather than the agency as a whole, and requires an ability to see behind one's back while looking at a shifting policy horizon.

Jim Watt's Rule

The agency head should rely primarily upon personnel management, rather than overly abstract or objective measures of efficiency. Cost-benefit analysis might be useful on occasion (in fact, it is required in regulatory matters), but the essential task is to comprehend the problem in its entirety, study the political environment, and understand the people involved in the process. To do this, the agency head must talk to those people, even down several levels into the organization, motivate and coordinate those who will help, and maneuver around those who pose a problem. Former Secretary of the Interior James Watt used what he called the "rule of three" to set his staffing policy for a subordinate unit. First, appoint a real leader as the head of the major sub-unit, one who can inspire and motivate. Then, appoint as his subordinate a deputy who has the administrative skills to get the job done. Finally, appoint a third person, who need not possess great technical expertise, whose primary job is to remind the other two why they were appointed: to carry out the president's agenda.

The critical issue for most agency heads is whether they will strive to manage effectively or give in to the environment and just enjoy the perks of office. Of course, this is not unique to government. Andrew Grove, president of Intel, says that managers are paid to elicit better performance, and there is no other way to do so than to assess what good personnel performance is and to measure progress toward that goal: "We managers need to stop rationalizing [how difficult this is] and stiffen our resolve and do what we are paid to do, and that is to manage." Jimmy Carter's one real legacy to government was his Civil Service Reform Act, which provided a technically sound performance appraisal system for the entire Civil Service and a pay-for-performance system for managers and executives.

A successful public-sector executive must rely upon such systems. He does not have that private-sector bottom line and therefore must give more attention to these less-than-optimal but nevertheless critical tools. If such management tools are as critical as Andrew Grove believes in a private sector, which has measurable cost centers, they are even more so in a process-oriented environment such as government.

No Bottom Line

Government management fundamentally differs from private-sector management. Decentralized management works in the private sector only because there is a bottom line, a quantifiable profit-and-loss, under which top management can evaluate progress. The underlying problem in government administration is that there is no equivalent, universally recognized measure of performance. Budgets and accounting statements, for example, cannot be relied on as indicators of success by managers of an agency. In fact, they at times give counter-indications and can mislead management. A government budget basically shows how much was spent last year and therefore how much more is "needed" this year because the problem remains unsolved. In other words, budgets are just the instrument by which the permanent bureaucracies in Congress and in the executive branch justify increased funding, no matter how ineffectively the funds may be spent. The only way to redirect the bureaucracy and its self-serving accounting is to build a loyal team that will establish more suitable evaluation systems and criteria to assess progress within the agency, using standards approved by the agency head.

Two noteworthy examples of effective management are ACTION, the coordinating agency for federally sponsored domestic volunteer activities, during President Reagan's first term and the Urban Mass Transit Administration (UMTA) during his second. In the former case, Tom Pauken became director of an agency that had been the plaything of the extreme left wing of the Democratic Party. Funds had been distributed with abandon to fringe political action groups, and no attempt had been made to assure that expenditures met either program or legal requirements. By the end of Pauken's first year, he and his team had established and implemented strict criteria, and ACTION's programs had been put back on track.

When the Reagan administration took office, UMTA had no systems in place to require accountability by its grantees. While progress was made during the first term, dramatic improvements began to occur when Alfred DelliBovi became deputy administrator and, ultimately, administrator. Over the protests of many local transit authorities, he refused to disburse additional grants until monies previously made available to grantees were properly accounted for.

The essence of agency management is personnel management through delegation to a loyal team. Its corollary is accountability. With the team in place, and the agenda, goals, and evaluation criteria established, people must be held accountable for progress or lack thereof. This is achieved through periodic reviews and critical assessments of the environment on an issue-by-issue basis. The frequency of reviews will of course depend on the nature of the issue and will vary from daily monitoring to weekly assessments or monthly evaluations. The essential point is to hold individuals accountable in exchange for the authority delegated, taking corrective actions as necessary. A high level of competence should be expected from every member of the management team, and poor performance should be dealt with forthrightly.

Issue Priorities

With a team and management system in place, the agency head can move towards implementation of his agenda. Necessarily, management methods in the public sector will differ from those in the private sector. In the private sector, goals, strategy, and tactics can normally be kept in the family until the desired moment. In Washington's fishbowl, one should assume that everything will be prematurely disclosed unless special steps are taken. Priorities should remain confidential until they are ready to be announced. Only the minimum number of people necessary should be involved, and one should not assume the issues that the internal bureaucracy says are the most critical are necessarily the ones the administration should be pursuing. The bureaucratic perspective may be statistically valid, but the analysis frequently lacks political

sensitivity or insight. The agency head must therefore personally set the major priorities and be involved in the creation of the secondary ones. Then, he needs to establish the strategy of when to go public, and periodically revisit his priorities to take advantage of opportunities that present themselves as the environment changes.

Sycophants and Hangers-On

Since the agency head is the president's most valuable asset, it is important to protect that resource. The most important fact to remember is that everything is public, and much of what is public is based on rumor and gossip. A great deal of information is traded on the cocktail circuit, at the ubiquitous "Washington reception," and other informal gatherings, which all feed the rumor mill. Character assassinations are rampant and everyone plays Washington's "gotcha" game.

Political executives will find an army of sycophants and hangers-on (some with powerful friends) but, unfortunately, few trustworthy allies. Even the president will demand much and give little, for he, too, has a job to do and cannot afford for the "Teflon" to be chipped away. This is all part of the job. Given this reality, it becomes clear why an agency head must pick loyal people to reinforce and project his own leadership.

Battles with OMB

Unfortunately, the burden on the political executive is increased by the problematic nature of the neutrality assumed to reside in the professional career service. Genuinely "neutral" instruments of government are very hard to find. Everyone is directly or indirectly affected by the government and has a point of view and an identifiable interest at stake. This is especially the case with federal agencies that are under fire for excesses or are targeted for budget cuts. But it also applies to supposedly neutral or nonpolitical institutions—including the General Accounting Office, the Congressional Budget Office, the FBI, the CIA, and even that paragon of professionalism and neutral competence, the career staff at OMB.

Nominally, it is OMB's job to help the president (and his surrogates—the agency heads) cut or control agency budgets. Through the budget process OMB has tremendous impact on agency programs and thereby an agency head's policy agenda.

OMB can be an ally on some budget battles with Congress and with a sometimes recalcitrant agency bureaucracy. But OMB is also the agency that will review and "clear" the agency's regulations and all congressional testimony and proposed legislation— "in the name of the president." There will be times when its views will reflect not the administration's position but its own historical prejudices and past experiences. After all, OMB is a bureaucratic institution itself, with institutional memory, and its employees may have scores to settle with an agency. The agency head may therefore find himself caught up in a conflict between governmental institutions, each protecting its authority or "turf."

Since OMB is administratively a part of the Executive Office of the President, disagreeing with it can easily lead to being accused of opposing "the president's position." It takes political astuteness and strength of character to identify the key policy elements involved in the issue and to challenge

OMB. The agency head must be able to defend his position in terms of the president's policies—which means knowing the president's position better than the OMB staff. When an agency head experiences a serious policy disagreement with OMB, he should take the issue first to the OMB director, then to the president's chief of staff, and as a last resort to the president himself.

The measures of success in Washington are as varied as the number of power centers and interest groups. Congress, the media, the bureaucracy, the special interests, even the White House, each has its own standards and expectations. There is no safe haven for the agency head in such an environment and the only fallback is personal integrity and strength of character. It is imperative, therefore, that the president select people with these attributes, not only for policy reasons, but for the sake of those he asks to make the tremendous sacrifices that come with public service.

CASE STUDY 13

The Judicial System

"Supreme Court Upholds Women's Right to Abortion"; "Court Strikes Down Quotas for the Admission of Minorities to Medical School"; "State Court Powers to Rule on Busing Limited"; "Nursing School Required to Admit Men"; "Supreme Court Upholds the Death Penalty in Florida." These newspaper headlines reveal that the federal judiciary is anything but a passive instrument of our political system. In the consideration of cases and controversies involving interpretation of the Constitution, laws, and treaties, the federal courts have had a profound impact upon governmental procedures and policy.

The judicial branch is bound by the Constitution to consider only cases and controversies that are brought to it for resolution. In order to achieve "standing" in court, parties must demonstrate a concrete adversary interest of the case, an interest that is distinguishable from the interest of the general public. And in challenging governmental action, persons must show injury from the challenged act.

Although the courts cannot initiate action and must, according to their own rules, resolve cases on the basis of the evidence or record before them, they operate in a political environment and make political decisions. Outside the area of private litigation, when government action is challenged important interests are always at stake. In these cases litigation is usually a group process, involving the resources and interests of powerful pressure groups seeking to overturn decisions of national or state governments. Courts are influenced not only by outside pressures but also by the experiences and beliefs of the judges themselves. Supreme Court judges can be described in many ways. Often they are viewed as being either "liberal" or "conservative." Liberal justices will tend to favor civil rights causes more than will their conservative brethren. More important, liberal justices will seek to involve the courts actively in the resolution of political conflicts, whereas conservatives tend to support judicial self-restraint in confrontation with other branches of the federal government and with state governments.

Although the Constitution set up an independent Supreme Court, it was well recognized at the time that the judicial branch would be highly political. The delegates recognized that an expanded federal judiciary, including not only the Supreme Court but inferior courts to be established by Congress, would be an important bulwark of national power. Some delegates, who feared an overly powerful national government, strongly objected to giving congress the authority to create new courts. With few exceptions, the most important political impact made by the Supreme Court and the federal judiciary has resulted from judicial review of *state* laws and actions.

The Constitution did not explicitly provide for either federal judicial review over the states or for review of *congressional* laws or presidential actions. The 1789 Judiciary Act, however, gave the Supreme Court the authority to review the decisions of the highest state court involving questions of conflict of federal and state laws. With regard to the authority to review congressional acts, the Supreme Court *assumed* it had that power even before Chief Justice John Marshall unequivocally stated it in *Marbury v. Madison* in 1803. The Court's power to interpret the Constitution and federal law subjected presidential decisions to judicial review as well. Thus the Supreme Court almost immediately became a potentially dominant political force.

THE FEDERAL COURT SYSTEM

The concept of "a government of law and not of men" is an ideal deeply rooted in Western political tradition. Belief in this ideal is basic to democratic political systems and distinguishes them from totalitarian ones. Under a system based on laws, government is not supposed to wield power according to the whims of those who govern but strictly according to preestablished rules. Conflicts that arise between individuals or between an individual and the government also are resolved by applying the law.

The Framers inherited their concept of judicial organization along with their concept of law largely from Great Britain. The establishment of an independent judiciary had long been recognized as an essential part of any government based on law. Since the British constitution was based largely on unwritten, or *common*, law, there had developed in Great Britain an independent body of judges whose sole function was to determine what the laws were and how they should be applied when specific controversies arose. But—as the experience of continental countries with all-written, codified laws has demonstrated—even the existence of written rules does not in itself mean that government will always act within the limits of such rules or that the rules will be applied impartially to all individuals.

The Framers realized that if a system of laws was to be preserved, there had to be an independent judiciary authorized to interpret and apply the laws in specific cases and controversies. This concept was embodied in the Constitution and is basic to the federal judicial system of the United States.

The Judicial System in the Constitution

The organization of the federal court system is derived from various provisions in the Constitution. The Framers made the national judiciary a separate branch of government because they recognized that the function to be performed by the courts was different from the functions of a legislature or an executive.

The judicial function. The nature of the judicial function of government sets it apart from legislative and executive functions. The legislative function involves *making* laws that usually pertain to the general community rather than to specific individuals. The exercise of judicial power, on the other hand, is concerned not with the general community but with specific parties and controversies. Whereas a judicial decision in a specific case may set a *precedent*—a standard that becomes applicable to the entire community because it governs subsequent judicial decisions—the exercise of judicial power presumably involves *interpreting* rather than making law. Another important distinction between the two functions is that legislating involves making *prospective*, or future, judgments, whereas adjudication hinges on the proper determination of *retroactive* facts pertaining to the activities and interests of the specific parties involved in a particular controversy. In a pure sense, legislation is highly political, while adjudication is not. However, in reality political factors may also shape judicial decisions. (The Supreme Court, in particular, takes notice of political realities.)

In the American political system, judicial functions have been delegated to parts of the bureaucracy, and federal court decisions increasingly have taken on the aspect of general governmental policies. However, in spite of this overlapping of functions in practice, the Framers did understand the judicial function as distinct from other functions of government. They affirmed this distinction in Article III of the Constitution by assigning the "judicial Power" specifically to the federal courts (Section 1) and by providing that judicial power should extend only to "Cases" and "Controversies" (Section 2).

Federal court jurisdiction. Any case or controversy that requires a judicial decision must be brought to the court that has the authority, or *jurisdiction*, to decide it. The jurisdiction of a particular court may be limited not only to a specific geographical location but also to cases and controversies that involve particular kinds of matters or parties.

Article III of the Constitution restricts the jurisdiction of the federal courts to cases and controversies that concern federal questions alone. Essentially this means that the federal courts can hear only cases that involve federal law. Cases that involve federal law are those "arising under [the] Constitution, the Laws of the United States, and Treaties." Also within federal court jurisdiction are cases affecting ambassadors and other public ministers, admiralty and maritime situations, controversies in which the United States itself is a party, and controversies between two or more individual states or between citizens of different states (Article III, Section 2). Other provisions for the jurisdiction of the federal courts are determined by Congress, which within limits is granted the power by Article III to determine judicial organization.

By limiting the jurisdiction of the federal courts to federal questions, Article III clearly separates the federal judicial branch from the judicial systems of the individual states. The organization and jurisdiction of state courts are determined by the states themselves; and cases and controversies that arise under the laws of a particular state must be settled by the courts of that state. Only when a case involves a conflict between a state law and a federal law or the federal Constitution does a state question become a matter for a federal court. In such instances appeals are taken directly—although there are some exceptions—from the highest court of the state to the Supreme Court of the United States.

Original and appellate jurisdiction. Most court systems, both state and federal, include a hierarchy of courts, each court having some degree of either original or appellate jurisdiction. A case is always decided first by a court that has *original jurisdiction*—that is, the authority to hear the case the first time a judicial decision is made. Although most decisions of such courts are final, sometimes one of the parties to a case decides to challenge the original court's decision. The party can then appeal to a higher court that has *appellate jurisdiction*—the authority to review the decisions of a lower court. Article III of the Constitution specifies certain types of cases over which the Supreme Court always has original jurisdiction, although it is not required to exercise it. The appellate jurisdiction of the Supreme Court and both the original and appellate jurisdictions of lower federal courts must be determined by Congress.

The courts of the federal judicial system are set up on three levels, which correspond to levels of original and appellate jurisdiction. The *district courts* are trial courts that have been given original jurisdiction for most federal cases; the *courts of appeals* are intermediate appellate courts that may review district court decisions; and the Supreme Court has final appellate jurisdiction for certain types of cases as assigned by laws of Congress (see Figure 15.1).

Whereas the 50 state court systems parallel the federal judicial system in some respects, the titles given to the various levels of state courts are not the same in every state. In California, for example, the highest state tribunal is called the supreme court; in New York State the trial court of original jurisdic-

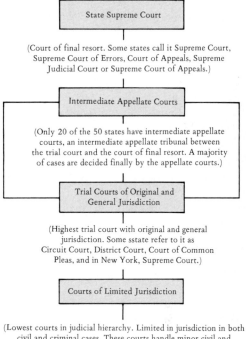

Federal Judicial System

Supreme Court
of the United States

U.S. Courts of Appeal
(13 Circuits)

U.S. District Courts with federal and local jurisdiction	Administrative Quasi-Judicial Agencies	U.S. District Courts with federal jurisdiction only
(Guam, Virgin Islands, Northern Mariana Islands)	(Tax Court, Federal Trade Commission, National Labor Relations Board, etc.)	(91 districts in 50 States; District of Columbia and Puerto Rico)

U.S. Court of Appeals for the Federal Circuit

Direct appeals from state courts in 50 states

U.S. Claims Court

U.S. Court of International Trade

State Judicial System

State Supreme Court

(Court of final resort. Some states call it Supreme Court, Supreme Court of Errors, Court of Appeals, Supreme Judicial Court or Supreme Court of Appeals.)

Intermediate Appellate Courts

(Only 20 of the 50 states have intermediate appellate courts, an intermediate appellate tribunal between the trial court and the court of final resort. A majority of cases are decided finally by the appellate courts.)

Trial Courts of Original and General Jurisdiction

(Highest trial court with original and general jurisdiction. Some sstate refer to it as Circuit Court, District Court, Court of Common Pleas, and in New York, Supreme Court.)

Courts of Limited Jurisdiction

(Lowest courts in judicial hierarchy. Limited in jurisdiction in both civil and criminal cases. These courts handle minor civil and criminal cases. Some states call these courts Municipal Courts, Police, Magistrates, Justice of the Peace, Family, Probate, Small Claims, Traffic, Juvenile Courts, and other titles.)

(Source: *Spring 1989 Guide to Current American Government*, p. 25. Reprinted with permission from Congressional Quarterly, Inc.)

FIGURE 15.1

tion is known as the supreme court, and the highest court is the court of appeals.

Civil and criminal cases. Cases decided in the courts involve either civil or criminal law. *Civil law* defines private rights and consists of rules that regulate the activities of private individuals with one another and with the government. Under civil law private parties may bring suits in court against adversary private or governmental parties. *Criminal law*, like civil law, regulates individual conduct; but criminal lawsuits always involve the government as the initiating party. Strictly speaking, criminal law offenses are offenses against the whole of society; therefore, the spokesman for

society—the government—is responsible for enforcing the law. Violations of criminal law, unlike violations of civil law, may carry penalties of loss of liberty or even life. A law that regulates the making of contracts between individuals is an example of a civil law. Laws that prohibit the selling of dangerous drugs, inciting riots, or conspiring to overthrow the government are examples of criminal laws.

There are two categories of criminal law: felonies and misdemeanors. *Felonies* are serious crimes, such as murder, arson, kidnapping, robbery, and forgery, and they are punishable by death or long-term imprisonment. *Misdemeanors* are minor criminal offenses, such as traffic violations, petty theft, and disorderly conduct, which are punishable by short jail terms or fines. At the federal level Congress defines criminal acts and determines the degree of punishment for such acts. Federal crimes, which cover such activities as counterfeiting, kidnapping, smuggling, bribery of federal officials, conspiracy to defy federal law, and attacks upon federal officials, are relatively limited in comparison to crimes as defined under state laws.

Civil cases may involve the government, private individuals, or groups. Usually, one party to such a case—the *plaintiff*—seeks judicial action against a second party—the *defendant*—for redress of a grievance or violation of law. The role of a court in a civil case is to determine whether the grievance of the plaintiff is valid and whether the defendant owes the plaintiff any *damages,* such as monetary compensation.

In a criminal case one of the parties is *always* the government acting as the *prosecutor* against a defendant who is accused of committing a criminal act. In such cases the purpose of the judicial process is to determine, first, whether the defendant is guilty of the crime of which he or she is accused and, second, what his or her punishment should be if guilty.

At the state level there may be separate courts that hear civil and criminal cases, but at the federal level all courts are involved in both areas of law. Although criminal cases must always be brought by the government, civil cases, even though they generally involve the redress of individual grievances, may also be brought by the government. Specific acts, such as the Sherman Antitrust Act and statutes governing the Internal Revenue Service, provide that the agencies enforcing these statutes, at their discretion, may bring either civil or criminal actions against individuals. For example, the Internal Revenue Service may seek civil damages from an individual for nonpayment of taxes, or it may seek imprisonment by bringing a criminal action.

Civil as well as criminal cases are decided at all levels of both the state and federal judicial systems, but the nature of the parties to any case and the laws involved determine whether a case is decided by a federal or a state court. If both plaintiff and defendant to a civil suit not involving federal law live in the same state, or if a defendant is accused of violating a state law, the case is heard in a state trial court. But if the plaintiff and defendant to a civil case are from two different states (known as a *diversity of citizenship* case) and the amount of damages claimed by the plaintiff is more than $10,000, the plaintiff can file his or her complaint in a federal district court, which, however, must apply pertinent state law. The $10,000 limit for federal jurisdiction has been set by Congress. State and federal courts have *concurrent jurisdiction* in civil cases involving more than this amount. That is, parties in such cases can agree to go to either a state or a federal trial court because Congress has given federal courts the authority to handle these cases concurrently with state courts. Any case involving a federal constitutional question, a federal law, or a United States treaty, whether civil or criminal in nature, goes first to a federal district court.

Consider the case of Mr. Jones who hires Mr. Smith to build a 10-room summer cottage. Mr. Jones later discovers that the wiring and plumbing of his new house are defective. If Jones decides to sue Smith for $15,000 and both men live in the same state, Jones will file a complaint in his state's trial court. But if Jones lives in New York and Smith lives in Connecticut, the suit probably will be filed in a federal district court unless both parties agree to a trial in the state court of New York.

Similar distinctions can be made for criminal cases. In most cases of robbery, the person accused of committing the crime is prosecuted by a state district attorney. But if a person is accused of robbing a federally insured bank, which is a federal crime, a federal attorney will prosecute the accused in a federal district court.

Constitutional and legislative courts. Congress, from the early days of the republic, expanded the federal judicial system beyond the Supreme Court, which was the only judicial body established by the Constitution. The authority of Congress to create courts is derived from two parts of the Constitution. *Constitutional courts* are those created by Congress on the basis of Article III, which grants judicial power to "such inferior Courts as the Congress may from time to time ordain and establish." Through the provision of Article I, which authorizes Congress to make whatever laws are necessary for carrying out its enumerated powers and the other powers of the federal government, Congress has established additional courts known as *legislative courts*. When Congress creates constitutional courts, its power to control the operations of such courts is limited by the provisions of Article III. In establishing courts under its powers in Article I, however, Congress has more discretion in determining the requirements for judges and the functions and jurisdiction of such courts.

Constitutional Courts

Although it provided for a Supreme Court, Article III of the Constitution left the entire organization of the lower federal judiciary to Congress. Besides the Supreme Court, other courts—the courts of appeals, the district courts, and three other special courts—have been created as constitutional courts.

Once a court is designated as "constitutional" under Article III, there are certain areas in which Congress cannot interfere. For example, Congress cannot alter the provisions pertaining to tenure and salaries of judges that are stated in Article III, Section 1:

The judges, both of supreme and inferior Courts, shall hold their Offices during good Behaviour, and shall, at stated Times, receive for their Services, a compensation which shall not be diminished during their Continuance in Office.

This section of Article III protects the judges of constitutional courts by making it almost impossible for Congress to remove a judge who has been appointed by the president with the advice and consent of the Senate. Judges can be removed only by impeachment. To date only four federal judges, all at the district level, have thus been impeached *and* removed from office.

Other limitations on Congress regarding constitutional courts are derived from the "Cases" and "Controversies" stipulations of Article III, Section 2. Article III, like most provisions of the Constitution, requires interpretation for clarification. For example, what exactly is a "case" and "controversy"? The Supreme Court has held that because of the case-and-controversy requirement of Article III Congress cannot authorize the federal courts to interpret the law or make judgments when specific cases and controversies are not involved. For example, Congress cannot authorize the courts to give *advisory opinions* to legislators or to the president about whether a bill under consideration is constitutional. Only after a law is passed and challenged by a specific party to a case can the federal courts render a judgment.

Another aspect of this limitation is that the federal courts cannot be authorized to make *declaratory judgments* unless controversies exist. A declaratory judgment is a court statement as to what the rights of parties are under such legal arrangements as statutes, contracts, or wills. Unlike most judgments, declaratory judgments are issued not after a lawsuit is filed for damages, but as a preventive measure before damages occur. Although its power over constitutional courts is thus restricted by Article III, Congress does have the power to determine the organization of these courts and most aspects of their jurisdiction as well.

District courts. The first Congress set up district courts as federal trial courts for various regions, and the number of district courts expanded as the nation grew. Today there is at least one federal district court for each state, and some of the larger states have as many as four. Altogether there are 89 district courts for the 50 states. There is also a district court, established by Congress as a legislative court under Article I, for the District of Columbia. In 1933 the Supreme Court ruled that this District of Columbia court is both constitutional and legislative and that its judges are protected by the stipulations for office in Article III.

Each of the federal district courts has from one to forty-three judges. As with all constitutional courts, the tenure of these judgeships is subject to the stipulations of Article III. Most district court cases are heard and decided by only one district judge, although Congress has provided that at least three judges be present to hear certain kinds of federal cases. These cases concern (1) crimes against the United States; (2) certain civil actions arising under the Constitution, statutes, and treaties (except where the Supreme Court has original jurisdiction); and (3) certain cases involving citizens of different states or citizens and aliens. Congress has also given the district courts the authority to review and enforce the decisions of certain administrative agencies.

Most district court decisions that are appealed are reviewed by a court of appeals. However, certain kinds of cases—the number of which is diminishing—may be appealed directly to the Supreme Court.

Courts of appeals. Congress set up the first courts of appeals in 1789 to relieve the Supreme Court of the need to review all cases that are appealed from the district courts. There are 10 constitutional courts of appeals, and each of the 50 states is assigned to one of the 10 *appellate circuits*, or areas of jurisdiction. The District of Columbia constitutes an eleventh circuit, and its court of appeals, like its district court, is both a legislative and a constitutional court.

Altogether there are 132 appellate judges for the 11 circuits. Each court has from four to twenty-six judges, depending on the amount of judicial activity within the circuit. For every case decided in a court of appeals, at least three judges preside at the hearings. (More judges may be present if there are more assigned to the court.)

The courts of appeals have appellate jurisdiction only. They may hear cases on appeal from the district courts within their circuits and from various legislative courts. Congress has also provided for the district and appellate courts to review cases of certain administrative agencies that exercise judicial functions. In some instances Congress has given the appellate courts authority to enforce administrative action by issuing appropriate judicial orders, or *writs*.

The Supreme Court. The number of *justices*, as judges on the Supreme Court are called, is determined by Congress and has ranged at various times from five to ten. At the present time there are nine justices on the Court: eight associate justices and one chief justice. Each justice is appointed to the Court by the president with the advice and consent of the Senate and cannot be removed except through impeachment and trial proceedings in Congress.

The Supreme Court devotes two weeks of each month to hearing arguments for various cases at sessions that are open to the public. For the remainder of each month the justices confer on the cases that have come before them, in order to arrive at their decisions. In addition, each justice is assigned to activities on at least one of the lower courts of appeals.

The Constitution gives the Supreme Court original jurisdiction "in all Cases affecting Ambassadors, other public Ministers and Consuls, and those in which a State shall be Party"; and Congress cannot alter the Court's original jurisdiction. Such cases were given to the highest court in the land because it was considered appropriate that the judgments on such cases should represent the highest judicial authority. It would hardly be suitable for a state court, or even for a lower federal court, to handle cases involving interstate controversy.

Very few cases of original jurisdiction reach the Supreme Court. In 1963 the Court had to resolve an interstate suit between Arizona and California concerning the amount of water from the Colorado River that could be used by California. Arizona sued California, as well as Nevada, New Mexico, Utah, and the United States, over the distribution of the Colorado River waters. Such a dispute, involving several states as well as the government of the United States, could not be tried in any court other than the Supreme Court. Cases of such magnitude are rare, but when they do arise the highest judicial authority must be invoked.

Most of the cases considered by the Supreme Court come to it through its appellate jurisdiction from lower federal and state courts. The appellate jurisdiction of the Supreme Court is limited in part by Article III, which authorizes Congress to make regulations concerning the Supreme Court's appellate authority.

Congress has passed laws granting the parties in certain types of cases the right to appeal to the Supreme Court, but it is a right subject to the Court's view of the issue as posing a "substantial federal question." In all other instances, cases reach the Court on appeal only if the members of the Court agree to hear them. Parties to such cases must first petition the Court to issue a *writ of certiorari,* which is an order issued to a lower court to send the record of a case to the higher court for review. The Supreme Court issues such orders on a very small percentage of the petitions it receives and only when it believes a case involves matters of far-reaching importance. It requires the votes of four justices to grant certiorari.

Special constitutional courts. During the 1950s Congress changed the status of three of the most important legislative courts and des-

ignated them as constitutional courts. These are the Court of Claims, the Customs Court, and the Court of Customs and Patent Appeals, which were originally established by Congress on the basis of its enumerated powers in Article I of the Constitution. The Court of Claims exercises nationwide original jurisdiction for cases that involve claims for compensation against the United States government. The Customs Court has original jurisdiction over cases involving tariff laws or other laws relating to imported merchandise. Most appeals from the Customs Court and all appeals from decisions of the Patent Office are made to the Court of Customs and Patent Appeals.

Although it is easy to distinguish legislative from constitutional courts in theory, it is more difficult to do so in fact. This may readily be seen in the case of *Glidden Company v. Zdanok,* decided by the Supreme Court in 1962. At issue was the status of the Court of Claims and the Court of Customs and Patent Appeals. The Court of Appeals for the Second Circuit (New York and Vermont) had upheld a lower court decision in a dispute between the Glidden Company and its employees. The panel of judges that decided the case for the court of appeals included judges of the Court of Claims and the Court of Customs and Patent Appeals who had been assigned to the panel under authorized procedure. The decision of the panel was appealed on the grounds that the legislative court judges who sat on the panel were not qualified to decide a case in a constitutional court.

In a confusing opinion the Supreme Court upheld the status of the disputed judges and thereby declared the Court of Claims and the Court of Customs and Patent Appeals to be essentially constitutional courts. Justices William O. Douglas and Hugo Black dissented, arguing that these courts performed functions and had status appropriate only to legislative courts, regardless of congressional enactments designating them as constitutional. Although the *Glidden* case did as much to confuse as to illuminate, it did illustrate that the problem of separating constitutional from legislative courts is not entirely one of definition.

Legislative Courts

The provisions in Article III that concern the judges and functions of constitutional courts do not apply to legislative courts. When Congress sets up legislative courts, it is free to establish whatever conditions it wishes regarding length of service and compensation of judges. It can change these conditions at any time and for any reason by simply amending the law establishing the court. In addition, the functions of legislative courts are not limited to making decisions on concrete cases and controversies. Courts created by Congress under the authority of Article I may be assigned nonjudicial functions and may engage in policy making at the same time that they make judgments in specific cases and controversies. For example, the Court of Military Appeals, which reviews court-martial cases, can, to a considerable degree, base its decisions on established military policy rather than on such judicial procedures and precedents as bind constitutional court decisions.

District of Columbia courts. The district and appellate courts of the District of Columbia were created by Congress through its constitutional power to govern the nation's capital. Established as legislative courts, the District of Columbia courts, unlike other district and appellate courts, have jurisdiction over local as well as federal matters within the District and can also perform certain nonjudicial functions. (As noted earlier, the Supreme Court has ruled that the courts of the District are at the same time both constitutional and legislative courts.)

Territorial courts. The Constitution, in Article IV, grants Congress the authority to govern the territories of the United States. On the basis of this authority, district courts have been established in the territories of Puerto Rico, Guam, the Virgin Islands, and the Panama Canal Zone. Like the constitutional district courts, the district court of Puerto Rico has jurisdiction for federal questions alone. The other territorial courts, however, also hear cases pertaining to local matters, since these jurisdictions do not have other court systems as do Puerto Rico and the states. A case decided in a territorial court may be appealed to the regular constitutional court of appeals to which the territorial court is assigned.

The Tax Court. The Tax Court of the United States is an independent agency that was officially designated by Congress to be a legislative court in 1969. Its functions are essentially judicial in nature. This court has jurisdiction over controversies involving taxpayers and the Internal Revenue Service. Sessions of the Tax Court are held at different locations throughout the country for the convenience of parties to the controversies before the court. Some of the Tax Court's decisions are final, whereas others are subject to review by the courts of appeals or the Supreme Court.

The Court of Military Appeals. In 1950 Congress created the Court of Military Appeals as a court of final jurisdiction in court-martial convictions. In rare cases involving constitutional questions, appeal lies directly to the Supreme Court.

Review of Administrative Decisions

The independent regulatory agencies, combined with other parts of the bureaucracy, also exercise a substantial amount of judicial power. Ordinarily, organizational charts of the American judicial system show direct lines of appeal between administrative agencies and the federal courts.

Although these routes of appeal exist, it is still extremely difficult to secure meaningful review of administrative judgments. The avenues of appeal are filled with obstacles and are frequently closed entirely. Judicial review of administrative action is automatically limited, because it is time-consuming and expensive. Moreover, the courts have exercised a great deal of self-restraint and have, more often than not, refused to interfere with the administrative process or to override the judgments of the bureaucracy.

The trend toward specialization. As American society grows more complex and as the need for judicial expertise increases, the judicial system is becoming more and more specialized. Federal and state courts of general jurisdiction handle a broad spectrum of cases. The tendency within many, though not all, state and local court systems is to create separate divisions or special courts to handle particular problems—traffic violations, small and large claims against individuals, divorce, probate (wills, estates), and so forth. On the federal level, administrative agencies act as such specialized courts when they judge cases arising within their particular jurisdictions.

This tendency toward a division of labor in judicial matters will undoubtedly continue to increase in the future. One of the probable consequences of such specialization will be that appeals from one court to another will be less readily obtained. The decisions of specialized courts with particular capabilities will probably be accepted as final by the parties coming before them, as well as by any designated appellate body.

JUDICIAL PROCEDURE

Regardless of which court has jurisdiction to resolve a particular matter, the basic judicial function of the court is always the same: to interpret the law and arrive at a fair decision for each particular case and controversy. The making of judicial decisions requires first that the judges be well-versed in the law. Second, there must be some procedure for examining all the facts pertinent to a case so that impartial judgments can be made.

Sources of Judicial Procedure

Probably more attention has been given to the development of logical and systematic procedures for the judicial process than to any other area of governmental decision making. The process of justice in the United States has evolved from the Constitution, the laws of Congress, and the decisions of the judicial system itself.

Many federal court proceedings, especially in the area of criminal law, are established by the Bill of Rights. For example, the Sixth Amendment guarantees an accused person in a federal criminal prosecution the right to a speedy and public trial by an impartial jury, as well as the right "to be confronted with the witnesses against him" and "to have the Assistance of Counsel for his defence." Many of these processes, including jury trials, have been extended to noncriminal cases as well, through legislation and court practice.

Congress establishes some judicial procedures not only when it creates various federal courts but also when it specifies how the courts should proceed if a case or controversy results from a particular statute. The Supreme Court has also played a significant role in setting precedents and making decisions that determine the procedures used by the lower federal courts. In addition, through its interpretation of the due process clause of the Fourteenth Amendment in specific cases, the Court has extended all but five more or less minor protections of the Bill of Rights, as well as many federal court practices, to the state court systems.

Although the rules of judicial procedure are somewhat standard, there is room for some degree of flexibility. The practical requirements for judging cases naturally cause a great many variations; and different courts and different judges will apply procedures in accordance with the particular needs of the cases before them. Some judges favor formal methods, whereas others adhere to informal techniques as much as possible.

Basic Elements of Judicial Decision Making

Court procedures vary from case to case and from one judge to another, but certain principles are basic to all judicial proceedings. Whether in the criminal or civil realm, the nature of judicial protocol pits one party against another. This is the *adversary process.* From the outset, all parties to a case are presumed to be equal. Thus the major elements of judicial decision making are those that provide for the

(From *Straight Herblock* [Simon & Schuster, 1964])

"You know what? Those guys act like they really believe that."
During the Warren era, the Supreme Court expanded constitutional protections of equality and civil rights.

examination of all facts pertinent to both sides of a case so that a fair decision can be reached.

Both parties to a case must therefore be able to gather the necessary facts and present them before impartial decision makers. Judicial decisions, in turn, should be based only on the record of facts presented, not on personal feelings or biases. In keeping with these requirements, all parties, regardless of their individual financial status, must be represented in criminal cases by attorneys (counsel), who are presumed to know the maze of judicial procedures and be able to present the facts of their clients' cases adequately. Parties may choose to represent themselves, even in criminal cases, but generally they act as their own counsel only in very minor cases, such as those tried in small claims or traffic courts.

Notice of the proceeding. The Sixth Amendment of the Bill of Rights stipulates that "in all criminal prosecutions" the accused has a right "to be informed of the nature and cause of the accusation." Although this constitutional right of notice applies only to federal criminal cases, it is used in civil as well as criminal proceedings.

A defendant in a dispute must be informed of the nature of the proceeding so that he can present his case accurately. A judicial proceeding conducted without adequate notice of the charge would be similar to a tennis match in which one person was asked to play without getting in shape. (The game would suffer as a consequence, and the best player might not emerge as victorious.)

The hearing. A fair settlement of a case requires that a hearing be held before a judge (and a jury, when the latter is required by law and requested by the parties) in order to present all the facts of the case. Such a hearing is open to all parties involved in the case and also to the public. This prevents decisions from being made in secret on the basis of personal friendships or biases. In this sense the purpose of the hearing within the judicial process differs considerably from that of a legislative hearing.

An open judicial hearing, where sufficient notice has been given, provides each party with knowledge concerning (1) the nature of his or her adversary and (2) who is to make the decision. It also provides each party with (3) the opportunity to present a record favorable to his or her point of view and (4) the opportunity to make use of certain procedures that may assist in developing his or her case. Through standardized hearing procedures, all parties can be treated equally and fairly. Yet, as with the presentation of notices, a great deal of variety exists in the conduct of hearings. (Hearings can even be dispensed with if the parties to a case agree to an informal settlement.)

Decisions based on the record. While the hearing is in progress, all proceedings are recorded word for word by a stenographer. (An exception is certain low-level state courts that are not considered courts of record.) This requirement is to preserve a complete record of the evidence upon which the final decision is based. Whether the decision is made by a judge or by a jury, it is supposed to be impartial, given only after the facts in the record have been considered and weighed carefully. Once the decision has been reached, it too is written into the record.

This written record is of utmost importance when a case is appealed to a higher court. Whenever the Supreme Court or a court of appeals reviews a lower court's decision, the appellate court must produce a written decision based on the evidence from the original trial court's record and any new evidence that is introduced.

Because judicial decisions are based on the record developed by the contending parties themselves, the manner in which they develop this information allows the parties to influence directly the decisions made in their own cases. They have the opportunity to bring in all the evidence they can muster in their own favor to affect the final judgment.

The right of appeal. A final ingredient of judicial decision making consists of the right of appeal. The actual record of the case compiled at the trial level of course stands, but appellate judges may apply the law differently than was done by the trial judge. This right is very important because it will in most cases allow persons with different values, who may view a given set of facts in another fashion, to be brought into the decision-making process. Giving parties the right of appeal reduces the probability of bias to a minimum and, insofar as it is humanly possible, permits an objective judgment of the facts.

(Reprinted by permission of *Saturday Review/World* and S. Harris; © by Saturday Review, Inc.)

"It's nothing personal Prescott. It's just that a higher court gets a kick out of overruling a lower court."

Contrary to this cartoon comment, a higher court cannot act on whim but must justify its decisions.

Procedures in Federal Civil Cases

The basic elements of judicial procedure are the same for civil and criminal cases that are settled in federal courts. However, civil cases are more apt to be settled informally or through simpler formal procedures than criminal cases. The most common civil cases at the federal trial court level include bankruptcy cases, in which individuals file for bankruptcy under federal law, and automobile damage cases involving citizens of different states when the amount in controversy exceeds $10,000.

In most civil cases, because the government itself is not usually a party, the original charge is made by the plaintiff, who brings suit against the defendant for the redress of grievances under civil law. The plaintiff, after filing the initial complaint, asks appropriate governmental authorities to serve a *summons* on the defendant. The summons constitutes the necessary notice of proceeding. It is signed by a judicial officer and includes the initial complaint with a requirement that the defendant appear in court. If the defendant ignores the summons, a verdict may be rendered automatically against the defendant, or he or she may be cited for contempt of court. A person who is in *contempt of court* has flouted the proper procedures of the court and can be punished by the court for interfering with the judicial process.

Once a civil case begins, the attorneys representing the plaintiff and defendant may enter their *pleadings* in writing and exchange relevant information. At this stage the defendant (or *respondent*, as the person is usually called in civil cases) is required to answer formally any charges that have been made against him or her in the pleadings of the plaintiff. Frequently, informal settlement of the case is made between the attorneys at this time. The case may be dismissed, or an informal agree-

(Drawing by Richter; © 1968 The New Yorker Magazine, Inc.

"These steps are killing me. I say we settle out of court."
A settlement out of court is usually based on expediency or a realization by one party that it cannot win.

ment may be reached on the exchange of money, if that is at issue. If agreement is not reached and the plaintiff insists, the case will be *docketed*, or scheduled, on the appropriate calendar of the court that has jurisdiction over the matter. Once the case is docketed, further informal proceedings will take place in the nature of pretrial conferences between the judge and the parties involved. These conferences provide another opportunity for settlement prior to a formal trial.

Formal trials in civil cases do not always involve juries. If the case primarily involves interpretation of law, the judge alone will decide the matter after the presentation of arguments by the attorneys for both sides. But if there are facts to be determined, such as the extent of an injury in an automobile accident case or whether a particular automobile manufacturer produced a faulty car or whether a doctor actually engaged in malpractice, a jury is necessary (unless this right is waived by both parties to the dispute). When a jury is to make the decision in a case, both sides have the right to approve the selection of jury members. This enables each side to exclude from the jury anyone who may be prejudiced against that side or who might contribute to an unfair jury decision.

During a trial the counsel for each side orally presents the facts relevant to the viewpoints of his or her client. Each attorney may also bring in witnesses and question them so as to bring out facts in support of the case. *Cross-examination* is a vital element in fair judicial procedure. It allows counsel for both the plaintiff and the defendant to question the witnesses for the other side and thus bring out facts possibly hidden by the opposition that may be advantageous to their own cases.

Sometimes, at the request of either party to a case, the court will serve a prospective witness with a *subpoena*—a court order requiring the person to testify at the trial or to provide certain information relevant to the case. Failure to respond to a subpoena is considered to be in contempt of court.

Once the testimony of the parties is completed, the judge or jury must deliberate over the final decision. If there is a jury, its members are given instructions by the judge before they leave the courtroom to discuss the record of the case. In federal courts the decision of the jury must be unanimous in both civil and criminal cases; but whereas a criminal case requires a jury of 12 persons, a civil one may be tried by a smaller number.

Eventually, the jury reaches a decision either for or against the plaintiff. If the decision is in favor of the plaintiff, the jury must also agree on the amount of damages owed by the defendant. After the jury announces its verdict before the court, it is the responsibility of the court to record the decision and to see that

it is carried out, unless the decision is to be appealed to a higher court.

Procedures in Federal Criminal Cases

Of the more than 200,000 cases begun in federal district courts each year, only a small proportion are criminal cases. Most criminal cases arise under state law and are therefore handled by state courts. Still, approximately 15 percent of the cases coming before the federal district courts are criminal.

The first step in a criminal case is for the government to bring a charge against a defendant for violating a specific criminal statute. This charge is made by a legal representative of the federal government, either the attorney general or one of the deputy attorneys general who serve throughout the country. After the defendant has been named, an arrest warrant is issued.

Pretrial procedures. There is always a pretrial process that begins once the defendant has been apprehended. These proceedings are very important to the ultimate fate of the defendant. In the first step of the pretrial stage the defendant is brought before a magistrate of the federal district court that has jurisdiction over the case.

The magistrate, an officer of the court, conducts a preliminary, informal pretrial examination to determine whether the defendant is to be released or is to be held to answer for the crime of which he or she is accused. If the magistrate decides that there is sufficient evidence for the defendant to be held, the magistrate must then determine whether the defendant is to be kept in custody or released on bail before the next step in the case takes place. (In certain minor cases United States magistrates may actually try a case and render a verdict, which may include a sentence of short-term imprisonment.)

After the preliminary investigation by the

federal magistrate, the defendant may be held over for a *grand jury* investigation. Grand jury proceedings, which are actually part of the pretrial process, are closed to the general public, although ordinary citizens serve as grand jurors. The function of a grand jury, which consists of from 12 to 23 members, is to determine whether the evidence against a defendant is sufficient to justify holding him or her for trial. Grand jury proceedings, which are constitutionally mandated for the federal level only and may be supplanted by the process of *information* on the state level, take place when the defendant has been accused of a serious crime. These proceedings are in the interest of the defendant if the charge against the person has been made on false or insufficient evidence. In such a case they can save the defendant from the tremendous cost and bad publicity of a public trial. At the federal level the charges in criminal cases are made so carefully that only about 10 percent of the defendants apprehended are released after preliminary hearings. At the state level approximately 50 percent are released in the pretrial stage.

If the members of the grand jury determine that there is evidence against the defendant, they will formally *indict*, or accuse, the individual. Once an accusation is made, the defendant is *arraigned*, which means that the official charges in the indictment are read. The arraignment constitutes the notice given to the defendant of the nature of the charges in his or her case. It also indicates to the defendant's attorney the basis of the government's charges and the points that the defense will have to answer at the trial. After the arraignment, the defendant is given a chance to plead guilty or not guilty. Usually, if a guilty plea is entered, the judge will dispose of the case by reaching a verdict without a jury trial. The same applies if the defendant pleads "no contest." If the defendant pleads not guilty, the trial then proceeds.

Trial proceedings. Before the start of the trial, a number of informal meetings may occur between the attorneys involved and the judge. In these meetings such procedural questions as whether the case might still be dismissed, whether there should be a change of *venue* (the place of the trial and the court of jurisdiction), a change in the pleadings, and so on, are discussed. The trial itself is conducted by the judge, with or without a jury. The right of the accused to a jury trial is guaranteed by the Constitution, both at the federal and at the state level, but the defendant may prefer to *waive*, or give up, this right if he or she believes that a judge will render a more favorable decision. The prosecution and the judge must agree to the waiver of a jury trial.

The trial procedure in criminal cases, as in civil cases, is adversary in nature. Both sides are presumed to be equal at the outset, even though the government itself is a party. Evidence must be introduced by the attorneys for both the prosecution and the defense to support their positions. The judge makes every effort to exclude the introduction of evidence not directly pertinent to the case at hand (for example, evidence about the defendant's past actions that a jury might consider to reflect adversely on his or her character).

Before the jury can reach a verdict, the judge's charge to the jury members must make clear to them the specific laws and corresponding punishments that are involved. In its deliberations the jury must then determine which, if any, of the charges against the defendant have been substantiated by the evidence presented. Although the jury decides whether the accused is actually guilty or not guilty, it is the trial judge who releases or sentences the defendant on the basis of the jury's verdict.

Obviously, if the verdict is "not guilty" the defendant is released. Otherwise, the judge determines what the punishment of the defendant should be in accordance with the laws that govern the charges upheld by the

(Drawing by Anthony; © 1982 The New Yorker Magazine, Inc.)

Judges and the attorneys who practice before them often view cases differently.

jury. If the defendant does not accept the verdict, he or she may appeal for review to the court of appeals that has jurisdiction over the case.

Cases on appeal. The review of a lower court decision, whether by a court of appeals or by the Supreme Court, is made by the judges of the court without a jury. An appeal is initiated when the attorney for a party to a case submits a petition for review to the higher court. The judges of the higher court may review the case by issuing a writ of certiorari to obtain the original record of the case from the lower court.

The appellate judges study not only the evidence presented at the trial court level but also the rulings and procedures followed by the lower court judge. They also consider the precedents set by similar cases and listen to arguments of the attorneys for the opposing sides. After weighing all these factors, the appellate court will issue a written opinion reversing or upholding the lower court's decision.

Decisions rendered by the courts of appeals or by the Supreme Court are not always unanimous. The written majority opinion of the court determines the outcome of the case and carefully explains the laws and other factors that have led to the decision. But also of significance are concurring and dissenting opinions. A *concurring opinion* is written by any of the judges on the appellate court who agree with the court's final decision but who base their decision on reasons not expressed by the majority opinion. A *dissenting opinion* may be submitted by one or more judges who disagree with the final decision reached by the majority. Concurring and dissenting opinions are important because they may be referred to in later cases and may influence subsequent court decisions.

Judicial Theory and Practice

When dealing with issues of law and the judicial process, it must be remembered that the actual way things are done does not always conform with the formal content of law or the formal organization for making judgments. Theoretically, all citizens are entitled to their "day in court," provided a proper case and controversy exists. But the fact of the matter is that access to the courts is very limited.

Time and expense are basic obstacles to the proper conduct of the judicial process both in the courts and in the administrative agencies. The main problem of the federal district courts, which now decide over 200,000 cases each year, is time. Rarely is a case heard sooner than six months from the time when it was filed before the court, and in many instances it takes years before a matter is finally adjudicated. In addition, the process of hiring attorneys and of appealing cases is very costly and often discourages individuals from utilizing the judicial process even though they might benefit from the results.

Time and expense are not the only factors limiting the accessibility of the courts. Judicial procedure itself is one of the most important ingredients in shaping the role of the courts. The courts are restricted by their own procedure in their ability to protect rights and supervise governmental activity. They can exercise judicial review only if the proper requirements have been met.

The extensive use of informal procedures renders the administrative agencies more accessible than the courts. Flexible rules readily allow individuals to file complaints and otherwise avail themselves of the administrative process. Thus agencies may initiate cases and settle matters through negotiation, rather than through the time-consuming adversary process. However, many crucial agency proceedings, such as those involved in licensing and rate making, remain highly formal, time-consuming, and, of course, expensive. In these cases the administrative process is favorable only to interest groups, practically excluding any individual participation.

The Views of Three Judges

In spite of all the rigid procedures and precedents that are embodied in the judicial process, a judicial decision involves a large element of personal judgment. Judges themselves have admitted to exercising personal discretion in reaching their decisions. Judicial decisions then, like laws, are as fallible as the people who make them.

The drama of the actual courtroom is not predictable. Unlike a television drama, the script cannot be written in advance. The outcome is determined in each case by the parties to the case, by the attorneys who present the facts for their clients, by the members of the jury who must reach a verdict, and by the judge who must interpret the laws.

At various stages in their careers as judges, three renowned Supreme Court justices—Oliver Wendell Holmes, Benjamin Cardozo, and Felix Frankfurter—described some of the human factors involved in the courtroom. The personal values and experiences of each are reflected in the three essays that follow. After several years as a professor of law, Holmes concentrates mainly on the importance of the study of law and other disciplines needed by the lawyer. Cardozo discusses the process by which judges reach decisions and the direction law should take. Frankfurter emphasizes the qualities of character necessary for a judge. Yet all three speculate from a similar perspective on the pressures and motivations that contribute to judicial decisions.

The Path of the Law / *Oliver Wendell Holmes*

When we study law we are not studying a mystery but a well known profession. We are studying what we shall want in order to appear before judges, or to advise people in such a way as to keep them out of court. The reason why it is a profession, why people will pay lawyers to argue for them or to advise them, is that in societies like ours the command of the public force is intrusted to the judges in certain cases, and the whole power of the state will be put forth, if necessary, to carry out their judgments and decrees. People want to know under what circumstances and how far they will run the risk of coming against what is so much stronger than themselves, and hence it becomes a business to find out when this danger is to be feared. The object of our study, then, is prediction, the prediction of the incidence of the public force through the instrumentality of the courts.

The means of the study are a body of reports, of treatises, and of statutes, in this country and in England, extending back for six hundred years, and now increasing annually by hundreds. In these [historic] leaves are gathered the scattered prophecies of the past. . . . These are what properly have been called the oracles of the law. Far the most important and pretty nearly the whole meaning of every new effort of legal thought is to make these prophecies more precise, and to generalize them into a thoroughly connected system. . . . The primary rights and duties with which jurisprudence busies itself again are nothing but prophecies. One of the many evil effects of the confusion between legal and moral ideas, . . . is that theory is apt to get the cart before the horse, and to consider the right or the duty as something existing apart from and independent of the consequences of its breach. . . . But, . . . a legal duty so called is nothing but a prediction that if a man does or omits certain things he will be made to suffer in

this or that way by judgment of the court:—and so of a legal right. . . .

The first thing for a businesslike understanding of the matter is to understand its limits. . . . You can see very plainly that a bad man has as much reason as a good one for wishing to avoid an encounter with the public force, and therefore you can see the practical importance of the distinction between morality and law. A man who cares nothing for an ethical rule which is believed and practised by his neighbors is likely nevertheless to care a good deal to avoid being made to pay money, and will want to keep out of jail if he can.

. . . The law is the witness and external deposit of our moral life. Its history is the history of the moral development of the race. The practice of it, in spite of popular jests, tends to make good citizens and good men. When I emphasize the difference between law and morals, I do so with reference to a single end, that of learning and understanding the law. . . .

. . . [T]hat distinction is of the first importance for the object which we are here to consider,—a right study and mastery of the law as a business with well understood limits, a body of dogma enclosed within definite lines. I have just shown the practical reason for saying so. If you want to know the law and nothing else, you must look at it as a bad man, who cares only for the material consequences which such knowledge enables him to predict, not as a good one, who finds his reasons for conduct, whether inside the law or outside of it, in the vaguer sanctions of conscience. . . . The prophecies of what the courts will do in fact, and nothing more pretentious, are what I mean by the law.

. . . In every system there are . . . explanations and principles to be found. It is with regard to them that a . . . fallacy comes in, which I think it important to expose.

Condensed from "The Path of Law" by Oliver Wendell Holmes, *Harvard Law Review* 10 (1897), p.39. Oliver Wendell Holmes was Justice, Massachusetts Supreme Judicial Court, 1882–1899; Chief Justice, Massachusetts Supreme Judicial Court, 1899–1902; and Associate Justice, U.S. Supreme Court, 1902–1932.

The fallacy to which I refer is the notion that the only force at work in the development of the law is logic. In the broadest sense, indeed that notion would be true. . . .The danger of which I speak is . . .the notion that a given system, ours, for instance, can be worked out like mathematics from some general axioms of conduct. This is the natural error of the schools, but it is not confined to them. I once heard a very eminent judge say that he never let a decision go until he was absolutely sure that it was right. . . .

This mode of thinking is entirely natural. The training of lawyers is a training of logic. The processes of analogy, discrimination, and deduction are those in which they are most at home. The language of judicial decision is mainly language of logic. And the logical method and form flatter that longing for certainty. . . .But certainty generally is illusion. . . .Behind the logical form lies a judgment as to the relative worth and importance of competing legislative grounds, often an inarticulate and unconscious judgment, it is true, and yet the very root and nerve of the whole proceeding. You can give any conclusion a logical form. You always can imply a condition in a contract. But why do you imply it? It is because of some belief as to the practice of the community or of a class, or of some opinion as to policy, or, in short, because of some attitude of yours upon a matter not capable of exact . . .measurement, and therefore not capable of founding exact logical conclusions. . . .We do not realize how large a part of our law is open to reconsideration upon a slight change in the habit of the public mind. No concrete proposition is self-evident, no matter how ready we may be to accept it. . . .

I think that the judges themselves have failed adequately to recognize their duty of weighing considerations of social advantage. The duty is inevitable. . . .When socialism first began to be talked about, the comfortable classes of the community were a good deal frightened. I suspect that this fear has influenced judicial action both here and in England, yet it is certain that it is not a conscious factor in the decisions to which I refer. . . .I cannot but believe that if the training of lawyers led them habitually to consider more definitely and explicitly the social advantage on which the rule they lay down must be justified, they sometimes would hesitate where now they are confident, and see that really they were taking sides upon debatable and often burning questions.

So much for the fallacy of logical form. Now let us consider the present condition of the law as a subject for study, and the ideal toward which it tends. . . .The development of our law has gone on for nearly a thousand years, like the development of a plant, each generation taking the inevitable next step, mind, like matter, simply obeying a law of spontaneous growth. . . .

. . .Most of the things we do, we do for no better reason than that our fathers have done them or that our neighbors do them, and the same is true of a larger part than we suspect of what we think. . . .Still it is true that a body of law is more rational and more civilized when every rule it contains is referred articulately and definitely to an end which it subserves, and when the grounds for desiring that end are stated or are ready to be stated in words.

At present, in many cases, if we want to know why a rule of law has taken its particular shape, and more or less if we want to know why it exists at all, we go to tradition. . . .The rational study of law is still to a large extent the study of history. . . .It is a part of the rational study, because it is the first step toward . . .a deliberate reconsideration of the worth of those rules. When you get the dragon out of his cave on to the plain and in the daylight, you can count his teeth and claws, and see just what is his strength. But to get him out is only the first step. The next is either to kill him, or to tame him and make him a useful animal. For the rational study of the law the blackletter man [master of print] may be the man of the present, but the man of the future is the man of statistics and the master of economics. It is revolting to have no better reason for a rule of law than that so it was laid down in the time of Henry IV. It is still more revolting if the grounds upon which it was laid down have vanished long since, and the rule simply persists from blind imitation of the past. . . .

. . .I look forward to a time when the part played by history in the explanation of dogma shall be very small, and instead of ingenious research we shall spend our energy on a study of the ends sought to be attained and the reasons for desiring them. As a step toward that ideal it seems to me that every lawyer ought to seek an understanding of economics. . . .We learn that for everything we have to give up something else, and we are taught to set the advantage we gain against the other advantage we lose, and to know what we are doing when we elect.

There is another study which sometimes is undervalued by the practical minded, for which I wish to say a good word. . . .I mean the study of what is called jurisprudence. Jurisprudence, as I look at it, is simply law in its most generalized part. Every effort to reduce a case to a rule is an effort of jurisprudence, although the name as used in English is confined to the broadest rules, and most fundamental conceptions. One mark of a great lawyer is that he sees the application of the broadest rules. . . .Theory is the most important part of the dogma of the law, as the architect is the most important man who takes part in the building of a house. . . .

The Nature of the Judicial Process / *Benjamin N. Cardozo*

The work of deciding cases goes on every day in hundreds of courts throughout the land. Any judge, one might suppose, would find it easy to describe the process which he had followed a thousand times and more. Nothing could be farther from the truth. Let some intelligent layman ask him to explain: he will not go very far before taking refuge in the excuse that the language of craftsmen is unintelligible to those untutored in the craft. . . .In moments of introspection . . .the troublesome problem will recur, and press for a solution. What is it that I do when I decide a case? To what sources of information do I appeal for guidance? In what proportions do I permit them to contribute to the result? In what proportions ought they to contribute? If a precedent is applicable, when do I refuse to follow it? If no precedent is applicable, how do I reach the rule that will make a precedent for the future? . . .Into that strange compound which is brewed daily in the cauldron of the courts, all these ingredients enter in varying proportions. I am not concerned to inquire whether judges ought to be allowed to brew such a compound at all. I take judge-made law as one of the existing realities of life. . . .The elements have not come together by chance. *Some* principle, however unavowed and inarticulate and subconscious, has regulated the infusion. It may not have been the same principle for all judges at any time, nor the same principle for any judge at all times. But a choice there has been . . .and the considerations and motives determining the choice, even if often obscure, do not utterly resist analysis. . . .There is in each of us a stream of tendency, whether you choose to call it philosophy or not, which gives coherence and direction to thought and action. Judges cannot escape that current any more than other mortals. All their lives, forces which they do not recognize and cannot name, have been tugging at them—inherited instincts, traditional beliefs, acquired convictions; and the resultant is an outlook on life, a conception of social needs . . .which, when reasons are nicely balanced, must determine where choices shall fall. In this mental background every problem finds its setting. We may try to see things as objectively as we please. None the less, we can never see them with any eyes except our own. . . .

We reach the land of mystery when constitution and statute are silent, and the judge must look to the common law for the rule that fits the case. . . .[H]ow does he set about his task?

The first thing he does is to compare the case before him with the precedents, whether stored in his mind or hidden in books. I do not mean that precedents are ultimate sources of the law. . . .Back of precedents are basic jural [legal] conceptions which are postulates of judicial reasoning, and farther back are the habits of life, the institutions of society, in which those conceptions have had their origin, and which, by a process of interaction, they have modified in turn. . . .Almost invariably, [the judge's] first step is to examine and compare [precedents]. If they are plain and to the point, there may be need of nothing more. . . .It is a process of search, comparison, and little more. Some judges seldom get beyond that process in any case. Their notion of their duty is to match the colors of the case at hand against colors of many sample cases spread out upon their desk. The sample nearest in shade supplies the applicable rule. But, of course, no system of living law can be evolved by such a process, and no judge of a high court worthy of his office views the function of his place so narrowly. If that were all there were to our calling, there would be little of intellectual interest about it. The man who had the best card index of the cases would also be the wisest judge. It is when the colors do not match, when the references of the index fail, when there is no decisive precedent, that the serious business of the judge begins. He must then fashion Law for the litigants before him. In fashioning it for them, he will be fashioning it for others. . . .

The final cause of law is the welfare of society. The rule that misses its aim cannot permanently justify its existence. "Ethical considerations can no more be excluded from the administration of justice . . .than one can exclude the vital air from his room and live." Logic and history and custom have their place. We will shape the law to conform to them when we may; but only within bounds. The end which the law serves will dominate them all. . . .I do not mean, of course, that judges are commissioned to set aside existing rules at pleasure. . . .I mean that when they are called upon to say how far existing rules are to be extended or restricted, they must let the welfare of society fix the path, its direction and distance. . . .

My analysis of the judicial process comes then to this, and little more: logic, and history, and custom, and utility, and the accepted standards of right conduct, are the forces which singly or in combination shape the progress of the law. Which of these forces shall dominate in any case must depend largely upon the comparative importance or value of the social interests that will be thereby promoted or impaired. . . .

If you ask how [the judge] is to know when one interest outweighs another, I can only answer that he must get his knowledge just as the legislator gets it; from experience and study and reflection; in brief, from life itself. Here, indeed, is the point of contact between the legislator's work and his. The choice of methods, the appraisement of values, must in the end be guided by like considerations for the one as for the other. Each indeed is legislating within the limits of his competence. No doubt the limits of the judge are narrower. He legislates only between gaps. He fills the open spaces in the law. . . .

. . .[Yet] the judge, even when he is free, is still not wholly free. . . .He is to draw his inspiration from consecrated principles. He is not to yield to spasmodic sentiment. . . .He is to exercise a discretion informed by tradition, methodized by analogy, disciplined by system, and subordinated to "the primordial necessity of order in the social life." Wide enough in all conscience is the field of discretion that remains. . . .

Our survey of judicial methods teaches us, I think, the lesson that the whole subject matter of jurisprudence is more plastic, more malleable, the moulds less definitively cast. . . .So also the duty of a judge becomes itself a question of degree, and he is a useful judge or a poor one as he estimates the measure accurately or loosely. He must balance all his ingredients, his philosophy, his logic, his analogies, his history, his customs, his sense of right, and all the rest, and adding a little here and taking out a little there, must determine, as wisely as he can, which weight shall tip the scale. . . .

The Judicial Process and the Supreme Court / *Felix Frankfurter*

Judges are men, not disembodied spirits. Of course a judge is not free from preferences, or, if you will, biases. . . .He will be alert to detect that though a conclusion has logical form it in fact represents a choice of competing considerations of policy, one of which for the time has won the day.

. . .For judges, it is not merely a desirable ca-

pacity "to emancipate their purposes" from their private desires; it is their duty. . . .It is asked with sophomoric brightness, does a man cease to be himself when he becomes a Justice? Does he change his character by putting on a gown? No, he does not change his character. He brings his whole experience, his training, his outlook, his so

This condensation from "The Judicial Process and the Supreme Court," by Felix Frankfurter, published in *Proceedings of the American Philosophical Society*, Vol. 98, No. 4 (1954), is reprinted by permission of the American Philosophical Society. Copyright 1954 American Philosophical Society. Felix Frankfurter was Associate Justice, U.S. Supreme Court, 1939–1962.

cial, intellectual, and moral environment with him when he takes a seat on the supreme bench. . . .

. . .To assume that a lawyer who becomes a judge takes on the bench merely his views on social or economic questions leaves out of account . . .the scope and limits of a judge's authority. The outlook of a lawyer fit to be a Justice regarding the role of a judge cuts across all his personal preferences for this or that social arrangement. . . .

Need it be stated that true humility and its offspring, disinterestedness, are more indispensable for the work of the Supreme Court than for a judge's function on any other bench? . . .

. . .The answers that the Supreme Court is required to give are based on questions and on data that preclude automatic or even undoubting answers. If the materials on which judicial judgments must be based could be fed into a machine so as to produce ineluctable [inescapable] answers, if such were the nature of the problems that come before the Supreme Court, and such were the answers expected, we would have IBM machines doing the work instead of judges. . . .

The core of the difficulty is that there is hardly a question of any real difficulty before the Court that does not entail more than one so-called principle. Anybody can decide a question if only a single principle is in controversy. . . .

This contest between conflicting principles is not limited to law. In a recent discussion of two books on the conflict between the claims of literary individualism and dogma, I came across this profound observation: "But when, in any field of human observation, two truths appear in conflict it is wiser to assume that neither is exclusive, and that their contradiction, though it may be hard to bear, is part of the mystery of things." But judges cannot leave such contradiction between two conflicting "truths" as "part of the mystery of things." They have to adjudicate. If the conflict cannot be resolved, the task of the Court is to arrive at an accommodation of the contending claims. This is the core of the difficulties and misunderstandings about the judicial process. This, for any conscientious judge, is the agony of his duty.

CHAPTER SIXTEEN

Judicial Policy Making

When Chief Justice John Marshall declared that the Supreme Court had the power to review acts of Congress and that "it is emphatically the province and the duty of the Judicial Department to say what the law is," he set the stage for the involvement of the judiciary in the political realm. By saying what the law is, judges actively enter into public policy making. Discussing this point, Harvard law school professor Paul Freund related the following anecdote:

A generation or two ago it was thought rather daring to insist that Judges make the law. Old Jeremiah Smith, who began the teaching of law at Harvard after a career on the New Hampshire Supreme Court, properly deflated the issue. "Do Judges make law?" he repeated, "Of course they do. Made some myself."[1]

In many ways the courts affect public policy today more than ever before. Government itself has expanded, bringing about an increased role for the judiciary in both the interpretation of laws and their enforcement. *Adjudication*, the judging of specific cases and controversies, necessarily includes more and more questions of public policy as the number of cases relating to problems of government expands. As the courts become increasingly involved in policy making, their decisions are subject to many of the same political pressures that affect other branches of the government.

---

[1] Paul H. Freund, *On Understanding the Supreme Court* (Boston: Little, Brown, 1949), p. 3.

THE MERGING OF JUDICIAL DECISIONS AND POLICY MAKING

It seems something of a paradox that the exercise of the judicial function in cases and controversies between specific parties can also produce public policy. This paradox is explained in part by the fact that many cases involve the government as a party or concern governmental matters, from state and federal laws to actions of the president and the bureaucracy. In all cases the federal judiciary is automatically brought into the policy-making process because in order to reach its decision it must interpret what the laws mean. In this merging of judicial decision making and policy making, no judicial institution plays a more significant role than the Supreme Court.

The Need to Interpret Law

Even if Chief Justice John Marshall had not determined in 1803 that it was the duty of the judges "to say what the law is," the courts would still have had to assume this duty. One of the major reasons for judicial involvement in public policy making is that law is usually vague. Ambiguous language, both in the Constitution and in congressional statutes, may be given as many different meanings as there are people who read it. For example, President Richard M. Nixon interpreted the Constitution as granting him executive privilege to withhold subpoenaed tapes of Oval Office conversations from a federal criminal trial of Watergate defendants. The Supreme Court disagreed with the President and in *United States v. Nixon* ordered him to deliver the tapes to presiding Judge John Sirica.[2] When controversies arise under either the Constitution or the statutes, it is the judicial system, and particularly the Supreme Court, that must resolve such issues by deciding what the laws mean. Because the decision of the Court in any one case may set a precedent for other cases, judicial interpretations of law are generally applicable and thus set federal policy. This has been true since the establishment of the Supreme Court.

Constitutional interpretation. Nothing was more significant in developing the framework of American government than the first dramatic interpretations of the Constitution by the Supreme Court in the early nineteenth century. Debates have continually taken place about the intent of the Framers concerning such important constitutional provisions as the enumerated powers given to Congress under Article I, the executive powers of Article II, and the nature of the judicial functions delegated in Article III. At a very early stage in the nation's development, the Supreme Court had to resolve disputes over the meaning of the commerce clause, the supremacy clause, and other provisions relating to the powers of the national and state governments. Even today, conflicts still arise over the intent of the commerce clause. In addition, there has always been disagreement over the meaning of the Bill of Rights and other constitutional amendments.

Some of the most significant policy-making decisions of the Supreme Court in the last few decades have been based on its interpretations of the Constitution. Through a number of cases the Court has expanded constitutional law regarding civil liberties and civil rights. While in the past the Court has exer-

---

[2]*United States v. Richard M. Nixon,* 418 U.S. 683 (1974).

(From *Herblock's Special for Today* [Simon & Schuster, 1958])

"Can you see me now?"
The Supreme Court strengthened individual rights through its interpretation of the Bill of Rights.

---

cised judicial self-restraint in these matters, today it tends to play a more positive role.

Much of the Court's intervention in the political process has been at the state level, based upon its interpretations of the "due process of law" and "equal protection of the law" clauses of the Fourteenth Amendment. Through such interpretation the high Court has developed guidelines governing state action in criminal proceedings as well as state responsibilities with regard to First Amendment freedoms, public education, and legislative apportionment.

Statutory interpretation. Like the Constitution, statutes are stated in vague terms, often because of the inability of elected politicians to reach concrete agreements on policy needs. Just as the bureaucracy has to make policy when it decides how such laws are to be enforced, the courts also set policy when they interpret the meaning of these laws to reach judicial decisions.

The Supreme Court has sometimes been able to establish a new federal policy by interpreting a vague law of Congress to mean something substantially different from the original intent of Congress. One instance of this was a 1937 decision in which the Supreme Court prohibited wiretapping on the basis of a provision in the Federal Communications Act of 1934. (Congress had passed the act to regulate radio broadcasting.)

The scope of the judiciary's role in policy making today can be seen by scanning the *dockets* (agendas) of cases being reviewed by the federal courts at the appellate level. They are filled almost entirely with questions of statutory interpretation. In cases involving the possible conflict of federal and state laws, the Supreme Court must often decide whether state laws conform to the requirements set forth in federal statutes and the Constitution.

Judicial Activism vs. Judicial Self-Restraint

From the debates at the Constitutional Convention of 1787 to the present, the role of the judiciary has been controversial. The debate over the role of the Supreme Court and the federal judiciary has always focused upon the appropriateness and even the constitutionality of judicial *intervention* in the activities of the political branches—Congress and the presidency—and, even more importantly, in matters that states' rights advocates have considered to be within state sovereignty. The Supreme Court historically has become embroiled in political controversy whenever it has taken an interventionist stance, holding federal or state laws to be unconstitutional. Presidents, too, have attacked the Court when it has failed to support their actions.

Both the president and Congress are bound by the same oath to uphold the Constitution as that taken by the Supreme Court jus-

tices. The Constitution, in Article VI, is declared to be the supreme law of the land and binds state judges to uphold its provisions. Moreover, the Constitution does not give the Supreme Court and the federal judiciary the authority to overturn congressional laws, presidential actions, or state laws by making judicial interpretations of its provisions superior to those of coordinate branches or state governments.

Regardless of the silence of the Constitution on judicial review, the Supreme Court assumed this power from the very beginning. The Court did not at first act against Congress, although it did refuse to exercise what it viewed as the nonjudicial authority that Congress had delegated to it. For example, Supreme Court justices refused to act as administrators with circuit court judges in determining pension claims for Revolutionary War veterans under a congressional law that would have made their decision subject to final approval by the secretary of war and Congress. The first chief justice, John Jay, held, in a circuit court case over which he presided (Supreme Court justices in the republic's early decades presided over circuit court cases along with circuit and sometimes district court judges), that "neither the legislative nor the executive branches, can constitutionally assign to the judicial [branch] any duties, but such as are properly judicial, and to be performed in a judicial manner."[3] Later, in *Marbury v. Madison* (1803), the Court held that Congress did not have the authority to grant it the power of mandamus in its original jurisdiction (see Chapter 2). In the *Marbury* opinion, Chief Justice John Marshall unequivocally declared that the Supreme Court had the authority to overturn acts of Congress that it deemed unconstitutional.

While the early Supreme Court did not directly overturn congressional legislation, it did not hesitate to overrule state laws found to be in conflict with the Constitution. Judicial activism was reflected in *McCulloch v. Maryland* (1819) and in *Gibbons v. Ogden* (1924), which

---

[3]In re Hayburn's Case, 2 Dallas 409, 410, fn. 2 (Circuit Court for the District of New York, 1792).

TABLE 16.1 FEDERAL, STATE, AND LOCAL LAWS DECLARED UNCONSTITUTIONAL BY THE SUPREME COURT BY DECADE, 1789–1987

Years	*Federal*	*State and local*
1789–1799	0	0
1800–1809	1	1
1810–1819	0	7
1820–1829	0	8
1830–1839	0	3
1840–1849	0	9
1850–1859	1	7
1860–1869	4	23
1870–1879	8	36
1880–1889	4	46
1890–1899	5	36
1900–1909	9	40
1910–1919	5	118
1920–1929	15	139
1930–1939	13	93
1940–1949	2	58
1950–1959	4	60
1960–1969	16	149
1970–1979	19	193
1980–1987	14	125
Total	120	1,151

Source: Lawrence Baum, *The Supreme Court*, 3d ed. (Washington, D.C.: Congressional Quarterly Press, 1989), 177, 180, in Harold W. Stanley and Richard G. Niemi, *Vital Statistics on American Politics*, 2d ed. (Washington, D.C.: Congressional Quarterly Press, 1990), p. 284. Reprinted with permission from Congressional Quarterly, Inc.

adopted an expansive view of national power and constraints upon state sovereignty.[4] Advocates of states' rights vehemently attacked the Court for these and other decisions. Their position was not only that the Court had misinterpreted the Constitution, but also that it should not have the authority to exercise judicial review over the states. Judicial review, however, has been a reality of the American political system from the beginning. The Supreme Court has always shaped the nation's law and helped to determine its destiny.

Judicial activism and judicial self-restraint have been cyclical phenomena. The Supreme Court has not always played an active or interventionist role by exercising review over the political or elected branches of the national and state governments or over state courts.

Whether by accident or by design, however, the Court has alternated activism with self-restraint in a way that has maintained its prestige and power. Attacks on the Court have always fallen short of their objective of crippling its power or of removing targeted justices by impeachment.

The Supreme Court does not make its decisions in a political vacuum. Justices are well aware of political pressures, and their opinions may implicitly include an assessment of the political climate. And politics is reflected in the Court itself, in divisions among the justices who rarely render unanimous opinions.

Judicial activism. The Supreme Court has boldly invaded the political arena periodically throughout its history. At the national level, however, with the important exception of the early New Deal Court, the justices have not often acted contrary to the clear will of a majority of Congress. Political scientist Henry J.

---

[4]See Chapter 4 for a discussion of the *McCulloch* and *Gibbons* cases.

Abraham has calculated that the Supreme Court has declared only "122 or 123 provisions of *federal* laws unconstitutional in whole or in part out of a total of over 85,000 public and private bills passed [through the fall of 1979]."[5] Over its history the Supreme Court has clearly been far more active in overturning state and local laws than in nullifying congressional legislation. (See Table 16.1.)

While judicial activism in the federal arena has been relatively limited in overturning congressional and presidential actions, the Supreme Court has unquestionably been an important influence in areas where it has chosen to intervene. In *Dred Scott v. Sandford* (1857), for example, it boldly held that Congress did not have the authority to regulate slavery in the Territories, a decision that some historians have argued helped precipitate the Civil War. The Court denied President Abraham Lincoln the authority to suspend unilaterally the writ of habeas corpus at the outset of the Civil War and later held that the President of the United States could not authorize military tribunals to try civilians in areas of the country where the civil courts were open and rebellion had not existed.[6] And after the Civil War the Court overturned the Civil Rights Act of 1875 on the ground that Congress did not have the constitutional authority to regulate private discrimination.[7]

Judicial activism at the national level surfaced in both the nineteenth and twentieth centuries in Court interpretations of the commerce power of Congress. At the beginning of the century Chief Justice John Marshall adopted an expansive view of the national commerce power. However, by midcentury the Court had narrowed its concept of commerce power, beginning a trend in judicial decision making that lasted well into the New Deal era.

The Court narrowly construed the commerce power of Congress in overturning much of Franklin D. Roosevelt's New Deal legislation, thereby precipitating a constitutional crisis. As the Court declared unconstitutional one New Deal law after another, the frustrations of Roosevelt and his advisers mounted until Roosevelt finally sought from Congress the authority to appoint one new justice for each septuagenarian justice on the Court (of which there were six at the time).[8] His message to Congress, containing his "Court-packing" plan, as his proposal was immediately labeled, was somewhat disingenuous. The message implied that justices over the age of 70 lacked the "full mental and physical vigor" to perform their duties and were "often unable to perceive their own infirmities." The message continued:

Modern complexities call also for a constant infusion of new blood in the courts. . . . A lowered mental or physical vigor leads men to avoid an examination of complicated and changed conditions. Little by little, new facts become blurred through old glasses, fitted, as it were, for the needs of another generation; older men, assuming that the scene is the same as it was in the past, cease to explore or inquire into the present or the future.[9]

Roosevelt more clearly expressed the political reasons for his Court-packing plan in a radio address to the people after he sent his message to Capitol Hill. He stated that the Court had no constitutional authority to strike down laws Congress considered to be in the national interest. The patriots who wrote the Constitution, he declared, had wanted to create a national government with expansive and flexible powers to meet the exigencies of the future. Above all, the Court should not thwart the will of the people. "We have," he con-

---

[5]Henry J. Abraham, *The Judicial Process*, 4th ed. (New York: Oxford University Press, 1980), pp. 296–297.

[6]See, respectively, Ex Parte Merryman, 17 Fed. Cases 9487 (1861), and Ex Parte Milligan, 4 Wallace 2 (1866).

[7]*Civil Rights Cases*, 109 U.S. 3 (1883).

[8]Roosevelt's plan extended to the entire federal judiciary, but his target was the Supreme Court.

[9]From Roosevelt's "Message to Congress," February 5, 1937, in *Guide to the U.S. Supreme Court* (Washington, D.C.: Congressional Quarterly, 1979), p. 965.

cluded, "reached the point as a nation where we must take action to save the Constitution from the Court and the Court from itself. ...During the past half century the balance of power between the three great branches of the federal government, has been tipped out of balance by the Court in direct contradiction of the high purposes of the framers of the Constitution. It is my purpose to restore that balance. You who know me will accept my solemn assurance that in a world in which democracy is under attack, I seek to make American democracy succeed."[10]

Roosevelt's plan was scathingly attacked on Capitol Hill, where the attitude among the more conservative Democratic committee chairmen merged with the Republican suspicions of the growing power of an "imperial presidency." Roosevelt's message, however, also helped to stir criticism of the Court, its justices, and the power of judicial review. The Washington columnist Drew Pearson, who later became Jack Anderson's mentor, wrote a critical inside account of the Court and its justices that in many ways was a predecessor to *The Brethren*.[11] The Pearson book, entitled *The Nine Old Men*, referred to the Court as "The Lord High Executioners" bent upon destroying the will of the people as expressed in the New Deal.

After Roosevelt had submitted his plan the Court, in "a switch in time that saved nine," abruptly shifted its position from a restrictive to an expansive view of congressional authority.

The Roosevelt attack on the Supreme Court on behalf of the political domains of the presidency and Congress was not unprecedented. The Federalists had tried to manipulate the lower federal judiciary in their favor by creating new judgeships that President John Adams could fill before leaving office in 1801; at the same time they reduced the number of justices on the Supreme Court from six to five to prevent incoming President Jefferson from appointing a Republican. The Republicans had responded by repealing the Federalist actions and impeaching the outspoken Federalist Supreme Court Justice Samuel Chase as an example of what would be done to judges who disagreed with the party in power.

Wide-ranging responses have been made by the political branches to what they view as a recalcitrant Court. Presidents long before Roosevelt attempted to "pack" the Court with agreeable justices. Most, however, would have agreed with President Harry S. Truman's remark that "packing the Supreme Court simply can't be done...I've tried and it won't work....Whenever you put a man on the Supreme Court he ceases to be your friend. I'm sure of that."[12]

While presidents attempt to control the Supreme Court through their authority to nominate justices for vacant seats, Congress, which also shares the appointment power due to the requirement for senatorial approval, has still other weapons to control the judiciary. It determines the *appellate* jurisdiction of the courts, including the Supreme Court. In the 1980s conservative forces led by North Carolina Republican Senator Jesse Helms attempted to remove Supreme Court jurisdiction over state cases involving abortion and busing to achieve racial balances. Helms was unsuccessful, but Congress in the past has in fact limited Supreme Court power by legislation, removing Court jurisdiction over particular categories of cases. For example, when the Court appeared about to rule on the constitutionality of the Reconstruction laws, Congress, believing the Court would overturn them, suddenly withdrew from the Court's jurisdiction a case that it had already heard and

---

[10]Roosevelt, "White House Broadcast," March 9, 1937, in *Guide to the U.S. Supreme Court*, pp. 968–969.

[11]Bob Woodward and Scott Armstrong, *The Brethren* (New York: Simon and Schuster, 1979). In this account the authors, investigative reporters, claimed a "first" in revealing behind-the-scenes activities of the Supreme Court.

[12]Henry J. Abraham, *Justices and Presidents* (New York: Oxford University Press, 1974), p. 63.

(Rollin Kirby; reprinted from *The New York Post*.)

The public will ultimately decide this.
A dilemma of judicial review is whether the Constitution or Congress is the real guardian of the people.

on which it was ready to pronounce an opinion. The petitioner in the case, a Mississippi newspaper editor who had been arrested and tried by a military commission under the first Reconstruction Act, contended that Congress did not have the authority to limit the Court's appellate jurisdiction. The Court, however, acquiesced in the congressional action, referring to the terms of Article III of the Constitution, which provide that the appellate jurisdiction of the Court is conferred "with such exceptions and under such regulations as Congress shall make." The Court concluded: "We are not at liberty to inquire into the motives of the legislature. We can only examine into its power under the Constitution; and the power to make exceptions to the appellate jurisdiction of this Court is given by express words."[13]

---

[13]Ex Parte McCardle, 7 Wallace 506 (1869).

While the Constitution grants Congress the authority to determine the appellate jurisdiction of the federal courts, most congressional efforts to use this power to bring the Supreme Court into line have failed. Usually a disgruntled congressional minority sponsors legislation to limit Supreme Court jurisdiction with no hope of success. However, Congress has also pressured the Supreme Court by introducing legislation or proposing constitutional amendments to overrule its decisions. Congress cannot legislatively overturn a Court decision based upon the Constitution, but it can overrule a judgment that has applied statutory law (law made by statutes, or legislation). Although many bills have been introduced to restrict or change Supreme Court interpretations of statutory laws, few have succeeded.

Congress has been most successful in changing unpopular Supreme Court decisions through proposing constitutional amendments that have later been adopted by the states. For instance, the Eleventh Amendment (1798), which makes states immune to suits brought within the original jurisdiction of the Supreme Court by citizens of other states for the collection of debts, overruled the Court's controversial decision in *Chisholm v. Georgia* (1793). The Fourteenth Amendment, adopted in 1868, was intended by its congressional sponsors to overturn the Court's decision in *Barron v. Baltimore* (1833), which held that the Bill of Rights was not applicable to the states. The Supreme Court, however, had the last word on that issue when it held in the *Slaughterhouse Cases* (1873) that the Fourteenth Amendment did not change the *Barron* ruling. When the Court held a congressionally imposed income tax to be unconstitutional in *Pollock v. Farmers' Loan and Trust Company* (1895), Congress proposed, and the states adopted, the Sixteenth Amendment in 1913, which overruled the decision. The Twenty-sixth Amendment (1971), which prohibited the United States or any state from denying citizens 18 years of age or older the right to vote, overturned a 1970 Court decision that upheld the authority of Congress to lower the voting age in federal but not in state and local elections.[14]

Members of Congress have unsuccessfully proposed other amendments to overrule Supreme Court decisions. Amendments have been introduced to overturn *Baker v. Carr* (1962), the ruling that gave the federal courts jurisdiction, under the equal protection clause of the Fourteenth Amendment, over the apportionment of state legislatures. Amendments have been introduced to allow prayer in public schools, contrary to the Court's ruling in *Engle v. Vitale* (1962). Also contrary to Court opinions, amendments to prevent school busing and to give the states authority to regulate abortions have been proposed.

Particularly since the New Deal, supporters of judicial independence, within and outside Congress, have prevented the success of most political incursions upon the Supreme Court. The reaction to North Carolina Senator Jesse Helms's proposals to cripple the Court, proposals which failed to gain any significant support in the Senate or the House, was one of deep concern for the constitutional system and the independent judiciary. Strong opposition to Helms's recommendations appeared both on Capitol Hill and elsewhere. The president of the American Bar Association and other prominent persons in the legal profession, including former attorneys general, solicitors general, and a former Supreme Court justice, sent a strongly worded message to Congress opposing legislation that would overturn prior Supreme Court decisions and restrict the Court's jurisdiction. The message stated, in part:

We are opposed to the pending legislative restrictions on the jurisdiction of federal courts to hear or grant remedies in constitutional cases involving such controversial issues as school desegregation and busing, prayers in public schools and abortion. We urge that Congress, in resolving these issues, not respond to dissatisfaction with particular Court decisions by attempting statutorily to rewrite constitutional law.

As individuals, we hold varying views on the substantive policy issues which are the subjects of these proposals, and as a group we take no position on them. But we are united in the belief that the proposals threaten our fundamental constitutional principles: the independence and supremacy in constitutional questions of the federal judiciary, the separation of powers, and the system of checks and balances.[15]

Colorado Senator Gary Hart (D.) expressed the views of a majority of his colleagues, as they debated the Helms proposal: "Concern about passage of the so-called Court-stripping bills is found among both Democrats and Republicans, liberals and conservatives, and it is not a partisan issue nor is it an ideological issue. It is at its very essence and at its foundation a constitutional issue. For the Constitution—our national charter—is at stake, and the Constitution belongs to all of us."[16]

For his part, Jesse Helms responded that Congress "may indeed interpret the Constitution differently from the Supreme Court and exercise its powers consistent with such interpretation." Forgetting John Marshall's statement of judicial power in *Marbury v. Madison*, Helms declared that the courts are not "the exclusive arbiter of the meaning of the Constitution." Helms furthermore cited nineteenth-century arguments in support of limited judicial power, including statements by Andrew Jackson and Abraham Lincoln.[17]

Judicial self-restraint. While the Supreme Court has often entered the "political thicket," to use Justice Felix Frankfurter's apt term, it has just as frequently exercised self-restraint

---

[14]*Oregon v. Mitchell*, 400 U.S. 112 (1970).

[15]*Congressional Record*, August 18, 1982, p. S10741.

[16]Ibid., p. S10743.

[17]Ibid., p. S10739.

in refusing to rule on controversial political issues. The Court has frequently applied the *political question doctrine* to support self-restraint. The doctrine proclaims that courts should not rule upon cases that are essentially political in nature, involving far-reaching questions of public policy that are more appropriately resolved by Congress, the president, state legislatures, and executives.

The Court applied the political question doctrine, for example, to support its refusal to rule in *Luther v. Borden* (1849) on the question of which of two contending political movements in Rhode Island was the legitimate government. The guaranty clause of the Constitution (Article IV, Section 4), stated the Court, which provides "the United States shall guarantee to every state in this Union a Republican form of government," must be enforced by Congress, not the courts.[18]

Chief Justice John Marshall had originally stated the political question doctrine in *Marbury v. Madison* (1803). "The province of the Court," he stated, "is, solely, to decide on the rights of individuals, not to inquire how the executive, or executive officers perform duties in which they have a discretion. Questions in their nature political, or which are, by the Constitution and laws, submitted to the executive, can never be made in this Court."[19]

The Court, using the political question doctrine, has refused to rule on a variety of cases, particularly presidential actions in foreign affairs. In the domestic political arena, the doctrine has been widely cited as the basis for the Court's early refusal to intervene in cases challenging state apportionment laws that determine the boundaries of congressional and state legislative districts.

Justice Felix Frankfurter, who thoroughly believed in judicial self-restraint, wrote the Court's plurality opinion in the 1946 case of

Colegrove v. Green, invoking the political question doctrine in declining to accept jurisdiction over a challenge to an Illinois congressional apportionment law. Frankfurter wrote:

We are of opinion that the petitioners ask of this Court what is beyond its competence to grant. This is one of those demands on judicial power which cannot be met by verbal fencing about 'jurisdiction.' It must be resolved by considerations on the basis of which this Court, from time to time, has refused to intervene in controversies. It has refused to do so because due regard for the effective working of our government reveals this issue to be of a particularly political nature and therefore not meet for judicial determination.[20]

When the Supreme Court accepted jurisdiction over electoral reapportionment cases in *Baker v. Carr* (1962), Justice Frankfurter expressed, in a dissenting opinion, his strong view that courts should not intervene in essentially political matters. Judicial activism in the political sphere, he wrote,

may well impair the Court's position as the ultimate organ of 'the supreme law of the land' in that vast range of legal problems, often strongly entangled in popular feeling, on which this Court must pronounce. The Court's authority—possessed of neither the purse nor the sword—ultimately rests on sustained public confidence in its moral sanction. Such feeling must be nourished by the Court's complete detachment, in fact and in appearance, from political entanglements and by abstention from injecting itself into the clash of political forces in political settlements.[21]

The political question doctrine is only one

---

[18]Howard 1 (1849).

[19]1 Cranch 137 (1803).

[20]328 U.S. 549 (1946). While the decision of the Court, on a 4–3 vote, was to decline jurisdiction in the *Colegrove* case, Justice John Rutledge, who voted with the majority, wrote a concurring opinion expressing his view that the Court did have jurisdiction over electoral reapportionment cases. Rutledge felt that since the *Colegrove* case arose in an election year, a judicial decision that would undoubtedly have overturned the Illinois apportionment scheme would disrupt the upcoming elections; therefore he voted to decline jurisdiction on a one-time basis.

[21]369 U.S. 186 (1962).

(Drawing by Dana Fradon; © 1979 The New Yorker Magazine, Inc.)

"Damn it, Fenton! We can't refuse to hear every case."
Courts may exercise judicial self-restraint under certain conditions by refusing to hear a case.

reason for judicial self-restraint. Courts have, particularly in reviewing the decisions of administrative agencies, claimed *judicial inexpertise* in factual matters and limited themselves to the review of legal and procedural questions. Courts may also exercise self-restraint by declining jurisdiction on the ground that a case and controversy *does not exist*, denying standing to a plaintiff. The Supreme Court also has discretion to *refuse the grant of a writ of certiorari*, or may limit a writ to specified issues, in exercising self-restraint.

Reviewing judicial activism and self-restraint, political scientist John P. Roche has concluded:

The power of the Supreme Court to invade the decision-making arena . . . is a consequence of that fragmentation of political power which is normal in the United States. No cohesive majority, such as formally exists in Britain, would permit a politically irresponsible judiciary

to usurp decision-making functions, but, for complex social and institutional reasons, there are few issues in the United States on which cohesive majorities exist.[22]

The Supreme Court is more likely to exercise self-restraint when it faces clearly defined political majorities. The New Deal Court, for example, changed its position from activism to self-restraint in reviewing economic legislation as it became clear that Roosevelt and Congress reflected an overwhelming political majority. The Burger Court limited the busing decisions of its predecessor as political opposition to busing mounted. The Court's abortion decision, while highly controversial, was supported, according to public opinion polls, by a majority of the people. Although the

---

[22]John P. Roche, "Judicial Self-restraint," *The American Political Science Review*, Vol. 49 (September 1955), p. 772.

Court continues to define the law and even occasionally to act as a "super legislature," in the long run it is limited, as are other branches of the government, by political forces.

Enforcement of Judicial Policy

Once the judicial branch has set public policy, the problem of carrying out its policy decisions still remains. Sometimes the Supreme Court delegates part of this task to the lower federal courts. For example, after deciding that segregation in public schools was unconstitutional in the 1954 case of *Brown v. Board of Education,* the Court handed down a second decision the following year that provided guidelines for implementing the first decision. In the *Brown* decision of 1955, the Court delegated to the district courts in the states where the defendants resided the responsibility of issuing any orders and decrees necessary to desegregate the school system in an orderly fashion. This delegation of responsibility did not give the lower courts the ability to initiate enforcement of the Supreme Court's decision in all public school systems, however. In order for the desegregation policy to be applied to school districts not involved in the *Brown* decision, cases had to be brought to the lower federal courts for trials.

As the Supreme Court extended its desegregation rulings to require, where necessary, the busing of schoolchildren to achieve racial balances, the district courts became deeply involved in shaping busing orders and even in the administration of school systems. In another area, that of electoral reapportionment, the district courts, once given jurisdiction over apportionment cases, in *Baker v. Carr* (1962), were deluged with challenges to state apportionment statutes. In state after state the courts had to determine whether or not apportionment schemes violated constitutional standards of equal protection. Whenever the Supreme Court announces a major change in constitutional interpretation (as when it up-

held a woman's right to have an abortion in *Roe v. Wade* [1973]) the lower courts must, whenever a case and controversy is brought to them, apply the new standards of constitutional law.

Enforcement of Supreme Court decisions may involve not only the lower courts but also the executive branch of government. After the Court's decisions in the two *Brown* cases, the district courts became involved in new cases concerning the desegregation of public school systems. When desegregation orders from the lower courts were not followed voluntarily, the chief executive stepped in to enforce them.

In one such incident, Arkansas Governor Orval Faubus prevented black students from entering Little Rock's Central High School by assigning the Arkansas division of the National Guard to keep them out. President Dwight Eisenhower then called out federal troops and nationalized the Arkansas National Guard to enforce the federal court order to desegregate the high school.

In addition to enforcing decisions of the Supreme Court, the lower federal courts also play some role in the enforcement of congressional policies. Through the enactment of various laws, Congress has provided for the involvement of the courts in the enforcement processes of such administrative agencies as the National Labor Relations Board and the Federal Trade Commission (FTC). However, when the courts do become involved in such enforcement, it is the executive branch or the bureaucracy that initiates the enforcement proceedings. For example, if the FTC, under authority granted by Congress, seeks an injunction to halt what it considers to be an unfair trade practice, the agency must secure such an injunction through a district court. The court must then determine whether the request of the agency is proper before the injunction can be issued.

Apart from being directly involved in the policy-enforcement activities of the bureaucracy, courts have general power of judicial review over administrative decisions. Although this power is strictly limited by congressional statute, administrative cases still comprise an important segment of the federal courts' work load. The courts generally do not become involved in substantive policy matters in reviewing administrative decisions, but limit themselves to procedural issues, making certain that the agencies have followed the procedures statutes have imposed upon them and have adhered to constitutional due process. In areas such as antitrust law, however, where the courts are an integral part of the enforcement process, their interpretations of statutory law (for example, of the meaning of what constitutes a "restraint of trade" as prohibited by statute) shape the policies that may be implemented.

INFLUENCES ON THE JUDICIARY

The Constitution supports a politically independent judiciary, but it does not isolate the federal courts from political influences. Courts are affected directly by the individuals and groups—including representatives of the other branches of government—who bring cases and controversies before them. Judges must consider and debate the written briefs and oral arguments presented to them. The courts are also influenced indirectly by the powers of Congress and the president to regulate their size and jurisdiction and make judicial appointments.

Cases that involve the government constitute most of the work load of the Supreme Court and courts of appeals. About 60 percent of the cases argued before the Supreme Court have the government as a party or as an amicus curiae (friend of the court).

The fact that government itself is the major source of demands made on the federal courts has had a profound effect. Many of the cases that resulted in policy-making decisions on civil rights and voting rights would not have been taken to the courts without the government's participation. Requests by government agencies to appeal lower-court decisions are often approved by the solicitor general so that the Supreme Court can set important public policy, even though the government itself might be overruled in such cases.

Direct Pressures on the Judiciary

The courts, unlike the other branches of government, cannot initiate action; they can only respond to the actions of others who bring matters before them. Moreover, it is quite difficult to gain access to the judicial system. It is necessary, first, that an actual case or controversy within the meaning of the law be involved; second, that the courts have jurisdiction under constitutional or statutory law to consider the case; third, that the parties requesting judicial action be "aggrieved" parties in the eyes of the law; and fourth, that the parties involved have the time to fight the case and the money to hire competent attorneys.

The influence of pressure groups. The requirements for obtaining judicial action tend to limit the number and sources of demands on the courts. Generally, pressure groups are more apt to possess the time, money, and skill necessary for taking legal action than are individuals.

The types of groups that are involved in the judicial process include large corporations, labor unions, and farm groups, as well as federal, state, and local governmental agencies, particularly law enforcement agencies. Some specialized groups, such as the American Civil Liberties Union (ACLU) and the National Association for the Advancement of Colored People (NAACP), help individuals bring cases to court to obtain their rights through the judicial process. Lawyers also have increasingly been involved in *pro bono* (for the public good) work that has increased the access of individuals to the courts. Even in the sphere of public interest law, however, litigation continues to be largely a group process. The Legal Services Corporation, a federal agency, makes grants to local agencies and groups that provide legal services for the poor. Ralph Nader has sponsored the Public Citizen Litigation Group, which may initiate court cases to protect consumer interests in such areas as health, environment, and transportation.

"Public interest" groups represent not only the individual consumer and the poor but also the conservative "public interest" views of corporations. For example, the Capital Legal Foundation, which receives contributions from corporations such as General Electric, Chase Manhattan Bank, and Exxon, litigates cases and monitors the activities of administrative agencies. The Washington Legal Foundation, the California-based Pacific Legal Foundation, and the Denver-based Mountain States Legal Foundation (of which Ronald Reagan's secretary of the interior, James Watt, was president until coming to Washington) are examples of conservative litigation groups.

The legal profession and the judicial process. America has become a litigious society. Lawsuits abound, and are initiated, it seems, at the drop of a hat. The legal profession is an important ingredient in the increasingly important role of the courts in resolving disputes requiring the interpretation of both statutory and constitutional law. Thousands of lawyers graduate from the nation's law schools each year, armed with the knowledge and possessing the incentive to put their new trade to work. Even before graduating they often have worked in their law schools' legal aid clinics, which provide free legal advice to the poor. Although most disputes handled by lawyers are settled out of court, the volume of litigation has grown to a point where justices, from the Supreme Court down, are calling for new courts and more judges to handle their work loads.

The legal profession—particularly its leaders and scholars—has had a profound influ-

ence on the courts beyond supporting, often unintentionally, litigation as a means of resolving disputes. The profession has developed and taught concepts of justice and fairness that have become an integral part of the law. The law schools have spawned judges and lawyers who have been trained in the art of advocacy, usually with an emphasis upon the importance of the protection of private interests and rights against governmental actions. It is the persons trained in the law who write the legislation that guarantees access to the courts, expands judicial review of administrative decisions, and generally helps to make the judiciary a major political force.

The role of the Justice Department. This executive department, under the supervision of the attorney general, provides legal counsel for the national government on judicial matters. The Justice Department also has been given the responsibility of enforcing various federal laws by initiating cases in the courts. In addition, the department aids the president and other executive departments and agencies in any matter that requires court action. Under the Taft-Hartley Act, for example, the president has the authority to seek delay of a strike that he feels is against the national interest. In such an instance the Justice Department may be asked to go before a federal district court in order to secure a court injunction against the union to halt the strike.

The solicitor general. Within the Justice Department, the solicitor general and his staff are responsible for arguing cases on behalf of the United States in almost all instances when the government is a party to a case, at any level of the court system. The solicitor general's office represents administrative agencies in the judicial process and may also file amicus curiae (friend of the court) briefs in all cases in which the government has an interest.

The Justice Department represents the president's views as well as the interests of administrative agencies. The Reagan administration, for example, wanted to use the federal courts to remold the "liberal" interpretation of prior judicial decisions that had supported busing and the right to abortion. Attorney General William French Smith called upon the courts to consider "the groundswell of conservatism evidenced by the 1980 election." The Justice Department filed a brief in an important busing case with the Fifth Circuit Court of Appeals, asking it to reconsider a district court order requiring busing in Louisiana's East Baton Rouge parish. The brief, filed in 1981, noted that under President Jimmy Carter the Justice Department had urged the opposite decision by supporting busing. But, urged the brief, "experience has shown court-ordered transportation generally to be a failed experiment [that] erodes community support for public education."[23]

The Reagan Justice Department also filed an anti-abortion brief, written by Solicitor General Rex Lee, a former dean of the Brigham Young University Law School. Lee had written a book that cited *Roe v. Wade*, the Supreme Court's 1973 decision upholding the right to abortion, as an example of "improper judicial intrusions into fundamental policy decisions that ought to be left to the legislature."[24] The brief repeated Lee's views that the Supreme Court should not intrude into policy-making arenas that are the proper province of state legislatures. (See Box 16.1.)

Since the government is a party to many cases, the solicitor general is involved in one-half of all major cases and approximately one-third of all cases that reach the Supreme Court. With a few exceptions, no administrative agency can appeal a case from a lower federal court to the Supreme Court without the approval of the solicitor general. The solicitor general's staff is also highly experienced in the judicial process. The solicitor general's

opinion is given more weight than those of most private attorneys, which makes him or her a potent legal force in the federal courts.

The solicitor general's office is subject to demands and supports, most of which come from the administrative agencies that make use of the office. The success of the solicitor general before the courts depends not only on the special skills of the solicitor general's own office but also on the validity of the cases initiated by the administrative agencies.

Antitrust Division. Numerous other divisions within the Justice Department also create inputs for the judiciary. In contrast to the solicitor general's office, the Antitrust Division of the Justice Department is essentially a separate administrative agency with specialized interests. A major activity of the division is that of filing suits against certain private parties to prevent mergers and business combinations that the agency considers to be restraints on trade in violation of antitrust laws.

Tax Division. The Tax Division of the Justice Department employs more than 200 lawyers to represent the United States in both civil and criminal cases arising under internal revenue laws. The Tax Division acts as counsel for the Internal Revenue Service in all cases in federal and state courts, with the exception of the federal Tax Court. The Treasury Department also employs lawyers to plead cases for the Internal Revenue Service before the Tax Court.

Other divisions. There are several other divisions within the Justice Department that represent the government in various kinds of court actions. The Land and Natural Resources Division, with more than a hundred lawyers, handles claims relating to the more than 750 million acres of land belonging to the federal government. Also within the department are the Internal Security Division and the Criminal Division. These divisions make direct demands on the courts by initiating certain kinds of prosecution proceedings.

The Civil Rights Division of the Justice De-

---

[23]Linda Greenhouse, "Busing Issue: New Attack," *The New York Times*, August 12, 1982, p. A25.

[24]Linda Greenhouse, "Abortion Brief Serves as a Roadmap," *The New York Times*, August 10, 1982, p. B6.

With pro- and anti-abortion groups rolling out their full legal firepower, the U.S. Supreme Court on November 30 tackled the most ticklish abortion issues it has faced in almost a decade.

The Justices heard arguments in Missouri, Ohio and Virginia cases that raise important questions about how far states and cities may go in regulating abortions, which have doubled in number to more than 1.2 million a year since the High Court legalized the procedure in 1973.

The suits, argued in a packed courtroom, stem from the contention of medical and pro-abortion groups that various state and local laws are "back-door" moves "to inhibit the right to choose" an abortion—a right the Supreme Court found to be implicit in the U.S. Constitution.

The rulings of the Justices—expected next spring—could affect dozens of laws being drafted or already on the books. [In 1983 the Court held, 6–3, that states could not restrict the right to abortion recognized in *Roe v. Wade* (1973), and ruled against each of the proposals to limit abortion presented in the oral arguments reprinted here.]

For a look at key issues the cases raise, from oral arguments and written briefs presented to the Court—

Who should have the leading role in determining curbs on abortion: Judges or legislators?

Solicitor General Rex Lee, speaking on behalf of the Reagan administration, told the Justices that state lawmakers should be able to enact reasonable limits on abortion. "The legislature

has superior fact-finding capabilities, is directly responsible to the public . . . and has greater flexibility than the courts," Lee declared.

Calling Lee's argument a "terrifying thought," Frank Susman, an attorney for the Planned Parenthood Association of Kansas City, said that under Lee's theory, "constitutional rights will be bargained away in legislatures." Susman accused abortion opponents of seeking to "thwart the free exercise of the right to an abortion."

May states and cities require that minors get parental consent before obtaining abortions?

The state of Missouri and the city of Akron, Ohio, say yes. Speaking for Akron, which applies such a rule to girls under 15 years of age, attorney Alan Segedy said that such girls "are not mature enough to make that decision. . . . The state can draw a line somewhere, as it does in other areas such as voting."

Responding for the Akron Center for Reproductive Health, lawyer Stephan Landsman asserted that such a law is too strict because it gives parents a "blanket veto" over all abortions involving young girls.

Is it reasonable for officials to make a woman wait 24 hours after requesting an abortion before it is performed?

Akron said that such a "cooling off" period gives a woman time to reconsider her decision, because as attorney Segedy put it, "clinics assume that abortion is always the best choice for a pregnant woman." He noted that women could use the extra time to obtain advice that they don't get during group counseling sessions offered by clinics.

Clinic lawyer Landsman responded that the requirement "poses a significant burden" on women seeking abortions, particularly low-income women from out of town who are forced to make a second trip or stay overnight. In addition, he said, the rule implies that "women are not to be trusted to make up their own minds."

May doctors be directed by government to warn women of the risks and consequences of an abortion?

Akron contended that its detailed seven-point statement on the subject enhances "freedom of choice" by making sure that pregnant women hear the pros and cons of abortion. Among other things, the law requires that women be told "the unborn child is a human life from the moment of conception," and that abortion "is a major surgical procedure which can result in serious complications."

Clinic lawyer Landsman declared in response that such language is "clearly slanted against abortion" and is "medically inaccurate." Compelling a doctor to read the statement, he added, "turns the physician into an adversary" of the patient.

Can women more than three months pregnant be required to have their abortions in hospitals?

Defending that Missouri rule, State Atty. Gen. John Ashcroft contended that "the state has the right to demand a margin of safety."

Ashcroft argued that many experts believe that after the 12th week of pregnancy, a woman having an abortion "belongs in a hospital" in case of complications.

Planned Parenthood lawyer Susman maintained that abortion techniques have become much safer in recent years and now can be used as safely in clinics as in hospitals. Susman said that many women who want abortions would be discouraged from seeking them if they had to go into hospitals.

May abortion be singled out among medical treatments when states enact criminal laws that apply to doctors?

Justice John Paul Stevens suggested that Virginia was doing so by restricting certain abortions to hospitals while placing no such limits on operations such as brain surgery.

Roy Lucas, attorney for a doctor sentenced to 20 days in jail for defying this requirement, agreed. He asserted that the state law unfairly puts doctors on the defensive, presuming them guilty unless they can prove that abortions performed in places other than hospitals are justified by "medical necessity."

Virginia Deputy Atty. Gen. William Broaddus defended use of criminal laws in abortion cases on the ground that "the state's interest in maternal health" is "compelling."

What the Supreme Court hears does not always determine what it decides, but both written briefs and oral arguments are important influences upon the justices.

partment handles cases arising under various civil rights laws. This division can file suits against certain officials or private persons who interfere with the right of citizens to vote. The Civil Rights Division can take similar legal action to enforce the regulations against racial discrimination in schools, hotels, and other public facilities covered by the civil rights laws.

Indirect Influences on the Judiciary

Federal judges who choose to remain on the bench cannot be removed from office except by impeachment. Moreover, the Constitution provides that their compensation cannot be reduced. In fact, they have tenure not unlike that enjoyed by a large number of university and college professors. Neither the president nor members of Congress, who are uninvolved in the day-to-day cases and controversies that must be settled by the courts, can directly affect judicial decision making. Each branch can, however, influence judicial decision making in the future. Congress can change the appellate jurisdiction of the courts and can propose constitutional amendments to overrule Supreme Court decisions (see pp. 441–442). And the president can use his constitutional authority to nominate Supreme Court justices and lower federal court judges to try to "pack" the judiciary.

Court appointments. The special preserve of the President of the United States is the appointment of justices to the Supreme Court, even though the Senate must give its advice and consent.

By the end of their terms of office all except four presidents have been able to appoint at least one of their nominees to the Court. After the administration of George Washington, in which of course the entire Supreme Court was appointed by Washington, only five presidents—Jackson, Lincoln, Taft, Franklin D. Roosevelt, and Eisenhower—were

able to appoint a majority of the Court during their administrations. Roosevelt had great difficulty with the Court until 1937, the year in which he was able to make his first appointment, that of Hugo Black, to the Court. By the end of Roosevelt's administration in 1945 all nine of the justices who had been on the court when he assumed the presidency in 1933 had either died or retired from office, and he was able to replace them with his own nominees.

Although presidents always try to appoint Supreme Court justices who share their broad political philosophy, particularly their views on the proper role of the Court in the political system, the White House is subject to a number of pressures in making Supreme Court appointments. These pressures are exerted by, among others, the important members of the Senate Judiciary Committee and other powerful senior senators, especially those of the president's party; by the American Bar Association, which feels it has a special interest in and is specially qualified to pronounce on judicial appointments (the ABA is most influential at the lower levels of judicial appointment); and by a broad spectrum of interest groups—all of which recognize the importance of the Supreme Court in the policy-making process.

Political pressures that affect Supreme Court appointments were illustrated in President Ronald Reagan's nomination of the first woman, Sandra Day O'Connor, to fill the Court seat vacated by Justice Potter Stewart, who had retired. Reagan had made a campaign pledge to appoint the first female justice, recognizing not only that it would be a historic act but also that it would increase his appeal to women's groups and pull in a larger segment of the female vote.

The nomination of O'Connor was cleared with the attorney general, Supreme Court justices, who strongly backed her, and with other prominent members of the legal profession. Nevertheless, the conservative New Right and anti-abortion groups opposed her. O'Connor, although personally opposed to abortion, had supported the repeal of an Arizona criminal statute against abortion when she had been a state legislator. Anti-abortion demonstrators marched in protest outside the Senate Office Building while the Judiciary Committee within was holding confirmation hearings. Conservative committee members were able to extract from O'Connor the opinion that abortion questions should be left to legislative bodies rather than determined by courts, but she refused to give them a pledge that she would vote to modify or reverse the 1973 Supreme Court decision upholding the right to abortion. In the end, the opposition to O'Connor proved to be largely symbolic, as her nomination was overwhelmingly approved by the Senate in a 99-to-0 vote.

Reagan again faced little opposition when he nominated another conservative, Antonin Scalia, to the Supreme Court. However, he encountered a political donnybrook when he nominated the highly conservative Judge Robert H. Bork to the Supreme Court in 1987, knowing that the Circuit Court judge and former Yale law school professor would face virulent opposition in the Democratic-controlled Senate. Senate Judiciary Committee Chairman Joseph Biden (D., Del.) joined with liberal colleagues such as Massachusetts Senator Edward Kennedy to spearhead what became a nationally organized liberal crusade to defeat Bork. After the Senate rejected Bork, by a vote of 58–42, Reagan was again embarrassed when he had to withdraw the nomination of Douglas Ginsberg to the high bench after revelations of marijuana use by the nominee in his youth. On his third attempt to fill his third Supreme Court vacancy Reagan succeeded in the appointment of Anthony M. Kennedy, who at the time was considered less conservative than either Bork or Ginsberg.

Reagan's defeats and embarrassments over Supreme Court nominations were certainly not without precedent. For example,

when the first vacancy during the Nixon administration occurred in 1969, the president's first two nominees (Clement Haynsworth and G. Harrold Carswell) were unacceptable to the Senate. Both nominees were vigorously attacked by liberal groups who claimed that the past records and personal conduct of the nominees, particularly in the sphere of civil rights policy, were unacceptable. Nevertheless, Nixon was able to make four appointments to the Court—Chief Justice Warren E. Burger and Associate Justices Harry A. Blackmun, Lewis F. Powell, and William H. Rehnquist—giving the Court a conservative tone that lasted into the Reagan administration.

Nixon's difficulties with the Senate were not unprecedented, nor were they explainable simply in terms of the party split between the White House and the upper body on Capitol Hill. Indeed, both of Nixon's rejected nominations had had the support of such powerful Democratic southern senators as James O. Eastland of Mississippi, chairman of the Senate Judiciary Committee, and John L. McClellan of Arkansas, as well as of the powerful Republican southerner on the Judiciary Committee, Strom Thurmond of South Carolina. Nor were Nixon's nominations overwhelmingly rejected. Haynsworth was turned down by a vote of 55 to 45, and Carswell—widely regarded as a bad appointment purposely made by Nixon to avenge Haynsworth's defeat—was surprisingly rejected by an even closer vote, 51 to 45.

In all, the Senate has rejected 12 of 145 Supreme Court nominations.[25] A number of presidential nominations, facing almost certain Senate rejection, were withdrawn. (See Table 16.2.) Henry J. Abraham has listed a number of reasons for senatorial rejection of nominees, including Senate opposition to the nominat-

---

[25]For an excellent discussion of the entire appointment process, see Henry J. Abraham, *Justices and Presidents* (New York: Oxford University Press, 1974).

TABLE 16.2 SUPREME COURT NOMINATIONS THAT FAILED

Nominee	Year	President	Action
William Paterson	1793	Washington	withdrawn
John Rutledge	1795	Washington	rejected, 10–14
Alexander Wolcott	1811	Madison	rejected, 9–24
John Crittenden	1828	J. Q. Adams	postponed
Roger B. Taney	1835	Jackson	postponed
John Spencer	1844	Tyler	rejected, 21–26
R. Walworth	1844	Tyler	withdrawn
Edward King	1844	Tyler	withdrawn
Edward King	1844	Tyler	withdrawn
John Read	1845	Tyler	postponed
G. Woodward	1846	Polk	rejected, 20–29
Edward Bradford	1852	Fillmore	postponed
George Badger	1853	Fillmore	postponed
William Micou	1853	Fillmore	postponed
Jeremiah Black	1861	Buchanan	rejected, 25–26
Henry Stanbery	1866	A. Johnson	postponed
Ebenezer Hoar	1870	Grant	rejected, 24–33
George Williams	1874	Grant	withdrawn
Caleb Cushing	1874	Grant	withdrawn
Stanley Matteys	1881	Hayes	postponed
W. B. Hornblower	1894	Cleveland	rejected, 24–30
Wheeler H. Peckham	1894	Cleveland	rejected, 32–41
John J. Parker	1930	Hoover	rejected, 39–41
Abe Fortas[a]	1968	L. Johnson	withdrawn
Homer Thornberry	1968	L. Johnson	withdrawn
C. Haynsworth	1969	Nixon	rejected, 45–55
G. H. Carswell	1970	Nixon	rejected, 45–51
Robert Bork	1987	Reagan	rejected, 42–58
Douglas Ginsburg	1987	Reagan	not submitted[b]

Note: Twenty-nine of the 145 presidential nominations have failed to obtain Senate confirmation. However, five nominees declined appointment after having been nominated (Harrison, 1789; W. Cushing, 1796; Jay, 1800; Lincoln, 1811; Adams, 1811) and two withdrew after being confirmed (W. Smith, 1837; Conkling, 1822).

[a]In 1968, Fortas, an associate justice, was nominated for chief justice.

[b]Publicly announced but withdrawn before the president formally submitted his nomination to the Senate.

Source: Harold W. Stanley and Richard G. Niemi, *Vital Statistics on American Politics*, 2d ed. (Washington, DC.: C.Q. Press, 1990), p. 269. Reprinted with permission from Congressional Quarterly, Inc.

ing president, controversy over the public policy positions of the nominee, a perception of the nominee as politically unreliable, and the nominee's clear lack of qualifications to sit on the bench of the nation's highest court. Although "senatorial courtesy" usually applies to nominees to the federal bench within the states, requiring presidential consultation with senior senators of the president's own party from those states before making the nominations, a general senatorial courtesy has also developed with respect to Supreme Court ap-

(Don Wright, *The Miami News*)

"When I hired Warren Burger he told me he'd never driven a bus in his life."
President Nixon's appointee for chief justice, Warren E. Burger, surprisingly upheld busing as a means of desegregating the schools.

pointments, as it has with regard to nominations to the top positions in the executive branch.[26] And the failure of presidents to consult adequately in advance with the Senate on their Supreme Court nominees is an important reason for Senate rejection.[27]

The fact that most presidents have not been able to appoint a majority of Supreme Court justices is indicative of the success of the constitutional provision for life tenure for the justices in insulating the Court from the political influence of the chief executive. In the twentieth century the continuity of the Senate Judiciary Committee, and of the Senate itself, gives the Senate far greater potential powers to influence the Supreme Court than is possessed by the White House.

Not only do presidents rarely have the opportunity to appoint more than a few justices to the Supreme Court but their judicial appointees, once having assumed the exalted

mantle of the high Court, may not always support the political philosophy of the president who appointed them. Once on the bench, justices need not bend to the whim of any individual, not even the president. Moreover, life tenure usually means that appointees remain on the Court for decades, and over time their political philosophy may change in a number of ways. Perhaps the most startling turnabout in the twentieth century was that of Chief Justice Earl Warren. President Dwight D. Eisenhower in 1953 appointed Warren to be chief justice, apparently expecting him to be a "middle-of-the-road" conservative like Eisenhower himself. The president was shocked when Warren, soon after his appointment, led the Supreme Court to its unanimous decision in *Brown v. Board of Education.*

Presidential appointment power over the Supreme Court, however limited, is greater than presidential appointment power over the lower federal judiciary—the district courts and the circuit courts of appeal. In the case of appointments to these lower federal courts, the president must consult not only with the senior senators of his party from the states involved but also with state party chairmen, governors, mayors, members of the bench, members of the bar, and appropriate leaders and committees of the American Bar Association. The nature of the Senate is such that powerful senior senators, even if they are not of the president's party, should be consulted by the White House when they represent the state in which lower judicial appointments are to be made.

Presidents, however, can have a significant influence in shaping the lower federal judiciary, regardless of the broad political considerations they must take into account. President Reagan, like presidents before him, used partisan loyalty as the basis of his federal judicial appointments. (See Table 16.3.) A Justice Department official involved in finding suitable candidates commented: "[Political] philosophy certainly has been a factor

---

[26]For a discussion of senatorial courtesy, see p. 368.

[27]See Abraham, *Justices and Presidents*, pp. 31–33 and passim.

TABLE 16.3 FEDERAL JUDICIAL APPOINTMENTS OF SAME PARTY AS PRESIDENT, PRESIDENTS CLEVELAND TO REAGAN

President	*Party*	*Percentage*
Cleveland	Democrat	97.3
Harrison	Republican	87.9
McKinley	Republican	95.7
T. Roosevelt	Republican	95.8
Taft	Republican	82.2
Wilson	Democrat	98.6
Harding	Republican	97.7
Coolidge	Republican	94.1
Hoover	Republican	85.7
F. Roosevelt	Democrat	96.4
Truman	Democrat	93.1
Eisenhower	Republican	95.1
Kennedy	Democrat	90.9
Johnson	Democrat	95.2
Nixon	Republican	93.7
Ford	Republican	81.2
Carter	Democrat	94.8
Reagan	Republican	97.8

Source: Harold W. Stanley and Richard G. Niemi, *Vital Statistics on American Politics,* 2d ed. (Washington, D.C.: Congressional Quarterly Press, 1990), p. 268. Reprinted with permission from Congressional Quarterly, Inc.

with regard to our appointments. I think it is entirely appropriate."[28] Political science professor Sheldon Goldman observed, "I think the Reagan administration has taken full advantage of the prerogatives of the presidency. They put on the bench those kind of people who are compatible with their ideology and political commitment. That was true of the Carter administration as well."[29]

While conservative groups applauded Reagan's appointments, groups representing minorities and women were disappointed because of what they viewed as a lack of fuller representation among the nominees. The Justice Department spokesperson for the Reagan administration declared: "We approach this from a different philosophy than the Carter administration. We did not adopt a view that we should strive for a quota or a goal of a particular number of women or minorities to be put on the federal bench. We wanted to first see that the people we nominated were of the highest possible quality."[30] However, the American Bar Association, which reviews the qualifications of presidential nominees, rated Reagan's appointees only slightly higher than the appointees of the Carter administration.

Presidents in the future will continue to take into account not only partisan but also other factors, including religion, race and ethnicity, and gender, in nominating federal district and appellate court judges as well as Supreme Court justices. Table 16.4 illustrates the different religious, racial, and gender

[28]*Congressional Quarterly Weekly Report*, Vol. 41, No. 2 (January 15, 1983), p. 83.

[29]Ibid.

Ibid., p. 84.

TABLE 16.4   **CHARACTERISTICS OF FEDERAL DISTRICT AND APPELLATE COURT NOMINEES, PRESIDENTS JOHNSON TO REAGAN (PERCENT)**

	Johnson nominees	*Nixon nominees*	*Ford nominees*	*Carter nominees*	*Reagan nominees*
District courts					
Religion					
Protestant	58.2	73.2	73.1	60.4	60.0
Catholic	31.1	18.4	17.3	27.7	30.4
Jewish	10.7	8.4	9.6	11.9	9.3
Race/ethnicity					
White	93.4	95.5	88.5	78.7	92.4
Black	4.1	3.4	5.8	13.9	2.1
Asian-American	0.0	0.0	3.9	0.5	0.7
Hispanic	2.5	1.1	1.9	6.9	4.8
Gender					
Female	1.6	0.6	1.9	14.4	8.3
Total number of nominees	122	179	52	202	290
Courts of Appeals					
Religion					
Protestant	60.0	75.6	58.3	60.7	55.1
Catholic	25.0	15.6	33.3	23.2	30.8
Jewish	15.0	8.9	8.3	16.1	14.1
Race/ethnicity					
White	95.0	97.8	100.0	66.7	97.4
Black	5.0	0.0	0.0	25.0	1.3
Asian-American	0.0	2.2	0.0	8.3	0.0
Hispanic	0.0	0.0	0.0	0.0	1.3
Gender					
Female	2.5	0.0	0.0	0.0	5.1
Total number of appointees	40	45	12	56	78

Source: Harold W. Stanley and Richard G. Niemi, *Vital Statistics on American Politics,* 2d ed. (Washington, D.C.: Congressional Quarterly Press, 1990), pp. 266–267. Reprinted with permission from Congressional Quarterly, Inc.

mixes of presidential nominees from Johnson to Reagan.

THE SUPREME COURT'S CONTINUING POWER

The Supreme Court has exercised remarkable power under a Constitution that on the surface confines the Court's power narrowly to the resolution of concrete cases and contro-versies arising under the Constitution, laws, and treaties. However, as John Marshall pointed out in *McCulloch v. Maryland* (1819), the Constitution was one of enumeration and not of definition, meaning that many of its provisions are vague and need to be clarified and defined by the Supreme Court and Congress. From the outset Supreme Court decisions implied the power of judicial review over congressional legislation, and Congress had in the Judiciary Act of 1789 explicitly given the high court the authority

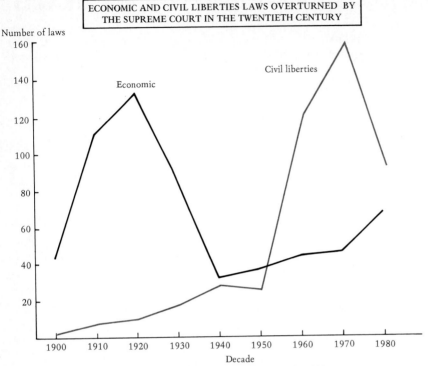

ECONOMIC AND CIVIL LIBERTIES LAWS OVERTURNED BY THE SUPREME COURT IN THE TWENTIETH CENTURY

Note: Civil liberties category does not include laws supportive of civil liberties. Laws include federal, state, and local. The figures for the 1980s are based on the actual numbers for 1980-1987, multiplied by 1.25 to create a ten-year "rate" for that decade.

(Source: Harold W. Stanley and Richard G. Niemi, *Vital Statistics on American Politics*, 2d ed. [Washington, D.C.: Congressional Quarterly Press], p. 285. Reprinted with permission from Congressional Quarterly, Inc.)

FIGURE 16.1

to exercise constitutional review of state actions.

Over its history the Supreme Court has clearly made many decisions that have had a profound impact upon the course of both national and state governments. However, the Supreme Court's power should not be exaggerated. In the early part of the nineteenth century the Court helped to expand national power not by taking an interventionist approach but by upholding congressional laws in such cases as *McCulloch v. Maryland* (1819) and *Gibbons v. Ogden* (1824). In fact, at the federal level, the Court has rarely overturned

congressional legislation, as Table 6.1 (p. 160) illustrates. The Court's most important impact has been in the area of state action where it has generally been far more active than at the federal level.

In 1937 the Supreme Court shifted from the position of activism in reviewing economic legislation to one of self-restraint in the economic sphere, while turning to a more interventionist stance in reviewing federal and state legislation affecting civil liberties and civil rights. As Figure 16.1 illustrates, however, it was not until the Warren era from 1953 to 1968 that the Court actively overturned legislation

"No breakout for me—I'll just sit back and wait for the right Supreme Court ruling to come along."

In recent decades, the Supreme Court has played a notable role in protecting the rights of the accused.

affecting civil liberties and civil rights. While the Court in the 1990s has become less active in reviewing civil liberties and civil rights legislation, its past decisions, defining, for example, the right to privacy in *Roe v. Wade* (1973), remain controversial as the Supreme Court, under the conservative influence of former President Reagan's appointees, begins to exercise more judicial self-restraint.

The question of judicial self-restraint versus judicial interventionism will continue to divide the Supreme Court justices as they grapple with the complex cases coming before them in the 1990s. Conservative justices, who in the past have been willing to inject their values into decisions to determine the fairness of national and state legislation, support self-restraint on the contemporary Court as they seek to reduce its role as a "super legislature," substituting its judgments for those that properly, in their view, should be reserved to the elected representatives of the people.

JUDICIAL SELF-RESTRAINT VERSUS JUDICIAL ACTIVISM IN THE 1990s

The Supreme Court occupies a unique position in our political system. Through its power of constitutional interpretation it in effect can declare what the law is and, in the process, can have a profound impact on the lives of all citizens. Supreme Court decisions have taken many twists and turns. Over its remarkable history the Court has alternated between judicial activism and judicial self-restraint. In the 1990s the Court, under the influence of conservative justices appointed by Ronald Reagan, appears to have taken the stance of judicial self-restraint, as the following case study illustrates.

Letting the People Decide / *Michael Barone with Ted Gest*

The Court Is Changing Rules in Ways That May Change the Country

For many years, the Supreme Court was the place where Americans who felt frustrated or aggrieved by the results of the political process sought relief,

asserting rights that they felt should be free from infringement. Under Chief Justice Earl Warren and, to the surprise of many, under Chief Justice Warren Burger, the Court often responded sympathetically to their claims. But this year, with Chief Jus-

Source: *U.S. News & World Report,* July 10, 1989, pp. 18–19. Copyright, 1989, U.S. News & World Report.

tice William Rehnquist rallying 6–3 and 5–4 majorities and the newest Justice, Anthony Kennedy, often casting decisive votes, the Court has been effectively overturning old decisions and rules. The result has been to turn over to politicians and voters decisions on issues on which Americans have passionate views and are often deeply divided.

Indeed, the Supreme Court this term has been changing the rules in ways that may turn out to change America. The result, says University of Virginia scholar A. E. Dick Howard, is a term that "tells us more about the Court and where it is likely to go than almost any term in 20 years" on civil rights and, some would add, on other issues as well. And as the week ended, the Court had yet to rule on the case that has attracted the most attention and raised the most apprehension—*Webster v. Reproductive Health Services*, the Missouri case in which the Court is reconsidering the 1973 *Roe v. Wade* decision that legalized abortion.

Caution should always be exercised by anyone tempted to declare that the Supreme Court has entered a new judicial era. Narrow majorities can be reversed, and Justices who come out on the same side in cases often depend on different reasoning. In the abortion case, the failure of the Court to decide the case last week, as widely expected, prompted rumors that the Justices were having difficulty putting together an opinion that could command majority support of the Court. As backers and opponents of the *Roe v. Wade* decision that was under attack stood outside the Court last week, their very presence was evidence that the Court's decisions, though sometimes written in dry legalese, penetrate public emotions at a time when there is little interest in conventional political issues.

The decision so far that has ignited the strongest feelings is, ironically, one in which the Court struck down the enforcement of a law—a Texas statute against flag desecration. It was a case in which two Reagan appointees, Justices Antonin Scalia and Kennedy, did not vote with Rehnquist. But opinion against the decision was so strong and so one-sided, among voters and on Capitol Hill, that the issue was thrust immediately into the political process, and the debate centered on whether it could be repealed by statute or whether it should be overturned by a constitutional amendment.

The political response to the Court's several decisions on civil rights has been slower. The Rehnquist Court did not hesitate to change the rules on a series of civil-rights issues. The Court's new and narrow majority insisted it was just interpreting the laws as Congress wrote them, and Justice Kennedy in one case emphasized that he was not "signaling 1 inch of retreat from Congress's policy to forbid discrimination." The Court, in various rulings, made it harder for a city to justify setting aside some of its contracts for minority firms, easier for white workers to challenge racial quotas, harder for minorities to prove racial discrimination in hiring and harder for minority workers to bring cases against what they consider racial harassment.

Technically, these decisions limit what governments or private businesses can be asked to do for minority contract seekers, job seekers and job holders. In practical terms, the decisions thrust back into the political arena issues that the politicians thought the courts had settled—and which arouse strong feelings on both sides. Many blacks and others expressed outrage at what they regarded as a reversal of progress in civil rights. But many other Americans fiercely resent racial quotas, preferences and set-asides.

The most vivid example of the Court's upholding laws that legislatures had already passed came in death-penalty cases. This is in contrast with the Supreme Court of the 1970s, which declared unconstitutional dozens of capital-punishment laws. The Court earlier had declared that it was acting in accordance with Americans' "evolving standards of decency." But in recent years, Americans have come to favor the death penalty by increasing margins. Justice Scalia, writing in the case that upheld death sentences for 16 and 17-year-olds, said "our job is to identify the evolving standards of decency . . .to determine not what they *should be* but what they *are.*"

Legislatures have passed death-penalty laws in most states, and legislators came within one vote of overriding Governor Mario Cuomo's veto of the death penalty last month in New York. Capital punishment remains a hot political issue, as it is in New York and may be again in states like Illinois and Pennsylvania, where portions of the death-penalty statutes have been overturned by courts. On one side, large majorities of voters strongly favor capital punishment. But sizable numbers of white liberals as well as black voters oppose the death penalty, as do governors like Cuomo and Michael Dukakis.

But this recent Court decision and another upholding death sentences for defendants who may be retarded are not likely to produce a rush to the death chamber for the 2,200 convicts now under death sentence. It is the courts, and not the executive branch, that administer this law, and the courts, led by the Supreme Court, have insisted on examining capital cases with a gimlet eye. Lawyers often find good ground to challenge death sentences. In one Florida murder case, a black defendant won a new trial when it was discovered that a police officer had neglected to report that an assault victim said the assailant was white. In another case, a death sentence was overturned when defense investigators showed that prosecutors presented false evidence to the jury. The very irreversibility of the death penalty once it is carried out makes it more likely that judges are going to reverse death sentences more often than lesser punishments. Nonetheless, the Court, in another 5–4 vote, ruled that the state need not pay for lawyers to give convicted criminals a second set of appeals, even though such appeals have resulted in reversal of the death sentence in 40 percent of the cases.

Taken one by one, each of these Supreme Court decisions may have only a marginal effect on the law or daily life. Taken together, they may signal a fundamental shift in direction for the Supreme Court. They show that the Court is ready to defer to the voters as they express themselves through their legislators and other elected officials and not let judges overrule their decisions. The era of judicial activism that began with the Warren Court outlawed school segregation in *Brown v. Board of Education* in 1954 and continued with the one-person-one-vote decisions of 1962 and 1964 and the criminal-procedure decisions culminating in *Miranda v. Arizona* in 1966 proved more durable than many critics expected. These rulings protected segments of society not fully represented in the political process—Southern blacks, criminal suspects, underrepresented voters—from unfair acts of government. Originally, all these decisions were fiercely opposed, but they came to be accepted even by their original targets.

President Richard Nixon, in appointing Warren Burger and other Justices, called for "strict construction" of the Constitution. But the Burger Court of the 1970s was activist in its own way, upholding massive school busing in 1971, legalizing most abortions in 1973 and throwing out much of the campaign-finance-reform law in 1976.

The difference was that not all of these decisions received such universal acceptance. The availability of abortions, systems of racial preference and capital punishment remain controversial: Strongly opposed by large numbers of Americans, strongly favored by large numbers as well. Politicians and voters protested them but could not summon up the massive support needed to pass constitutional amendments to overturn some of them. Marginal changes were prevented by rulings of the Court.

Now, the Rehnquist Court seems to be making such challenges easier by in effect removing some decisions from the judiciary and giving them to the political process. This is not the first time the Supreme Court has turned away from judicial activism. In the first years of this century, the Court often overturned laws that interfered with economic freedoms, including the income tax, minimum-wage-and-hour regulations and child-labor laws. In the 1930s, it declared unconstitutional several major New Deal programs. This prompted Franklin Roosevelt's 1937 Court-packing proposal, which was rejected but which got one elderly Justice to retire, and after 1937 the Court that had been so active in overturning economic regulation never overturned a major piece of economic legislation again. Later, when the Warren Court began its judicial activism phase, Justice Felix Frankfurter, in stinging dissents, said that the Court should leave the acts of other branches of government, on both economic and noneconomic issues, undisturbed except in the clearest cases of constitutional violations. This theory of judicial restraint was kept alive in the Warren and Burger years in the writings of the late Prof. Alexander Bickel, who had been one of Frankfurter's law clerks, and of Bickel's good friend, former federal Judge Robert Bork, whose nomination to the Supreme Court was rejected by the Senate in 1987. Ironically, key votes for judicial restraint this year were cast by the man who won confirmation to the seat Bork was denied—Justice Kennedy.

It is too soon to say that today's Supreme Court has gotten out of the business of social legislation. But it has given the politicians more leeway—or has put them out in the open, where they must make decisions on issues on which their constituents have strong and often conflicting feelings. In the next few weeks, Congress will be grappling with the flag-burning issue, on which strong opinions are almost all on one side. But for some time to come, this year's Supreme Court decisions will force politicians in Washington and across the country to confront other, tougher, issues such as racial preference, capital punishment and abortion. These issues cut to the quick of Americans' lives and rouse passions on both sides. The new majority of the Court may believe it is depoliticizing jurisprudence by leaving decisions to elected legislators. But at a time when the politicians are dwelling on issues like the budget deficit and congressional ethics that do not stir many emotions, the decisions the Court has reached this year, by thrusting hot issues into the political process, have done anything but depoliticize the country.

CASE STUDY 15

The Media: The Fourth Estate

The First Amendment to the Constitution stipulates that "Congress shall make no law . . .abridging the freedom of speech or of the press. . . ." The fight for freedom of the press has been long and bitter. Both Great Britain and its American colonies had strict sedition laws that enabled the government to suppress political criticism. Governor William Berkeley of Virginia perhaps best expressed the view of the colonial governments during the seventeenth century, when there was no press in most colonies and no freedom of the press:

But, I thank God, there are no free schools nor printing; and I hope we shall not have these [for a] hundred years; for learning has brought disobedience, and heresy, and sects into the world, and printing has divulged them, and libels against the best government. God keep us from both![1]

The press, banned in the seventeenth century in many colonies, began to flourish during the eighteenth century and was to exert an important influence in shaping the political attitudes of the colonists in the direction of the Revolution. Newspapers and pamphlets throughout the colonies, particularly in Boston, Philadelphia, New York, and in the states of Maryland and Virginia, spurred and helped to lead the fight of the beleaguered colonists against Great Britain.

A free press and political freedom were considered inseparable in eighteenth-century America. An anonymous correspondent forcefully expressed the prevailing attitude of the colonists in a letter written in 1734 to John Peter Zenger, the publisher of the *New York Weekly Journal*, shortly before his trial for seditious libel:

The *Liberty of the Press* is the *Foundation* of all our other *Liberties*, whether *Civil* or *Religious* and whenever the Liberty of the Press is taken away, either by *open Force*, or any *little, dirty infamous Arts*, we shall immediately become as *wretched*, as *ignorant*, and as *despicable* SLAVES, as any one Nation in all *Europe*.[2]

Zenger's acquittal in 1735 spurred the expansion of freedom of the press.

The present-day adversary relationship between the government and the press stems from the circumstances surrounding the rise of a free press in the eighteenth century. No government likes criticism of its actions, which may undermine public confidence and lead to change either peacefully or by revolution. Most governments in the world continue to suppress the press because they agree with the sentiments expressed by Governor Berkeley over three hundred years ago. Modern totalitarian regimes, however, recognizing the importance of the press, control it and use it as an instrument of suppression. When the adversary relationship between the press and the government changes to one of collusion

---

[1]Clinton Rossiter, *Seedtime of the Republic* (New York: Harcourt Brace, 1953), p. 29.

[2]Ibid., p. 31.

and mutual support, political freedom vanishes.

The contemporary role of the press is profoundly shaped by history, traditions, customs, and by the Constitution as well.

THE CONSTITUTIONAL CONTEXT

Freedom of the press, protected by the First Amendment, was not always given the elevated status accorded to it today. Ironically, both the common and statutory laws of seditious libel that so easily enabled the government to punish those who publicly criticized it were tacitly, if not openly, supported by the Founding Fathers and prominent members of the political elite of the time. Before the Revolution liberty of the press resulted in criticism of Great Britain and its colonial governors. Colonial legislatures, too, even though elected, came in for their fair share of criticism. From the standpoint of those who governed, liberty of the press was considered dangerous. However, from the viewpoint of the government's critics, freedom of the press was considered imperative to liberty and democracy.

Virtually all of the state constitutions drafted after the Revolution contained provisions protecting freedom of the press. The Revolutionists who controlled the new state legislatures knew only too well the colonial practice of suppression of free speech and press. "In colonial America," writes historian Leonard Levy, "as in England, the common law of criminal libel was strung out like a chicken wire of constraint against the captious and the chancy, making the open discussion of public issues hazardous, if not impossible, except when public opinion opposed administration policy." Colonial governors and assemblies considered immunity from criticism a prerogative of office. Levy describes the result:

Zealously pursuing its prerogative of being immune to criticism, [a colonial] Assembly might summon, interrogate, and fix criminal penalties against anyone who had supposedly libeled its members, proceedings, or the government generally. Any words written, printed, or spoken, which were imagined to have a tendency of impeaching an Assembly's behavior, questioning its authority, derogating from its honor, affronting its dignity, or defaming its members, individually or together, were regarded as a seditious scandal against the government, punishable as a breach of privilege.[3]

While the Revolutionists considered liberty of the press to be essential and embodied it in their state constitutions, the Founding Fathers did not insert a word in defense of a free press in the national Constitution. The subject was mentioned, but never discussed, during the Philadelphia debates of 1787. However, the First Amendment was added to the Constitution as part of the Bill of Rights, which many state conventions insisted upon as a condition of ratification.

The Meaning of Freedom of the Press

In concrete terms, the original state and national constitutional protections of freedom of the press meant very little. The simple insertion of liberty of the press into a constitution did not by itself supersede the common law of seditious libel. Moreover, state legislatures passed their own sedition laws providing for the punishment of persons who by speech or in writing spread falsehoods or defamed the government.

Alexander Hamilton, in *The Federalist*, chided those who wanted freedom of the press added to the Constitution. Addressing

---

[3]Leonard W. Levy, *Legacy of Suppression* (Cambridge, Mass.: Belknap Press of Harvard University Press, 1960), pp. 19–21.

himself to the people of New York in *The Federalist*, No. 84, he wrote:

On the subject of the liberty of the press, as much as has been said, I cannot forbear adding a remark or two: In the first place, I observe, that there is not a syllable concerning it in the Constitution of this state; in the next, I contend that whatever has been said about it in that of any other state amounts to nothing. What signifies a declaration that 'the liberty of the press shall be inviolably preserved'? What is the liberty of the press? Who can give it any definition which would not leave the utmost latitude for evasion? I hold it to be impracticable; and from this I infer that its security, whatever fine declarations may be inserted in any constitution respecting it, must altogether depend on public opinion, and on the general spirit of the people and of the government.

Hamilton's point was well taken and proved accurate with respect to the First Amendment's protections of freedom of speech and press. Early presidents, congressmen, and judges criticized what they often considered to be a scandalous and libelous press, which threatened to undermine the very foundations of the new government. Congress incorporated the English law of seditious libel into the Sedition Act of 1798, making it a crime to write or assist in writing attacks on the government.

The Sedition Act was a Federalist law vigorously enforced by Federalist judges to repress political criticism. The Republicans opposed this law largely because they felt that control of the press should be within the jurisdiction of the states. When Thomas Jefferson became the first Republican president he urged state officials and judges to take swift and firm action against what he believed had become a "licentious" press. Jefferson wrote to the governor of Pennsylvania that the lying and licentious newspapers of the country had produced

a dangerous state of things, and the press ought to be restored to its credibility if possible. The

restraints provided by the laws of the states are sufficient for this if applied. And I have therefore long thought that a few prosecutions of the most prominent offenders would have a wholesome effect in restoring the integrity of the presses. Not a general prosecution, for that would look like a persecution; but a selected one . . .if the same thing be done in some other of the states, it will place the whole band more on their guard.[4]

Jefferson decried the press attacks upon his administration in his second inaugural address on March 4, 1805:

During this course of administration, and in order to disturb it, the artillary of the press has been leveled against us, charged with whatsoever its licentiousness could devise or dare. These abuses of an institution so important to freedom and science, are deeply to be regretted, inasmuch as they tend to lessen its usefulness and to sap its safety; they might, indeed, have been corrected by the wholesome punishments reserved and provided by the laws of the several states against falsehood and defamation; but public duties more urgent press on the time of public servants, and the offenders have therefore been left to find their punishment in the public indignation.[5]

To the early governors of the nation, including the drafters of the First Amendment, freedom of the press clearly meant the freedom to act *responsibly* in relation to the government. Political criticism was to avoid false and defamatory statements, under the threat of punishment for seditious libel. The political leaders of the new nation found the adversary press a thorn in their sides, an attitude that is shared by many of their counterparts today.

---

[4]Paul L. Ford, ed., *The Writings of Thomas Jefferson*, Vol. VIII (New York: Putnam, 1897), pp. 218–219.

[5]Adrienne Koch and William Peden, eds., *The Life and Selected Writings of Thomas Jefferson* (New York: Random House, Modern Library Edition, 1944), pp. 342–343.

The Development of Freedom of the Press

Freedom of the press developed as much from the customs and traditions of our society as from the First Amendment. During the early years of the republic a free press flourished in the face of government attempts to curb it. Thomas Jefferson himself, while trying to contain press criticism of his administration, pardoned those who had been punished under the 1798 sedition law, which itself had been discredited by most political leaders by the time of the administration of Andrew Jackson in the 1830s.

However, both national and state governments continued to seek suppression of hostile press criticism when compelling circumstances, from the governmental viewpoint, seemed to require it. For example, national and state governments attempted to curb the abolitionist press before the Civil War. Every Southern state government except Kentucky enacted measures limiting freedom of the press; and in the North, too, abolitionist publishers were often attacked by mobs with the tacit support of government authorities. Both the government of the Union and of the Confederacy took strict measures to suppress seditious speech during the Civil War. President Abraham Lincoln ordered newspapers that were critical of the government barred from the mails. The courts, which in the twentieth century were to become the guardians of freedom of the press, were not sought out to intervene in governmental attempts to regulate the press during the nineteenth century.

Contemporary Constitutional Doctrines of Freedom of the Press

Today the government continues to define liberty of the press in its own terms. The twentieth century has witnessed a variety of national and state governmental attempts to con-

trol the press, always undertaken for the declared purpose of protecting the national or public interest. Government efforts to curb the First Amendment freedoms of speech and press have raised challenges involving the Supreme Court in a series of cases, beginning with *Schenck v. United States* in 1919, that have defined the permissible extent of governmental authority under the Constitution.

The fundamental freedom of expression. Liberty of the press is one of the freedoms of expression in the First Amendment, which also protects freedom of speech, association, and the freedom to petition government for the redress of grievances.

The Supreme Court recognized the fundamental importance of freedom of speech and press in *Gitlow v. New York* (1925), when it declared that liberty of speech and press was protected by the due process clause of the Fourteenth Amendment.[6] Several years later the Court emphasized, in *Near v. Minnesota* (1934), that government could not, except under the most compelling circumstances, engage in *prior* restraint or censorship of the press. Protection against prior restraint is deeply rooted in the Anglo-American political tradition and is one of those historical and fundamental freedoms considered by the Supreme Court to be essential to the preservation of liberty and democracy. The great English jurist Sir William Blackstone had pointed out as long ago as 1768, in his famous *Commentaries on the Laws of England*, that "the liberty of the press is indeed essential to the nature of a free state; but this consists in laying no *previous* restraints on publications, and not in freedom from censure for criminal matter when published. Every freeman has an undoubted right to lay what sentiments he pleases before the public; to forbid this is to destroy the freedom of the press: but if he publishes what is improper, mischievous, or

_____

[6]See Chapter 4.

illegal, he must take the consequences of his own temerity."[7]

New York Times Co. v. United States (1971). The constitutional ban on prior censorship of the press, derived from historical custom and from interpretation of the First Amendment, is not, in theory at least, absolute. Justice Charles Evans Hughes wrote, in the Court's majority opinion in *Near v. Minnesota* (1931), that "the protection even as to previous restraint is not absolutely unlimited."[8] But, Hughes declared, prior restraint can be permitted only in the most exceptional cases, as in those where such action is required to protect the national security during wartime. Prior censorship may also be constitutionally permissible to ban obscene publications, protect the community against violence, and prevent the forceable overthrow of the government. However, the presumption against prior censorship always places a heavy burden of proof upon the government to demonstrate a compelling need for it.

An important modern case involving prior censorship occurred in 1971, when the government attempted to prevent the *New York Times* and other newspapers from publishing a classified Pentagon study concerning United States involvement in Vietnam that was unsparing in its criticism of government policies, from the Eisenhower through the Johnson administration. Defense Secretary Robert McNamara had appointed a special group within the Defense Department to conduct the study, which was intended for his eyes only. However, Daniel Ellsberg, working at the Rand Corporation in Santa Monica, California, at the time, and a strong opponent of the war, saw a copy of the report, which he thought it would be in the public interest to divulge. Ellsberg photocopied the study and "leaked" it to the *New York Times*, which be-gan to publish its contents in serial form. The Justice Department immediately stepped in and sought a court injunction which, although denied by the federal district court, was sustained on a temporary basis by the Court of Appeals pending a determination of the merits. The *New York Times* considered the temporary restraining order upon publication to be inimical to its interest and to that of the public, and appealed immediately to the Supreme Court. The High Court in turn hastily granted review in an unusual procedure that bypassed the Court of Appeals. A majority of Supreme Court justices felt that the importance of the matter, which affected not only the *New York Times* but the *Washington Post* and other newspapers, required its immediate attention and decision.

The Supreme Court squarely confronted the issue of prior restraint upon publication in the *New York Times* case, for the government was attempting to prevent the publication of further contents of the Pentagon Papers. The majority of the Supreme Court agreed that the government had not demonstrated a sufficiently compelling public interest to justify the prior censorship it sought. Each of the justices wrote a separate opinion, but even the three justices who dissented—primarily on the grounds that the decision had been rendered too hastily without allowing the lower court to hear the cases on the merits—recognized that prior governmental restraint of the press was generally forbidden. Chief Justice Warren Burger, one of the dissenters, wrote that there is "little variation among the members of the Court in terms of resistance to prior restraints against publication."

Justice Hugo Black, one of the majority justices who held that the government had not met the heavy burden of proof required to justify prior restraint of the press, stated bluntly: "To find that the President has 'inherent power' to halt the publication of news by resort to the courts would wipe out the First

---

[7]Blackstone, *Commentaries* (Boston: Beacon Press, 1962), Vol. 4, pp. 151–152. Emphasis added.

[8]283 U.S. 697 (1931).

Amendment and destroy the fundamental liberty and security of the very people the government hopes to make 'secure.'" William O. Douglas, another justice in the majority in the case, wrote: "Secrecy in government is fundamentally anti-democratic, perpetuating bureaucratic errors. Open debate and discussion of public issues are vital to our national health. On public questions there should be 'uninhibited, robust, and wide open' debate."[9]

Protection of the press from libel suits. Historically, the most common threat against a free press has been laws that permit publishers and journalists to be sued for seditious libel and defamation of the character of public officials. To the extent that such suits are permitted, press criticism of the government is stifled.

The *New York Times* was again involved in a historic case in which the Supreme Court was asked to rule on the permissible scope of state libel laws that permitted public officials to sue the press for criticism of their actions. The case involved an Alabama law that as interpreted by the state supreme court made a publication libelous per se "where the words published tend to injure a person libeled by them in his reputation, profession, trade, or business, or charge him with an indictable offense, or tend to bring the individual into public contempt."[10]

Under the law, the state courts of Alabama had awarded $500,000 in damages to L. B. Sullivan, a police commissioner of the city of Montgomery, who had sued the *New York Times* and several black clergymen and civil rights leaders because of an advertisement that appeared under their names in the paper on March 29, 1960. The advertisement appealed for funds for the civil rights movement and for the legal defense of Dr. Martin Luther King, Jr., who was involved at that time in a perjury case in Montgomery.

The advertisement, entitled "Heed Their Rising Voices," stated that although the civil rights movement was peaceful, it had met with violent opposition in the South. The alleged libelous statements in the advertisement were contained in two paragraphs. The first stated:

In Montgomery, Alabama, after students sang "My Country Tis of Thee" on the state Capitol steps, their leaders were expelled from school, and truckloads of police armed with shotguns and teargas ringed the Alabama State College campus. When the entire student body protested to state authorities by refusing to reregister, their dining hall was padlocked in an attempt to starve them into submission.

The second allegedly libelous paragraph stated:

Again and again the Southern violators have answered Dr. King's peaceful protests with intimidation and violence. They have bombed his home almost killing his wife and child. They have assaulted his person. They have arrested him seven times—for 'speeding,' 'loitering,' and similar 'offenses.' And now they have charged him with 'perjury'—a *felony* under which they would imprison him for ten years.

The paragraphs singled out by the plaintiff, Sullivan, in the libel case did not mention him by name, but he charged that the word "police" in the first of the paragraphs singled him out for attack and referred to him, and that by implication the second paragraph also referred to the police in its charge that "they have arrested him [Dr. King]."

The Supreme Court unanimously reversed the judgment of the Alabama Supreme Court in the *New York Times* case. The Court was particularly concerned that the Alabama law as interpreted by its state courts could be used to suppress criticism of public officials. Laws that cast such a "chilling effect" upon the First Amendment freedoms of speech and press are clearly unconstitutional. Justice Brennan's opinion for the Court noted:

---

[9]403 U.S. 713 (1971).

[10]*New York Times Co. v. Sullivan*, 376 U.S. 254 (1964).

[W]e consider this case against the background of a profound national commitment to the principle that debate on public issues should be uninhibited, robust, and wide-open, and that it may well include vehement, caustic, and sometimes unpleasantly sharp attacks upon government and public officials. The present advertisement, as an expression of grievance and protest on one of the major public issues of our time, would seem clearly to qualify for the constitutional protection.

However, does the First Amendment protect criticism of public officials that inadvertently contains false statements that allegedly defame them? The Court concluded: "Just as factual error affords no warrant for repressing speech that would otherwise be free, the same is true of injury to official reputation." Erroneous statements honestly made are protected by the First Amendment where criticism of the government is involved. "The constitutional guarantees [of the First Amendment] require," stated the Court, "a federal rule that prohibits a public official from recovering damages from a defamatory falsehood relating to his official conduct unless he proves that the statement was made with 'actual malice'—that is, with knowledge that it was false or with reckless disregard of whether it was false or not." The effect of the *New York Times* case was to make it almost impossible for public officials to suppress press criticism of their actions, for the burden of proof is upon them to demonstrate that their critics acted with malice or reckless disregard of the truth.

Limits on Press Freedom

While the First Amendment generally protects the press from limitations on its rights to expression, its freedoms are not absolute. The Court has held in a number of cases that the constitutional freedoms of speech and press may be curtailed when there is a clear and present danger to the nation. Moreover, state and local communities are permitted rea-

sonably to restrict freedom of expression in pursuit of the legitimate protection of the public order and morality. Finally, the requirements of the Sixth Amendment right to a fair trial may curtail press access to criminal trials and compel reporters to reveal their sources of information when a trial judge considers it necessary for a fair verdict.[11]

On balance, however, the Constitution gives the press extraordinary leeway for the criticism of public officials and the expression of ideas. Only the most extraordinary circumstances permit limitations upon the press. The broad boundaries of liberty of the press have fostered a resource that plays a critical role in the political process. The government relies upon the media to interpret its actions favorably to the public, while the public depends on a free and independent press to keep it informed in a critical way of official activities and the meaning of government policies.

IMPACT OF THE MASS MEDIA

Until television came into widespread use in the 1950s, the only communications media capable of reaching a mass audience nationwide were newspaper chains, such as the one owned by William Randolph Hearst; certain national magazines, such as *Life* and the *Saturday Evening Post*; and national network radio, which was prominent in the 1930s and 1940s.

Changing Patterns of Journalism

Television's coming of age in politics occurred with the televising of the national presidential nominating conventions in 1952 and the presidential campaigns of Dwight D.

---

[11]Limitations on freedom of the press in court trials are discussed in Chapter 4.

Eisenhower and Adlai Stevenson. From that time on, Marshall McLuhan's later statement that "the medium is the message" became an increasingly apt description of the influence of television on politics. Although television has brought about profound change in the way in which people view the drama of politics, it should always be remembered that even before television the mass media were, through image manipulation, able to make emotional appeals to people. The "yellow journalism" that often characterized the Hearst newspapers helped to stir popular support for the Spanish-American War during the administration of Theodore Roosevelt, and virtually all of the newspapers during World War I helped to fortify jingoism and stimulate an emotional hatred of the Germans that, among other results, cause the term "liberty cabbage" to be used for a while in place of "sauerkraut."

Most of the journalism profession today would be aghast at the extreme news-slanting techniques that were a commonly accepted practice from colonial times through at least the end of World War II and even beyond. The result was a great deal of misinformation being conveyed to people; mass emotions were constantly being manipulated, which of course helped shape the political demands on government for action of one sort or another.

The generation of journalists that came to maturity in the 1930s and 1940s, both in newspapers and in radio, forged new standards of integrity and responsibility for the news media. Names such as Walter Lippmann and Edward R. Murrow come immediately to mind as pacesetters in newspaper and radio journalism, respectively. Lippmann, who never fully trusted public opinion, helped establish the standard that it is the duty of journalism to report the facts to the American people and to be the constant objective guardian of the public weal by overseeing and constantly scrutinizing government.

Edward R. Murrow set standards for radio journalism, which eventually he and others transferred to the medium of television, that reflected Lippmann's views. The young Murrow, reporting from war-torn London in the early 1940s, helped to mold public opinion in support of the war by making its ghastly realities apparent to the American people. In the 1950s Murrow transferred his talents to television and, through his series "Edward R. Murrow Reports" highlighted important issues of public policy and raised the consciousness of the American people about important problems confronting the nation.

Of course, while the new standards of journalism that in part evolved from Lippmann and Murrow were supposed to be as objective as possible, reporting always of necessity has a large subjective element. At the threshold, the choice of topics to be covered is itself highly significant, and the way in which those topics are presented necessarily requires subjective choices. Objectivity may be the goal, but subjectivity inevitably surfaces. When Edward R. Murrow in the 1950s made the demagoguery of Senator Joseph McCarthy the subject of one of his reports, the bias was obvious. Similarly, when he chose the plight of sharecroppers for another of his reports, the medium indeed became the message, for the mere depiction of the life of sharecroppers inevitably caused a sympathetic response in a large portion of the audience.

Today, the impact of televised newscasts cannot be overstated. The topics selected and presented on national network news help to shape the views and, perhaps more important, the *images* people have of government. Television newscasters are, after all, more trusted than politicians by the American people. (If Walter Cronkite had run for president, it is highly likely that he would have swept the nation!)

Television clearly has its own unique impact not only on popular images of politics but also on political leaders who themselves want to *appear* dignified, statesmanlike, and, above all, acceptable to their television audience.

(Drawing by Dana Fradon; © 1982 The New Yorker Magazine, Inc.)

"Bring me my pipe, my bowl, my fiddlers three, and my pollster."
Political leaders are keenly interested in public opinion.

Television widens the constituencies of political leaders from their immediate electoral and power base to the viewing audience of the television shows on which they appear.

Newspapers and Reader Selectivity

The impact of a newspaper on readers and, in turn, on governmental policy is measured not only by the size of the paper's circulation but also by the identity of its readers. The kinds of readers, their power in the community, and the possibility that potential decision makers will be influenced by what they read are all more important criteria for measuring the impact of a newspaper than sheer numbers of readers. Which segment of the public is reached is the important consideration. Papers such as the *New York Times, Washington Post, Wall Street Journal, St. Louis Post-Dispatch, Los Angeles Times,* and *Louisville Courier-Journal* may reach smaller numbers of readers than a paper like the New York *Daily News,* but the readers of these papers are more likely to be in influential positions in business and government. The *New York Times* and the *Washington Post* are read by many of the highest officials in Washington. Sometimes these papers even serve as a means of communication within government itself, because officials are not always kept informed about happenings in other departments.

A common thread runs through the news because there is an interconnective network of reporting among all the media. An important linkage among newspapers as well as in radio and television broadcasting is the Associated Press (AP) and United Press International (UPI), vast networks of reporters located throughout the world supplying the same information to all of their newspaper and broadcasting subscribers. This linkage results in a certain amount of uniformity of reporting. While such substantial papers as the *New York Times* and the *Wall Street Journal* and the major networks are not dependent upon AP and UPI nearly as much as smaller papers and independent broadcasters, they are nevertheless constantly looking over one anothers' shoulders, and stories that appear in one leading newspaper or network are likely to surface elsewhere, not only in the newspaper and broadcasting world but also in the mass-circulation magazines. The effect of this on the formulation of political opinion is important because it means that even though there is diversification within the media, there are common sources of information and a tendency to "follow the leader" when one reporter has written about something that seems particularly newsworthy.

Readers' opinions are, of course, partially shaped by the kind of information that reaches them. Most readers may not be swayed by the editorial page, where opinions are clearly expressed and identified as opinions. They will, however, be influenced subconsciously by the way in which the paper sifts information and thereby determines the reader's knowledge about a particular subject. When, for example, the *New York Times*, the *Washington Post*, and other newspapers decided to give front-page coverage to the Pentagon Papers, the public was given a critical slant on United States involvement in Vietnam. The *Washington Post* ran scores of front-page stories on the Watergate break-in, eventually tracing it and the cover-up attempt to the highest circles in the Nixon administration. During President Ronald Reagan's second term in the 1980s, newspapers ran similar stories revealing the involvement of top White House staffers in the illegal diversion of funds from the sale of arms to Iran to the Nicaraguan contras.

The press influences politics not only by the kind of straightforward investigative reporting that was done in the Pentagon Papers and Watergate cases but also through direct and indirect image building around the personalities of political leaders. Constantly in search of newsworthy stories, newspaper, magazine, and television reporters seek to portray the personality characteristics of politicians in an interesting light; in doing this they help to mold the views of the public and leaders alike on the character of politicians who find themselves in the spotlight. Reporters also have a "herd instinct" that makes them follow the lead of reporters who have hit "pay dirt" in their portrayal of political personalities. An excellent example of image molding by the press occurred in 1976, when Jimmy Carter began to be portrayed by reporters for such newspapers as the *Wall Street Journal* and the *Washington Post* as an interesting personality with an outside chance for the presidential nomination. Even before the primary season began, reporters recognized a good story in the "Jimmy Carter phenomenon," and reporters from all the media jumped on the Jimmy Carter "personality bandwagon." In this sense Carter was at least in part a creation of the press and television.

Backgrounds and Attitudes of the Media Elite

There is inevitably an element of bias in coverage of politics by all media. First, editorial writers and columnists consider it their professional responsibility to present their opinions and views without fear of retribution. The liberal stance of the *Washington Post*, for example, is countered by the conservative views expressed on the editorial pages of the *Wall Street Journal.* Television coverage also includes political editorials. Moreover, commentators as Bill Moyers was on the CBS National News, anchored by Dan Rather, freely express their opinions on political matters. Second, newspapers and the electronic media can and do inject subjective values on political issues simply by their choice of topics to be covered and the format used. News executives, producers, bureau chiefs, department heads, anchor persons, and even film editors slant the news in many ways. Determining what is newsworthy in the first place is a matter of subjective choice. It must also be remembered, however, that competition in the mass media marketplace dictates the coverage of many major news stories, such as presidential press conferences and trips, major congressional committee hearings, and political demonstrations.

A major shift in media elite attitudes has occurred since the 1930s and 1940s when a largely conservative and Republican-oriented press, as reflected in newspapers throughout the country, dominated the media scene. Today, a New York–Los Angeles–Atlanta (CNN) television network nexus, complemented by a host of younger journalists with liberal views, is the dominant media force. And generally media leaders hold more liberal views on many social and political issues than are accepted by a cross section of the electorate. However, newspaper endorsements continue to favor Republican over Democratic candidates, although an increasing number of newspapers are in the neutral column during presidential elections. (See Figure 17.1.)

Mass Media and Public Opinion

There is little evidence that the media, for all their apparent power, can easily sway the political attitudes of the public. The media, particularly television, have the power to boost the name recognition of political candidates among voters. However, factors such as educational level and socioeconomic status determine the political persuasion of most of the electorate. Voters tend to read newspapers and magazines and view political commentaries on television that have political slants similar to their own. For example, the majority of *Wall Street Journal* readers are undoubtedly politically conservative. They enjoy Robert Bartley's highly conservative editorials, which serve to reinforce their views.

The effects of various media. The University of Michigan Center for Political Studies measures *issue familiarity* by analyzing the responses of its election sample to a number of questions on prominent issues. *Political participation* is measured by determining the extent to which respondents vote, give money to political parties, go to political meetings and rallies, work for political clubs and parties, wear campaign buttons, put stickers on their cars, and so forth.

It has been found that magazine readers have the greatest familiarity with issues and the highest level of political participation. This is a selective audience. Next in line are those who rely on combinations of two or more media, such as newspapers and radio or magazines and television. Newspaper readers are third. Those who rely primarily on television or radio alone for information exhibited lower indexes of issue familiarity and political participation.

The Role of Mass Media

The role of the mass media in the political process depends mostly on how they affect various groups. In most cases the media are a primary source of information. In others the media are especially important because they offer contrasting viewpoints on the same subject. National elections would be virtually impossible without exposure of the candidates through the various media. Door-to-door can-

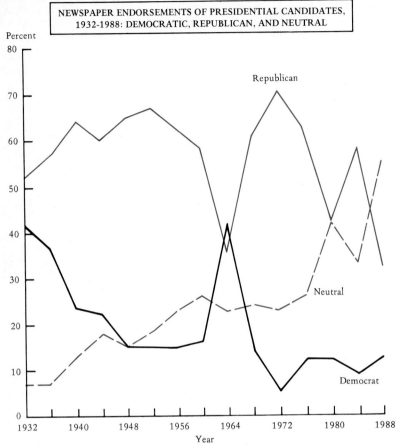

NEWSPAPER ENDORSEMENTS OF PRESIDENTIAL CANDIDATES,
1932-1988: DEMOCRATIC, REPUBLICAN, AND NEUTRAL

(Source: Harold W. Stanley and Richard G. Niemi, *Vital Statistics on American Politics*, 2d ed. [Washington, D.C.:
Congressional Quarterly Press, 1990], p. 73. Reprinted with permission from Congressional Quarterly, Inc.)

FIGURE 17.1

vassers and mail campaigns can reach only a small number of people. To communicate a candidate's message to a nationwide constituency, the mass media have been better equipped to develop a common language that is easily understood by all the potential voters.

Usually, however, when media operate on a mass scale, there is a *dilution of information.* That is, the information presented to the public may not be given in its entirety; or it may be tailored or slanted so that it appeals to the greatest number of people. Commercial considerations account for some of this dilution. After all, newspapers have to sell to

the greatest possible number of readers in order to attract advertisers and remain profitable. And television broadcasters do not want to anger their viewers, who may show their displeasure by not buying the products advertised.

The mass media can be thought of as the common denominator of ideas. American democracy must span a broad continent inhabited by many types of people. There must be some bond between the people as a whole and the government that is supposed to represent all the divergent subgroups within the nation. The mass media can help to provide

"You know, I've been keeping a record, and in the last year I've agreed with eight hundred and sixty 'Times' editorials, disagreed with three hundred and thirty-five of them, and had no opinion on two hundred and sixty-five."

This cartoon presents a basic question: Do people buy a newspaper because they agree with its opinions?

---

a unifying link between the people and their government.

A comparison of recent presidential campaigns with those of the past illustrates this aspect of the mass media quite vividly. Years ago, before there were such continent-spanning mass media as television and radio, presidential candidates had to traverse a long campaign trail in order to carry their programs to the public. Although local newspapers and magazines aided the campaigns by bringing the candidates to the public's attention, it was still impossible for presidential aspirants to come before all the American populace.

Television compared to other media. The pervasiveness of television, including the fact that a vast majority of people gain most of their news and views of political candidates from it, makes it the most significant medium in shaping political views.

Perhaps the most important impact of television, particularly at the national level and in presidential politics, has been the expansion of coverage of the "horse race" and candidate personalities, particularly during the primary season. (See Table 17.1.) To paraphrase Marshall McLuhan: Where television is the medium, what is *seen* is important, not what is heard or what substantive viewpoints are presented. At least the public relations advisers of political candidates have succeeded in convincing them that this is so—that it is their image, embodied in their personality and style, that will sway voters. Thus every effort

DOONESBURY   by Garry Trudeau

Pollsters and reporters are often relentless in their pursuit of public opinion.

TABLE 17.1   FOCUS OF TELEVISION NEWS COVERAGE, 1988 PRESIDENTIAL ELECTION

Period	*Horse race (percent)*	*Campaign issues (percent)*	*Policy issues (percent)*	*Number of stories*
Primary				
1987 (2/8–12/31)	33	48	19	258
Iowa (1/1–2/8)	39	38	22	238
New Hampshire (2/9–2/16)	70	22	7	108
Super Tuesday (2/17–3/8)	58	23	18	130
Midwest (3/9–4/5)	82	8	10	148
New York (4/6–4/18)	56	22	22	59
California (4/19–6/7)	41	15	43	123
Primary total	50	29	20	1,064
General election				
Pre-convention (6/8–7/21)	11	55	33	248
Conventions (7/22–8/18)	18	43	38	200
First debate (8/19–9/25)	11	51	38	296
Second debate (9/26–10/13)	18	45	37	184
Final 25 days (10/14–11/7)	33	35	33	309
General election total	19	46	36	1,237
Primary and general election total	33	38	29	2,301

Note: "Horse race" coverage focuses on the contest—who's ahead, who's behind; "campaign issues" concern candidate character; "policy issues" involve concerns such as those detailed in Table 2.7.

Source: Harold W. Stanley and Richard G. Niemi, *Vital Statistics on American Politics*, 2d ed. (Washington, D.C.: Congressional Quarterly Press, 1990), p. 57; Center for Media and Public Affairs content analysis of the ABC, CBS, and NBC evening news from February 8, 1987, through November 7, 1988. Reprinted with permission from Congressional Quarterly, Inc. and the Center for Media and Public Affairs.

is made to "sell" the candidate to the public much as a product is sold in the marketplace.

Has television helped or hindered the democratic political process? Certainly politics in the television age has produced leaders of a quality and effectiveness equal to those in the past. Moreover, while television makes the personalities and the styles of political candidates of paramount importance, there is no evidence that this has not always been the case. Indeed, television may make it more difficult for candidates and their advisers to manipulate the public than could be done through other media in which candidates are less exposed.

For candidates, the main difference between television and the other media is the amount of public exposure they receive. They have to be more consistent before the television audience, both in speech and in appearance. With newspapers, magazines, or radio, the audience is not so vast, and certain inconsistencies on the part of a candidate will not be detected. But under the eye of the television camera, which projects a person's image into millions of living rooms at the same time, a candidate cannot change the presentation or alter the program to suit a particular audience. Thus candidates are more apt to talk in generalities before the television camera. They must concentrate on broad ideas that appeal to the greatest number of voters.

While there is little doubt that television accentuates the styles and personalities of political candidates, it can also transmit ideas and contrasting positions on public policy to vast numbers of people. It has the potential to strengthen rather than weaken democracy. Moreover, assessing candidates on the basis of their styles and personalities is not necessarily undesirable, because these characteristics can be very important to effective political leadership. However, whether television emphasizes those attributes of style and personality that contribute to effective leadership is questionable. Television can certainly mask

character traits that under the pressures of political office fail to produce responsible action. And television can be a more effective manipulator of public opinion than the other communications media.

Television will loom ever more important in the political campaigns of the future. The images conveyed by political personalities will inevitably become more important as public relations advisers to candidates compete with one another in their attempts to mold public opinion.

The media's role in the transmission of information and opinions to the public makes them essential not only to political campaigning but to the ongoing process of government.

THE PRESS AND GOVERNMENT: CRITIC AND ALLY

The press and the government, while often seemingly at odds with each other, actually are linked together in a relationship of mutual dependency. The press depends upon the government, which is a major news source, for much of its sustenance. The government in turn relies upon the press to publicize, hopefully in a supportive way, its multiple and various activities.

The Press as Critic

The dramatic growth in the size and activities of the national government beginning with Franklin D. Roosevelt's New Deal in the 1930s spawned a similarly dramatic growth in the size of the Washington Press Corps. (See Figure 17.2.) Thousands of Washington reporters cover the activities of government and politics in depth, from the White House and the executive branch to Capitol Hill and the Supreme Court. No part of the government is immune from press scrutiny. For the most part government actions are taken in public,

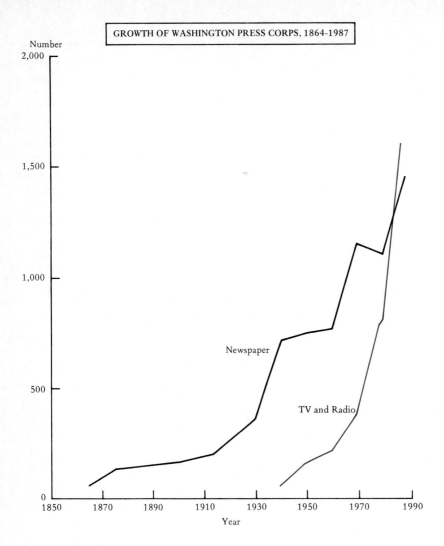

GROWTH OF WASHINGTON PRESS CORPS, 1864-1987

Number

2,000

1,500

1,000

500

0

1850   1870   1890   1910   1930   1950   1970   1990

Year

Newspaper

TV and Radio

(Source: From Harold W. Stanley and Richard G. Niemi, *Vital Statistics on American Politics*, 2d ed. [Washington, D.C.: Congressional Quarterly Press, 1990 , p 52. Reprinted with permission from Congressional Quarterly, Inc.)

FIGURE 17.2

and secrecy is almost impossible to maintain even in areas of national security. Over the years, the White House has been particularly concerned with "leaks" to the press that reveal what has taken place at secret meetings, including those of the National Security Council. However, Washington reporters of long standing, particularly investigative columnists, such as Jack Anderson, have "sources" throughout the government who keep them supplied with inside information.

At the top of the political reporter's creed is the principle of open access to all government decision-making forums. Congress seemingly accepted the importance of virtually unlimited public access to the inner sanctums of government by the passage of the Freedom of Information Act (FOIA) in 1966, which makes it extraordinarily difficult for administrative agencies to deny reporters and the public information about government activities. The government may withhold purely "internal" memoranda, matters pertaining to national security, trade secrets, and information that would invade personal privacy from inquisitive reporters and others seeking information under the law; however, the FOIA has made it impossible for the government to maintain the kind of secrecy that was commonplace before passage. (The executive branch, understandably, has sought to narrow the FOIA.) In addition to the FOIA, the executive branch is covered by a "sunshine law" that requires most administrative proceedings to be open to the public. And moreover, Congress itself has adopted sunshine resolutions that encourage committees to conduct most of their hearings and markup sessions openly.

The FOIA and the mandate that the government operate openly make it far more difficult than formerly for executive agencies and "the powers that be" on Capitol Hill to conceal their activities. This was not always the case. Douglass Cater, in his remarkable book on the press, *The Fourth Branch of Government*, has described how some agencies, particularly those concerned with national security and intelligence, in the past routinely concealed information from inquisitive reporters:

Many times the agencies of organized intelligence operate to conceal or distort the issues for the reporter. The Atomic Energy Commission, for example, has released handouts about its "Operation Sunshine," designed to create bright illusions about a deadly dark business. Life and death facts about radioactive fallout have been casually and belatedly made public by means of a commissioner's speech which was too technical to capture public notice until someone like Dr. Ralph Lapp, a scientist-turned-reporter, made the necessary translation. The AEC at times has pretended to tell everything while explaining

nothing. Since no satisfactory safeguards exist to make sure the government will freely communicate its organized intelligence even to appropriate officials within government itself, the reporter still has the job of investigating and describing the closest approximation to the truth that he can discover.[12]

Political reporters continue to have to dig for the facts, and the government, although perhaps less inclined to do so than in previous times, continues to try to shape the truth in its own interest. The Nuclear Regulatory Commission, for example, the successor to the Atomic Energy Commission, continues to stress the safety of nuclear power, paying scant attention, at least publicly, to the considerable evidence of its dangers. The Defense Department and most other agencies of government deluge the media with propaganda favorable to their points of view. The White House, understandably, tries to emphasize facts favorable to the president's position in order to put him in a good light.

The job of the political journalist as critic is to ferret out the truth, and give the public a balanced critique of what the government is doing. Sensational examples of the way in which the press performed this role were the publication of the Pentagon Papers, which revealed the long involvement of the United States in Vietnam, and the *Washington Post*'s publication of a series of investigative articles on the Watergate break-in, which eventually led to impeachment proceedings against Richard M. Nixon and finally to his resignation.

Government reaction to press criticism. The government attempted to suppress the publication of the Pentagon Papers, and the Watergate revelations caused near-hysteria in the White House. Those were extreme cases. The cumulative effect of more mundane revelations and investigations tends to produce a kind of paranoia in government officials. But

---

[12]Douglass Cater, *The Fourth Branch of Government* (Boston: Houghton Mifflin, 1959), p. 173.

(Drawing by Lorenz; © 1982 The New Yorker Magazine, Inc.)

"My son, you have survived the ordeal by fire and the ordeal by water. You now face the final challenge—ordeal by media."
Aspiring political leaders must learn how to deal with the media.

government criticism is the grist of the political reporters' mill as they strive to come up with newsworthy stories that will make the front page, or, in television reporting, that will be on the nightly news.

In a conversation with David Gergen, President Ronald Reagan's assistant for communications, and Jody Powell, Jimmy Carter's press secretary, Ben Wattenberg of the American Enterprise Institute asked them: "In the post-Vietnam, post-Watergate era, do reporters—unless they have clear reason to think otherwise—start from the presumption that the government is lying or that the United States is the bad guy? Is this in our media culture now? Doesn't it make it difficult to govern?" Gergen's reply reveals the adversary character of the relationship between the White House and the press. "That feeling is obviously still there," he noted. "I don't know what the roots are. Clearly, Vietnam and Watergate had a great deal to do with it but it does seem to me that it has dissipated somewhat from the height of Watergate."

Reporters from the Watergate era, continued Gergen,

are often in the old frame of mind. They will come at you hammer and tongs on the *assumption* that somehow you've shaded it. But that is not necessarily characteristic of the overall White House press corps. There is a willingness now to give you the benefit of the doubt the first time around. It differs from individual to individual. One of the problems Reagan's

National Security Adviser [Dick Allen] ran into was a suspicion they had about him before this issue of the Japanese gifts ever broke. [Allen was accused of accepting gifts and money from Japanese businessmen, an accusation that eventually led to his resignation.] Some [reporters] automatically assumed that there must be something more to it. They were never willing to give him the benefit of the doubt.[13]

The spotlight of the press focuses more upon the president than on any other aspect or figure of the government. White House reporters go through a "honeymoon" with a new president, giving him initially the benefit of the doubt and often building up his public image. The press, like the public, has high expectations at the outset of a presidential administration. However, disillusionment inevitably sets in as it becomes evident that the president is unable to solve many of the nation's problems that are beyond his control.

David Gergen observed: "One unfortunate tendency we've seen in the press in three of our most recent presidencies is for them to bring the fellow up larger than life—to make him some kind of superhuman—only to find out that he is, in fact, an ordinary mortal. Then they tear him down." And Jody Powell noted: "Most reporters don't have a direct professional or personal interest in breaking the President. But because they feel they have to keep themselves on the newsstands and on the air, there is a bias—subconscious for the most part—against any institution that is being covered on a full-time basis. The result is the same. In fact, the result may be even worse for it not being a matter of malice or intent, but of the way the process works."

David Gergen concluded, "I question whether the George Washingtons and Ben Franklins and Thomas Jeffersons could have survived as popular figures under the klieg lights of national television." And Jody Powell added, "I happen to believe—and this may be

one of the few times I'll argue on behalf of the fourth estate—that it makes sense for the President to be exposed on a frequent and regular basis to that sometimes foolish, sometimes ill-mannered, but also sometimes enlightening questioning by the people who cover the President day-in and day-out."[14]

The press as the "opposition party." Douglass Cater interestingly refers to the role of the press as that of an "opposition party" in the British sense, which implies a press incentive to "put the government on the spot."[15] In Great Britain, the opposition party has the opportunity each week during the "question period" in the House of Commons to query the prime minister and the cabinet about their government activities and policies. Questioning is often sharp, and the sessions raucous. Other Commonwealth countries also have question periods, and some, as in Canada, are even televised. Whether reported by the press or on television, question periods between disciplined government and opposition parties help to keep the government on its toes and the public informed.

In the United States, while cabinet secretaries are subjected to intense questioning before congressional committees, the president is not.[16] The closest analogy to a question period is the presidential press conference, in which reporters often take the role of the opposition, sharply questioning the president and sometimes even attempting to embarrass him. President Harry S. Truman compared the presidential press conference with the question period: "I think an analogy to [the Question Period] in Britain is our public press conference which the President faces, and at

---

[13]*Public Opinion*, December/January 1982, p. 12.

[14]Ibid., p. 10.

[15]Cater, *The Fourth Branch of Government*, pp. 142–155.

[16]The lack of disciplined political parties makes congressional questioning of administration witnesses more sporadic and expressive of the views and interests of individual legislators than in Great Britain and other Commonwealth countries with disciplined parties.

which he answers the same sort of questions he would answer if he were on the Floor of the Congress. I don't think it's practical under our system to have that take place in the Congress of the United States. George Washington tried it one time and he got so disgusted with the way they treated him that he went back to the White House and never went down there anymore."[17] The press has become so effective as a White House adversary that contemporary presidents have disbanded the practice of regular press conferences, which began during the administration of Franklin D. Roosevelt. Presidents, who often feel besieged by a hostile media, agree with the remark made by John F. Kennedy about the press even before he became president: "Always remember that their interests and ours ultimately conflict."[18]

President Dwight D. Eisenhower reportedly considered abandoning the presidential press conference altogether, but it was not until the latter years of the administration of Lyndon B. Johnson that presidents began to use direct television appeals to the people to supplant communication with them through the intermediary of the press. Presidents know well that a hostile press can destroy their efforts to create a favorable public image. President Ronald Reagan's deputy press secretary, Larry Speakes, recalled that during the Reagan administration, "Underlying our whole theory of disseminating information in the White House was our knowledge that the American people get their news and form their judgments based largely on what they see on television. We knew that television had to have pictures to present its story. We learned very quickly that when we were presenting a story or trying to get our viewpoint

across, we had to think like a television producer. And that is a minute and thirty seconds of pictures to tell the story, and a good solid sound byte with some news." Speakes admitted, "Reagan did hold far fewer full-fledged press conferences than most of his predecessors, and there's a good reason for it: press conferences no longer serve the presidency or the press, and are in danger of becoming obsolete unless reporters decide to use them as information-gathering sessions, which is what they're intended to be."[19]

The Reagan administration's attempt to manage the news was nothing new. President Richard Nixon considered himself an expert in press relations and news management. Moreover, Nixon expressed the views of many presidents in his outspoken criticism of White House reporters.

Publicly, Richard Nixon disingenuously refuted a comment, attributed to him by John Ehrlichman, that White House reporters ask "dumb and flabby" questions during news conferences. Nixon addressed this allegation during an informal Oval Office meeting with reporters:

question: Mr. President, is Mr. Ehrlichman correct when he says that you sometimes get irritated with us for our dumb and flabby questions, so-called?

the president: You are not dumb and flabby. No, I noted that comment and expected a question on it. I am afraid if I begin to characterize the questions you will begin to characterize my answers, but you probably will anyway. In any event, as far as questions are concerned, I think what Mr. Ehrlichman was referring to was the tendency in the big East Room conferences for questions to come in from all over the place and no follow-up, as there can be in a conference like this.

Sometimes the questions may appear somewhat less relevant. I have found, for example, although we do not rule out the big

---

[17]CBS television program "Small World," November 30, 1958, cited in Cater, *The Fourth Branch of Government*, p. 142.

[18]William Safire, *Safire's Political Dictionary* (New York: Random House, 1978, p. 397.

[19]Larry Speakes, *Speaking Out* (New York: Scribner's, 1988), pp. 220, 234.

conference where everybody gets to come, I have found that these smaller sessions do provide an opportunity for members of the regular White House press, who study these issues day by day and who know what is relevant and what is not relevant and who can follow up, I think that the possibility of dumb and flabby questions is much less and I don't, frankly, complain about it.

The other point that I should make is this: in looking over the transcripts of various press conferences, I have not seen many softballs, and I don't want any because it is only the hardball that you can hit or strike out on.

Privately, Nixon told Ehrlichman about the press: "They are biased, of course. Kicking the press is an art. Your flabby-and-dumb crack was good. You let them have it without rancor. That's what you have to do."[20]

The views of Nixon and his aides about the press, while they may seem extreme, are generally characteristic of all modern presidential administrations, which view "the Fourth Estate" with suspicion and distrust at the same time that they attempt to use the media to put themselves and their policies in a favorable light. Some presidents, such as John F. Kennedy and Ronald Reagan, skillfully used press conferences, which they often treated with a sense of humor, to build support for their programs. But Kennedy, Reagan, and other presidents with the skill to turn press conferences to their own purposes nevertheless can never be immune from criticism. Kennedy remarked in the spring of 1962, when asked what he thought of the press, "Well, I am reading it more and enjoying it less—[laughter]—and so on, but I have not complained, nor do I plan to make any general complaints."[21] Kennedy's successors did not treat the press with his sense of humor, and Johnson, Nixon, and Carter in par-

ticular complained bitterly about their treatment by the press while they often tried desperately to manage the news.

George Reedy, Lyndon B. Johnson's press secretary, explained the antagonism that so frequently exists between presidents and other politicians and the press: "It is an article of faith with most politicians that any newspaper item even remotely touching upon the government was written through partisan inspiration, not just because it happened. The concept that there are professional standards which determine news leads and news placement is alien to their view of society." The politician "refuses to concede that there are events which will find their way into the newspapers without any partisan help whatsoever. Moreover, he is incapable of crediting newsmen with the ability to make simple deductions unassisted by people with an axe to grind."[22]

Reedy incisively analyzed why all presidents consider the press to be the enemy:

Since the press as a whole cannot be 'won over' by tactics which political leaders regard as legitimate, it is inevitable that newspapermen eventually become the 'enemy.' In addition, they also become the personification of all the frustrating forces that make the life of a President so difficult. Therefore, over a period of time, it is certain that the political leader will vent his spleen against the press, never realizing that what he is really doing is venting his spleen against the whole intractible environment that surrounds him.[23]

Reporting on the White House is focused on the president and a few of his top aides. The president's daily activities and the policy issues that concern him are automatically front-page news. White House reporters have little difficulty in filing their daily stories. Of-

---

[20]Ibid., p. 161.

[21]Arthur M. Schlesinger, Jr., *A Thousand Days* (Boston: Houghton Mifflin, 1965), p. 719.

[22]George E. Reedy, *The Twilight of the Presidency* (New York and Cleveland: World Publishing, 1970), pp. 111, 112.

[23]Ibid., pp. 116–117.

ten a handout from the president's press secretary suffices, amplified, perhaps, by remarks made during the daily briefings given by the press secretary in the West Wing. Journalists, usually those outside the White House, who choose to adopt the role of critic know their adversary. Whether in simple reporting or in criticism, the White House is always newsworthy.

While the presidency is the major focus of the press, journalists are also busy covering the other branches of the government. The linkage between the press and Congress, the bureaucracy, and the Supreme Court differs from the relationship between the press and the president.

(Copyright 1983 by Herblock in *The Washington Post*.)

"Damn media! You should know better than to report all the dopey things he says."
Presidents are often embarrassed later by their remarks to the press.

Congress and the press. Approximately 300 journalists cover Congress on a regular basis, a larger contingent than routinely covers the White House. The congressional press, however, has received far less attention than the presidential press corps.

Reporters on Capitol Hill have a highly diverse menu from which to select their topics. Congress is not focused. There are no daily briefings, although the Speaker of the House and the Majority Leader of the Senate may hold press conferences on a fairly regular basis. Such conferences are not particularly important to the aspiring reporter, who is constantly seeking stories that will please his or her editor and be placed as far to the forefront of the newspaper as possible or, in the case of the electronic media, appear along with the reporter on the network or local news.

However, while covering the White House is prestigious, many reporters find Capitol Hill more challenging. "Every journalist ought to have a chance to cover the White House," commented Phil Jones of CBS News, "It's a hell of a trip. But once done, they should move on. It has ruined more good journalists than it has made." Jones preferred his Capitol Hill beat to the White House. "Up here," he observed, "there are 535 sources, most of them eager and available to the press, and their aides, thousands of them. At the White House, you work from your little booth and you're confined to a specific area. Here, you can spread your wings. I can walk down and ask the doorkeeper to speak to a senator. He'll come out, I'll ask my questions and we'll shoot the breeze."[24]

Press coverage of Congress falls into two distinct categories: national media coverage, and local media reporting. The national media are distinctly more critical of Congress than is the press from a member's district. Because press coverage of House incumbents is

---

[24]*National Journal*, May 1, 1982, p. 769.

generally carried out by local newspapers, it is for the most part favorable and has been a significant factor in the increase in their electoral safety. The critical national press focuses more upon the Senate, making incumbency there far less secure than in the House.

One Capitol Hill press official explained the difference between the national and local press coverage of Congress:

I'd say yes [the national media] are tougher. The nationals represent great powerful forces. Conversely, the regional guy, the little and small town guy is concentrating on . . .half a dozen, maybe a dozen members. And he sees them day in and day out. Consequently, . . .he has to be invited back in. His demeanor and his attitude [are] somewhat different. It's more flexible, more on a personal basis now. He knows he's there to do a reporting job and that the congressman is there to get whatever publicity he can. The [nationals] say, so he [the member] doesn't like me. He needs us. We're big. We're powerful. We can publicize him [nationally]. So if he doesn't like us—the hell with him.[25]

There is a general perception on Capitol Hill that the press has become highly critical and reporters more effective investigators since Watergate. "The press is getting tougher," is the prevailing view. But the most widely read coverage of Congress, that done by journalists working for state and local newspapers and media, is supportive and serves the members' interests. The national press, while sporadically uncovering Capitol Hill scandals that embarrass individual members, for the most part confines its criticism to Congress as an institution. The low repute of Congress in the minds of the public may very well be attributed to typical comments such as that made by David Brinkley on the nightly news to an audience of millions: "It is widely believed in Washington that it would

take Congress thirty days to make instant coffee."[26]

The press and the bureaucracy. Press coverage of the bureaucracy ranks a poor third to reporting on the presidency and Congress. The major news networks mention the bureaucracy more frequently than newspapers do, but coverage is sporadic at best.

Major news bureaus, such as Associated Press (AP) and United Press International (UPI), the networks, and the larger newspapers assign reporters to the major departments of government, such as Defense, State, and Justice. The *New York Times*, the *Washington Post*, and the *Wall Street Journal* are among the few top newspapers that maintain broad coverage of the bureaucracy with an investigative bent. But the Washington press continues to focus more on personalities than on issues, and the most interesting personalities are generally to be found in the White House or Congress.

The *Wall Street Journals*'s Washington bureau chief, Norman C. Miller, admitted that his staff of 36 professionals had a difficult time covering the bureaucracy, although the bureau had increased its efforts in that direction. "We took over the bureau in 1973," commented Miller. "We used to have one person covering the [Federal Reserve Board], Treasury and Commerce, but because of interest in economic affairs, we now have four people covering economics, [one] who specializes in international economics, [and] we have also increased our coverage of national affairs and national security policy from two to three people."[27]

Jack Nelson, when he was the Washington bureau chief of the *Los Angeles Times*, admitted that the tendency of the press is to focus on personalities rather than on issues, particularly on the president, resulting in diminished coverage of major areas of the bu-

---

[25]Cited in Michael J. Robinson, "Three Faces of Congressional Media," in Thomas E. Mann and Norman Ornstein, eds., *The New Congress* (Washington, D.C.: American Enterprise Institute, 1981), p. 77.

[26]David Brinkley, NBC "Nightly News," February 3, 1976.
[27]*National Journal*, April 17, 1982, pp. 666, 668.

reaucracy. The president's every move, Nelson noted, is "on the evening news every night, so we have to have it on page 1. It may be overplayed, but everybody reads it." While the *Los Angeles Times* adequately covers the White House and Congress, there is little reporting on significant areas of public policy implemented by the bureaucracy. For example, Nelson explained, "California is a big farm state, but we don't have anybody covering agriculture, and we don't do enough on urban problems and transportation."[28]

Administrative agencies and their heads occasionally do become involved in newsworthy stories, especially when there are hints of scandal or dereliction of duty. Numerous scandals involving top Reagan administration officials, including Attorney General Edwin Meese, whetted the media's appetite for newsworthy stories and helped fill many front pages and network news programs. The media also became preoccupied with the Iran-contra scandal involving top Reagan White House aides during the president's second term. Press accounts of scandals in the White House always are more newsworthy than coverage of improprieties by bureaucrats.

The most comprehensive information about the bureaucracy is not gathered by the traditional press or the media but by newsletters that focus upon narrow segments of the executive branch and are aimed at the special interests and publics. The array of newsletters is truly dazzling. Their specialized character is reflected in their titles: *The Energy Daily, Cardiac Alert, Political Gun News, Joy of Travel, Sludge, The Whale Report, Hazardous Waste News, The Underwater Letter, Space Letter, Higher Education Daily, Employee Benefit Cases*, and *Air Pollution Control* are examples of the more than 500 Washington newsletters.[29] While newsletters provide specialized information, they do not help to keep the public informed in a critical way about the activities of the bureaucracy.

The press and the Supreme Court. Press coverage of the Supreme Court and the lower federal judiciary is minimal. Major Supreme Court decisions are reported on the nightly news and are published in major newspapers such as the *New York Times*. In general, however, reporting on the activities of the judiciary is scanty and often inaccurate. Relatively few reporters understand the complexities of the law and judicial procedure, and editors understand even less, which contributes to the confusion in the reporting of court decisions. The courts and the law have often been shrouded in mystery, comprehensible only to members of the legal profession. Lay reporters not only find it difficult to explain the meaning and impact of court decisions, but also find that the public is not particularly interested. Supreme Court decisions are newsworthy, but those of the lower judiciary are rarely considered of sufficient importance to be reported in most newspapers.

Supreme Court justices have perennially complained about inaccurate and scant press coverage. Justice William O. Douglas, who served on the Court from 1939 until 1975, forcefully expressed the views of his colleagues concerning the press:

The Court, I discovered, got very poor news coverage for several reasons. There were few reporters who made the history of the Court their profession. That is to say, the reporters were bright but uninformed men who were doing the best they could with complicated and technical material. Moreover, the appetite of the news services for spot news put tremendous pressures on the newsmen to write their stories in a few minutes and get them on the wires. The result was usually news stories which the author of the Court opinion would hardly recognize as descriptive of what he had written. That's why the public got strange and distorted views of the Court and its rulings. In the forties I pleaded with Henry Luce to give a few solid pages of his magazines to intelligent reporting of Court

[28]Ibid., p. 673.

[29]See *National Journal*, April 17, 1982, for a listing and discussion of the phenomenon of Washington newsletters.

decisions. He made a feeble effort, but no magazine or newspaper was faithful to the task.

Douglas recalled that Justice Felix Frankfurter wanted to get newsmen to study law at his alma mater, Harvard Law School, before they undertook to report on the Court. Douglas recalls that some reporters heeded Frankfurter's wish, notably Anthony Lewis (who became the Supreme Court reporter for the *New York Times,* and who wrote *Gideon's Trumpet*), "one of the ablest journalists of my time." While Frankfurter encouraged reporters to study law, he was not always tolerant of their stories. Douglas relates one incident involving a *Washington Post* reporter who was meticulous and unbiased, but who at the end of each term

put into tables the production of each justice in opinions for the Court, concurring opinions and dissenting opinions. Frankfurter despised those columns, since they showed, truthfully, that he wrote fewer opinions for the Court than any other justice. He ranted and inveighed against Stokes [the reporter] in the precincts of the Court, denouncing anyone who would even intimate that writing a few opinions was not equal to writing many opinions. 'Cases are not fungable,' he would shout. Finally he induced Phil Graham, his former law clerk and publisher of the *Post,* to remove Stokes from the assignment. It was rather sad, because Stokes had more insight into Court problems and more knowledge of Court history than any other reporter before or since."

To increase the accuracy of press reporting on the Supreme Court, the justices in 1971 instructed the Court Reporter to include brief, explanatory headnotes for each case. This procedure "measurably helped increase the accuracy of reports sent over the wires on opinion days." Douglas added, "To aid the newsmen we gave up making Mondays the exclusive opinion days, handing down opinions throughout the week when the Court was hearing arguments. In this way the burden on newsmen was somewhat lightened.

Yet by and large, mediocrity in reporting continued to be the norm."

That Supreme Court justices often have the same jaundiced view of the press that so frequently characterizes the attitudes of the White House and Capitol Hill toward the fourth estate, is reflected in Douglas's conclusion that the press "is by and large a mimic, not an original research group. It prints handouts from government and from industry and expresses its opinions on those items. But the basic facts are seldom mined; the press does not have the initiative or the zeal to ferret out the original from the false or pretended."[30]

The antagonism that often exists between the Court and the press is by no means one-sided. Reporters feel that the "secrecy" of the Court makes it extremely difficult for them to run to ground the facts behind actions and decisions. *Washington Post* reporters Bob Woodward and Scott Armstrong wrote, in their introduction to *The Brethren,* "The Court's deliberative process—its internal debates, the tentative positions taken by the justices, the preliminary votes, the various drafts of written opinions, the negotiations, confrontations, and compromises—is hidden from public view."[31] The Court, they concluded, "has developed certain traditions and rules, largely unwritten, that are designed to preserve the secrecy of its deliberations." Woodward and Armstrong set out to give a behind-the-scenes account of the Court in *The Brethren,* a book as widely publicized and acclaimed as attacked. (Reportedly, it caused considerable discomfort on the Court, which had never been subjected to Watergate-style reporting.)

The Press as the Ally of Government

From reading the acerbic comments made about the press by presidents, their aides, con-

---

[30]William O. Douglas, *The Court Years: 1939–1975* (New York: Random House, 1980), pp. 205–207.

[31]Bob Woodward and Scott Armstrong, *The Brethren* (New York: Simon & Schuster, 1979), p. 1.

gressmen, and Supreme Court justices, one would conclude that the press is always a thorn in the side of government. However, the news media are far more a part of government than they are a critical and independent force. That is why Douglass Cater has referred to the press as "the fourth branch of government."

Jonathan Daniels, Franklin D. Roosevelt's press secretary and a person of long Washington experience, recalled that by the time of the New Deal the press had become part of the Washington establishment. He wrote:

It would be difficult to find a body of men who more clearly represent Washington than the gentlemen of the press who report it. There are notions, carefully cultivated, that they are in Washington but not of it, and that they stand in scrutiny but also in separation. Actually, of course, they are probably more representative of the good and the bad on the capital scene than any other body of bureaucrats. As they stay in Washington, which most of them hope to do, they are at least as remote from the country as the administrators are."[32]

Upon arriving in Washington, journalists may have every intention of standing apart from the government in order to view it with a disinterested and a critical eye, reporting "all the news that's fit to print" and exposing government actions against the public interest, wherever they occur. But the government, which lives by publicity, strives mightily to co-opt the press so that it can be used for its own purposes.

Publicity and power. Politicians, to be effective, need publicity that will enhance their reputations for power and that will generate favorable support within and without government for their causes. The press is potentially one of the most important allies of ambitious politicians, who know that if they can dominate the news their reputations for power will be enhanced. Presidents, legislators, and as-

piring bureaucrats want the press not only to project a favorable image of them, but one that reflects their power. They want to be on the front page, on the nightly news, on "Meet the Press" and "Face the Nation," on "60 Minutes," and "20/20," and "Nightline" because the mere appearance in such forums symbolizes stature and power.

The president's press office, press aides on Capitol Hill, and public relations personnel throughout government are there to create favorable media images for their bosses and their programs. Political entrepreneurs flourish in a government that lacks hierarchical power arrangements and disciplined political parties. Power seekers who play the political game most effectively know how to use the media to keep themselves foremost in the minds of their constituents within and without government.

A politician's power is measured in large part by the success of his or her policies, and no policy has much chance of passage through the labyrinth of government without publicity. "No one," wrote Douglass Cater, "who has been in on the development and growth of a major policy is likely to minimize the publicity consciousness which must guide its course every step of the way." Reporters can play an important role in policy outcomes by their selection of what is newsworthy. "News standards," declared Cater, "go to the very core of policy formulation by officials. As a program moves from the tentative planning stage in the executive department through the long wearisome process of legislative enactment, appropriations, further enactment, and still further appropriation, there is an inevitable tendency to accentuate those aspects which are newsworthy and deemphasize—sometimes causing atrophy—those aspects which are not newsworthy." Cater concluded: "The competitive news advantage of one policy over another has great bearing on the com-

[32]Jonathan Daniels, *Frontier on the Potomac* (New York: Macmillan, 1946), p. 159.

[33]Cater, *The Fourth Branch of Government*, pp. 15–17.

(Drawing by Bernard Schoenbaum; © 1982 The New Yorker Magazine, Inc.)

"Why haven't some of my private cogent off-the-cuff remarks found their way into the media?"
Politicians strive to gain media attention.

parative ease with which each survives the legislative process."[33]

Those in the upper stratum of government use the media to boost themselves and their programs, but this opportunism is by no means one-sided. Reporters who win the confidence of politicians are invited into their "inner sanctums" and are given titillating tidbits of information that will please their editors and help to boost their reportorial reputation. Thus journalists often find that they can best advance themselves through cooperation rather than conflict with those in government.

Presidential use of the press. Theodore Roosevelt, who thought of the presidency as a "bully pulpit," was the first president to give press reporters White House quarters.[34] Roosevelt recognized the linkage between leadership and publicity, and from the days of his administration presidents have tried to orchestrate the news. From these beginnings the presidential press conference became a major channel of communications between the president and the people. Moreover, today the prominence of television news gives the president an additional vehicle to tell "his side of the story" to the electorate. Direct televi-

---

[34]The adjective *bully* is used in the sense of first-rate or admirable. Thus "bully pulpit" refers to the "active use of the presidency's prestige and high visibility to inspire or moralize." Safire, *Safire's Political Dictionary*, p. 83.

TABLE 17.2   PRESIDENTIAL NEWS CONFERENCES WITH WHITE HOUSE CORRESPONDENTS, 1929–1989

President	Average number of press conferences per month	Total press conferences
Hoover (1929–1933)	5.6	268
Roosevelt (1933–1945)	6.9	998
Truman (1945–1953)	3.4	334
Eisenhower (1953–1961)	2.0	193
Kennedy (1961–1963)	1.9	64
Johnson (1963–1969)	2.2	135
Nixon (1969–1974)	0.5	37
Ford (1974–1977)	1.3	39
Carter (1977–1981)	1.2	59
Reagan (1981–1988)	0.5	47
Bush (1989)[a]	1.9	8

[a]As of May 31.

Source: Harold W. Stanley and Richard G. Niemi, *Vital Statistics in American Politics,* 2d ed. (Washington, D.C.: Congressional Quarterly Press, 1990), p. 53. Reprinted with permission from Congressional Quarterly, Inc.

sion addresses to the people have replaced press conferences as the principal means of communication with the people for the modern presidency.

Successive presidents have increasingly reduced the number of press conferences they hold, but they cannot disband the practice entirely without incurring the wrath of the fourth estate, which would accuse the White House of attempting to undermine freedom of the press. While press conferences are always unpredictable, presidents attempt to maintain control of them somewhat by preparing careful answers to questions they think will be asked and by recognizing more friendly than unfriendly reporters. President Reagan used a television monitor to refresh his memory of reporters' names and affiliations. He also often called on reporters by their first names, creating a friendly and disarming rapport with his questioners. President George Bush also cultivated a friendly style with the White House press corps, one that was more informal than Reagan's. But Bush continued the trend of modern presidents toward holding fewer and fewer press conferences knowing that the White House could easily get its views across to the Amer-

ican people directly through nationally televised addresses. (See Table 17.2.)

Presidential aide John Ehrlichman illustrated one manipulative technique employed by Richard Nixon:

During the years I worked for him, Nixon was usually capable of a passionless and penetrating analysis of his press opportunities. He was a talented media manipulator. I often watched him successfully plan how he or his spokesmen would dominate the evening news, capture the headlines and right-side columns of the front page of the *Washington Post,* or the lead story in *Time* or *Newsweek.* Richard Nixon could think like an editor. . . .[He] was convinced that the vast majority of reporters and commentators would be unfair to him if left to their own devices. They had to be prevented from airing their biased views, therefore, by whatever means were available."[35]

The Reagan White House assigned over 40 aides to work on press communications. When the press began to criticize the President and question his programs and capabilities to carry them out, the Reagan press office responded by deluging reporters with

---

[35]Ehrlichman, *Witness to Power,* pp. 263–264.

information. One aide noted, "We have intentionally blitzed [the press] with news and numerous briefings." The theory was that "a busy press is one that is unlikely to cause mischief."[36]

The White House press secretary speaks for the president and attempts as much as possible to use the daily press briefings to cast the president in a favorable light. Richard Reeves once cynically commented that the White House press briefings are "an adult day-care center" and the job of the press secretary is to keep the reporters "occupied, dumb and happy." Helen Thomas, who served in the White House for years as the correspondent for United Press International, commented: "We're pretty tightly managed and controlled. On the other hand, they do it in a nice way; there is none of the hostility and antagonism which sometimes existed before. Even when Reagan flays the press, it doesn't have the same atmospherics. There is a certain amount of civilized feeling on both sides." Thomas pointed out how the White House press typically tries to control the reporters: "They plan the day's story and try to keep our eye on that ball. We have only limited access to the President. We can go for days without seeing him. They seem to think that it is bad manners to ask him questions except under certain controlled conditions. Every day, they calculate what we do and how we jump."[37]

The critical role of the White House press has been modified by successful presidential efforts to manage the news. Significantly, the most stunning revelation about the White House in the twentieth century—Watergate—was turned up, not by the White House press corps, but by two *Washington Post* reporters on local beats. Since Watergate, members of the White House press have dreamed of being the first to uncover a new Watergate-like episode. But White House reporters have become in many respects part of the president's team, co-opted by him to serve his purposes. The incentives and access of White House reporters limit their role as independent and even unbiased investigators. They can comfortably do their job within the news world simply by reporting the information fed to them by the press office and by respectfully questioning the president during news conferences.

Congressional use of the press. As Douglass Cater has pointed out,

The member of Congress is uniquely creator and creature of publicity. It is the nature of his job to be concerned with that amorphous substance known as public opinion, and with the processes by which the public attention is attracted and public opinion shaped. He lives in a state of intimacy with the newspaperman baffling to outsiders who mistake this vital relationship for pure cronyism. He employs his highest-paid assistant to diagnose and fill the prescriptive needs of the press. For the lone congressman, the ideal is so to affect his press relations that back in his constituency the news is ever presented on a 'me and the President' basis. The more ambitious members seek to extend the constituency to which this image is projected."[38]

The goal of "me and the President," of course, varies in accordance with the popularity of the president and his party affiliation in relation to the legislator. But by whatever means, members of Congress seek to use the press to bolster their images back home and their status on Capitol Hill.

Members of Congress can help reporters get good stories, and in return they expect respect and appreciation. Colorful congressional personalities are stories in themselves. "The business of Congress," wrote Douglass Cater, "is the stuff of which good news reporting is made. . . . Its battles can be described in terms of colorful personalities rather than amorphous issues that may confound the copy

---

[36]*National Journal*, May 1, 1982, p. 769.

[37]Ibid., pp. 768–769.

[38]Cater, *The Fourth Branch of Government*, p. 47.

desk and confuse the reader. Washington is a highly fragmented capital city in which it is not always simple for the reporter to follow the thread of his story. But it is possible for him to glimpse the image of the total story in the congressional mirror, indeed to see its outlines in a bold relief that may not be so apparent on direct view."

A major reason for congressional power to co-opt the press is the reporter's reliance on close and friendly ties with the delegation he or she covers to provide the earliest possible access to whatever is going on—and thereby to avoid being "scooped." State delegations are covered by more than one newspaper, whose editors place strong demands upon their Capitol Hill reporters to be the first to obtain breaking news. Reporters who have incurred the wrath of the members they are assigned to cover are left out in the cold on important breaking stories. In the relationship between the press and members of Congress there is "a degree of protectionism that comes into play. Powerful pressures dissuade the reporter from being as zealous an exposer of Congress itself as he is of the executive department. His stock in trade in terms of news 'exclusives' depends upon the preservation of a chummy relationship with members of Congress. A great amount of news is dispensed to him as a favor and must be regarded as such. There is not quite the same camaraderie about news gathering in the more austere precincts of the executive."[39]

Reporters from a member's state or district particularly avoid becoming an irritant, for they, more than their counterparts in the national press, depend upon the relatively narrow "sources" of their state delegations. Scandal and wrongdoing on Capitol Hill generally are revealed by the national rather than the local media. Once, however, even the national press corps protected members of Congress who were involved in the most egregious scandals. Commenting on the 1940s and 1950s, Douglass Cater wrote:

The reporter knows there is slim likelihood of any followup on his initiative should he publish evidence of corruption or wrongdoing on the Hill. For one who turns up malfeasance in the executive branch, there is always a congressional committee standing by eager to pick up and pursue the matter. In fact, the publication of the expose and the commencement of the committee probe have sometimes been carefully coordinated in advance. Reporter and committee counsel work hand in glove to reap its full benefits. The congressmen are seldom as prone to examine one another. Nor is the executive branch always alert to bear down on congressional abuses. It has no publicity mechanism comparable to the congressional committee probe for airing such abuses.[40]

After Watergate, however, the *national* press began more boldly to take an adversary position to Congress and expose wrongdoing. Michael Robinson cites the example of Congressman Dan Flood, who was indicted for bribery in 1978 with widespread accompanying publicity in the national press and the media. Only nine years before, the national press had given virtually no publicity to a similar indictment of Senator Daniel Brewster (D., Maryland). The Brewster and Flood cases presented a stark contrast in the way they were reported on network television news. Robinson notes:

Flood was referred to in fifty-nine different news stories, while Brewster was mentioned in eight. More incredible, Flood was the principal news focus or a secondary news focus for 4,320 seconds of network time, while stories about Brewster amounted to only 170 seconds. Flood-related stories received 25 times as much network news attention as did Brewster-related items, even though Brewster was a senator and Flood "only a representative."

---

[39]Ibid., pp. 53–54.

[40]Ibid., p. 55.

The Dan Flood case also illustrates that the local press is less critical of Capitol Hill scandals than the Washington media. The Wilkes-Barre, Pennsylvania, *Time-Leader,* the largest newspaper in Flood's district, reported the facts of his indictment and trial for conspiracy, bribery, and perjury but emphasized the congressman's strong support in his district. Only 7 percent of the Flood stories in that newspaper were on the front page. The *Washington Post,* on the other hand, put news of Flood on the front page in 42 percent of its stories and emphasized constituent support of Flood in only two stories. One network correspondent stressed the tendency of the local press to support congressmen, using the Flood case and that of Wilbur Mills, who was involved in a drinking and sex scandal:

The classic case is Dan Flood. He is God back home. I was home when it all broke open. What they were getting back home [in the media] was they're picking on our boy Dan. The same was true with Wilbur Mills. The papers back home said Wilbur's in trouble and we've got to rally around our boy Wilbur.[41]

The Congress member's incentives for reelection, power on Capitol Hill, influence in the broader world of Washington, and "good public policy" are all served by the press. Members rely upon the media for advertising and for the publicizing of their credit-claiming and position-taking activities, all of which are essential for reelection.[42] *Within* Congress, a "good press" helps a member's prestige and can be used to bolster a legislator's reputation for power. Stories about the winners and losers in the congressional political game are always good copy, and it behooves the Congress member who is seeking to build his or her reputation for power to be cast as a winner by the media. Finally, members who want to achieve policy goals know they must sell not only themselves, but their programs to the media. Jack Kemp, for example, might have remained virtually unknown as a congressman, although he had achieved fame as the quarterback for the Buffalo Bills, a National Football League team. However, billed by the media as a former professional-quarterback-turned-congressman he was newsworthy. The nationally televised CBS program "60 Minutes" featured Kemp and the "supply-side economics" that he espoused, which later was to become part of the operating philosophy of the Reagan administration.

Bureaucratic entrepreneurs and the press. J Edgar Hoover, the late FBI director, and Admiral Hyman Rickover immediately come to mind as bureaucratic entrepreneurs who knew the value of publicity in gaining support within and without government for themselves and their programs. Henry Kissinger, as Richard Nixon's national security advisor and secretary of state, also used the media effectively to enhance his reputation for power. The most effective political entrepreneurs at the top levels of the executive branch carefully cultivate the press, planting stories about themselves and their programs to advance personal power and achieve backing on Capitol Hill, in the White House, and among special interest groups for their policies. The media in turn like colorful personalities in the executive branch as well as in other parts of the government, considering them to be newsworthy and excellent vehicles for journalistic advancement.

Perhaps the paradigm of the bureaucratic entrepreneur was FBI Director J. Edgar Hoover. In 1924, at the age of 29, Hoover became the director of the Bureau of Investigation (in 1935 renamed the Federal Bureau of Investigation) in the Justice Department, with a mandate to make the agency (which had fallen into disrepute) a reputable and effective law enforcement body. Hoover moved cautiously at first and for almost a decade and a

---

[41]Robinson, "Three Faces of Congressional Media," in Mann and Ornstein, *The New Congress,* pp. 74, 77–79.

[42]See Chapter 10.

half carefully solidified his power within government, cultivating good relationships with the White House and Capitol Hill while paying close attention to every detail of the Bureau's operation. The first stage of his carefully laid plan, to give himself and his agency credibility *within* government, was complete after he had convinced the president and key members of Congress and the Justice Department that "his" agency was essential in the fight against political subversion and crime.

Hoover then turned his attention to public relations in the early 1940s in order to broaden public support for the FBI. Over the next several decades he mounted what was to become the most effective public relations campaign ever carried out by an administrative agency. Senator George Norris (R.) of Nebraska, who served in the Senate from 1913 until 1943, recognized the significance of Hoover's early public relations efforts and called him the "greatest publicity hound on the American continent today." Hoover used all the media to build the public image he wanted for himself and for the FBI. He gave sympathetic journalists access to the agency to help them write books praising the agency's fight against subversion and crime. These best-selling books led to radio, television, and motion picture productions that increased public support for the agency to a point where its director became politically invincible.

J. Edgar Hoover took every opportunity to manipulate the media. His objectives seemed to be nothing less than the socialization of the entire nation into acceptance of his version of the FBI. Those with long memories cannot forget the more than 400 half-hour radio programs produced between 1945 and 1953 entitled "The FBI in Peace and War" and "This Is Your FBI." Both radio series were based upon popular books written with the cooperation of the agency, and Hoover himself helped to shape the program "This is Your FBI." The FBI's cooperation with authors, producers, and directors was conditioned on the agency's approval of the final product. The Washington bureau chief of the *New York Herald Tribune* in 1955 was granted a request to write a history of the Bureau, which became *The FBI Story*, a ranking best-seller. Hoover's assistant, Louis B. Nichols, provided the author with the necessary information from the Bureau's files and carefully read the manuscript before its publication. "Whitehead made a few mistakes," Nichols said later, "but by going over the manuscript we were able to put him back on the right track . . . we corrected a few of his facts, but we never interfered with his conclusions." When Whitehead's book later became a popular film, starring James Stewart as its protagonist, Hoover, who had written the foreword of the book, was so thrilled with the film that he reportedly "wept with joy at its premier."[43]

J. Edgar Hoover and his agency were perhaps the supreme media manipulators, but others have done almost as well, particularly Admiral Hyman Rickover, who used the media to help defy Navy tradition and secure approval for his nuclear submarine program. Rickover operated much in the same way as Hoover, carefully cultivating the press and Capitol Hill to build his empire and run it outside the formal channels of bureaucratic command. Rickover faced a crisis in 1952 when a Navy Selection Board for the second time passed him over for promotion from captain to rear admiral. Both his career and his dream of a nuclear submarine fleet seemed over. However, writes journalist Jonathan Alter:

Rickover was smart enough to know that if he could create enough interest outside the Navy, he might have a fighting chance after all. In part because he had a sexy project . . . he caught the attention of the press, particularly a young Pentagon correspondent for *Time* named Clay Blair. Blair knew a good story when he saw one, and Rickover knew how to be cooperative—he

---

[43]Sanford J. Ungar, *FBI* (Boston: Little, Brown, 1975), pp. 373, 374.

even lent the use of his office and his wife's editing skills for the book Blair eventually wrote about him. In later years, once safely ensconced, Rickover shunned reporters, but when it counted he played them masterfully, especially those journalists like Edward R. Murrow whom he knew could endow him with some of their own respectability."[44]

Henry Kissinger, in his memoirs, perhaps best sums up the relationship of mutual dependence between the ambitious bureaucrat and the press:

Washington is like a Roman arena. Gladiators do battle, and the spectators determine who survives by giving the appropriate signal, just as in the Coliseum. Barely noted by the rest of the country, leaks to media serve Washington as clues to power and influence. . . .Reputations can be damaged, or made, by leaks that find no rebuttal from the powerful, even if untrue. A particularly subtle version is the untrue leak that is permitted to run its course uncontested by those in a condition to rebut it, and is denied only when the news cycle has passed it by. This has the advantage of damaging the victim almost as much, while preserving the reputation of the source.

Leaks, of course, always involve the press and the media. Kissinger also comments:

The journalists act simultaneously as mutual conduits and a tribunal, shielding their witnesses by the principle of 'protection of sources' and often determining the outcome by the emphasis they choose to give competing versions. The press is thus both spectator and participant. The people may have 'a right to know'—but only what the press chooses to tell it. In bureaucratic in-fighting, masking the identity of the leakers is frequently a suppression of the most significant part of the story. The journalist may strive for objectivity, his competitors may have an incentive to knock down his story, but leakers can only initiate a drama that creates its own momentum through the reactions of the victim

and the power brokers. Rarely, it seems, does anyone worry about the motives of the source, though there are serious ethical problems when the journalist's interest in a scoop and the source's self-interest coincide, as in some "investigative" journalism. It becomes difficult to determine who is using whom."[45]

THE INTERNAL WORLD OF THE PRESS AND POLITICAL REPORTING

Political reporters and their editors work in organizations that are as highly "political" as the government they cover. Games of power and status are played in the newspaper and media world as in politics. Reporters want to advance within their organizations, which is best done by pleasing their editors, who in turn, must protect themselves in a rigid editorial hierarchy.

Newspaper Politics

The best-selling author Gay Talese achieved his reputation by writing the story of the *New York Times* in a book whose title, *The Kingdom and the Power*, reflects the highly charged political atmosphere of the newspaper world. The book portrays the often fascinating and always ambitious editors and reporters who vied for power within the *New York Times* organization. The story of the *New York Times* makes the interactions portrayed on the old television series "Lou Grant" seem like kindergarten politics. The *New York Times* is at the top of the "major league" newspapers, making the stakes higher there for the organizational climbers than in other newspapers. However, editors and reporters in all major newspapers intensely play the game of organizational politics.

The internal structure of newspapers. Large newspapers have "desks," or coverage

---

[44]Jonathan Alter, "The Powers That Stay," *The Washington Monthly*, March 1982, p. 14.

[45]Henry Kissinger, *Years of Upheaval* (Boston: Little, Brown, 1982), pp. 421–422.

areas, that vie with each other for recognition within the organization. There are generally three desks: national, metropolitan, and city. Each desk is given jurisdiction over the area implied by its name. The national desk covers national news, the metropolitan desk takes in the entire circulation area of the newspaper, and the city desk reports on the city or cities within the circulation area. An editor is assigned to each desk, and competition among editors can be intense. The editor of the national desk stands apart from the others and is higher in prestige, reporting only to the managing editor, who stands above all the desks. The city desk editor generally reports to the metropolitan editor. State editors who do not technically have "desks," oversee the state capital bureau and the state political reporters. Newspapers with wide circulations also have regional and international editors. For example, the *New York Times* has regional editors that cover the South, the Midwest, and the West. A foreign desk covers international news in conjunction with bureaus throughout the world. Whether running desks or not, editors are always in competition with each other for internal prestige, which causes them to defend their respective turfs from incursions by other editors and their reporters. Editors want the reporters under them to distinguish themselves against other reporters both within and without the newspaper. (Nothing is more embarrassing to an editor than to have one of his or her reporters "scooped" by another newspaper.)

Gay Talese describes the kind of infighting that frequently occurs among editors. "In 1965," he wrote, "the New York desk blocked an attempt by the *Times'* national political correspondent, David S. Broder, stationed in Washington, to cover President Johnson's speech in Princeton, New Jersey, because Princeton was part of the New York desk's territory. In possible retaliation, the national desk refused to let the New York reporter who had covered Johnson's speech make a trip to Hot Springs, Arkansas, to report on the National Young Republican Board's action on the New Jersey Rat Fink case. Instead David Broder was ordered to Arkansas by Sitton [the national news desk editor]. Broder wrote his story from there and filed it with the New York desk, and it was killed after one edition."[46] (Broder was so frustrated by the bureaucratic infighting at the *Times* that he resigned in 1966 and went to the *Washington Post*, where he is today a nationally syndicated columnist.)

The effect of newspaper politics. The power of editors and the advancement of reporters depend upon a constant flow of newsworthy stories. Thus reporters have an incentive to cultivate good relationships with their sources. Washington correspondents, then, tend to be sympathetic to the government they report about, and stories coming out of the national news bureaus are often "puff pieces" that portray their subjects uncritically. National reporters and their editors particularly like personality profiles of prominent politicians who are making their mark on the Washington political scene. Such portrayals are always positive in tone, for not only is the cooperation of the subjects necessary to do the stories, but there is nothing newsworthy in subjects who are political failures— unless they are involved in scandals. Reporters seek out the ambitious and successful politicians to write about, in the process boosting the politician's reputation and their own as well.

A simple glance at national reporting on Congress reveals the generally laudatory view reporters take of the members they cover. "All Eyes on Russell Long" was a title typical of feature stories written about Capitol Hill personalities, this one by John Pierson of the *Wall Street Journal*'s Washington Bureau. Pierson joined the chorus of journalistic praise for Long, whom reporters built up as one of the

---

[46]Gay Talese, *The Kingdom and the Power* (New York and Cleveland: World Publishing, 1966), p. 384.

most powerful legislators ever to ply the political craft on Capitol Hill when he was chairman of the Senate Finance Committee. Pierson's piece on Long was characteristic of the journalistic praise of the senator and concluded: "Huey Long made it to the Senate. But unlike Russell, Huey was too ambitious for higher office and too much a rabble-rouser to reach the Senate's inner circle. The father knew how to move the people. The son knows how to move at least 51 of the people's representatives. What a team they would have made!"[47]

Other national press coverage typical of Congress is represented by headlines such as: "Baker, Making Mark as a Leader in Senate, Builds His Prospects"; "O'Neill Orchestrates the Vote to Save Politically Risky Raise"; "Proxmire Thrives in His Chosen Role as Senate Maverick"; "How Representative Foley Played a Key Role in Shaping Disputed Farm Bill"; "Republicans Are Turning to Conable as Their Spokesman in Congress."

White House reporters, and those who cover the executive branch, also find they can most readily produce the newsworthy stories their editors want by maintaining cordial and often uncritical relations with their sources. From inside the White House the press appears overly critical and often vicious. However, reality belies the White House perspective of the press, which for the most part uncritically transmits information to the national editors who in turn, because the stories concern the president, are able to command front-page space. White House reporters generally find that they can most easily perform their jobs and gain recognition with their newspapers by reporting uncritically on the activities of the president and his family. *Washington Post* reporters Bob Woodward and Carl Bernstein, whose investigation led to the Watergate revelations, sig-

nificantly were not part of the White House press corps, nor were they working for the national desk of the *Post*. (Woodward was a general assignment reporter on the *Post*'s local staff, and Bernstein was a police reporter.)

Peer pressure. Bill Kovach, when he was the Washington editor of the *New York Times*, emphasized peer pressure as another factor internal to the newspaper world that may reduce the critical role of the press. "There is a constant effort by Washington reporters to seek the approval of their peers," he commented. "The bulk of the press corps members reinforce each other's views. It is a closed system, a herd instinct. They look to each other for reinforcement; they develop their own jargon. Journalists are the last people to exercise their talent that way. It's hard to break out of. Sometimes editors won't let them for fear of being out of step."[48]

One of the deans of Washington journalism, Eric Sevareid, points to the self-importance of the press. "The media feeds on itself," he comments. National political reporters, journalists, and electronic media personalities have become stars. They have been invited into the inner sanctums of Washington power and have become part of the Capital's establishment. Michael Novak of the American Enterprise Institute commented: "The statement of public policy that comes through our public institutions comes through the media. Those reporters and the analysts who give us our picture of ourselves are now themselves among the top ten percent, by education, by income, and by status. They tend to present a picture of this country that reflects themselves rather than the other 90 percent."[49]

Publishers, too, are often linked directly or indirectly with the Washington political es-

---

[47]*Wall Street Journal*, August 14, 1978, p. 12.

[48]*National Journal,* April 17, 1982, p. 673.
[49]Ibid.

(Drawing by Lorenz; © 1982 The New Yorker Magazine, Inc.)

"And as the campaign heats up, the latest poll shows the Dan Rather news team running slightly ahead of the Peter Jennings news team, with the Tom Brokaw team just two points back and gaining."

The networks compete vigorously to raise their ratings during presidential campaigns.

tablishment. Jack Anderson, who writes one of the liveliest and most provocative investigative columns in the country, feels that investigative reporting has "cooled off. Publishers don't like investigative stories because generally we're criticizing their friends. Many editors like it less because it causes them problems. They know they have to respond to complaints from the publisher, their sources, the object of the investigation and so forth."[50]

The world of the electronic media. Television correspondents, like their counterparts in the press, strive to get their stories on the nightly network news (for which they are paid bonuses) or on the local stations' news programs. Their editors and the heads of television news departments are involved in much the same kind of power game within

[50]Ibid., p. 672.

the organization that characterizes newspapers. Ratings are critical to the survival of the heads of news departments and their reporters and anchorpeople. Television news is viewed more as entertainment than are the "hard" news stories that appear in major newspapers. Television news editors seek dramatic and entertaining material and, for the ends of their programs, news stories with happy endings that will leave their audiences minimally engaged and content. Television news has neither the purpose nor the time for in-depth coverage, let alone for the presentation of a critical view of the political process. Television reporters, to get their stories on the news, must focus upon imagery with very little substance.

THE IMPACT OF TELEVISION ON POLITICAL REPORTING

Television news is big business with a Hollywood flair. The anchorpeople for national network news are stars making well over a million dollars a year. Even local anchorpersons, especially in major cities such as Los Angeles and Boston, where local news competition is intense, may receive annual salaries of a million dollars or more. Network and local news are a major source of station revenues, and only a few rating points can make a significant difference in the amount of money that can be charged for advertising. Network and station news executives and producers stress style, glamour, drama, and human interest stories to capture large viewing audiences.

Network news producers focus on Washington and try to find in the Capital's daily events drama that will be of interest to their audiences. All of the major news networks maintain large Washington bureaus. News programs feature presidential press conferences and White House news briefings, congressional hearings, and interviews with members of congress who are engaged in "newsworthy" activities, such as spearheading important legislation.

Wide audiences make television the principal means of communication between politicians and their constituents. Just as Richard Nixon "used to sit around figuring out how he could get a minute and a half on the evening news," senators, representatives, and even heads of executive departments plan daily activities that they feel will be attractive to television news reporters and producers. Political candidates in particular rely upon television for fund raising and, comments *Washington Post* columnist David Broder, "their speeches are tailored for TV, the strategy being to control as much as possible a 90-second or 2-minute time bite. They reduce all their other activities to get on the evening news programs." The result, according to Broder, is to force "journalists to do other things and to spend more time away from the candidates, looking at other parts of the campaign. That's to the good."[51]

Competition between Television and Newspapers

Television and newspaper reporters operate in different worlds, but they often cover the same political events, which to an extent puts them into competition. Traditionally there has been a great deal of competition between the two camps. As television news became more prominent and TV reporters more ubiquitous, newspaper journalists often disparaged their TV counterparts. One CBS correspondent even admitted: "A lot of TV reporters are not really reporters at all. They've come up from local radio and TV stations, and they really don't know much about politics.

---

[51]*National Journal*, April 24, 1982, p. 721.

But all they have to do is run around and dredge up a minute and a half of thought. It makes no difference if they're ignoramuses because there's no space on the program anyway."[52]

Timothy Crouse described the mixed feelings that journalists—or "printmen," as he called them—had towards television reporters in his lively account of the role of the press in the Nixon-McGovern presidential contest in 1972:

The printmen on the bus did admire a few TV reporters, mostly correspondents who covered Washington full-time, such as Doug Kiker (who was a refugee, after all, from the old *Herald Tribune*), Dan Rather, Cassie Mackin, Roger Mudd, and Dan Schorr. These people were good, they dug for news; but still, how could you take seriously a person whose daily output lasted two minutes on the air? In newspaper terms, the TV news amounted to putting out a paper that contained only ten stories every day, with only four paragraphs to each story. In fact, if you put a whole transcript of a network news show into newspaper type, it covered only a third of the front page of the *New York Times*.[53]

Print journalists recognize, often somewhat jealously, the importance and prominence of TV news. Columnist Joseph Kraft commented, "I have to keep abreast of TV and watch it because that is what most Americans watch." For their part, the network executives and bureau chiefs for television news insist television reporting and news programs are as important and informative as newspaper reporting. Former NBC Washington Bureau Chief Sid Davis remarked, "We can cover stories as well as the good newspapers. Look how often TV is quoted. We initiate stories on our own and I never felt we had a lack of ideas. We broke stories on the failed rescue raid on Iran, the defection of a Soviet general, stepped-up aid to El Salvador, the Libyan hit team, and the five Americans hidden in the Canadian Embassy in Iran."[54]

ABC Washington Bureau News Chief William Knowles assessed the relative importance of newspapers and television news: "We obviously all read the newspapers; it is still a major source of news that we recommend viewers to read. But we don't subscribe to the premise that if it is not in the *Post* or the *New York Times*, it is not news. We read the *Post* bulldog edition every night, as we have ever since Watergate. We keep our eyes open to the wire services and we get a lot of news from our affiliates." Knowles added, "Our quintessential correspondent can hold his own with the top print journalists; on top of that he has to use pictures properly, write to them, and explain them and not fight them. That takes a mixture of narrative and reportorial writing."[55]

Whatever may be the lasting effects of television, there is no doubt that it has added an important new dimension to political reporting. The existence of television has forced all participants in the political process to think far more in terms of images than was the case in the pre-television era. Even reporters themselves are directly affected. In the view of James Deakin, a former White House correspondent for the *St. Louis Post-Dispatch*, television has changed presidential press conferences: "There are none of the rough exchanges that occurred in the pre-television era. It's like a teaparty. Everybody is an actor playing up to millions of viewers and all are on their best behavior."[56] In other respects, too, television has had an impact. Bill Kovach of the *New York Times* commented: "The lead stories in a paper are seldom a surprise, so in large measure in response to television, you have to ask 'What can I do to help the reader a little more?' We try to publish as much detail

---

[52]Timothy Crouse, *The Boys on the Bus* (New York: Ballantine, 1976), pp. 150–151.

[53]Ibid., p. 151.

[54]*National Journal*, April 17, 1982, p. 669.

[55]Ibid.

[56]Ibid.

as possible but also to do something special, usually an analytical piece that runs on the front page and is marked 'News Analysis.'"[57]

The Significance of the Media

The press, always a major force in American politics, has become even more important as it has expanded with the nation's capital to become an important ally of government, as well as its critic. Modern government depends upon the media to publicize and gain support for its programs. In an open society such as ours, those who play the political game depend

---

[57]Ibid., p. 664.

upon the press and the media to enhance their positions and support their policies. Although the press and the media often act collusively with government for their mutual benefit, there is no damper upon the free exchange of ideas and the constant flow of information to the citizenry. The media are not a monolithic force, but are as pluralistic as the political system itself. That pluralism may not always be felt due to the "pack instinct" of many reporters, who follow the same stories and report them in the same way, but it is most certainly a protection against government control of information. Freedom of the press remains one of the most important underpinnings of our democratic system.

The Media Revolution and the New Politics

The ubiquitous character of the media and the communications revolution has transformed democratic politics. Media advisers are the top honchos on political campaign staffs, and political consulting has become a big business. The media make it possible for democratic politics to flourish as the flow of information between candidates and the electorate increases, giving voters the opportunity to decide more rationally which candidates will best serve their interests. However, it is "common knowledge" that media campaigns often stress images more than issues, distorting the rational linkage between candidates and voters that democratic theory posits. The author of the following case study takes a fresh look at the way in which the modern media revolution has affected politics, and the way in which democracy is supposed to work.

The New Media and the New Politics / *Jeffrey Abramson*

Governance and Grass-Roots Lobbying
Campaigns and elections are the means of democratic politics, not its end. After the last hurrah comes governance and the difficult task of translating the temporary mobilization of voters during an election into the more permanent loyalties that governing and its hard choices require.

Here we come to a paradox about the communications revolution that is only now coming clear: the easier the new media make it to campaign, the harder they make it to govern. We are at a point in our history, I believe, where a virtual chasm is opening up between what it takes to win a presi-

dential election and what it takes to govern. There are three reasons for this.

First, elections used to test voter loyalty to a candidate in a manner that was likely to survive the election. Up through the New Deal, voting was an act of swearing allegiance to a party as well as to a personality. To vote was to express not just one's politics but also one's ethnic, sectional, and occupational loyalties. Moreover, a vote for a candidate was typically also a vote for the party boss or ward leader who marched alongside the candidate and who was in a position to exert continued pressure on the candidate if elected. All in all,

Source: *Aspen Institute Quarterly*, Spring 1990, pp. 25–28. Reprinted with permission of the Aspen Institute Quarterly and Jeffrey B. Abramson.

through much of our history candidates could only gain a party's nomination by striking deals with the interests these bosses and ward leaders wanted government to serve after the election. That left the party nomination process far from democratic. But at least the general election then presented the voters with a coherent choice. To vote for a candidate who campaigned on the basis of interests made the vote a decent prediction of continued support after the election.

Ever since the advent of television, the communications revolution has been working to destabilize these traditional sources of voter loyalty. Candidates today advertise themselves, not their party label, and they do so directly, campaigning on a one-to-one basis in our living rooms, as it were. They seek our vote not primarily because of their group (Democrat or Republican) or ours (Irish or Italian or labor) but because we happen to agree with their solution to the deficit or their position on the death penalty or their promise not to raise taxes. This makes the modern campaign ever so more focused on the issues than its nineteenth-century counterpart (a point wholly missed by most commentators). But when I owe allegiance to a politician only because I agree with his views, that loyalty melts away as soon as a mistake calls the candidate's views into question (witness the overnight fall of Gary Hart) (Schneider 1989). Moreover, if my vote expresses agreement with the candidate only on a single issue that is particularly important to me, then the candidate cannot count on my support after the election on any other issue. The paradox results that the communications revolution, by permitting candidates to appeal more directly than ever to individual voters, makes it more difficult for the winner to count on the continued support of the troops after the campaign. To put the same point another way: the ability to win votes one by one avoids the need to build the kind of coalitions or strike the kind of deals that governance has always required.

A second reason for the growing gulf between the art of campaigning and the art of governing has to do with another child of the communications revolution: grass-roots lobbying via computer. Traditionally, lobbyists attempted to influence legislation by talking to legislators or their staff. But today's Washington lobbyist is more likely to bypass the legislator in favor of direct mail communication with the constituents back in the district. The hope is that constituents can be aroused to do the "lobbying" of their representatives themselves. Almost every organized interest group, whether of the left or the right, from the National Rifle Association to Common Cause, is in the business today of using computerized direct mail to make of politics a kind of permanent, emotional, divisive election—but now an election or referendum on particular pieces of legislation or committee actions rather than an election of candidates.

Recent examples of this kind of "governance out-of-doors" include the grass-roots lobbying done to influence the votes of senators on the Tower confirmation vote for secretary of defense or on the Bork confirmation vote for a seat on the Supreme Court. Most recently, a direct-mail campaign by prochoice forces helped turn out 300,000 persons in Washington to "lobby" the Supreme Court, in a manner of speaking, on the abortion issue. These are all examples of the new media being used by groups to bring public opinion to bear more directly and intensely on the deliberations of governmental bodies.

In the view of the organizers of these lobbying events, democracy is served when the magic of electronics is used to bring the views of the people to bear on the Senate or Supreme Court. But in the classical vision of democracy, plebiscitary schemes for referring particular matters of legislation to the people were rejected in favor of the need for independent representatives to deliberate on the merits of a proposal, sometimes out of the public eye (this was the case with the Constitutional Convention of 1787). For democracy, at best, is not just a matter of registering or adding up the preconceived interests and opinions of individuals; it is a matter of engaging citizens in collective conversation about the common good—the kind of conversation that puts at risk one's opinions as matters come to be viewed in a public, rather than personal, light.

The computer has turned grass-roots lobbying into a political tool at odds with these classical views about independent representatives and the art of governing. Insofar as the idea of an independent representative rested on the technological impossibility of a representative's knowing what his constituents wanted on each and every pending bill, the computerization of polling makes just such knowledge possible. And this is where grass-roots lobbying comes in. Computerized data services now permit groups to retrieve instant information about any pending bill or committee hearing in Congress. When Congressional action touches on the group's arena of interests, they use their computers to analyze a mass of demographic and public opinion data, isolating potential supporters who then become a target for a narrowly focused, often emotionally phrased rallying cry to action.

Because the mailing is only to presumed sympathizers and concerns only one issue, there is, as we already saw in the context of campaigns, less need for broad-based appeals and more focus on stimulating immediate, emotional responses. To aid in the emotional appeal, the computer and laser printer will personalize the letter ("Dear Professor Abramson, As a fellow professor on the East Coast who shares my believe in . . ."). State-of-the-art laser printers can do 20,000 personalized letters an hour! They can even make the letter look as if it is in the candidate's own handwriting (Peterson 1988: 118). And, as a final aid in the immediate mobilization of troops, preprinted "telegrams" or "ballots" can be inserted that I just have to sign and send back to my representative.

In another place I have already criticized at length the "pseudodemocracy" accomplished by confusing direct mail with direct democracy (Abramson, Arterton, and Orren, 1988: 164–177). It is true that the computer empowers groups to lobby more effectively at the mass level, thereby bringing public opinion to bear more immediately and more frequently on the acts of our representatives. But this kind of electrification of democracy, without more, short-circuits or bypasses the kind of deliberations and meetings and debates and considerations of opposing views that alone give democratic substance to the act of registering an opinion on an issue. Democracy demands a concern for, and a familiarity with, the views of others. When electronic democracy is envisioned as a way of permitting individuals, isolated in their own homes, to respond to direct mail stimuli while avoiding the meetings and conversations that alone permit an individual to find his interests in a public context, then the communications revolution threatens democracy with the historic ills of faction and balkanization—different interests competing for power with no sense of community or a common good, the winners bearing no responsibilities for the life of the losers in their midst.

PART FOUR

The Nature and Distribution of Government Responsibilities

A major purpose of government is to enact public policies that meet the needs and interests of the people. Interest groups, parties, political, social, and economic elites, and public opinion are constantly pressuring government for action. Public policy is formulated in many ways: Congress, the president, the bureaucracy, and the courts all have important roles to play, as do the multitude of state and local governments. National, state, and local governments all have their own constituencies and constitutional powers; this division of responsibilities inevitably shapes the policy process and the nature of law. By dividing power among the branches of the national government and the state governments, the Framers of the Constitution ensured that America's government would be richly pluralistic. And, by making all governments responsible both to the higher law of the Constitution and to the people, they guaranteed that it would be truly democratic.

CHAPTER EIGHTEEN

Government Policies: Their Nature and Scope

"President Bush Offers Economic Development Loan to New Polish Government"; "Senate Votes for 'Hazardous Waste Fund' to Help Clean Up Environment"; "House Votes Funds for New Weapons Systems"; "Commerce Secretary Mediates with Japanese to Lift Import Trade Barriers"; "IRS Vows Tougher Enforcement on Tax Delinquents"; "American Troops Ordered to Saudi Arabia."

These headlines give a small sampling of the wide range of government policies. Constantly changing political demands, as well as changing national and international conditions, continuously shape the nature and scope of policies. For example, substantial government regulation of the economy arose out of political demands at the end of the nineteenth century and intensified through nearly three-quarters of the twentieth century, particularly during the administrations of Franklin D. Roosevelt in the 1930s and Lyndon B. Johnson during the 1960s. However, this regulatory trend began to wane in the late 1970s, and, in response to new political pressures throughout the 1980s, "deregulation" became the trend. Democrats joined Republicans in sponsoring legislation to decontrol the airline and trucking industries and to reduce the amount of governmental regulation in other areas as well.

What are the constitutional bases and limits that shape the nature and scope of governmental policies? Within the broader context of national conditions and political demands, how are specific policies initiated and shaped? Are there important differences among the types of policies that our government undertakes, and among the kinds of political activities they involve? This chapter provides some fundamental perspectives for understanding the answers to these questions.

THE CONSTITUTIONAL CONTEXT OF PUBLIC POLICY

The Framers of the Constitution, in addition to their interest in creating a strong national government within the framework of a separation of powers and checks and balances system, had substantive policy concerns. They were particularly interested in creating a national government that could effectively regulate commerce among the states and provide for the national defense. They were also of course anxious that the new national government have revenue-raising capabilities (through the power of taxation) that would enable it to sustain itself and spend for the public good. These policy concerns led to the establishment of the three most important policy-making powers of the national government: (1) the regulation of commerce among the states, (2) the power to raise and support armies and provide for the national defense, and (3) the authority to tax and spend for the general welfare.

The Regulation of Commerce

Article I of the Constitution gives Congress the authority to "regulate commerce among the several states." The need for a national commerce power was a major underpinning of the Union. A year before the Philadelphia Convention in 1787, Alexander Hamilton and James Madison, who were so important in shaping the Constitution itself, called for a meeting of the states in Annapo-

lis. The aim of this conclave was to strengthen the powers of the Confederacy to end the commercial wars among the states, which threatened to end the fragile Union under the Articles of Confederation. Only 12 delegates attended the Annapolis convention—from New York, New Jersey, Pennsylvania, Delaware, and Virginia. The convention was adjourned due to the failure of more states to attend, and a new convention was planned for the next year in Philadelphia, principally to deal with the problem of national regulation of commerce but also to amend the Articles of Confederation to generally secure a more perfect Union.

Alexander Hamilton explained, in *The Federalist,* the purpose of the commerce power

(Drawing by Richter; © 1982 The New Yorker Magazine, Inc.)

Government officials may not always succeed in persuading skeptical citizens that their taxes are well spent.

that had been given Congress under the Constitution. He wrote in *The Federalist*, No. 22, that the government under the Articles of Confederation was "altogether unfit for the administration of the affairs of the Union." As Hamilton saw it, the lack of a national commerce power had "already operated as a bar to the formation of beneficial treaties with foreign powers, and . . .given occasions of dissatisfaction between the states." The delegates to the Philadelphia Convention generally agreed that a new national power to regulate commerce was necessary. James Madison, in *The Federalist*, No. 45, wrote: "The regulation of commerce, it is true, is a new power; but that seems to be an addition that few oppose and from which no apprehensions are entertained."

During the early part of the nineteenth century the supporters of states' rights began to have very strong apprehensions about the scope of the national commerce power, which they saw as a constitutional provision potentially fatal to their cause. They wanted the commerce clause of the Constitution to be interpreted "strictly," or "narrowly," essentially in order to limit the authority of the national government to the regulation of commerce that was carried out *between* the territorial boundaries of the states. Under this doctrine the states not only would have been permitted to regulate commerce concurrently with the national government, but their laws would have nullified conflicting national legislation that touched upon *intrastate* commerce. The Supreme Court, in the historic case *Gibbons v. Ogden* (1824), rejected the arguments of the states' rights advocates. The Court interpreted the national commerce power broadly and unequivocally proclaimed national supremacy in commercial regulation (see Chapter 3).

Providing for the National Defense

The Constitution supported a strong national government that would provide for the national defense. Alexander Hamilton wrote in *The Federalist*, No. 23: "The principal purposes to be answered by Union are these—the common defense of the members; the preservation of the public peace, as well against internal convulsions as external attacks; the regulation of commerce with other nations and between the states; the superintendence of our intercourse, political and commercial, with foreign countries."

Hamilton expressed strong views on the breadth of the constitutional power needed to provide for the national defense. Again, in *The Federalist*, No. 23, he wrote:

The authorities essential to the common defense are these: to raise armies; to build and equip fleets; to prescribe rules for the government of both; to direct their operation; to provide for their support. These powers ought to exist without limitation, *because it is impossible to foresee or to define the extent and variety of national exigencies, and the correspondent extent and variety of the means which may be necessary to satisfy them.* The circumstances that endanger the safety of nations are infinite, and for this reason no constitutional shackles can wisely be imposed on the power to which the care of it is committed.

Hamilton wrote more extensively on the necessity for a strong national defense in *The Federalist* than on any other subject. His views were representative of the nationalists at the Philadelphia Convention of 1787, who saw a weak national defense as a major deficiency of the government under the Articles of Confederation. Above all, the Framers did not want state sovereignty to diminish the capability of the federal government to provide for the national defense. "Security against foreign danger is one of the primitive objects of civil society," Hamilton wrote in *The Federalist*, No. 41. "It is an avowed and essential object of the American Union. The powers requisite for attaining it must be effectually confided to the federal councils."

Expansion of the congressional war power. Under the Constitution the congressional war power, like the authority to regulate commerce among the states, is complete. The implied powers clause, which grants Congress the authority "to make all laws which shall be necessary and proper for carrying into execution the foregoing [enumerated] powers [of Article I]," makes explicit the intent of the Framers to construe congressional power broadly. Congress has over the years passed many measures to deal with wartime emergencies, and such legislation has rarely been challenged on constitutional grounds. On the several occasions when challenges have been raised, the Supreme Court has indicated its willingness to grant Congress wide-ranging discretion under its war powers.

During wartime, the Court has taken a particularly lenient view of congressional war powers. For example, in *Korematsu v. United States* (1944) a congressional law authorizing the exclusion of Japanese-Americans from the West Coast, passed after the president had issued an exclusionary order, was upheld. "We are unable to conclude," stated the Court, "that it was beyond the war power of Congress and the Executive to exclude those of Japanese ancestry from the West Coast war area at the time they did."[1] The circumstances of the case had been extraordinary. President Franklin D. Roosevelt and his military commanders and advisers had decided that persons of Japanese ancestry were a threat to the nation, could not be trusted in the war against Japan, and therefore should be excluded from their West Coast homes and relocated in the more interior parts of the country. The Court admitted that the exclusionary order and its subsequent congressional enactment discriminated on the basis of race, which would normally be constitutionally fatal. But the interests of the government, concluded the Court, outweighed the constitutional rights of the Japanese-American citizens. In supporting the exclusion order, the Court used the same reasoning it had applied in a previous case upholding a congressional enactment that authorized the president and his military commanders to impose a curfew upon Japanese-

Americans: "We cannot say that the war-making branches of the government did not have ground for believing that in a critical hour such persons could not readily be isolated and separately dealt with, and constituted a menace to the national defense and safety, that demanded that prompt and adequate measures be taken to guard against it."[2]

The president's war power. President Harry S. Truman set an important precedent by his unilateral decision to engage American troops in the defense of South Korea after it had been invaded by North Korea in 1950. Truman consulted with congressional leaders, gaining their support, but the decision was his own. His action represented the first time that a president had involved the country in a major conflict without a congressional declaration of war. President Lyndon B. Johnson, following Truman's example, escalated the Vietnam War far beyond the intent of the Gulf of Tonkin resolution, which had authorized him "to take all necessary measures to repel any armed attack against the forces of the United States and to prevent further aggression" in Southeast Asia. President Richard Nixon continued the Vietnam War and secretly ordered the bombing of Cambodia without consulting Congress. Twentieth-century presidents from Truman to Nixon in effect made war while Congress acquiesced, whereas nineteenth-century presidents, with the exception of Abraham Lincoln, had always acted in concert with Congress in exercising the war power.

Ironically, the War Powers Resolution of 1973, which its sponsors hoped would restore the constitutional balance between the president and Congress in making war, was more a recognition of the president's war-making power than a limit upon him. It required the president to obtain a congressional declaration of war or a specific authorization for the commitment of the armed forces to military action abroad after 60 days. But while limiting the

---

[1]323 U.S. 214 (1944).

[2]*Hirabayashi v. United States*, 320 U.S. 81 (1943).

(Drawing by Dana Fradon; © 1982 The New Yorker Magazine, Inc.)

"Hey! After we spend the Russians into the ground, if there's any money left let's give a little party!"

Defense spending is still seen as a necessary response to the Soviet Union, despite recent treaties to limit armaments.

president, it was in fact an explicit congressional recognition of the president's war-making prerogative. A *New York Times* editorial correctly pointed out, after the resolution had been passed: "The War Powers bill itself is not the revolutionary measure that Mr. Nixon and other critics attempted to make it out to be. It does not in any way curtail the President's freedom, as commander-in-chief, to respond to emergency situations. If anything, it gives the Chief Executive more discretionary authority than the framers of the Constitution intended in order to deal with foreign contingencies that they could not have foreseen."[3]

The most important constraints upon the president as commander in chief are political, as demonstrated by White House decisions to finally deescalate the Vietnam War in the face of growing congressional and public opposition. White House response, however, had been slow in coming, as in the meantime Presidents Lyndon Johnson and Richard Nixon, respectively, continued to take whichever uni-

[3]*The New York Times*, November 8, 1973.

lateral military positions they considered appropriate. During President Reagan's second term, Congress explicitly forbade the President from providing financial aid to "Contra" rebel forces that were fighting a Communist-dominated regime in Nicaragua. Yet members of the president's National Security Council continued to provide aid to the Contras in a variety of ways. Colonel Oliver North was brought before a congressional committee in national televised hearings to account for his secretly providing funds to the Contras against the express wishes of Congress. (However, the American public seemed to regard North as a political hero for carrying on his efforts against the Nicaraguan government.)

Although twentieth-century presidents have seized the war-making initiative, Congress remains an important force in determining the nation's defense posture. Presidents formulate defense budgets, but Congress must approve them. The Armed Services committees and the Defense Appropriations subcommittees are deeply involved in the formulation and determination of defense policies and budgets. And they do not simply rubber-stamp administration proposals. Their close linkage with the Defense Department generally leads them to cooperate with its recommendations, which consistently are for increases in defense expenditures.

Taxation and the General Welfare

Both taxation and the promotion of the general welfare were subjects of intense interest to the Founding Fathers. The promotion of the general welfare was one of the stated purposes of the new national government in the Preamble to the Constitution. The power to tax was of course necessary not only to promote the general welfare, but also to provide for the national defense and in general to enable the government to perform its constitutional responsibilities as listed in Article I and

elsewhere. The authors of *The Federalist* wrote about both taxation and the general welfare in broad terms, emphasizing that revenue needs and concepts of the public good would change over time.

The origin and nature of the tax power. All governments must of course have the authority to tax in order to sustain themselves. Moreover, taxes can be used by the government to redistribute the wealth, to take from the rich and give to the poor, or, as is more commonly practiced, to take from those in the upper income levels and redistribute to those in the middle or lower levels. Regardless of the reasons for taxation, no one would disagree that the power to tax is the power to destroy. Thus the politics of taxation is broad and intense and may even lead, as in the case of the American colonies, to revolution.

The unhappy experience of the colonists with what they considered to be unfair taxation was an important backdrop to the deliberations at the Constitutional Convention over the extent of the taxing authority of the new government and the governmental process that would determine tax policy. The Founding Fathers made certain that both the taxing authority and the procedures involved in setting taxes would be carefully circumscribed, knowing that the states would never ratify a constitution that would enable the new government to impose heavy tax burdens upon their citizens. Moreover, the Framers represented an affluent class that did not want its wealth redistributed through popularly inspired tax policies.

Limits on taxing authority. Congress was given the authority to impose uniform *indirect taxes,* such as sales taxes or taxes on the privilege of doing business. But it could levy *direct taxes* upon property only if the taxes were apportioned among the states according to their populations.

The scope of the national taxing power was not seriously tested until after the Civil War. The first income tax law, enacted during the Civil War, was challenged on the ground that it was a direct tax requiring apportionment. However, the Court rejected the argument, holding that the tax was an excise or duty.[4] Meanwhile, Congress had repealed the tax in 1872, but in 1894 it passed a second income tax law. This time the Court upheld a challenge to the law, on the ground that it was a direct tax that failed to meet the constitutional apportionment requirement.[5] The Sixteenth Amendment, adopted 18 years later in 1913, finally overturned the Court's decision by providing that "the Congress shall have power to lay and collect taxes on incomes, from whatever source derived, without apportionment among the several states, and without regard to any census or enumeration."

The spending power and the general welfare. Article I, Section 8, which gives Congress the taxing power, also provides that it shall have the power "to pay the debts and provide for the common defense and general welfare of the United States." This provision, which delegates the spending power to Congress, has been of the utmost importance in providing a constitutional underpinning for wide-ranging defense and welfare policies, such as the Social Security Act of 1935. Congress has also used its taxing authority in conjunction with its spending power to enact regulatory laws—to discourage gambling and the sale of harmful drugs, for example.

The meaning of the Constitution for public policy. The Constitution and its early interpretation by the Supreme Court emphasized the importance of a broad and flexible national power to regulate commerce, provide for the national defense, and levy taxes in order to raise revenue. The Supreme Court restrained the federal commerce and tax powers during the late nineteenth and early twentieth centuries, but by the late 1930s it

once again supported the expansive view of federal power that had shaped its decisions in the early decades of the republic. Moreover, the Court interpreted the spending authority of Congress broadly to support general welfare policies.

There are few *constitutional* impediments to public policy today. Alexander Hamilton's philosophy in support of a strong national government with the wide powers to enact policies for the public good prevails. Hamilton wrote in *The Federalist*, No. 34:

Constitutions of civil government are not to be framed upon a calculation of existing exigencies, but upon a combination of these with the probable exigencies of ages, according to the national and tried course of human affairs. Nothing, therefore, can be more fallacious than to infer the extent of any power proper to be lodged in the national government from an estimate of its immediate necessities. There ought to be a *capacity* to provide for future contingencies as they may happen; and as these are illimitable in their nature, so it is impossible safely to limit that capacity.

The virtually unlimited policy-making authority of the national government has not created a government without restraint. The Constitution continues to impose important limits on government in the area of civil liberties and civil rights. Moreover, both elected and appointed policy makers must be responsive to political forces both within and without government.

THE POLITICAL CONTEXT OF PUBLIC POLICY

Within the constitutional framework that allows great latitude for government policy making, what determines the nature and extent of the policies undertaken? What explains the activity of the national government in the formulation of policies of defense, social wel-

---

[4]*Springer v. United States*, 102 U.S. 586 (1881).

[5]*Pollock v. Farmers' Loan and Trust Company*, 158 U.S. 601 (1895).

fare, the economy, and civil rights from one historical period to another? The answer in great part lies in the broader political context, in the political forces that impinge upon government from the outside and that shape from within the behavior of government institutions. Within the broader political context, however, what explains the sources of specific policy initiatives, how they are formulated and become law, and how they are implemented?

Models for Explaining the Origins of Public Policy

Political scientists have developed a wide variety of models for explaining how and why policies originate within the broader political context. These various models might be summarized in the following categories.

Elite preference. Policies can be viewed as the expression of the preferences of a small, powerful economic and social elite. *Elite theory* divides the community into two classes: leaders and followers. The leaders have the means and the incentives to control the avenues and positions of power in the political system. Their motivations are diverse and may be based, for example, upon the desire to protect their wealth, position, and power within the economic and political sphere. Elites may also be motivated by the spirit of noblesse oblige, advocating policies they consider to be in the broader national interest.

Gaetano Mosca, the Italian political scientist, set the tone of all future elite theory in his classic early nineteenth-century book *The Ruling Class:*

Among the constant facts and tendencies that are to be found in all political organisms, one is so obvious that it is apparent to the most casual eye. In all societies—from societies that are very meagerly developed and have barely attained the dawnings of civilization, down to the most advanced and powerful societies—two *classes* of people appeared—a class that rules and a class that is ruled. The first class, always the less numerous, performs all political functions,

monopolizes power and enjoys the advantages that power brings, whereas the second, the more numerous class, is directed and controlled by the first, in a manner that is now more or less legal, now more or less arbitrary and violent, and supplies the first in appearance, at least, with material means of subsistence and with the instrumentalities that are essential to the vitality of the political organism.[6]

C. Wright Mills was one of many later elite theorists who took up Mosca's theme and applied it to the American political system. Mills mocked traditional democratic theory:

The people are presented with problems. They discuss them. They formulate viewpoints. These viewpoints are organized and they compete. One viewpoint "wins out." Then the people act on this view, or their representatives are instructed to act it out, and this they promptly do.

Such are the images of democracy which are still used as working justifications of power in America. We must now recognize that description as more a fairy tale than a useful approximation. The issues that now shape man's fate are neither raised nor decided by any public-at-large.[7]

Circulation of elites is an important component of elite theory. Elite theory is not entirely antidemocratic, and the dominant economic and social classes, which provide a continuity of leadership, are not closed but accept new members who meet their conditions. Circulation of elites and the necessity for political leaders to maintain a consensus of the people over time prevent elite rule from getting out of touch with the broader political concerns of the public.

[6]Gaetano Mosca, *The Ruling Class* (New York: McGraw-Hill, 1939), p. 50. The Italian edition of this work first appeared in 1895, and was subsequently revised in 1923. Emphasis added.

[7]C. Wright Mills, "The Structure of Power in American Society," *The British Journal of Sociology*, Vol. 9, No. 1 (March, 1958). Reprinted in Irving Louis Horowitz, ed., *Power, Politics, and People* (New York: Ballantine, 1963).

Elites make the decisions of war and peace. The small group of "the best and the brightest" surrounding Presidents John F. Kennedy and Lyndon B. Johnson was instrumental in the formulation of policies that escalated the Vietnam War. Elites, in both the North and the South, have always been important in the formulation and implementation of civil rights policies. A black elite, led by Martin Luther King, Jr., and others, was instrumental in the civil rights movement of the 1960s. Prior to that period the Supreme Court, the National Association of Colored People, and others drawn from the elite stratum of society single-handedly brought about the decision to desegregate public education in 1954, which was a major civil rights policy change of the twentieth century.

Interest-group dynamics. In the *group model*, public policy is explained as the outcome of conflicts and accommodations among organized special interest groups (see Chapter 9). Organized groups collectively represent the political interests of all individuals. Potential groups always exist under the surface of society and become organized as new political interests arise. Special interests extend to the inner recesses of government and are represented in political institutions. They are the constituencies of government, determining the policies made by the president, the bureaucracy, Congress, and the courts. In this model the national interest is not defined as necessarily separate from the interests of special groups, and the political compromises among groups ultimately determine what is in the public interest.

The importance of interest-group politics in the determination of public policy is visible in many areas. For example, all of the "iron triangles" of government, formed by the close linkage among congressional committees, administrative agencies, and special interests, reflect the power of groups in the policy-making process. The "military-industrial complex," to use President Dwight D. Eisenhower's term, is an iron triangle encompassing Congress, the Pentagon, and the armaments industry that is a major influence on defense policy. (Alternatively, this same triangle could be interpreted in terms of the elite model.)

Rational problem solving. The *rational model* views policies as an attempt to solve societal problems or resolve issues on the basis of an objective analysis of the best available information. Politics is reduced to a minimum in rational problem solving, as experts attend to the needs of government and society. The Federal Center for Disease Control in Atlanta, Georgia, illustrates rational problem solving when it uses its scientific and medical resources to solve a public health problem such as Legionnaires' disease. The scientific community was engaged in rational problem solving in the Manhattan Project which developed the atomic bomb during World War II.

Institutionalism. The activities of government institutions determine public policies in the *institutional model*. The president, administrative agencies, Congress and its committees, and the courts become the focus of attention in seeking to understand the origin of policies. The different characters of institutions are examined—including their contrasting constituencies, which are so important in determining political incentives.

Presidential policies, for example, are seen as the result of the constitutional, political, and administrative character of the office. The institutional context of the White House shapes the policies that emanate from it. The institutional character of Congress, its multitude of committees, weak party organization, leadership styles, parliamentary procedures, reelection incentives, and constituencies all explain why congressional policies are different from those of the White House. Similarly, the institutional nature of the courts and administrative agencies determines the policies they originate.

Incrementalism. The *incremental policy model* suggests that public policies are generally the next small step upon a well-charted path that policy makers have followed. The budgetary process of government, for example, that is so important to policy, is often viewed as an incremental one in which small additions tend to be made each year to past allocations. Incrementalism maintains the political status quo, building upon but not diverging sharply from what has been done previously.

Each of the policy models presented helps to explain the origins of public policy. No single explanation, however, accurately portrays the making of public policy generally. The models should not be considered exclusive interpretations of policy making, even though advocates often offer their favorite as a single explanation for all policies. Students of the policy process should keep all the models in mind to see which and how many are at work in the various areas of public policy.

Types of Public Policies

Even as many models have been developed to explain the *origins* of public policies, others have been created to differentiate among *types* of policies and their effects on society and on the political process itself. As with the models devised to explain the origins of policy, those that distinguish different types and effects, although useful, are not fully satisfactory in accounting for all distinctions among individual policies.

Political scientist Theodore Lowi has developed one of the most stimulating and useful ways of looking at the political importance of different types of policy.[8] He divides policy into redistributive, distributive, and regulatory categories and points out that the outcomes in each area distinguish three contrasting political arenas.

Redistributive policies. Government may take some of the benefits enjoyed by one class of society and *redistribute* them to other classes. Redistributive politics, which occurs mostly in the economic realm, involves broad

classes of persons. Political parties often provide the linkage between government and the people in the redistributive arena. All the components of government are included in redistributive politics. The president and the Congress must work together to make major changes in economic policies, and the courts in turn must be concerned with assuring that redistributions are in accord with civil rights and liberties.

Examples of redistributive policies include the progressive income tax, welfare programs, and food stamps. In each of these policy spheres the government has been involved in redistributing the wealth of the community. The rich pay proportionately more tax than the poor, the higher-income groups more than middle-income classes. The poor usually receive far more benefits through welfare payments and food stamps than they have paid, proportionately, in the taxes that fund such programs.

Redistributive politics primarily involves economic policies, but redistribution can also occur in other areas. The government's attempt to remedy the effects of past discrimination through affirmative action programs was a good example of a redistributive policy. Affirmative action required institutions of higher learning, employers, labor unions, and other groups to give up some of their freedom in hiring or admitting members in order to remedy racial and gender imbalances.

Political elites play an important role in redistributive politics, even though broad classes of persons are ultimately involved. Franklin D. Roosevelt and his New Deal Brain Trust devised, in the spirit of noblesse oblige, the redistributive policies of the era that benefited so many middle- and lower-income groups. A handful of experts formulated the Social Security Act of 1935, which passed Congress with little opposition. The Great Society programs of Lyndon B. Johnson and the redistributive policies that evolved from the civil rights movement were also inspired and formulated by elites.

---

[8]Theodore Lowi, "American Business, Public Policy, Case-Studies and Political Theory," *World Politics*, Vol. 16 (July, 1964), pp. 673–715.

The role of elites in redistributive politics is, however, always complemented by a broader-based politics, which often becomes most intense and evident *after* government action has been taken. Franklin Roosevelt forged a broad coalition of labor, farmers, intellectuals, and others who would benefit from New Deal legislation to give him the backing he needed in Congress. Once his programs were enacted, powerful groups then coalesced to support them.

The redistributive policies that began with the New Deal and culminated in the Great Society helped the poor, minorities, and the middle class as well. Redistribution *downward* was the goal of these programs. By contrast, and in reaction to the policies of the past, the administration of Ronald Reagan took an entirely different redistributive tack. It enacted programs that disproportionately benefited those with relatively high incomes as well as many segments of the business community. Social programs were cut, and the tax structure was changed to limit downward redistribution. Federal programs to protect civil rights, while not abandoned, were softened during the Reagan administration and in later years by decisions of a U.S. Supreme Court that was dominated by justices who had been appointed by President Reagan.

Distributive policies. "Pork barrel" legislation (which provides government money for dams, river dredging, federal buildings, and other federal projects in local districts) and government subsidies to business, agriculture, and other segments of the economy are examples of *distributive policies*, which hand out the largess of government to narrow sectors of the community. Virtually every part of the business community has benefited over time from subsidies, including the energy, transportation, defense, and health care industries. Farm price supports have buttressed the agricultural community ever since the New Deal. Other special interests, too, such as education and real estate development, have been the recipients of direct government aid.

Distributive politics reflects the special interests that are involved. "Iron triangles," composed of congressional committees, administrative agencies, and special interests, coalesce to form independent policy arenas. In the broader political system subsidy policies are not viewed as a zero-sum game; that is, subsidies given to one group do not preclude aid to other interests. The separate distributive policy sectors, then, largely determine for themselves the amounts of the subsidies to be given. In "pork barrel" politics the rule followed by Congress is that there is enough government largess to go around. Presidents periodically try to veto funds for local projects and cut back on subsidies, but they generally find it difficult, if not impossible, to penetrate the iron triangles of Washington politics.

The continuity of distributive policies, regardless of presidential attempts to control them, is apparent in many areas. Presidents, for example, have tried to limit veterans' benefits and veto the special veterans' bonuses that Congress has passed from time to time, but the coalition of the Veterans Affairs committees on Capitol Hill, the American Legion, the Veterans of Foreign Wars, and the Veterans Administration has consistently thwarted the White House. This coalition was sufficiently strong to create a new, Cabinet-level Department of Veterans Affairs, established in 1989.

During his two terms Ronald Reagan made one of the more concerted efforts in recent decades to curtail government subsidies, only to find, after some initial successes, that traditional political alliances once again reared their heads and protected special interests. And even Reagan did not attempt to challenge one of the most powerful iron triangles, that consisting of the agriculture committees of Congress, the Department of Agriculture, and special agricultural interests, which has long operated to sustain commodities subsidies, such as those for the tobacco industry.

Regulatory policies. Though the government regulates conflicting group interests mostly *within* narrow economic sectors, it also regulates them *across* the economic spectrum and in other areas as well. *Regulatory policies* determine the rights and obligations of private parties. For example, the conduct of business may require the prior approval of a government agency, and a business practice may be subject to government control. A corporation cannot sell its securities to the public without registering them with the Securities and Exchange Commission, which imposes disclosure requirements in order to protect the investing public. The Federal Trade Commission defines and prevents deceptive business advertising and practices as well as unfair competition. The National Labor Relations Board regulates labor unions as well as businesses, preventing unfair labor practices and protecting the right of unions to organize. All utility rates are regulated, as are some transportation rates, such as those charged by railroads to shippers.

Regulation also controls access to markets. Companies often must receive licenses from the government in order to do business. For example, the Nuclear Regulatory Commission licenses nuclear power plants, which must meet government safety requirements. The Federal Communications Commission licenses broadcasting companies, requiring them to meet "public interest, convenience, and necessity" standards. There has been some deregulation of access control in recent years, for example in the airline and trucking industries, where companies now are free to choose the markets they wish to serve.

Regulatory policies "are distinguishable from distributive in that in the short run the regulatory decision involves a direct choice as to who will be indulged and who deprived."[9] Group competition for the favors and protection of government characterizes regulatory politics. Agricultural interests, for example, sought the protection of Congress against

what they considered to be the unfair business practices of the railroads in the 1880s. Congress responded by passing the Interstate Commerce Act of 1887, creating the Interstate Commerce Commission to regulate railroad rates. Labor groups were instrumental in the passage of the National Labor Relations Act of 1935, under which the National Labor Relations Board protects unions and their members from unfair labor practices. Presidential initiatives have also been important in the creation of regulatory agencies, such as the Securities and Exchange Commission, established in 1933 to protect members of the public engaged in securities transactions.

Policy Types and the Political Process

The way in which policies are made differs in the redistributive, distributive, and regulatory arenas, reflecting the contrasting politics of each area.

The redistributive policy process. The president and Congress always become involved in formulating redistributive policies because these affect the entire nation, and the response of voters to them is reflected in electoral judgments of presidential and congressional performance. Redistributive policies are part of a zero-sum game on a national scale, with broad classes of persons as the winners or losers. Redistributive outcomes shape patterns of political support, often determining the balance of electoral power between the two major parties.

The visibility of redistributive policies requires politicians to "stand up and be counted." They cannot, as they would often like to do, hide behind the smoke screen of arcane congressional procedures and committees, whose activities often befuddle the public. Redistributive policies are not attached as obscure amendments to appropriations bills or other legislation. Redistributive legislation is complex, but its general import is understood not only by its makers but by the gen-

---

[9]Lowi, "American Business, Public Policy," pp. 690–691.

eral public, who can smite politicians at the polls for their misjudgments of the will of the majority in their respective political constituencies.

President Ronald Reagan's tax and general welfare policies illustrate the way in which redistributive politics works. The President's tax and budget-cutting proposals were at the top of his political agenda and were initially formulated by David Stockman, his first director of the Office of Management and Budget, who worked in consultation with the White House and the Cabinet. Reagan's redistributive agenda soon became that of Congress, and virtually every committee on Capitol Hill, including the congressional leadership of both parties, became involved. The press and national television kept the public informed to every twist and turn taken in the tortuous route to final passage of the major redistributive tax and welfare legislation. Every voter knew where his or her representative and senators stood on the issues, and the pros and cons of Reagan's upwardly redistributive policies were hotly debated throughout his two terms. President Bush, and his first director of the Office of Management and Budget, Richard Darman, began the Bush presidency vowing to avoid new taxes, and these men showed no sign of initiatives in the area of redistributive policies.

The distributive policy process. In contrast to the redistributive arena, the politics of distributive policy is far narrower and almost invisible to the general public. Congressional committees and special interests largely determine the scope and amount of subsidies that will be granted to the different segments of the private sector. Neither the president nor even the congressional leadership is deeply involved in subsidy policies, although the White House makes sporadic, and usually unsuccessful, attempts to control subsidy levels.

Distributive policies are not national campaign issues, although members of Congress always take great care to claim credit for subsidies that benefit the special interest groups

in their constituencies. Republican Senator Jesse Helms, for example, broadcasts his support for tobacco subsidies loudly and clearly in his home state of North Carolina. Members of the House who are concerned with reelection strive to become members of committees, such as Agriculture, Energy and Commerce, Interior, and Insular Affairs, that have important jurisdiction over subsidy policies and pork barrel projects.

The regulatory policy process. The bureaucracy is the primary policy maker in the regulatory realm. Congress, confronted with conflicting political demands for regulation in areas demanding specialization and expertise, solved both the political and practical problems before it by delegating broad authority to administrative agencies to regulate in the "public interest, convenience, and necessity," and on the basis of "just and reasonable" considerations. The great and abiding incentive of Congress in the regulatory realm is to transfer both the political and practical burden of resolving group conflict to the bureaucracy. No advantage accrues to members of Congress for making regulatory decisions, which can only get members into trouble by antagonizing the groups that are the losers in the regulatory game.

Regulatory issues are not part of the political mainstream. Regulatory, like distributive, politics is played out in a wide variety of separate arenas. Regulatory issues are complex, and although they affect the general public, they remain the principal concern to the special interests that are directly involved. Regulatory policies often become *protective* of private interests as regulatory agencies increasingly draw upon the latter for political support. The Interstate Commerce Commission (ICC), for example, originally created at the behest of agricultural interests to regulate the railroads, eventually protected railroad interests, which in turn strongly supported the ICC on Capitol Hill. The National Labor Relations Board protected union interests from its inception. The Civil Aeronautics Board, when it had regulatory authority, shielded the airline industry from cut-throat competition. The deregulation of the airlines in the early 1980s brought about more than one bankruptcy.

Predictably, deregulation was generally opposed by most regulated groups, such as the larger airlines and the trucking industry, which stand to lose their protection when agencies can no longer control the market entry and pricing that, in effect, allows quasi-monopolies to exist. The deregulation of the airline and trucking industries demonstrated that the group theory model of policy making, particularly its idea that "iron triangles" of pressure groups and administrative agencies control policy in conjunction with congressional committees, is not always accurate. Presidents Ford and Carter—along with a few key members of Congress—originated deregulation and raised enough support to pass it.

While the distinctions between redistributive, distributive, and regulatory policies are not always perfectly clear, the use of these categories in analyzing the policy process helps greatly to clarify how public policies differ and the contrasting ways in which they are made. That public policy is often a mixture of the three categories should always be kept in mind. Moreover, some extremely important policy areas, such as national defense, have unique characteristics that do not neatly fit into any category but their own.

BALANCING NATIONAL AND SPECIAL INTERESTS

How to define and balance national needs with special interests is a central dilemma that confronts government policy makers. Every elected politician and top-level appointed official knows that his or her political future depends upon the satisfactory accommodation of constituent interests, which consist not only of ordinary voters but of a wide range of special interests within and without government. Political demands, from whatever source, provide the grist for the hundreds of policy-making mills throughout government.

Defining the National Interest

The concept of *national interest,* a term that generally is loosely bandied about, is one of the most difficult to come to grips with in analyzing policy making. Over the ages political philosophers have attempted to define the public interest, which understandably is interpreted differently, depending upon the viewpoint of the individual explaining it.

The pluralistic character of America's political system, in which each branch of the government and a host of private interest groups vie for power, makes it extremely difficult to agree on what the national interest is in the different policy arenas. Group theorists, who argue that a free process of group interaction is the basis of democracy, have categorically stated that there is no single national interest apart from the interests of various political groups. (There were even groups that opposed World War II, a time of extraordinary national consensus in support of the government.)

The Framers of the Constitution, although generally concerned with substantive public policy in their support of a strong national defense, the effective regulation of commerce, and the promotion of the general welfare, purposely created a government that would represent different views of the national interest. The perspectives of the president and Congress, and of the House and Senate, obviously were tied to their different political constituencies. Congress was to be the primary initiator of public policy, but the approval of the president was required to enact legislation unless it had the backing of two-thirds of the legislature. The Supreme Court, too, as the system evolved, claimed and exercised the power of judicial review over legislation, although throughout history very few provisions of fed-

(© 1990 Rob Rogers. Reprinted by permission of United Features Syndicate, Inc.)

Executive departments fight presidential proposals to cut their budgets.

eral laws have been declared unconstitutional. Historically, with the exception of the New Deal period, the Supreme Court decisions that have had the most profound effect on public policy have been those that interpreted, and often declared unconstitutional, state laws and actions.

The president and Congress remain the principal sources that define the national interest, a power that the bureaucracy shares to some extent, especially in the arenas of regulatory policy. The branches of the government have as much difficulty as ever in reaching agreement as to what constitutes the national interest. The policy debates of the 1980s illustrated the ever-present political conflict over the national interest. President Ronald Reagan, for example, proposed significant increases in defense expenditures, supported

of course by the Defense Department and the armaments industry. Reagan clearly felt the national interest required the enactment of his recommendations. But Congress, including some members of the president's party, disagreed that the national interest supported all of the presidential proposals. Capitol Hill turned down Reagan's plea to fund the installation of MX missiles near Cheyenne, Wyoming, in a so-called "dense-pack" formation.[10] Congress also did not agree with all the President's tax- and spending-reduction recommendations. The Congress

---

[10]The missiles were to be placed so close together, in a "dense-pack," that incoming Soviet missiles, in order to hit the target would—hypothetically, at least—destroy each other.

of the Reagan years, like those before it, fulfilled its constitutional responsibility of checking the White House by advancing and often implementing its own views of the national interest.

Political leaders, regardless of the mixture of national and special interests in their policy decisions, confront the overriding reality of *limited government resources*. Occasionally, as during the Great Society era of Lyndon B. Johnson, the president and Congress have seemed to forget that sooner or later government programs—whether in defense or social services—must be paid for out of the federal treasury, which in turn receives its money from taxes or from borrowing in the financial markets. Federal spending can also be supported by inflation if the Federal Reserve Board is willing to cooperate by taking various measures to increase the money supply, but inflation ultimately imposes one of the harshest "taxes" upon private citizens.

The experience of the Reagan administration illustrated the difficulties of balancing national and special interests while staying within the limits of what government can do financially. When Ronald Reagan entered office in 1981 he predicted that the federal budget would be balanced in 1983 or 1984. By the time he left office in 1989, the annual deficit in the federal budget (excesses of expenditures over revenues) was $163 billion. The budget itself was $1.149 trillion (or $1,149 billion). The yearly interest that the government had to pay out of this budget to finance the cumulative national debt was $169 billion, or about 15 percent of the total budget. Defense spending, in part due to President Reagan's efforts to build up the military, had reached $298 billion, or 26 percent of the budget. And despite President Reagan's efforts to cut back social programs, they accounted for 40 percent of the budget. In short, as President Bush took office, just three categories of spending—interest on the debt, defense, and social welfare—added up to 81 percent of the budget.

(Source: *Newsweek*, February 12, 1990, p. 17. ©1990 by Herblock in *The Washington Post*.)

"What an irresponsible thing to do when we're trying to save money on electricity!"
Critics, led by New York Senator Daniel Patrick Moynihan, have attacked the government's practice of using Social Security trust funds to offset budget deficits.

SOCIAL WELFARE POLICIES

Government social welfare policies are important components of federal spending, covering a wide spectrum: Social Security; Medicare; food stamps; child nutrition; Medicaid; Aid to Families with Dependent Children (AFDC); and Supplemental Security Income (SSI) for the blind, the disabled, and the poor elderly. Together, these programs accounted for about $480 billion of the 1990 budget total

Twenty-five years ago today, several hundred Government officials and community leaders faced Lyndon B. Johnson as he signed into law the Economic Opportunity Act of 1964, launching the "war on poverty." Today, it is painfully clear that the war has not been won.

The Rose Garden ceremony provided an exhilarating moment, one of great expectations, not so much for the specific provisions of the law but because of its commitment "to eliminate the paradox of poverty in the midst of plenty."

President Johnson issued a prescient warning: "The war on poverty is not fought on any single, simple battlefield and it will not be won in a generation. There are too many enemies: lack of jobs, bad housing, poor schools, lack of skills, discrimination; each intensifies the other."

Today, the ranks of the poor are again swelling. It is particularly disturbing that more than 13 million children—one out of five—are poor, and that black unemployment, especially among the young, continues to be two to three times as high as that for whites.

These and other statistics have led careless observers to conclude that the war on poverty failed. No, it has achieved many good results. Society has failed. It tired of the war too soon, gave it inadequate resources and did not open up new fronts as required.

Large-scale homelessness, an explosion of teen-age pregnancies and single-parent households, rampant illiteracy, drugs, and crime—these have been both the results of and causes of persistent poverty.

While it is thus inappropriate to celebrate an anniversary of the war on poverty, it is important to point up some of the big gains.

The key elements in the package enacted in 1964 have been so successful that they have been continued, albeit not generously enough, by every Administration since Mr. Johnson's: Head Start, Job Corps, Vista, Upward Bound, Foster Grandparents, Community Action. Ask millions of beneficiaries whether the war has been lost.

The initial effort sparked other programs that have significantly helped the poor: Medicare and Medicaid, food stamps, low-income housing, manpower training, minimum-wage improvements, aid to education, beneficial tax-law changes.

of $1.6 trillion that President Bush submitted to Congress.

Most government spending for social welfare is redistributive in character, and much of it provides benefits to citizens who are needy. Medicaid is a federal health insurance program for low-income persons that is administered and partially financed by the states. And recipients of food stamps, AFDC, and SSI must have incomes and assets below a specified level in order to be eligible for government aid. These programs are financed through general tax revenues of the federal government.

Other social programs, chiefly authorized through the Social Security Act, work on a "social insurance" principle. These programs are redistributive, too, but they pay benefits on the basis of terms of eligibility other than an income or asset test. Social Security provides public benefits to persons on the basis of their work histories during which they have paid payroll taxes—under the Federal Insurance Contribution Act (FICA)—into three trust funds. The Old Age and Survivors Insurance Trust Fund pays income benefits to retirees and to dependent survivors of workers who have paid FICA taxes. The Disability Insurance Trust Fund makes income payments to

A new consciousness—and conscience—about America's poor has been evident. Even conservative Ronald Reagan acknowledged the need for a social "safety net."

Did every program of the 60's work? Was every dollar used to its maximum potential? Should every Great Society program be reinstated or increased? Of course not.

But we must also ask these questions: Has every defense contract yielded a perfect product, at minimum cost? Has every cancer project brought a cure? Has every space launching succeeded? Has every diplomatic initiative brought peace?

Why should a less than perfect record for social programs be less tolerable to society than failed economic, military or diplomatic policies?

Every day, thousands of babies are being born who—if we fail to take the necessary actions, public and private—are doomed to be poor for the rest of their lives. They may well be the parents of another generation of impoverished children 25 years hence.

Can we afford a renewed war on poverty? Is it even thinkable at a time of huge Federal deficits?

First, we cannot afford not to resume the war. One way or another, the problem will remain expensive. Somehow, we will provide for the survival needs of the poorest: welfare, food stamps, beds and roofs for the homeless, Medicaid. The fewer poor there are, the fewer the relief problems. Getting people out of poverty is the most cost-efficient public investment.

Second, if the additional public funds required for adequate education and training and housing programs cannot come from increased or diverted Federal funds, taxes must be raised.

In 1939, a quarter century before Presidents John F. Kennedy and Johnson declared war on poverty, Franklin D. Roosevelt gave us a sound basis for judging our national character. "The test of our progress," he said, "is not whether we add more to the abundance of those who already have much; it is whether we do enough for those who have too little."

Twenty-five years from today, will we be able to say we have met that test?

---

persons who are permanently disabled and unable to work. A Health Insurance (Medicare) trust fund is used to reimburse hospital-related health care costs for persons aged 65 and older, disabled persons, blind persons, and patients who are suffering from "end-stage" renal disease (kidney failure).

Social Policies and Poverty

National social policies have always been based on the philosophy that the government should help those who cannot help themselves. Both conservatives and liberals, Republicans and Democrats, agree that social security is an important government goal. That agreement did not come until the 1950s, for conservatives generally strongly opposed New Deal social programs. But Republican President Dwight D. Eisenhower initiated significant increases in social security coverage, which reflected the emerging bipartisan support for the program.

Social security, however, was originally limited to retirement benefits, unemployment compensation, and minimal public assistance to the poor. Conservatives might agree with those objectives, but they normally opposed the vast expansion in the level of government social services that occurred in the 1960s under the leadership of Lyndon Johnson.

Ronald Reagan undertook to dismantle Johnson's War on Poverty, and his efforts succeeded in many respects. He achieved substantial budgetary cuts in a number of social programs and managed to eliminate specific programs and agencies, such as the Community Services Agency (originally the Office of Economic Opportunity when established during the Johnson administration).

While cutting back social programs, President Reagan promised that the government would continue to provide a "safety net" that would assure minimum economic and social protection for poor persons, or, as he termed them, "the truly needy." The position of the Reagan administration was that full and free rein should be given to the economy to promote growth and solve many of the nation's social problems. A healthy private sector, Reagan believed, was the real clue to providing social security in the broadest sense.

At the end of the Reagan administration, however, both Republicans and Democrats still regarded poverty as a major problem. In particular, attention focused upon the 20 percent of American children who were estimated to be in poverty in spite of the ongoing welfare program of Aid to Families with Dependent Children. A consensus developed among liberals and conservatives that welfare payments alone were an inadequate means of lifting poor families and their children out of poverty.

In 1988 Congress enacted a new approach to the problems of welfare and poverty called the Family Support Act. This policy, implemented in 1990, emphasizes education and job training that will secure lasting employment, rather than long-term welfare payments, for persons who are welfare recipients. It requires the states to ensure that all parents receiving welfare who have children over three years old are enrolled in job training or education programs. Any welfare recipient under age 20 must be enrolled in a high school equivalency program if he or she is not already a graduate. The more a state succeeds in eventually securing long-term employment for former welfare recipients, the greater is its reward in federal funds.

Crisis and Continuity in Policies

An important fact about many of the social (and other) policies of government is that they are firmly entrenched, both politically and legally, making it very difficult to change them. All government policies, whether redistributive, distributive, or regulatory, have strong political proponents within Congress, special interest groups that benefit from them, and a bureaucracy that is ready to fight to preserve them.

These forces for continuity are especially present in programs of the Social Security Act. The Act spells out a vast array of "entitlements" that are due to tens of millions of citizens. Moreover, these citizens are present in significant numbers within every Congressional district in the nation. Yet, even with respect to such programs, economic and political circumstances can engender a perceived "crisis" that sets an agenda for substantial reform.

The Social Security Reform Act of 1983. At the outset of President Reagan's first term the major social policy "crisis" in Washington was the financial condition of Social Security's trust fund for paying Old Age and Survivors Insurance (OASI) benefits. The Social Security payroll tax was not yielding enough revenue to enable the government to meet its obligations for paying OASI benefits in the years immediately ahead. High inflation rates, incorporated in Cost of Living Adjustments (COLAs) for Social Security benefits, were threatening to widen further the gap between revenues and obligated payments.

The President created a bipartisan Commission on Social Security Reform and charged it to come up with a solution. Both President Reagan and Congress were well aware that 17 percent of those who vote in national elections are persons 65 years of age and older, and that the interests of this constituency were most threatened by the possibility that Old Age Insurance benefits might not be paid. At the same time changes were also required in the Social Security system to assure the younger working generation that it, too, would some day be able to receive retirement and survivor benefits. The Commission's report in early 1983, quickly adopted by Congress, was a masterpiece of compromise. It presented a solution comprised of minor changes across the board, leaving the basic structure of the program intact. (See Box 18.2.)

The crisis in health care costs. In the 1990s the principal social policy "crisis" perceived in Washington, and throughout the country, is a rapid escalation in the costs of health care—at an annual average rate of 12 percent, which is three to four times greater than the general rate of inflation. The nation's annual health care expenditures total about $600 billion, exceeding 12 percent of the gross national product of the United States (the total economic value of all our goods and services).

The national government, state governments, and large corporations—the entities that pay for an overwhelming proportion of American health care—are attempting to limit their financial obligations in this sector. National policy efforts put forth to deal with this issue primarily focus on reforming the Medicare program of health insurance for the elderly, the disabled, and patients with kidney failure. Medicare is a focal point for cost-containment efforts because it is one of the larger government spending programs and is the biggest single source of payment for health care in America (about $100 billion annually). It also has substantial leverage on the various elements of our health care system; for example, over 40 percent of the patients in hospitals have their costs partially insured by Medicare.

The challenge of containing health care costs in the 1990s involves at least as much political conflict with vested interests and constituents as attempts to reform policies in any other arena. The some 33 million Medicare recipients naturally resist attempts to narrow the entitlements for which they are insured under the program. And they are equally sensitive to proposed changes that ask them to share a greater burden of the costs (see Case Study 17). Whereas physicians initially opposed the enactment of Medicare in 1965 because they thought it might lead to "socialized medicine," they now recognize that it is a major source of their income and thus fight attempts to cut it back. Hospitals, nursing homes, medical equipment and supply companies, pharmaceutical companies, and others in the health care industry also have a strong economic dependence upon Medicare reimbursements.

There is no easy solution to this problem of health care expenditures. In fact, even as the federal government is attempting to hold down the costs of an existing policy—the Medicare program—it is being pressured from many quarters to expand government health insurance to cover an estimated 37 million additional Americans who have no health insurance at all. But the possibility of such an expansion is lessened by the presence of strong organized interests of the private health insurance industry.

The tax, spending, and entitlement issues that President Bush and Congress grappled with in the health care arena in the early 1990s are typical of the political and economic thicket that characterizes most policy arenas. Politics and policies of the past shape those of the present and future. Political leaders can promise change, but they cannot easily alter the politics of public policy that is rooted in economic, social, and other environmental forces beyond their control.

Following are the major provisions of the Social Security rescue plan signed into law April 20, 1983 (PL 98-21).

Enhanced Tax Revenues
• Increase employer and employee payroll taxes. Would be .3 percent less for employees than for employers in 1984. Difference to be made up by income tax credit.
• Increase payroll taxes for self-employed individuals by 33 percent to equal the combined tax paid by employers and employees.
• Tax as regular income the Social Security benefits with adjusted gross income over $25,000; $32,000 for a married couple filing a joint return.

COLA Cuts, Adjustments
• Delay the July 1983 cost-of-living allowance six months.
• Adjust the annual COLA indexation to lesser of wages and prices whenever Old Age and Survivors Insurance (OASI) or Disability Insurance (DI) reserve ratios fall below 15 percent (20 percent after 1988).

Increasing Retirement Age
• Gradually increase the retirement age from sixty-five to sixty-seven by 2027.
• Liberalize the penalty currently placed on retirees with outside earnings.
• Increase the benefit bonus individuals receive for delaying retirement.
• Require the secretary of health and human services to study the effects of the retirement age change on those who are forced to retire early because of physically demanding work.

Accounting
• Require the Treasury to credit the Social Security trust funds at the beginning of each month with all payroll taxes expected that month.
• Allow the three Social Security trust funds—OASI, DI, and Hospital Insurance (HI)—to borrow funds from each other through 1987.
• Permanently reallocate payroll taxes from the DI trust fund to the OASI trust fund.
• Remove the Social Security system from the "unified" federal budget, beginning in fiscal year 1992.

• Require the Social Security Board of Trustees to inform Congress in its annual report if the system is in danger of falling short of funds (before general Treasury revenues can be tapped).

• Require state and local governments to turn over payroll taxes to the Treasury more rapidly. Before the law, such employers could hold the funds for thirty days.

Extension of Coverage

• Require Social Security coverage of all new federal civilian employees, current and future members of Congress, the president, the vice president, sitting federal judges, top political appointees, and civil servants by January 1, 1984.

• Require Social Security coverage of nonprofit organization employees.

• Prohibit state and local governments already under Social Security from withdrawing.

Miscellaneous

• Add two public members to the Social Security Board of Trustees.

• Require a study by April 1, 1984, on how to turn the Social Security Administration into an independent agency.

• Reduce the so-called "windfall benefit" some retirees—most often former government employees—receive when they work under Social Security for only a short time by cutting the base retirement benefit.

• Change the investment procedures of Social Security trust funds to address criticisms that past investments have yielded low returns.

• Credit the Social Security trust funds with certain military benefits and uncashed Social Security checks.

• Restrict benefits for survivors and dependents of nonresident aliens and for convicted felons.

• Include certain elective fringe benefits in the wage base subject to Social Security payroll taxes.

• Eliminate a credit now allowed certain individuals under age sixty-five, who collect government pensions, to compensate them for the fact that their pension income does not include tax-free Social Security benefits.

• Liberalize benefits designed especially to help widowed, divorced, and disabled women; eliminate certain sex distinctions in the law.

Source: *Aging in America: The Federal Government's Role.* Washington, D.C.: Congressional Quarterly, Inc., 1989, pp. 30–31. Reprinted with permission from Congressional Quarterly, Inc.

THE POLITICS OF TARGETING TAXPAYERS

Even though the government was attempting to contain health care costs in 1988, Congress enacted a limited expansion of Medicare, the federal health insurance program that primarily covers persons aged 65 and over. The Medicare Catastrophic Coverage Act of 1988, among its provisions, insured all persons eligible for Medicare for the possibility of a lengthy and catastrophically expensive stay in a hospital.

President Reagan and Congress, sensitive to the sizable annual deficit in the federal budget, agreed to make this program expansion "revenue neutral." They did this by financing the expanded coverage through a complicated structure of new taxes levied on Medicare program participants themselves. This targeting of taxes to a specific segment of the population was relatively unprecedented. In effect, it was a "potential user's tax."

Neither Congress nor interest groups representing older persons did a very good job of interpreting the legislation for their constituents prior to its enactment. When the nature of the new benefits and, particularly, the amount and character of the tax mechanism became known to older persons—who were both beneficiaries and selected taxpayers for the policy—the protests to Congress and to organized representatives of the elderly were loud and long-lasting.

In the following case study Martin Tolchin provides an illustrative overview of what can happen when a policy is enacted without "trial balloons" and effective prior interpretation for the constituents who will be affected by it. The law was repealed by Congress in 1989.

Expansion of Medicare Is Painful for Congress / *Martin Tolchin*

The Congressional recess has brought the nation's lawmakers scant relief from the anger of older Americans who resent being taxed for new Medicare benefits intended to protect them against catastrophic medical expenses.

Representative Dan Rostenkowski, the chairman of the House Ways and Means Committee, was pursued in his Chicago district by elderly people shouting "liar!" and "impeach!" In Tulsa, Okla., Representative Mike Synar, a Democrat, was accosted by elderly constituents, and in his Spokane, Wash., office, Speaker Tom Foley received a petition of protest with 10,000 signatures.

Thus Congress is now hearing from one side in a debate that seems politically insoluble as the costs of medical care for the elderly increase far faster than inflation. With the proportion of older Americans rising quickly, too, health costs are expected to increase to 15 percent of G.N.P. in 2000, from 6 percent in 1965. At issue is not only

which generation shall pay, but also whether the more affluent elderly should subsidize the poor elderly.

Last year, it seemed that one decision had been made: President Reagan and the Democratic Congress agreed that the extended insurance would be financed entirely by its beneficiaries. The Administration and Congress received praise then, but now recriminations are coming from the very group they sought to benefit.

"There will be a change in the program," Mr. Foley said last week, "because it's been very substantially and heavily criticized."

The anger focuses on the surtax that finances the mandatory program. The surtax of $22.50 for every $150 in Federal income taxes begins in the $15,000-to-$20,000-a-year range. The maximum surtax is $850, paid by most of those with individual incomes over $35,000.

The program, intended to prevent older Amer-

The bills rise. . .

Health care expenditures per capita for Americans 65 and older, with breakdown by source of payment.

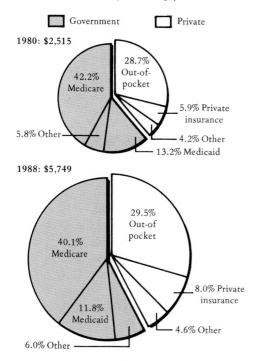

☐ Government   ☐ Private

1980: $2,515

- 42.2% Medicare
- 28.7% Out-of-pocket
- 5.9% Private insurance
- 4.2% Other
- 13.2% Medicaid
- 5.8% Other

1988: $5,749

- 40.1% Medicare
- 29.5% Out-of-pocket
- 8.0% Private insurance
- 4.6% Other
- 11.8% Medicaid
- 6.0% Other

Source: House Select Committee on Aging

. . . And so does the Individual's burden

Average personal health expenditures as a percentage of income for people 65 and older. Includes out-of-pocket payments for medical services and insurance premiums.

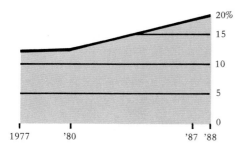

1977	'80 '87 '88

20%
15
10
5
0

Source: House Select Committee on Aging

FIGURE 18.1

icans from being pauperized by medical expenses, will pay for hospitals, doctors, and half the expense of prescription drugs, but not for long-term nursing care. Except for deductibles, there are no limits on the benefits.

Most Medicare beneficiaries already had supplemental private insurance, called Medigap policies, and had paid less for it. Although their benefits fell far short of those in the new law, many contend that it was their right to decide how much protection to buy.

Some in and out of Congress believe that this protest reflects the ingratitude of a group that has grown prosperous with the help of Government programs and whose political clout exceeds its social conscience. "With 37 million Americans without health insurance, why should we pay the health costs of a Bob Hope or a Malcolm Forbes?" asked Dr. Warren Greenberg, professor of health services at George Washington University.

The Medicare Catastrophic Coverage Act had the support of most groups representing the elderly, including the American Association of Retired Persons, which has taken searing criticism from its members but has not backed away. "Everybody trusted the representation of the retirees," an aide to the Senate Finance Committee said. "They viewed the benefits as extremely desirable and were concerned about abuses in Medigap policies and people paying too much for too little."

The bill passed by a lopsided 86 to 11 in the Senate and 328 to 72 in the House.

Congress usually begins a program by providing benefits and then presenting the charges for them. But this time, Congress postponed some of the benefits. The law provided a ceiling of $560 a year on a patient's payments for Government-approved hospital bills, beginning last January; but not until next January do Government payments for doctor bills, with a deductible of $1,370, begin, and prescription drug benefits start in 1991.

A Better Deal

Many Medicare recipients thought they could do better, a view supported by Congressional Budget Office studies. Its studies found that this year the value of the new Medicare benefits was $62, while the new premiums averaged $145. By 1993, when the entire program is in place, the estimated value of new benefits is $322, and average new premium $331.

But overall, Medicare remains a bargain, with total benefits this year valued at $3,192 and average premiums of $480. By 1993, the benefits will be valued at $4,834, with average premiums of $720. Those paying the maximum surtax will pay only 32 percent of the value of the total benefits.

Lawrence S. Lewin, president of Lewin/ICF, a health policy consulting firm, said that had the bill been sold as a way to help the poorer elderly, "It would have been harder to pass the legislation, but there would not be this sense of anger and betrayal."

The Congressional Budget Office estimates that only 36 percent of the elderly pay any surtax. But the cost to the 5 percent who pay the maximum surtax is 14 times the value of the catastrophic-care benefits. In addition, those at the top end of the income scale are likely to have health plans already through former employers. And many of these taxpayers believe that the health costs of the poor should be borne by the population as a whole.

There are only a few ways to revise the program: reduce both costs and benefits, for example, or rearrange the premiums. The House Ways and Means Committee chose the second option shortly before the recess, voting to halve the surtax and increase the flat premium that all individuals pay, from $48 a year to $58.80. This would increase the cost for low-income individuals, while reducing it for those earning $15,000 to $45,000. The committee plan would also make the program voluntary.

The Senate Finance Committee will address the issue this fall. "The issue is, who should pay?" said an aide to the committee. "Should the cost be paid by society at large, or those who stand to benefit?

CASE STUDY 17

The Distribution of Government Responsibilities: State and Local Governments

"Governor Seeks Federal Aid from Bush"; "State Lottery Voted by Legislature"; "Mayor Vows War on Street Gangs"; "Port Authority Plans New Terminal"; "County Hospital to Close." These headlines illustrate the pluralistic nature of America's political system, reflecting the division of powers and responsibilities among national, state, and local governments.

As indicated in Chapter 5, the distribution of responsibilities among governments in the United States has been changing throughout the more than 200 years of our nation's history. In recent years, during the two terms of President Reagan's "New Federalism" policy in the 1980s, state and local government responsibilities increased and the role of the federal government diminished. President Bush apparently has maintained this policy, but the weight of responsibilities could shift again, toward Washington, under future presidents.

The national government of the United States is but one of the approximately 80,000 distinct governments in America. Not all are of equal importance, yet they are all interdependent. No understanding of America's political system can be complete without at least a brief overview of state and local governments, and their constantly changing linkage with each other and with the federal government.

STATE GOVERNMENTS

Since the states served as models for the national government, it is hardly surprising that the constitutions and political structures of the states resemble those of the national government. Like the national Constitution, state constitutions include bills of rights that set forth the rights of the individual that are to be preserved against infringement by the state. They also provide for the formal separation of powers and distribution of authority among the states' legislative, executive, and judicial branches.

State Constitutions

A notable feature of most state constitutions is that they usually contain a far larger 531 number of provisions than the national Constitution. Alabama's constitution includes approximately 174,000 words, and New York's about 80,000. (Compare this with the approximately 7,000 words now in the U.S. Constitution.)

Most state constitutions are long because they contain very specific stipulations about the operation of government, rather than defining powers and limitations in a general way. For example, whereas the national Constitution simply provides that "Congress shall have Power To lay and collect Taxes, Duties, Imposts and Excises . . .," many state constitutions include thousands of words on taxation and finance.

Although such specific provisions often become outdated, they can be altered by constitutional amendment. The constitution of Hawaii, for example, has been increased by 78 amendments since 1950; that of New York by 205 since 1895; and that of Texas by 304 since 1876.

The adoption of a constitutional amendment in most states requires the approval of the voters of the state in a statewide balloting known as a *referendum.* An amendment can be proposed to the voters in one of two ways. Through the *initiative* procedure, private individuals can have an amendment proposal placed on an election ballot after first collecting a required number of signatures on a petition. In some states, however, an amendment is first proposed by the state legislature and then submitted to the voters.

Extensive constitutional revision or the adoption of an entirely new constitution requires the calling of a constitutional convention or commission. In some states voter approval is necessary before such a convention can be called. Once a new constitution is drafted, it too requires the approval of the state's electorate in order to be adopted. In some instances, major constitutional changes worked out over many years by constitutional conventions or commissions have been re-jected when finally submitted to popular vote. Proposed new or revised constitutions were rejected in the 1970s by voters in Maryland, New York, Rhode Island, and Idaho. Georgia voters, on the other hand, approved a new constitution in 1983.

State Legislatures

Although state constitutional provisions are similar to one another in broad outline, great variations exist in specific details. State legislatures differ in size, in the terms and salaries of their members, in the length of their legislative sessions, and in their procedures.

Size of legislatures. With the sole exception of Nebraska, all the states have bicameral legislatures. Although the Supreme Court's equal apportionment ruling requires that state legislators be apportioned equally among the voters, the total number of legislators so apportioned by a state is determined by the state itself in its constitution. Thus state legislatures differ markedly in size.

New Hampshire, for example, with a population of only 977,000 has 399 representatives in its lower house and 24 members in its senate. California, on the other hand, has 80 representatives in the lower house and 40 members in its senate, representing more than 25 million people.

Terms and salaries of state legislators. In most state legislatures, members of the upper house are elected for four-year terms; members of the lower house, for two-year terms. There are some exceptions. Members of the state's senate serve for only two years in Arizona, Connecticut, Georgia, Idaho, Maine, Massachusetts, New Hampshire, New York, North Carolina, Rhode Island, South Dakota, and Vermont. In Alabama, Louisiana, Maryland, and Mississippi, on the other hand, state representatives are elected for four years; so are members of Nebraska's unicameral legislature.

The salaries of state legislators also vary widely from state to state. At one extreme is

New Hampshire, where a legislator receives a salary of $100 per year. In contrast, New York legislators receive an annual salary of $57,500, and those in Pennsylvania get $47,000 a year.

In states where financial compensation is very small, the legislators do not, of course, depend on their public office for a living. But even in New York the salary and other financial rewards of legislators are modest when compared with those of members of Congress, who receive an annual salary of $89,500 and many other financial benefits officially related to their work.

Legislative sessions and procedures. Unlike the Congress, state legislatures do not necessarily meet every year. In some states, sessions are held only every other year, although the annual session is now becoming more common. Some state constitutions place limitations on the length of sessions as well.

The operation of state legislatures is similar in some ways to that of Congress. All state legislatures have standing committees that deal with specialized legislative matters. Hearings are held to gather information necessary for passing legislation. In almost all state legislatures, bills are referred to committees by a "speaker of the house" in the lower house and by a "president of the senate" in the upper house.

Other aspects of legislative procedure vary markedly among the state legislatures. Committee assignments, for example, are made in a number of different ways. Rules regarding the authority of the committees vary, too. In some states committees must report all bills (make recommendations on them to the full legislature), although this is not usually the case. There are also different time limits on the introduction of bills: some states allow presession filing of bills; others prohibit this practice.

In most states bills are passed by majority vote of the legislators present when the bill is voted; in a few states a majority of the entire membership of the legislature is required. Exceptions to the rules of the legislature may be made by extraordinary majority vote, usually a two-thirds vote.

Bills must be read three times before enactment in almost all states, and the readings must take place on separate days. However, the entire bill does not have to be read literally, although this is usually required for one of the readings. Generally, then, the formal procedures followed by state legislatures are similar, although important differences do exist.

State Executives

In most respects the functions of the chief executive of a state—the governor—parallel those of the president at the national level. All the governors except North Carolina's have veto power over legislation, for example. Most governors also possess the authority to veto specific items in certain bills without overturning the entire bill. This power, which is called the *item veto,* is a power that the president does not possess. The item veto provides considerable discretionary power to the governor, who may confine the gubernatorial veto to unfavored portions of an appropriations bill. In most cases it is almost impossible for a state legislature to raise enough votes—usually from a two-thirds to a three-fourths majority of the legislature—to override a governor's veto.

Another important power that all governors possess is the ability to call special legislative sessions for consideration of problems that the legislature has been unable or unwilling to solve. Frequently, the threat of such a special session will force a legislature to take action on a bill it has been avoiding.

State executives also have broad authority over the administrative branches of their respective states. Many can reorganize the bureaucratic agencies of the state, just as the president can reorganize agencies at the national level. In the past, state legislatures have passed some very restrictive measures curbing executive authority over state administrative agencies. The trend in recent years, though, has been toward streamlining administrative organization and generally giving the governor responsibility for the bureaucracy.

In most states the governor not only has authority over administrative offices but also to fill vacancies in elective offices that occur between elections due to the death, resignation, or removal of a state-elected official or even of a United States senator.

State Bureaucracies

The administrative structures of the different states are as varied as the number of states in the Union. There are some official titles, however, that are found in most state structures. Forty-two of the states have a lieutenant governor, who acts as a deputy governor when the governor is incapacitated or out of the state. Each state has a secretary of state, who maintains records of the governor's and the legislature's official acts and keeps official documents. There is a state treasurer in each state, although this office may have another title, such as director of finance or commissioner of taxation and finance. An attorney general heads the legal structure in every state. And often a state school administrator has charge of the educational system.

There are, in addition, a number of boards and commissions that handle other functions. Within each state, such activities and services as agriculture, health, highways, banking, public utilities, schools, mental institutions, and prisons are supervised by specific agencies: a state board of health, a state public utilities commission, a state board of hospitals, a state commission on prisons, and so forth. A number of other agencies issue licenses for driving, for serving liquor, or for hunting and fishing.

Patterns of bureaucratic change. During the past two decades there has been growing concern in many states that the agencies, bureaus, and commissions that administer various state functions are inefficient and disorganized. One result has been increased pressure to reorganize the state bureaucracies and institute better planning and coordination.

One of the most significant features in the reorganization of state bureaucracies has been the trend toward centralized budgeting. This method of budgeting requires agencies to submit outlines of their program proposals to a central agency (usually controlled by the governor), which tries to improve coordination of administrative activities. Where centralized budgeting agencies are controlled by the governor, this method of course increases gubernatorial authority over the bureaucracy, especially over the policy-planning activities of the administrative agencies.

Another feature of contemporary state government reorganization has been a trend toward the establishment of "cabinet-level" departments, administered by "secretaries" who report directly to the governor. These departments, state-level counterparts to such federal entities as the U.S. Department of Health and Human Services, oversee and coordinate the programs of clusters of agencies that have related or complementary missions. Reflecting the bureaucratic and political histories of particular states, the names of these entities vary somewhat from state to state, even when they are similar in programmatic responsibilities. Florida, for example, has a Department of Health and Rehabilitative Services, while Delaware has a Department of Health and Social Services. States also differ as to whether a cabinet-level department is desired to administer a particular program area. Massachusetts, for instance, has had a cabinet-level department administered by a Secretary of Elder Affairs since the 1970s. But programs for older persons in many states are run by agencies that do not report directly to the governor.

Still another pattern of bureaucratic change brought about by some state legislatures in recent years has been the establishment of so-called sunshine procedures. *Sunshine laws* have been passed, requiring bureaucratic units to carry out many of their activities in sessions that are open to the public, and to make most public records readily available to citizens upon their request. The thinking behind these requirements, of course, is that the open conduct of public business increases pressures upon bureaucracies to be efficient and accountable.

State Court Systems

Since each state is a sovereign entity, it has the authority to set up whichever type of court system it wants. Basically the nature of a state's court system is stipulated in the state's constitution, just as the broad outlines of the federal judicial system are determined by Article III of the Constitution. At the state level as at the federal level the legislatures possess additional constitutional authority to determine the nature of the judicial system.

State courts handle all cases arising under state constitutions and state laws. The procedures used in state courts are similar to the general procedures pertaining to civil and criminal cases in federal courts.

Tremendous variations exist among the states in the organization of the judiciary. Like the federal judiciary, every state judicial system includes a hierarchy of courts. But the number of tiers in the state hierarchies varies between three and five. In some states there are two levels of the court system that have original jurisdiction—the power to hear cases when they are first adjudicated. Only about half the states have intermediate appellate courts—where the decisions of original-jurisdiction courts are first subject to review before reaching the highest state court.

The decisions of a state court of last resort are final on all questions of state law.

Only when a federal question is at issue can an appeal be made from these courts to a federal court. In such instances, appeals go directly to the United States Supreme Court.

Selection of judges. The most important difference between the federal judicial system and the state systems is that whereas the judges in the federal courts are appointed, judges in the state and local courts are often selected in other ways. Many are elected. Some are nominated by special judicial councils and then appointed by the governor. Some are appointed by the governor with the approval of special commissions. Some are appointed by the governor with the advice and consent of the state senate, much as federal judges are appointed by the president and approved by the Senate.

Very rarely are judges at the state level appointed or elected for life, as they are at the federal level. They usually serve for terms, which may range from four to fifteen years.

Direct Democracy

In many states the voters can directly propose, accept, or reject state laws through procedures known as initiative and referendum. Through the *initiative* procedure, thousands of voters' signatures are collected on a petition proposing a specific measure of state legislation or a constitutional amendment. There are two types of initiative: direct and indirect. Under *direct initiative* a proposed law is placed directly on a ballot for the approval of the state's voters. Under *indirect initiative* a proposal is first sent to the state legislature. If the legislature does not enact the proposal, it is placed on a statewide ballot. Through the *referendum* procedure the voters have an opportunity to approve or veto legislation already passed by the state legislature; to register views on matters not yet acted on by the legislators; or (in some states) to create directly a new law, which state officials are then required to carry out.

(Tony Auth; © 1978, The Philadelphia Inquirer/Washington Post Writers Group)

The enactment of an amendment to the constitution of California in 1978, through the initiative and referendum Proposition 13, challenged some rather basic assumptions about taxes.

These forms of direct democracy do not exist in all states; but in a number of states they are frequently used tools through which the public can express opinions and even directly make policy. In a large state like California as many as twenty proposals may be presented to the voters for approval at election time.

A landmark example of direct democracy was a proposal, Proposition 13, placed on a California election ballot through the initiative procedure and enacted as a constitutional amendment by the voters of that state in a referendum held in 1978. Through this initiative and referendum process, the citizens of California were able to reduce substantially the real estate taxes they would have been obliged to pay their local governments, starting in 1979 and throughout the many years since. Inspired by this California event, citizens of many other states have subsequently used initiative and referendum procedures to limit their state and local taxes, too.

Every year, the electorates of almost every state are given the opportunity to vote on such important issues of public policy. These votes may be as binding as the implementation of an amendment to the state constitution, or they may merely provide the electorate with an opportunity to advise the state legislature in its consideration of bills for the upcoming legislative session. Sometimes they may simply be expressions of broad sentiment, as when issues such as nuclear disarmament are placed on the ballot.

State Politics

For many years, before reapportionment was ordered by the federal courts in 1962, the composition of some state legislatures was heavily weighted with representatives of rural constituents at the expense of the more numerous urban and suburban constituents. When the Supreme Court insisted on the "one man, one vote" doctrine for both state and national legislatures, it was assumed that reapportionment would change the political scene. Actual effects of the reapportionment ruling, however, have not been clear. Some studies suggest that there has been no marked difference in policies at the state level since reapportionment went into effect.

The forces that are most meaningful in state politics do not come from the voters at large but rather from small, influential groups of political party leaders, interest-group leaders, and community leaders. In some states powerful industrialists, labor leaders, and publishers of newspapers are apt to have more influence in the state government than are large numbers of voters. Thus reapportionment may be relatively meaningless in changing the balance of influence within a state.

Characteristics of State Political Parties

As at the national level, the political parties at the state level serve as the foremost instruments for expressing public opinion and thus making demands on the state governments. On a smaller scale, state political parties have exactly the same kinds of challenges as exist in national parties. They must bridge the gap between the people and the state government by providing party programs that the voters will support and by carrying out these programs once their candidates are elected.

State political party organizations are composed of numerous factions, each struggling to control the party apparatus. Each faction has a different program, so that the electorate of the state is just as confused with regard to state party programs as it is over national party policies. Because of this fragmentation of political parties, few party demands that are made at the state level have the complete support of all the party members.

Factionalized within themselves, state political parties also are almost entirely free of control by any national organization. A major reason for the independence of state parties is that they draw financial support from their own sources. In addition, state parties have their own patronage to distribute among loyal party followers at the state level. Even at the national level, state parties have considerable influence on the distribution of jobs. As leader of his party at the national level, the president must respond to patronage demands of congressional and state party leaders in order to maintain their support.

Regional party strength. State party politics in certain portions of the country tend to conform to regional patterns. The "Solid South" is a well-known feature of American politics. In many states of that region, as a longstanding aftermath of the Civil War, the political scene was dominated by the Democratic party for decades. The Solid South has been broken to some extent in recent years with the reemergence of Republican parties in many southern states. However, this breakdown of one-party domination has occurred primarily during presidential elections rather than in the context of state party politics. Conflict is not absent in such one-party states, but it exists within the framework of the single dominant party, rather than among different parties. Such internal conflict within a party can provide the electorate with a choice among opposing candidates in a primary election.

There are states outside the South that also tend to conform to a sectional political pattern. Politics in certain states of New England and the Midwest have been dominated by the Republican party. However, one-party rule has not been as strong in these regions as it has been in the South.

The most significant pattern of two-party conflict in state politics occurs in the heavily populated, industrialized states, where there are large numbers of urban voters. In such states as California, Illinois, Michigan, and New York there is a split between the rural and urban electorates. This is usually reflected in a conservative-liberal division, with the rural voters of these states supporting the Republicans and the urbanites aligning with the Democrats.

Interest Groups in State Politics

Interest groups operate in state politics in more or less the same way that they do at the national level. They lobby legislators, governors, and administrators, and they institute court cases that are in the interests of their members.

The federal system, which has left much formal power in the hands of state governments, greatly strengthens the potential influence of interest groups. If a goal is unobtainable at the national level, there may be an additional opportunity at the state level to achieve whichever policy best serves the interests of a group. Lobbies can be especially effective in areas where the economic stability of the community or region is dependent on the industry or profession represented by the interest group. A representative in the state legislature from such a community must take the wishes of the interest group into consideration or lose its support and possibly his or her seat in the state government. Therefore, major oil companies and their lobbies have influence on the state governments of California, Texas, and Louisiana, where oil is a major industry, but not on the state governments of Nebraska, Vermont, or Idaho, where oil is not a significant industry. Aircraft manufac-

turers, likewise, are important to the states of Washington and California and especially to the economies of Seattle and Los Angeles. Agricultural pressure groups have more influence in the state governments of Kansas and Idaho than in those of New Jersey or Rhode Island. It is to be expected that such interest groups have effective access to the governments in these cities and states.

Nevertheless, despite the seemingly overwhelming influence of some pressure groups at the state level, the electorate serves as a countervailing force that prevents domination by any one group. The voters have the opportunity at least to resist any policy that appears to benefit a single group, by defeating in the next election representatives who support that policy or, in some cases, by rejecting the policy itself in a referendum.

State Policies

The states have the authority to make laws whenever the subject of the policy is not exclusively within the jurisdiction of the national government. Therefore, the states pursue many policies concurrently with the national government. (See Box 19.1.)

Any list of state governmental activity would include important policies dealing with public education from kindergarten through graduate school, transportation, natural resources, recreation, crime, regulation of business, control over liquor and drugs, and health and welfare. States also enact laws dealing with marriage and divorce, traffic regulation, and voting requirements. Another important concern of the states is the allocation of state money to local governments for such pressing needs as education, housing, and mass transportation.

As might be expected, certain industrial states can afford to spend far more money than can other states. The leading states in total direct expenditures are California, New York, Texas, Illinois, Pennsylvania, and Ohio.

Those spending the least are Vermont, South Dakota, Delaware, New Hampshire, North Dakota, and Idaho.

Since each state has different populations and physical characteristics, and each establishes its own social and economic objectives, there is substantial variety among the states in their priorities for spending. Massachusetts, which is tenth in total expenditures and seventh in public welfare aid, ranks only twenty-third among the states in funds spent on highways. Texas, which ranks third in total expenditures, is ninth in the spending of welfare funds. Wyoming, which outspends only six other states in total dollars, outranks eleven states in the funds it devotes to health and hospitals.[1]

Economic policies. Like the federal government the states regulate many aspects of economic life within their borders. They grant licenses and set qualifications for such professions as teaching, the law, and medicine. Private businesses are legalized through incorporation or licenses granted by state government, and various business activities are subject to state regulation. Wide variation exists among the states in their attitudes regarding the regulation of business. Some states provide tax concessions or other benefits to encourage businesses to locate within their borders. Many states also set minimum wages, maximum hours, and other standards regulating the working conditions of their labor forces.

Many businesses are subject to both state and federal regulation. Although the Federal Communications Commission regulates long-distance telephone rates, for example, telephone rates charged for calls within a state come under the jurisdiction of that state's public utility commission. The rates set by state commissions for intrastate telephone and other public utilities vary considerably from state to state.

LOCAL GOVERNMENTS

Just as the nation is divided into state jurisdictions, each of the 50 separate states is divided into innumerable units of government. These are the counties, towns, townships, cities, villages, boroughs, school districts, and special districts. Each of these local governments has a specific set of powers for serving the people or regulating the activities within its boundaries.

No local or regional government has sovereignty or power in its own right. These units of government are not even mentioned in the national Constitution. They exist because they have been created by the states as instruments to help carry out state governmental responsibilities. Some local governments have been created by state constitutions; others have been created by specific acts of state legislatures; still others have originated through special compacts or agreements between two or more states. The characteristics and purposes of these units show considerable variation.

Since each state creates its own local government, their powers, officers, and other features of these units vary throughout the country even when they have the same name. Some city governments, for example, have control over local police, whereas others do not. Since the boundaries of local governments frequently overlap or are entirely contained within other units, it is difficult to draw clear lines separating the jurisdictions of these structures. School districts may serve one or more counties or towns. Townships may lie within counties, towns within townships, and so forth. In some rural areas counties are the sole instruments of local government. In New York City five counties are coextensive with five borough governments. In other cities,

---

[1] U.S. Bureau of the Census, *Statistical Abstract of the United States, 1988* (Washington, D.C.: U.S. Government Printing Office, 1988), pp. 264–265.

In a pioneering program that is being closely watched in Congress, the state of Washington this week began providing medical insurance to working people who cannot afford it.

The state will pay up to 90 percent of the cost of health insurance for selected families whose incomes are less than double the poverty level. About 30,000 Washingtonians, 4 percent of those who have no medical insurance, will be covered in the first five years, and state officials say they hope to expand the plan if it proves successful.

As Congress prepares to debate proposals to help the 37 million Americans who do not qualify for Government assistance yet cannot afford private health insurance, officials here and in several other states say they can no longer wait for Federal help and are going ahead on their own.

'We're Not Waiting'
"We've decided that some of the states like ourselves are going to pioneer these projects and then share the information with other states," said Gov. Booth Gardner of Washington. "We're not waiting in this state."

Representative-elect James McDermott, a Seattle Democrat who was a leading advocate of the plan when he was a State Senator, said it could help bridge the gap between no insurance and the Federal programs being debated in Congress.

"State legislatures are the laboratory of democracy," said Dr. McDermott, who is also a child psychiatrist. "If the states can get it rolling, they can point the way for the Federal Government."

The Washington pilot project is fundamentally different from a Massachusetts plan that has attracted more attention. Where the Washington program puts most of the financial burden on the state government, the Massachusetts law, signed in April by Gov. Michael S. Dukakis, requires all employers of more than five people to pay at least half the cost of health insurance for their workers.

Burden on Employers
Under the Massachusetts law, employers who do not comply must pay up to $1,680 per employee per year into a state health insurance pool. The program is taking effect in phases; right now it covers about 7,600 people.

In Washington State, a family of four making $23,300 or less, double the Federal Government's poverty line, would qualify for state-subsidized coverage. Nearly half of those who meet the requirements are under 25 years old, state officials say; many are children of working parents too poor to buy health insurance. In its first phase, the coverage is being offered only to families in two populous counties, King and Spokane.

Without the state subsidy, private insurance would cost a family of four about $250 a month. With it, individuals will pay $7.50 to $38, depending on income and family size, and the state will pay the rest.

such as Chicago, city and county units govern almost the same territory.

Counties

There are slightly more than 3,000 counties in the entire nation. In Connecticut and Rhode Island they are merely geographical designations and have no governmental structures. In all the other states, counties are governmental units as well as territorial subdivisions of the state. (In Louisiana they are called parishes; in Alaska, boroughs.)

Long-Term Saving Predicted

The plan is expected to cost $66 million in its first two years, but state officials say it will reduce other costs in the long run. They say people without health insurance often put off seeing a doctor until a problem becomes serious, at which point they may turn up in a hospital emergency room. Because they cannot afford the costs of treatment, their bills may be written off by the hospital and passed on to other patients, or they may be financed by the taxpayers under the Medicaid program for the indigent.

Some uninsured patients manage to pay their own medical bills, but officials say the cost can force them onto the welfare rolls.

"There is an expectation," said Thomas Kobler, director of the Washington program, "that if people come in to be treated for wellness" —shots, and dietary advice—instead of illness, then your costs will be less in the long run."

Mr. Kobler said he saw the Washington experiment as a chance to find out whether a taxpayer-financed health insurance program would work and how much it would cost.

Although the plan was opposed by conservatives, it carried the State Legislature with support from both parties. McDermott said health care for lower-middle-class citizens has become a nonpartisan issue, as unemployment was in the 1930's.

Plans in Other States

Meanwhile, other states continue to plan on their own.

The Pennsylvania Legislature is expected to vote on a health care package in the 1989 session. Similar to the Washington plan, it would also provide state subsidies for small concerns that have trouble paying for employee health insurance.

In California, voters in November approved an increase in the state cigarette tax to 35 cents a pack from 10 cents. The proceeds, estimated at $650 million a year, are to be used to pay hospitals and doctors who care for people with no health insurance.

Hawaii is considering expansion of a program requiring most employers to provide health insurance to their workers.

New York is setting up two small pilot programs to allow some low-income families and small businesses to buy subsidized health insurance.

Biggest Question: the Cost

Although the Washington State plan won approval from business groups and the medical establishment, it could run into political trouble if the costs of expanding the program get out of hand. It faces renewal by the Legislature every two years.

Washington, Massachusetts, and other states are experimenting with their own health insurance programs, even as Congress debates a new national health insurance program.

Counties are also extremely varied with respect to population and territorial size. Los Angeles County in California has over 7 million people; Galatin County in Kentucky, 4,800. Counties range in area from the 22 square miles of New York County (Manhattan) to the 20,131 square miles of California's San Bernardino County.

Counties as governmental units differ from one another in their powers and characteristics mainly because they have developed in different regions of the country, in different periods of time, and in different social, economic, and political contexts. Still, several general purposes are common to most counties.

The various activities that can be performed by counties are extensive. Counties in some areas, such as New England, carry out only a handful of these functions, whereas counties in Western states such as California provide a broad range of facilities and services.

Most of the officials in charge of these county functions are elected directly by county voters. As a result, they are relatively independent of one another.

Counties as agents of state governments. One general purpose of a county is to carry out state functions in a specific geographical section of state territory. Among the typical activities carried out by a county are the issuance, recording, and maintenance of such legal documents as marriage and birth certificates, mortgages, wills, and deeds to property. A *county recorder* or *register of deeds* enrolls and maintains the official records of mortgages, wills, deeds, and other documents concerning property ownership and transactions. Sometimes these records are kept by a *county clerk,* but usually the clerk is more concerned with the recording and filing of personal records such as birth, marriage, and death certificates. The clerk also issues licenses required by state law for marriages, hunting, and fishing. The state itself authorizes these legal documents, and the counties act as agents for the state in administering these activities.

The major law enforcement officer of every county is the *county sheriff,* whose general duties are to carry out the orders of the county courts, to detect and arrest suspected lawbreakers, to prevent the violation of laws, and to maintain peace and safety in the county.

The *county coroner* or *county medical examiner* has the responsibility of investigating the circumstances surrounding a mysterious or violent death. With the aid of a *coroner's jury*

made up of county citizens, this official reviews the medical and other circumstances of any unusual death.

Counties as providers of local services. A second general purpose of counties is to provide local services and facilities. These are not part of statewide programs, but are undertaken to meet strictly local needs through the authority granted to counties by a state. Thus a county road may be built because of a county government's decision to have it for a specific local purpose. The taxes to finance the building of such a road would be levied and collected by the county government only from residents of that county, not from citizens in other parts of the state.

Prior to the 1960s it was only in relatively rural areas that counties provided important services of local government. In many rural areas, in fact, states have made the counties the sole instruments for local government. In such areas counties are the only political structures people can turn to for essential local facilities and such services as schools, fire and police protection, and sanitation systems.

In other, heavily populated or urbanized areas the states have usually created additional bases for local government—the city, village, borough, or town. These bases have become far more important than counties as instruments of local government in urban areas. As cities become the focus of urban citizen needs, the counties in these areas are bypassed.

Specific local functions. The activities of county officials have to do with carrying out local functions related to education, fire prevention and protection, health services and disease prevention, welfare services, public works, and the levying, collection, and expenditure of taxes.

Although the office of *county superintendent of schools* exists in many states, public education is a county responsibility only in relatively rural areas where there is no other unit of local government. Cities, towns, townships, and special school district governments are responsible for education in heavily settled areas. But the county superintendent, along with the county school board, is responsible for schools that do not fall within the boundaries of any other unit of local government. The same is generally true of the county's role in preventing and fighting fires. These functions fall to the county only when other units of government are not available to carry them out.

Health and welfare may be important county functions in urban as well as in rural areas. In the city of Chicago, for example, Cook County Hospital is the main public hospital. In rural areas it is necessary for the county to handle health and welfare, because there are no other local governments to do it. In urban areas this role is largely a matter of historical accident.

Most counties also have public works departments that build bridges and roads, control insects by draining swamps and spraying foliage with pesticides, and survey property lines. In some counties, public works departments even build airports and run power, water, and sewage-disposal systems.

Regardless of the range and character of county activities, one function is common to most county governments—the levying, collection, and expenditure of taxes from the county's residents to finance the county's activities. While they also receive funds from the state and federal governments, one of the direct ways in which counties raise revenue is by taxing property holders in proportion to the value of the property they own (in contrast to an income tax, which provides the federal government with most of its revenue).

A complete list of activities undertaken by counties throughout the United States would be virtually endless. Some maintain museums, zoos, parks, forest preserves, and other recreational areas. Others engage in soil conservation and agricultural research. The specific functions and responsibilities of a given

county are related to the history and shifting demands of the local communities that lie within and around it.

The powers and functions of county boards. Unlike the federal, state, and city governments, most counties lack a chief executive. There is no single official comparable to a president or governor. The most powerful organ of county government is usually a *county board*. In small or rural counties it tends to be a *board of commissioners* of from three to seven members, elected at large by the voters of the county. In large or urban counties there is often a *board of supervisors* consisting of a dozen or more members, each of whom is elected by a district within the county. Members of both types of boards are generally part-time officials.

The board of commissioners or supervisors has the only legislative powers of a county. Of prime importance is a county board's authority to levy taxes, issue bonds, and stipulate the ways in which taxes may be spent. Through this authority the board retains an important measure of control over the activities of such other elected officials as the county sheriff.

The other legislative powers of the board are relatively limited. Some county boards are empowered by the state to regulate the purposes—residential, commercial, industrial, or agricultural—for which various areas of land may be used in the county. Some boards are empowered to regulate the sale of alcoholic beverages and to license public accommodations and places of entertainment.

The board also has administrative power over county activities for which there is no elected executive official. In virtually every county, the county board administers the health department and appoints the county director of health. Although the board is not authorized by the state to enact legislation regulating or affecting health in the county, it can take whatever administrative actions it deems necessary to carry out general state laws concerning health. Some counties have attempted to centralize executive activities and administration in the hands of a full-time professional, the *county manager*, hired by the county board.

County boards also have one limited judicial function in certain states. They serve as boards of review or appeal for taxpayers wishing to protest the value that a county assessor has assigned to property as a basis for determining taxes.

New England Towns and Townships

For historic, social, and commercial reasons, other units of government have developed within the counties. In densely populated areas, municipalities such as towns, villages, boroughs, and cities have been incorporated by the states to serve as local governing units. Incorporation is accomplished when a state grants a charter to a locality in response to a request by people living there.

There are, however, in New England and in some Middle Atlantic and midwestern states, forms of local government—towns and townships—that differ from municipalities in that they have not been incorporated by the state. These units and their governmental structures developed before incorporation became prevalent. Altogether, there are nearly 17,000 of these units in America.

New England towns. The New England town originated during the colonial era as the principal instrument of local government in that region. Within the territories of the chartered colonies, compact clusters of settlements grew up around the churches, the stockades, and the common pastures and fields. As a matter of course, the settlers met to consider common problems and ways to deal with them. This was the origin of the New England town meeting.

By the time the New England colonies had become sovereign states, much of their territory had already been subdivided into towns.

These existing towns were given the responsibilities of handling decentralized state functions. They were able to meet the needs that would be fulfilled by the county governments in other states at a later time. Even when counties were later established in New England, the towns retained most of their original functions.

Despite the fact that towns existed prior to states in New England, the legal governing powers of these towns are now derived from the authority of the state. The towns are permitted to undertake only those activities authorized by the state. For the most part, these activities are the same as those carried out by the counties of other states: education, police and fire protection, garbage collection, health and welfare services, construction of roads, taxation, and so on.

A unique local governmental feature of the New England towns is the *town meeting*—an annual gathering of the town's adult citizens. The town meeting possesses all the necessary legislative powers to run the town. Often described as the purest form of democracy, the town meeting makes decisions by simple majority vote.

In some New England towns where populations have greatly increased, the traditional town meeting has undergone changes. When a town has 20,000 residents, an annual meeting of all voting citizens becomes an unwieldy affair. As a result many large New England towns have changed their form of government by incorporating as municipalities and now hold *representative* or *limited* town meetings. Representatives are elected to conduct the town meeting on behalf of the whole population. Depending on the size of the town, there may be from 50 to 100 representatives.

Townships. Townships did not originate in as haphazard a manner as the town meeting type of government. Townships were planned units. In 1785 the Continental Congress provided for a survey of the national territories in the regions beyond the Appalachians to facilitate legal transactions and the identification of land to be settled. The survey marked off squares measuring six miles on a side. The total thirty-six-square-mile parcel became known as a "congressional township" or a "geographical township."

As these territories of the Northeast and North Central parts of the country became settled and states were formed, it was a simple matter to utilize the old boundaries of these districts as subunits of county government and to authorize them to provide local services and facilities. The state empowered them as *civil townships* with political and governing functions.

The townships modeled their governments after the New England towns. And like the New England towns, the townships perform local governmental functions and act as agents of the states for selected activities. However, despite the township's formal similarity to the New England town, it is a far less vital unit of government. Because it was created artificially rather than in relation to population clusters, it has rarely become a major focus for the demands of local citizens.

The main function of most modern townships is the maintenance of local roads. But even this activity is gradually shifting to counties and municipalities. Most annual township meetings are so poorly attended that often there is not an official quorum (a minimum number of citizens who must be present if there is to be a vote on an issue). Still, they remain part of the American local political scene, and a few are very effective governmental entities.

Municipal Corporations: Cities, Villages, Boroughs, and Towns

For the majority of Americans who live in heavily settled areas, the best-known and most important units of local government are the city, the village, the borough, and the town. Known as *municipalities*, these units, which number close to 18,000 in all, have been created by the states specifically to serve the needs of dense population clusters. The common feature of municipalities that differentiates them from counties, townships, or New England towns is the legal basis of their powers—their charters of incorporation.

Some municipalities are located within counties; others overlap county boundaries. As a community becomes densely populated and the state provides it with a municipal charter, a large proportion of the local services and facilities formerly provided by the county are taken over by the newly incorporated government. Usually, the county government continues to provide local services in rural areas where the citizens have no other government to answer their needs, but the residents of the more urbanized communities direct their demands to the newer municipal structures. In some instances, however, a county and a municipality perform services of a duplicate nature in the same community.

Although the terms *city, village, borough,* and *town* are widely used labels for municipal entities, these terms are not used in the same way throughout the country. The particular term applied to a municipality depends on the criteria used by the state that sets it up. In some older, Eastern states, local tradition and custom have determined the nomenclature. For the most part, the size of a municipality's population is the primary factor determining its designation.

In general, *city* is the term applied to municipalities with populations of several tens of thousands. Smaller municipalities are usually designated villages, boroughs, or towns. However, there are exceptions to this rule. A city in Kansas, for example, may have as few as 200 residents, whereas the village of Oak Park, Illinois, has more than 60,000 inhabitants. Moreover, a "town" in New England has a very different type of government from a town in Louisiana, California, or Texas.

TYPES OF MUNICIPAL GOVERNMENT ORGANIZATION

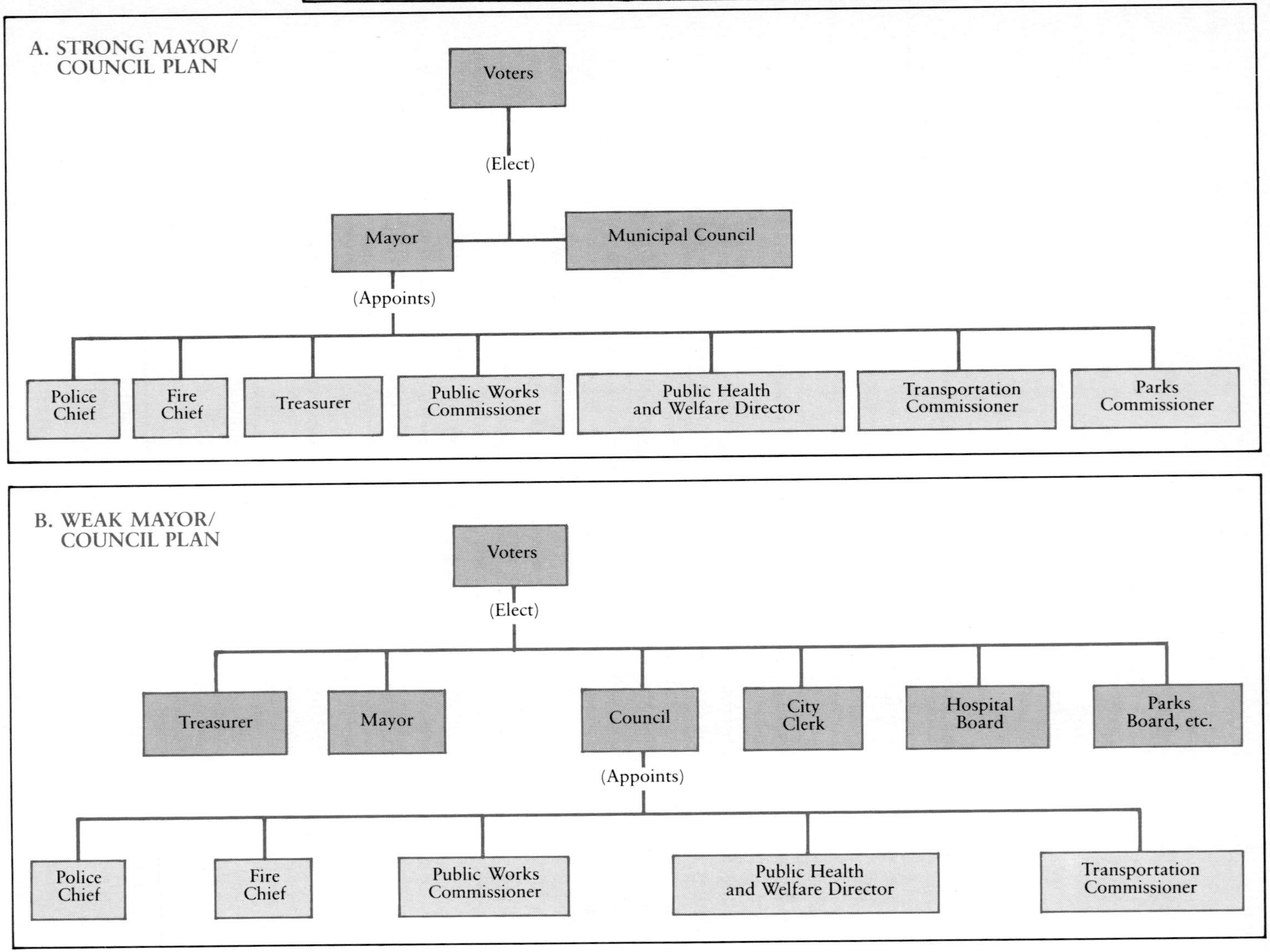

A. STRONG MAYOR/ COUNCIL PLAN

Voters

(Elect)

Municipal Council

Mayor

(Appoints)

Police Chief

Fire Chief

Treasurer

Public Works Commissioner

Public Health and Welfare Director

Transportation Commissioner

Parks Commissioner

B. WEAK MAYOR/ COUNCIL PLAN

Voters

(Elect)

Treasurer

Mayor

Council

City Clerk

Hospital Board

Parks Board, etc.

(Appoints)

Police Chief

Fire Chief

Public Works Commissioner

Public Health and Welfare Director

Transportation Commissioner

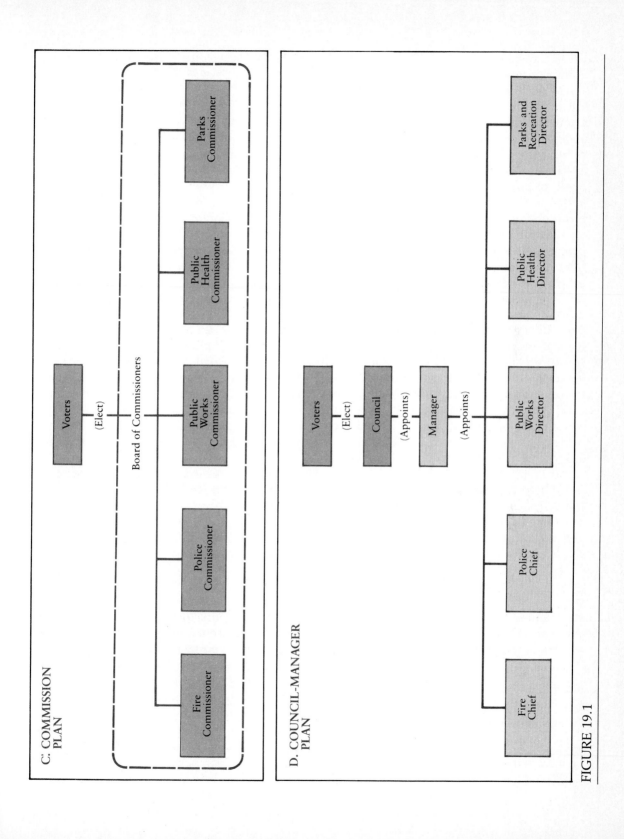

C: COMMISSION PLAN

Voters

(Elect)

Board of Commissioners

Fire Commissioner

Police Commissioner

Public Works Commissioner

Public Health Commissioner

Parks Commissioner

D. COUNCIL-MANAGER PLAN

Voters

(Elect)

Council

(Appoints)

Manager

(Appoints)

Fire Chief

Police Chief

Public Works Director

Public Health Director

Parks and Recreation Director

FIGURE 19.1

Clearly, the meaning of the label attached to a municipality varies from state to state.

Municipal charter of incorporation. Cities, villages, boroughs, and towns are local governments known legally and technically as *municipal corporations.* Just as a business becomes incorporated to carry on certain legal and financial transactions, a city, village, borough, or town is given legal status as a "corporate body" through a municipal charter of incorporation.

The state has full authority over municipalities unless it imposes limitations on itself through an amendment to its constitution. In some states, therefore, the state government can, whenever it wishes, alter the major features of the municipal corporation. For example, without the agreement of any other party, the state government can change the municipal corporation's powers, officers, territorial jurisdiction, and requirements for such activities as borrowing money. Many states, however, have constitutionally or legislatively adopted the principle of *home rule,* by which the establishment, alteration, or elimination of any municipal charter requires the approval of local residents.

Whenever there is doubt about what a municipal corporation can or cannot do, the courts are inclined to interpret municipal powers strictly according to the language of the charter. In the early twentieth century an Iowa judge, John F. Dillon, summarized the approach taken by the courts in interpreting municipal power. Known as *Dillon's Rule,* his statement is still acknowledged as an accurate summary of the situation regarding the legal powers of municipalities. Dillon stated:

It is a general and undisputed proposition of law that a municipal corporation possesses and can exercise the following powers and no others: First, those granted in express words; second, those necessarily or fairly implied in or incident to the powers expressly granted; third, those essential to the accomplishment of the declared objects and purposes of the corporation—not

simply convenient, but indispensable. Any fair, reasonable, substantial doubt concerning the existence of power is resolved by the courts against the corporation, and the power denied.[2]

The persistence of Dillon's Rule and of court rulings against broad interpretations of municipal powers are in direct contrast to the Supreme Court's broader interpretations of the national Constitution and the consequent expansion of the federal government's powers.

Types of municipal charters. A *municipal charter of incorporation* may be a single document that enumerates such specific items as the powers of the corporation, its governing officials, and how they are chosen. Or it may consist of a series of statutes, each of which defines specific municipal offices and powers in elaborate detail. These statutes may have been enacted by a state legislature over many years and may not even be compiled in any comprehensive order. The exact meanings of the multiple provisions in such piecemeal charters are determined only when lawyers and courts have practical reasons for attempting to resolve specific issues regarding the powers and offices of a municipality.

The types of charters and governing structures that exist for different municipalities vary considerably (see Figure 19.1). Most often there is an executive officer, either a *mayor* or a *city manager*, and a policy-making body, such as a *city council* or a *commission*. The executive officer of a municipality, whether mayor or manager, presents an annual budget to the municipal government. The budget indicates the proposed programs to be undertaken by the various departments, their estimated costs, and the amount of taxes that will have to be levied to meet costs. The legislative body (the council or commission) officially enacts

_____

[2] John F. Dillon, *Commentaries on the Law of Municipal Corporations* (Boston: Little, Brown, 1911) Vol. 1., p. 448.

this budget by levying taxes and appropriating funds to the various departments. It also has the power to enact local laws, known as *ordinances*, within the specific areas of power granted by the state legislature. The municipal legislature may enact ordinances concerning such matters as traffic, land use, and pollution; but it does not pass laws concerning felonies, divorce, inheritance, and a host of other matters that are dealt with directly by state governments. The general categories of municipal legislative powers are often referred to as the local "housekeeping" functions. In this way they are distinguished from broader matters over which the state reserves jurisdiction to itself. In short, the activities carried out by municipalities include the local government functions typical of counties, New England towns, and townships: police and fire protection, public works, maintenance of official records, and so on. The dollars needed to carry out these activities come from a variety of places. Major sources of funds are taxes levied on local real estate and the grants-in-aid provided by the state and federal governments. Some of the nation's larger cities also levy taxes on retail sales and on payrolls. A comparatively small proportion of funds comes to the municipal treasury from fees and licenses for dogs and cars, the operation of public accommodations and amusement facilities, and various other sources.

For two centuries the *real estate tax* or *property tax* was the principal source of revenue for municipalities, as well as for counties, towns, and townships. As late as 1955 that tax provided over two-thirds of the funds of local governments in the United States. Now, near the end of the century, the property tax is providing only about one-third of the revenue of local governments, with slightly more than one-third coming from the states, close to one-tenth from the federal government, and the remainder from local fees, charges, and miscellaneous taxes.

SPECIAL DISTRICT AND METROPOLITAN GOVERNMENTS

As vast numbers of people have migrated from rural areas to the cities during the twentieth century, American urban centers have literally burst at the seams and spilled into surrounding suburbs and counties. This phenomenon has produced the densely populated regions known as *metropolitan regions.*

In spite of the many needs and problems that all parts of a metropolitan region may share in common, the political fragmentation within these regions tends to make common solutions difficult if not impossible. Most of the communities within a metropolitan area are governed by distinct local municipalities. Each local political system has its own governing structures and public officials that respond to local community demands.

Due to such political fragmentation, it is difficult for the many governments that have jurisdiction within a metropolitan area to undertake coordinated action. Thus the many problems needing governmental action have tended to persist and to become increasingly acute. Housing shortages, traffic congestion, and high property taxes, for example, continue to drive people out of the central cities. As families and businesses move out of the cities, the city governments lose the tax support they must draw upon to solve these problems and to meet the costs of such essential services as mass transportation and police and fire protection. Although some of these central-city services benefit residents of outlying communities, people who live in these outlying communities are taxed at higher and higher rates by their own local governments and have no desire to pay for curing the ills of the cities as well.

The scope of metropolitan needs and problems and the limitations of traditional municipal structures and patterns of finance have prompted the search for new urban governing structures. The establishment of special district governments to cope with specific problems has been one popular solution. But attempts to place metropolitan communities under the political umbrella of single, multipurpose governing units are naturally resisted by the political forces in each locality that want to keep their political independence intact.

Special Districts

One widespread response to local demands has been the establishment of *special districts*—units of local government that carry out specialized kinds of tasks. Like other forms of local government, special districts are created by the states. Unlike other types of governing units, such as municipalities and counties, however, each special district is a government devised to handle one specific kind of activity. Although school districts are technically special district governments, the origins and major features of school districts are different from those of most other special districts.

Most special district governments are essentially problem-engendered governments. They have been created in response to citizen demands for solutions to specific local problems that municipalities, townships, and counties could not handle. With the exception of school districts, most special districts have been created since World War I, although a handful were established in the nineteenth century, and one even as early as 1790 in Philadelphia.

Special districts can be found today in each of the 50 states and in both urban and rural areas. Altogether there are about 24,000 of them, not including school districts. More than half are concentrated in just eight states: California, Illinois, Kansas, Nebraska, New York, Pennsylvania, Texas, and Washington.

Functions of special districts. The functions performed by special district governments fall into three broad categories. First, there are some special districts that are re-

sponsible for developing and maintaining *facilities*, such as bridges, tunnels, airports and other transportation terminals, parks, and forest preserves. One of the best-known examples of this type of special district is the Port of New York Authority, which was established in 1921 to develop port facilities in the harbor area of New York and New Jersey. The creation of the authority required joint action by the New York and New Jersey legislatures, as well as ratification by Congress because the undertaking clearly involved interstate commerce.

Another common function of special districts is to perform specific *services*, such as removing garbage, furnishing public health services, and supplying water, gas, electricity, or mass transportation. Examples of such districts include the Metropolitan St. Louis Sewer District, the Massachusetts Bay Transportation Authority, the Indianapolis Utilities District, and the Metropolitan Water District of Southern California.

A third general function of special district governments is to undertake *regulatory activities* for achieving such objectives as flood control and pollution abatement. The Los Angeles Air Pollution Control District is a representative example.

Financial flexibility. The impetus for creating many special district governments has been the need to circumvent state laws that impose limits on the amount of money municipalities can borrow. Suppose the citizens of a community are completely united in their demands on city officials to build an airport. Even though the mayor and councillors also favor the plan, such an undertaking cannot be financed if the city is close to its state-imposed debt ceiling. In such an instance, the community might turn to the state legislature for the establishment of a new airport district government. The new structure would have its own borrowing power granted to it by the state and would be able to sell bonds to investors for financing an air terminal. The boundaries of special districts created under circumstances of this kind often coincide with the boundaries of a single city or town.

Territorial scope. The territorial and jurisdictional limitations of municipalities and counties are also responsible for the creation of special districts. Demands for special services, facilities, and regulations cannot always be confined within the boundaries of a single city, town, or county.

The demand for mass transportation in the Boston area, for example, was expressed throughout the approximately 80 cities and towns in the metropolitan region. A network of 80 separate transit systems, requiring coordination among dozens of municipal governments, would be an unwieldy operation. Instead, the area's mass-transit system is operated by the Massachusetts Bay Transportation Authority, a special district that encompasses within its jurisdiction all these cities and towns. For similar reasons the Port of New York Authority was created as a special district with jurisdiction over parts of two states and 1,400 local governments.

The jurisdictional boundaries of a special district do not always result from simply combining the territories of the cities, towns, and counties to be served. In some districts, only the portions of communities that are to be served or developed are included. Sometimes, owing to the peculiar logistics of a problem, the jurisdiction of a special district government may cover territories that are geographically separated from one another. A classic illustration is the Metropolitan Water District of Southern California. Created in 1928, it serves Los Angeles, San Diego, and adjoining towns by bringing water to them from the Colorado River, more than 250 miles away. Consequently, the district has jurisdictional authority in these widely separated locales.

Some special district boundaries must be regional in scope because of the areawide nature of a problem, not simply for motives of efficiency. Consider the problem of air pollution. If a pollution control district were set up in Hollywood, California, and if Los Angeles was excluded from the district, it is doubtful that the air over Hollywood would become any purer. Therefore, it is not surprising that Los Angeles, Glendale, Pasadena, and other municipalities of the area are all within the Los Angeles Air Pollution Control District.

Political detachment. Sometimes special district governments are created because state legislators or local citizens want to remove a particular activity from local partisan politics. Although no structure of government can be entirely removed from the competing political demands that are constantly made on it, the creation of a special district can limit the control of a dominant local political party or faction over a specified area of activity. For example, a municipal airport may be run by officials who have obtained their jobs as patronage from the local party machine and are therefore highly responsive to party needs in making decisions about airport operation. But the state legislature can take this entire function out of local party hands by creating a special district government to run the airport, with commissioners or directors appointed by the governor.

Structure, powers, and finances. Generally, the governing structures of special districts are set up as multimember boards or commissions. Unlike the governing officials of municipalities and counties, the officials of most special district governments are not directly responsible to the voting public. Special district officials are usually appointed rather than elected. One reason is that the officials who create such districts want to keep them out of the hands of local political factions. There is also a generally accepted notion that since special districts are created to provide specialized services, district officials should be selected on the basis of their qualifications for performing the necessary tasks rather than their public popularity.

The governing officials of some special

districts are appointed by the state. In other special districts, officials are appointed by public officials of the municipalities and counties within the district's jurisdiction. And sometimes, appointive powers are shared by the state and localities.

To perform the specific tasks for which they are established, special district governments are granted powers similar to those of other local governments. They can acquire property through eminent domain. Once such land has been acquired, a special district has the authority to maintain, develop, and dispose of it. Special districts can construct facilities, hire personnel, promulgate and enforce regulations, and bring suit or be sued in court. Some special districts even have their own district police forces, as do the Chicago Park District and the Metropolitan District Commission in the Boston area.

Most types of special districts finance their activities through some means other than levying direct taxes. Many special districts borrow money by selling interest-bearing bonds to investors. When the New Jersey Turnpike Authority wishes to finance the building of a bridge, for example, it can issue bonds—with the approval of the federal Securities and Exchange Commission and the corresponding state agencies—for sale to the investing public.

Another common source of funds for special districts is the collection of tolls or fees from citizens who use district services. A district that supplies water, electricity, or some other utility may simply charge each user for the amount of water or electricity he or she consumes.

Sometimes, however, local property taxes are used indirectly to finance special district services that cannot be entirely sustained from fees and bond issues. The fares charged by the Massachusetts Bay Transportation Authority (MBTA) for the use of subways, buses, and streetcars, for example, do not bring in sufficient revenue to provide for the personnel, facilities, equipment, and maintenance of the system. Thus each year approximately 80 cities and towns are billed for a portion of the MBTA deficit, with the city of Boston paying the lion's share. The cities and towns customarily meet this obligation from revenue derived from property taxes.

School districts. Although school districts in some areas of the country are merely administrative subdivisions of other local governments, most are properly classified as special district governments. About 16,000 of them have been created to perform a particular category of functions and are not general-purpose governments as are municipalities and counties. School districts, however, are not problem-engendered governments created to get around financial and territorial limitations of other structures. They have been set up as autonomous units by state governments to assure local control of education, to make school facilities easily accessible to children of each community neighborhood, and in principle to keep the function of education separate from politics. In recent years, of course, public schools have been at the heart of heated political controversies about racial balancing and busing of pupils.

Unlike other types of special districts, school districts have traditionally been dependent upon property taxes as their source of funds. Many school districts have the power to levy taxes themselves. The bonds that they market to investors are paid off through property taxes rather than through the collection of fees or service charges. Although school districts receive some funds from federal and state aid programs, they have been more dependent on property taxes than has any other type of government. As a consequence, they are in big trouble.

Compared to other types of special districts that are notable for their financial strength, school districts have severe financial problems. In central cities, for example, where the assessed value of property has declined, the resulting decrease in tax revenues has put an even greater strain on school districts than on municipal governments. This financial strain has had an impact on the size of teachers' salaries, the frequency with which curriculum materials can be updated, and the capacity to construct new facilities.

The financial problems of school districts are compounded by various constitutional restrictions that limit their powers. Even when the governing board of a school district is strongly committed to the construction of new schools, for example, there may be state constitutional limits on the rate of property tax the school district can levy. State constitutional requirements also often force a district to submit proposals for bond issues and tax increases to the voters in local referendum elections. Such proposals are defeated more often than not in many communities and may be submitted to voters four or five times over a period of 10 to 12 years without being approved. These difficulties have led to steadily increasing financial assistance to education from the federal and state governments, as well as to cutbacks in school programs. In some instances in recent years, some schools have even been shut down during the semester when their districts have run out of funds.

General-Purpose Metropolitan Governments

Although special districts have coped effectively with some individual metropolitan needs, as single-purpose governments they are unable to deal in a comprehensive way with the wide range of metropolitan problems. Many reform-minded citizens, therefore, are continuously seeking ways to provide metropolitan areas with all-inclusive, general-purpose governing structures. These governing structures would have the multifunction characteristics of municipal governments, but they would encompass entire metropolitan regions within their respective jurisdictions.

Attempts to create multipurpose metropolitan governments have been somewhat successful in Indianapolis, Minneapolis-St.

Paul, Nashville, Miami, Jacksonville, and other urban areas where there are relatively few incorporated municipalities. The more complex a metropolitan region, the more difficult it is to set up a government over it. Proposals for structural change in more complex regions often include plans for dividing government functions between metropolitan structures and the structures of older municipalities.

A common contemporary approach to metropolitan reorganization is *city-council consolidation*. Through this method, a city and the surrounding county are merged into a single unit of government. City-county consolidation is far from a new idea. It was used as early as 1813 in New Orleans. The approach has been applied in recent decades to the consolidation of Baton Rouge and East Baton Rouge Parish in Louisiana, of Nashville and Davidson County in Tennessee, and, more recently, of Jacksonville and Duval County in Florida.

Under city-county consolidation, an entire metropolitan area is governed by an elected mayor and a metropolitan county council. The entire county is included in a *general services zone,* while the areas of the former municipalities become part of an *urban services zone.* The general services zone provides areawide services for the whole county (such as recreational facilities and fire and police protection) for which all county residents are taxed. The urban services zone provides typically local services (such as street lighting and sewage disposal), for which only the residents of the urban district are taxed. The territory of an urban services zone can be expanded in time, with the approval of the metropolitan mayor-council government.

There are several reasons why city-county consolidation is of limited usefulness as a general instrument for metropolitan structural reorganization. First, city-county consolidation is possible only where metropolitan regions are still encompassed within an existing county. There are few metropolitan regions, however, that do not exceed the boundaries of a single county. Furthermore, even where metropolitan areas are contained within county boundaries, city-county consolidation tends to be unpopular with voters of suburban communities. Whereas the city-county consolidations of the nineteenth century were accomplished through state legislative action, state laws today generally require voter approval for city-county consolidation. Central-city residents tend to approve such plans, but suburban voters for the most part prefer local autonomy and vote against them.

For metropolitan areas that are confined within the boundaries of a single county, an alternative to city-county consolidation is the *comprehensive urban county plan.* Such a plan calls for the reassignment of governmental functions rather than the merging of municipal and county governments. Ordinarily, a countywide referendum is held for the adoption of a charter that transfers areawide functions from municipal and local special district governments to the county government. Existing municipal structures retain those functions that are strictly local in nature.

The first successful adoption of a comprehensive urban county scheme was the metropolitan Miami area of Dade County, Florida, established in 1957. Voters of the entire state first had to approve a state constitutional amendment granting home rule to Dade County. Once the amendment was passed, the new charter was drafted and submitted to the Dade County voters. Adoption of the charter required only the approval of a countywide popular majority rather than majorities within the 26 separate municipalities. With a heavy turnout of voters from the central city of Miami, the new Dade County charter was adopted by a narrow voter majority.

The Dade County government was given the power to administer numerous county activities as well as to prepare and enforce plans for the county's development. The county government can construct and operate expressways and mass-transit systems, can provide training and communication for fire and police protection, and can administer programs for the control of air pollution, floods, and beach erosion. The county government also has the authority to set and enforce zoning and business regulations and uniform building codes throughout the county. It can also set minimum standards for those functions and services still provided by the municipalities, and it must approve any alterations in municipal jurisdiction.

In spite of its broad range of governing authority, the governing structure of Dade County has had mixed success in meeting areawide problems. It has provided more efficient coordination of some areawide operations and services. It has been more successful in setting up plans and regulations for county land use, however, than it has been in enforcing them. In addition, resistance from political forces within the county has blunted the county government's powers to regulate municipal activities.

Attempts to establish comprehensive urban counties have been undertaken in Cleveland, Houston, Louisville, and other metropolitan areas. Most of these attempts have failed, however, due to legal and political obstacles to the adoption and implementation of such plans. In many states constitutional amendments must be passed before comprehensive urban county governments can be authorized. Furthermore, incumbent county officials and other politicians who benefit from existing structures of county government form a potentially formidable barrier to the adoption of any change. In addition, some state constitutions impose such rigid financial limitations on the county governments that any transfer of new functions to these counties is virtually impossible. The state constitution can be amended, but this is always a difficult task without the support of a substantial portion of the electorate.

Despite these legal and political obstacles to the adoption of comprehensive urban county structures, the plans may continue to have some appeal. Where metropolitan areas coincide with county boundaries, the transfer of functions from one level of government to another is bound to be more acceptable to many localities than relinquishing their autonomy entirely.

Where an urban area spreads beyond the boundaries of one or more counties, city-county consolidation and comprehensive urban county proposals are obviously unsuitable. A more appropriate plan for such an area is the *metropolitan federation.*

In a metropolitan federation, existing municipal, and even county, governments are retained to perform local functions. These local governments are linked together under a new unit of government that combines certain features both of special district governments and of urban counties. Like the special district governments, the metropolitan federation has boundaries specially drawn to include the total area to be served. Like the urban county, it is a multipurpose structure.

Throughout the twentieth century, a number of urban areas in the United States have tried unsuccessfully to set up metropolitan federations. Because the adoption of such plans usually requires the approval of voter majorities in each separate municipality to be included in the proposed federation, proposals have been defeated whenever submitted to voters in referendums. As with other types of urban reorganization, the adoption of a metropolitan federation ordinarily requires prior passage of a constitutional amendment in many states.

The only successful adoption of a metropolitan federation in North America has been metropolitan Toronto, in the province of Ontario, Canada. Since its inception in 1953 the experience of the Toronto federation, known as the Municipality of Metropolitan Toronto, has been watched with interest in the United States by many persons who seek new governmental solutions to urban problems. Its performance so far has been quite creditable— far better than that of Dade County, established at about the same time.

FEDERAL IMPACT ON STATE AND LOCAL GOVERNMENTS

The development and expansion of a direct role for the federal government in state and local affairs has been largely a phenomenon of the twentieth century. Yet, as indicated earlier, the distribution of constitutional authority between the national and state governments has evolved continuously since the Constitution was adopted in 1789. Similarly, the actions of the national government have been indirectly affecting local communities and governments since the founding of the republic. Consider the profound impact that national immigration policies have had since the eighteenth century in shaping the growth and character of urban centers. The protective tariffs and other national economic policies of the nineteenth century that promoted the growth of American industry and commerce certainly contributed to the development of cities where these activities thrived.

Like other developments that have occurred within America's political system, the federal government's conscious concern with state and local affairs has come about gradually. It has been only during the twentieth century that the national government has played a direct role in financing and shaping the policies of state and local governments when these latter structures have had difficulty in meeting the demands of their citizens.

The Growth and Scope of Federal Aid

Since the New Deal of the 1930s, Congress has passed many laws providing *grants-in-aid* of federal funds to states and localities that are willing to develop and administer certain kinds of programs. Public welfare programs, intrastate highway systems, public housing, urban renewal, vocational education, and job-training programs are just a few of the many state and local programs that have received major boosts from these grants-in-aid. The dollar-total of these programs remained insignificant until the mid-1950s; by the early 1980s federal aid to states and localities had jumped from about $3 billion in 1955 to over $100 billion annually.

The purposes for which federal aid can be used are usually restricted by very specific categorical requirements attached to each program. Some of the major program functions or types of aid can be described as follows (with the approximate percentages of federal aid they have accounted for in recent years in parentheses): Medicaid, health care insurance for low-income persons (21 percent); welfare payments for mothers with dependent children, disabled persons, the blind, and the aged, plus home energy assistance for low-income persons (12 percent); transportation, including highway funds (10 percent); low income housing assistance (5 percent); community development (4 percent); compensatory education (3 percent); environmental protection (3 percent); and employment training (2.5 percent).

State and local governments have become increasingly involved in starting new policies or expanding old ones to take advantage of available federal funds. Programs initiated in Washington often have guidelines that states must follow in order to qualify for federal funds. When energy conservation became an issue of national concern in the mid-1970s, the national government stipulated that only states that reduced their speed limits to the desired 55 miles per hour would be eligible for certain highway grants. Similarly, to be eligible for federal Medicaid funds, states must agree to provide health care reimbursement to all persons described in federal regulations as being needy. After such requirements have been met, however, the programs are designed and administered by the states themselves. States, for example, are free to extend the populations to whom Medicaid reimbursement is available, and share the costs. Under the federal highway program the national government paid 50 percent of the cost of building interstate highway systems. In turn each of the state governments had to provide its matching 50 percent share of road construction costs and had to devise policies for maintaining and administering highways built through the program. Most federal grants require that state governments put up a matching share of funds before they are eligible for federal aid.

The federal formulas for providing grants to the states and for requiring state matching funds have varied with different legislated programs. Many of these formulas lead to substantial differences in the amounts of federal aid provided to each of the states through a specific grant mechanism. In fiscal year 1988, for instance, California received $24.8 million and New York $20.8 million under a population-based formula for implementing the Title III-B Supportive Services program of the Older Americans Act; under the same formula, Alaska, Delaware, New Mexico, Rhode Island, and a dozen other states received under $2 million. Such differences in federal allotments lead the states to take different approaches to implementing federally initiated programs. Variations among the states in the administration of federal grant programs are also influenced, of course, by local needs, conditions, and the policy priorities that states have developed.

Block Grants

Recognition of potential variation in state and local priorities and needs has sometimes been undertaken through the consolidation of existing categorical grants into larger groupings, or *block grants*. For example, the Housing and Community Development Act of 1974 established a new block grant by combining several previously established federal assistance programs—urban renewal, model cities, water and sewer facilities, open spaces, neighborhood facilities, rehabilitation loans, and public facility loans—into a single program.

This consolidation, which was part of President Richard Nixon's "New Federalism" initiatives, was designed to enable state and local governments to use federal funds with greater flexibility and discretion than had been possible under the previous seven categorical programs. Today, the Community Development Block Grant program provides $2 billion in grants, through a population-based distribution formula, to metropolitan cities and urban counties. An additional $900 million goes to other local governmental units through a competitive process.

On a larger scale, when President Reagan took office in 1981 he initially proposed, as part of *his* "New Federalism," the consolidation of some 500 specific categorical programs into 6 unrestricted block grants—2 for education, 2 for health, 1 for energy and emergency aid, and 1 for social services. While this proposal was a bit too bold for Congress to accept, before the year was out 57 federal categorical programs had been consolidated into 9 block grants. One of these, for example, is the Social Services Block Grant program. In fiscal 1989 it distributed $2.7 billion in aid to the states for such diverse activities as child day care, home-based services for the elderly, protective and emergency services for children and adults, family planning, transportation, staff training, and program planning.

Changing the Distribution of Responsibilities

The Social Services Block Grant program illustrates a major element of the "New Federalism" philosophy that characterized President Reagan's two terms in office. For the first time under a social service grant-in-aid program, states were given the responsibility of designing their own mix of services and establishing their own eligibility requirements. The nature of this shift in responsibilities from the federal government to the states can be appreciated by considering one of the previous programs that was consolidated into the Social Services Block Grant program—Title XX of the Social Security Act.

Title XX provided 75 percent federal financing for most social services (except family planning, which was 90 percent federally funded) and required the balance to be funded by the states. The law required that at least half of each state's federal allotment be used for persons who were receiving welfare or eligible for Medicaid (low-income) health insurance. The remaining funds could be used to provide services to anyone whose income did not exceed 115 percent of the median income of persons in the state. All services provided by a state had to be tied to at least one of five federally legislated goals that related to self-sufficiency and self-support. At least one service had to be provided pursuant to each of the five goals. And further, Title XX required states to offer at least three services for aged, blind, and disabled persons receiving welfare payments.

Most of these restrictions were eliminated when Congress incorporated Title XX into the Social Services Block Grant. States are no longer required to provide a minimum level of services for welfare and Medicaid recipients, and no income limits are imposed on service eligibility. States are no longer required to match federal funds with their own. And federal quality standards for child day care services were dropped.

This type of shift in responsibilities from the federal government to state and local governments is what Reagan had in mind when he announced, early in his administration:

In the recent past, as the Federal Government has pushed every city, county, and state to be more like every other, we have begun to lose one of our greatest strengths: our diversity as a people. . . .Federal bureaucrats now dictate where a community may build a bridge or lay a sewer system. We have lost the sense of which problems require national solutions and which are best handled at the local level.[3]

---

[3]*The New York Times*, July 14, 1982, p. A21.

One effect of this consistent emphasis on reducing the role of the federal government during the Reagan presidency, however, may be that state and local governments are now being stretched to the limits of their capacities to handle responsibilities (see Case Study 18).

President Reagan clearly changed the trend that started in the New Deal era, through which the federal role in state and local affairs had grown steadily for about 50 years. President Bush, sharing the philosophical outlook of his predecessor, is also inclined to limit the role and responsibilities of the federal government.

Most state and local officials have always been supportive of the philosophy espoused by Presidents Reagan and Bush—that federal officials should not use national purse strings to dictate local policy—and they will undoubtedly remain supportive of this "New Federalism" as long as it does not extend to severe cuts in the funds available from the federal purse through grants-in-aid. In the last half of the twentieth century, state and local governments have become highly dependent on federal funds to support many of their basic, ongoing functions.

THE CHANGING ROLE OF STATE LEGISLATORS

Although many presidents since Franklin D. Roosevelt's New Deal in the 1930s have proposed sweeping changes in intergovernmental relations, President Ronald Reagan's push for a "New Federalism" during the 1980s was particularly bold. In broad outline, Reagan reversed a 50-year trend through which Washington had increasingly assumed state and local decision-making responsibilities by attaching highly specific requirements to federal grants-in-aid regarding how state and local governments could spend such funds. The consolidation and reduction of federal requirements in grant programs that took place in the 1980s also appears to be having an impact upon state legislatures.

The following case study highlights a trend in many states, through which it is becoming increasingly difficult for legislators to have another business, profession, or job while holding a seat at the statehouse. Particularly in larger states, the demands of being a state legislator may be transforming the elected position from a part-time to a full-time job, like the jobs of U.S. Senators and Representatives.

As Workload Grows, Number of Part-Time Legislators Falls / *Elizabeth Kolbert*

The "citizen" legislator, who spends one season in the state capital and returns home to tend to a business in the next, is becoming a rare breed.

The movement away from the part-time legislature is transforming state government from here [Albany, N.Y.] to Sacramento, Calif. Reasons for the change include the expanding responsibilities state governments had to take on in the Reagan years and the growing number of lobbies making demands on state legislators.

The movement is most notable in populous states like New York, California and Pennsylvania, where many state legislators already consider lawmaking a full-time job. But experts say that even legislatures in smaller states are finding themselves dealing with more complex issues and taking more time to do so.

"About two-thirds of the states are moving inexorably in the direction of a full-time legislature," said Alan Rosenthal, director of the Eagleton Institute of Politics at Rutgers University. "This is the trend."

Changes Over 2 Decades

Even in those states that constitutionally limit the number of days the legislature can meet, lawmakers are spending much more time on legislative business than they did two decades ago, meeting with constituents, attending hearings and raising money for the next campaign.

At the same time, the composition of state legislatures has changed markedly. From 1976 to 1986, the number of legislators who described lawmaking as their profession quadrupled, a survey by the National Conference of State Legislatures shows.

In that period the number of lawyers, historically the most heavily represented profession among legislators, dropped by one-quarter. Nationwide lawyers still make up the largest group of state legislators, 16 percent. The conference attributed the decline in lawyers largely to the difficulty of balancing a law practice against the time demands of holding office.

But there is still little consensus that a full-time legislature is worthwhile. While supporters say the full-time legislature reduces conflicts of interest between lawmakers' official duties and their outside employment, opponents assert that without jobs in their districts, lawmakers will lose touch with their communities.

Legislators' Conflicting Feelings

"In most states, there's a very strong desire to try to maintain a part-time legislature," said Rich Jones, director of legislative programs for the National Conference of State Legislatures. "But it's becoming more and more difficult."

Lawmakers themselves often voice conflicting sentiments on the issue.

Since he was elected 27 years ago, Matthew J. Ryan, the minority leader of the Pennsylvania House of Representatives, has watched the legislative calendar extend from a few months a year in the early 1960's to a year-round one today. Although he has not seen much change in the number or the quality of new laws, he said the public's access to the process has dramatically increased.

"There are a lot more public hearings than there used to be," Mr. Ryan said. "And people are getting a great deal more personal attention."

The Statehouse As a Second Job

Percentage of state legislators holding other jobs, from a survey in 1986.

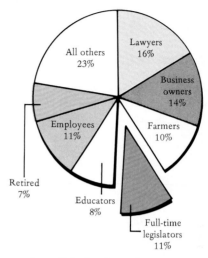

Source: National Conference of State Legislatures

(Source: National Conference of State Legislatures)

FIGURE 19.2

Most Pennsylvania legislators now have district offices and newsletters, which they did not have 20 years ago. And more than half the lawmakers, who earn $47,000 a year, list the Legislature as their sole occupation.

Here in New York's capital, a debate has been raging about whether lawmakers, who now earn $57,500 a year, should move to a full-time session. But many experts say that in fact the decision has already been made: last year the Legislature was in session for at least part of every month but October.

In California, where the Legislature has met year round for almost two decades, more than a third of the lawmakers say they have no outside job and rely on their $40,816 salary.

Experts characterize the legislatures in California, Illinois, Massachusetts, Michigan, New York, Ohio and Pennsylvania as virtually full-time bodies. Although many lawmakers continue to hold outside jobs in those states, the length of the legislative sessions, at least six months and usually more, makes most outside careers impossible.

States heading toward a full-time legislature include Missouri, New Jersey and Wisconsin. In all those states, the number of legislators who call lawmaking their full-time career has increased dramatically over the last decade. A new breed of lawmaker has also emerged, one who has had no career other than politics.

For example, Robert K. Sweeney, a first-term member of the New York State Assembly, has spent his entire adult life in government. Before coming to Albany, he was a village clerk.

"It's my belief that this is and should be a full-time job," said Mr. Sweeney, a 39-year-old Democrat from Lindenhurst, L.I.

Full-time lawmakers who have no outside career make up 11 percent of the legislators nationwide, business owners 14 percent and farmers 10 percent. The rest are divided among a wide range of occupations.

Proponents of a full-time legislature stress that it eliminates conflicts that have historically plagued statehouses, where members often must act on bills that could affect their private businesses or law practices. They also say a more professional legislature can provide an important check on the governor and the executive bureaucracy. Many legislators also say mastering the complicated problems that state governments face demands lawmakers' full attention.

'Cannot Afford to Lose'

John Vasconcellos, chairman of the Ways and Means Committee of the California State Assembly, said, "I wouldn't claim to understand the subtle issues that I have to deal with if I weren't here full time."

But some politicians worry that as more legislators have come to rely on an elective office for their livelihood, they have become more vulnerable to all sorts of political pressure.

"Now you've got a lot of people who have no other profession besides the legislature," Gov. Mario M. Cuomo of New York said. "Now people cannot afford to lose."

Statistics on legislative turnover indicate that as membership has moved toward a full-time occupation, members are becoming more reluctant to give up their seats. In New York, 31 percent of the seats in the Legislature changed hands in 1972, when almost all lawmakers had outside careers. In 1986 only 9 percent of the seats changed hands.

Several experts said state lawmakers themselves helped to create the conditions that have led them to spend more time in the state capitals. And as legislators have taken on more responsibility and hired more full-time staff members, there has been a snowball effect.

"One fed the other," said Robert Hendershot, co-director of the Pennsylvania State Legislature's Bipartisan Management Committee. "The demand on the State Legislature became greater and greater. They increased the staff and the pay and the benefits to members." The staff of the Pennsylvania Legislature has grown almost ten-fold since lawmakers began moving toward a year-round session in the mid-1960s.

In New Jersey, where the Legislature is a "commuter" body and lawmakers rarely spend the night in the capital, legislators' staff allotment has increased almost twelvefold in two decades.

Even in states where the legislature meets every other year, lawmaking is becoming a time-consuming job.

In Oregon, for example, the legislature is in session for only six months out of every two years. But lawmakers found they were spending so much time dealing with constituents' complaints in the 18 months between sessions that each member was recently granted $600 a month to hire a staff assistant for the interim.

In Nevada, where the Legislature also has a session every two years, legislators are expected to meet in Carson City through June of this year, even though by law they stopped receiving their $130-a-day salary in late March.

Still, there are several states where lawmaking remains decidedly part time.

In New Hampshire there is a $100 constitutional limit on legislators' salaries—$125 for the leader of each house—and a 45-day limit on the length of the annual session. For the 400 members of the House of Representatives, one of the few perquisites of power is a locker in the Statehouse.

The Constitution of the United States of America

We the People of the United States, in Order to form a more perfect Union, establish Justice, insure domestic Tranquility, provide for the common defence, promote the general Welfare, and secure the Blessings of Liberty to ourselves and our Posterity, do ordain and establish this Constitution for the United States of America.

Preamble: The people ordain and establish the Constitution.

ARTICLE I

CONGRESS

SECTION 1. All legislative Powers herein granted shall be vested in a Congress of the United States, which shall consist of a Senate and House of Representatives.

Legislative power, bicameralism

SECTION 2. The House of Representatives shall be composed of Members chosen every second Year by the People of the several States, and the Electors in each State shall have the Qualifications requisite for Electors of the most numerous Branch of the State Legislature.

Membership of the House
voter qualifications

No person shall be a Representative who shall not have attained to the Age of twenty-five Years, and been seven Years a Citizen of the United States, and who shall not, when elected, be an Inhabitant of that State in which he shall be chosen.

qualifications for representatives

[Representatives and direct Taxes shall be apportioned among the several States which may be included within this Union, according to their respective Numbers, which shall be determined by adding to the whole Number of free Persons, including those bound to Service for a Term of Years, and excluding Indians not taxed, three fifths of all other Persons.]* The actual Enumeration shall be made within three Years after the first Meeting of the Congress of the United States, and within every subsequent Term of ten Years, in such Manner as they shall by Law direct. The Number of Representatives shall not exceed one for every thirty Thousand,† but each State shall have at Least one Representative; and until such enumeration shall be made, the State of New Hampshire shall be entitled to chuse three, Massachusetts eight, Rhode-Island and Providence Plantations one, Connecticut five, New-York six, New Jersey four, Pennsylvania eight, Delaware one, Maryland six, Virginia ten, North Carolina five, South Carolina five, and Georgia three.

apportionment of representatives and taxes

When vacancies happen in the Representation from any State, the Executive Authority thereof shall issue Writs of Election to fill such Vacancies.

filling vacancies

Source: U.S. Government Printing Office, 1968. House Document #308. This book presents the Constitution and all amendments in their original form. Items which have since been amended or superseded, as identified in the footnotes, are bracketed.

*Changed by Section 2 of the Fourteenth Amendment.

†Ratio in 1979 was one to over 450,000.

The House of Representatives shall chuse their Speaker and other Officers; and shall have the sole Power of Impeachment.

choosing the Speaker
impeachment

SECTION 3.   The Senate of the United States shall be composed of two Senators from each State, [chosen by the Legislature thereof,]* for six Years; and each Senator shall have one Vote.

Membership of the Senate
equal representation

Immediately after they shall be assembled in Consequence of the first Election, they shall be divided as equally as may be into three Classes. The Seats of the Senators of the first Class shall be vacated at the Expiration of the second Year, of the second Class at the Expiration of the fourth Year, and of the third Class at the Expiration of the sixth Year, so that one-third may be chosen every second Year; [and if Vacancies happen by Resignation, or otherwise, during the Recess of the Legislature of any State, the Executive thereof may make temporary Appointments until the next Meeting of the Legislature, which shall then fill such Vacancies.[†]

one-third of the Senate
elected every two years

No Person shall be a Senator who shall not have attained to the Age of thirty Years, and been nine Years a Citizen of the United States, and who shall not, when elected, be an Inhabitant of that State for which he shall be chosen.

qualifications of senators

The Vice President of the United States shall be President of the Senate, but shall have no Vote, unless they be equally divided.

president of the Senate

The Senate shall chuse their other Officers, and also a President pro tempore, in the absence of the Vice President, or when he shall exercise the Office of President of the United States.

choosing Senate officers

The Senate shall have the sole Power to try all Impeachments. When sitting for that Purpose, they shall be on Oath or Affirmation. When the President of the United States is tried, the Chief Justice shall preside: And no Person shall be convicted without the Concurrence of two thirds of the Members present.

trying impeachments

Judgment in Cases of Impeachment shall not extend further than to removal from Office, and disqualification to hold and enjoy any Office of honor, Trust or Profit under the United States; but the Party convicted shall nevertheless be liable and subject to Indictment, Trial, Judgment and Punishment, according to Law.

judgment authority in
impeachment cases

SECTION 4.   The Times, Places and Manner of holding Elections for Senators and Representatives, shall be prescribed in each State by the Legislature thereof; but the Congress may at any time by Law make or alter such Regulations, except as to the Place of Chusing Senators.

Regulating Senate
elections

The Congress shall assemble at least once in every Year, and such Meeting shall [be on the first Monday in December,][‡] unless they shall by Law appoint a different Day.

Convening Congress

SECTION 5.   Each House shall be the Judge of the Elections, Returns and Qualifications of its own Members, and a Majority of each shall constitute a Quorum to do Business; but a smaller number may adjourn from day to day, and may be authorized to compel the Attendance of absent Members, in such Manner, and under such Penalties as each House may provide.

Rules of Congress
judgment of member
qualifications

Each House may determine the Rules of its Proceedings, punish its

Expulsion of members

---

*Changed by Section 1 of the Seventeenth Amendment.

†Changed by Clause 2 of the Seventeenth Amendment.

‡Changed by Section 2 of the Twentieth Amendment.

Members for disorderly Behavior, and, with the Concurrence of two thirds, expel a Member.

Each House shall keep a Journal of its Proceedings, and from time to time publish the same, excepting such Parts as may in their Judgment require Secrecy; and the Yeas and Nays of the Members of either House on any question shall, at the Desire of one-fifth of those Present, be entered on the Journal.

Journal requirements

Neither House, during the Session of Congress, shall, without the Consent of the other, adjourn for more than three days, nor to any other Place than that in which the two Houses shall be sitting.

single House adjournment limitations

SECTION 6. The Senators and Representatives shall receive a Compensation for their Services, to be ascertained by Law, and paid out of the Treasury of the United States. They shall in all Cases, except Treason, Felony and Breach of the Peace, be privileged from Arrest during their Attendance at the Session of their respective Houses, and in going to and returning from the same; and for any Speech or Debate in either House, they shall not be questioned in any other Place.

Salaries for members of Congress

No Senator or Representative shall, during the Time for which he was elected, be appointed to any civil Office under the Authority of the United States, which shall have been created, or the Emoluments whereof shall have been encreased during such time; and no Person holding any Office under the United States, shall be a Member of either House during his Continuance in Office.

Limits on outside employment

SECTION 7. All Bills for raising Revenue shall originate in the House of Representatives; but the Senate may propose or concur with Amendments as on other Bills.

House origination of revenue bills

Every Bill which shall have passed the House of Representatives and the Senate, shall, before it becomes a Law, be presented to the President of the United States; If he approve he shall sign it, but if not he shall return it, with his Objections to that House in which it shall have originated, who shall enter the Objections at large on their Journal, and proceed to reconsider it. If after such Reconsideration two thirds of that House shall agree to pass the Bill, it shall be sent, together with the Objections, to the other House, by which it shall likewise be reconsidered, and if approved by two thirds of that House, it shall become a Law. But in all such Cases the Votes of both Houses shall be determined by Yeas and Nays, and the Names of the Persons voting for and against the Bill shall be entered on the Journal of each House respectively. If any Bill shall not be returned by the President within ten Days (Sundays excepted) after it shall have been presented to him, the Same shall be a Law, in like Manner as if he had signed it, unless the Congress by their Adjournment prevent its Return, in which Case it shall not be a Law.

Presidential signature requirement; veto power; veto override

Every Order, Resolution, or Vote to which the Concurrence of the Senate and House of Representatives may be necessary (except on a question of Adjournment) shall be presented to the President of the United States; and before the Same shall take Effect, shall be approved by him, or being disapproved by him, shall be repassed by two thirds of the Senate and House of Representatives, according to the Rules and Limitations prescribed in the Case of a Bill.

Congressional-presidential concurrence

SECTION 8. The Congress shall have Power To lay and collect Taxes, Duties, Imposts and Excises, to pay the Debts and provide for the common Defence and general Welfare of the United States; but all Duties, Imposts and Excises shall be uniform throughout the United States;

Enumerated powers of Congress
taxation, defense, and general welfare

To borrow money on the credit of the United States;

borrowing money

To regulate Commerce with foreign Nations, and among the several States, and with the Indian Tribes;

regulation of commerce

To establish an uniform Rule of Naturalization, and uniform Laws on the subject of Bankruptcies throughout the United States;

naturalization; bankruptcies

To coin Money, regulate the Value thereof, and of foreign Coin, and fix the Standard of Weights and Measures;

coinage of money; weights and measures

To provide for the Punishment of counterfeiting the Securities and current Coin of the United States;

punishing counterfeiting

To establish Post Offices and post Roads;

post office

To promote the Progress of Science and useful Arts, by securing for limited Times to Authors and Inventors the exclusive Right to their respective Writings and Discoveries;

copyrights and patents

To constitute Tribunals inferior to the supreme Court;

establishing courts

To define and punish Piracies and Felonies committed on the high Seas, and Offenses against the Law of Nations;

punishing piracy

To declare War, grant Letters of Marque and Reprisal, and make Rules concerning Captures on Land and Water;

declaring war

To raise and support Armies, but no Appropriation of Money to that Use shall be for a longer Term than two Years;

raising armies and a navy

To provide and maintain a Navy; To make Rules for the Government and Regulation of the land and naval Forces;

To provide for calling forth the Militia to execute the Laws of the Union, suppress Insurrection and repel Invasions;

calling up and regulating the militia

To provide for organizing, arming, and disciplining the Militia, and for governing such Part of them as may be employed in the Service of the United States, reserving to the States respectively, the Appointment of the Officers, and the Authority of training the Militia according to the discipline prescribed by Congress;

To exercise exclusive Legislation in all Cases whatsoever, over such District (not exceeding ten Miles square) as may, by Cession of particular States, and the acceptance of Congress, become the Seat of the Government of the United States, and to exercise like Authority over all Places purchased by the Consent of the Legislature of the State in which the Same shall be, for the Erection of Forts, Magazines, Arsenals, dock-Yards, and other needful Buildings;—And

government of the District of Columbia

To make all Laws which shall be necessary and proper for carrying into Execution the foregoing Powers, and all other Powers vested by this Constitution in the Government of the United States, or in any Department or Officer thereof.

implied powers clause

SECTION 9. The Migration or Importation of such Persons as any of the States now existing shall think proper to admit, shall not be prohibited by the Congress prior to the Year one thousand eight hundred and eight, but a tax or duty may be imposed on such Importation, not exceeding ten dollars for each Person.

Restrictions on powers of Congress
importation of slaves

The privilege of the Writ of Habeas Corpus shall not be suspended, unless when in Cases of Rebellion or Invasion the public Safety may require it.

habeas corpus

No Bill of Attainder or ex post facto Law shall be passed.

no bill of attainder

No capitation, or other direct, Tax shall be laid, unless in Proportion to the Census or Enumeration herein before directed to be taken.*

apportionment of direct taxes

No Tax or Duty shall be laid on Articles exported from any State.

no export taxes

No preference shall be given by any Regulation of Commerce or Revenue to the Ports of one State over those of another: nor shall Vessels bound to, or from, one State, be obliged to enter, clear, or pay Duties in another.

free trade among states

---

*But see the Sixteenth Amendment.

No Money shall be drawn from the Treasury, but in Consequence of Appropriations made by Law; and a regular Statement and Account of the Receipts and Expenditures of all public Money shall be published from time to time.

appropriation of money

No Title of Nobility shall be granted by the United States: And no Person holding any Office of Profit or Trust under them, shall, without the Consent of the Congress, accept of any present, Emolument, Office, or Title, of any kind whatever, from any King, Prince, or foreign State.

prohibition of titles of nobility

SECTION **10**.   No State shall enter into any Treaty, or Confederation; grant Letters of Marque and Reprisal; coin Money; emit Bills of Credit; make any Thing but gold and silver Coin a Tender in Payment of Debts; pass any Bill of Attainder, ex post facto Law, or Law impairing the Obligation of Contracts, or grant any Title of Nobility.

Restrictions on powers of the states

contract clause

No State shall, without the Consent of the Congress, lay any Imposts or Duties on Imports or Exports, except what may be absolutely necessary for executing its inspection Laws; and the net Produce of all Duties and Imposts, laid by any State on Imports or Exports, shall be for the Use of the Treasury of the United States: and all such Laws shall be subject to the Revision and Controul of the Congress.

prohibition of state imposts or duties

No State shall, without the Consent of Congress, lay any duty of Tonnage, keep Troops, or Ships of War in time of Peace, enter into any Agreement or Compact with another State, or with a foreign Power, or engage in War, unless actually invaded, or in such imminent Danger as will not admit of delay.

prohibition of state armies

ARTICLE II

THE EXECUTIVE

SECTION **1**.   The executive Power shall be vested in a President of the United States of America. He shall hold his Office during the Term of four Years, and, together with the Vice-President, chosen for the same Term, be elected, as follows.

Executive power

Each State shall appoint, in such Manner as the Legislature thereof may direct, a Number of Electors, equal to the whole Number of Senators and Representatives to which the State may be entitled in the Congress: but no Senator or Representative, or Person holding an Office of Trust or Profit under the United States, shall be appointed an Elector.

[The Electors shall meet in their respective States, and vote by Ballot for two persons, of whom one at least shall not be an Inhabitant of the same State with themselves. And they shall make a List of all the Persons voted for, and of the Number of Votes for each; which List they shall sign and certify, and transmit sealed to the Seat of the Government of the United States, directed to the President of the Senate. The President of the Senate shall, in the Presence of the Senate and House of Representatives, open all the Certificates, and the Votes shall then be counted. The Person having the greatest Number of Votes shall be the President, if such Number be a Majority of the whole Number of Electors appointed; and if there be more than one who have such Majority, and have an equal Number of Votes, then the House of Representatives shall immediately chuse by Ballot one of them for President; and if no Person have a Majority, then from the five highest on the List the said House shall in like Manner chuse the President. But in chusing the President, the Votes shall be taken by States, the Representation from each State having one Vote; a quorum for this Purpose shall consist of a Member or Members from two thirds of the States, and a Majority of all the States shall be necessary to a Choice. In every Case, after the Choice of the President, the Person having the

Electors

greatest Number of Votes of the Electors shall be the Vice President. But if there should remain two or more who have equal Votes, the Senate shall chuse from them by Ballot the Vice-President.]*

  The Congress may determine the Time of chusing the Electors, and the Day on which they shall give their Votes; which Day shall be the same throughout the United States.
Time of choosing electors

  No person except a natural born Citizen, or a Citizen of the United States, at the time of the Adoption of this Constitution, shall be eligible to the Office of President; neither shall any Person be eligible to that Office who shall not have attained to the Age of thirty-five Years, and been fourteen Years a Resident within the United States.
Qualifications for president

  [In Case of the Removal of the President from Office, or of his Death, Resignation, or Inability to discharge the Powers and Duties of the said Office, the same shall devolve on the Vice President, and the Congress may by Law provide for the Case of Removal, Death, Resignation or Inability, both of the President and Vice President, declaring what Officer shall then act as President, and such Officer shall act accordingly, until the Disability be removed, or a President shall be elected.]†
Presidential seccession

  The President shall, at stated Times, receive for his Services, a Compensation, which shall neither be encreased nor diminished during the Period for which he shall have been elected, and he shall not receive within that Period any other Emolument from the United States, or any of them.
Presidential compensation

  Before he enter on the Execution of his Office, he shall take the following Oath or Affirmation:—"I do solemnly swear (or affirm) that I will faithfully execute the Office of President of the United States, and will to the best of my Ability, preserve, protect and defend the Constitution of the United States."
Presidential oath of office

SECTION 2. The President shall be Commander in Chief of the Army and Navy of the United States, and of the Militia of the several States, when called into the actual Service of the United States; he may require the Opinion in writing, of the principal Officer in each of the executive Departments, upon any subject relating to the Duties of their respective Offices, and he shall have Power to Grant Reprieves and Pardons for Offenses against the United States, except in Cases of Impeachment.
Powers of president
commander-in-chief

chief administrator

pardons

  He shall have Power, by and with the Advice and Consent of the Senate, to make Treaties, provided two-thirds of the Senators present concur; and he shall nominate, and by and with the Advice and Consent of the Senate, shall appoint Ambassadors, other public Ministers and Consuls, Judges of the supreme Court, and all other Officers of the United States, whose Appointments are not herein otherwise provided for, and which shall be established by Law: but the Congress may by Law vest the Appointment of such inferior Officers, as they think proper, in the President alone, in the Courts of Law, or in the Heads of Departments.
treaties

appointments

  The President shall have Power to fill up all Vacancies that may happen during the Recess of the Senate, by granting Commissions which shall expire at the End of the next Session.
filling vacancies

SECTION 3. He shall from time to time give to the Congress Information of the State of the Union, and recommend to their Consideration such Measures
State of the Union message

---

*Superseded by the Twelfth Amendment.

†This clause has been modified by the Twenty-fifth Amendment.

as he shall judge necessary and expedient; he may, on extraordinary Occasions, convene both Houses, or either of them, and in Case of Disagreement between them, with Respect to the Time of Adjournment, he may adjourn them to such Time as he shall think proper; he shall receive Ambassadors and other public Ministers; he shall take Care that the Laws be faithfully executed, and shall Commission all the Officers of the United States.

Convening and adjourning Congress

Receiving ambassadors
Chief executive clause

SECTION 4. The President, Vice President and all civil Officers of the United States, shall be removed from Office on Impeachment for, and Conviction of, Treason, Bribery, or other high Crimes and Misdemeanors.

Impeachment

ARTICLE III

THE JUDICIARY

SECTION 1. The judicial Power of the United States, shall be vested in one supreme Court, and in such inferior Courts as the Congress may from time to time ordain and establish. The Judges, both of the supreme and inferior Courts, shall hold their Offices during good Behaviour, and shall, at stated Times, receive for their Services, a Compensation, which shall not be diminished during their Continuance in Office.

Supreme Court; lower federal courts

Tenure of judges
Guaranteed compensation

SECTION 2. The judicial Power shall extend to all Cases, in Law and Equity, arising under this Constitution, the Laws of the United States, and Treaties made, or which shall be made, under their Authority;—to all Cases affecting Ambassadors, other public Ministers and Consuls;—to all Cases of admiralty and maritime Jurisdiction;—to Controversies to which the United States shall be a Party;—to Controversies between two or more States;—between a State and Citizens of another State;*—between Citizens of different States;—between Citizens of the same State claiming Lands under Grants of different States, and between a State, or the Citizens thereof, and foreign States, Citizens or Subjects.

Jurisdiction of courts

In all Cases affecting Ambassadors, other public Ministers and Consuls, and those in which a State shall be Party, the supreme Court shall have original Jurisdiction. In all the other Cases before mentioned, the supreme Court shall have appellate Jurisdiction, both as to Law and Fact, with such Exceptions, and under such Regulations as the Congress shall make.

original jurisdiction of the Supreme Court

appellate jurisdiction

The trial of all Crimes, except in Cases of Impeachment, shall be by Jury; and such Trial shall be held in the State where the said Crimes shall have been committed; but when not committed within any State, the Trial shall be at such Place or Places as the Congress may by Law have directed.

Jury trial

SECTION 3. Treason against the United States, shall consist only in levying War against them, or in adhering to their Enemies, giving them Aid and Comfort. No Person shall be convicted of Treason unless on the Testimony of two Witnesses to the same overt Act, or on Confession in open Court.

Definition of treason

The Congress shall have Power to declare the Punishment of Treason, but no Attainder of Treason shall work Corruption of Blood, or Forfeiture except during the Life of the Person attainted.

Punishment for treason

ARTICLE IV

THE STATES

SECTION 1. Full Faith and Credit shall be given in each State to the public Acts, Records, and judicial Proceedings of every other State. And the Con-

Full faith and credit

---

*Restricted by the Eleventh Amendment.

gress may by general Laws prescribe the Manner in which such Acts, Records and Proceedings shall be proved, and the Effect thereof.

SECTION **2**.   The Citizens of each State shall be entitled to all Privileges and Immunities of Citizens in the several States.

Privileges and immunities

A Person charged in any State with Treason, Felony, or other Crime, who shall flee from Justice, and be found in another State, shall on demand of the executive Authority of the State from which he fled, be delivered up, to be removed to the State having Jurisdiction of the Crime.

Extradition

[No Person held to Service or Labour in one State, under the Laws thereof, escaping into another, shall, in Consequence of any Law or Regulation therein, be discharged from such Service or Labour, but shall be delivered up on Claim of the Party to whom such Service or Labour may be due.]*

Return of fugitive slaves

SECTION **3**.   New States may be admitted by the Congress into this Union; but no new State shall be formed or erected within the Jurisdiction of any other State; nor any State be formed by the Junction of two or more States, or parts of States, without the Consent of the Legislatures of the States concerned as well as of the Congress.

Admission of new states

The Congress shall have Power to dispose of and make all needful Rules and Regulations respecting the Territory or other Property belonging to the United States; and nothing in this Constitution shall be so construed as to Prejudice any Claims of the United States, or of any particular State.

Regulation of federal territory and property

SECTION **4**.   The United States shall guarantee to every State in this Union a Republican Form of Government, and shall protect each of them against Invasion; and on Application of the Legislature, or of the Executive (when the Legislature cannot be convened) against domestic Violence.

Guaranty clause

ARTICLE V

AMENDMENTS

The Congress, whenever two-thirds of both Houses shall deem it necessary, shall propose Amendments to this Constitution, or, on the Application of the Legislatures of two thirds of the several States, shall call a Convention for proposing Amendments, which, in either Case, shall be valid to all Intents and Purposes, as part of this Constitution, when ratified by the Legislatures of three-fourths of the several States, or by Conventions in three-fourths thereof, as the one or the other Mode of Ratification may be proposed by the Congress: Provided that no Amendment which may be made prior to the Year One thousand eight hundred and eight shall in any Manner affect the first and fourth Clauses in the Ninth Section of the first Article; and that no State, without its Consent, shall be deprived of its equal Suffrage in the Senate.

Proposal of amendments

Ratification of amendments

ARTICLE VI

EFFECTS OF CONSTITUTION

All Debts contracted and Engagements entered into, before the Adoption of this Constitution, shall be as valid against the United States under this Constitution, as under the Confederation.

National debts

This Constitution, and the Laws of the United States which shall be made in Pursuance thereof; and all Treaties made, or which shall be made, under the Authority of the United States, shall be the supreme Law of the Land;

Supremacy clause

---

*Superseded by the Twelfth Amendment.

and the Judges in every State shall be bound thereby, any Thing in the Constitution or Laws of any State to the Contrary notwithstanding.

 The Senators and Representatives before mentioned, and the Members of the several State Legislatures, and all executive and judicial Officers, both of the United States and of the several States, shall be bound by Oath or Affirmation, to support this Constitution; but no religious Test shall ever be required as a Qualification to any Office or public Trust under the United States.

Oaths of office

No religious test for office

ARTICLE VII

RATIFICATION

 The Ratification of the Conventions of nine States shall be sufficient for the Establishment of this Constitution between the States so ratifying the Same.

Done in Convention by the Unanimous Consent of the States present the Seventeenth Day of September in the Year of our Lord one thousand seven hundred and Eighty seven and of the Independence of the United States of America the Twelfth. In Witness whereof We have hereunto subscribed our Names.

Go WASHINGTON
Presidt and deputy from Virginia

New Hampshire.

John Langdon
Nicholas Gilman

Connecticut.

Wm Saml Johnson
Roger Sherman

Massachusetts.

Nathaniel Gorham
Rufus King

New York.

Alexander Hamilton

New Jersey.

Wil: Livingston
David Brearley
Wm Paterson
Jona: Dayton

Maryland.

James McHenry
Danl Carroll
Dan: of St Thos Jenifer

Pennsylvania.

B Franklin
Robt. Morris
Thos. FitzSimons
James Wilson
Thomas Mifflin
Geo. Clymer
Jared Ingersoll
Gouv Morris

Virginia.

John Blair
James Madison Jr.

North Carolina.

Wm Blount
Hu Williamson
Richd Dobbs Spaight

Delaware.

Geo: Read
John Dickinson
Jaco: Broom
Gunning Bedford jun
Richard Bassett

South Carolina.

J. Rutledge
Charles Pinckney
Charles Cotesworth
 Pinckney
Pierce Butler

Georgia.
William Few
Abr Baldwin

Attest:

william jackson, *Secretary.*

Articles in Addition To, and Amendment Of, the Constitution of the United States of America, Proposed by Congress, and Ratified by the Legislatures of the Several States, Pursuant to the Fifth Article of the Original Constitution.*

AMENDMENT I. (1791)†

Congress shall make no law respecting an establishment of religion, or prohibiting the free exercise thereof; or abridging the freedom of speech, or of the press; or the right of the people peaceably to assemble, and to petition the Government for a redress of grievances.

Freedoms of expression

AMENDMENT II. (1791)

A well regulated Militia, being necessary to the security of a free State, the right of the people to keep and bear Arms, shall not be infringed.

Right to bear arms

AMENDMENT III. (1791)

No Soldier shall, in time of peace, be quartered in any house, without the consent of the Owner, nor in time of war, but in a manner to be prescribed by law.

Quartering of soldiers

AMENDMENT IV. (1791)

The right of the people to be secure in their persons, houses, papers, and effects, against unreasonable searches and seizures, shall not be violated, and no Warrants shall issue, but upon probable cause, supported by Oath or affirmation, and particularly describing the place to be searched, and the persons or things to be seized.

No unreasonable search and seizure

AMENDMENT V. (1791)

No person shall be held to answer for a capital, or otherwise infamous crime, unless on a presentment or indictment of a Grand Jury, except in cases arising in the land or naval forces, or in the Militia, when in actual service in time of War or public danger; nor shall any person be subject for the same offence to be twice put in jeopardy of life or limb; nor shall be compelled in any criminal case to be a witness against himself, nor be deprived of life, liberty, or property, without due process of law; nor shall private property be taken for public use, without just compensation.

Grand Jury indictment; double jeopardy; self-incrimination; due process of law; just compensation

---

*Amendment Twenty-one was not ratified by state legislatures, but by state conventions summoned by Congress.

†The dates in parentheses are the dates when the amendments were ratified.

AMENDMENT VI. (1791)

In all criminal prosecutions, the accused shall enjoy the right to a speedy and public trial, by an impartial jury of the State and district wherein the crime shall have been committed, which district shall have been previously ascertained by law, and to be informed of the nature and cause of the accusation; to be confronted with the witnesses against him; to have compulsory process for obtaining witnesses in his favor, and to have the Assistance of Counsel for his defence.

Rights of accused during trial

AMENDMENT VII. (1791)

In suits at common law, where the value in controversy shall exceed twenty dollars, the right of trial by jury shall be preserved, and no fact tried by a jury, shall be otherwise reexamined in any Court of the United States, than according to the Rules of the common law.

Jury trial in civil cases

AMENDMENT VIII. (1791)

Excessive bail shall not be required, nor excessive fines imposed, nor cruel and unusual punishments inflicted.

No excessive bails and fines; no cruel and unusual punishments

AMENDMENT IX. (1791)

The enumeration in the Constitution, of certain rights, shall not be construed to deny or disparage others retained by the people.

Effect of enumerated rights

AMENDMENT X. (1791)

The powers not delegated to the United States by the Constitution, nor prohibited by it to the States, are reserved to the States respectively, or to the people.

Reserved powers

AMENDMENT XI. (1795)

The Judicial power of the United States shall not be construed to extend to any suit in law or equity, commenced or prosecuted against one of the United States by Citizens of another State, or by Citizens or Subjects of any Foreign State.

Suits against states

AMENDMENT XII. (1804)

The Electors shall meet in their respective states and vote by ballot for President and Vice-President, one of whom, at least, shall not be an inhabitant of the same state with themselves; they shall name in their ballots the person voted for as President, and in distinct ballots the person voted for as Vice-President, and they shall make distinct lists of all persons voted for as President, and of all persons voted for as Vice-President, and of the number of votes for each, which lists they shall sign and certify, and transmit sealed to the seat of the government of the United States, directed to the President of the Senate;— The President of the Senate shall, in presence of the Senate and House of Representatives, open all the certificates and the votes shall then be counted;— The person having the greatest number of votes for President, shall be the President, if such number be a majority of the whole number of Electors ap-

Electoral vote for president and vice-president

pointed; and if no person have such majority, then from the persons having the highest numbers not exceeding three on the list of those voted for as President, the House of Representatives shall choose immediately, by ballot, the President. But in choosing the President, the votes shall be taken by states, the representation from each state having one vote; a quorum for this purpose shall consist of a member or members from two-thirds of the states, and a majority of all the states shall be necessary to a choice. [And if the House of Representatives shall not choose a President whenever the right of choice shall devolve upon them, before the fourth day of March next following, then the Vice-President shall act as President, as in the case of the death or other constitutional disability of the President.—]* The person having the greatest number of votes as Vice-President, shall be the Vice-President, if such number be a majority of the whole number of Electors appointed, and if no person have a majority, then from the two highest numbers on the list, the Senate shall choose the Vice-President; a quorum for the purpose shall consist of two-thirds of the whole number of Senators, and a majority of the whole number shall be necessary to a choice. But no person constitutionally ineligible to the office of President shall be eligible to that of Vice-President of the United States.

AMENDMENT XIII. (1865)

SECTION 1.   Neither slavery nor involuntary servitude, except as a punishment for crime whereof the party shall have been duly convicted, shall exist within the United States, or any place subject to their jurisdiction.

Abolition of slavery

SECTION 2.   Congress shall have the power to enforce this article by appropriate legislation.

AMENDMENT XIV. (1868)

SECTION 1.   All persons born or naturalized in the United States, and subject to the jurisdiction thereof, are citizens of the United States and of the State wherein they reside. No State shall make or enforce any law which shall abridge the privileges or immunities of citizens of the United States; nor shall any State deprive any person of life, liberty, or property, without due process of law; nor deny any person within its jurisdiction the equal protection of the laws.

Citizenship for former slaves

Due process and equal protection requirements extended to states

SECTION 2.   Representatives shall be apportioned among the several States according to their respective numbers, counting the whole number of persons in each State, excluding Indians not taxed. But when the right to vote at any election for the choice of electors for President and Vice-President of the United States, Representatives in Congress, the Executive and Judicial officers of a State, or the members of the Legislature thereof, is denied to any of the male inhabitants of such State, being twenty-one years of age, and citizens of the United States, or in any way abridged, except for participation in rebellion, or other crime, the basis of representation therein shall be reduced in the proportion which the number of such male citizens shall bear to the whole number of male citizens twenty-one years of age in such State.

Apportionment of representatives

---

*Superseded by Section 3 of the Twentieth Amendment.

SECTION 3. No person shall be a Senator or Representative in Congress, or elector of President and Vice-President, or hold any office, civil or military, under the United States, or under any State, who, having previously taken an oath, as a member of Congress, or as an officer of the United States, or as a member of any State legislature, or as an executive or judicial officer of any State, to support the Constitution of the United States, shall have engaged in insurrection or rebellion against the same, or given aid or comfort to the enemies thereof. But Congress may by a vote of two-thirds of each House, remove such disability.

Former rebels prohibited from holding public office

SECTION 4. The validity of public debt of the United States, authorized by law, including debts incurred for payment of pensions and bounties for services in suppressing insurrection or rebellion, shall not be questioned. But neither the United States nor any State shall assume or pay any debt or obligation incurred in aid of insurrection or rebellion against the United States, or any claim for the loss or emancipation of any slave; but all such debts, obligations and claims shall be held illegal and void.

Rebel debts repudiated

SECTION 5. The Congress shall have power to enforce, by appropriate legislation, the provisions of this article.

AMENDMENT XV. (1870)

SECTION 1. The right of citizens of the United States to vote shall not be denied or abridged by the United States or by any State on account of race, color, or previous condition of servitude

Blacks given right to vote

SECTION 2. The Congress shall have power to enforce this article by appropriate legislation.

AMENDMENT XVI. (1913)

The Congress shall have power to lay and collect taxes on incomes, from whatever source derived, without apportionment among the several States, and without regard to any census or enumeration.

Congressional authority to levy income taxes

AMENDMENT XVII. (1913)

The Senate of the United States shall be composed of two Senators from each State, elected by the people thereof, for six years; and each Senator shall have one vote. The electors in each State shall have the qualifications requisite for electors of the most numerous branch of the State legislatures.

When vacancies happen in the representation of any State in the Senate, the executive authority of such State shall issue writs of election to fill such vacancies: *Provided,* That the legislature of any State may empower the executive thereof to make temporary appointments until the people fill the vacancies by election as the legislature may direct.

This amendment shall not be so construed as to affect the election or term of any Senator chosen before it becomes valid as part of the Constitution.

Direct popular election of senators

AMENDMENT XVIII. (1919)

[**SECTION 1.** After one year from the ratification of this article the manufacture, sale, or transportation of intoxicating liquors within, the importation thereof

Prohibition of alcoholic beverages

into, or the exportation thereof from the United States and all territory subject to the jurisdiction thereof for beverage purposes is hereby prohibited.

[SECTION 2.   The Congress and the several States shall have concurrent power to enforce this article by appropriate legislation.

[SECTION 3.   This article shall be inoperative unless it shall have been ratified as an amendment to the Constitution by the legislatures of the several States, as provided in the Constitution, within seven years from the date of the submission hereof to the States by the Congress.]*

AMENDMENT XIX. (1920)

The right of citizens of the United States to vote shall not be denied or abridged by the United States or by any State on account of sex.

Congress shall have power to enforce this article by appropriate legislation.

Women given right to vote

AMENDMENT XX. (1933)

SECTION 1.   The terms of the President and Vice President shall end at noon on the 20th day of January, and the terms of Senators and Representatives at noon on the 3d day of January, of the years in which such terms would have ended if this article had not been ratified; and the terms of their successors shall then begin.

Presidential term begins January 20

SECTION 2.   The Congress shall assemble at least once in every year, and such meeting shall begin at noon on the 3d day of January, unless they shall by law appoint a different day.

Congress convenes January 3

SECTION 3.   If, at the time fixed for the beginning of the term of the President, the President elect shall have died, the Vice President elect shall become President. If a President shall not have been chosen before the time fixed for the beginning of his term, or if the President elect shall have failed to qualify, then the Vice President elect shall act as President until a President shall have qualified; and the Congress may by law provide for the case wherein neither a President elect nor a Vice President elect shall have qualified, declaring who shall then act as President, or the manner in which one who is to act shall be selected, and such person shall act accordingly until a President or Vice President shall have qualified.

Emergency presidential succession

SECTION 4.   The Congress may by law provide for the case of the death of any of the persons from whom the House of Representatives may choose a President whenever the right of choice shall have devolved upon them, and for the case of the death of any of the persons from whom the Senate may choose a Vice President whenever the right of choice shall have devolved upon them.

SECTION 5.   Sections 1 and 2 shall take effect on the 15th day of October following the ratification of this article.

---

*Repealed by Section 1 of the Twenty-first Amendment.

SECTION 6. This article shall be inoperative unless it shall have been ratified as an amendment to the Constitution by the legislatures of three-fourths of the several States within seven years from the date of its submission.

AMENDMENT XXI. (1933)

SECTION 1. The eighteenth article of amendment to the Constitution of the United States is hereby repealed.

Prohibition repealed

SECTION 2. The transportation or importation into any State, Territory, or possession of the United States for delivery or use therein of intoxicating liquors, in violation of the laws thereof, is hereby prohibited.

SECTION 3. This article shall be inoperative unless it shall have been ratified as an amendment to the Constitution by conventions in the several States, as provided in the Constitution, within seven years from the date of the submission hereof to the States by the Congress.

AMENDMENT XXII. (1951)

SECTION 1. No person shall be elected to the office of the President more than twice, and no person who has held the office of President, or acted as President, for more than two years of a term to which some other person was elected President shall be elected to the office of the President more than once. But this Article shall not apply to any person holding the office of President when this Article was proposed by the Congress, and shall not prevent any person who may be holding the office of President, or acting as President, during the term within which this Article becomes operative from holding the office of President or acting as President during the remainder of such term.

President may serve only two terms

SECTION 2. This article shall be inoperative unless it shall have been ratified as an amendment to the Constitution by the legislatures of three-fourths of the several States within seven years from the date of its submission to the States by the Congress.

AMENDMENT XXIII. (1961)

SECTION 1. The District constituting the seat of Government of the United States shall appoint in such manner as the Congress may direct:

A number of electors of the President and Vice President equal to the whole number of Senators and Representatives in Congress to which the District would be entitled if it were a State, but in no event more than the least populous State; they shall be in addition to those appointed by the States, but they shall be considered, for the purposes of the election of President and Vice President, to be electors appointed by a State; and they shall meet in the District and perform such duties as provided by the twelfth article of amendment.

District of Columbia electors

SECTION 2. The Congress shall have power to enforce this article by appropriate legislation.

AMENDMENT XXIV. (1964)

SECTION 1.   The right of citizens of the United States to vote in any primary or other election for President or Vice President, for electors for President or Vice President, or for Senator or Representative in Congress, shall not be denied or abridged by the United States or any State by reason of failure to pay any poll tax or other tax.

Poll taxes prohibited

SECTION 2.   The Congress shall have power to enforce this article by appropriate legislation.

AMENDMENT XXV. (1967)

Presidential succession

SECTION 1.   In case of the removal of the President from office or of his death or resignation, the Vice President shall become President.

removal, death, or resignation of president

SECTION 2.   Whenever there is a vacancy in the office of the Vice President, the President shall nominate a Vice President who shall take office upon confirmation by a majority vote of both Houses of Congress.

vacancy in vice-presidency

SECTION 3.   Whenever the President transmits to the President pro tempore of the Senate and the Speaker of the House of Representatives his written declaration that he is unable to discharge the powers and duties of his office, and until he transmits to them a written declaration to the contrary, such powers and duties shall be discharged by the Vice President as Acting President.

presidential disability

SECTION 4.   When the Vice President and a majority of either the principal officers of the executive departments or of such other body as Congress may by law provide, transmit to the President pro tempore of the Senate and the Speaker of the House of Representatives their written declaration that the President is unable to discharge the powers and duties of his office, the Vice President shall immediately assume the powers and duties of the office as Acting President.
    Thereafter, when the President transmits to the President pro tempore of the Senate and the Speaker of the House of Representatives his written declaration that no inability exists, he shall resume the powers and duties of his office unless the Vice President and a majority of either the principal officers of the executive department or of such other body as Congress may by law provide, transmit within four days to the President pro tempore of the Senate and the Speaker of the House of Representatives their written declaration that the President is unable to discharge the powers and duties of his office. Thereupon Congress shall decide the issue, assembling within forty-eight hours for that purpose if not in session. If the Congress, within twenty-one days after receipt of the latter written declaration, or, if Congress is not in session, within twenty-one days after Congress is required to assemble, determines by two-thirds vote of both Houses that the President is unable to discharge the powers and duties of his office, the Vice President shall continue to discharge the same as Acting President; otherwise, the President shall resume the powers and duties of his office.

independent declaration of presidential disability

AMENDMENT XXVI. (1971)

SECTION **1**. The right of citizens of the United States, who are eighteen years of age or older, to vote shall not be denied or abridged by the United States or any state on account of age.

Voting age lowered to 18

SECTION **2**. The Congress shall have the power to enforce this article by appropriate legislation.

The Student Researcher

The Student Researcher directs you to both primary and secondary sources for further information about the facets of America's political system covered in the text. You will find the Researcher particularly useful in writing papers as well as in expanding your knowledge of American government.

Reference and government documents sections of libraries contain primary reference materials as well as some of the more important secondary sources, such as the invaluable Congressional Quarterly reports and guidebooks. The books about American government listed as secondary sources are available not only in most libraries, but also in bookstores, where many can be purchased in paperback.

The Ideological Foundations: Philosophies of Constitutional Democracy

PRIMARY SOURCES

The great philosophical works that provided the theoretical underpinnings of America's political system, John Locke's second treatise *On Civil Government** (1690) and Baron de Montesquieu's *Spirit of the Laws** (1721), are available in many editions. The classic work of American political theory is *The Federalist* (1788), a collection of 85 essays by Alexander Hamilton, James Madison, and John Jay, which explained and urged the adoption of the new Constitution. Clinton Rossiter, ed., *The Federalist Papers* (New York: New American Library, Mentor Books, 1961),* is the best edition; it contains an excellent introduction and an invaluable index and appendix, which cross reference ideas and the provisions of the Constitution to *The Federalist*.

Alexis de Tocqueville's *Democracy in America* (1835) published originally in French, is available in many English translations. Phillips Bradley's edition (New York: Knopf, 1945) is a standard version. De Tocqueville's work is a fascinating view of America's political system in the early nineteenth century from a foreign perspective.

SECONDARY SOURCES

Early American political thought is conveniently summarized in Clinton Rossiter, *Seedtime of the Republic* (New York: Harcourt, Brace and World, 1955). Louis Hartz, *The Liberal Tradition in America* (New York: Harcourt, Brace, 1955),* emphasizes the uniqueness of the American experience, particularly the lack of a feudal past, and how this background influenced political ideas. Edward S. Corwin, *The "Higher Law" Background of American Constitutional Law* (Chicago: University of Chicago Press, 1953),* describes in detail the idea that a "higher law" or natural law should govern relationships among citizens, which was so important in colonial and revolutionary America. Garry Wills provocatively examines the origins and meaning of the Declaration of Independence in *Inventing America* (Garden City, N.Y.: Doubleday, 1978).*

The Constitutional Framework

PRIMARY SOURCES

Max Farrand, *The Records of the Federal Convention of 1787*, rev. ed., 4 vols. (New Haven, Conn.: Yale University Press, 1966),* includes James Madison's notes of the debates of the Federal Convention of 1787 as well as other accounts of the convention. Its comprehensive index pinpoints convention discussions of every aspect of the Constitution. The intentions of the Framers are most lucidly set forth in *The Federalist*.*

*Available in paperback.

SECONDARY SOURCES

Charles Warren, *The Making of the Constitution* (Cambridge, Mass.: Harvard University Press, 1947), is a lively and comprehensive account of the convention proceedings, and the political and social environment of the time. John P. Roche, "The Founding Fathers: A Reform Caucus in Action," *American Political Science Review*, Col. 61 (December, 1961), pp. 799–816, describes the politics of the convention. R. A. Rutland, *The Ordeal of the Constitution: The Anti-Federalists and the Ratification Struggle of 1787–1788* (Norman: University of Oklahoma Press, 1966), examines the ratification campaign.

The anticipation and celebration of the bicentennial of the Constitution in 1987 resulted in a number of volumes that sought to shed new light on the origins and development of the American system of government. Among the most interesting are Robert A. Goldwin and William A. Schambra, eds., *How Democratic Is the Constitution?* (Washington, D.C.: American Enterprise Institute, 1980);* Goldwin and Schambra, eds., *How Capitalist Is the Constitution?* (Washington, D.C.: American Enterprise Institute, 1982);* Charles R. Kesler, ed., *Saving the Revolution: The Federalist Papers and the American Founding* (New York: Free Press, 1987); and Sarah Baumgartner Thurow, ed., *Constitutionalism in Perspective: The United States Constitution in the Twentieth Century* (Lanham, Md.: University Press of America, 1988).*

Civil Liberties and Civil Rights

PRIMARY SOURCES

Both constitutional and statutory law determine the civil liberties and rights of Americans. The Civil Rights Act of 1964 is particularly important, and can be found in the *United States Statutes at Large,* the compilation of all laws passed by Congress, published annually. The *United States Statutes* are usually available in the reference or government documents sections of libraries. Individual laws are cited by volume and page numbers. The Civil Rights Act is cited as 78 stat. 252 (1964), i.e., volume 78, page 252 of the *Statutes.*

The official texts of Supreme Court decisions are published annually, in the *United States Supreme Court Reports,* abbreviated simply as "U.S." in case citations. [A case cited as 438 U.S. 265 (1978) can be found in volume 438 of the *Reports,* beginning on page 265, for example.]

Information on discrimination and the status of minorities, women, and the elderly may be found in a number of government documents. *The Social and Economic Status of the Black Population in the United States* is an annual report on the income, education, family characteristics, housing, health care, employment, voting participation, and distribution of the black population. (Order from the U.S. Government Printing Office, Washington, D.C. 20402, under the title *Current Population Report,* Series P-23.) *Social Indicators of Equality for Minorities and Women* provides data on the employment, income, housing, and education of these groups. (Order from the Office of Information and Publications, Commission on Civil Rights, 1121 Vermont Ave., N.W., Washington, D.C. 20425.)

Annual reports of the Equal Employment Opportunity Commission and the Commission on Civil Rights are invaluable sources of information on discrimination in employment, housing, and other areas (Washington, D.C.: U.S. Government Printing Office). The status of the Hispanic population is analyzed in *Characteristics of Persons and Families of Mexican, Puerto Rican and Other Spanish Origin,* published by the U.S. Census Bureau under the title, *Current Population Reports,* Series P-20 (Washington, D.C.: U.S. Government Printing Office). For the position of the elderly see *The Age Discrimination Study* (Washington, D.C., Commission on Civil Rights) Whitcombe Washburn, *The American Indian and the United States: A Documentary History* (New York: Random House, 1973), is a four-volume study that includes the reports of the Commissions of Indian Affairs, congressional debates and laws, bureaucratic proclamations, and court decisions that have affected Indians. *Indian Courts and the Future* examines the civil rights of Indians on reservations (available from the Bureau of Indian Affairs, Judicial Services Officer, 1951 Constitution Avenue, N.W., Washington, D.C. 20425).

SECONDARY SOURCES

Henry J. Abraham, *Freedom and the Court,* 4th ed. (New York: Oxford University Press, 1982),* is the standard survey of key civil liberties and civil rights cases. Allan P. Sindler, *Bakke, De Funis, and Minority Admissions* (New York: Longman, 1978),* is a comprehensive analysis of the *Bakke* case and the use of racial quotas in affirmative action. For general coverage of the issue of obscenity and pornography see *Report of the Commission on Obscenity and Pornography* (New York: Bantam Books, 1970).* Earl Latham, *The Communist Controversy in Washington—From the New Deal to McCarthy* (Cambridge, Mass.: Harvard University Press, 1959), discusses the problem of subversive activities. Allan F. Westin, *Privacy and Freedom* (New York: Atheneum, 1967), is the classic work on privacy. Walter F. Murphy, *Wire Tapping on Trial* (New York: Random House, 1965),* examines the problem of wiretapping and constitutional rights. Abigail M. Thernstrom, *Whose Votes Count: Affirmative Action and Minority Voting Rights* (Cambridge: Harvard University Press, 1987), provides a thorough and provocative examination of the history of the 1965 Voting Rights Act.*

Case studies of interest include Felix Frankfurter, *The Case of Sacco and Vanzetti* (Boston: Little, Brown, 1962)*; Jason Epstein, *The Great Conspiracy Trial* (New York: Random House, 1970),* on the trial of the "Chicago Seven" during the 1960s; Allan F. Westin and Barry Mahoney, *The Trial of Martin Luther King* (New York: Crowell, 1974).

The Structure of Federalism

PRIMARY SOURCES

The Book of the States, published biennially, provides up-to-date information on the structure, operation, and financing of state governments (available from the Council of State Governments, Iron Works Pike, Lexington, Ky. 40511). Every five years the Census Bureau of the U.S. Department of Commerce issues the *Census of Governments,* which contains data on state and local government organizations and functions, public employment, and finances (Washington, D.C.: U.S. Government Printing Office). The Community Services Administration for the Executive Office of the President annually issues the *Geographical Distribution of the Federal Funds,* which gives statistics on federal outlays and the comparative demographics of the states.

SECONDARY SOURCES

William H. Riker, *Federalism: Origin, Operation, Significance* (Boston: Little, Brown, 1964),* is a classic work on the theory of federalism; Riker analyzes federalism from historical and comparative perspectives. Aaron Wildavsky, ed., *American Federalism in Perspective* (Boston: Little, Brown, 1967),* contains essays on various aspects of federalism by a number of authors. Richard H. Leach, *American Federalism* (New York: Norton, 1970),* discusses federalism in theory and analyzes intergovernmental relations, state and local governments, and problems of metropolitan government. *American Federalism: Toward a More Effective Partnership* (Washington, D.C.: Advisory Commission on Intergovernmental Rela-

tions, 1975), contains essays on all aspects of federalism by Daniel P. Moynihan, Daniel J. Elazar, Robert E. Merriam, Harlan Cleveland, and Edmund Muskie, among others. Daniel J. Elazar, *American Federalism: A View from the States,* 3rd ed. (New York: Harper & Row, 1984), gives a sympathetic analysis of the historical development and present character of American federalism.

Michael D. Reagan and John G. Sanzone, *The New Federalism* (New York: Oxford University Press, 1981); and Timothy Conlan, *New Federalism: Intergovernmental Reform from Nixon to Reagan* (Washington, D.C.: Brookings Institution, 1988),* look at important developments in federalism during the past two decades, including changes in grants-in-aid, revenue sharing, and block grants. Martha Derthick, *The Influence of Federal Grants* (Cambridge: Harvard University Press, 1970); George E. Hale and Marian Palley, *The Politics of Federal Grants* (Washington, D.C.: Congressional Quarterly, 1981);* and Paul Peterson, Barry Rabe, and Kenneth K. Wong, *When Federalism Works* (Washington, D.C.: Brookings Institution, 1986)* review the political aspects of intergovernmental relations.

Political Attitudes

PRIMARY SOURCES

George Gallup in Princeton, New Jersey, Louis Harris and Associates in New York, and Elmo Roper in Storrs, Connecticut, head three of the main American polling organizations. The Gallup and Harris surveys are available in report form in most university and college libraries. In addition, many universities and colleges are members of the University of Michigan's political consortium and receive the survey data gathered by the University's Center for Political Studies.

The Commerce Department's Bureau of the Census conducts surveys and collects data on social and economic activities, and population characteristics. The Bureau and its extensive library are located at Suitland and Silver Hills Rds., Suitland, Md. (mailing address: Washington, D.C. 20233).

SECONDARY SOURCES

Raymond E. Wolfinger and Steve J. Rosenstone, *Who Votes?* (New Haven, CT: Yale University Press, 1980);* and Frances Fox Piven and Richard Cloward, *Why Americans Don't Vote* (New York: Pantheon, 1988),* examine the effect of socioeconomic status, age, sex, and such factors as registration laws on voting and voter turnout. A classic early work in the field is V. O. Key, Jr., *Public Opinion and American Democracy* (New York: Knopf, 1961), which analyzed the 1950s surveys of the Center for Political Studies. See also Angus Campbell, Philip E. Converse, Warren Miller, and Donald Stokes, *The American Voter* (Chicago: University of Chicago Press, 1980; originally published in 1960),* which documents the importance of partisan loyalties as a referent for political attitudes and behavior. Norman H. Nie, Sidney Verba, and John R. Petrocik, *The Changing American Voter,* enlarged edition (Cambridge: Harvard University Press, 1979),* traces the important shifts in American voter attitudes since 1960. Seymour M. Lipset and William Schneider, *The Confidence Gap: Business, Labor, and the Government in the Public Mind,* revised edition (Baltimore: Johns Hopkins University Press, 1987),* reveals the declining support for major institutions in the United States during the past two decades. The American Enterprise Institute's journal, *Public Opinion,* publishes current survey data and analyzes the effects of public opinion on government.

American Political Parties

PRIMARY SOURCES

Guide to U.S. Elections (Washington, D.C.: Congressional Quarterly, 1975) is a rich source of historical data on the development of political parties. It includes listings of the political party affiliations of Congress and the president from 1789 to 1973, along with census data and immigrants by country.

Information on party organization, rules, procedures, positions, and financing may be obtained from a variety of sources. For questions about the Democratic party, contact the Democratic National Committee (1625 Massachusetts Avenue, N.W., Washington, D.C. 20036); the Democratic Conference (1411 K St., N.W., Washington, D.C. 20005), which represents liberal Democrats interested in party and primary reforms; the House Democratic Study Group (1422 Longworth House Office Bldg., Washington, D.C. 20515), a group of moderate and liberal Democrats that assists similarly minded colleagues in developing positions and conducting campaigns; the Women's National Democratic Club (1526 New Hampshire Ave., N.W., Washington, D.C. 20036), a political action committee that presents positions to party and congressional leaders on issues of particular concern to women; the Young Democratic Clubs of America (1625 Massachusetts Ave., N.W., Washington, D.C. 20036), a

federation of youth (ages 18–35) organizations in the Democratic party that encourages participation in party affairs and assists Democratic candidates.

Information on the Republican party may be obtained from the Republican National Committee (310 First St., S.E., Washington, D.C. 20003), and the College Republican National Committee (at the same address), which arranges lectures, debates, conferences, and conventions on college campuses; the Ripon Society (800 18th St., N.W., Washington, D.C. 20006), a moderate Republican group that publishes a newsletter and is interested in recruiting young people; the Young Republican's National Federation (310 First St., S.E., Washington, D.C. 20003), a federation of Republican youth organizations that recruits campaign workers for Republican candidates.

SECONDARY SOURCES

James MacGregor Burns, *The Deadlock of Democracy: Four-Party Politics in America* (Englewood Cliffs, N.J.: Prentice-Hall, 1963), is a valuable study of party history and politics; Burns argues that the Madisonian model of the separation of powers has been a major factor in preventing unified parties at the national level. William J. Crotty and Gary C. Jacobson, *American Parties in Decline* (Boston: Little, Brown, 1980), examines the thesis popular among political scientists that the influence of political parties has decreased. Henry Fairlie, *The Parties: Republicans and Democrats in This Century* (New York: Simon & Schuster/Pocket Books, 1978),* is a readable account of party politics in the twentieth century. Everett C. Ladd, Jr., *Where Have All the Voters Gone?* (New York: Norton, 1978),* discusses the growing fragmentation of political parties. Edwin O'Connor, *The Last Hurrah* (Boston: Little, Brown, 1956),* is an entertaining fictional account of an urban political boss.

Not all scholars agree that party decline is inevitable and irreversible. Among the works that offer an account of how the national Democratic and Republican parties have successfully adjusted to new political conditions are Cornelius Cotter, James L. Gibson, John F. Bibby, and Robert J. Huckshorn, *Party Organizations in American Politics* (New York: Praeger, 1984); Xandra Keyden and Eddie Mahe, Jr., *The Party Goes On* (New York: Basic Books, 1985);* Larry J. Sabato, *The Party's Just Begun* (Glenview, Ill.: Scott, Foresman, 1988);* and Paul Herrnson, *Party Campaigning in the 1980s* (Cambridge: Harvard University Press, 1988). Martin P. Wattenberg, *The Decline of American Political Parties, 1952–1984* (Cambridge: Harvard University Press,

1986),* suggests that the strengthening of parties organizationally at the national level has failed to regenerate partisan loyalty among the voting public.

Nominations, Campaigns, and Elections

PRIMARY SOURCES

Congressional Quarterly's *Guide to U.S. Elections* (see above) is a rich source of information on election results and party nominating conventions. A chronology of nominating conventions from 1831 to 1972 is given, along with key nominating convention ballots and a complete list of party nominees. Also included are electoral and popular vote returns in presidential elections, and primary vote returns as well. The gubernatorial, Senate, and House elections are also covered. Richard Scannon, ed., *American Votes*, published every two years by Congressional Quarterly, gives statistics on presidential, congressional, and gubernatorial elections, including the results of presidential primaries and maps of congressional districts.

Factual Campaign Information (Washington, D.C.: U.S. Government Printing Office), a compilation of constitutional and statutory provisions governing federal elections and a list of state primary elections by date, is issued three times a year by the U.S. Senate Library. The Federal Election Commission (1325 K St., N.W., Washington, D.C. 20463), publishes periodically *Federal Election Campaign Laws*, a compilation of all federal statutes governing campaigns. The Commission also issues an annual report reviewing campaign financing and the contributions of political action committees and other groups.

Kirk Porter and Donald Johnson, *National Party Platforms, 1840–1976* (Urbana: University of Illinois Press, 1978), is a two-volume compilation of the platforms of major and minor parties.

SECONDARY SOURCES

Many lively accounts of presidential elections have been written over the years. Theodore H. White's books, beginning with *The Making of the President, 1960* (New York: Atheneum, 1961) are the most notable, and were published after each presidential election through 1972. His books describe in colorful detail the presidential campaigns, from primaries through the general election. The phenomenal success of White's books spawned numerous progeny. In 1976 White decided to bypass his traditional account, but virtually every major political journalist who covered the campaign wrote a book about it. Jules Witcover, *Marathon: The Pur-*

suit of the Presidency, 1972–1976 (New York: Viking, 1977), is typical of the many excellent books on Carter's campaign. Journalist accounts of presidential campaigns were quite prevalent during the 1980s. Among the more interesting on the 1988 campaign are Jack W. Germond and Jules Witcover, *Whose Broad Stripes and Bright Stars* (New York: Warner Books, 1989); and Elizabeth Drew, *Election Journal* (New York: William Morrow, 1989). Gerald M. Pomper et al., *The Election of 1988* (Chatham, N.J.: Chatham House, 1989);* and Michael Nelson, ed., *The Elections of 1988* (Washington, D.C.: Congressional Quarterly, 1989),* give a more scholarly view of the contest. Classic accounts of presidential campaigns are Honores Thompson, *Fear and Loathing on the Campaign Trail* (New York: Quick Fox, 1973),* an account of the McGovern primary campaign in 1972; and Joe McGinniss, *The Selling of the President, 1968* (New York: Trident Press, 1969),* a lively account of the 1968 Nixon campaign.

Stephen J. Wayne, *The Road to the White House,* 3rd ed. (New York: St. Martin's, 1988), examines the electoral college system, campaign financing, the delegate selection process, and campaign strategies, tactics, and organizations. Conventions are the topic of Paul T. David et al., *The Politics of National Party Conventions* (Washington, D.C.: Brookings Institution, 1960),* and of Richard Reeves, *Convention* (New York: Harcourt Brace Jovanovich, 1977),* a journalist's view of the 1976 Democratic convention. Walter D. Burnham focuses on parties and elections in *Critical Elections and the Mainsprings of American Politics* (New York: Norton, 1970).* Nelson W. Polsby and Aaron Wildavsky, *Presidential Elections*, 7th ed. (New York: Scribner, 1988),* is an excellent general analysis of political strategies, structures, and problems of reform in the presidential election process.

Frank J. Sorouf, *Money in American Elections* (Glenview, Ill.: Scott, Foresman, 1988)* is an excellent source on campaign finance laws and practices. Two recent collections of essays by scholars and journalists provide comprehensive treatment of elections in the United States: Kay L. Schlozman, ed., *Elections in America* (New York: Allan and Unwin, 1987);* and A. James Reichley, ed., *Elections American Style* (Washington, D.C.: Brookings Institution, 1987).*

Interest Groups

PRIMARY SOURCES

Many government agencies, congressional committees, and private groups track the political activities of special interest groups. The Federal Election

Commission regulates and reports on direct and indirect campaign contributions made by interest groups. Each candidate must report all contributions and expenditures for both primary and general election campaigns, and the FEC's files on the candidates are public information. The Clerk of the House of Representatives (Office of Records and Registration, 1036 Longworth House Office Bldg., Washington, D.C. 20515), receives the reports of campaign receipts and expenditures of House candidates and committees, as well as the registration statements of all Washington lobbyists who must file reports giving the names of their employers, the legislation in which they are interested, and their expenditures. The reports are open to the public. The Secretary of the Senate (Office of Public Records, 623 Senate Annex, Washington, D.C. 20510) receives the corresponding reports and registrations for the Senate.

Common Cause's Campaign Finance Monitoring Project (2030 M St., N.W., Washington, D.C. 20036) tracks the expenditures of special interest groups and evaluates their importance in the legislative process. Its findings are published six times a year in the magazine *Common Cause*. The *Congressional Quarterly Weekly Report* and the *National Journal* are invaluable sources of information on interest group activities. Michael Barone's biennial publication, *The Almanac of America's Politics* (Washington, D.C.: Barone and Co., 1989), gives interest-group ratings of members of Congress.

SECONDARY SOURCES

David B. Truman, *The Governmental Process*, 2nd ed. (New York: Knopf, 1971),* is a classic work on interest groups first published in 1951. It is a modern version of Arthur F. Bentley's *The Process of Government* (Cambridge, Mass.: Harvard University Press, 1908). Theodore Lowi, *The End of Liberalism*, 2nd ed. (New York: Norton, 1979),* criticizes the premises of group theories presented in Truman and Bentley's works. Edgar Lane, *Lobbying and the Law* (Berkeley: University of California Press, 1964), is a valuable history of the legal regulation of lobbying that began at the state level in the nineteenth century.

There are numerous case studies of pressure group politics. Among the more interesting are Robert Engler, *The Politics of Oil* (Chicago: University of Chicago Press, 1961);* Oliver Garceau, *The Political Life of the American Medical Association* (Cambridge, Mass.: Harvard University Press, 1941); and Arthur Maass, *Muddy Waters* (Cambridge, Mass.: Harvard University Press, 1951), a classic study of the Army Corps of Engineers and its influence on

Congress. More recent case studies include David Howard Davis, *Energy Politics*, 2nd ed. (New York: St. Martin's, 1978);* A. Lee Fritschler, *Smoking and Politics*, 2nd ed. (Englewood Cliffs, N.J.: Prentice-Hall, 1975);* Erwin Krasnow and Lawrence Longley, *The Politics of Broadcast Regulation*, 2nd ed. (New York: St. Martin's, 1978);* Andrew McFarland, *Common Cause: Lobbying in the Public Interest* (Chatham, N.J.: Chatham House, 1984);* Martha Derthick and Paul Quirk, *The Politics of Deregulation* (Washington, D.C.: Brookings Institution, 1985);* Jeffrey Birnbaum and Alan S. Murray, *Showdown at Gucci Gulch* (New York: Random House, 1987);* and Richard A. Harris and Sidney M. Milkis, *The Politics of Regulatory Change: A Tale of Two Agencies* (New York: Oxford University Press, 1989). Kay Lehman Scholozman and John T. Tierney, *Organized Interests and American Democracy* (New York: Harper & Row, 1986);* and Jeffrey M. Berry, *The Interest Group Society*, 2nd ed. (Glenview, Ill.: Scott, Foresman, 1989),* provide useful overviews of recent developments in interest group politics in the United States.

Congress

PRIMARY SOURCES

The *Biographical Directory of the American Congress* (Washington, D.C.: U.S. Government Printing Office, 1971), provides biographies of all members of Congress from 1789 to 1971. It was compiled by the Joint Committee on Printing of Congress. Michael Barone, *The Almanac of American Politics* (Washington, D.C.: Barone and Co., 1989;* published biennially) includes biographies of current members of Congress, profiles of their districts, and "snapshots" of their congressional activities, including committee assignments and voting records. A similar almanac is also published every two years by Congressional Quarterly, under the title *Politics in America*.

The publications of Congressional Quarterly (1414 22nd St., N.W., Washington, D.C. 20037) are indispensable to students of Congress. The *Congressional Quarterly Weekly Report*, published since 1945, follows the daily activities of Congress and its relations with the President, the bureaucracy, the courts, interest groups, political parties, and constituents. Each year the Congressional Quarterly publishes an *Almanac* that covers congressional and other political activities of the preceding year. Five Congressional Quarterly volumes entitled *Congress and the Nation*, covering 1945–1964, 1965–1968, 1969–1972, 1973–1976, 1977–1980, and 1981–1984, give a historical account of congressional activities and politics. See also Congressional Quarterly's *Guide to Congress* (1982).

The daily floor proceedings of the House and the Senate are reported in the *Congressional Record* (Washington, D.C.: U.S. Government Printing Office). The *Congressional Monitor* is a daily report on congressional committee and floor schedules, including an advance schedule of committee hearings, published by Congressional Quarterly.

House procedures are set forth in a biennial publication of the Parliamentarian of the U.S. House of Representatives: *Constitution, Jefferson's Manual and Rules of the House of Representatives of the United States*. The Senate Rules and Administration Committee also issues a manual of Senate rules every two years under the title *Senate Manual*. Both are available from the U.S. Government Printing Office. See also, Floyd Riddick, *Senate Procedure: Precedents and Practices, a Publication of the U.S. Senate Parliamentarian* (Washington, D.C.: U.S. Government Printing Office, 1974). The rules of standing, joint, and select committees may be found in *Rules Adopted by the Committees of Congress* (Washington, D.C.: U.S. Government Printing Office, 1977), a compilation prepared by the House Select Committee on Congressional Operations and the Senate Committee on Rules and Administration.

The Congressional Information Service (7101 Wisconsin Ave., N.W., Washington, D.C. 20014) publishes the *CIS Index to Congressional Hearings, Documents, and Reports*. The Index gives lists of witnesses and abstracts of their testimony. It is issued monthly and quarterly and in a two-volume annual edition. The Cis also publishes on microfiche the texts of all congressional bills, hearings, reports, and other documents. The Commerce Clearinghouse (4025 W. Peterson Ave., Chicago, Ill. 60646) publishes the *Commerce Clearinghouse Congressional Index*, a weekly guide to legislation that has been introduced in Congress.

SECONDARY SOURCES

Richard F. Fenno, Jr., *Homestyle: House Members in Their Districts* (Boston: Little, Brown, 1978),* describes the personal electoral styles of members in their districts. Morris P. Fiorina, *Congress: Keystone of the Washington Establishment*, 2nd ed. (New Haven: Yale University Press, 1989),* links the growing electoral security of congressional incumbents to the effectiveness of their pork barreling and casework activities. Arthur Maass, *Congress and the Common Good* (New York: Basic Books, 1984), gives a more positive account of congressional institutions and practices.

Barbara Hinckley, *Congressional Elections* (Washington, D.C.: Congressional Quarterly, 1981),* discusses congressional elections in terms of voters, incumbency, the effects of party, the candidates, issues, presidential coattails, and midterm elections. Gary C. Jacobson, *The Politics of Congressional Elections* (Boston: Little, Brown & Co., 1983),* also covers congressional elections, and examines congressional candidates, campaigns, and voters.

William J. Keefe, *Congress and the American People* (Englewood Cliffs, N.J.: Prentice-Hall, Inc., 1980),* is a brief overview of congressional politics. John W. Kingdon, *Congressmen's Voting Decisions*, 2nd ed. (New York: Harper & Row, 1981),* is a seminal work on the forces that influence voting decisions in Congress. Thomas E. Mann and Norman J. Ornstein, eds., *The New Congress* (Washington, D.C.: American Enterprise Institute, 1981),* is a collection of articles by leading congressional scholars on the context of Congress, including the media, the nature of the institution, and the policy process. Norman J. Ornstein, ed., *Congress in Change* (New York: Praeger, 1975),* focuses on the nature and importance of congressional reform during the 1970s. Rochelle Jones and Peter Woll, *The Private World of Congress* (New York: Free Press, 1979), examines the internal world of Capitol Hill and the importance of the members' drive for power and status within Congress.

Harrison W. Fox, Jr., and Susan Webb Hammond, *Congressional Staffs, The Invisible Force in American Lawmaking* (New York: Free Press, 1977),* discusses the historical and contemporary roles of committee and personal staffs in Congress. Michael J. Malbin, *Unelected Representatives* (New York: Basic Books, 1979),* is a firsthand account of congressional staff. Two excellent case studies of congressional policymaking are: Eric Redman, *The Dance of Legislation* (New York: Simon and Schuster, 1973);* T. R. Reid, *Congressional Odyssey* (San Francisco: W. H. Freeman, 1980).*

Philip Brenner, *The Limits and Possibilities of Congress* (New York: St. Martin's Press, 1983),* contains case studies of congressional foreign and domestic policymaking. The possibilities of congressional reform are assessed. Lawrence C. Dodd and Bruce J. Oppenheimer, eds., *Congress Reconsidered*, 4th ed. (Washington, D.C.: Congressional Quarterly, 1988),* is a recent collection of studies on congressional politics.

The Presidency

PRIMARY SOURCES

The authors of *The Federalist* explained the constitutional basis of the presidency in great detail. See especially *Federalist,* No. 64 (John Jay), on the President's treaty-making power, and Nos. 67–78 (Alexander Hamilton), on the structure and responsibility of the presidency.

Presidential memoirs afford behind-the-scenes glimpses of the White House. Every president since Harry S. Truman has written his memoirs. See, for example, Lyndon B. Johnson, *The Vantage Point: Perspectives on the Presidency, 1963–1969* (New York: Popular Library, 1971); Richard M. Nixon, *The Memoirs of Richard Nixon* (New York: Grosset & Dunlap, 1978);* Gerald R. Ford, *A Time to Heal* (New York: Harper & Row/Reader's Digest Press, 1979);* and Jimmy Carter, *Keeping the Faith* (New York: Bantam, 1982).* Presidential papers are also available, but far less accessible. They may be found in the Library of Congress, and in special presidential libraries throughout the country.

The texts of presidential press conferences, veto messages, State of the Union addresses, and other documents are available in the *Congressional Quarterly Weekly Reports* and yearly *Almanacs.* The *Federal Register* (Washington, D.C.: U.S. Government Printing Office) contains the texts of all official presidential actions and messages.

SECONDARY SOURCES

Edward F. Corwin, *The President: Office and Powers,* 4th ed. (New York: New York University Press, 1957), is the classic work on the constitutional framework of the presidency. Clinton Rossiter, *The American Presidency,* 2nd ed. (New York: Harcourt, Brace and Jovanovich, 1960),* and Richard Neustadt, *Presidential Power* (New York: Wiley, 1980),* give contrasting views on the presidency; Rossiter believes its strengths are intrinsic, while Neustadt argues its powers are entirely political. Thomas E. Cronin, *The State of the Presidency,* 2nd ed. (Boston: Little, Brown, 1980),* and Benjamin I. Page and Mark P. Petracca, *The American Presidency* (New York: McGraw-Hill, 1983), are excellent general texts on the presidency.

Michael Nelson, ed., *The Presidency and the Political System,* 3rd ed. (Washington, D.C.: Congressional Quarterly, 1990), offers an up-to-date collection of studies on the presidency in all its aspects. A number of recent texts have shed light on the historical development of the executive office. For examples, see James Ceaser, *Presidential Selection: Theory and Development* (Princeton: Princeton University Press, 1979);* Jeffrey Tulis, *The Rhetorical Presidency* (Princeton: Princeton University Press, 1987);* and Sidney M. Milkis and Michael Nelson, *The American Presidency: Origins and Development, 1776–1990* (Washington, D.C.: Congressional Quar-

terly, 1990). Richard Nathan, *The Administrative Presidency* (New York: Wiley, 1982);* and Peri Arnold, *Making the Managerial Presidency, 1905–1980* (Princeton: Princeton University Press, 1986), examine the nature of the institutionalized presidency. Fred Greenstein, ed., *Leadership in the Modern Presidency* (Cambridge: Harvard University Press, 1988),* includes a number of well-written and interesting essays on individual presidents spanning Franklin D. Roosevelt to Ronald Reagan. Charles O. Jones, ed., *The Reagan Legacy* (Chatham, N.J.: Chatham House, 1988); and Sidney Blumenthal and Thomas Edsall, eds., *The Reagan Legacy* (New York: Pantheon, 1988), give accounts of the important political developments of the Reagan years.

James D. Barber, *The Presidential Character: Predicting Performance in the White House,* 3rd ed. (Englewood Cliffs, N.J.: Prentice-Hall, 1985),* links presidential performance to the character of the man who occupies the office. The book presents stimulating and often provocative accounts of presidents from Woodrow Wilson to Jimmy Carter. Theodore C. Sorenson, *Decision Making in the White House* (New York: Columbia University Press, 1963),* discusses the nature of the presidency and the demands made upon the office. Robert F. Kennedy describes the Cuban Missile Crisis and the presidential reaction to it in *Thirteen Days,* rev. ed. (New York: Norton, 1971).* Arthur M. Schlesinger, Jr., *The Imperial Presidency* (Boston: Houghton Mifflin, 1973),* examines what he and many other presidential scholars viewed at the time to be an overextension of presidential power during the Nixon administration. Henry Kissinger's memoirs, *White House Years* and *Years of Upheaval* (Boston: Little, Brown, 1979, 1982), are weighty but important and fascinating accounts of presidential foreign policymaking during the Nixon years. Zbigniew Brzezinski, *Power and Principle* (New York: Farrar Strauss & Giroux, 1983), is a memoir of foreign policymaking during the Carter administration, as is Cyrus Vance, *Hard Choices* (New York: Simon & Schuster, 1983), which offers a contrasting view of how foreign policy should be made. Seyom Brown, *The Faces of Power* (New York: Columbia University Press, 1983);* offers a well-written and carefully argued discussion of foreign policy from Harry Truman to Ronald Reagan.

The Bureaucracy

PRIMARY SOURCES

The *Government Organization Annual* (Washington, D.C.: U.S. Government Printing Office), published annually, lists each administrative agency, its enabling statute, responsibilities, officers, and provides organizational charts. The *Federal Register,* published daily by the U.S. Government Printing Office, contains all executive orders, and the rules and regulations of administrative agencies. The *Washington Information Directory* and the *Federal Regulatory Directory* (Washington, D.C.: Congressional Quarterly), are comprehensive guides to agency sources of information, policies, procedures, and personnel, published every two years.

SECONDARY SOURCES

Ralph P. Hummel, *The Bureaucratic Experience,* 2nd ed. (New York: St. Martin's, 1982),* examines bureaucratic organization, recruitment, and the relations between administrative agencies and citizens. David Nachmias and David H. Rosenbloom, *Bureaucratic Government USA* (New York: St. Martin's, 1980), gives an overview of bureaucratic power and organization, including a discussion of private-sector bureaucracies. Harold Seidman and Robert Gilmour, *Politics, Position and Power* (New York: Oxford University Press, 1986),* investigates the dynamics of federal organization and emphasizes the politics of the bureaucracy. Peter Woll, *American Bureaucracy* (New York: Norton, 1977),* discusses the political basis and functions of the bureaucracy, and includes an overview of the legal framework and implications of administrative power.

Recent accounts of the expansion of administrative power and its consequences include Stephen Skowronek, *Building a New American State: The Expansion of Administrative Capacities, 1877–1920* (Cambridge: Cambridge University Press, 1982);* Francis Rourke, *Bureaucracy, Politics and Public Policy* (Boston: Little, Brown, 1984);* John Rohr, *To Run a Constitution: The Legitimacy of the Administrative State* (Lawrence, Kan.: University Press of Kansas, 1986);* and James Q. Wilson, *Bureaucracy* (New York: Basic Books, 1989).

The Judicial System

PRIMARY SOURCES

Supreme Court opinions are contained in the *United States Supreme Court Reports* (see above, p. 578). The first ninety volumes are cited by the names of their reporters. Lower federal court reports through March 1880 are available in the *Federal Cases.* From March 1880 until October 1932, the *Federal Reporter* gave the lower court decisions. Beginning in October 1932, the *Federal Reporter,* 2nd

ser. gave the opinions of the federal circuit courts of appeal, and a new *Federal Supplement* (F. Supp.) reported the decisions of the district courts.

Philip P. Kurland and Gerhard Casper, eds., *Landmark Briefs and Arguments of the Supreme Court of the United States* (Arlington, Va.: University Publications of America, 1975) is a compilation of written briefs filed with the Supreme Court in important cases. *Landmark Briefs* should be available in the reference sections of university and college libraries. Students who have access to law libraries may also obtain transcripts of the oral arguments before the Supreme Court. Both briefs and oral arguments are indexed by case names, such as *Baker v. Carr,* 369 U.S. 186 (1962).

SECONDARY SOURCES

An excellent and comprehensive work on the judicial system is Henry J. Abraham, *The Judicial Process,* 5th ed. (New York: Oxford University Press, 1986).* A classic work on judicial procedure is Benjamin Cardozo, *The Nature of the Judicial Process* (New Haven, Conn.: Yale University Press, 1921). See also, Herbert Jacob, *Justice in America: Courts, Lawyers, and the Judicial Process,* 3rd ed. (Boston: Little, Brown, 1978).*

Supreme Court history is covered in Charles Warren, *The Supreme Court in United States History,* rev. ed., 2 vols. (Boston: Little, Brown, 1947). A perspective on the early Supreme Court is also in Charles G. Haines, *The Role of the Supreme Court in American Government and Politics, 1789–1835* (New York: Da Capo, 1944). Robert H. Jackson, *The Struggle for Judicial Supremacy* (Cambridge, Mass.: Harvard University Press, 1941),* discusses the role of the Supreme Court during the New Deal. Alexander M. Bickel, *The Least Dangerous Branch: The Supreme Court at the Bar of Politics* (Indianapolis: Bobbs-Merrill, 1962), and *Politics and the Warren Court* (New York: Da Capo, 1965), examine the Warren Court and the political controversies that surrounded it. Henry J. Abraham, *Justices and Presidents* (New York: Oxford University Press, 1974), discusses the history and politics of appointments to the Supreme Court. Bob Woodward and Scott Armstrong, *The Brethren* (New York: Simon & Schuster, 1979),* is a behind-the-scenes account of Supreme Court justices in action.

Anthony Lewis, *Gideon's Trumpet* (New York: Random House, 1964),* is the classic study of the Supreme Court's decision to nationalize the right to counsel. Alan F. Westin, *The Anatomy of a Constitutional Law Case* (New York: Macmillan, 1968),* is a fascinating account of the famous steel seizure case of 1952. Alan F. Westin and Barry Mahoney, *The Trial of Martin Luther King* (New York: Crowell, 1974), takes the reader behind the scenes of the trial of Martin Luther King for contempt of court after refusing to obey its order prohibiting parading without a permit in Birmingham.

A number of recent works have examined the constitutional and policy implications of judicial activism. Among the best are Donald L. Horowitz, *The Courts and Social Policy* (Washington, D.C.: Brookings Institution, 1977); R. Shep Melnick, *Regulation and the Courts* (Washington, D.C.: Brookings Institution, 1983);* and Jeremy Rabkin, *Judicial Compulsions* (New York: Basic Books, 1989). For a comprehensive, up-to-date treatment of the Supreme Court in all its aspects, including an intelligent discussion of the Reagan legacy, see William Lasser, *The Limits of Judicial Power: The Supreme Court in American Politics* (Chapel Hill: University of North Carolina Press, 1988).*

Government and the Media

PRIMARY SOURCES

The *Washington Post, New York Times,* and the *Wall Street Journal* are national newspapers that have an important influence on government and political elites. You should refer not only to the political reporting of the newspapers, but also to their editorial pages. The ABC, CBS, and NBC nightly news programs are eagerly followed not only by the President of the United States and Washington politicians, but also by millions of citizens throughout the country. Local press and media should also be followed to note the contrasting styles and content of political reporting at the national and local levels.

SECONDARY SOURCES

The *Washington Journalism Review* and the *Columbia Journalism Review* contain popular and academic articles, respectively, on political journalism.

Douglass Cater, *The Fourth Branch of Government* (Boston: Houghton Mifflin, 1959), is the classic, seminal work on political reporting and the Washington press corps. Doris A. Graber, *Mass Media and American Politics,* 3rd ed. (Washington, D.C., Congressional Quarterly, 1988),* discusses the impact of the media on government and citizens. Hoyt H. Purvis, *The Press: Free and Responsible?* (Austin, Tex.: Lyndon B. Johnson School of Public Affairs, 1982),* presents the discussions of a sym-

posium of leading media and government figures on freedom and responsibility.

William L. Rivers, *The Other Government: Power and the Washington Media* (New York: Universe Books, 1982), examines the media in Washington, from investigative reporters to government flacks, from the White House to the Supreme Court. Larry J. Sabato, *The Rise of Political Consultants* (New York: Basic Books, 1981), examines media consultants and their political influence. Gay Talese, *The Kingdom and the Power* (New York: World Publishing, 1966),* is a fascinating inside account of the politics of the *New York Times.* Judy Woodruff, *This is Judy Woodruff at the White House* (Reading, Mass.: Addison-Wesley, 1982), is a light but delightful account of NBC's leading woman correspondent.

Timothy Crouse, *The Boys on the Bus* (New York: Random House, 1972),* is an entertaining and informative account of the press following the McGovern campaign of 1972. Jeff Greenfield, *The Real Campaign* (New York: Summit Books, 1982), argues that the media missed the real story of the 1980 presidential campaign. Jeffrey B. Abramson, F. Christopher Arterton, and Gary R. Orren, *The Electronic Commonwealth* (New York: Basic Books, 1988), examines the impact of new media technologies on democratic politics in the United States.

Government Policies: Their Nature and Scope

PRIMARY SOURCES

The *Budget of the United States* (Washington, D.C.: U.S. Government Printing Office), published yearly, lists all government programs and briefly describes them.

The *Congressional Quarterly Weekly Reports* focus particularly on congressional policies and policymaking, but also cover the Supreme Court and the Executive branch. Special Congressional Quarterly publications, such as the yearly *Almanac,* and *Congress and the Nation* volumes should also be consulted. The *Annual Journal* (Government Research Corporation, 1730 M Street, N.W., Washington, D.C. 20036), is an additional invaluable source of information on government policies and processes.

Congressional Committee Hearings and Reports, summarized in the CIS Index (Congressional Information Service, 7101 Wisconsin Ave., N.W., Washington, D.C. 20014), examines special areas of public policy in accordance with the jurisdiction of the different committees. Appropriations and authorization hearings should be consulted along with general legislative hearings and reports.

The Congressional Quarterly's *Washington Information Directory*, published biannually, lists sources of information for all government policies.

SECONDARY SOURCES

James E. Anderson, *Public Policy-Making*, 3rd ed. (New York: Holt, Rinehart and Winston, 1984),* gives an overview of the policy process, including discussions of policy makers, policy formation, and the implementation of policy. Thomas R. Dye, *Understanding Public Policy*, 2nd ed. (Englewood Cliffs, N.J.: Prentice-Hall, 1975), is a standard work that gives models of policymaking and examples of public policy. Charles E. Lindblom, *The Policy Making Process*, 2nd ed. (Englewood Cliffs, N.J.: Prentice-Hall, 1980),* describes the rational approach to policymaking and its limits. Deborah A. Stone, *Policy Paradox and Political Reason* (Glenview, Ill.: Scott, Foresman, 1988),* offers a fresh approach to the study of public policy that emphasizes the place of politics in the formulation and development of government programs. Aaron Wildavsky, *The Politics of the Budgetary Process*, 4th ed. (Glenview, Ill.: Scott, Foresman, 1984),* examines budgetary choices and how they are made; the same author's *Speaking Truth to Power* (Boston: Little, Brown, 1979) is a broad examination of policy analysis and politics.

David A. Caputo, ed., *The Politics of Policy Making in America* (San Francisco: W. H. Freeman, 1977), includes case studies on the Equal Rights Amendment, energy policy, campaign finance reform, housing, and foreign policy. A number of recent volumes have attempted to provide a comprehensive review of the important changes in federal policymaking during the past two decades. See, in particular, the following: John Chubb and Paul Peterson, eds., *Can the Government Govern?* (Washington, D.C.: Brookings Institution, 1988); Richard A. Harris and Sidney M. Milkis, eds., *Remaking American Politics* (Boulder, Colo.: Westview Press,

1989); and Anthony King, ed., *The New American Political System*, 2nd version (Washington, D.C.: American Enterprise Institute, 1990).

State and Local Governments

PRIMARY SOURCES

See the sources listed under Federalism (p. 580).

SECONDARY SOURCES

Claude E. Barfield, *Rethinking Federalism: Block Grants and Federal, State, and Local Responsibilities* (Washington, D.C.: American Enterprise Institute, 1981), is a clear and concise review of the development of federal grants to state and local governments, and various proposals for sorting out governmental responsibilities in the 1980s. How local governments cut back their expenditures when their resources are limited is examined in Charles H. Levine, Irene S. Rubin, and George G. Wolohojian, *The Politics of Retrenchment: How Local Governments Manage Fiscal Stress* (Beverly Hills, Calif.: Sage Publications, 1981). David B. Walker, *Toward a Functioning Federalism* (Cambridge, Mass.: Winthrop Publishers, 1981), is a critique of the current state of American federalism, arguing that intergovernmental relations are hopelessly "overloaded" by political, fiscal, judicial, and administrative burdens. David Osborne, *Laboratories of Democracy* (Boston: Harvard Business School Press, 1988), gives a more optimistic account of intergovernmental relations.

A broad and well-organized selection of articles on state and local government and politics can be found in Robert L. Morlan and David L. Martin, *Capitol, Courthouse, and City Hall* (Boston: Houghton Mifflin, 1981). A rich case study of federal judicial intervention in local school politics can be found in Emmett H. Buell, Jr., *School Desegregation and Defended Neighborhoods: The Boston Controversy* (Lexington, Mass.: D. C. Heath, 1982).

Glossary

Absentee voting State and federal laws permit persons to vote within the states and districts of their residence while they are away from home. Absentee voting takes place before the regular voting day, and absentee ballots are counted after regular ballots are tabulated.

Administration A particular regime, usually meaning the president and his cabinet and other political appointees.

Advance man A person who goes ahead of a political candidate to check schedules, transportation, hotel reservations, locations of appearances, and to arrange for publicity. "Advancing" a trip involves making arrangements for it.

Advice and consent Article II, section 2 of the Constitution requires the President to obtain the advice and consent of the Senate to make treaties (which need the concurrence of two-thirds of the Senate to go into effect), and to appoint ambassadors, public ministers and consuls, and Supreme Court justices. Congress may and has extended the advice and consent requirement to presidential appointments of a wide range of executive and military officers.

Administrative law judges (ALJs) Independent hearing officers within administrative agencies that conduct initial formal rule-making and adjudicatory proceedings. Their decisions may be overruled by the agencies, but the evidence they have gathered must be taken into account.

Administrative Procedure Act of 1946 (APA) Legislation that imposes judicial-type procedural requirements upon formal administrative rule-making and adjudicatory proceedings. The APA also made hearing officers independent of the agencies. Later amendments added Freedom of Information requirements that permit citizens to obtain certain information from agency files.

Adversary process The process by which opposing parties contest each other's claims; it is characteristic of all judicial and many administrative proceedings.

Affirmative action Practices to remedy the effects of past discrimination by granting special benefits to members of the groups which have suffered discrimination. An affirmative action program that involved quotas for the representation of minorities in a medical school's student body was ruled unconstitutional by the Supreme Court in *Regents of the University of California v. Bakke* (1978). However, the Court's majority held that race could be taken into account in a school's admission process.

Appellate jurisdiction The judicial authority to review the decisions of a lower court. Congress determines the appellate jurisdiction of the Supreme Court and lower federal judiciary, and may limit it unless constitutional questions are involved.

Appropriations Congress provides money through appropriations bills for programs it has already authorized. Appropriations, in effect, put money into the government's checking account at the Treasury for specific programs.

Arraignment The formal notice of the charges against a defendant, followed by the defendant's plea of guilty or not guilty.

Authorization Congress authorizes money to be spent for particular programs through authorization bills that place ceilings on how much money can be spent. Appropriations must be within the limits set by authorization bills.

Back-bencher In the British House of Commons a back-bencher is a party member who sits on the back benches behind the party leaders; hence, a back-bencher is a person of low seniority and party rank.

Backgrounder A press conference held by a government official "on the record," but on condition that the official's name not be revealed. (Reporters then attribute their stories to "a high government source," "a senior government official," and so on.)

Bagman The intermediary person who carries a bribe to a government official.

Baker v. Carr The 1962 case that applied the one   589

person–one vote rule to state legislative apportionment laws.

Balanced ticket A slate of candidates designed to appeal to a wide variety of political voters. In Presidential races a balanced ticket is one in which the presidential and vice-presidential candidates are from different regions of the country and represent different wings of the parties.

Ballot A printed list of political candidates; as a verb, the act of voting.

Bandwagon The symbol of a political movement, usually a winning one, causing politicians to "jump on the bandwagon" lest they be left behind. The "bandwagon effect" is the political instinct to be on the winning side.

Bicameral Composed of two houses, used in reference to legislatures.

Bill Proposed legislation. Public bills pertain to matters of concern to the public at large; private bills concern individual claims against the government, immigration cases, and similar matters.

Bill of attainder A legislative act that condemns and punishes a person without a trial. Congress is prohibited by the Constitution from passing bills of attainder.

Bipartisan Agreement and cooperation between the two major parties on public policy issues, as in bipartisan foreign policy.

Boss A political party leader, often in large cities, who exercises tight control over party organization, which is called a *political machine*. City bosses arose in the nineteenth century, capitalizing on the needs and loyalties of new immigrants for whom the machines provided important services.

Bureaucracy The administrative departments and agencies of government, most of the personnel of which are civil service employees and not subject to direct political control. Bureaucracies are traditionally hierarchical structures with a chain of command from the top to the bottom and a chain of responsibility from the bottom to the top. Because bureaucracy is often associated with red tape, delay, and bungling of all kinds, it is a pejorative in political language.

Calendar (legislative) A listing of bills in the House or the Senate. There are five calendars in the House: the Union Calendar for bills to raise or spend money; the House Calendar for other major legislation; the Consent Calendar for noncontroversial legislation; the District of Columbia Calendar for bills dealing with the District; and the Private Calendar for private legislation. There are only two calendars in the Senate: the Calendar of General Order for all legislation except treaties and nominations; the Executive Calendar for treaties and nominations requiring the advice and consent of the Senate.

Cabinet The heads of the 13 executive departments (Agriculture; Commerce; Defense; Education; Energy; Health and Human Services; Housing and Urban Development; Interior; Justice; Labor; State; Transportation; Treasury), who are appointed by the president and advise him on public policy.

Casework The work of members of Congress in which they handle constituent complaints and requests that usually concern administrative agency actions. Casework buttresses the reelection chances of incumbents.

Caucus A special group, usually political party members or members of the legislature, that meets to take positions on public policy issues or to endorse candidates. (See also **Congressional Caucus**.)

Certiorari, writ of A written order by a higher court to a lower court or administrative agency to send the record of a case to the higher court for review. Writs of certiorari are appropriate only where judicial or quasi-judicial proceedings have produced a written record, which is usually but not always the case.

Chief administrator The president's role as head of the bureaucracy, derived from his responsibility under Article II to see that the laws are faithfully executed.

Chief executive The president's role as head of the executive branch, based upon his responsibility under Article II to see that the laws are faithfully executed.

Chief legislator The president's role, derived from Article II, to recommend legislation to Congress and to keep the legislature informed of the state of the Union. As chief legislator the president helps to set the congressional agenda.

Chief of state The president's ceremonial role as the head of the nation and its symbol both at home and abroad.

Coattails A presidential candidate's ability to draw votes to other party candidates.

Civil liberties The freedoms of speech, press, association, and religion that cannot be infringed by the government unless justified by a compelling public interest.

Civil rights The rights of citizens—such as the right to vote, the right to protection against self-incrimination, and the right to a jury trial—that the government is required to protect.

Civil service system The system under which government employees are hired on the basis of merit and guaranteed their tenure so long as the job continues and their performance is adequate.

"Clear and present danger" First announced by Justice Oliver Wendell Holmes in *Schenck v. United States* (1919), the standard allows the government to suppress freedom of expression if it constitutes a clear and present danger to the security or other legitimate ends of government.

Clerk of the House The administrative officer of the House of Representatives.

Closed primary A primary in which voters must be members of a particular party in order to vote for its candidates.

Closed rule A House rule that restricts floor debate on legislation by prohibiting amendments. (The only exceptions are made, with the approval of the House, for members of the committee that sponsored the legislation.)

Cloture Senate Rule 22, requiring the approval of 60 senators before debate on legislation can be closed.

Commander-in-chief The president's role under Article II as the supreme commander of all the armed forces.

Commerce clause Congress's Article I authority to regulate commerce among the states, which became the basis for far-reaching national power and supremacy over the states.

Common law Judge-made law, based upon the decisions of courts, as distinguished from legislative enactments. The common law, derived from the English common law, is applied in every state except Louisiana.

Committee of the whole The entire House resolves itself into a committee to enable it to debate and discuss legislation informally.

"Community standards" Part of a judicial formula that permits local communities to apply their own standards in obscenity cases. Community standards may not, however, violate constitutional principles.

Concurrent jurisdiction Under the Constitution federal and state governments have concurrent jurisdiction over certain areas of policy, such as commerce and taxation. State laws, however, are void if they conflict with federal legislation.

Concurrent resolution A resolution passed by both houses of Congress that does not have the power of law and does not require the president's signature.

Conference committee A committee composed of members of both the House and Senate that has the purpose of arranging a compromise between the houses when they have passed different versions of a bill.

Congressional intent The expression of congressional policy objectives in laws delegating authority to administrative agencies.

Connecticut Compromise The agreement at the Constitutional Convention of 1787 that resulted in a bicameral Congress; each state would have two representatives in the Senate and House representation would be in proportion to state population. Also called the "Great Compromise."

Congressional caucus Sometimes referred to as legislative service organizations, congressional caucuses represent special interests, such as the Black Caucus, Women's Caucus, and Tourism Caucus.

Congressional district The local district from which a representative is elected.

Congressional record Published daily while Congress is in session, the *Record* includes floor debate, members' remarks, and whatever material members choose to insert.

Constitutional democracy A government of popular participation limited by law.

Critical election An election which initiates a long-term realignment of voters from one party to another. The last critical election was in 1932, when the Democrats replaced the Republicans as the majority party.

De facto segregation Segregation that exists in fact but not by law.

Defendant The party against whom a legal action is brought.

De jure segregation Segregation required by law.

Delegate-at-large Delegate awarded to a state as a whole by the delegate-selection formulas for presidential nominating conventions.

Delegated power Legislative power delegated by Congress to the president or the bureaucracy.

"Deliberate speed" The Supreme Court's standard in *Brown v. Board of Education* (1954) requiring school districts segregated by law to segregate their facilities "with all deliberate speed."

Deviating election An election in which there is a temporary shift in the party allegiance of the electorate as the result of personalities or temporary issues.

Direct democracy A government in which people participate directly, and in which the majority rules without constitutional restraints. The Framers of the Constitution were careful to create an indirect form of democracy in which the voice of the people would be filtered and checked. (See *The Federalist*, Nos. 10, 47, 48, 51.)

Direct lobbying Attempting to influence the actions of legislators on pending bills. Contrasts with indirect or grass-roots lobbying that attempts to raise ground swells of public opinion for or against pending or proposed legislation. The Federal Regulation of Lobbying Act of 1946 regulates direct but not indirect lobbying.

Direct primary A political process that involves rank-and-file members in the nomination of candidates to run for office. Direct primaries often reduce the power of party leaders and bosses, although powerful bosses can manipulate them for their own ends.

Discharge petition In the House, if a committee does not report a bill within 30 days after referral, a member may file a discharge motion—which requires the signature of 218 members—asking that the committee be discharged of the legislation. If a simple majority of the House votes in favor of the motion, the committee is discharged. In the Senate, any senator may introduce a motion to discharge legislation from the committee, which, if passed by a majority vote, removes the bill from the committee's jurisdiction.

Due process of law Procedural protections afforded to individuals whose life, liberty, or property is at stake. The Fifth and Fourteenth Amendments contain due process clauses. Historically, due process requires fair trials, especially for criminal defendants. The meaning of due process has varied over time as judicial views of what constitutes fair and reasonable government action changed.

Editorialize Journalists' expression of subjective viewpoints on the news they report.

Electoral College The body that elects the president and vice-president; each state is represented by the same number of members as in its congressional delegation. Originally, the members of the Electoral College were selected in the manner prescribed by their state legislatures and had some discretion in making their choice. Now the 538 members (including, since 1961, three from the District of Columbia) have only a pro forma function: each state delegation is legally bound to vote as a bloc for the presidential candidate who received a plurality of the state's votes.

Elite model The view that economic, political, and social elites determine public policy.

Engrossed bill The final copy of a bill approved by one chamber of Congress that is sent to the other chamber.

Enrolled bill The final copy of a bill approved by both the House and the Senate in identical form, printed on parchment, and sent to the House

Speaker, the Senate President, and the President of the United States for signature.

Enumerated powers The powers of Congress under Article I, including the commerce power, taxing authority, and the war power.

Equal protection of the laws The Fourteenth Amendment's equal protection clause prohibits states from denying equal protection to their citizens, and the due process clause of the Fifth Amendment proscribes discrimination by the national government. Only the most compelling government needs permit discrimination in any form, as in *Korematsu v. United States* (1944), which upheld discriminatory treatment of Japanese-Americans during World War II.

Errand boy A denigrating title given to members of Congress when they perform casework handling the grievances of constituents.

Executive agreement A presidential arrangement with a foreign nation made outside of the framework of a formal treaty and thus not subject to Senate approval.

Executive department A cabinet department, headed by a secretary nominated by the president and approved by a majority of voting senators. (See **Cabinet.**)

Executive function The implementation of existing programs and policy standards by the president and the bureaucracy.

Executive power The president's authority under Article II to carry out the law.

Executive privilege The president's privilege of withholding information from Congress on the ground that disclosure would interfere with the exercise of executive power and the constitutional responsibilities of the president. *United States v. Nixon* (1974) upheld the concept of executive privilege, but denied Nixon's specific claim of privilege, made on tenuous grounds, to withhold information from a pending criminal investigation.

Faction A special interest group or political party, defined by James Madison as intrinsically opposed to the national interest (*The Federalist*, No. 10).

Favorite son A presidential candidate, popular in his or her home state, who goes to the national convention with the backing of most of the state's delegates, but has little chance of gaining the nomination.

Federalism A government system in which constitutional authority is divided between a central government and state or provincial governments.

Felony A crime—such as murder, rape, or burglary—that is considered to be more serious than a misdemeanor and is punishable by a harsher sentence.

Filibuster Derived from a Dutch word meaning "freebooter" or pirate, the word began to be used in the eighteenth century to describe the tactics of senators who, under a rule allowing unlimited debate, were able to delay or kill bills by talking them to death. Senate Bill 22, which originally required a vote of two-thirds of the entire Senate membership to close debate, was changed in 1975 to require the approval of only 60 senators. Historically, both conservative and liberal senators have used filibusters to get their way.

Fireside chats Originally, informal radio addresses from the White House, initiated by President Franklin D. Roosevelt in 1933 to explain his New Deal policies. Presidents have revived fireside chats on many occasions since the New Deal. President Ronald Reagan made regular radio broadcasts to explain his policies.

"Fishing expedition" Generally refers to a Senate or House committee investigation which has no specific legislative goal, particularly the investigations conducted by the House Committee on Un-American Activities during the 1940s and 1950s.

Floor manager A member of Congress, generally the chairman or ranking members of committees that have reported legislation, who attempts to steer a bill through floor debate to a final vote.

Foggy Bottom The State Department, because the department's office buildings occupy a swamplike area of Washington close to the Potomac River which, because of its persistent fogginess, was originally called Foggy Bottom.

Fourth branch of government The bureaucracy.

"Fourth estate" The press and the media. Historically, the estates of European nations such as France and England were classes of citizens (generally clergy, nobility, and commoners), which had distinct political rights and separate government representation. Referring to the press as the fourth estate in the context of America's political system makes the interests represented by Congress, the president, and the federal judiciary the first three estates.

Freedom of Information Act (1966) A law that allows citizens to obtain information from government agencies.

Germaneness rule House rules require that all amendments to a bill be germane (i.e., relevant). Senate rules require germaneness of amendments to general appropriations bills, and bills being considered under cloture or under a unanimous consent agreement to limit debate. Both House and Senate germaneness rules are often waived by suspension of the rule (which requires a two-thirds vote of the members present), or by unanimous consent of the members on the floor.

Gerrymander To draw the lines of political districts to favor particular groups, usually the political party in power. The term is derived from Governor Elbridge Gerry of Massachusetts, who signed legislation in 1811 that adjusted legislative districts to favor Democrats over Federalists. One district was dubbed a salamander because of its resemblance to the creature, and hence the word gerrymander was born to refer to politically redrawn districts with odd shapes. The Supreme Court has allowed political gerrymandering, but forbids racial gerrymandering. Moreover, while districts may be gerrymandered, they must be equal in population under the one person–one vote rule applied to state legislative districts in 1962 and to congressional districts in 1964.

GOP Republican party, derived from "Grand Old Party," a common reference to the Republicans in the late nineteenth century.

Government The instrument by which people within a society establish standards (legislative power), the means of carrying them out (executive power), and methods for resolving disputes (judicial power), so that all elements of society will be regulated by the same general rules.

Government corporation A type of administrative unit that is analogous in its structure to a private corporation but has a public responsibility and accountability, such as the Tennessee Valley Authority.

Governmental interest group The different branches of the government, and their components, such as administrative departments and agencies, can be viewed as interest groups within government, which strive to benefit themselves and their constituencies.

"Government of laws and not of men" A shorthand description of constitutional government in which the rulers are bound by the higher law of a constitution.

Grant-in-aid A grant of money from the federal government to the states or local communities with strings attached, requiring grant recipients to adhere to designated national standards.

Grass roots The base or root of political power; in a democracy, the people; in a political party, the rank-and-file members.

"Great Society" President Lyndon B. Johnson's slogan, adopted in 1964 for his programs to eliminate poverty and achieve equality and prosperity.

The Great Society programs went far beyond the New Deal in supporting federal intervention in the economic and social life of the country.

Habeas corpus, writ of A court order to a government official detailing a person to produce the body of a prisoner before it and state the cause for the detention, after which judgment is rendered on whether or not the confinement violates the prisoner's due process. Because of its overriding importance for the protection of individual rights in the English common-law system, the writ became known as the "Great Writ of Liberty."

Hardball Political tactics that are tough, competitive, and aimed at winning at all costs. ("Hardball" is one of the many sports terms that have been adapted to political language.)

Hearings Formal, judiciallike proceedings conducted by administrative agencies and congressional committees to gain information pertaining to individual cases or broader public issues.

Higher law In the Western political tradition, the law of nature from which immutable principles of government and the inalienable rights of the individual are drawn.

Hill (the) Congress, derived from Jenkins Hill, on which the Capitol is located.

Honeymoon period The brief period after a new president takes office when he and his programs are given the benefit of the doubt by Congress and the media. Presidents usually have their greatest successes with Congress during honeymoon periods.

Hopper The box on the clerk's desk of the House of Representatives in which members deposit bills they wish to introduce.

Ideology A system of ideas, based upon the values and aspirations of those who believe in them, that often becomes, particularly outside of the United States, the foundation of political movements.

Imperial presidency A dominant presidency: the president stretches the Constitution in the exercise of prerogative powers, such as Chief Executive and Commander-in-Chief, and ignores the wishes of Congress. The term was first used by Arthur Schlesinger, Jr., in *The Imperial Presidency* (1973), which attacked what the author viewed as the unconstitutional extension of executive power under Richard M. Nixon.

Implied powers Powers of Congress that are not specifically enumerated in Article I of the Constitution but may be implied if they are "necessary and proper" to the exercise of enumerated powers.

Incumbent A person holding office, particularly an elected official such as a member of Congress or the president.

Incumbency effect The tendency of incumbents to be reelected, particularly members of the House of Representatives who build electoral support in their districts through advertising to increase their name recognition, credit-claiming for concrete benefits given by the federal government, taking positions that appeal to a majority of voters, nurturing ongoing political organizations to garner votes, and by adopting attractive personal styles.

Independent regulatory commissions Multi-headed administrative agencies whose members are appointed by the president by and with the advice and consent of the Senate, but that are independent of direct presidential control in their exercise of quasi-legislative and quasi-judicial functions. Examples of independent regulatory commissions are the Federal Communications Commission, the Nuclear Regulatory Commission, and the Securities and Exchange Commission.

Indictment Formal accusation against a defendant, usually made by a grand jury.

Indirect representation A style of representation in which legislators act in what they consider to be the national interest and the interests of constituents rather than simply transmitting constituents' views.

Informal Forces, organization, and behavior that occur outside of official institutional channels. The formal structure of government is complemented by a vast informal network of political power and influence.

Informal administrative adjudication Agency proceedings to settle cases by negotiation rather than through formal hearings.

Informal administrative rule-making The formulation of agency rules through "notice and comment" proceedings. Rules are published in the *Federal Register* and interested parties are given an opportunity to comment on them before they go into effect.

Infrastructure The internal administrative apparatus of an organization, such as the presidency, Congress, and executive departments. The White House staff, for example, is part of the infrastructure of the presidency.

Inner Club A term coined by the journalist William S. White (in *Citadel: The Story of the U.S. Senate,* 1956), to refer to the collegial elite that controlled power within the Senate. As power became more dispersed in the Senate in the 1960s and

1970s, the influence of the Inner Club, or the Senate Establishment, as it was also known, gradually declined.

Item veto Proposed presidential authority to veto portions of legislative bills without having to veto the entire legislation. The president does not have the constitutional authority to exercise an item veto, which the White House has long sought in order to be able to turn down riders, which often involve increased federal spending, attached to important legislation.

Joint committee A congressional committee, usually investigative in nature, created by law, which includes members from both the House and Senate. There are four standing (permanent) joint committees of Congress: Economic, Library, Printing, and Taxation. The chairmanship alternates between the senior House and Senate majority party member every two years, coinciding with the beginning of a new Congress.

Joint resolution A resolution approved by both the House and the Senate that becomes a law upon the signature of the president. Such joint resolutions are the same as laws, although they are usually narrower in scope. Joint resolutions may also be used to propose amendments to the Constitution, which do not require a presidential signature and are adopted upon the approval of three-fourths of the states.

Journal The Constitution requires Congress to keep a journal of its proceedings to record its votes and actions. The *Journal* is separate from the *Congressional Record*, which, unlike the *Journal*, records floor debate and a vast array of other material.

Judicial review The authority of the higher courts to review the decisions and actions of the legislative and executive branches of the government and of the lower courts. This authority can be exercised only when challenges to government action arise within the framework of "cases and controversies." Judicial review may result in laws being overturned as unconstitutional, or in declarations that executive actions are unconstitutional or beyond executive authority under statutory law.

"Junket" A congressional "fact-finding" trip abroad that appears to have no direct legislative purpose. Junkets are vacations at public expense, and junketeering is a pejorative term.

Jurisdiction The extent of the legal authority of a governmental body, usually used in reference to a court or administrative agency. Congress determines the jurisdiction of administrative agencies and of the lower federal judiciary.

Justice department Headed by the Attorney General, the Justice department acts as the attorney for the government, prosecuting federal criminal cases and pursuing civil actions as well. (The FBI is an agency of the Justice department.)

Keynote address A highly partisan speech given at the outset of national nominating conventions to stir up the party faithful and set the theme.

Lame duck A defeated officeholder whose term has not yet expired.

"Last hurrah" The end of a political career, from Edwin O'Connor's novel, *The Last Hurrah* (1956), a fictionalized account of the career of Boston Mayor James Curley.

Left wing Radical political views, such as communism and socialism, proposing the use of government to redistribute income and manage the economy. The left wing of a political party or organization consists of those who hold more radical views than the majority. The ideological spectrum from left to right consists of communists, socialists, liberals, moderates, conservatives, and reactionaries.

Legal brief A legal argument made in court by one of the parties to a case or controversy.

Legislation Laws that apply to all persons within the jurisdiction of the legislative body enacting them. Congress is the primary lawmaker for the nation, but administrative agencies may exercise quasi-legislative power that has been delegated to them by Congress. State and local legislative and administrative bodies also make law.

Legislative apportionment The distribution of population among the legislative districts. The Supreme Court has required congressional districts to be equally apportioned, and has imposed the one person–one vote rule as well upon districting for both branches of state legislatures.

Legislative day The time between meeting and adjournment of either branch of Congress. The House usually adjourns each day, so that legislative and calendar days coincide. Senate legislative days usually include more than one calendar day, however.

Legislative veto Congressional action, authorized by law, overturning administrative decisions. Legislative veto provisions usually allowed either the House or the Senate, by a simple majority vote, to overturn administrative action. The legislative veto was declared unconstitutional by the Supreme Court in 1983.

Legislative Service Organization (LSO) A special

congressional caucus, such as the Black Caucus, Women's Caucus, and Tourism Caucus. Caucuses often provide staff assistance to members.

Liberal A person who is left of center in the American ideological spectrum, and who generally supports government social programs to aid the poor and, within limits, to redistribute wealth.

Library of Congress A comprehensive library and adjunct to Congress, containing the Congressional Research Service that provides staff assistance to legislators. Thomas Jefferson's book collection launched the library.

Lobby As a verb, to pressure members of Congress. As a noun, a group that seeks to influence Congress. Under the terms of the Federal Regulation of Lobbying Act of 1946 lobbyists must register with the Clerk of the House of Representatives and the Secretary of the Senate. Although lobbying was originally confined to legislative bodies—the influence seekers gathered in the lobbies of legislative chambers—vigorous attempts are now made to influence executive departments and administrative agencies as well.

Logrolling The trading off of votes by legislators in support of each other's projects, mostly economic, to aid their districts. Logrolling was once described as, "You scratch my back and I'll scratch yours."

Loyal opposition In Great Britain, the official name of the party out of power; it acts as a critic of the ruling party, but does not advocate a radical change in the constitutional system. Acting as a "loyal opposition" is the responsibility of the party out of power in a constitutional democracy.

Machine A disciplined local party organization headed by a political boss.

Mandamus, writ of A judicial writ that directs executive or administrative officials, or lower-court judges, to perform their duties under the law.

Maintaining election An election that reelects the majority party. (See also **Critical** and **Deviating elections.**)

Majority Leader In the House and the Senate, the leader chosen by the majority party. The Majority Leader of the Senate is relatively more powerful than the House Majority Leader, who is overshadowed by the Speaker.

Majority rule Control of government by the majority of citizens, but without the constitutional restraints that the Framers of the Constitution were so careful to provide.

Marbury v. Madison The 1803 Supreme Court case that established the authority of the Supreme Court to exercise judicial review over congressional laws.

Markup Congressional committees meet to deliberate and amend bills, literally changing and adding to them in "markup" sessions.

Managed news Information or news released by the government to put it in a favorable light.

McCulloch v. Maryland The 1819 Supreme Court case that upheld the supremacy of federal over state law and stated the doctrine of implied powers.

Media The press, television, and radio. The press is often distinguished from the "electronic media," which is primarily television.

Medicaid A joint federal and state program run by the states to pay for medical care for the needy.

Medicare A federal program that pays some of the costs for health care for persons over the age of 65.

Merit system Under the merit system, federal employees are hired and promoted on the basis of their skills as measured by testing and objective evaluations. In the federal bureaucracy the merit system replaced the **spoils system** in 1883.

Military-industrial complex The "iron triangle" of the Defense Department, Armed Services, and Defense Appropriations subcommittees on Capitol Hill, and the armaments industry that often determines defense policy. President Eisenhower warned the nation about the growing power of the military-industrial complex before he left office.

Minority Leader In the House and the Senate the leader elected by members of the minority party. Minority leaders help develop party positions and guide their party's actions.

Miranda v. Arizona The 1966 Supreme Court case requiring criminal suspects to be told of their rights to remain silent and to consult counsel.

Misdemeanor A minor crime, punishable by a fine or a short prison term other than in a penitentiary.

Multiparty system A political system composed of more than two parties, which usually requires a coalition among parties to form a government.

National supremacy The doctrine established in *McCulloch v. Maryland* (1819) that the Constitution, federal laws, and treaties are the supreme law of the land and void conflicting state action.

Natural law The "higher law" derived from the proper relationships among persons in a state of nature.

Natural rights Rights derived from natural law, such as the right to life, liberty, and property. John Locke, in his *Second Treatise, Of Civil Government*

(1689), set the theme for the Anglo-American political tradition which holds that natural rights, being inalienable, cannot be taken away from the individual by government without due process of law.

Near v. Minnesota   The 1931 Supreme Court case that for the first time declared a *state* law to be unconstitutional under the due process clause of the Fourteenth Amendment because the law allowed prior censorship of speech and the press.

New Deal   President Franklin D. Roosevelt's program, adopted in 1933 and subsequent years during the depression, to bring economic prosperity and social security through government intervention.

New Federalism   First announced by President Richard M. Nixon in 1969, New Federalism encompasses programs whose purpose is to transfer responsibilities from the federal government to state and local governments. Part of Nixon's New Federalism was *revenue sharing,* under which federal money was given to the states without strings attached. President Ronald Reagan proposed to extend New Federalism by replacing grant-in-aid programs with block grants the states could spend as they wished.

Nominating convention   The gathering of party delegates for the purpose of choosing candidates. By the Jacksonian era of the 1830s, national nominating conventions had replaced the congressional caucuses of the parties as the bodies that nominated presidential and vice presidential candidates.

Nonpartisan   Without regard to party politics or positions, in contrast to partisan, in which parties predominate, and bipartisan, which involves cooperation between the parties. Nonpartisan elections and government are common only at the local level.

Nullification   A state's invalidation—within its jurisdiction—of a federal law. The doctrine was frequently invoked by Southern politicians before the Civil War. It surfaced again in the mid-twentieth century as Southern politicians sought ways of defying what they viewed as the overextension of Supreme Court power in the 1954 desegregation decision, *Brown v. Board of Education.*

Office of Management and Budget (OMB)   An arm of the executive office of the president created in 1970 by executive order; originally the Bureau of the Budget, established in 1921 and made part of the executive office in 1939. OMB develops, in conjunction with executive departments and agencies, the executive budget and acts as a clearinghouse for the legislative proposals of the bureau-

cracy. OMB is directly accountable to the president and acts as his agent.

Off-the-record   Information given by public officials to reporters, but not for publication.

Off year   Non-presidential-election years.

Ombudsman   An official who acts as an intermediary between citizens and the government. The ombudsman's office is a Scandinavian institution that became popular in the United States—primarily at the local level of government—in the late 1960s. Congressmen perform an ombudsman's function in doing casework for constituents.

One man (person)–one vote   The requirement established by the Supreme Court's decision in *Baker v. Carr* (1962) that electoral districts for a given institution be apportioned to be equal in population.

Open convention   A political convention in which no candidate initially has a majority of the delegates.

Open primary   A type of primary, now rare, in which any registered voter may vote, regardless of party affiliation.

Open rule   Made by the House Rules Committee, an open rule permits floor amendments to legislation. In contrast, a *closed rule* prohibits or restricts floor amendments.

Opinion leader   A person, usually a member of the political, economic, or social elite, who can influence the views of others. Opinion leaders include the media elite, and interest-group and political party leaders.

Original jurisdiction   The authority to hear a case the first time it is raised, i.e., to hold the trial that determines the facts of the case. The original jurisdiction of the Supreme Court is specified in the Constitution. Congress determines the original jurisdiction of the lower federal judiciary, and has set up the district courts as the original or trial courts.

Out party   The party that does not control the White House.

Oval Office   The president's formal office, used as a synonym for the president and his closest advisors.

Overlapping group membership   The condition, in a pluralistic political system, of individual membership in a variety of groups whose interests do not coincide. The law of the imperfect mobilization of political interests, based upon overlapping group membership, states that no pressure group can claim the complete loyalty of its members for more than a single cause.

Oversight   The legislative responsibility to supervise the programs implemented by administrative departments and agencies. Specific oversight functions are assigned to congressional committees which periodically conduct oversight hearings. The House Government Operations Committee, for example, oversees the efficiency of the federal bureaucracy.

Pairing An agreement between two legislators on opposite sides not to vote, so that they can be absent from the chamber but have their position a matter of record.

Partisan As a noun, a loyal member of a political party (also in the generic sense, one who holds strong views on political issues, a militant member of a group or faction); as an adjective, as in a partisan position, in support of the party viewpoint.

Party discipline Voting the party line after policy positions have been taken.

Party followers The rank and file members of a party.

Party leaders Those at the upper echelons of a party organization who play an active role in developing policies and strategies.

Party platform A statement of party positions, developed by a platform committee and adopted by national nominating conventions. American party platforms reflect the diverse viewpoints within each party, which often requires that positions be stated in broad terms.

Party ticket A list of party candidates for elective offices.

Pendleton Act The 1883 legislation that created the Civil Service Commission and began the Civil Service System in the United States. The Office of Personnel Management and the Merit System's Protection Board replaced the Civil Service Commission in 1979.

Pigeonholing A congressional committee's retention of legislation; the committee can kill a bill by refusing to report it for consideration by the whole chamber.

Plaintiff The person who initially brings a court action against a defendant.

Plank Part of a party platform, stating a position on a given issue.

Pluralism The existence of a variety of groups in the political process.

Plurality A greater number of votes than those of any other candidate, but not necessarily more than those of all other candidates combined.

Pocket veto A presidential veto of legislation by refusing to sign it within 10 days of congressional adjournment.

Political apathy Lack of interest in politics; failure to vote and participate in the political sys-

tem. Some political scientists have suggested that a certain degree of apathy is a desirable reflection of contentment with the system. Others argue that apathy reflects alienation and despair among those who fail to participate, a potentially dangerous situation.

Political constituency The individuals and groups upon whom the power of governmental officials depend. Those who vote for an elected official are part of his or her political constituency, but politicians must also heed a variety of other forces, such as Political Action Committees, which may be national in character. Once elected, politicians have to deal with constituencies within government. For example, Congress and the bureaucracy are an important part of the president's political constituency, and vice versa.

Poll tax A fee levied upon voters in Southern states to discourage blacks and poor whites from voting. The tax was abolished by the Twenty-Fourth Amendment, adopted in 1964.

Political party A group, composed of leaders, activists, and followers, which is formed to field candidates for elective office and to advance general or specific public policies.

Political science The systematic study of government and politics to determine the nature of political behavior.

Political socialization The process of passing on political values from one generation to another; also the process of assimilation of values, for example by immigrants.

"Potomac fever" Caught by Washington politicians and their aides, causing an insatiable taste for the political and social life of the nation's capital. The result is that even after defeat politicians and their staffs stay on along the banks of the Potomac, undertaking new political endeavors, often becoming lobbyists.

Power broker Individuals, such as local party bosses and labor union leaders, who control blocks of votes and exercise influence on the selection of political candidates. Also, those who act as intermediaries in the formation of political coalitions.

Power elite A term popularized by sociologist C. Wright Mills to describe the political, corporate, and military elites that, in the view of elite theorists, determine the nation's fate.

Precedent A judicial opinion that, under the rule of *stare decisis* (adhere to or abide by the decision), is followed in future cases of a similar nature. The rule of *stare decisis* is not necessarily applied, and precedent tends to be used only where it conveniently fits the views and standards judges want to impose.

President pro tempore The presiding officer of the Senate in the absence of the vice president, elected by the body and by tradition the most senior member of the majority party.

Presidential commission A group of experts appointed by the president to investigate and report on a specific problem. Conflict in Central America, Social Security, crime, drugs, and pornography have been recent subjects of presidential commissions.

Press secretary A person who is in charge of media relations for politicians.

Private bill A law granting special benefits to named individuals.

Private calendar A list of private bills in the House, which pertain to individuals in such matters as immigration and claims against the government. The bills are taken up in order on the first and third Tuesday of each month.

Privilege See **Executive privilege.**

Procedural rights Protections and processes guaranteed to the individual by the Constitution, statutory law, and administrative rules in judicial, prosecutorial, administrative, and other government proceedings.

Proportional representation The allocation of seats in a representative body according to the proportion of the total vote received by each party. Since it does not require that a party receive a plurality of votes in any electoral district in order to win a seat, proportional representation is beneficial to third parties.

Prosecutor A government official, usually a district attorney, who brings actions against individuals in the name of the government for violations of the law.

Public bill A law that applies to the community as a whole.

Quasi-judicial Administrative functions of a judicial nature that determine the rights and obligations of individuals under the law, performed mostly by regulatory agencies.

Quasi-legislative Administrative rule making that has the force of legislation under a congressional delegation of authority (which indicates congressional intent but gives broad leeway to agencies to define the public interest).

Quorum The minimum number of members who must be present in a legislative or other body to conduct business. In the House and the Senate a majority of members constitutes a quorum.

Quota Where persons are concerned, an allotment assigned to a particular group. See **Affirmative action.**

Rank and file In political parties, the broad membership as opposed to the leaders.

Reactionary One with extremely conservative political views, who wants to return to the economic and political system of the past.

Recess A temporary suspension of House or Senate proceedings that, unlike adjournment, does not terminate the legislative day. The Senate tends to recess at the end of a calendar day, leaving its legislative day intact; the House generally adjourns from day to day.

Red tape Burdensome and inefficient administrative procedures, including paperwork, that cause delay and result in citizen frustration and inconvenience.

Reinstating election An election in which the long-term party allegiances of voters reassert themselves and the majority party is returned to power. It occurs after a deviating election, which is determined by transitory factors such as the charismatic personality of the victor.

Report A statement of the legislative intent of a congressional committee on a bill it recommends, with the dissenting views, if any, of the minority members who did not favor the legislation.

Republic A constitutional form of representative government. The term republic was originally used to describe governments that were not monarchies.

Resolution A measure passed by the House or the Senate dealing with the rules and other internal affairs of the bodies, or expressing sentiments on political issues or personal matters. Resolutions are exclusively within the authority of the House or the Senate, and do not have to be approved by the other body or signed by the president.

Rider A nongermane amendment to a bill, more common in the Senate than in the House.

Roe v. Wade The 1973 Supreme Court decision upholding the right of a woman to abortion as part of the liberty protected by the due process clause of the Fourteenth Amendment.

Rule of law A political system in which the responsibilities and limits of the government and the rights and obligations of citizens are determined by a constitution and statutory law.

Rules Committee The legislative gatekeeper of the House, an arm of the Speaker, that determines the procedures under which most legislation is debated and amended on the floor.

Schechter Rule Derived from the 1935 Supreme Court case *Schechter v. United States*, the rule held that Congress could delegate its primary legislative authority to the president or the executive branch. Congress can delegate quasi-legislative authority provided it clearly states its intent for the guidance of administrators.

Secretary of the Senate   The chief administrative officer of the body, who directs employees, receives lobbyists' registration statements, and administers oaths.

Security risk   A term developed in the late 1940s and used particularly frequently in the 1950s in reference to individuals, mostly government employees, who because of political beliefs, associations, or personal habits, past or present, were thought to endanger national security. Denied security clearance, these individuals could not hold sensitive government positions where they would have access to classified information.

Select committee   A special committee of the House or the Senate created for a specific purpose, usually investigative in nature, and for a limited period of time. However, many select committees have continued from one session of Congress to another, making them permanent in character.

Senatorial courtesy   Courtesy extended by senators to a colleague who calls for the nonconfirmation of a presidential appointment within his or her state. (By custom, the senior senator of the president's party must approve presidential appointments of judges within the senator's state.)

Seniority rule   The custom, which arose in the twentieth century, under which committee chairmanships in Congress are automatically assigned to the most senior member of the majority party on the committee. In the early 1970s, House Democrats set a new precedent by turning down several senior committee members for chairmanships because of their unpopularity and unresponsiveness to the Democratic caucus. Nevertheless, the seniority rule remains largely intact, particularly on standing committees.

Separation of powers   The partial division of legislative, executive, and judicial authority among the three branches of the national government.

Shared functions   The interlinking of powers and responsibilities among the three branches of government, so that each has some influence on the others, resulting in checks and balances.

Single-choice ballot   A ballot that is arranged by party, permitting voters to choose one party's candidates for all offices by pulling a single lever or by a single mark.

Single-member district   An electoral district represented by only one candidate who receives a plurality of votes.

Smith Act   The 1940 law that made it a crime to teach or advocate the duty or necessity of overthrowing the government of the United States or any state and its subdivisions by force or violence, or to organize and associate for such purposes. The Supreme Court, in *Dennis v. United States* (1951), upheld the law against a First Amendment challenge, the Court stating that the government has the authority to suppress expression that may constitute a clear and present danger to it.

Smoke-filled rooms   The hideaways and back rooms where party bosses meet to select candidates. The term has a pejorative connotation, suggesting intrigue, political machinations, and lack of responsiveness to the people.

Social Security Act   The 1935 law establishing the first social insurance program that provides retirement benefits, survivors' benefits, aid to disabled workers, as well as federal-state unemployment insurance.

Solicitor general   The officer of the Justice department who is responsible for arguing cases in which the United States is a party. The solicitor general is particularly important in determining which government cases will be appealed to the Supreme Court when lower federal courts have ruled against government agencies. The solicitor general has, over the years, been a particularly important influence upon the Supreme Court, which pays close attention to his arguments and often incorporates them into its opinions.

"Solid South"   Largely a phenomenon of the past, when Southern congressional representatives and convention delegates acted as a bloc, particularly in opposition to the federal imposition of civil rights standards and the candidates who supported an enlarged federal role in the protection of civil rights. The Solid South was also thought to be an important reason for the success of Democratic presidential candidates when it voted as a bloc; however, in the twentieth century the votes of the Solid South were rarely necessary for a Democratic presidential victory.

Sovereignty   The supreme authority to rule. In a democracy sovereignty resides in the people and is exercised by their elected representatives.

Speaker of the House   A constitutional officer, elected by the membership, who presides over the body. He is always the leader of the majority party in the House.

Split ticket   A ballot cast by a voter who ignores party slates, choosing candidates from different parties for different offices.

Spoils system   When the nonelective offices of government become the "spoils" or fruits of political victory, and are filled by the winning party on the basis of partisan considerations. The spoils system was the norm in the federal bureaucracy until 1883, when it was replaced by the **merit system.**

Staffer An assistant or aide, usually to an elected or formerly elected public official. The term is used most often to refer to Capitol Hill aides.

Standing committee A permanent, major committee of the House or the Senate, with the authority to recommend legislation, the expenditure of money, and the appropriation of funds (appropriations committees).

State of the Union message The president's annual report to Congress, required by the Constitution, that outlines his legislative program. While the first two presidents, George Washington and John Adams, personally delivered their State of the Union messages (called Annual Messages until 1947), from 1797 until 1913 the messages were given in writing. Woodrow Wilson revived the practice of delivering the message personally, and since then all presidents have followed his example.

State sovereignty The supreme authority of states, which has been narrowly defined by the Supreme Court since the outset of the Republic.

Statutory law The body of law made up of all legislation enacted by Congress and state legislatures.

Straw poll Originally, a nonscientifically conducted poll of opinion, for example when newspapers ask their readers to register their preferences for political candidates. Increasingly, the term is being used to include scientific polls, in which systematic sampling techniques are used, as well as informal straw votes.

Strict construction Judicial interpretation of the Constitution by the letter of the law, limiting national authority to the powers explicitly granted to the national government, resulting in a restrictive rather than expansive view of national power.

Succession Act (1947) Established the order of succession to the presidency in the event of the president's death or disability: vice-president, Speaker of the House, president pro tempore of the Senate, and members of the Cabinet in the order of the seniority of their departments.

Sunset laws Laws providing for the termination of government programs after they have been in operation for a predetermined period of time, usually three to five years. Sunset legislation has been enacted in various states, and proposed for national programs.

Sunshine laws Legislation that opens government proceedings to the public. "Government in the sunshine" is a feature of both national and state governments.

Supply-side economics The theory that increasing consumer demand for products and services by lowering the tax rate leads to economic prosperity. New York Republican congressman Jack Kemp became a leading proponent of the theory in the 1970s, along with economists such as Arthur Laffer. The Reagan administration adopted the theory and pushed through major tax cuts in 1981.

Tammany Hall New York's city Democratic party machine that ran the city from approximately 1850 to 1950. The term evokes backroom, corrupt bossism at its worst. (The Tammany Tiger was the symbol of the machine.)

Task force An appointed group of experts, assigned to a special project. Task forces often operate under presidential or congressional commissions, investigating domestic and foreign policy problems, such as crime, pornography, and Central America.

Teller vote In the House of Representatives, a vote taken by having members file past tellers, who count those for and against a measure but do not record the names of those voting.

Third party In presidential politics, a party outside of the two major political parties that fields candidates for the presidency and vice-presidency. Third parties are often splinter groups from one of the two major parties whose interests are not represented by them. The most successful third party was Theodore Roosevelt's Bull Moose party in 1912.

Ticket A slate of candidates, almost always from the same party, who run for office as a team. For example, presidential and vice-presidential candidates of the same party comprise a ticket.

Totalitarianism A system in which the government has total control over the people and unlimited authority to achieve what it thinks best.

Trade-off In political negotiations, to sacrifice an expendable proposal in exchange for a concession from the other side.

Trial balloon Information concerning proposed action released by a government official other than the person responsible for the proposal so that the latter can avoid blame if the balloon is shot down by adverse reaction within or without government.

"Trickle-down" theory The belief that the wealth and prosperity of corporations and individuals inevitably "trickle down" to benefit lower income groups.

Turnout The number of voters who go to the polls on election day. Turnout is higher in presidential than in congressional elections, and although the vast majority of *registered* voters vote, less than 60 percent of those *eligible* vote in national elections.

Ultra vires   Beyond legal authority. Action taken by a governmental official that is outside the boundaries of his or her constitutional or statutory authority is *ultra vires,* and upon a determination of such by a court it becomes null and void.

Umbrella party   Applied to American political parties, a loose confederation of interests joined together under the wide party "umbrella."

Unanimous consent   A Senate procedure under which the rules are suspended and the conduct of business is facilitated. Unanimous consent agreements are also used to determine the rules of government floor debate on important legislation.

Unicameral   Refers to a one-house legislature. Nebraska is the only state with a unicameral legislature.

Union Calendar   Lists appropriations and revenue bills in the House.

Unit rule   Binds a group to abide by the decision and position of the majority.

Veto   Rejection by one government body of the action of another body. For example, under the Constitution the president may veto congressional legislation; only a two-thirds vote by both houses of Congress can override a presidential veto. In 1983 the Supreme Court ruled that Congress may not provide for a legislative veto of executive action, however.

Voice vote   In the House or the Senate, when the presiding officer calls for the "ayes" and "nays," and gives the decision to the louder chorus.

War on Poverty   President Lyndon B. Johnson's programs in the mid-1960s to help the poor.

Watergate   In politics, the scandal triggered by the break-in at the Democratic National Committee Headquarters in the Watergate complex in Washington, D.C., in 1972 by employees of the Republican Committee to Re-elect the President. President Nixon and his aides tried to cover up their involvement, but, when the cover-up was discovered, impeachment proceedings were instituted against Nixon; he resigned on August 9, 1974. "Watergate" has become synonymous with political corruption.

Wednesday Club   A group of moderate House Republicans.

Welfare state   A system under which the government takes positive action to ensure the economic welfare of its citizens. In American political rhetoric the term has a pejorative connotation, often implying socialism. Sweden is the model of the modern welfare state.

Whip   A legislative party leader, selected by the party caucus, who keeps members informed of the position of the party leadership on crucial issues and ensures that party members are present to vote the party line.

Whistle-blower   A government employee who exposes mismanagement and corruption by informing the media.

White House   In political language, the president and his staff. For example, typical headlines read: "The White House pressures Congress to enact its programs."

Write-in   Refers to voting for a candidate who is not officially listed on the ballot, by writing his or her name in a blank space. Write-in voters are rarely successful; they are usually used to register a protest against a party's candidate or slate.

Zero-sum game   In politics, a game in which victory for one side means defeat for the other.

Index